# Money, Banking, and Financial Markets

# Money, Banking, and Financial Markets

**J. WALTER ELLIOTT**
*University of Wisconsin-Milwaukee*

**WEST PUBLISHING COMPANY**
*St. Paul    New York    San Francisco    Los Angeles*

**Cover Photo**

The cover photo combines the buildings of the New York City skyline with the image of the Statue of Liberty. Copyright © 1982 B. Carter. Photo reprinted by the permission of the Image Bank, Chicago.

COPYRIGHT © 1984 By WEST PUBLISHING CO.
50 West Kellogg Boulevard
P.O. Box 3526
St. Paul, Minnesota 55165

**LIBRARY OF CONGRESS CATALOGING IN PUBLICATION DATA**

Elliott, Jan Walter.
  Money, banking, and financial markets.

  Bibliography: p.
  Includes index.
  1. Money.    2. Banks and banking.    3. Finance.
4. Money—United States.    5. Banks and banking—United
States.    6. Finance—United States.    I. Title.
HG256.E45  1984          332          83-17007
ISBN O-314-77985-X

# CONTENTS

# 5
## THE SPECIAL LANGUAGE OF FINANCIAL MARKETS 75

# 6
## BANKING INSTITUTIONS—PAST AND PRESENT 105

**PART II**

## THE U.S. BANKING AND FINANCE INDUSTRY 103

# 7
## THE STRUCTURE OF BANKING INSTITUTIONS 119

**8**
ASSETS AND LIABILITIES OF DEPOSITORY INSTITUTIONS  127

**9**
MANAGING BANK ASSETS AND LIABILITIES  139

**PART III**

THE FEDERAL
RESERVE
SYSTEM
157

**10**
GROWTH AND GOVERNANCE
OF THE FEDERAL RESERVE SYSTEM  159

**21**
# ECONOMIC POLICY   375

**22**
# THE ONGOING ECONOMIC POLICY DEBATE   393

# To the Instructor

This book has been inspired by two important developments in the field. The first is the rapid advancement of macroeconomic theory over the past several years, moving these ideas into a "post-monetarist debate" era. The second important development is the massive institutional change associated with the enactment of the 1980 banking law. These two changes are inadequately reflected in existing texts, being largely incorporated by add on material. The overall concept of this book is to present major themes in the field of money and banking in a comprehensive way that builds upon the important theoretical and institutional changes of recent years.

## STYLE AND PEDAGOGY

One of the reviewers of this book provided a one sentence description of its style which captured what I had in mind when I began writing this book. He said, "The language in the book is simple, but the ideas are not." This is exactly what I sought to do. I wanted to present the major themes of money and banking in a complete yet simply described manner. To this end:

**1.** jargon has been replaced by common language wherever possible,

**2.** some pruning has been done in the interest of keeping the flow of the main thoughts clear,

**3.** the writing style is kept informal,

**4.** chapter summaries are provided at the end of each chapter, along with discussion questions and suggestions for further reading.

The book incorporates several pedagogical innovations. Among these are the use of *Memos* and *Memorandums*. The *Memo* at the start of each chapter introduces the chapter to the student and provides a perspective on what the student is about to read. The *Memorandums* in the body of the chapters contain material that is either of a "high interest" nature or is a technical supplement.

A second pedagogical innovation in the book is the *Feature Sections* that are at the end of the book's six major parts. These *Feature Sections* deal with topics designed to stimulate the student's general interest in the subject matter. Accordingly, the *Feature Sections* cover: (I) how to read the Wall Street Journal, (II) problems banks have in managing their reserve position on a day-to-day basis, (III) a look at the process of the FRB setting targets and hitting them, (IV) a three act play starring a Keynesian, a monetarist, and a truck driver, (V) a description of major speculative episodes in history, including the tulip-bulb craze, the nifty fifty, and the new issues market, and (VI) a look at the role of the FRB in the international economy.

## FLEXIBLE ORGANIZATIONS

The chapter-by-chapter layout of the book enables it to be used in a number of ways. Part I is an introductory section that should normally be read by all students. It contains the basics on the role of money in the economy, a primer on the Federal Reserve System, the basics of the banking system and the money supply process, an introduction to the major economic statistics that surround us, and a presentation on the language of financial markets. Only the fundamentals are covered in each of these chapters. For courses that give heavy emphasis to one or more of these areas, more advanced material is included in later chapters.

In Part II, it is possible to pick any combination of the four chapters on banking institutions and structure. They are written so that one does not necessarily precede the other. The same is true of the three chapters that comprise Part III. Any subset of them can be read without a sequencing problem.

Part IV on monetary theory and policy does have some sequencing to be taken into consideration in using the book. For those who want to use the IS–LM structure, Chapters thirteen through fifteen present that material, which should be read in order. For those who want to use the IS–LM to develop a simple aggregate demand and supply framework, Chapters thirteen through fifteen should be followed by Chapters sixteen and seventeen. Then, beyond Chapter seventeen, it is possible to "pick from the menu" provided by Chapters eighteen through twenty-two on inflation, monetarism, policy, and the Keynesian-monetarist debate.

For those who want to cover the classical-monetarist model in lieu of the IS–LM approach, Chapters thirteen and fourteen, (which present the simple Keynesian Cross model) can be followed by Chapter eighteen which presents the natural rate hypothesis and loanable funds theory. This can be followed by Chapter twenty which presents the quantity theory. Chapter twenty-one on economic policy then can be read in this sequence.

Part V contains three chapters on financial markets that can be read in any combination and which do not greatly depend on the theory sequence chosen. Part VI on the international economy, contains three chapters that also can be selected "menu-style" with no sequencing problems. There are more specific suggestions on sequencing contained in the instructor's manual that accompanies this book.

## ACKNOWLEDGEMENTS

Many people have helped this book come to life. Mary Schiller of West must be given much credit. She contributed solid ideas on pedagogy and style as well as infectious enthusiasm for the whole project. The book had the advantage of excellent reviewers. I want to especially thank each of the following individuals who provided countless insightful suggestions throughout the development of this manuscript.

| | |
|---|---|
| Peter Alonzi | Maryann Keating |
| Maclyn Clouse | Timothy Koch |
| Donna Dial | John Rea |
| Clifford Fry | John Silvia |
| Robert Harris | Philip Wiest |
| Barry Keating | |

Finally, students at the University of Wisconsin-Milwaukee have contributed by forcing the fuzziness out of early drafts by asking all the right questions.

J. Walter Elliott
University of Wisconsin-Milwaukee

# To the Student

This book focuses on how the economy, the banking system, and financial markets all work. In the world we live in, these themes are highly intertwined. It is difficult to understand how the economy works without understanding the framework of the banking system that stands at the center of economic activity.

Similarly, financial markets represent the nationwide arena where the banking system and the economy carry out the many transactions that determine the thousands of interest rates we see in newspapers and other periodicals. Ignoring these markets when discussing banking and the economy would be to ignore the *real world* locations where much of "the action" involved in the subject actually occurs. Therefore, studying the economy, banking, and financial markets as related subjects is not an arbitrary approach but a highly logical one.

As you study money and banking, why not make it as enjoyable as possible? Start reading business publications such as the *Wall Street Journal, Business Week,* and *Fortune,* as well as general news publications like *Time* and *Newsweek.* Become curious about what you read. Ask questions, and try predicting how changing national and world events will affect banking, the economy and financial markets. In a word, as you read and study the subject, get involved in it. It's easy to do, because in the 80's the subject matter of this book is often front page news.

The book in your hands is laid out a bit differently from the usual textbook, and some explaining is in order. The most noticeable difference is that you will find *Memos* and *Memorandums* spread throughout the chapters written by me to you. These boxes deal with topics and issues I think you will find interesting. The *Memos* and *Memorandums* amplify the mainstream ideas you read about in the text of each chapter.

Another difference you will find is that each of the book's six major parts is followed by a *Feature Section* that explores a particular topic not taken up in the part proper. For example, at the end of Part I there is a *Feature Section* that looks at reading the financial pages of the *Wall Street Journal*. This is included because it has been brought to my attention by many students that the normal person is not born knowing how to do that. Yet, it is something that is interesting to know.

Other *Feature Sections* deal with famous speculative episodes in financial markets throughout history and the growing role of the Federal Reserve in the international economy. There is even the script of a play for you to peruse at the end of Part IV. This play stars a Keynesian, a monetarist, and a truck driver.

Finally, now is an exciting time to study money and banking. The 1970's were a challenging and stimulating time to study the subject with interest rates reaching all time highs along with inflation, and with the U.S. banking system undergoing more changes than it had for the preceding four decades. But, hard as that act is to follow, the 1980's promise to be an even more dynamic time to learn about and get involved with money and banking. During this decade, we can expect changes to occur in banking at a rate faster than new computers are being developed. In all likelihood, you will be talking about things in class that happened yesterday, last week, or last month.

Unfortunately, the dizzy pace of change in financial markets and in banking will make parts of this book outdated by the time it reaches your hands. Do not worry. The book's major themes will remain intact and the news media will keep you informed of specific institutional changes as they occur.

J Walter Elliott
(JWE)

# Money, Banking, and Financial Markets

# PART I

# FIRST
# THINGS FIRST

## CHAPTER 1

# Money:
# What and Why

## CHAPTER OUTLINE

## IMPORTANT TERMS

medium of exchange
store of value
unit of account
Gresham's Law
fiat money
share drafts
demand-type deposits

currency
M1
barter system
inflation
recession
depression

## MEMO

To:        All readers
From:     JWE

This first chapter is about the concept of money. As you begin this book, it is important to do some thinking about the concept of money and its role in the economy. In this chapter you will read about the essential economic functions of money and about the historical connection between money and precious metals. You will also read about how money is officially defined in the United States.

You can learn something important about the essential role of money in our economy by thinking about what the world would be like without money. A moneyless economy? It is far-fetched, but within the realm of reason. In this chapter you can take a trip to a futuristic moneyless United States. This trip shows the essential role money plays in inflations and in recurring recessions.

Finally, with this chapter, you are practicing the rare and difficult art of making a beginning. Take heart. You cannot possibly finish until you begin.

---

Bob Ellis was doing ten years on a forgery rap. Bill Kraus was up for eight on a white-collar swindling charge. They were in Bob's cell conducting the most important business of the week. "I'll give you 4 packs," said Bob. "It's worth more than that, you crook," replied Bill. Bob shot back, "Not to me it isn't. And, watch who you're calling a crook."

Later in the day the deal was closed. Bob paid Bill three and a half packs of cigarettes for Bill's two fresh nine-volt batteries. Although neither would admit it, both men were happy with the deal. Bob now had batteries for his electronic football game. With the game back in operation, he could win an easy ten to fifteen packs of cigarettes by betting on games in his cell block. Bill added the three and a half packs from the transaction to his stash, which now totaled almost thirty packs. He had big plans for this nestegg. One of the guards had offered him an FM radio for thirty packs and Bill was now ready to make the buy.

## MONEY IS WHAT MONEY DOES

You just took a peek into a prison economy. There is something simple yet basic and important about what is going on there. In prisons, dollars do not officially circulate. Yet, almost without exception, inmates in prisons invent something that acts as money. This is not accidental. Rather, prison money arises out of a need for the services money provides.

Cigarettes are serving as money in this prison example. As such, they perform three important and essential functions required of any type of workable money.

First, the cigarettes are the prison's *medium of exchange*. By this term we mean that the cigarettes are the go-between enabling prisoners to trade one thing for another at different times or places. Let us say Bob sold something on Monday, stored the cigarettes he got in payment until Wednesday, and then bought the batteries with those cigarettes. Although he has done nothing more during this three-day period than trade one good for another, he has used money as a medium to facilitate this exchange. Thus, we use the term medium of exchange to describe this function of the prison's cigarette money. Notice that dollars do the same thing for people who live in the outside world.

Closely related to this function is money's function as a *store of value*. The cigarettes Bob got on Monday were durable enough to last until Wednesday. And, they were still recognized as being as valuable and worthy of exchange on Wednesday as they were on Monday. In Bill's case, cigarettes were being saved up to make one big buy. This store-of-value aspect is required of any money. Suppose the prisoners used fresh peaches rather than cigarettes as their money. The peach money would have to be exchanged fairly rapidly, or it would become rotten, stinky, and lose its value in exchange. So, peach money probably would not be successful.

Peaches and dollars in our pockets during a time of rising prices have something in common. The longer we hold dollars when prices are rising, the less valuable they are in exchange for goods. Consequently, during periods of rising prices, people often behave as if their wallets contain rotting peaches.

The final function of the inmates' cigarettes is that of a *unit of account*. The worth of anything traded in the prison can be measured in terms of the number of packs of cigarettes for which it can be exchanged. This simplifies the pricing system in the prison. Without this standard unit of account, the inmates would need to have an exchange ratio of every good they buy and sell with every other good. It would be cumbersome to have to keep track of a large number of exchange ratios for everything traded in the prison. And, of course, if the complexities of it gave rise to some inconsistencies and unfairness, someone could wind up with a knife in the back.

## PRECIOUS THINGS AND MONEY

One logical (if not actual) reason a prison economy might settle on cigarettes as its money is that the supply of cigarettes is controlled.

There is presumably a cigarette ration of a certain number of new packs each week. There is also a certain number of packs smoked by inmates. Yes, some people are actually smoking up their money! The difference between cigarettes supplied and those consumed is the change in the prison money supply. If 200 new packs of cigarettes are issued in a typical week and only 190 of them are smoked, the stock of cigarettes in the prison goes up by 10 packs.

Any increase in the stock of cigarettes is an increase in the total buying power of the inmates. Suppose the supply of goods the inmates trade with each other does not change for a period of six months or so, but the stock of cigarettes goes up by a hundred packs per week. In this case, it will take an increasing number of cigarettes to buy the goods available in the prison. The reasoning is as follows. If more and more purchasing power is placed in the hands of the inmates, but no additional goods are available for purchase, the prisoners will be willing to bid more for the goods they want. Accordingly, the price of all prison goods will go up.

To see the pressures involved here, think of a room full of buyers at an auction with a table of a hundred items for sale. The items are to be auctioned off to the highest bidder. Now suppose the total of all the money in the buyers' pockets is $800. If we ran the auction, and everyone spent their money, the average price of the goods would be $800/100 = $8 per item. Now, let us pass out $200 more to these same buyers and rerun the auction. If they now spent a total of $1,000, the 100 items would bring an average price of $1000/100 = $10 per item. The 25 percent increase in purchasing power at the auction resulted in a 25 percent higher price. The moral of this story for auction-goers is that the more money at the auction, the higher the prices of the goods sold. It is not much different in the prison economy, and not completely different in the real world.

For example, can you imagine the result if the prison were flooded with new cigarettes? Suppose the supply of cigarettes were doubled. If the inmates had twice the purchasing power to buy the same amount of goods, the price of prison goods would double.

There is a powerful and simple lesson here. The result of flooding any economy with money is an explosion in the prices of everything exchangeable for money. It is no accident that money in the real world, as well as money in the prison, *must have a controlled supply*. It cannot be something that people can manufacture on their own (counterfeiters aside). If we all could take a couple of hours and print up or otherwise produce 10,000 dollars, we would suddenly discover that everyone would be doing it, and the value of each dollar would be declining at an astonishing rate.

The need to control the supply of money explains in large part why many countries originally chose a precious metal such as gold or silver for their money. The supply of a precious metal is naturally controlled by its scarcity. Expanding the supply of gold or silver by a large amount in a short time period is impossible. Therefore, many countries in the past minted their official money from precious metals.

To: Readers interested in money floods in the real world
From: JWE

The world is not without examples of the result of flooding the economy with money. During and after World War I, several eastern European countries did just this. In Poland, the government increased the supply of money at a runaway rate just by printing it to pay the nation's wartime bills. During one twenty-month period, the supply of money increased by an unbelievable 10,000 percent. (If you are not used to dealing with such large figures, do some calculating with pencil and paper to see for yourself the increase involved.)

Prices rose by the same 10,000 percent. It is hard to appreciate an inflation of this magnitude without living through it, but maybe some of the famous fables of the period will help give you an impression. Money was said to be depreciating so rapidly that it was cheaper to burn it in wood-burning stoves than to use it to buy firewood. The problem of carrying it around was reported to have required shoppers to use wagons and wheelbarrows to get their purchasing power to the grocery!

The United States is no exception. Gold and silver coins were the heart of the stock of circulating money in the United States when our nation first began minting its own money in 1792. The twenty-dollar gold piece was at one time the symbol of conspicuous wealth because of what twenty dollars could buy. Now, it is again, because of the market value of that much gold.

Gold coins were not without their problems. They were unwieldy to carry around. Also, gold and silver are soft metals that are easily damaged. Coins made from them soon took on the appearance of ten-year-old cars driven exclusively in New York City. The picture of the U.S. statesman on the coins soon resembled Jack the Ripper. Therefore, the coins had to be reminted frequently.

Another more serious problem with the coins had to do with the gold and silver content of the U.S. coins compared with the gold and silver content of the coins of other nations. For example, the U.S. silver dollar was slightly lighter than the Spanish silver dolar. However, citizens of the West Indies were unimpressed by the difference in silver content and traded Spanish silver dolars one for one with U.S. dollars. This meant that there was more than one U.S. dollar's worth of silver in one Spanish dolar. As a result, U.S. speculators went to the West Indies with U.S. silver dollars, traded them for an equal number of Spanish dolars, brought the coins back to the United States, and melted them down. The amount of silver that resulted was worth more than the dollars the speculators started with, so they made a profit. However, this meant that U.S. dollars were flowing out of the country.

# Memorandum

If you are wondering how the dollar got its name, and what that has to do with pieces of eight, you are reading the right memo. In the revolutionary-war period, Spanish coins circulated freely in the United States partly because of the absence of U.S. money. (We did not officially invent our money until 1792.) The most common of these coins was the Spanish dolar. (The Spanish dolar has only one *l*.) Spanish dolars were called pieces of eight because they were scored so they could be broken into eight pie-shaped pieces, called bits. These bits were used in making change, each having the value of one-eighth of a dolar. These coins gave rise to the term two bits, which refers to a quarter.

One wonders whether the heritage of the Spanish dolar also explains why stock prices are denominated in one-eighths of a point on the New York Stock Exchange. In any event, popular acceptance and familiarity with the Spanish dolar were principal reasons why Thomas Jefferson recommended in 1786 that the silver dollar be made our standard monetary unit.

The dollar was officially designated the monetary unit by the Coinage Act of 1792. At that time, the new U.S. mint was authorized to make gold eagles ($10.00), half-eagles ($5.00), quarter eagles ($2.50), silver dollars, half-dollars, quarter-dollars, dismes (later the *s* was dropped), half-dismes (later changed to nickels), copper cents, and half-cents. The double-eagle, or twenty-dollar gold piece, came along later. Thus, the quarter in your pocket has a heritage going all the way back to 1792.

Similar problems were also affecting the U.S. gold coins, which were winding up in France and England in large quantities. As a result, President Jefferson suspended the coinage of silver dollars in 1806, fourteen years after they had first been minted. The United States was learning that it was difficult to keep coins made from precious metals in circulation in a world where the value of precious metals in coins of various nations changes frequently. Whenever the gold or silver value of U.S. coins became greater than that of some other nation's coins, the U.S. coins would disappear from U.S. circulation. This tendency was dubbed *Gresham's Law*, following the thesis of Professor Gresham who pronounced that "bad" or undervalued money always drives out of circulation "good" or overvalued money.

It was difficult if not impossible, for the United States to adjust quickly enough and in the right direction to prevent recurring undervaluation of the U.S. coins. Therefore, there were chronic problems keeping the coins in circulation. Paper money offered an apparent solution to this problem.

But how would the public react to paper money? What value would people see in it compared with the obvious value of gold or silver?

By the time the United States became interested in issuing paper money, the public had already had some experience with privately issued paper money. Bank IOUs had been in limited circulation in the United States for some time. However, the acceptance of private bank money was usually confined to the town or region where the bank was located. The holders of such money usually could see and walk into the bank issuing the IOU, which probably helped in its acceptance. But paper money issued by a faraway federal government was something else. When the government eventually began issuing paper money it was in essence asking the public to take the IOU and use it as if it were gold or silver coins. Now, there are limits to how trusting the American public can be expected to be. But the government had a plan. Much of the early U.S. paper money carried with it the promise that it could be redeemed in gold or silver whenever the owner of the paper chose.[1] That promise was backed up by the law, which stated that gold-backed paper money could be issued only up to the limits of the government's gold stock. With that provision, the paper money became essentially a warehouse receipt giving its owner a claim to gold stored there. (Fort Knox was established as the actual warehouse.)

The period from the mid-1800s to the depression of the 1930s was one of recurring issues of paper money, usually exchangeable for gold or silver. Although the United States experienced a civil war and a world war along with several economic crises, the period was generally one in which public acceptance of paper money was established.

The year 1933 was possibly the worst of the Great Depression in terms of jobs and the well-being of the American people. It was also the year that a fundamental change was made in the nature of U.S. paper money. For many decades prior to 1933, the U.S. government made good on its promise to exchange most paper money for gold whenever any of its citizens so requested. That period had established among the public a strong feeling of confidence in paper money. Indeed, by 1933, the U.S. dollar was largely seen *as* the paper money, not the gold behind it. A growing fraction of the population was only dimly aware that the dollar could be exchanged for gold.

In early 1933, the U.S. government felt a need to expand the supply of money significantly, as a move to try to do something about the depression. That meant either finding a mountain full of new gold or changing the rules governing the issuing of paper money. President Roosevelt opted for the latter. In the spring of that year, the legal requirement for gold to back paper money was cut from the existing 100 percent to 25 percent. At the same time, all U.S. citizens were legally prohibited from holding gold coins or bars (jewelry and tooth

1. Some paper money was redeemable in gold and some in silver. This meant that the United States had two precious metals backing its money. This is called a bimetallic system. The United States is described as having been on a bimetallic standard from 1792 until 1861, when the pressures of the Civil War caused the issuance of nonbacked "greenbacks," or essentially unsecured IOUs.

fillings were allowed). By the stroke of a pen, paper money was no longer a warehouse receipt on the contents of Fort Knox. But what was it? Since people could no longer hold gold, the dollar could not be exchanged for it. What could the "new" dollar be exchanged for? The answer is simply another dollar, or two fifty-cent pieces, et cetera. Before 1933, people widely believed that the dollar was a receipt for a precious metal in which value resided. After the change, the dollar itself was the object in which the value of the currency resided. But, would it be accepted? Would the public agree with the government's contention that nothing had substantially changed? Would they heed the government's call to treat the dollar as usual? Helped by the government's new pledge that paper currency would only be issued up to the limit of four times the government's stock of gold (so that gold is at least 25 percent of currency), most store owners, consumers, and other citizens did treat the new dollar much the same as the old.

The transformation of the dollar that began in 1933 was completed in 1968 when all the backing of currency by gold was eliminated by a stroke of another presidential pen. The 25 percent gold backing behind the most common type of paper money, Federal Reserve Notes, was removed. With this change, the U.S. government removed the limit on the growth of currency represented by the value of the U.S. stock of gold. Again this was done in response to a pressing problem. By 1968 the U.S. gold stock was beginning to decline while the needs of the economy for currency were growing. It was again time either to discover more gold or to change the rules. And, again, the U.S. government chose to change the rules. As a result of the 1968 change in law, the maximum amount of paper dollars the government can issue is set by Congress. Congress can and periodically does change this ceiling. The pressure to legislate this change usually occurs when the actual supply of currency approaches the maximum[2] permitted by existing law.

After 1968, the U.S. paper dollar had no further connection with gold as far as U.S. citizens were concerned.[3] This established the U.S. dollar as *fiat money*, meaning money backed by the confidence of the public rather than by a precious metal. Actually, *fiat* in Latin means "Let it be done." Fiat money, therefore, is money deemed so by government decree, money about which the government has said, in effect, "Let it be money!"

## MONEY IN THE UNITED STATES

Even though the supply of paper dollars is all that the U.S. government has officially decreed to be money, it is not all that is officially

2. All this is a reminder that changing the rules on how the supply of paper money related to the gold stock and changing the rules on the maximum amount of paper money that can be issued are largely the same thing.

3. However, foreigners were for a further period of time treated differently, as we shall see in a much later chapter.

counted as money in government statistics kept by the Federal Reserve System. Banks, thrift institutions, and credit unions give individuals and firms checkable accounts, such as bank checking accounts, checkable savings accounts, and share-draft accounts. (A *share draft* is a checklike document drawn on an account containing shares of an investment fund. It authorizes an agent to transfer share ownership to the person presenting it.) Holders of checkable accounts routinely pay their bills with checks; checks and share drafts are widely accepted as a means of payment. Also, checkable accounts allow individuals and firms to hold immediate purchasing power. In these ways, checks and share drafts are close, if not perfect, substitutes for paper money. The resemblance is close enough for the government's keepers of official statistics, who define all checkable accounts and paper money as the two components of official U.S. money. Checkable accounts are called *demand-type deposits.* The term reflects the idea that they are deposits (which the public has made in a financial institution) that are redeemable upon demand by the depositor. (In other words, people owning a balance in a checkable account can have their paper money back whenever they want.) Paper money is officially and more eloquently called *currency.* The official money supply, called *M1,* therefore, consists of currency plus checkable demand deposits.[4]

Besides M1, there are several more measures of monetary-type assets, which include other kinds of financial assets as well as demand and other checkable deposits and currency. In chapter 5, we examine these additional monetary measures.

## LIFE WITHOUT MONEY—BARTER IN THE TWENTY-FIRST CENTURY

Now that we have briefly examined the functions, historical background, and current definition of money, let us imagine life without money. What would happen if we suspended its use? Would we all be back in the caves? To form some impressions on these questions, have a hypothetical peek at life in a future moneyless society—the United States in the year 2056.

Yoda Yassaf works a standard twenty-three-hour week in a shirt factory. Today is payday. Yoda examines his pay statement. It shows the total number of shirts produced in the factory that week, and it shows Yoda's share of this production. It had been a good week. The factory produced 488 shirts, a good 10 percent higher than normal. "Ohhh," said Yoda, "that's good." He thought that such a good week was probably the result of very little downtime. All the droids had operated at 100 percent efficiency during the week, even that lemon R4–D7. Yoda's share of the production was his usual 4.89 percent. He felt good. When he started at the factory, he made only 2.14

4. In this official definition, checkable deposits do not include deposits made by foreign-official deposit holders. The definition also includes traveler's checks.

percent of output, but he had advanced quickly to a more responsible and productive job. One more promotion and his share would be up to 5 percent. Then he could afford a new ground-effects machine.

The bottom line on Yoda's pay statement showed his weekly earnings: 488 shirts $x$ .0489 = 23.86 shirts credited to his account. That is the most Yoda had added to his account in any week since the cashless system was set up twenty-one years ago. At that time, the one surviving credit-card company had proposed the change as a way of simplifying its accounting methods. With government sponsorship, a large computer system was set up in Iowa (approximately the geographic center of the country) that could handle the pay records of all members of the work force, including laborers, management, and government workers. Everyone that earned income had an account set up in the Iowa computer. Then, companies began paying their payrolls by giving managers, workers, and others a share of the output produced rather than a dollar amount. The transition had not been that difficult, Yoda recalled. If a worker earned $400 per week and the company had production of $20,000, the worker would receive 400/20,000 = .02 or 2 percent of the company's output. If the firm made 4,000 cases of beer during the week, the worker would be credited with 4,000 $x$ .02 = 80 cases of beer for the week.

But, what—you ask—would such a worker do with eighty cases of beer during one week and still be alive to tell about it? That's where the Iowa computer comes in. The computer holds the accounts of everyone getting credit for producing anything. The sum of all the accounts in Iowa is the total of all goods and services produced during the week. The computer handles the mammoth job of accounting for the exchange of these goods among the nation's workers. Even though the system was no longer new, Yoda still marveled at the way it worked.

He decided to have a celebration drink at the corner bar while he marveled. By the time he reached the bar, his Iowa account had already been credited with his weekly share of shirt production. Yoda ordered a double whoozout. When he paid for the drink, he presented his account card to the bartender as he did for any transaction anywhere. When the bartender punched the drink sale into his countertop computer terminal, the terminal displayed the current exchange ratio between the account-holder's product, shirts, and the product being purchased, a double whoozout. Today that ratio stood at .198 shirts per double whoozout. The amount in Yoda's account was reduced by .198 shirts. At the same time, the bartender had 1.0 drinks credited to his account—his production. Yoda remembered his earlier confusion over how the system worked from this point. He knew that in a moneyless system, he was essentially trading goods for goods in all his transactions—but what if the bartender did not happen to want his shirt just because Yoda happened to want the bartender's drink?

Fortunately, the computer had worked out that problem long ago. All products offered in exchange (such as Yoda's .198 shirt) went into a temporary limbo state called the product float. And, if a bartender anywhere in the country had recently purchased anything, he would have "paid" for it with drinks, which also would have been put into the float. Upon Yoda's purchase, one of these drinks would have been removed from the float and replaced by its equivalent, .198 of a shirt. So Yoda was indeed trading part of a shirt for a drink. It just did not happen to be that particular bartender's drink involved in the trade. The economy was big enough that there were usually products of all kinds available in the float. But what if there were none?

The system had provisions for the situation where the float was "dry" for particular products. In such a case, the float would go into a net borrowed or "red" position until some drinks were added to it by bartender expenditures. A red position for a product was the signal to the computer to change the exchange ratios for that product. For example, if the float was dry relative to drinks, it meant that either those producing drinks were not presently spending their credits, or that not enough drinks were being produced relative to the number being consumed. The computer's response to this would be to raise the value of a drink compared to all other products. If this had happened in Yoda's case, he might have found that the next drink cost .20 of a shirt instead of .198.

This change in the exchange ratio accomplishes two things. First, it makes all other products cheaper for those who are producing drinks. This should stimulate the bartender's consumption of other items, which would add more drinks to the float. Second, it makes drinks more valuable in terms of all other goods, which should stimulate the production of drinks. Some bartenders may decide to stay open longer at these higher exchange ratios. The computer would keep inching the drink exchange ratios upward until the red condition was eliminated.

The computer also worked in the opposite direction. If a glut of a certain product began appearing in the float, the computer would begin lowering the exchange ratio. A glut would appear if those who produced one type of product were consuming a lot of other things in a short period of time (a mass shopping spree) or if there was very little demand for the product by others, as would happen if a product went out of fashion. In either event, the computer would lower the exchange ratio until the glut had been eliminated. This usually corrected the problem, because a lowered exchange ratio meant that those producing the product would be able to buy less of other things with a week's production. Times would be bad in that industry. Usually, some firms would stop producing the item, preferring to switch to other more profitable products. And the lower exchange ratio made the product cheaper, since the computer had essentially put it on sale, compared to all other goods. This usually helped reduce the glut.

Yoda looked at his chronograph. He punched one button and got the time, and another and got the up-to-the-minute exchange ratio between double whoozouts and shirts. It had dropped to .195. "Ohhh," exclaimed Yoda, "not only do I have time for another drink, but the computer has put them on sale. Bartender, fix me another double whoozout!''

## IS MONEY WORTH ITS COST?

Yoda's world has some advantages over ours. Let us focus on those having to do specifically with the role of money in both worlds. First, is Yoda's economy really a *barter system*? Is there something functioning as money? Well, if you think that it really is a barter system, you are right. But if you think Yoda's account card is in fact money because he can buy a drink with it, keep this in mind; the computer would have kicked his card back if Yoda's account had had insufficient shirts in it. The card is just an accounting device. In Yoda's world as in any real barter system, *goods trade for goods with no medium of exchange.* Although the Iowa computer system helped goods trade against goods, we are stretching the point to say that in so doing, Yoda's world has computer money in it. The computer only did with lightning speed and high technology what natives in primitive societies did in a more pedestrian way—traded the products they produced with one another directly, haggling endlessly over the ratios of exchange.

How does Yoda's system compare to ours? In Yoda's system there is no opportunity for a general inflation to occur, where *Inflation*, is defined as a persistent increase in the general level of prices. With inflation so serious in our world, a contention like this deserves further discussion. Think about the purchasing power in Yoda's economy. Purchasing power is the sum of all credits in the accounts of workers throughout the country. But they gain these credits by working and producing products and services. The accounts are credited with the total quantity of products produced. So production creates the economy's purchasing power. Moreover, *the total purchasing power and the total products available for purchase are the same.* There can be no situation where the general purchasing power *exceeds* the available goods. Never will there be the equivalent of flooding the prison with cigarettes.

Even if some workers do not use up all their purchasing power in a single week (that is, they save), there can be no difference between purchasing power and production, as long as those who end a week with a balance in their account are willing to allow the computer to lend it out at interest to others who want to spend more than they are currently producing. We can suppose that the computer could evolve an interest rate that would always equate total borrowing and lending in each period—thus the purchasing power exercised would always be equal to the total current production. Thus, there can never be a general deviation of purchasing power from products produced.

As if the impossibility of excess purchasing power is not enough to thwart inflation, there is another aspect of a barter system that prevents it. Inflation is a continued increase in the general price level. The prices of average consumer goods rise during inflation. In barter, there is no such thing as a general price level, and it is impossible for the price of goods to be rising. Why? Because rather than having fixed prices, barter systems have only ratios of exchange. In Yoda's world, there are exchange ratios for every product compared with every other product, but no concept of general prices. The Iowa computer contains a gigantic matrix that has all the available products listed in both the vertical and horizontal directions. The entries in the matrix are the exchange ratios of everything against everything else. When one of these ratios goes up, another automatically comes down. More shirts per drink means, by definition, fewer drinks per shirt.

Moreover, the Iowa computer is always adjusting these ratios in response to market demands. Whenever a product is in heavy demand, its exchange ratio rises compared with other goods. The product will be relatively scarce, heavily sought after, and thus increasing in value. But this increase in value will be relative to other goods for which it is exchanged, whose ratios will be falling. There can be no general increase in the prices in this system, because they are *relative to each other*.

In a moneyless system, there are no general recessionary or depressionary periods. A *recession* is defined as a period in which output, jobs, and spending fall off. A *depression* is a very severe recession. In Yoda's economy production, by definition, creates an equal amount of purchasing power (the products themselves). If all of the currently earned purchasing power does not get exercised, there will be a falloff of demand for products, and production will decline, that is, a recession will occur.

But if the Iowa computer is vigilant in continually adjusting the interest rate so that all unspent current production is lent to those who want to buy beyond the limits of their current production, then all the purchasing power produced by current production will be exercised. Only if no one wants to borrow unspent production will there be a problem. And as long as the computer is an effective auctioneer of available excess purchasing power, this will not happen. A general recession will be impossible.

This is not to say that in Yoda's system all individual industries and firms will always produce at capacity. Quite the contrary. Firms and industries producing products that the general population does not want will experience hard times. The exchange ratios of their products with others will fall as long as they produce beyond the market's demand. Those working in, managing, and owning factories in the blighted areas will find their products are able to buy less and less of other things. They will eventually decide to switch to other uses of their resources; but in the meantime they will see their output decline and will suffer losses. But there will not be a general recession. Product demand will be strong in other areas, and the profitability of producing in those areas will be on the rise as the exchange ratios move in their favor.

To: Readers interested in barter in the present—day United States
From: JWE

The idea of a barter system in the United States is not totally unrealistic. As reported in the *Wall Street Journal*, there is at least one not-so-small corporation called Barter Systems, Inc., that arranges barter as its line of business. In 1980, this company arranged more than 100 million dollars of barters, up from only 0.9 million dollars four years ago. Helping others to do business without money is a growth industry! The firm recently helped a tire company trade a jet airplane for 1.3 million dollars worth of coal. In a separate development, the *Detroit Free Press* recently offered readers a free three-line advertisement proposing barter exchanges. One reader wanted to swap dog grooming for plumbing. Another offered religious instruction in exchange for food. And, recently, the Civil Aeronautics Board granted airlines permission to barter airline tickets for goods and services they use. We do not have the big computer in Iowa, but is all this interest and activity an early sign of it?

The peek into Yoda's world shows that money is a necessary condition for inflation and depression. This is not to say that in a world with money we *must* have inflation and depression. But, we would not have problems of inflation or depression without money. Money exposes us to two disabling economic viruses. Is it worth this basic cost?

If we had the hypothetical Iowa computer fully operating, the answer probably would be, "No, it isn't." But the Iowa computer is not a reality. And in the absence of such a computer, money lets us live in a way that roughly resembles the world of Yoda. It enables easy exchange of goods, allows the storage of purchasing power, and gives a uniform value to everything by a simplified set of money prices. Money enables a modern, specialized, and industrialized society to function smoothly, efficiently, and at a high level of activity. At present, this powerful function outweighs the costs of a money society. Part of the answer to the question, "Is money worth its cost?" is associated with the issue of whether we can effectively control the problems of inflation and recession associated with money.[5]

**Important Ideas in This Chapter**

1. Money has three essential functions. It functions as a medium of exchange, allowing one good to be exchanged for another at different points in time and in different places. Money is a store of value in this regard, enabling the value of goods exchanged to be accumulated

5. The emphasis in this sentence is on *can*. We have not always controlled inflation and depression in the past. But that may be the result of not doing what we should have done. The economic question is whether we *can* do it. Whether we *will* do it is a political question.

and carried over in time. Money also is a standard unit of account that enables a comparable value to be placed on diverse goods and services.

**2.** Gold and silver in the past have been the basis for money because of their intrinsic value, because of the immediate faith in them held by the public, and because of their naturally controlled supply. In the United States, the development of money has steadily deemphasized the role of precious metals to the point where there is at present no connection between U.S. money and gold and silver.

**3.** In a barter system, money is not present. Goods trade for goods. Because of this, the total amount of goods produced becomes the total purchasing power. There is always just enough purchasing power available to buy what has been produced, because goods are directly exchanged for goods.

**4.** A barter system eliminates the possibility of inflation, recession, and depression. Inflation is not possible because, among other reasons, there is no general level of prices in barter, so that it is impossible for the price of things to rise.

**5.** Depression is impossible under barter as long as a credit market operates to channel savings into the hands of borrowers.

**6.** The costs of a money economy are essentially the potential for inflation and depression. The benefits are those of convenience and efficiency associated with a modern industrialized society.

**Discussion Questions**

**1.** The chapter talks about the use of cigarettes as money in a prison. Can you think of other examples from the real world in which things other than currency were or are used as money?

**2.** If checks are considered money under the government's definition, why not credit cards? After all, in some retail stores, in order to pay by check you have to show a credit card. Where do credit cards fit in?

**3.** Can you see any disadvantages of Yoda's barter system? Would you want to live under it?

**4.** What would happen in a barter system if the exchange ratios could not change over time? Would the result be advantageous?

**5.** If Yoda gets a raise from 4.89 percent to 5 percent, does this mean that some other worker gets less? Is it true that for one person's share of real production to rise, another's must fall? What are the implications for wage increases in the United States?

**Suggested Readings**

Interested in the history of the development of money in the United States? A good source of facts and figures is Paul Studenski and Herman E. Kroos, *Financial History of the United States*, 2d ed., New York: McGraw-Hill, 1963.

For an analysis of the stock of money and its individual components, plus something of a history of the Federal Reserve, see Milton Friedman and Anna Schwartz, *Monetary History of the United States*, New York: National Bureau of Economic Research, 1956.

## CHAPTER 2

# Banking in the United States—Some Basics

CHAPTER OUTLINE

IMPORTANT TERMS

commercial banks
banking institution
balance sheet
net worth
demand deposit
financial intermediary
default risk

interest-rate risk
Federal Reserve Board
reserve ratio
required reserve ratio
check-clearing process
deposit multiplier
float

## MEMO

To:      All readers
From:    JWE

These days, banks are not the only ones doing banking. Savings and loan associations, mutual savings banks, and credit unions are joining conventional banks as institutions where banking functions are performed. What are these banking functions and how are they performed? These questions are the initial concern of this chapter. In it, you can read and think about the economic functions performed by banking institutions.

Banking institutions are responsible for issuing a large part of the nation's money supply. In this chapter, you will read about how this is done. To understand how banking institutions create money, you will read about the role of bank reserves in money creation and how the government regulates and oversees the process. And finally, you will learn about bank float, an intriguing and important facet of modern banking.

Conventional banks, such as Chase Manhattan, are referred to as *commercial banks*. In 1980, sweeping changes were made in U.S. banking laws that have resulted in savings and loan associations and mutual savings banks assuming a new role that is quite similar to that of commercial banks.

As a result of this entry of new institutions into the business of banking, it is a growing problem to pinpoint which financial institutions are banks and which are not. The most enduring approach to the problem is to define a *banking institution* as one that performs certain essential banking functions. Then we can answer the question "What is a bank?" by deciding whether these essential functions of a banking institution are being performed.

Just what are these essential functions? There is no better way to find out than to ask a couple of bankers. We now join a hypothetical interview with two bank managers, Richard Schnell and Mary Wehrley.

## WHAT DO BANKING INSTITUTIONS DO?

*Interviewer:* Mr. Schnell, what do you see as the essential functions your bank performs?

*Mr. Schnell:* Let's go back to the beginning. My great grandfather started this bank in Deadwood, North Dakota in the days of the Wild West. In those days, one of the important functions of a bank was to provide a safe place to store money. With so many pistol-carrying outlaws roaming around, it was not a good idea to carry around much silver or gold coin or dust (all of which were used as money in those days) unless you were prepared to fight for it. So the bank was originally a place where people could safely keep their money.

*Interviewer:* But why were banks willing to do this? Did they enjoy fighting with bank robbers?

*Mr. Schnell:* No, some charged a fee. However, banks found they could safely lend out some of the money that people brought in. This way, banks could earn interest on the townsfolk's money being stored in their vaults.

*Interviewer:* But what if the people wanted this money back?

*Mr. Schnell:* Well, our bank soon got a pretty good idea of the amount of new money coming in compared with the amount people wanted to withdraw. And great granddaddy just had to make sure that he had enough on hand for this purpose. Now, if more withdrawals than deposits occurred on a steady basis, our bank would have had to reduce the amount of loans we extended. As loans came due, we would not renew them. By not renewing a loan, we convert it back into money. Actually, having enough gold on hand was seldom much of a problem from what I am told.

*Interviewer:* Why is that?

*Mr. Schnell:* The flow of gold coin was largely a closed loop. Let me illustrate. Suppose a rancher comes in to borrow a hundred dollars to buy lumber to build a new corral. Our bank arranges a loan and the rancher walks out with five twenty-dollar gold pieces. He takes this money to the Deadwood Lumber Company and buys the lumber with it. That same evening, Jed Smith, owner of the Deadwood Lumber Company, brings the hundred dollars in to the bank to be deposited to his account for safekeeping. So, by nightfall, our bank has the five twenty-dollar gold pieces back that it loaned out that morning. We were, after all, the only bank in town.

*Interviewer:* I'm not sure I completely follow your example.

*Mr. Schnell:* I was afraid of that. It's because you don't think in terms of balance sheets as we bankers do.

*Interviewer:* I'm afraid I don't know what a balance sheet is all about.

*Mr. Schnell:* A *balance sheet* shows the assets, liabilities, and net value of a business at a set point in time. Let me illustrate by describing how my great granddaddy started the Deadwood Bank and how his balance sheet looked when he did it. First, he got on a stagecoach to Deadwood with $800 he had inherited. For $750 he bought a building, some cabinets, equipment, and a vault. (Things were cheaper then.) He had $50 in gold coin left, which he put in his new vault. The next day, he opened for business. Figure 2.1 shows his balance sheet as it looked when he was about to open for business. The bank's assets are the value of the building, equipment, and the gold coin. At this point, the bank has no debts or other obligations, and therefore has no liabilities. Great granddaddy's original $800 is called net worth. *Net worth* is the difference between total assets and total liabilities. Because net worth is defined as the difference between assets and liabilities, total assets will always be equal to liabilities *plus* net worth. It's true by definition. So balance sheets always balance.

On the first day of business, the townsfolk brought in $600 in gold coin to be stored in the bank's vault. In return, they got deposit receipts entitling them to retrieve their money whenever they wanted. As far as balance sheets go, these deposits are called *demand deposits,* where the "demand" part refers to the idea that the townsfolk's gold is redeemable upon demand. Demand deposits are assets to the townsfolk, but liabilities to the bank, because the bank owes this money to its depositors upon their demand.

How the balance sheet looked at the end of opening day is shown in figure 2.2. Assets now include the new $600 in gold, while new liabilities in the form of the accompanying $600 in demand deposits now balance off that entry.

*Interviewer:* I get the picture, but where do loans come in?

*Mr. Schnell:* Glad you asked that. Let's suppose that the $100 loan we talked about earlier was the first the bank made. Here's how the balance sheet would change. When the rancher got the $100, the following entries would be made on the asset side of the balance sheet:

| ASSETS | | LIABILITIES AND NET WORTH |
|---|---|---|
| Gold coin in vault | − $100 | |
| Loan | + $100 | |

Keep in mind that the loan is an asset for our bank. It is an IOU that we own, and it has a market value. Loans can be bought and sold by financial institutions much like used cars. So a loan is just as much an asset to us as your car is to you. In fact, a loan earns income while gold in the vault doesn't earn a penny. So shifting assets out of money and into a loan represents a profitable move for the bank.

*Interviewer:* How about the closed loop and Jed from Deadwood Lumber?

| ASSETS | | LIABILITIES AND NET WORTH | |
|---|---|---|---|
| Gold coin in vault | $50 | Net Worth | $800 |
| Building, equipment | $750 | Total liabilities and net worth | $800 |
| Total Assets | $800 | | |

FIGURE 2.1.
Pre-Opening Balance
Sheet.

*Mr. Schnell:* When Jed brings the $100 he got from the rancher into the bank for deposit, here's how we handle the books.

| ASSETS | | LIABILITIES AND NET WORTH | |
|---|---|---|---|
| Gold coin in vault | +$100 | Demand deposits (Jed) | +$100 |

At the end of the day, we incorporate these pluses and minuses into our balance sheet (figure 2.3). Notice that the gold in the vault is the same at the end of the day as at the start. (We got our gold back.) However, we now have a new asset, a $100 loan, and we have increased a liability, the demand deposit, by the same amount.

*Interviewer:* It looks to me as if you could have accomplished the same thing by just giving the rancher a deposit in his account rather than the five gold pieces. Then he could have signed the deposit over to Jed who could have put it in his account at the bank. The gold could have stayed in the vault. It would have been much safer than having the rancher and Jed traveling those dangerous streets of Deadwood with all that money jingling in their pockets.

*Mr. Schnell:* How perceptive. That's exactly what we started doing some time later. Even now, when we make loans, we do so by just adding funds on paper to a customer's checking account. (A checking account and a demand deposit are two names for the same thing.) Then the customer spends the newly borrowed money by writing a check drawn on his or her account. After that . . .

*Ms. Wehrley:* Sorry to interrupt, Rick, but you are passing over a second fundamental function of banking institutions, which is what this gentleman asked about in the first place.

*Mr. Schnell:* What are you talking about?

*Ms. Wehrley:* That of creating money.

| ASSETS | — | LIABILITIES AND NET WORTH | |
|---|---|---|---|
| Gold coin in vault | $650 | Demand deposits | $600 |
| Building, equipment | $750 | Net worth | $800 |
| Total assets | $1,400 | Total liabilities and net worth | $1,400 |

FIGURE 2.2.
Balance Sheet after
Opening Day.

FIGURE 2.3.
Balance Sheet after a
Loan Is Made.

| ASSETS | | LIABILITIES AND NET WORTH | |
|---|---|---|---|
| Gold coin in vault | $650 | Demand deposits | $700 |
| Loan | $100 | Net worth | $800 |
| Building, equipment | $750 | Total liabilities and net worth | $1,500 |
| Total assets | $1,500 | | |

*Interviewer:* Pardon, but I'm not following this, Ms. Wehrley. Could you explain?

*Ms. Wehrley:* Sure. We define money to be currency plus demand deposits. When banks write entries in people's checking accounts in order to make a loan to them, they are bringing about an increase in the amount of money outstanding. The point is, if banking institutions are creating and giving to people demand deposits that are being used to pay bills, then banking institutions are creating money. The result is no different than if banks minted up gold coins. Creating money is an important function of banks.

*Interviewer:* Can banks do this whenever they want?

*Ms. Wehrley:* No, an agency of the government called the Federal Reserve regulates the amount of demand deposits we can issue. But *we* do the issuing, not the government.

*Mr. Schnell:* The Federal Reserve is an institution somebody should do something about. Let me tell you . . .

*Ms. Wehrley:* Sorry to interrupt again, Rick, but the third of the major functions of banking institutions will go unnoticed if you get going on the Federal Reserve system. This gentleman can find out more about the Federal Reserve on his own, by reading a book on money and banking. The third main function of banking institutions is to act as a *financial intermediary* between households and business. Households are the only sector of the U.S. economy that regularly save a portion of their income. And most households want to invest their savings in very safe and highly liquid ways. They typically do not want to take risks with their savings. On the other hand, business usually wants to borrow funds to finance new building and equipment projects as well as to support inventories and customer credit. These business loans are somewhat less liquid in that they are not easily sold if the need arises. They are also risky in that the business borrowers sometimes go bankrupt and thus cannot pay the loans back. We banking institutions are in the middle. We take the savings that households bring us in return for safe and liquid deposits that we originate. Then we invest these savings in the more risky and less liquid securities of business and the government. Now keep in mind that commercial banks such as ourselves don't do much long-term financing of business money needs. That is left to other banking and financial institutions, most notably insurance companies and some mutual funds and financial investment trusts. We are more into financing the short-term needs of business. But the principle is the same. We obtain our funds in a way that gives no risk to households, but we invest it in a way that involves taking some risk on our part. Banking institutions are fundamentally in business to bear this kind of risk.

*Interviewer:* Very interesting, but could you be a little more specific.

*Ms. Wehrley:* Sure. Figure 2.4 shows a contemporary balance sheet for Rick's Deadwood Bank. Notice that the balance sheet has gotten more complex in the years since 1870, but it isn't fundamentally different. Assets now include reserves (required by law), short-term notes and bonds, business loans, home mortgages, and buildings and equipment. Besides demand deposits, liabilities include time deposits (such as savings accounts) and certificates of deposit, which are longer-term savings accounts. There are two key things to note about this balance sheet. First, the sources of money to us are basically our liabilities. Second, the sources of our liabilities are about the same as they were in the days of the Wild West. They come mostly from households. We use these funds to buy assets. So our assets basically show what we have done with the household savings that have been deposited with us. As you see, we have invested in the securities of government and business, as well as in home mortgages.

In making such investments with our depositors' funds, we bear a sizable risk. Here's why. The money households deposit with us can be claimed by them either when they want it (demand deposits), after a short waiting period (savings accounts), or immediately upon forfeiture of some interest (certificates of deposit). The government even insures these deposits against default by us. So households take no risk that they will lose the funds they deposit with us. The *default risk,* or risk that we will not make good on our promise to repay, is zero. By contrast, we get no such guarantee from most of those to whom we loan money.

| ASSETS | | LIABILITIES AND NET WORTH | |
|---|---|---|---|
| Reserves | $210,000 | Demand deposits | $1,400,000 |
| Currency | 105,000 | Time deposits | 2,001,000 |
| Short-term notes | 1,200,000 | Certificates of deposit | 840,000 |
| Government bonds | 900,000 | Net Worth | 930,000 |
| Business loans | 1,209,000 | Total liabilities and | |
| Home-mortgage loans | 800,000 | net worth | $5,171,000 |
| Building, equipment | 747,000 | | |
| Total assets | $5,171,000 | | |

FIGURE 2.4.
Balance Sheet—
Deadwood Bank.

Besides shouldering the default risk on the loans and other notes we hold, we bear another kind of risk as well, called *interest-rate risk*. This is the risk that we will have to sell a bond or note at a loss before it matures. Let me illustrate. If we own a government bond and the rate of interest in the market goes up, our bond goes down enough in price that it yields the same as newly issued bonds. If we have to sell it during such a time, we take a loss.[1] The chance of this loss is our interest-rate risk.

Fundamentally, we create highly liquid default-free accounts for households in the form of demand deposits, time deposits, and certificates of deposit, and we buy less-liquid, non-default-free securities such as government bonds, mortgages, and business loans on which we may have to take losses. Bearing both default and interest-rate risks is a fundamental function of banking institutions in the United States.

*Interviewer:* Let me see if I understand this. We have talked about three essential functions of banking institutions. The first is to provide a safe place for the public to store money. The second is to actually create money in the form of demand deposits. The third is to function as a financial intermediary—that is, to bear the risk associated with issuing safe and liquid deposits to households in return for their savings, and to invest the money in the more risky securities of business and government. Is that about it?

*Mr. Schnell:* That's it exactly. I certainly wish the Federal Reserve had thinkers such as you. Then . . .

*Ms. Wehrley:* Rick, please.

*Interviewer:* Thank you both. I think I have it.

## HOW BANKING INSTITUTIONS CREATE MONEY

Modern banking institutions create money in the same general way as the old Deadwood Bank. However, the specifics differ markedly. To understand how it is done in the contemporary United States, you must be familiar with a few key characteristics of our modern system. The first such characteristics is that the *Federal Reserve Board* (the main government body that regulates banking) requires as a matter of law that all banking institutions keep funds either as cash in the vaults or on deposit with them (in a checking account) to back the demand deposits that the institutions have outstanding. For any banking institution, the amount of this required holding of cash and Federal Reserve deposit is determined as a fraction of its demand deposits. Therefore, a key ratio for any banking institution is its *reserve ratio*, defined as follows:

1. You can read more about this in chapter 5.

$$\text{Reserve ratio} = \frac{\text{Vault cash plus reserves at the Federal Reserve}}{\text{Demand deposits}}$$

The Federal Reserve establishes a minimum value that banking institutions must maintain for this reserve ratio, called the *required reserve ratio*.

For larger commercial banks, the required reserve ratio is in the general neighborhood of 12 to 15 percent. At 15 percent, a bank with one million dollars of demand deposits must keep $150,000 either as cash on hand or on deposit with the Federal Reserve. Through the required reserve ratio, the Federal Reserve gains some control over deposit expansion (that is, money creation) by banks. If the Federal Reserve Board feels that banks are expanding demand deposits too rapidly, it has the option of increasing the required reserve ratio, thus requiring banks to either increase the size of their reserve deposit or reduce their demand deposits. The result is that banks must reallocate funds away from assets such as loans and securities and into reserves. As loans fall, so do demand deposits. We discuss this process in more detail in the next section.

Control over demand deposits is not the only function of required reserves. These reserves also provide a means for banks to settle claims against each other. Unlike the Deadwood example of only a single bank, there are typically several banks in the same geographic area, each regularly receives checks drawn on other banks. Consider two banks, which we will call Bank A and Bank B. When a person walks into Bank A and deposits to his account a $100 check written on an account in Bank B, Bank A gives the person credit for $100. But how does Bank A get reimbursed? Does Bank A present the check to Bank B for payment? The answer is no, but the Federal Reserve branch office accomplishes the same thing; and not just for Bank A but for all the other banks in its area of responsibility. Here is where each bank's reserve deposit comes in. Bank A sends the check drawn on Bank B to its district Federal Reserve office where the reserve account of Bank B is reduced by the amount of the check, and the reserve account of Bank A is increased by the amount of the check. When this happens, the following entries are made to the balance sheets of Banks A and B:

**BANK A**

| ASSETS | | LIABILITIES AND NET WORTH | |
|---|---|---|---|
| Reserves | +$100 | Demand deposits | +$100 |

**BANK B**

| ASSETS | | LIABILITIES AND NET WORTH | |
|---|---|---|---|
| Reserves | −$100 | Demand deposits | −$100 |

The reserve accounts of banking institutions are thus used to settle claims arising from the normal practice of banks honoring each other's checks. This process of settling up is called the *check-clearing process.* Our example illustrates a general point. When a bank receives more checks drawn on other banks than its depositors are presenting to other banks, the bank's reserves and demand deposits both rise. However, nothing happens to the total reserves or deposits of all banks combined as a result of this check-clearing process. As in our example, deposits and reserves are repositioned by the check-clearing process, but their total is not changed.

## New Reserves and New Money

The check-clearing process transfers reserves between banking institutions. Some individual bank's reserve ratios rise while others fall. When a bank's reserve ratio rises above the required value, it can reallocate some reserves into profitable uses. Banking institutions usually want to reallocate extra reserves, for the simple reason that their reserve account at the Federal Reserve Bank earns zero interest while the alternative, a short-term bond or a loan, earns the going rate of interest. Profitable banks want to keep their reserve deposit down to the minimum required by law. However, in the case of check clearing, some banks are able to expand their loans while others must contract theirs. For a *net expansion* of loans, demand deposits, and thus, money, to take place, *new reserves must flow into the banking system from an outside source.*

A major source of outside reserves is the Federal Reserve system itself. When the Federal Reserve writes a check to a private citizen, who then deposits it in a bank, that bank's reserves go up when the check is cleared. *But no other bank's reserves go down.* So new reserves are added to the banking system when the Federal Reserve originates a check. Here are the entries made to the balance sheets of the bank receiving the check and the Federal Reserve Bank, assuming that (1) the Federal Reserve bought $500,000 of government bonds from a private bond dealer and paid for them with a check, and (2) the bond dealer deposited the check in Bank A:

**BANK A**

| ASSETS | | LIABILITIES AND NET WORTH |
|---|---|---|
| Reserves | + $500,000 | Demand deposit—bond dealer + $500,000 |

**FEDERAL RESERVE BANK**

| ASSETS | | LIABILITIES AND NET WORTH |
|---|---|---|
| Holdings of bonds | + $500,000 | Reserve deposit—Bank A + $500,000 |

The entries for Bank A are the same as for any check clearing. The bank's reserves and demand deposits go up. However, since the Federal Reserve did the check writing, the other part of the transaction is different from our earlier example. The Federal Reserve Bank shows an increase in an asset (holdings of bonds) of $500,000. It also shows an increase in a liability (reserve deposit of Bank A) by the same amount. Are you surprised that Bank A's deposit at the Federal Reserve is a liability to the Federal Reserve? Keep in mind that a liability is something you owe. Those deposits are money that legally belongs to banks but is being held by the Federal Reserve. So it is a liability just as the deposits of the Deadwood townspeople were liabilities of the Deadwood Bank.

This Federal Reserve transaction has added $500,000 of new reserves to the account of Bank A. How can we expect Bank A to react? One thing is clear. If Bank A formerly had just the required amount of reserves on deposit with the Federal Reserve Bank (before the Federal Reserve's bond purchase) it has more reserves than it needs now. Undoubtedly, Bank A's managers will want to move funds out of their reserve account and into some type of interest-earning investment. This is where the process of expanding the money supply begins to occur.

Suppose Bank A has a backlog of qualified loan applicants to whom it can loan money if it wishes. Our balance sheet entries show that the bank has $500,000 in new deposits and the same amount of new reserves. With a required reserve ratio of 15 percent, Bank A must hold $.15 \times \$500,000 = \$75,000$ of reserves against the new deposit. Thus, $\$500,000 - \$75,000 = \$425,000$ of reserves may be moved out of the bank's reserve account and into a loan. To do this, Bank A negotiates with a borrower a loan for $425,000, opens a checking account for the borrower, and makes a deposit in it of $425,000. The balance-sheet entries for this loan transaction are as follows:

**BANK A**

| ASSETS | | LIABILITIES AND NET WORTH | |
|---|---|---|---|
| Loans | + $425,000 | Demand deposits | + $425,000 |

This transaction is only the beginning of the process of money expansion initiated by the introduction of $500,000 in new reserves. The next move we may expect to take place is on the part of the borrower. The borrower of the $425,000 presumably will spend these funds. Virtually no one borrows just so his checking account will be enlarged. It is a safe assumption that anyone who arranges to borrow money does so to finance the purchase of something. So the next step in this process is that the borrower writes a check for the amount borrowed, using it to buy something such as a new machine or an expansion of factory space. Let us further suppose that the check written by the borrower is deposited in Bank B. Now Bank B sends the check to the Federal Reserve for clearing. When the check clears, Bank B's reserves go up by the amount of the check while Bank A's reserves are reduced by the same amount. The balance-sheet entries are:

**BANK A**

| ASSETS | | LIABILITIES AND NET WORTH | |
|---|---|---|---|
| Reserves | −$425,000 | Demand deposits | −$425,000 |

**BANK B**

| ASSETS | | LIABILITIES AND NET WORTH | |
|---|---|---|---|
| Reserves | +$425,000 | Demand deposits | +$425,000 |

So the $425,000 increase in Bank A's demand deposits was only temporary, going down as fast as it went up. But it was not without impact. Before tracing it further let us sum up the net effect of all three of the transactions made by Bank A. They are grouped together in the following balance-sheet format:

**BANK A—CONSOLIDATED ENTRIES**

| ASSETS | | LIABILITIES AND NET WORTH | |
|---|---|---|---|
| Reserves | +$500,000 | Demand deposits | +$500,000 |
| Loans | +$425,000 | Demand deposits | +$425,000 |
| Reserves | −$425,000 | Demand deposits | −$425,000 |

The net effect on the balance-sheet position of Bank A is thus:

**BANK A—NET CHANGE**

| ASSETS | | LIABILITIES AND NET WORTH | |
|---|---|---|---|
| Reserve | +$75,000 | Demand deposits | +$500,000 |
| Loans | +$425,000 | | |
| Total change | +$500,000 | Total change | +$500,000 |

So Bank A has accomplished what it set out to do—it has moved $425,000 out of reserves and into loans, leaving $75,000 in new reserves to back the new deposit of $500,000. But the story is not finished. Bank B now has $425,000 of new reserves. Its managers do not want to keep these funds in its reserve account any more than Bank A's managers did. So further adjustments take place. Bank B's managers reason that they can safely loan out all but 15 percent of these new reserves, keeping the remainder to back the new $425,000 deposit. So Bank B makes a new loan for $(1 − .15) \times \$425,000 = \$361,250$ by creating a demand deposit as follows:

### BANK B

| ASSETS | | LIABILITIES AND NET WORTH | |
|---|---|---|---|
| Loans | + $361,250 | Demand deposits | + $361,250 |

When Bank B's borrower spends the $361,250, a third round in this process is initiated. Suppose the borrower's check is deposited in a third bank, Bank C. Bank C presents the check for clearing, and upon clearing, it now has the new reserves formerly credited to Bank B. The entries of both banks are:

### BANK B

| ASSETS | | LIABILITIES AND NET WORTH | |
|---|---|---|---|
| Reserves | − $361,250 | Demand deposits | − $361,250 |

### BANK C

| ASSETS | | LIABILITIES AND NET WORTH | |
|---|---|---|---|
| Reserves | + $361,250 | Demand deposits | + $361,250 |

Grouping the entries made on Bank B's books, we have:

### BANK B—CONSOLIDATED ENTRIES

| ASSETS | | LIABILITIES AND NET WORTH | |
|---|---|---|---|
| Reserves | + $425,000 | Demand deposits | + $425,000 |
| Loans | + $361,250 | Demand deposits | + $361,250 |
| Reserves | − $361,250 | Demand deposits | − $361,250 |

The net effect on the balance-sheet position of Bank B is thus:

### BANK B—NET CHANGE

| ASSETS | | LIABILITIES AND NET WORTH | |
|---|---|---|---|
| Reserves | + $ 63,750 | Demand deposits | + $425,000 |
| Loans | + $361,250 | | |
| Total change | + $425,000 | Total change | + $425,000 |

At this point, Bank B is content with the situation, having increased its lending by $361,250 while keeping reserves equal to 15 percent of its new deposit of $425,000. But Bank C has the situation of too many reserves. Accordingly, Bank C increases its lending via demand-deposit creation, keeping 15 percent of the new reserves it acquired, and passing the rest along to a new bank, which continues the process. How far does it go? Since each bank retains 15 percent of the reserves being passed around, the surplus reserves eventually dwin-

dle to nothing, and the process stops. But along the way, a considerable amount of money has been produced.

To calculate the total amount by which demand-deposit money
expands as a result of this process, you could construct a table as
follows:

| Step | Increase in Demand Deposits |
|------|------------------------------|
| 1 (Bank A) | $500,000 |
| 2 (Bank B) | $.85 \times \$500,000 = \$425,000$ |
| 3 (Bank C) | $.85 \times \$425,000 = \$361,250$ |
| . . | . . . |
| . . | . . . |
| . . | . . . |
| $n$ . | . . . |
| Total increase in demand deposits | = $3,333,333 |

Or you could do it an easier way, by taking advantage of some added
insights about this process of demand-deposit expansion viewed from
the perspective of the whole banking system.

### Reserves and Demand
### Deposits—View from the Top

In following $500,000 of new Federal-Reserve-supplied reserves from
bank to bank, we just saw that each bank obtained the new reserves
in the course of obtaining new deposits. Thus, each bank could not
pass along all of the reserves it had obtained, but needed to retain
some to back the new deposit. If each bank kept just enough reserves
to back its new deposits, then when the process had run its course,
the new reserves put into the banking system would be 15 percent
of the total new deposits created. If the newly introduced reserves
were more than 15 percent of the deposits created, then some banks
would have more reserves than they needed, and demand-deposit
expansion would continue. So we may safely reason that by the time
the new reserves are fully absorbed into the banking system, the
following relationship will hold:

$$\Delta reserves = (r_d) \times \Delta demand\ deposits$$

where the symbol $\Delta$ refers to the "change in" and $r_d$ refers to the
required reserve ratio. This equation simply says that upon full adjustment, the amount of any new reserves put into the banking system
will be just adequate to fulfill legal reserve requirements, which are
given by $(r_d) \times \Delta demand$ deposits. If this is not the case, then
demand-deposit expansion will continue. Since we usually know the
amount of new reserves put into the system and the required reserve
ratio, it is the amount of demand-deposit expansion that we want to
determine. Solving for $\Delta demand$ deposits, we obtain:

$$\Delta demand\ deposits = \frac{1}{r_d} \times \Delta reserves$$

So for our example where we had initial new reserves of $500,000 and a required reserve ratio of .15, the amount of demand-deposit expansion is $(1/.15) \times \$500,000 = \$3,333,333$.

The term in parentheses $(1/r_d)$ is sometimes referred to as the *deposit multiplier*, since it shows by how much demand deposits can expand when reserves expand. Do not forget that demand deposits are part of the money supply. When banks expand demand deposits, they are by definition expanding the nation's official money supply.

One important aspect of the process of money expansion is that bank lending expands along with it. Banks have no interest per se in expanding the nation's money supply. They do have an interest in maintaining the lowest legal reserves they can, and making new loans is one way to transfer funds out of zero-earning reserves and into interest-earning accounts. The creation of demand deposits comes about as a by-product of the banking industry's use of new reserves to expand lending and credit. Generally (as in our example), credit expansion and money expansion go hand in hand.

## Deposit Contraction

So far, this discussion has been exclusively about expansion of demand-deposit money as a response to more bank reserves. What about the other side of the process—that of contracting money when bank reserves fall? To trace through a deposit contraction, suppose the Federal Reserve sells $500,000 of government bonds from its portfolio to a private bond dealer, receiving a check drawn on Bank A in payment. The check says "Pay to the order of the Federal Reserve five hundred thousand dollars." To whom does the Federal Reserve present this check for payment? The answer is, nobody; instead it reduces Bank A's reserve account by the amount of the check. Bank A now has $500,000 less in reserves. If Bank A held no reserves in excess of its requirements prior to this transaction, it is now deficient in reserves. The balance-sheet entries for the bond sale are:

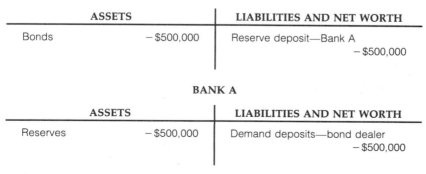

**FEDERAL RESERVE BANK**

| ASSETS | | LIABILITIES AND NET WORTH | |
|---|---|---|---|
| Bonds | $-\$500,000$ | Reserve deposit—Bank A | $-\$500,000$ |

**BANK A**

| ASSETS | | LIABILITIES AND NET WORTH | |
|---|---|---|---|
| Reserves | $-\$500,000$ | Demand deposits—bond dealer | $-\$500,000$ |

How can Bank A's managers respond to this situation of deficient reserves? Basically, they can reduce their level of total lending. Bank

A, like other banks, can be presumed to have some loans maturing each week. At the same time, Bank A makes some new loans each week. When the number of new loans Bank A makes is more than the number of loans that mature, total lending expands. When there are less new loans than maturing loans, total lending falls.

But how does reducing loans help reserves? Suppose Bank A has a $600,000 loan maturing at the beginning of this week. Its managers look over the situation, noting that reserves have fallen by $500,000 along with demand deposits. The fall in demand deposits reduced required reserves by $.15 \times \$500,000 = \$75,000$. So required reserves are deficient by $\$500,000 - \$75,000 = \$425,000$. Suppose at the beginning of the week the bank receives a check from the borrower for $600,000 drawn on Bank B in full payment of the maturing loan. Alternatively, the borrower could have put the $600,000 in his account in Bank A and written a check on it. The results are the same.[2] Bank A's reserves will go up by $600,000 when the check from Bank B clears the Federal Reserve. The balance-sheet entries are:

**BANK A**

| ASSETS | | LIABILITIES AND NET WORTH |
|---|---|---|
| Loans | − $600,000 | |
| Reserves | + $600,000 | |

**BANK B**

| ASSETS | | LIABILITIES AND NET WORTH | |
|---|---|---|---|
| Reserves | − $600,000 | Demand deposits | − $600,000 |

Bank A's managers now conclude that the $425,000 reserve deficiency has been more than offset by the $600,000 in new reserves from the maturing loan, allowing new loans to be made in the amount of $\$600,000 - \$425,000 = \$175,000$.[3] When these loans are made (by opening new checking accounts), the balance-sheet entries are:

**BANK A**

| ASSETS | | LIABILITIES AND NET WORTH | |
|---|---|---|---|
| Loans | + $175,000 | Demand deposits | + $175,000 |

2. Or the bank could just reduce the borrower's checking account by the amount of the maturing loan.

3. The simplist (and most unrealistic) possibility would be that the maturing loans equal $425,000, exactly the amount of the reserve deficiency. Then no new loan extensions are made.

When the newly borrowed funds are spent, and the resulting check deposited in Bank B and cleared through the Federal Reserve, the further entries are:

### BANK A

| ASSETS | | LIABILITIES AND NET WORTH | |
|---|---|---|---|
| Reserves | − $175,000 | Demand deposits | − $175,000 |

### BANK B

| ASSETS | | LIABILITIES AND NET WORTH | |
|---|---|---|---|
| Reserves | + $175,000 | Demand deposits | + $175,000 |

By now Bank A and Bank B have had a number of balance-sheet adjustments, which have cured Bank A's reserve deficiency. Consolidating the changes shows how.

### BANK A—CONSOLIDATED ENTRIES

| ASSETS | | LIABILITIES AND NET WORTH | |
|---|---|---|---|
| Reserves | − $500,000 | Demand deposits | − $500,000 |
| Loans | − $600,000 | Demand deposits | + $175,000 |
| Reserves | + $600,000 | Demand deposits | − $175,000 |
| Loans | + $175,000 | | |
| Reserves | − $175,000 | | |

The net change on the books of Bank A is:

### BANK A—NET CHANGE

| ASSETS | | LIABILITIES AND NET WORTH | |
|---|---|---|---|
| Reserves | − $75,000 | Demand deposits | − $500,000 |
| Loans | − $425,000 | | |

From this, we see that Bank A has cured its reserve deficiency by reducing its lending. Because the $600,000 maturing loan has been replaced by only $175,000 of new loans, the amount of loans outstanding has gone down by $425,000. With $425,000 of new reserves raised by loan contraction, the net fall in reserves is reduced to $75,000. And reserves could legally fall by $75,000 since demand deposits have fallen by $500,000. So Bank A's reserve position is in balance.

But what about the ripple effects? Let us look at the entries in the books of Bank B.

**BANK B—CONSOLIDATED ENTRIES**

| ASSETS | | LIABILITIES AND NET WORTH | |
|---|---|---|---|
| Reserves | − $600,000 | Demand deposits | − $600,000 |
| Reserves | + $175,000 | Demand deposits | + $175,000 |

**BANK B—NET CHANGE**

| ASSETS | | LIABILITIES AND NET WORTH | |
|---|---|---|---|
| Reserves | − $425,000 | Demand deposits | − $425,000 |

Now Bank B has inherited Bank A's reserve deficiency, only the amount is $425,000 instead of $500,000. Because of the fall in demand deposits, Bank B's required reserves have gone down by .15 × $425,000 = $63,750. But Bank B's actual reserves have gone down by $425,000. So Bank B's reserve deficiency is $425,000 − $63,750 = $361,250. This is the amount by which Bank B must reduce its lending in order to raise reserves to cover this deficiency. When Bank B cuts its lending by this amount and clears the resulting checks through the Federal Reserve, its net change in balance-sheet position is:

**BANK B—NET CHANGE**

| ASSETS | | LIABILITIES AND NET WORTH | |
|---|---|---|---|
| Reserves | $63,750 | Demand deposits | − $425,000 |
| Loans | − $361,250 | | |

Now some other bank has the problem of deficient reserves. This bank will now have to reduce its lending, and so forth.

The picture that emerges is the mirror image of the process of deposit and lending expansion. In the former case, the excess reserves were passed from bank to bank, eventually all being absorbed as required reserves to back demand deposits. In the case of deposit contraction, the reserve deficiency is passed from bank to bank, until the total decline in demand deposits eliminates the deficiency. In either case, the change in reserves touches off bank actions that lead to magnified changes in demand-deposit money in the same direction. In our example, the initial Federal Reserve action lowered demand deposits by $500,000. The reaction of Bank A to this situation resulted in Bank B's demand deposits falling by $425,000. Bank B's reaction resulted in demand deposits of another bank falling by $361,250, and so forth. Thus, the deposit multiplier works in the negative direction also, leading to a total contraction in demand-deposit money equal to the fall in reserves multiplied by the reciprocal of the required reserve ratio.

## Complications in
## Deposit Expansion
## and Contraction

To make the process of money expansion and contraction as easy as possible to see, we have assumed that some of the complicating factors involved in deposit changes in the real world are either constant or changing by small amounts. To gain a fuller appreciation of how the process works, you should be aware of these factors.

The first has to do with deposits other than demand deposits. Banks in the United States actually have to hold reserves against time deposits, savings deposits, and other forms of liabilities. In other words, besides the reserve requirements established for demand deposits, there are reserve requirements for other bank liabilities. The reserve account of banks must cover all these requirements. For example, when time deposits go up, banks need more reserves to cover them. In the examples you are reading about, no provision is made for changes in these other accounts. This amounts to assuming that they will remain the same when demand deposits and loans are being changed in response to changes in reserves. This is not at all unreasonable, but it is also far from a sure thing. To incorporate all this into the analysis would produce a more complex money multiplier and would require assumptions about how time deposits and other reservable liabilities behave when demand deposits change. Incorporating these additional factors would complicate the process of deposit changes, but it would not change the essentials of it.

The second factor omitted in our analysis of deposit expansion relates to the possibility that banks will want to hold extra reserves that enter the system rather than convert them into earning assets. The assumption so far is that banks hold no idle reserves. If idle reserves are held by banks, the process would not work as described. However, with pressures to earn profits, banks have little incentive to just "sit" on idle reserves. Thus, the assumption of fully used reserves that underlies this discussion is quite realistic in the United States.

The third omitted factor deals with the public's demand for currency. If people want to hold more currency, they simply cash more checks and put the money in their wallets. Banks find their supply of currency falling, and they have to "order" more from the Federal Reserve. When they do this, the Federal Reserve gives them more currency but reduces their reserve account in payment. So changes in the public's demand for currency have an impact on bank reserves. In this analysis of demand-deposit expansion, no mention has been made of the effect of changes in the public's desire to hold currency. By building this into the money-multiplier model, we introduce an additional complexity. Again, however, no important changes occur in the essentials of the process by introducing this impact.

## Bond Purchases and Deposit Expansion

The examples of demand-deposit expansion and contraction have assumed that banks react to either excess or deficient reserves by making changes in loans. But what if banks do not have qualified new applicants or do not have sufficient loans maturing to use loans as a way to transfer funds out of reserves into profitable assets? Answer: If banks expand assets other than loans, the ultimate effect is the same, although there are some differences in the way the process works.

Suppose a bank with excess reserves decides to invest the excess in government bonds. To do this, the bank writes a check to a dealer or other private seller of bonds. When the bank's check is deposited in another bank and clears, reserves are transferred to the other bank and the demand deposits of that bank expand by the amount of the deposit. The process proceeds from here just as in our earlier example. The same is true of any other type of earning asset into which unneeded reserves are shifted. So our use of bank loans as an example should be taken as representative of any assets into which banks may wish to expand when surplus reserves are present.

## Bank Float and Deposit Expansion

One point made several times in this discussion of deposit expansion and contraction is that when a bank receives a check drawn on another bank, its reserves go up. Although this is absolutely true, it does not happen immediately in the real world. Actually, it takes a few days for a bank such as our illustrative Bank A to forward a check to the Federal Reserve and for the Federal Reserve to do the necessary accounting to shift funds from one bank's reserve account to another bank's account. Meanwhile, it is still necessary for the bank's books to balance. To get them to do so, banks have an accounting category called "Cash Items in Process of Collection" or what bankers call *float*. What actually happens when Bank A receives a $1,000 check drawn on Bank B is as follows:

### BANK A

| ASSETS | LIABILITIES AND NET WORTH | |
|---|---|---|
| Cash items in process of collection +$1,000 | Demand deposits | +$1,000 |

No changes are made on the books of Bank B at this point because Bank B's managers are unaware that a check has been written by one of their depositors and presented to Bank A. After the check has been processed by the Federal Reserve, it is sent back to Bank B. At this point, Bank B learns that a depositor has written a check and that its reserve account has been reduced. Bank B then makes the following entries:

**BANK B**

| ASSETS | LIABILITIES AND NET WORTH |
|---|---|
| Reserves at the Federal Reserve −$1,000 | Demand deposits        −$1,000 |

At the same time, Bank A learns that Bank B's check has cleared. It makes these entries:

**BANK A**

| ASSETS | LIABILITIES AND NET WORTH |
|---|---|
| Cash items in process of collection −$1,000 Reserves            +$1,000 | |

That is, when the check clears the Federal Reserve's processing operation, Bank A is informed that the check has been credited to its reserves. At this time, Bank A subtracts the money from its float account and adds it to its reserve account. So the float is a temporary holding tank for funds the bank knows will be added to reserves but are not yet officially a part of reserves.

The bottom line is that checks received by a bank and drawn on other banks do add to that bank's reserves, but they do not do so immediately. First they add to float, then to reserves.

**Important Ideas in This Chapter**

1. In the United States, institutions that perform banking functions extend beyond conventional banks to include savings and loan associations and others.

2. A banking institution is best defined in terms of what it does rather than by its title. Three essential functions are performed by banking institutions. They are (1) to provide a safe place to store money, (2) to create money, and (3) to sell highly liquid securities to households, buying the more risky securities of ultimate business borrowers, and assuming the risk involved in doing so.

3. A demand deposit is a liability to banking institutions and an asset to the depositor. It is an account that is payable upon the demand of the depositor, and is accessible by writing checks.

4. Demand deposits are the bank-created component of the nation's money supply.

5. The Federal Reserve Board is the principal governmental body regulating the operation of the nation's banking institutions. This board exerts control over the amount of demand deposits that banking

institutions create, and regulates the credit advanced by these institutions. It also provides for the clearing of checks among banking institutions.

**6.** When new reserves enter the banking system, banks can expand the existing amount of demand deposits by a multiple of the reserves. When reserves are withdrawn from the banking system, deposits must contract by a multiple of the lost reserves.

**7.** The deposit multiplier shows by how much demand deposits can change when reserves change. It is given basically by the reciprocal of the required reserve ratio.

**8.** The deposit-multiplier process works regardless of whether banking institutions originate loans as a means of disposing of surplus reserves, or invest the funds in some other way. Any normal method of shifting funds from reserves to earning assets involves an expansion of demand deposits.

**9.** The bank float is an account used by banks to show the amount of checks due them that are in process of collection at the Federal Reserve. The float is an asset to banks. When a check clears the Federal Reserve collection process, the float drops and reserves increase.

**Discussion Questions**

**1.** Based on what you have read in this chapter, do U.S. commercial banks deserve to make profits as much as, say, a manufacturer of machine tools? Explain.

**2.** What are the "products" sold by a modern banking institution? Explain.

**3.** If the required reserve ratio is 10 percent, how much can money expand when four billion dollars in new reserves are added to the economy by the Federal Reserve?

**4.** If one bank is deficient in reserves, what can it do to correct the situation? Explain.

**5.** If banks in general are deficient in reserves, can they successfully do the same things a single bank in the same situation can do? Explain.

**Suggested Readings**

A more detailed technical discussion of the money-multiplier process can be found in Jerry L. Jordan, "Elements of Money Stock Determination," *Monthly Review*, Federal Reserve Bank of St. Louis (October 1969): 10–19. For a definitive treatise on the subject, see Albert E. Burger, *The Money Supply Process*, Belmont, Calif.: Wadsworth, 1971.

## CHAPTER 3

# A Primer
# on the Federal Reserve

IMPORTANT TERMS

Federal Reserve system
Federal Reserve Board
regional Federal Reserve banks
Federal Reserve districts
open-market operations
open-market policy

discount window
discount rate
"real bills" doctrine
bank panic
The Federal Reserve Bulletin

---

## MEMO

To:       All readers
From:     JWE

The Federal Reserve. It does not refer to the way government employees are supposed to behave. Instead, it is the name of the government body that regulates the U.S. banking industry. The Federal Reserve is the link between the government and its policies and the private banking industry and its profit objectives.

In this chapter, you will read about how the Federal Reserve system is put together. Then, the policy-making activities of the Federal Reserve are discussed. The term *Federal Reserve policy* means the actions taken by the Federal Reserve to influence production, employment, prices, and interest rates in the economy.

The important day-to-day activities of the Federal Reserve are also discussed here. Basically, the Federal Reserve takes care of much of the monetary mechanics that allow the business of banking to proceed smoothly.

In general, this chapter provides you with an overview of how the Federal Reserve works. In terms of the old "forest and trees" analogy, this chapter is a sketch of the whole forest. In later chapters, you will have a chance to examine each tree.

---

Almost every industrialized nation has a governmental agency responsible for the control and guidance of its banking activities. In some countries, banks are run by the government. In others, banks are privately operated but regulated by a governmental body usually called the central bank. In the United States, banks are private corporations set up for profit, owned by shareholders, and regulated by the government.

In that banks are private profit-seeking corporations, the banking industry is not unlike the automobile or textile industries. However, the banking industry is different in one fundamental way. Firms engaged in banking create money in the form of demand deposits. The money-creating function of the banking industry has tended to mingle the public's interest with that of bank shareholders, primarily because of the impact the overall supply of money has on the economy. A specific governmental unit has evolved to regulate banking in a way that looks out for the interests of all involved parties. The governmental body that regulates the U.S. banking industry is called the *Federal Reserve system*.

# JUST WHAT IS THE FEDERAL RESERVE?

The Federal Reserve system has two major parts. The first is the Federal Reserve Board of Governors, or as it is usually called, the *Federal Reserve Board*. The board is a group of seven appointed officials who are responsible for deciding on the policies and regulatory actions to be taken by the Federal Reserve system. Members are appointed for fourteen-year terms by the President of the United States with the advice and consent of the Senate. This procedure is designed so that the members of the board, in making their decisions on Federal Reserve policy, are independent of any particular presidential administration and largely free from political considerations.

The second major part of the Federal Reserve system is the group of *regional Federal Reserve banks* that carry out many of the actions decided on by the board. There are twelve such regional banks, each of which takes care of Federal Reserve business in its geographic area. These areas are called *Federal Reserve districts*. The regional banks do not do banking business with the public. Instead, the regional Federal Reserve banks deal mostly with private banking institutions. Because of this, the regional Federal Reserve banks are sometimes called "bankers' banks."

The activities of the Federal Reserve system fall into two broad categories. First, the Federal Reserve Board decides on and initiates policy regarding the nation's money supply, interest rates, and credit expansion. It then develops and monitors statistical data to see how that policy is being carried out. Second, the regional Federal Reserve banks provide a range of services important for the smooth working of the nation's banking industry.

# POLICY MAKING BY THE FEDERAL RESERVE

The Federal Reserve Board got its charter through a series of banking laws dating back to 1913. At present, the board's policy is directed largely toward regulating the money-creating and credit-expansion capacity of the banking industry. The board uses three tools to carry out this policy.

## Policy Tool 1: Setting Required Reserves

In chapter 2, you read about how the required reserve ratio influences the amount of money that banking institutions can create. The higher the required ratio, the smaller amount of money that banking institutions can create for a certain volume of reserves. The Federal Reserve Board has the power to change the required reserve ratio within

limits established by Congress. Actually, there are several bank liabilities against which reserves must be held, including demand deposits, time deposits, and certificates of deposit. There are reserve
requirements for each of these liabilities. These requirements vary
depending on the size of the banking institution, with larger institutions generally having higher reserve requirements. So the Federal
Reserve Board can make changes in one or more of these required
reserve ratios, and in doing so will influence the amount of money
expansion by banking institutions.

Changing the required reserve ratio can have a powerful impact
on the nation's money supply. To see this, suppose the required
reserve ratio against demand deposits is 15 percent and is increased
by the Federal Reserve Board to 16 percent. Also, suppose that outstanding demand deposits total $200 billion. And assume that when
the required reserve ratio was 15 percent, no excess reserves were
present. Thus, actual and required reserves are .15 × 200 = $30
billion. When the required ratio is raised to 16 percent, these $30
billion of reserves now will support only 30 ÷ .16 = $187.5 billion
in demand deposits. Banks must reduce demand deposits by $12.5
billion. (They would do this by a process similar to that described in
chapter 2). Thus, a small change (1 percent in our example) in the
required reserve ratio brings about a comparatively large change ($12.5
billion in our example) in demand deposits.

This magnified effect of changes in the required reserve ratio makes
it one of the Federal Reserve's most potent policy tools. By changing
required ratios, the Federal Reserve can immediately make the existing level of reserves either more than or less than that legally required.
When a reserve ratio is increased, banks can be forced to scramble to
obtain the newly required reserves. This can be costly, as it may mean
selling securities at possible losses or bidding aggressively for available new funds. In any event, it is bound to be disruptive to the
smooth operations of banks. Perhaps for this reason, changes in required reserve ratios have been made only infrequently (say, less than
once a year) by the Federal Reserve Board.

### Policy Tool 2: Open-Market Policy

In constructing the foundations of the modern Federal Reserve system
in 1913, Congress gave the system the right to accumulate a portfolio
of U.S. government securities. This is not to enable the Federal Reserve to buy all the government debt, thereby keeping government
financing "in-house." Neither is it designed to make the government
wealthy by enabling government to speculate in its own securities.
The legislation has a more fundamental purpose in mind. It is to give
the Federal Reserve Board the power to add or subtract bank reserves
by its purchases and sales of securities from its portfolio. The activities
of buying and selling government securities from the Federal Reserve's portfolio are called *open-market operations*. Decisions on whether

to buy or sell at a particular time constitute the Federal Reserve Board's *open-market policy.*

How do open-market operations work? Why does buying or selling securities from the Federal Reserve's portfolio change the level of bank reserves? You have seen most of what is involved in answering this question in chapter 2, in the discussion of how banks expand and contract the money supply. But that was looking at the picture from the perspective of banking institutions. We now wish to examine the process from the perspective of the Federal Reserve Board.

The key to seeing how security purchases and sales impact on reserves is to understand the way the Federal Reserve pays for them when they buy them, and what they do with payments received when they sell them. When the Federal Reserve buys a security, it writes out a check payable to the seller, exactly as you or I would do upon purchase of the same security. However, the Federal Reserve's check is fundamentally different from ours in its impact on the banking system. When the Federal Reserve's check finds its way to a bank and is presented to the Federal Reserve for clearing, the reserves of the bank presenting it go up, and no other bank's reserves go down. In the case of our check, an increase in one bank's reserves is accompanied by a decrease in the reserves of another. But because the Federal Reserve's check makes no such decrease, total bank reserves rise by the amount of the Federal Reserve's check. The Federal Reserve's books still balance after such an open-market transaction. To see how, suppose the Federal Reserve buys 10 billion in government securities from several different dealers and brokers. Suppose the checks the Federal Reserve wrote in payment are presented to thirty different banks. When they are forwarded to the Federal Reserve for payment, the following entries are made to the balance sheet of the Federal Reserve:

**FEDERAL RESERVE**

| ASSETS | | LIABILITIES AND NET WORTH |
|---|---|---|
| Securities held | + 10 billion | Reserves of thirty banks   + 10 billion |

These balance-sheet entries show that the Federal Reserve expands bank reserves whenever it adds to its holdings of government securities.

When the Federal Reserve sells securities from its portfolio, it receives checks drawn on private banking institutions in payment. When these checks are cleared, the reserves of banks on which they are drawn are reduced. As holdings of U.S. government securities in the Federal Reserve's portfolio are decreased, total bank reserves go down.

It is of some consequence whether the Federal Reserve buys government securities from the public or from the U.S. Treasury in its open-market operations. If the Federal Reserve buys newly issued securities from the Treasury, bank reserves will not be directly increased. This is because the Treasury keeps its checking accounts at the Federal Reserve. The Federal Reserve's check made out to the Treasury will just wind up back at the Federal Reserve to be deposited to the Treasury's account. However, when the Treasury spends the funds in its account (a logical expectation), then the check it originates flows into a commercial bank and adds to bank reserves. So in the case of a security purchase from the Treasury, reserves go up when the Treasury spends the funds. Thus, for the Federal Reserve's security transactions to impact directly on bank reserves, the transactions must be with private holders of securities.

## Policy Tool 3: The Discount Rate

Besides adding or subtracting bank reserves by open-market operations, the Federal Reserve also lends to banks with deficient reserves. Under recent changes in the banking laws, all banking institutions that hold reserves with the Federal Reserve have the privilege of borrowing from the Federal Reserve itself. Banks that borrow from the Federal Reserve are said to be using the *discount window*. The discount window is not an actual window through which the loan is handed to a banker by a Federal Reserve official. The term denotes a loan between the two parties. The Federal Reserve charges interest on such loans.

The rate of interest on Federal Reserve loans to banks is called the *discount rate*. The term evolves from the way bank loans were and still are made by the Federal Reserve. When the Federal Reserve began making loans to banks years ago, it required banks to put up collateral as a condition of the loan. In this arrangement, the Federal Reserve was not willing to loan the full value of securities offered as collateral by a bank, but "discounted" this value in arriving at the maximum loan it would extend. A bank with $500,000 of securities to offer as collateral might only get a loan of $475,000. Thus, the Federal Reserve "discounted" the value of the collateral securities, giving rise to the term *discount rate*.[1]

The discount window provides a way for banks to borrow reserves needed to satisfy reserve requirements. Here is how it works. When such a loan is made, say for $500,000 to Bank A, the balance-sheet entries are:

**FEDERAL RESERVE BANK**

| ASSETS | | LIABILITIES AND NET WORTH |
|---|---|---|
| Loan to Bank A | + $500,000 | Bank A's reserve account<br>+ $500,000 |

1. In fact, often the borrowing bank would offer securities that it had bought at discount. In lending, the Federal Reserve would rediscount the securities. This practice often led to the Federal Reserve's lending rate being called the rediscount rate.

BANK A

| ASSETS | | LIABILITIES AND NET WORTH |
| --- | --- | --- |
| Reserve | + $500,000 | Loan payable to Federal Reserve + $500,000 |

In other words, the Federal Reserve adds the amount of money borrowed directly to the borrowing bank's reserve account, offsetting this added liability with a new loan. The borrowing bank shows its reserves going up along with its liabilities in the form of the new Federal Reserve loan.

These entries show that the discount window is a way that banks can add to their reserves in much the same way that the Federal Reserve can through open-market policy.

However, if the Federal Reserve is not interested in having the new reserves in the banking system, it can take actions that reduce the attractiveness of borrowing reserves, and by doing this can discourage banks from using this way to expand reserves.

The most important tool the Federal Reserve has to change the attractiveness of borrowing at the discount window is the discount rate. The Federal Reserve Board can change it whenever it wishes, and thus alter banks' cost of borrowing. In recent years, another device has been used as well—the surcharge. The Federal Reserve attached a surcharge to the cost of borrowing for large banks and others designated as "frequent users," thus making the interest rate to them several percentage points higher than the rate to smaller banks. This policy was directed toward discouraging large banks from using the window while not scaring off smaller banks that might be in need of borrowed reserves.

A second tool related to the discount window has to do with "attaching strings" to loans made through it. The Federal Reserve can give more than just the new reserves when it makes a loan to a bank. If it sees what it thinks are inappropriate loan policies on the part of the bank, it can issue informal directives or advice along with the loan, or it can attach conditions to the loan relating to a bank's lending policies. Usually, such conditions are concerned with moving the bank's lending policies in a more conservative direction. Upon experiencing this type of counseling, some bank managers contend that when a bank borrows from the Federal Reserve, it not only gets the reserves, but it gets the Federal Reserve Board as an office-mate as well.

## Federal-Reserve Policy, Bank Reserves, and the Money Supply

You have now read about three main policy tools available to the Federal Reserve. They all head in one main direction—influencing

To: Readers interested in the ''real bills'' doctrine
From: JWE

In the past, the Federal Reserve used the discount window as a way to influence the kind of investments banks made. The Federal Reserve did this by placing restrictions on the bank-held securities that banks could use for collateral in borrowing from the Federal Reserve. This in turn was an inducement for banks to invest in the type of security that could be discounted at the Federal Reserve in case the need to borrow at the discount window arose.

The "real bills" doctrine was one of the more specific of these Federal Reserve attempts to influence bank lending policies. Essentially, the goal was to induce banks to lend to business only for what the Federal Reserve called short-term, self-liquidating loans that contributed directly to current production. A self-liquidating loan is one made to business to help it get through a temporary cash flow problem. The normal activities of the business are expected to generate the funds for its repayment. An example of such a short-term, self-liquidating "productive" loan is one made to support a seasonal buildup in inventories, such as a retailer would normally have between Thanksgiving and Christmas. Once the seasonal bulge passed, inventories would be reduced and the money raised would be used to liquidate the loan. The Federal Reserve's policy was that only bank-owned notes and securities arising from such "productive" loans were eligible for discounting. Such securities were referred to as "real" bills, and the Federal Reserve's policy was called the "real bills" doctrine. In recent years, this policy has been abandoned, and the securities eligible for discounting have expanded to include most of the short-term assets held by banks.

how much money banks can create. This is done by either changing the amount of reserves that must be set aside to meet legal requirements, changing the reserves available in the banking system, or changing the cost of borrowed reserves. Changing the required reserve ratio is a way of immediately causing bank reserves either to be free for new lending and deposit expansion (if the ratio is lowered) or to be deficient, requiring a contraction of deposits and lending (if the ratio is raised). Through open-market policy, the Federal Reserve introduces new reserves into the banking system or withdraws existing reserves from it. Changing the discount rate is a way of making bank borrowing of reserves more or less attractive, thus changing the amount of borrowed reserves.

Reserves are the raw material from which banking institutions create money. Thus, the Federal Reserve's tools are all directed toward influencing the amount of money available in the economy. The Federal Reserve's interest in controlling the supply of money stems from the belief by the members of the Board of Governors that the amount of money in the economy plays an important role in determining the pace of inflation, the level of interest rates, and the amount of production taking place in the nation's factories, shops, and mills. Exactly how money relates to these other economic variables is a subject that will have to wait until later. But it is inflation, interest rates, and production that the Federal Reserve Board has its sights set on when it applies the three principal tools available to it.

## NON-POLICY FUNCTIONS OF THE FEDERAL RESERVE

Besides turning policy dials and levers in order to influence the supply of money in the nation, the Federal Reserve system performs four other essential financial functions on a day-to-day basis.

### Providing a Payments Mechanism

The first and most basic of the Federal Reserve's daily activities is to act as the hub of the nation's payments system. About 90 percent of the value of economic transactions that routinely occur each day in the United States are made by check. The remainder are made by using currency. The Federal Reserve system provides check-clearing services that enable check transactions to occur. Each of the regional Federal Reserve banks clears the checks in its district. Check clearing is a massive but virtually unnoticed function performed by the Federal Reserve on an almost round-the-clock basis.

The Federal Reserve issues all of the presently outstanding currency in the form of Federal Reserve Notes. If you look at a bill in your wallet, you will see on it the words, "Federal Reserve Note." This bill was issued by the Federal Reserve and is backed by the assets of the Federal Reserve system. Thus, besides clearing checks, the Federal Reserve provides currency for the remaining cash transactions. It does this at the request of banks, which order currency when they need it for their vaults much as you and I would cash checks. The Federal Reserve is constrained in issuing currency by limits set by Congress.

### Acting As The Treasury's Banker

Besides functioning as the hub of the nation's payments system, the Federal Reserve acts as the fiscal agent for the U.S. Treasury. In other words, the Federal Reserve is the Treasury's banker. The Federal Reserve holds the Treasury's basic bank accounts, and performs banking functions for it much as commercial banks do for the public.

### Supervising Bank Operations

In addition to its other duties, the Federal Reserve system is charged with the responsibility of supervising and overseeing the operations of the nation's banking institutions. In carrying out this duty, the Federal Reserve sees to it that banks are not investing in assets that are too risky for the well-being of depositors. The Federal Reserve continually monitors the liquidity of banks, by maintaining a watchful eye over the assets banks are invested in and the liabilities they have created. If a bank does get into financial trouble and bankruptcy is threatened, the Federal Reserve has the authority to direct the bank to merge with another bank, or even to remove the bank's managers and run the bank itself until a more permanent solution can be found.

These supervisory powers are given to the Federal Reserve to enable it to act as watchdog over the banking system so that the kinds of excesses in lending and investing that led to bank panics (in the early 1900s and during 1929 and 1930 in particular) are avoided. A *bank panic* occurs when the public enmasse comes to believe that its money is not safe in the bank. When most depositors try to draw out their funds over a short time period (say a couple of days), even well-managed banks cannot liquidate enough of their assets to cover the withdrawals. When such "runs" occur on banks, the system crumbles like a house of cards.

In the late 1920s, some banks used depositors' funds to purchase highly speculative stocks. When the value of many such stocks collapsed during late 1929 and early 1930, banks incurred losses which meant that the banks had insufficient funds to cover their deposit liabilities. The Federal Reserve system's present governance over banks is designed to prevent such occurrences long before they erupt in defaults and runs. To further guard against runs on banks, the Federal Reserve system is buttressed by a number of independent deposit insurance corporations that insure deposits against loss. The biggest of these is the Federal Deposit Insurance Corporation (FDIC) which insures bank deposits. Others are the Federal Savings and Loan Insurance Corporation (FSLIC) which insures the deposits of savings and loan associations, and the National Credit Union Association (NCUA) which insures the deposits of credit unions. With the current level of governance by the Federal Reserve and the protection of deposit insurance, there is much less reason for bank "runs" to occur in the contemporary U.S. economy than during the past, when such safeguards were not present.

## Providing Financial Data to the Public

A final function of the Federal Reserve is to provide financial information to the banking and investment community. The Federal Reserve collects and maintains a broad range of financial information, much of which is published in its monthly publication, *The Federal Reserve Bulletin*. The *Bulletin* contains information on the Federal Reserve system, and on the assets and liabilities of banks, savings and loans companies, life insurance companies, and other financial institutions. It contains data on the components of the money supply and bank reserves, and a range of information on the amount of short-term credit issued by firms and by banks. The *Bulletin* also contains information on reserve requirements, the discount rate, and the status of the banking industry concerning actual versus required reserves. Information on interest rates for a broad range of short-term and long-term securities is given, along with data on overall stock and bond prices. In short, the *Bulletin* is a wealth of financial data that is compiled and published as a service of the Federal Reserve system.

**1.** The central bank in the United States is called the Federal Reserve system. It is composed of two main parts. The first is a group of seven appointed officials that make up the Federal Reserve Board of Governors, the main policy-setting and decision-making body for the nation's monetary policy. The second part is a group of twelve regional banks that carry out the functions of the Federal Reserve system.

**2.** The Federal Reserve performs two classes of functions. The first is to set monetary policy regarding a number of key factors that affect the money supply. The second is to provide a range of nonpolicy monetary services.

**3.** The Federal Reserve Board sets the required reserve ratios for various banking-institution deposits within boundaries specified by the U.S. Congress. The required reserve ratio is one of the most potent policy tools available to the Federal Reserve.

**4.** Open-market operations are a major way in which the Federal Reserve Board implements its policies toward money growth. Open-market operations refer to the buying and selling of government securities by the Federal Reserve. When this occurs, bank reserves are either increased (in the case of a purchase) or decreased (in the case of a sale). By open-market operations, the Federal Reserve can directly impact on the amount of reserves in the banking system.

**5.** The Federal Reserve loans reserves to banks through the discount window at an interest rate called the discount rate. Banks with deficient reserves may borrow from the Federal Reserve by this means. The Federal Reserve scrutinizes these loans and the lending practices of the borrowers, and influences lending activities among borrowing banks. The Federal Reserve can raise or lower the discount rate, thus changing the attractiveness of borrowing in order to provide reserves.

**6.** Each of the Federal Reserve's main policy tools impacts on bank reserves, either directly or indirectly. Bank reserves in turn are the raw material that governs the amount of bank-created money. The Federal Reserve's goal in affecting reserves is to impact on production, employment, prices, and interest rates through the influence its policies have on the supply of money in the economy.

**Important Ideas in This Chapter**

7. The Federal Reserve has four major nonpolicy functions that it performs daily. They are: (1) to provide a payments mechanism for the nation's economic transactions; (2) to function as the fiscal agent for the U.S. Treasury; (3) to oversee and govern the operations and management of the nation's banking industry; and (4) to provide a range of financial information to the public.

**Discussion Questions**

1. From what you read in this chapter, if one of the Federal Reserve's three main policy tools had to be eliminated (for whatever reason, which one should it be, if the objective is to reduce the Federal Reserve's power by the smallest amount? Explain.

2. What do you suppose happens when a particular security being held in the Federal Reserve's portfolio matures? What are the balance-sheet entries? How would you expect the Federal Reserve to respond?

3. Is the discount rate higher or lower than rates at which banks lend funds? Look this up in either the *Wall Street Journal* or *The Federal Reserve Bulletin*. What do you make of what you found, as far as bank-management practice is concerned?

4. Judging from what you read in current periodicals, what is the current policy of the Federal Reserve Board? Be as precise as possible.

5. What is the ultimate objective of Federal Reserve policy? That is, what is the most important economic outcome that Federal Reserve actions influence? Defend your answer.

**Suggested Readings**

A treatise on the functions of the Federal Reserve that comes from the "horse's mouth" is *The Federal Reserve System, Purposes and Functions*, Washington, D.C.: Federal Reserve Board of Governors, 1974. A good history of banking under the Federal Reserve appears in an article by Philip Cagan, "The First Fifty Years of the National Banking System," in *Banking and Monetary Studies*, ed. Deane Carson (Homewood, Ill.: Norton), 1969. An encyclopedic treatise on the history of U.S. banking and monetary activities can be found in Milton Friedman and Anna Schwartz, *A Monetary History of the United States, 1867–1960*, Princeton, N.J.: Princeton University Press, 1963.

## CHAPTER 4

# Taking a Reading on the Economy

## CHAPTER OUTLINE

## IMPORTANT TERMS

National Income Accounting (NIA)
  system
Gross National Product (GNP)
services
nondurable goods
durable goods
structures
personal-consumption spending
gross private domestic investment
government spending
net exports
final sales
total labor force
total employment
unemployed
unemployment rate

full employment
Consumer Price Index (CPI)
inflation
deflation
noninflationary
real GNP
GNP deflator
Price of Consumer Expenditures
  (PCE)
recession
expansion
nominal GNP
cyclical GNP
noncyclical GNP

/VIEMO

To:          All readers
From:        JWE

Many people have rather vague notions about what it means to say the economy is going up or down. What does it really mean? And what about inflation? How do we measure it? What is the cost of living you hear so much about? What is the unemployment rate that policy makers seem so concerned about? How do we define a recession, and what happens when the economy goes into one?

Earthshaking questions? Maybe not. But understanding the actual statistical measures involved with inflation, unemployment, and the Gross National Product is important in helping to push back the shroud of mystery that too often accompanies these terms. Much of macroeconomic theory is directed toward understanding how the stock of money relates to prices, employment, and recessions. In this chapter, you can learn about the specific measures used to convert these vague terms into statistical facts. In the process, you can sharpen your understanding of how we define the GNP, inflation, recession, unemployment, and full employment.

Do you sometimes wonder what it really means when an economist says the economy is "going up" or "going down"? What is this thing called "the economy," and how do we know whether it is rising or falling? An economist's fable tells us that before the 1930s government leaders in large cities measured the state of their local economy by counting the number of factory smokestacks in use. The concern of citizens and government leaders about the economy during the depression years of the 1930s stimulated an interest in doing a more precise job of assessing the state of the economy than counting smokestacks. The result was the introduction of the *National Income Accounting* (NIA) system in the United States in the mid-1930s. The national income accounts constitute an array of measures describing the level of total production, income, and spending in the United States. Since their introduction, citizens and government leaders have relied on them heavily to make judgments about whether the economy is going down or up, and what sectors are contributing to the trend. The centerpiece of the NIA system is a measure of overall economic activity called the *Gross National Product,* or more simply, the GNP.

# THE GNP AND ITS PARTS

The GNP is an estimate of the market value of current domestic final production of goods and services. This sentence is packed full of meaning. Let us unpack it and look at it, idea by idea. The *market value* part means that those doing the estimating of the GNP do not quibble over whether things are worth what people are paying for them. If a new car is sold for $9,500, the GNP system assumes its value is precisely that. The word *current* here means that the GNP is designed to reflect production currently taking place. Sales of goods produced in an earlier period are not part of the GNP. This means the sale and purchase of used goods are not reflected in the GNP. However, if a used good is reconditioned or embellished so that its value increases, *the increase* in value is part of the GNP and is considered to be current production.

The word *domestic* in the definition means that the GNP focuses on production in U.S. factories only. The GNP counts how much production is taking place in U.S. work places regardless of who buys the products. Thus, when a U.S. consumer buys a foreign car, the car does not count as part of the GNP; but when a foreign consumer buys a U.S.-produced car, it does count as part of the GNP.

The word *final* in the definition means the GNP is concerned with measuring the volume of production sold to the final user only. Goods such as raw materials or components that are bought for further processing are not part of the GNP. Because of this, the GNP reflects economic activity only when finished products are sold to end users.

## Production Equals Income

There is a simple rule governing the kind of economic activity that contributes to the GNP. *Any activity that produces current income for people, firms, or the government adds to the GNP.* As far as the GNP definition is concerned, production takes place when incomes are earned. Think about the sale of a new car for $10,000. From the car buyer's standpoint, it is an expenditure, and a big one. But from the standpoint of the car dealer, the company that produced it, and the workers who assembled it, it is income. From the standpoint of the GNP accounts, it is production. A hypothetical breakdown of the car's $10,000 purchase price might be as follows:

| | | |
|---|---|---|
| 1. | Wages, salaries | $6,000 |
| 2. | Sales commissions | 700 |
| 3. | Profits: factory | 1,000 |
| | dealer | 500 |
| 4. | Interest, rent | 900 |
| 5. | Depreciation of equipment used in production | 400 |
| 6. | Taxes | 500 |
| | Total incomes | $10,000 |

From this list, you can see that the term *income* in the NIA system does not just mean a person's paycheck. Instead, NIA income means any claim on current production. Accordingly, from the NIA standpoint the government earns "income" when it takes a part of the sales price of the car in the form of a sales tax.[1] Depreciation write-offs associated with the machinery used in production are part of the total income generated by the production of the car, because they represent a claim made on production by those who own the machinery and equipment used.

The logic of this example applies to the entire economy. The GNP is simultaneously a measure of (1) the total production of final goods and services taking place in the United States, and (2) the total income currently generated in the economy.

Statisticians charged with the job of measuring the GNP take advantage of the equality of production and income by building measures of each and cross-checking the two. Specifically, data on incomes earned by all parties are gathered largely from the tax system. These data are used to build an income estimate of the GNP. Figure 4.1 shows how the GNP was distributed as income from 1950 to 1980. The bottom line in the graph shows the amount of income earned as wages and salaries. The next line represents the amount of profits earned by corporations and by noncorporate business. The small sliver of income that comes next is interest income. The uppermost category in figure 4.1 contains depreciation, sales taxes, social-security payments and receipts, and other miscellaneous distributions of production. The top line showing the total of these income components represents the GNP.

The GNP is also broken down into categories according to the kinds of products produced. Figure 4.2 shows this approach. In this graph, the bottom line shows the amount of services produced. *Services* are defined as products used up immediately (or nearly so) upon production. By definition, services cannot be taken home and stored on a shelf. Examples of services are medical treatment, recreational spending, rents, transportation, government functions, and educational programs. Paying for a ski trip is officially counted as buying a consumer service (recreational spending) whereas the cost of the local police force is counted as a governmental service.

The next category of production shown in figure 4.2 is called *non durable goods*. These are goods that last a short period of time, generally less than one year. Unlike a service, they can be taken home and temporarily stored. Nondurable goods include food, clothing, shoes, drinks, cosmetics, home-care products, and personal-care products.

---

1. The income taxes paid by those who earned income in categories 1 through 4 in the list are considered to be a distribution of the income the people earned, and thus are not to be mistaken for the sales tax in category 6.

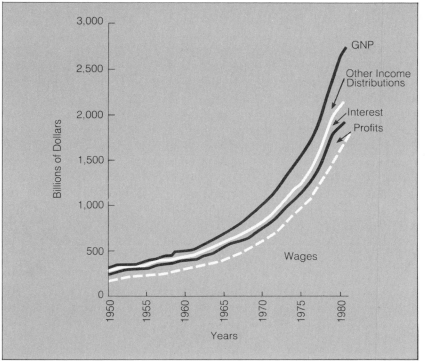

**FIGURE 4.1. Distribution of the GNP To Income Earners.**

The next category in figure 4.2, *durable goods*, includes those products which last upward of a year. Their long service lives and usually high value cause them to be thought of as "possessions" by their owners. Durables include consumer durables such as automobiles, motorcycles, bicycles, furniture, stereo equipment, and appliances. Business-type durable goods include machinery, equipment, and furniture. Finally, durables also include defense equipment bought by the government.

The last line in figure 4.2, *structures*, shows the production of new houses and apartments, business factories, and office buildings. Production of these structures is not included as part of durable goods. They are so much more durable than other durable goods (often having useful lives of thirty years or more) that to add them to durables would be combining two quite dissimilar types of production. Therefore they get their own heading.

The total of services, nondurables, durables, and structures produced adds to the GNP, just as does the sum of wages, profits, interest, and other income distributions. In terms of the graphs, the top line in figure 4.1 and the top line in figure 4.2 are the same. Total final goods and services produced and income earned are indeed the same.

FIGURE 4.2.
Composition of the
GNP by Type of
Production.

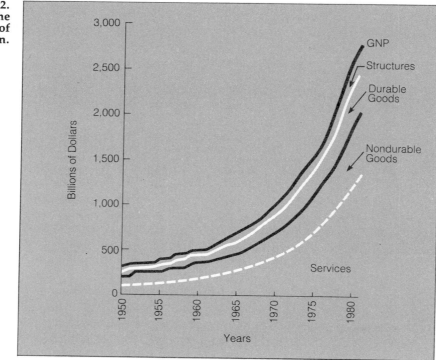

The GNP and Total Spending

Another important part of the NIA system is a bank of data showing who buys the products and services included in the GNP. The groups that buy the nation's production are consumers, business firms, government, and net foreign consumers. Figure 4.3 shows the composition of the GNP broken down by these main spending groups. The first category, *personal consumption spending*, includes the total spent by consumers on durable goods, nondurables, and services. The second category, investment spending, has a more formal name in the NIA system. It is called *gross private domestic investment*. It contains (1) all the spending by business on factories, machinery, and equipment, (2) all the spending on new houses, apartments, and other residential structures, and (3) the amount of inventory change. The change in business inventories is considered to be new investment in working capital. *Government spending* includes all the spending on durable and nondurable goods by federal, state, and local governmental units, plus the cost to all governmental units of the services they provide.

The last category of spending, *net exports*, shows the amount of U.S. production purchased by foreign consumers minus the amount of foreign production bought by U.S. consumers. Production by U.S. firms is what the GNP measures. Net exports makes the necessary import-export adjustment.

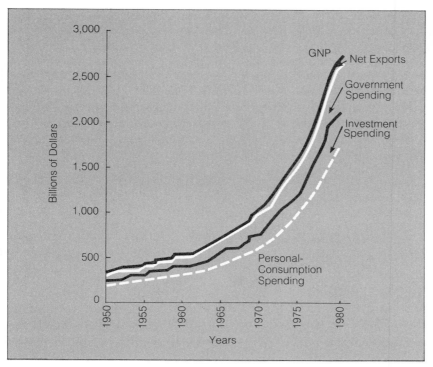

**FIGURE 4.3.
Composition of the
GNP by Spending
Groups.**

The total of personal consumption spending, investment spending, government spending, and net exports makes up the GNP, as does the total of all incomes and the total of all types of products produced. Total spending on the GNP is thus always equal to total production. This does not mean all production will necessarily be sold. Accounting systems cannot equate sales and production.

To illustrate, suppose that consumer spending, government spending, investment spending, and net exports total 2,500 billion dollars during some particular time period, while production of all types of goods and services is 2,550 billion dollars worth over the same period. The GNP counts what was produced. Production was 2,550 billion dollars worth, so that is the GNP. Buyers took home only 2,500 billion dollars worth. The other 50 billion that was produced but not sold accumulated as inventories, largely by default.[2] Now recall that part of the spending category called gross private domestic investment is inventory change. Actual sales to customers were 2,500 billion, but inventory change was 50 billion. Therefore, when inventory change is included as part of investment, then total spending on the GNP equals the GNP. By defining inventory change as part of spending, the designers of the NIA system have created this equality.

2. I say "largely" because producers want to make some inventory investment in order to support expanding sales, or because it is necessary to have more "work-in-process" inventories to support larger production levels. These are intended changes in inventories. Therefore, a portion of any inventory change is "intended," with the remainder being "unintended."

The GNP shows the amount produced. However, because inventory change is added, the GNP does not show how sales across the economy are going. Total production and total sales often vary substantially when recessions are close at hand. *Final sales* is a  measure of total sales of GNP products. It is derived by simply subtracting from the GNP the amount of inventory change. Accordingly, the final-sales measurement shows ups and downs in the combined buying patterns of consumers, firms, governments, and net foreign consumers more directly than the GNP. Economic analysts often use final sales as an early warning signal of changes in the production of GNP goods and services.

## THE UNEMPLOYMENT RATE

The GNP statistics tell a lot about what we are producing, how it is divided up among income earners, and who is buying it. But the GNP data do not touch upon the topic of how many people are at work. Neither does it reveal how many are seeking jobs but not finding them. These are important concerns of U.S. policy makers. Such concerns have given rise to another family of economic statistics designed to measure employment and unemployment. These data are compiled by the U.S. Department of Labor's Bureau of Labor Statistics (BLS).

Figure 4.4 shows the major parts of the BLS data on employment. The starting point in understanding these data is the top line. This shows the total U.S. population over the age of sixteen. Until the start of 1983, members of the military were excluded from this group and from the other employment measures as well. Designers of the statistics did not want military buildups to be a factor in increasing employment. However, the move to an all-volunteer military in the United States has changed this and all eligible people are now included.

The second line from the top in figure 4.4 is what the BLS calls the *total labor force*. It measures the number of people over age sixteen who are seeking jobs. The graph shows that the labor force is calculated by subtracting the group of over-sixteen people not seeking jobs from the total over-sixteen population.

The lowest line in figure 4.4 shows the number of people over sixteen who are employed. This number, called *total employment,* shows how many of those in the labor force have been successful in finding a job. The difference between the labor force and total employment is what the BLS calls *unemployed. The unemployment rate* is the fraction of the labor force that is unemployed.

The unemployment rate is perhaps the most widely publicized of all the BLS statistics. It deserves a second look. Do you see that the unemployment rate is a fraction of the job seekers rather than a fraction of the over-sixteen total population? Therefore, 7 percent un-

To: Chart readers
From: JWE

In looking over figures 4.1, 4.2, and 4.3, did you notice that: (1) the biggest share of the total incomes earned in the United States is in the form of wages and salaries, (2) the biggest category of GNP product produced is services, and (3) the largest amount of the GNP is bought by consumers? Is there any doubt that basically: (1) the U.S. economy is dominated by the economic activities of those who work for a paycheck, (2) we are an increasingly service-oriented economy, with the production of services of one kind or another accounting for about 50 percent of the GNP in 1980, up from about 30 percent in 1950, and (3) we are a consumer-oriented economy in that consumers buy about 60 percent of all that is produced?

Are you surprised that government accounts for a comparatively small share of total spending on the GNP? Well, there is more to government than what you see here. First, about half of the government spending in figure 4.3 is by the federal government. Second, the federal government transfers a large volume of funds from some citizens to others in the form of social-security payments, medicare payments, welfare programs, and interest on government bonds. These transfers are not without impact. It is generally believed that transfer payment recipients spend more of the money than taxpayers would have spent had taxpayers not paid taxes.

employed means that 7 percent of all those seeking jobs are unsuccessful, not 7 percent of the total eligible population. Do you also see the dependence of the unemployment rate upon the size of the non-job-seeking group? These non-job seekers are all the men and women who are of working age but are not looking for work. Some members of this group are (1) students, (2) those with full-time child-care responsibilities, (3) those "finding themselves," (4) those whose spouse is earning enough to give them a choice about whether to work, and (5) those whose accumulated wealth enables them to forsake work as a life's project (sigh). One thing is clear about this non-job-seeking group. For some of its members, being a job seeker or a non-job seeker is a choice that is subject to rapid and frequent change. For some, it is a state of mind that may change between 9:00 A.M. and 5:00 P.M. This makes the measurement of non-job seekers a difficult undertaking, and it makes the resulting measures of the labor force and the unemployment rate fragile economic statistics.

Figure 4.4 shows some broad patterns among job seekers that have significantly altered the meaning of unemployment in the United States. Notice that the growth in the labor force was noticeably slower in the period 1950 to 1964 than in the years 1965 to 1980. Before 1965, the labor force was growing more slowly than the civilian over-sixteen

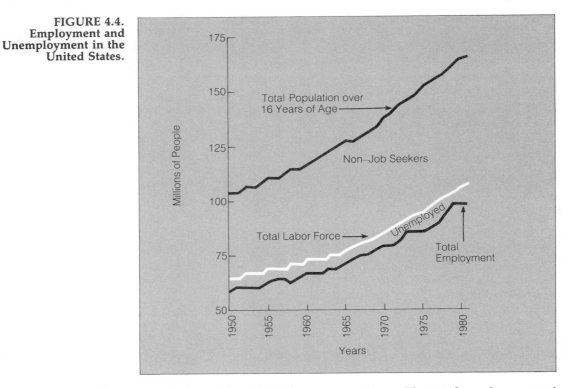

population. After 1965, the reverse is true. The total employment of people grew at a greater rate after 1965 than before, but because of the rapid growth in the labor force, the unemployment rate generally rose in the latter period. Some economists have recently argued that an unemployment rate of 5.75 percent in 1980 is comparable to an unemployment rate of 4 percent in the pre–1965 period, primarily because of the increasing numbers of women entering the labor force in the later period. In other words, a significant increase has occurred in the size of the female job-seeking group.

*Full employment* is a term that comes up frequently in discussions of economic policy, whether such discussions appear in the local newspaper or in a college textbook on money and banking. What does it mean? We can think of full employment as a level of employment where all job seekers are employed except (1) those who are out of work for temporary reasons, such as those who are between jobs, (2) those who are seasonally unemployed, such as pickers or professional athletes, (3) those who lack training sufficient to compete for available jobs, and (4) those who have marketable skills but are geographically immobile.[3] This definition makes it clear that some unemployment will exist at "full" employment. Thus, the term refers

3. This is not the only way full employment can be defined. One of my favorites is that full employment occurs when the number of unfilled jobs equals the number of unemployed people.

to a level of employment that is as good as the economy can do given the level of training, the patterns of work, and the mobility of the work force. It is increasingly difficult to assign a number to the unemployment rate that corresponds to full employment. In the 1960s, numbers close to 4 percent commonly accepted but arbitrary. Some economists have suggested that a comparable full-employment rate for the early 1980s is in the 5.5–6.0 percent range.[4]

## Measuring Inflation

Inflation is one of the most serious economic problems of our time, and is the object of much discussion later in this book. Now, our concern is with seeing how inflation is measured. The primary measure of prices, used to calculate inflation, is the *Consumer Price Index*, or CPI. It is calculated by the *Bureau of Labor Statistics*. What better way to see how the government estimates inflation than to peek in on a talk being given on the subject by a government economist to a group of students.

*Government Economist:* I want to talk with you for a few minutes about how the government measures inflation, and to examine with you that experience that people in the United States have had with inflation since World War II. Let's first define inflation. Who knows how to define *inflation?*

*Student A:* It's when the government is creating too much money.

*Government Economist:* Not really. This is more nearly what *causes* it.

*Student B.* It's when it costs more to live.

*Government Economist:* No, this is a consequence of inflation rather than the definition of it. Inflation is simply a period when prices are rising in a persistent manner and by significant amounts.

*Student A* (whispering to Student B): That's just great. What does it mean? The words *persistent* and *significant* can mean anything.

*Student B* (whispering back to Student A): I agree, but listen—I think he's getting to that.

*Government Economist:* Of course, for this definition to be applied we need some agreement on what constitutes a "persistent" price rise and what "significant means. A rule of thumb that works well is

---

4. The rise is often accounted for by noting that the rapidly growing female part of the labor force is less mobile geographically than the average job seeker. Thus, a higher unemployment rate evolves as a result of greater overall geographic mismatches between job seekers and jobs.

that rising prices for more than a year are considered persistent and that prices rising at more than a 4 percent rate are rising significantly. So, basically, a pattern of continuing price increases at a rate of 4 percent or more is a good working definition of inflation.

*Student C:* Do you mean a 4 percent annual rate?

*Government Economist:* Yes. If prices actually rise by .5 percent over a month, we multiply that by twelve months to get an annual rate. Thus, the .5 percent in a month translates into a 6 percent annualized inflation rate. When you hear the newspaper reports on the latest Consumer Price Index, this is the procedure followed. The CPI, as it is called, is calculated every month. So, if it rises by 1 percent from month to month, this is reported as a 12 percent inflation rate.

*Student B:* What is the CPI exactly?

*Government Economist:* It is the main index of the prices of consumer goods used by the government and others to calculate the cost of living. When it rises by 10 percent, the cost of living is assumed to rise by 10 percent. The CPI is defined to be the price tag for a large basket of goods (several hundred items) that is regularly bought by a representative urban consumer.

*Student D:* Is the CPI the number used to figure out if the cost of living has gone up in the case of labor contracts that have cost-of-living adjustment clauses?

*Government Economist:* Yes, and it is also used by the Social Security office to adjust payments for changes in the cost of living. It has been recently estimated that more than forty million Americans' paychecks are affected by the value of the CPI. It may also have been of importance in electing two or three presidents since the severity of inflation is a topic of vital public concern.

*Student D:* How does the CPI measure cost of living?

*Government Economist:* The representative items in the consumer's basket of goods are priced each month at a number of different locations around the country. These are weighted by the proportion of the consumer's budget normally spent on them, and a weighted average of all the prices is formed. This weighted average price is the index.

*Student A:* How are these prices determined? Does the Department of Labor go around and dicker with the retailers? I am asking this because I just bought a car and I can tell you that determining the price of the car was no easy matter. It took about four days, several trips back and forth to the dealer, and even some theatrics.

*Government Economist:* Well, you have hit on one of the limitations of the CPI as a measure of inflation. The CPI measures everything at list prices, and does not account for sales or special bargains. In the case of your car, the CPI would figure it in at the sticker price. The only exception to this is a recent change that allows the introduction of factory rebates into the calculations. There may be more such changes to come. Personally, I hope so, because we are observing a clear pattern of merchandising in which discounts from list price are being used more and more as a sales tool. How often do we hear from shopkeepers that next year's prices are going up, so now is the time to buy at 60 percent of next year's price? These patterns may often mean that the actual prices which consumers are paying are going down while the list prices are going up. The CPI would incorrectly show a rise in such cases.

*Student B:* This business about the car raises some other questions about the CPI. Cars change every year. What do the statisticians do about this?

*Government Economist:* Well, the people who go out and gather information on prices have the option of pricing an equivalent item if the item in the official basket is no longer available. One of the official cars in the CPI is a four-door Chevy Impala. Over the years the actual car that is used to estimate car prices varies from the official definition. Every ten years or so, the basket is redefined on the basis of a new survey of consumer purchases.

*Student D:* Every ten *years?* Isn't that a bit silly? People change their purchase habits much more often than that. Why, I'll bet that half the things I buy now weren't even invented ten years ago.

*Government Economist:* Well, the point you raise is a problem with the index. The basket of goods is defined on the basis of a survey. But it takes a number of years to do this survey and to fully analyze and process the results. So a new survey doesn't affect the CPI until several years later.

*Student F:* The more I hear about our main measure of inflation, the less I like it. You have now told us that it measures list prices rather than the actual prices people are paying, that it doesn't take into account sales or special promotions, that the actual goods priced are from a supposedly representative basket that is outdated and inflexible, and that the products used to represent the ones in the representative basket can be changed by the surveyor.

*Government Economist:* Actually, there is still another major limitation of the index. That has to do with the method of handling changes in quality. Suppose the field worker who is pricing toothpaste walks into the sample store for this month's price and finds that the toothpaste is now "new and improved." What to do? If it is in fact new and improved, it is a higher-quality product. If a higher-quality product sells for the same price as the old one, is the price in effect cut? If the new and improved toothpaste now costs twenty cents more, is this increase really an increase in price, or does it correspond to the value of the improvement in quality? This is a tough call for the statisticians making up the CPI, and it is fair to say they account for quality changes only imperfectly.

*Student F:* Why do we settle for such a crude measure of inflation when it has such a potent economic influence—referring to your statement about the paychecks of forty million Americans and the election of two or three presidents?

*Government Economist:* There have been several attempts in Congress to totally overhaul the CPI to make it a more acceptable measure of changes in the cost of living. But, they have been scuttled. There seems to be little support in Congress for spending the money required to calculate a better inflation index. It would cost several million dollars to fix up some of the cruder parts of the CPI. Also, neither business nor labor has shown much of an interest in such legislative changes. So, CPI bills have had no real lobbying support. Probably it will eventually happen. But meanwhile we have to live with the CPI, so we should keep in mind that it is at best a crude measure of inflation.

But, on to a different subject. You all have before you figure 4.5, which is a plot of the annual rate of change in the CPI calculated over successive six-month periods from 1948 to 1982.

*Student D:* Why six-month periods?

*Government Economist:* A compromise. Annual periods seem to me to average out too much that goes on during a year. Shorter periods such as a quarter would show more of this detail as well as more vagarious fluctuations in the inflation rate that may not mean much. Besides, quarterly periods would make the graph longer than the paper.

**FIGURE 4.5.
Annual Rate of
Change in Consumer
Prices in the
United States.**

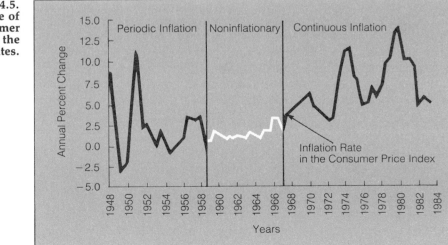

*Student A*  (whispering to Student B): Oh, brother, he's worried about the graph being longer than the paper.

*Student B*  (whispering back): Hey, these economists live in their own little worlds. Quiet down now, I think he's talking about some important stuff.

*Government Economist:*  Notice in figure 4.5 that the U.S. experience breaks roughly into three periods over the years shown. The period from the end of World War II to about the end of 1958 was one of periodic or intermittent inflation. It was a time of sharply rising prices followed by declines in prices. For example, in 1949 and 1954, consumer prices fell, so that we had a negative rate of inflation.

*Student A:*  Is there a special name for a negative rate of inflation?

*Government Economist:*  Yes, it's called *deflation.* Returning to the graph, you see that 1948 and 1951 were periods of rapid rises in prices, with the inflation rate reaching almost 12 percent in the first half of 1951. But inflation quickly returned to lower levels in 1952.

The period starting in the last half of 1958 and ending in the first half of 1967 was *noninflationary.* Prices increased at about a 2 percent average rate over this period. The beginning of 1967 dates the start of the longest period of persistently rising prices in the history of the United States.

*Student D:*  Why is this happening?

*Government Economist:*  Well,—oh, I see we are out of time. I've got to catch . . . my plane back to Washington.


One point our government economist did not cover is that the CPI is not the only measure of inflation available. An alternative government measure of inflation is produced as part of the NIA system. In estimating the GNP, statisticians gather data on dollars spent and prices paid for hundreds of categories of consumer goods, capital goods, and government services. The prices are collected to adjust the GNP estimate for the effect of inflation. For each class of products in the GNP, such as consumer goods or machinery and equipment, the estimate of dollars spent on each product is divided by its price, which produces an estimate of the quantity of the product purchased. These estimates of the quantity of products purchased are called constant-dollar expenditures. When the constant-dollar expenditures are added together for all products, they form a constant-dollar GNP. This constant-dollar GNP is called the *real GNP.*

The prices collected as part of the GNP system allow calculation of a separate index of inflation. The price index for each category of GNP goods and services is weighted by the amount of spending in that category to form a weighted index of the price of all the goods and services in the GNP. This index is called the *GNP deflator.* The word *deflator* in this context refers to the use of the index to convert, or deflate, the current dollar GNP into the real GNP.

The GNP deflator is much broader than the CPI in its coverage. Besides consumer goods, it encompasses prices of capital goods and government services. The GNP deflator is not directly comparable to the CPI, but an index is extracted from the deflator that is directly comparable to the CPI. It is formed by taking the GNP prices for only consumer goods (durable, nondurable, and services) and weighting them by the amounts purchased in each category. The resulting index is called the *Price of Consumer Expenditures,* or PCE. The PCE index measures the prices paid for the consumer goods that people are actually buying as part of the GNP. There are no fixed weights in the PCE as in the case of the CPI. The weights attached to each item in the PCE change each calendar quarter corresponding to the changes in the amounts that people are spending on consumer goods.

The PCE is not the answer to all our difficulties in measuring inflation. It shares with the CPI the imperfections about how actual prices are measured. But, measuring the prices of goods and services people are buying each quarter (the PCE) is not the same thing as measuring the prices of items in an unvarying basket of goods (the CPI). All in all, many economists prefer the PCE to the CPI as a measure of inflation.

## RECESSIONS AND EXPANSIONS

A *recession* is a period of time when the amount of final goods and services produced in the entire nation declines. As the amount produced falls, employment usually declines. Therefore, a recession is a time of falling employment and a rising unemployment rate. Recessions are often defined in terms of movements in the real GNP. A rule of thumb often used by economists is that two successive quarterly declines in the real GNP constitute a recession.[5] Similarly, an *expansion* in the economy is when the real GNP is rising over two or more quarterly periods.

Figure 4.6 shows the quarterly movements in the real GNP from 1970 to 1981. Notice the vertical axis is labeled "Billions of 1972 Dollars." This is the result of 1972 being arbitrarily chosen as the year when the GNP deflator had a value of 1.0, or a value of 100 index points. If, for 1976, the deflator had a value of 125 index points or 1.25, it would mean that prices in 1976 were 25 percent higher than in 1972.

5. The National Bureau of Economic Research (NBER) is a publicly funded private organization that tracks a wealth of economic data and is concerned with dating the precise starting and ending points of recessions. Its findings are widely accepted as being the "official" dates of recessions. Through the years, there has been a close correspondence between the NBER's recessions and the "two-quarters of declining real GNP" rule of thumb.

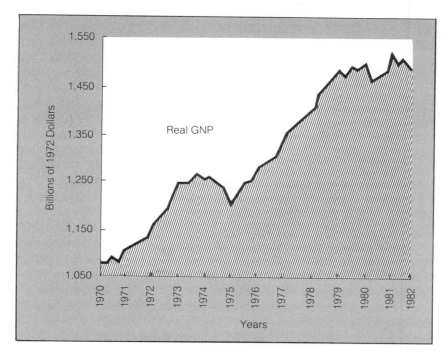

**FIGURE 4.6.**
**Quarterly Movements**
**in the Real GNP.**

Thus, "1972 dollars" means that if prices had stayed constant at their 1972 levels, the GNP produced would have been as shown in figure 4.6.[6] The pattern in figure 4.6 shows that a recession took place between the fourth quarter of 1973 and the first quarter of 1975. Production over this period declined from about 1,260 billion constant dollars to about 1,180 billion constant dollars, a fall off of about 6.5 percent. The situation in 1979–1980 is not as clear-cut. In this latter period, production fell, but not for two successive quarters. However, the overall pattern of weakness over this period leads many to the conclusion that a recession took place despite our rule of thumb.

Figure 4.6 shows two periods of economic weakness. Now, if you went back to figure 4.1 and tried to find these recessions in the unadjusted or *nominal* GNP charted there, you would not be successful. The reason the recessions do not show up in the nominal GNP is that in both periods, prices increased faster than the real GNP fell. For example, the 6.5 percent decline in production over 1973–1975 was accompanied by an increase in prices of more than 30 percent. As a result, the nominal GNP rose by more than 24 percent. This is why recessions are defined in terms of the real GNP rather than the nominal GNP.

6. The base year for price indices is changed from time to time, and it is not the same for all economic statistics. The differences mean little, since any price index can be "rebased" just by dividing each value in it by the new base year. Doing this makes that base year have a value of 1.0 (index value of 100), and all other years being measured are relative to it.

## The Cyclical GNP

When a recession occurs, all parts of the economy are not equally affected. Some parts of the economy have severe cyclical fluctuations while others are highly insulated from the general recession. In other words, the GNP can be broken into a cyclical part and a noncyclical part. The *cyclical GNP* consists of the production of capital goods such as machinery and equipment, factories, houses, apartment buildings, consumer durable goods such as automobiles and appliances, and the change in business inventories. In other words, the cyclical GNP is equal to all of the NIA category called Gross Private Domestic Investment plus consumer durable goods.

It is logical that this part of the GNP is cyclical. Almost all the goods included in it are assetlike. As assets, these goods have long lives. People can postpone purchasing such as asset just by using the existing asset longer. For example, it is easy to put off buying a new car as long as you an still drive the old one. The same is true with residential construction and with construction of business structures. Also, credit is a factor in the purchase of most assets. When credit is either unavailable or too costly because of high interest rates, spending plans for durables and capital goods can be postponed. Even the attitude of the public is influential in markets for cyclical goods. When the mood of consumers and business becomes pessimistic, spending plans are often postponed or canceled. These factors add up to an unstable level of production. As a result, the cyclical GNP category definitely has its ups and downs.

To see some of these ups and downs, take a look at figure 4.7. It shows production of cyclical goods in constant dollars. The picture

**FIGURE 4.7.**
**The Cyclical GNP.**

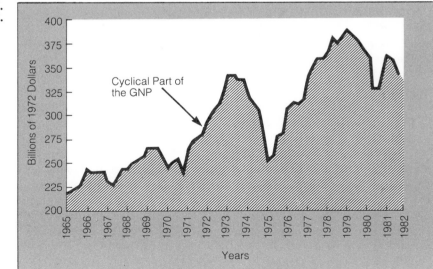

is clearly one of substantial periodic fluctuations. Notice the decline from the start of 1973 to the start of 1975. During that time, the real GNP dropped by 6.5 percent. But the cyclical part dropped by more than 26 percent. While the entire economy had a recession, cyclical markets experienced disaster. Fortunately for the overall stability of the economy, the entire economy is not cyclical.

## The Noncyclical GNP

The *noncyclical GNP* consists of consumer nondurables and services plus government spending. The largest part of the noncyclical GNP is consumer nondurables and services. These goods and services are the everyday purchases that support the lifestyle of U.S. households. Experience shows that they are highly insulated from recessionary periods. U.S. households do not want to downgrade their living habits unless absolutely necessary. The remaining part of the noncyclical GNP, government purchases, actually tends to rise slightly during recessions because of the impact of income-assistance programs triggered by rising unemployment.

Figure 4.8 shows the time path of the noncyclical GNP. You can see that the pattern is one of steady and nearly unbroken upward movement. This is the base of stability in the United States that keeps the violent movement in the production of cyclical goods from shoving the entire economy into equally violent fluctuations. And, it is a large base. In 1980, the noncyclical part of the real GNP was about 1,100 billion 1972 dollars, whereas the cyclical part was about 355 billion 1972 dollars.

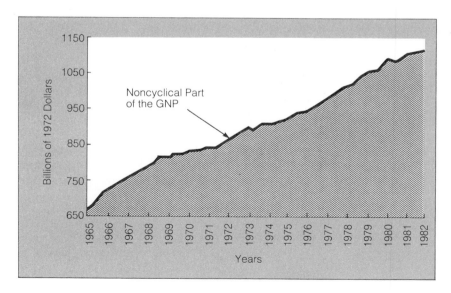

**FIGURE 4.8.**
**The Noncyclical GNP.**

**Important Ideas in This Chapter**

1. The GNP is an estimate of the market value of current domestic final production of goods and services.

2. Economic activity that generates current income is counted as production and adds to the GNP. Therefore, total GNP production and total income originated are always equal.

3. The GNP is estimated by adding together incomes earned by wage earners, profits, interest payments, and nonincome distributions such as depreciation and sales taxes. The GNP is also calculated as the total production of durable goods, nondurable goods, services, and structures.

4. The GNP is also broken down into categories showing how much spending took place by consumers, business firms, governments, and net foreign consumers. The sum of this spending also equals the GNP, once inventories are properly taken into consideration.

5. When total sales and total production are not the same, inventories either rise or fall to account for the difference. However, because inventory change is considered to be part of the GNP, total expenditures *on the GNP* always equal the GNP itself. Final sales is a statistic formed by subtracting inventory change from the GNP. Final sales is thus a measure of the actual sales of goods and services to final customers. It will not equal the GNP unless inventories are constant.

6. The labor force is the group of work-age people looking for jobs. Total employment is the number of people in the labor force that are successful. The unemployment rate is the percentage of the work force that is looking for work but has not found it.

7. Full employment occurs when the unemployment rate is pushed down to a level where all job seekers are employed except those who are temporarily between jobs, those who are seasonally unemployed, those who lack training sufficient to allow them to compete for a job, and those who are geographically immobile.

8. Inflation is a period in which prices are rising in a persistent manner and by significant amounts. Usually, if prices are rising at 4 percent or better for more than a year, we think of this period as being inflationary.

9. The Consumer Price Index is a measure of the cost of purchasing a particular basket of consumer goods. The goods are thought to be representative of the spending of a representative urban consumer.

10. The CPI is the most widely used measure of the cost of living, impacting on the salaries of many millions of Americans who have cost-of-living adjustments in their incomes.

11. The CPI has clear limitations, relating to the treatment of list prices, quality adjustments, and revision of the basket of goods sampled. For these reasons, it is a crude measure of consumer prices.

**12.** When the GNP is corrected for price changes, the resulting constant-dollar measure is called the real GNP. To measure the real GNP, statisticians collect price data on the goods and services included in it. These data enable computation of a second price index for consumer expenditures that overcomes some of the shortcomings of the CPI. This measure is called the Price of Consumer Expenditures index. The PCE index is in increasing use as an alternative to the CPI.

**13.** A recession is a period where the real GNP falls for two quarters or more. Unemployment rises during a recession. An expansion is when the real GNP rises for two quarters or more, and is accompanied by falling unemployment rates.

**14.** It is important to think of recessions and expansions in terms of the real GNP rather than the nominal GNP because the effects of inflation often cause the dollar amount of production to rise during recessions, even though the amount of goods and services falls.

**15.** The cyclical GNP is the part of production that tends to rise and fall with expansions and recessions. It consists of the production of business factories, offices, and equipment; consumer durable goods; houses and apartments; and inventory change. These parts of the GNP tend to have exaggerated movements when general business fluctuations occur.

**16.** The noncyclical GNP is the part of production that is highly insulated from economic fluctuations. It consists of consumer nondurable goods and consumer services, plus government spending. These parts of the economy seldom decline, even during severe overall recessions. The noncyclical part of the GNP provides a stable base for the overall economy.

**Discussion Questions**

**1.** Suppose a used-car dealer buys a car for $400, reconditions it at a cost of $150, and sells it for $700. What is the contribution to the GNP associated with this activity?

**2.** Are there any differences in the way the GNP is affected in the following examples: (1) Ford Motor Company giving its employees a raise while holding its prices constant, and (2) the federal government giving its employees a raise? Explain.

**3.** Which do you think gives the earliest warning of an upcoming recession: changes in the real GNP, changes in final sales, or changes in the nominal GNP? Explain.

**4.** Explain fully how the rising fraction of female job seekers has impacted on the employment and unemployment statistics.

**5.** Make an argument that the CPI overstates the actual cost of living. Now make an argument that it understates the cost of living. Which argument do you think is the more convincing?

**Suggested Readings**

Precise definitions of all the NIA components including all those in the GNP are found in the biannual supplements to *The Survey of Current Business,* published by the U.S. Department of Commerce. For a continuing analysis of how well the CPI does in measuring the cost of living, look through some recent issues of the *Review of the Federal Reserve Bank of St. Louis.* Current analyses of cyclical trends in the economy can be found in *Business Conditions Digest* and the *Federal Reserve Bulletin.*

## CHAPTER 5

# The Special Language
# of Financial Markets

## CHAPTER OUTLINE

## IMPORTANT TERMS

financial markets
financial instrument
primary market
secondary market
short-term financial instruments
long-term financial instruments
credit instruments
equity instruments
Treasury bills
commercial paper
default risk
prime commercial paper
repurchase agreements
overnight repurchase agreements
banker's acceptances
certificates of deposit
small-denomination CD
large-denomination CD
negotiable
savings account
money-market certificates
money-market mutual funds
credit lines
prime rate
money-market deposit account

eurodollar deposits
eurodollar loans
eurodollar market
corporate bonds
coupon rate
debenture
mortgage bond
U.S. Treasury bonds
U.S. Treasury notes
federal-agency bonds and notes
municipal bond
common stock
board of directors
preferred stock
convertible bonds
callable bonds
call price
coupon equivalent yield
time value
present value
yield to maturity
real interest rate
realized real rate
expected real rate
M1, M2, M3, L

## MEMO

To:      All readers
From:    JWE

Modern financial markets do have their special language. Without it, you would not know what to call the unique kinds of "goods" being bought and sold in these markets, and you would have a difficult time understanding how financial markets work. This chapter acquaints you with the language of finance. In it, you can read about the names and characteristics of the major financial instruments used by investors to buy and sell investment funds.

Markets in short-term financial assets are often called money markets in the United States, indicating that they are markets for assets that are close to money in their characteristics. Longer-term markets where corporations raise most of the funds used to finance expansion and modernization of facilities and equipment are called capital markets, indicating that business financial capital flows from lenders to borrowers in these markets.

The rate of interest is the principal measure of the price of goods sold in money and capital markets. In this chapter, you can also read about how interest rates are defined and calculated in both types of markets. In addition, the real or inflation-adjusted interest rate is an increasingly important topic explored in this chapter; it will help you understand the workings of financial markets during inflations.

With these topics under your belt, you will be speaking finance fluently. Just think, when you have mastered the essentials of the language, you will be able to come up with entire sentences that are incomprehensible to even the brightest of outsiders.

Consider these excerpts which you might find in your local newspaper on any given day: "Today in the world of high finance," "Wall Street insiders explained that the rise in the stock market was due to technical reasons relating to the market's short position," and "financial experts interpreted the move in interest rates as reflecting the heavy calendar of corporate offerings." Statements such as these are cause to wonder if there is any common ground between the "world" of finance and the one in which you live. There is much common ground. Financial markets are not difficult to understand, if you know the language.

The world of finance revolves around financial markets. *Financial markets* are where lenders and borrowers come to do business with each other. They may not physically gather to do their business, but may get together by telephone, telegram, or wire service. Financial markets are the communication link between borrowers and lenders. The data produced in these markets inform all parties of the offers of other parties. For example, if a firm wants to borrow $50,000 and is willing to pay 8 percent interest for it, a financial market sees to it that this information is available to lenders.

The goods bought and sold in financial markets are called financial instruments. A *financial instrument* is an IOU written by a borrower and given to a lender in return for the lender's check. Borrowers create and issue financial instruments. Lenders buy them. The word *instrument* refers to the role of the IOU as an instrument by which a borrower and a lender produce a transaction.

A *primary market* is one where newly issued financial instruments are bought and sold. In primary markets, new funds are raised for investment purposes by ultimate borrowers (usually firms). A *secondary market* is one in which previously issued financial instruments are exchanged. When 40,000 shares of General Motors stock are traded on a secondary market for stocks, the company does not receive any funds. Instead, some existing owners of the stock decide to exchange their shares for cash while others holding cash decide to exchange it for shares. However, when General Motors initially issued the stock in the primary market, it received funds in exchange for its shares.

There are many different kinds of financial instruments in use in U.S. financial markets today. To grasp the language of finance, you must know what these instruments are and how they are used. After all, they are the "nouns" in the language of finance. There are two basic categories of financial instruments: short-term and long-term. *Short-term financial instruments* are those having maturities of one year or less. *Long-term financial instruments* have maturities greater than one year. Short-term instruments are all *credit instruments,* meaning they are vehicles by which a lender advances funds to a borrower in return for the borrower's IOU. Long-term instruments may be either credit instruments or *equity instruments,* the latter being vehicles by which investors supply permanent financing to firms or other borrowers. Those who invest in equity instruments are part owners of the firm in which they have placed their funds.

## SHORT-TERM FINANCIAL INSTRUMENTS

*Treasury bills* are government-issued IOUs with maturities of between three months and one year. The three-month and six-month Treasury Bills (or T-Bills as they are called) are the most widely issued. A new issue is sold each week by the Treasury. T-Bills are sold at a discount from their redemption price, and bear no interest coupon. Investors in T-Bills earn a return by bidding for and buying a bill at less than its redemption or "face" value and recovering the face value when the bill reaches maturity. Most T-Bills are bought from the Treasury by dealers in securities, who plan to resell the bills at higher prices than they paid for them. There is an active secondary market for existing T-Bills where owners can sell them prior to their maturity, and where buyers can find bills having precisely the maturities called for by their investment plans. For example, if a firm knows it has $150,000 of cash that will be available for a period of twenty-four days, it can in all likelihood find for sale in the secondary market 150,000 dollars worth of T-Bills that have approximately twenty-four days until maturity. The bills the firm buys might have been either three-month, six-month, or even one-year bills when newly issued in the primary market. As they approach maturity, they effectively become shorter and shorter bills as far as investors in the secondary market are concerned.

The fact that there is an active secondary market for T-bills means that the bills can be easily sold prior to maturity if the need for cash arises. The T-Bills' "nearness to cash" causes those in financial circles to refer to them as highly liquid. Thus, T-Bills are highly liquid short-term financial instruments. (In case you did not notice, you've just read your first sentence written entirely in "finance"!)

*Commercial paper* is a corporation-issued short-term IOU having a maturity generally in the range of three to nine months. Like T-Bills, commercial paper is fully discounted, bearing no coupon. Also, a growing secondary market exists for commercial paper. In both these ways, commercial paper is much like a corporate version of the government's T-Bills. However, there is one major difference. In the case of T-Bills, the IOU says words to this effect: "The United States of America promises to pay the holder upon maturity a sum of $10,000." In the case of commercial paper, the same promise is made, only by a corporation. Generally, the government's promise is thought to be more of a sure thing than a corporation's promise. *Default risk* is the chance that a borrower will not make good on a promise to pay. Although both commercial paper and T-Bills have low default risk, that of T-Bills is lower.

Of course, all commercial paper does not have the same default risk. For all practical purposes, the commercial paper of large, profitable, and growing corporations may have little more risk of default than T-Bills. However, all corporations issuing commercial paper do not fall into this category. Some are less financially stable than others. To provide information to investors on the stability of the corporations issuing commercial paper, several agencies, most prominently *Moody's Investor Service*, rate the commercial paper of most corporations that issue it, often grading it on an A to C scale. Commercial paper rating the highest (that with the lowest default risk) is referred to as *prime commercial paper*. As with prime cuts of meat, prime commercial paper brings the highest prices in the financial marketplace.

Since it is sold on a discount basis, the highest price means the lowest interest rate to the investor and the lowest financing cost to the issuer. Suppose two issues of twelve-month $10,000 commercial paper are made at the same time, one of which is rated as prime and the other graded B. Further, suppose that the prime paper brings a selling price of $9,300 whereas the B-rated paper brings only $9,200. The return— that is, the ratio of profits to invested funds—on the commercial paper is ($10,000 − $9,300)/$9,300 = 7.53 percent, whereas the return on the B-rated paper is ($10,000 − $9,200)/$9,200 = 8.7 percent. In this illustration as in most financial markets, investors are willing to pay more for the prime paper and settle for a lower return than they would get on lower-graded paper, because they attach a value to the lower default risk of the prime paper.

The firms issuing commercial paper are for the most part corporations that make consumer loans for the purchase of automobiles, TV sets, furniture, and appliances. The finance companies owned by major automobile producers are leading issuers of commercial paper, as are consumer finance companies. When a new-car buyer finances a purchase through the car dealer, the funds have usually been raised by an issue of commercial paper by the automobile firm's finance subsidiary. In recent years, a growing number of nonfinancial corporations have found that they can successfully raise funds by issuing commercial paper. For large, well-established firms, such an alternative can provde to be superior to bank loans as a means of raising short-term capital.

*Repurchase agreements* are arrangements made in connection with short-term IOUs; they give the holder of the note the option of selling it back to the issuer at a set price after part or all of the time period of the note has expired. Maturities of repurchase agreements range from several days to a year or more. However, most have maturities below six months. The name of this instrument refers to the agreement by the seller of the note (the borrower) to repurchase the note at a prearranged price after a fixed time has elapsed.

Repurchase agreements usually involve other financial instruments. An example of this occurs regularly in the T-Bill market. Dealers who bid for and obtain newly issued T-Bills often sell them to the Federal Reserve, with a repurchase agreement to buy them back after a few days. Doing this helps the bond dealer keep inventories of T-Bills low (thus minimizing invested funds) while still having a known supply of T-Bills available for resale at a known future date. In this case, the bond dealer who uses repurchase agreements is in effect borrowing from the Federal Reserve a portion of the funds required to buy newly issued Treasury Bills from the Treasury. The dealer must pay interest on the funds borrowed in this way. At the same time, the dealer receives interest on the T-Bills that have been "repo'd." When the interest on the repo is above that of the associated T-Bills, the dealer is paying a carrying cost to finance this standby inventory. Dealers call this "negative carry." If the repo rate is less than the associated T-Bill rate, it would be referred to as "positive carry." Positive carry represents a situation where the dealer is making a profit on the repo transaction.

Banks use repurchase agreements to give holders of their IOUs more flexibility, thus making the bank's notes more attractive to firms. A bank may arrange to borrow funds from a firm for ninety days but give the firm a repurchase agreement allowing the firm to sell the note back to the bank after thirty days at the firm's option.

*Overnight repurchase agreements* are contracts between banks and nonfinancial firms that provide for the firm to buy an interest-earning deposit from the bank each afternoon before the close of the bank's business. The firm pays for the deposit with the funds in its checking account. The bank then agrees to buy this deposit back the next morning, putting the funds back into the firm's checking account. The result of this overnight repurchase agreement is that funds are transferred out of the firm's checking account each evening into an interest-bearing account. They are then transferred back into the checking account for the next day's business. Overnight repurchase agreements are clearly of interest to firms because firms can in effect earn interest on their checking account between the close of one day's business and the start of another. Are you wondering why banks would be interested in issuing them? Basically, it is because banks are not required to hold reserves against overnight funds, whereas they would be required to hold reserves against the associated demand deposit. Thus, transfers of demand deposits into and out of overnight accounts free up reserves that banks can use to make profitable loans or investments.

*Banker's acceptances* are short-term, fully discounted IOUs issued by corporations, but backed for a fee by banks—thus the name. By agreeing to pay the note in case the issuing firm defaults, the bank greatly lowers the default risk of the firm's IOU. Banker's acceptances historically have been written to finance imports. The bank's backing helps produce a secondary market for these notes, which gives them roughly the same liquidity as commercial paper. Generally, firms issuing banker's acceptances are not as financially strong as those which issue commercial paper. Commercial-paper issuers do not need the backing of banks to sell their IOUs in the market. Firms that choose to sell banker's acceptances usually could not successfully sell commercial paper.

A *certificate of deposit* (CD) is the primary type of IOU issued by banks as well as savings and loan institutions. A *small-denomination CD* is considered to be one that is less than $100,000 in amount, and is bought predominantly by households with savings. They are issued in maturities ranging from a few months to several years. A *large-denomination CD* is one of $100,000 and up. They are bought predominantly by business and by investment funds. The main distinctions between large and small CDs are: (1) the rate of interest on large CDs is unregulated and is set in financial markets, whereas for small CDs, maximum rates are fixed by law[1] and (2) a secondary market exists for large-denomination CDs but not for small CDs. That is, holders of large-denomination CDs have the option of selling their certificates in a secondary market prior to maturity. Large-denomination CDs are called *negotiable*, meaning that the bank's obligation to repay the amount of the certificate can be transferred from one holder to another. For a negotiable CD, the issuing bank is obliged to pay the face amount of the certificate to whoever owns it when it matures. Unlike T-Bills, commercial paper, and banker's acceptances, large-denomination CDs are sold at or near their face value and carry a set coupon payment. Thus, large CDs are not discounted as are other short-term financial assets.

A *savings account* is a special type of certificate of deposit in which money can be drawn out almost on demand by the depositor and which has no set maturity date. Most savings accounts give the issuing bank or savings and loan institution the option of requiring notice prior to withdrawal. However, in practice this option is rarely used. In contrast, CDs have fixed maturity periods, and funds can be withdrawn earlier only by payment of a penalty.

*Money-market certificates* are six-month notes issued by banks, savings and loan associations, and other financial institutions. Such notes carry rates of interest set in accordance with the six-month T-Bill rate. The rates of interest on these certificates fluctuate each week according to the rates established at the T-Bill auction.

Money-market certificates were an innovation of the late 1970s. They were designed to retain and attract savers to thrift institutions during the record-high interest rates of the latter half of the 1970s. Prior to the certificates, an alarming number of households took funds out of savings accounts and small CDs and invested them in T-Bills. And why not? In buying T-Bills, savers could earn better than 10 percent, whereas if they invested in traditional savings accounts or small-denomination CDs of six-months' maturity, they would earn only 5 to 6 percent.

*Money-market mutual funds* are pools of funds invested in short-term financial instruments. The pool of funds is accumulated by selling shares and is invested by fund managers in securities such as T-Bills, commercial paper, banker's acceptances, and large-denomination CDs. Each shareholder in a money-market mutual fund owns a portion of the combined assets of the fund, and receives a proportionate share of the interest earned on the financial instruments owned by the fund.

Although money-market mutual funds were available to large investors in the early 1970s, the development of funds designed for household savers did not occur until late in the same decade. When the household money-market funds began to grow, the money-market certificates had already reversed the pattern of households shun-

1. These maximum rates are being slowly phased out under banking legislation passed in 1980.

ning thrift institutions. Almost immediately, the money-market mutual funds diverted a considerable amount of the newly acquired funds away from thrift institutions and into the assets acquired by the funds. It was no accident. The funds offered households a better deal. The funds had lower minimum denominations than the certificates. Most certificates are issued in minimum denominations of $10,000, just like the T-Bills with which they were intended to compete. The money funds have minimum denominations of $2,000 or less. The money funds allow immediate and free withdrawal privileges in contrast to the fixed six-month period and heavy penalties of the certificates. Many of the funds allow shareholders to write check-line drafts on their shares, giving holders high liquidity, whereas the certificates have no such feature. However, a drawback of the money-market funds is that they are not insured by the federal government, whereas the certificates are. This proved to be of little consequence to many savers, as funds quickly accumulated in the money-market mutual funds during the late 1970s and early 1980s.

In mid-December of 1982, banks and thrift institutions introduced another innovation along the lines of the money-market mutual funds and the money-market certificates. This account, called the *money-market deposit account* (MMDA), has no minimum maturity, allows limited check-writing privileges, and pays a rate of interest that compares with that paid by money-market mutual funds. As with money-market mutual funds, the rate of interest on the MMDAs varies each week, depending on the rates being offered by the money-market mutual funds. The MMDAs have a minimum deposit of $2,500, which makes them compare favorably with the money-market certificates for smaller savers.

The concept of the MMDA is to give banks and thrift institutions a ''product'' that allows them to effectively compete with the money-market mutual funds. The biggest ''plus'' associated with the MMDA is that it is insured by an agency of the federal government, and thus offers more solid protection against loss than the money-market mutual fund.

*Eurodollar deposits* are various types of IOUs issued by European and United Kingdom banks and held by both United States citizens and investors in other nations. These overseas IOUs are denominated in dollars rather than in the currency of the European or United Kingdom bank in which they are held. The dollars that foreign banks receive in return for eurodollar deposits are used to make dollar-denominated loans to European and United Kingdom borrowers. Foreign borrowers of dollars usually want the funds in order to buy goods in the United States. Dollar-denominated loans made by European and United Kingdom banks are called *eurodollar loans*. The market in which eurodollar lending takes place is called the *eurodollar market*.

Eurodollar deposits have been an attractive investment for U.S. investors because the generally high rates of interest on eurodollar loans have motivated foreign banks to offer similarly high interest

To: Readers interested in the prime rate
From: JWE

Did you know that business firms were using the equivalent of credit cards long before consumers had them? Years before VISA, firms routinely negotiated arrangements with their banks for *credit lines* authorizing them to overcharge on their checking accounts by an amount not to exceed a prearranged limit. Under a credit-line arrangement, when a firm goes into the "red" on its checkbook balance, it begins paying interest on the credit balance. The interest rate paid by a firm on line-of-credit borrowing is typically tied to the bank's published lending rate on credit lines, called the bank's *prime rate*. The prime rate is the rate on short-term (mostly credit-line) borrowing that the bank's biggest and most secure customers can obtain. Specific credit-line arrangements for firms other than prime-rate borrowers are usually negotiated at interest rates scaled to the prime rate. For example, a firm's line-of-credit agreement may specify that the firm may borrow up to ten million dollars at a half point above the bank's prime rate. When the bank changes its prime rate, the interest rates on all loans tied to it automatically change. How often do banks change their quoted prime rates? In the volatile financial markets of the late 1970s and early 1980s, fifteen prime-rate changes in a year would not have been uncommon.

Credit lines are not a market-traded financial instrument such as commercial paper. Accordingly, the prime rate is not a market-determined rate as is the commercial-paper rate. However, the prime rate is highly influenced by short-term rates such as the commercial-paper rate and the rate on large CDs. Why? Because many large firms have a realistic option of whether they borrow from banks in the form of credit lines or issue commercial paper, thus borrowing in the market for short-term capital. If the prime rate is out of line with rates such as the commercial-paper rate, firms will take their borrowing business elsewhere. Thus, banks generally seek to keep the prime rate in line with interest rates on short-term financial assets.

rates to attract U.S. depositors. Money-market mutual funds have been important buyers of eurodollar deposits in recent years. In addition, U.S. banks have been frequent borrowers of eurodollars, particularly when reserves have been under pressure.

## LONG-TERM FINANCIAL INSTRUMENTS

*Long-term financial instruments* are those with maturities of upward of a year, used primarily by firms to raise funds for new capital investments. The useful life of factories and machinery typically is greater than ten years; as a rule, firms seek long-term financing when they make capital investments.

*Corporate bonds* issued by firms, are long-term IOUs that entitle the holder to regular interest payments. The term *bond* denotes a financial instrument having a set rate of interest, called the *coupon rate,* which the firm pays at fixed intervals. At the maturity date of the bond, the firm is obliged to pay the face amount shown on the bond. Most bonds are issued in thousand-dollar units. Thus, a ten-year corporate bond with a 9 percent coupon rate is a note promising to pay the owner 9 percent of a thousand dollars (ninety dollars) each year for ten years, followed by repayment of the thousand dollars when the bond is retired.

A *debenture* is a corporate bond that is not secured by any specific collateral. Instead, a debenture is backed by the general assets of the firm that issues it. By contrast, a *mortgage bond* is a corporate note secured by giving the holder a claim on the firm's buildings and equipment in case of default. Because mortgage bonds are backed by tangible marketable assets, they have a lower default risk than debentures.[2]

Government bonds are long-term coupon-bearing IOUs issued by the federal, state, and local governments. They are issued with maturities ranging from one year to twenty-five years or more. *U.S. Treasury bonds* and U.S. *Treasury notes* are federal-government debt instruments issued by the Treasury to finance federal budget deficits or to refinance prior debt issues. Other federal agencies have issued separate notes in recent years. Agricultural-support agencies, mortgage-assistance agencies, and other housing-related agencies have been among those issuing *federal-agency bonds and notes.* Although not issued by the Treasury, federal-agency debt is backed by the same assets as Treasury debt. Agency debt tends to be treated by investors as largely the same as Treasury debt. Federal-agency bonds are seen by investors as having the lowest default risk among all the bonds traded in long-term financial markets. Presumably, the thinking is that if the federal government cannot pay its obligations, the economic climate will be such that corporations or local governments will be in even worse shape. In any event, federal-agency bonds usually carry a somewhat lower interest rate than other bonds, indicating the lower risk that is attached to them by investors.

*Municipal bonds* are the coupon-bearing IOUs of state, county, and city governments, and other local governmental units. They vary widely in maturity, ranging from one to twenty or more years. Municipal bonds are unique in that the interest earned on them is exempt from federal income tax. Selling these tax-free municipals is the primary way local governments raise funds to finance the construction

2. Debentures also come in different classes. Subordinated debentures do not receive payment in case of default until all nonsubordinated debentures have been retired. Many debentures stipulate that as long as they are outstanding, no debt can be issued that is entitled to a prior claim on the firm's assets. There are many variations on the specific provisions a debenture can carry in terms of what happens in case of default.

of roads, hospitals, sewers, and so forth. Because the interest earned on them is exempt from federal taxes, municipal bonds can effectively compete with federal bonds for the funds of investors, particularly those in high tax brackets.

The *common stock* of a corporation represents the owner's investment in the company. Those who hold shares of a corporation's common stock are its legal owners. The corporation's *board of directors* is a committee elected by the firm's common-stock holders to represent them in top-level management decisions facing the firm. The board of directors makes major strategic decisions such as whether to merge with another firm, whether to move into new products or industries, and whether to replace the firm's president or other senior officers. Common-stock holders influence these decisions by electing the board.

Bonds have specific maturity dates. Common stock does not mature and has no provision for being retired. When a firm issues new common stock, it need not make plans to repay the funds raised. Instead, the funds raised by common-stock offerings are permanent financing, and can be viewed as the ownership capital of the firm. Common stock pays no fixed coupon payment as do bonds. Even though many common stocks pay dividends as regularly as bonds pay interest, there is an important difference between dividend payments on common stock and interest payments on a bond. The bond interest payments are income to which the bondholder is legally entitled. Dividend payments on common stock occur only when the board of directors declares them. Common-stock holders are not legally entitled to them. When a corporation is doing poorly, its board of directors may vote to omit the dividend. On the other hand, the board can vote to declare an extra dividend if profits are unusually high. Thus, the dividends from common stock are less certain than the interest from bonds.

*Preferred stock* is a hybrid of bonds and common stock. Although most of it is issued without provision for retirement, some preferred stock has a specific redemption date at which time the company will retire it at a price stated in the preferred-stock certificate. The dividend arrangements on preferred stock are something of a cross between stocks and bonds. However, if the company does not earn enough profit to pay the preferred dividend, most preferred stocks allow the dividend to be omitted or deferred. Thus, the dividend payments on preferred stock are not as much of a sure thing as bond interest payments, but they are more secure than common-stock dividend. The other distinguishing feature of preferred stock is that it usually does not carry the voting rights associated with common stock.

A *convertible bond* is a financial butterfly. It starts out life as a bond, and at a fixed time it may be converted into common stock. In their initial state as bonds, convertibles pay a fixed coupon payment. The conversion of the bonds into stock is written into the bond agreement as a ratio of a unit of bonds for a set number of shares of common stock. Conversion is usually at the option of the holder. Typically, the conversion ratio is set at a level that does not make conversion attractive at current prices of the stock. If the company's profits grow and its stock price increases, then conversion becomes attractive to the bondholders, and the debt is converted into stock. For example, suppose a thousand-dollar convertible bond converts into fifty shares of common stock. Suppose the stock is selling for fifteen dollars per share. Bondholders would not profit by converting at this share price, as they would realize only $15 \times 50 = $750$ for their $1,000 bond. But if the stock price goes up to $25, then conversion yields $25 \times 50 = $1,250$, and conversion becomes attractive.

A *callable bond* gives the issuing firm the option of retiring the bond prior to its maturity at a price stated in the bond. This price is identified as the *call price,* and the action of exercising the call privilege is referred to as "calling" the bond. Call prices are usually set somewhat above the issue prices of the callable bonds. Callable bonds give the issuing firm the flexibility of refinancing its debt if interest rates should fall after the bonds are issued. When interest rates fall, the prices of existing bonds go up. Therefore, falling interest rates move the price of callable bonds toward the call price, at which point the firm can retire the bonds and reissue new bonds at a lower interest rate.

## MEASURING THE RATE OF RETURN

The rate of return on a financial asset is usually referred to as its interest rate. The interest rate on a financial asset is closely related to its price. To see how they are related (a requisite of speaking fluent "finance"), you need to understand how interest rates are calculated for various financial assets. The method of calculating interest rates differs depending on whether the financial asset is a discounted bill or a coupon-bearing bond.

### Interest Rates on Discounted Bills

When buyers and sellers of discounted bills negotiate their deals, they usually do not directly haggle over the interest rate. Rather, the price of the bill is the figure on which the bargain is struck. The agreed-upon price for the bill easily converts into its interest rate, and we may rest assured that both buyer and seller are well aware of the interest rates into which prices translate.

To see how prices translate into interest rates, consider this example from the T-Bill market. Suppose at one particular T-Bill auction, the average price paid for thirteen-week T-Bills is $97,000 for each $100,000 of future redemption value (or face value, as it is called). This means that investors are willing to pay $97,000 for a T-Bill that the Treasury promises it will redeem for $100,000 after thirteen weeks. Calculating the rate of return on this T-Bill issue requires forming a ratio of profits

## Memorandum

*The Wall Street Journal* recently reported on some interesting financing plans by PepsiCo, Incorporated. The firm announced plans to sell an unusual bond having thirty years to maturity on which no interest is to be paid. Instead, PepsiCo's bond will be a fully discounted long-term note. It will be issued at a price of about $270 for each $1,000 face amount. PepsiCo will receive about $6,750,000 in the financing and will repay $25,000,000 after thirty years.

Although most short-term money-market instruments such as T-Bills, commercial paper, and banker's acceptances are routinely sold on a fully discounted basis, long-term bonds rarely are designed this way. One important advantage of these proposed new bonds for the investor is that they offer security against being redeemed prior to maturity, since PepsiCo will have to redeem them at their face value. On the other hand, greater default risk attaches to the bonds because the entire return accrues in the form of price increases, so that in the case of default, the investor is left with less total return than with a traditional bond. For PepsiCo, the major advantage is that the bonds require no cash outlay until maturity. Thus, cash-flow problems are greatly eased.

to funds invested (a rate of return) and then converting this ratio to an annual basis. In this example, the profits are $100,000 − $97,000 = $3,000. The investment is $97,000 for each $100,000 of T-Bills. So, the ratio of profits to investment is $3,000 ÷ $97,000 = .0309, which shows that investors will earn 3.09 percent over the thirteen-week period in which their funds are invested.

To speak correct "finance," we must convert this thirteen-week return to an equivalent annual return. Putting all rates on an annual basis allows the return on financial assets having different maturities to be compared most directly. In this case, the period of the investment is 91 days (13 weeks × 7), while a year is conventionally considered to be 365 days. Thus, there are 365 ÷ 91 = 4.011 thirteen-week periods in a conventional year. Multiplying the thirteen-week yield of 3.09 by 4.011 gives the annualized yield of 12.39 percent. We can summarize this calculation by the following expression:

$$(5.1) \quad r = \left[ \frac{F - P}{P} \right] \times \left[ \frac{365}{D} \right]$$

where $r$ is the annualized interest rate on the discount bill, $F$ is the face or redemption value of the bill ($100,000 in our example), $P$ is the price paid for the bill ($97,000 in our example), and $D$ is the number of days until the bill matures (91 days in our example). The Treasury Department and the *Wall Street Journal* refer to the interest rate on bills calculated by equation 5.1 as the *coupon equivalent yield*, indicating it is comparable to measures of interest rates on coupon-bearing bonds.[3]

Equation 5.1 can be used to translate prices into yields for all non-coupon-bearing discounted securities, including T-Bills, commercial paper, and banker's acceptances. The equation reveals something about how short-term interest rates change in U.S. financial markets. If the number of buyers seeking lenders of short-term financial assets increases while the supply of these assets does not, bidding for the assets intensifies, and their prices are driven up. This lowers short-term interest rates according to equation 5.1.

## Interest Rates on Coupon-Bearing Bonds

Measuring the interest rate on a coupon-bearing bond presents a new problem. The profit from investing in a coupon-bearing bond is in the form of periodic interest payments in addition to profits (or losses) resulting from any differences between the amount paid for the bond and the redemption price. Whereas discounted bills are always sold at prices below their redemption value, coupon-bearing bonds are typically sold at prices that are close to their redemption value. Thus, most of the profits from investing in a coupon-bearing bond are typically in the form of the bond's interest payments. These payments are spaced out through time, which is where the problem arises. A dollar to be received today is worth more than a dollar to be received in a year. Today's dollar can be invested at interest, thus producing more than a dollar in a year. Interest receipts have a *time value*, with current receipts being worth more than distant receipts. The time value of money means that the successive coupon payments from a bond cannot simply be added together to determine the total profits from a bond investment. Instead, coupon payments from different time periods must be converted to their equivalent value at a common point in time in order to be added together. The point in time, conventionally chosen for equating future interest flows, is the current period. The *present value* of a future interest receipt is the amount of funds required today to reproduce that future interest receipt.

For example, suppose you are to receive a hundred dollars in five years. To find the present value of this (or any) future income, we need to know the rate of interest at which funds can be invested over the next five years. Suppose this interest rate is 10 percent. Define $X$ to be the amount of money you need now to produce a hundred

3. The Treasury Department has a second way of calculating yields on T-Bills that is not directly comparable to other financial-asset returns. It is similar to equation 5.1 except that $F$ is used in the denominator instead of $P$, and a 360-day year is assumed instead of a 365-day year. (Yes, it appears that the Treasury does live in its own world of 360-day years.) When the results at T-Bill auctions are announced, the interest rate is calculated from both equation 5.1 and this unworldly modification of it.

dollars after five years. If you deposit $X$ dollars in an account earning 10 percent per year for five years, here is what the balance in the account will be after each year:

| after year number: | the account balance is: |
|---|---|
| 0 | $X$ |
| 1 | $X(1.1)$ |
| 2 | $X(1.1)^1 (1.1) = X(1.1)^2$ |
| 3 | $X(1.1)^2 (1.1) = X(1.1)^3$ |
| 4 | $X(1.1)^3 (1.1) = X(1.1)^4$ |
| 5 | $X(1.1)^4 (1.1) = X(1.1)^5$ |

The initial balance of $X$ in this account increases by 10 percent during year 1 to end the year at 1.1 times its original value. After year 2, this amount is increased by another 10 percent to $X(1.1)^2$. After five years, the amount in the account equals $X(1.1)^5$. This is the amount we want to be equal to $100. Thus, we can solve for the unknown $X$:

$$X(1.1)^5 = \$100,$$

and

$$X = \frac{\$100}{(1.1)^5} = \$62.09$$

Thus, if $62.09 is deposited today, it will grow to $100 after five years. Here is the account on a year-by-year basis:

| after year number: | the account balance is: |
|---|---|
| 0 | $62.09 |
| 1 | 68.30 |
| 2 | 75.13 |
| 3 | 82.64 |
| 4 | 90.91 |
| 5 | $100.00 |

The example illustrates this general point: future interest to be received after year $t$ (where $t$ stands for some future year) can be converted to its present-value equivalent by dividing it by the factor $(1 + r)^t$, where $r$ is the current interest rate. Therefore, if a regular coupon payment of $100 on a bond is to be received each year for five years, the present value of this interest stream is the sum of all the present-value equivalents, and is given by:

$$\frac{100}{(1 + r)} + \frac{100}{(1 + r)^2} + \frac{100}{(1 + r)^3} + \frac{100}{(1 + r)^4} + \frac{100}{(1 + r)^5}$$

In general, the present value of the coupon payments, $C$, on a bond having $n$ years to go until maturity is given by:

$$(5.2) \quad \frac{C}{(1 + r)} + \frac{C}{(1 + r)^2} + \ldots + \frac{C}{(1 + r)^n}$$

For any specific bond, equation 5.2 gives the amount of funds required to reproduce the coupon payments for each of $n$ years, when the earning rate is $r$. Accordingly, equation 5.2 shows the present value of the stream of coupon payments. However, the present value of the coupon payments does not include the present value of the funds to be received when the bond matures after $n$ years. If we denote the value of the bond at maturity as $F$ ($F$ for face value), the present value of this receipt is $F \div (1 + r)^n$. If we add the present value of the maturity value to the present value of the coupon flow given by equation 5.2, the result is the *present value of the bond*. The present value of the bond shows how much the bond is worth in the market when the earning rate is $r$.

However, we know how much any bond is "worth" just by looking at its market price. What we do not know is $r$, the interest rate on the bond. Notice that the present values of both the coupon stream and the redemption prices are influenced by $r$. The higher the value of $r$, the lower the present value and vice versa. It is possible to find a value of $r$ that equates the present value of the bond with its price.

Moreover, the value of $r$ that equates the two has special significance. If a bond's price is higher than its present value when calculated at $r$, investors would be better off putting their funds into an account earning $r$, for they could withdraw the same coupon and principal payments that the bond offers but with a smaller investment. If the bond's price were lower than the present value, the opposite is true, and the bond is preferred. Therefore, associated with the price of a bond is an implied earning rate (a value of $r$) that makes the present value of the bond exactly equal to its market price. This specific value of $r$ is called the bond's *yield to maturity*. If we denote the yield to maturity by $i$ and the price of the bond by $P$, the following expression can be solved for $i$:

$$(5.3) \quad P = \frac{C}{(1 + i)} + \frac{C}{(1 + i)^2} + \ldots\ldots + \frac{C}{(1 + i)^n} + \frac{F}{(1 + i)^n}$$

In equation 5.3, we know the market price, $P$, the bond's coupon, $C$, the maturity of the bond, $n$, and the redemption price, $F$. We can find a specific interest rate that makes the left-hand side (the present value) equal to the right-hand side (the price).

Sounds easy. However, calculating $i$ from equation 5.3 is a difficult problem because of the polynomial expression in the denominator. One approach is to assume various values for $i$, and use them to calculate the present value of the bond. These present values can then be compared with the price. The assumed value of $i$ that equates the price with the present value is the solution. This trial-and-error method can produce a close approximation to $i$. For example, suppose you are contemplating buying a five-year, $1,000 bond at a selling price of $963 that pays a coupon of 10 percent per year. In terms of equation 5.3, $P = \$963$, $F = \$1,000$, $C = .10 \times \$1,000 = \$100$ per year, and

$n = 5$. If trial $i$ values of .09, .10, .11, and .12 are used, the following present values result:

| present value at: | $i =$ |
|---|---|
| $1,039 | .09 |
| 1,000 | .10 |
| 963 | .11 |
| 927 | .12 |

Notice that a value of $i = .11$ makes the present value of the bond equal to its price of $963. The bond's yield to maturity is thus .11. Smaller values of $i$ result in present values that are too high, whereas larger values reduce the present values of the bond below its price.[4]

This trial-and-error process can be long and tedious. A reasonably close approximation to the yield can be obtained with a one-step calculation using the following formula:

$$(5.4) \quad i = \frac{C + \dfrac{F - P}{n}}{\dfrac{F + P}{2}}$$

For our example:

$$i = \frac{100 + \dfrac{1,000 - 963}{5}}{\dfrac{1,000 + 963}{2}} = .1094$$

Thus, by using equation 5.4, we get a yield of 10.94 percent, compared to an exact yield to maturity of 11 percent. For many uses, this may be a close enough approximation.[5]

## REAL INTEREST RATES

Jim finally saved the last of the $10,000 required to buy that sportscar he had always wanted. But now it is decision time. He is impressed by high current interest rates. Maybe he should wait a year for the

4. Notice also that a trial rate of .10 makes the present value of the bond equal to its face value of $1,000. In this case, the yield and the coupon rate are the same. If the prevailing interest rate on similar bonds was .10, then a bond paying a coupon of this amount would sell at its face value. In general, when the price and the redemption value of a bond are equal, the yield to maturity equals the coupon rate.

5. This approximation will deteriorate in accuracy when the selling price of the bond varies substantially from the face value.

car, and put the money into a one-year note on which he could earn 13 percent. In a year, he would be richer. Then he would buy the car. The decision is made. Jim waits a year, putting his $10,000 into a one-year 13 percent note.

When the year is up, Jim cashes his note and heads for the car dealership. To his chagrin, he finds the price of the sportscar has gone up from $10,000 to $12,500. Even by throwing in his "profits" from the note Jim is still short. He is, in fact, worse off for having loaned his $10,000 for a year. The resulting $11,300 he has now will buy less of what Jim wants than his $10,000 would have bought one year ago. Jim delayed buying the product he wanted because of his expectations that he would be able to buy it and more in a year. In other words, he gave up his command over products (his $10,000) in the present because of his expectations that he could increase his command over products in the future.

Fundamentally, all lending is motivated by the lender's expectation of an increase in purchasing power over the period of the loan. Logic dictates that lenders expect to earn enough interest to offset the effect of inflation and still be left with some increased ability to purchase products. In Jim's case, $2,500 in interest would have been required just to cover the cost of inflation for the specific product he wanted. For Jim to have made a real gain, the interest payment would have had to exceed $2,500. Only then could Jim have bought more products in a year than at present.

The *real interest rate* is the inflation-adjusted interest rate that shows how much the lender's purchasing power is expected to go up. As long ago as the early 1900s, the great American economist Irving Fisher specifically defined the real interest rate to be the observed (or nominal) interest rate minus the rate of inflation expected over the period of the financial contract. Notice the word *expected* here. As in the case of Jim, lenders do not know what the upcoming inflation rate will be when they commit their funds to a loan. Therefore, investors cannot know with certainty whether they will realize an increase in purchasing power when they lend their money. All lenders operate on the basis of expectations in this regard. Expectations of the upcoming inflation rate translate into expectations of the real interest rate. The following expression summarizes the relationship:

**(5.5)** $R^* = i - p^*$

where $R^*$ stands for the expected real interest rate, $i$ is the nominal interest rate, and $p^*$ is the expectation of inflation in the period ahead. In Jim's case, the nominal interest rate on the one-year note was 13 percent. It is logical to assume that Jim's willingness to buy the note was based on his belief that the price of the product he wanted would go up by less than 13 percent. As it turned out, Jim's inflation index (the price of a sportscar, in his case) went up by 25 percent, resulting in a negative value for the real rate of interest *after the fact*. Jim realized a real return of 13% − 25% = −12%. This achieved real return is called the *realized real rate*, whereas the real return that investors expect is called the *expected real rate*.

Realized real rates can be directly measured. In contrast, expected real rates can only be inferred from assumptions made about inflationary expectations. On the basis of studies of realized real rates and studies that construct measures of expected rates, many economists have concluded that real rates are more stable than nominal rates. According to this view, the main reason observed interest rates fluctuate is that the expectation of inflation, $p^*$, fluctuates.

## HOW THE FEDERAL RESERVE DEFINES MONEY

The last part of this language lesson deals with how the Federal Reserve Board officially defines money. It is an advanced topic in "finance" because some of the monetary definitions are completely incomprehensible without a working knowledge of the language. In early 1980, the Federal Reserve announced a massive overhaul of its money definitions.[6] At this writing, the Federal Reserve has four definitions of money, each of which adds additional financial assets to the previous definition. The definitions are as follows:

M1 = currency + demand deposits + traveler's checks + other checkable deposits

M2 = M1 + overnight repurchase agreements and eurodollars + money-market mutual-fund shares held by individuals + money-market deposit accounts + savings accounts + small-denomination CDs

M3 = M2 + large-denomination CDs + repurchase agreements (longer than overnight) + money-market mutual fund shares held by institutions.

L = M3 + eurodollar deposits (longer than overnight) + U.S. savings bonds + short-term treasury securities[7] + banker's acceptances + commercial paper

The first of these definitions, M1, is described as the "narrow" definition in that it includes only financial assets that are being used as a medium of exchange. Besides currency, demand deposits, and traveler's checks, the definition incorporates most forms of interest-bearing accounts upon which checks can be drawn. These include Negotiable Order of Withdrawal (NOW) and Automatic Transfer Ser-

6. See *The Federal Reserve Bulletin*, February, 1980.

7. Includes T-Bills and all U.S. coupon-bearing bonds having eighteen months or less until maturity. U.S. savings bonds are fully-discounted notes sold in small-denominations ($25 and up) and largely to households. These money supply definitions are as given in the *Federal Reserve Bulletin*, February, 1983.

vice (ATS) accounts, both of which allow checks to be drawn on savings accounts. The "other checkable deposits" category also includes share-draft accounts held in mutually owned thrift institutions. (A mutually owned thrift institution is one where the depositors are the owners, and accordingly where their deposits are in the form of shares in the company. Such an account is made checkable by allowing the holder to write drafts authorizing the liquidation of shares in the account, with payment of the proceeds to the person presenting the draft.)

M2 begins to add to this narrow definition a group of financial assets the Federal Reserve feels are close enough to the medium of exchange that they should be added to it for some purposes. M3 continues this progression by adding a second group of financial assets that have high liquidity and are close to the medium of exchange because of their easy transferability into checking accounts. Finally, L adds still more short-term financial assets, resulting in a broad measure of short-term liquidity in the economy. Indeed, the financial assets included in L encompass most of the financial instruments that are traded in short-term financial markets in the United States.

Why so many definitions? It is a recognition of the rapid state of change in U.S. financial institutions. In efforts to both survive and prosper in the environment of high and volatile interest rates of the late 1970s, banking institutions rapidly produced innovations in the financial arrangements they make and the instruments they deal with. Some of these new instruments, such as the overnight repurchase agreement, have many of the properties of money. Whether they should be added to our official definitions is a complex question requiring considerable research to resolve. Meanwhile, the Federal Reserve has chosen to involve an exhaustive number of financial assets in their official definitions.

**Important Ideas in This Chapter**

1. Primary markets are those for newly issued securities, and secondary markets are markets in existing securities.

2. Short-term financial markets are those for assets with maturities of less than one year, whereas long-term markets are for assets having longer maturities, or in the case of stocks, infinite maturities.

3. Treasury Bills, commercial paper, and banker's acceptances are important short-term financial instruments in current U.S. financial markets. Each is sold on a fully discounted basis.

4. Repurchase agreements are arrangements made in connection with short-term notes. These agreements give the holder the option of selling the note back to the issuer at a set price after a set time has passed.

5. Overnight repurchase agreements are contracts that transfer funds from the checking accounts of firms to certificates of deposit on an overnight basis, returning the funds for the next day's business.

**6.** Certificates of deposit are IOUs issued mostly by financial institutions. Large-denomination CDs are negotiable, meaning they can be traded in a secondary market.

**7.** Money-market certificates are a recent innovation introduced by thrift institutions providing Treasury-Bill rates of interest to households willing to commit savings for six-month periods.

**8.** Money-market mutual funds and Money-Market Deposit Accounts (MMDA's) are recent innovations that have superseded money-market certificates in attracting household savings. Money-market funds and MMDA's offer advantages of liquidity and checkability not offered by certificates.

**9.** Eurodollar deposits are accounts denominated in dollars and held in non-U.S. financial institutions by U.S. citizens. They have grown in popularity in recent years because of the high interest rate often available on them.

**10.** Corporate bonds are long-term IOUs of corporations. Debentures are unsecured corporate debt, whereas mortgage bonds are secured by buildings or equipment.

**11.** The U.S. Treasury and other agencies of the federal government issue federal bonds, which are the long-term debt instruments of the national government.

**12.** Municipal bonds are the debt instruments of state and local governments. Their distinguishing feature is that the interest on them is exempt from federal taxes.

**13.** The ownership certificates in corporations are called common stock, and entitle the holder to vote in the election of the board of directors and other major corporate-policy decisions.

**14.** Preferred stock is a cross between bonds and common stock; it has some of the properties of debt and some of the properties of equity.

**15.** Convertible bonds are debt instruments that convert into common stock. They are a way for a firm to issue debt that later converts into ownership capital.

**16.** Callable bonds are bonds that can be redeemed at a specified price prior to maturity.

**17.** The interest rate on a short-term note can be easily calculated from the price of the note by using a standard formula.

**18.** The yield to maturity on a long-term coupon-bearing bond is the discount rate that equates the present value of the bond and principal payments with the market price of the bond. The yield to maturity is the specific term declaring the interest rate on a bond.

**19.** The real interest rate is the inflation-adjusted interest rate that shows how much the lender's purchasing power is expected to go up. Irving Fisher defined it to be the difference between the nominal rate of interest and the expected rate of inflation.

**20.** The Federal Reserve's money definitions encompass a broad spectrum of financial assets in a series of money measures, each more inclusive than the last. The two most popular are M1 and M2. M1 includes currency and all checkable deposits whereas M2 adds overnight repurchase agreements and eurodollars, money-market mutual funds, savings accounts, and small-denomination CDs.

**Discussion Questions**

**1.** Do Treasury Bills always have a lower interest rate than commercial paper? Check out some recent data to find out about this. Explain the reasons for what you have found.

**2.** What would be the result of a new Federal Reserve rule stating that banks have to hold the same ratio of required reserves on overnight repurchase agreements as they hold on checking accounts? Explain.

**3.** Explain carefully the difference between investing in a money-market certificate and investing in a money-market mutual fund.

**4.** Does logic suggest that a municipal bond should have a higher or lower interest rate than a Treasury bond? Find out what the relationship is between the yields on these two kinds of bonds. Explain why you observe the pattern you found.

**5.** Explain in your own words the difference between the expected real interest rate and the realized real interest rate on a Treasury Bill.

**Suggested Readings**

Further reading about the language of finance can take the direction of a good corporate finance book. One popular text is James Van-Horne's *Financial Management* (Prentice-Hall, latest edition). A definitive account of the working of money markets is given in Marcie Stigum's *Money Markets: Myth, Reality, and Practice*.

# Accent on Reading
# the Wall Street Journal

Even the best college-level preparation in literature does not prepare a person of above-average brightness to read certain parts of the *Wall Street Journal*. Many things that cannot be learned in the classroom can be picked up by imitation. But, this too is difficult in the case of the *Journal*. Even though you may creep up on an experienced reader of the *Journal*, peek over the person's shoulder, and observe for hours, you probably will still not be able to figure out what information is being gleaned from the blizzard of numbers contained in the last part of this, the world's foremost financial daily paper.

What is a person to do? Read this feature section, and you will have a start on becoming an experienced *Journal* reader. Here, I will present a key to reading parts of the *Journal* that are difficult to understand. To read this section properly, you must have a copy of the *Journal* to accompany the discussion. The date is not important, because the format of the paper stays the same.

Open the *Journal* to the second section, next-to-last page—the one with the graphs labeled "The Dow Jones Averages." The *Dow Jones industrials* are a group of thirty large firms that the Dow Jones company has been following for many years.[1] The *Dow Jones*

*Industrial Average* is based on the average price per share of the common stock of the thirty industrial firms involved. When the Dow Jones company first started to calculate this average, it simply added together the thirty per-share prices of the firms, and divided by thirty to obtain an average price. Then, each day the average price was recomputed. Changes in it gave an indication of general price movements in the broad class of stocks represented by the thirty firms in the sample. But, at some point, complications set in. Some firms split their stock, two shares for one, meaning they gave out two new shares for each one of the old shares outstanding. When this is done, the price of the new split shares quickly moves to about half the old price. After all, if you own 100 shares of General Motors (GM) worth $40 per share of $4,000 total market value, and GM replaces your 100 with 200 newly split shares, it is logical that the market value of your holdings should still be $4,000 or $4,000 ÷ 200 = $20 per share. When this happens, an adjustment has to be made in calculating the average. Otherwise, the index would incorrectly conclude that GM stock fell in value from $40 to $20 on the day of the split. Through the years, many hundreds of such adjustments have been

1. The specific firms in the Dow Jones Industrial Average are Allied Corporation, Aluminum Company, American Brands, American Can, American Telephone and Telegraph, Bethlehem Steel, DuPont, Eastman Kodak, Exxon, General Electric, General Foods, General Motors, Goodyear, Inco,

IBM, International Harvester, International Paper, Johns-Mansville, Merck, Minnesota Mining and Manufacturing, Owens-Illinois, Proctor and Gamble, Sears, Standard Oil of California, Texaco, Union Carbide, United Technologies, U.S. Steel, Westinghouse, and Woolworth.

incorporated into the index. At present, the divisor corrected for splits and other similar changes is about 1.3. Accordingly, the "average" is almost a sum of the prices of the thirty stocks, since we are dividing the sum by only 1.3. Doing this keeps the average comparable to its value in earlier years.

The other two Dow Jones averages are for transportation and utility firms. They are constructed the same way as the industrial average. Although there are three Dow Jones averages, the one that is most prominently reported is the industrial average. When you hear that the stock market went up by ten points, it usually means that the Dow Jones Industrial Average rose by ten points from one day to the next. From the chart on the next to last page of the *Journal,* you can track the path of the Dow Jones Industrial Average for the last several months.

Now, look across the page to the "Market Diary" table. The first row shows how many stocks (issues) were bought and sold during the previous five days of trading. The next row shows how many of these went up, how many went down, and how many were unchanged. The last two rows labeled "new highs" and "new lows" show the number of issues that reached high or low prices compared with their prices in the last twelve months. The number of advancing and declining stocks, along with the new highs and lows, give a broad indicator of the path of the market during the previous five trading days. On a day of a rapidly advancing market, it is not uncommon to see advancing issues leading declining issues by a three or four to one ratio. In a rapidly declining market, it is also not uncommon to see these ratios reversed.

Now, look below the "Market Diary" table to the one labeled "Other Market Indicators." In this table, the *Journal* presents alternative measures (to the Dow Jones average) of overall market behavior. The *NYSE composite* is listed first. It is a considerably broader measure of overall market activity than the Dow Jones average, encompassing most of the stocks traded on the market in the previous day. It is also an average that is adjusted as necessary for stock splits, and so on. The NYSE composite contains all firms whose stock was traded in the previous day, whereas the Dow Jones Industrial Average is composed of mostly large, secure (called blue chips) firms.

A second important index listed under "Other Market Indicators" is the *Standard & Poor's 500 stock index.* It is an index of the stock prices of five hundred firms and is similar in construction to the Dow Jones average. Part of the importance of the Standard & Poor's 500 stock index is its long historical availability, dating back to the early 1900s. By contrast, the NYSE composite dates back only to the latter part of the 1960s.

The last of the graphs on this page of the *Journal* shows the volume of trading on the New York Stock Exchange. The numbers shown are in millions of shares traded. Recent years have seen a staggering increase in the volume of trading in stocks. Many would agree that without the assistance of large-scale computers, trading on the stock exchange would be confined to about half of what the chart shows. Maybe you have not picked up on it yet, but a fair amount of money changes hands each day on the stock exchange. With 45 million shares traded at an average price of about 50 dollars per share, about $2.25 billion changes hands each day on the New York Stock Exchange alone.

Turn now to the second-to-last page labeled "NYSE—Composite Transactions." This is the page that is awash in numbers. To understand what the title "Composite Transactions" means, we must digress a little. There are various stock exchanges around the country where corporate stocks can be traded. The largest two are in New York, with the *New York Stock Exchange* (NYSE) being by far the biggest. The *American Stock Exchange* (Amex), also in New York, ranks second in size and number of shares traded. Other smaller exchanges are located in Boston, Philadelphia, and San Francisco. When a corporation reaches a sufficient size, it can apply for "listing" on one of these exchanges. Once the firm obtains a stock-exchange listing, its shares will be traded on that exchange. Generally, the NYSE has the most stringent listing requirements regarding size and financial stability, so this exchange tends to deal in the stocks of large, well-established corporations. Firms have an incentive to seek listing on the largest possible exchange because their shares get the maximum investor exposure. Although almost every daily newspaper carries the prices of NYSE stocks, not all carry Amex prices, and few carry prices of shares traded only on other exchanges. Firms can "graduate" from smaller to larger exchanges. Many NYSE firms were previously listed on the Amex. In recent years, firms listed on either the NYSE or the Amex have also been traded on other exchanges simultaneously. For a time, this practice created some confusion because there were different prices reported for the same stock traded on different exchanges. Recently, the exchanges began publishing a composite transactions table for the NYSE and the Amex that adds the stock transactions made on other exchanges to those made on the exchange where the stock is listed. Thus, the "NYSE—Composite Transactions" table in front of you includes all transactions made in stocks listed on other exchanges.

Let us dive into the sea of numbers on this page. Pick any stock you like. (The names are abbreviated, but most of them are easy to figure out.) The first two numbers to the left of the firm's name show the highest and lowest prices the stock has reached in the previous fifty-two weeks, ending with the current trading day. Each day, this fifty-two week backdrop changes, deleting the most distant day and adding the latest day. The two numbers give the reader a moving picture of the price fluctuations of the stock in the latest time period.

The first number to the right of the firm's name shows the indicated dividend payment per share per year. A figure of 2.00 means that if the firm continues to pay dividends for the entire year at the rate it actually paid for the most current quarter, it will have paid $2.00 per share per year. Usually, firms pay dividends at quarterly intervals, or four times per year. In the case of a 2.00 figure, this means that the firm paid $2.00 ÷ 4 = $.50 per share during the last quarter.

The second number to the right of the firm's name is the annual *dividend yield*. It is calculated by dividing the indicated yearly dividend by the current price of the stock. If a stock paying a $2.00 per year dividend is selling at $25.00 per share, then the dividend yield is 2 ÷ 25 = .08 or 8 percent. The table would show it as 8.0, since the entries are in percentages. The third number to the right of the firm's name is the stock's *price-earning ratio* or PE ratio. The PE ratio is the result of dividing the current price of the stock by the firm's earnings per share in the last fifty-two week period. *Earnings per share* (EPS) is the result of dividing the firm's earnings available to common stockholders (essentially after-tax

profits) by the number of shares outstanding. EPS shows the amount of corporate profits per share of common stock. Investors are usually concerned with evaluating the price of a firm's stock in relation to its earnings. The PE ratio is a convenient measure of this key relationship. Suppose a firm earned $3.00 per share profits during the last year and its stock currently sells for $30.00 per share. The PE ratio is $30 ÷ $3 = 10. The stock is said to be selling at ten times its earnings. At current prices, investors believe that one dollar of earnings of a firm is worth ten dollars of market price.

The fourth number to the right of the firm's name summarizes the number of shares of the stock traded during the previous trading day. Specifically, the figure in the table shows the amount of trading in *hundreds of shares*. Thus, a number of 120 in this slot means that 120 hundred-share lots, or 12,000 shares, were traded during the previous day.

The last four entries in the table give price information on the day's trading in the stock. The first two of these numbers show the high and low prices attained by the stock during the day's trading. The next number (the second from the right) gives the closing price for the stock during the day. Finally, the right-hand figure in the table gives the change in the stock's closing price from the previous day.

Look at the left-hand column on the "NYSE—Composite Transactions" page. The table labeled "Most Active Stocks" lists the fifteen stocks that had the highest volume of trading during the day of all those listed. Why the interest in the heaviest traded stocks? Investors want to know where the "action" is, and a quick review of the stocks having the heaviest volume of shares traded often provides an indication of this. It is not unusual to find several stocks from the same industry on the most active list when new information comes to light on the profit prospects for that industry. For example, if a major new development has occurred affecting the oil industry, five or six of the most active stocks might very well be oil stocks.

Turn your *Journal* to the page labeled "New York Exchange Bonds." Stocks are not the only security traded on organized exchanges. The *New York Bond Exchange* is the best known market for bonds. Pick a row in this table. The first entry in the row gives the firm's abbreviated name. Just after the name are two numbers grouped together. The first of these shows the annual coupon rate on the bond, and the second shows the last two digits of the year in which the bond matures. For example, a particular row might read: "Ford 8 1/8 90." This refers to the Ford Motor Company bonds carrying a coupon of 8⅛ percent per year and maturing in 1990.

The first number to the right of the coupon-maturity data is the approximate yield to maturity on the bond, measured in percent. However, some bonds have the letters *cv* in place of a yield. This means that the security is convertible, and indicates that a conventional yield-to-maturity calculation is not meaningful.

The next number in the row (the second one to the right of the coupon-maturity data) is the volume of trading in the bond, measured in units. Each unit is $1,000 of face value of the bond. Thus, an entry of 112 means that $112,000 of face value of the bond was traded during the previous day.

The remaining numbers in the table show the high, low, and closing prices for the bond during the day's trading. The final number shows the change in the closing price from the previous day's trade.

Turning back further, you will come to the page labeled "Amex Composite Transactions." This page shows the same numbers for Amex-listed stocks that the NYSE composite page showed for NYSE-listed stocks. As with the NYSE data, the trades of Amex stocks on all exchanges are added together for this composite table.

Leaf back through your *Journal* until you find the page labeled "Over-the-Counter Markets." This page gives stock price information for stocks that are not listed on any exchange. Instead, such stocks are bought and sold "over the counter" (OTC) by brokers and dealers. These dealers quote both a bid and an asking price for the stocks in which they deal. The bid price is the dealer's offer to buy shares, whereas the asking price is the dealer's selling price for the shares. The dealer's profit on over-the-counter stocks is represented by the spread between bid and asking prices.

In the OTC table, the first entry in each row gives the name of the stock, followed by the indicated annual dividend. Next, the sales volume of the stock is given, again in

hundreds of shares as with the NYSE and Amex volume data. The next three numbers show the dealer's bid price, asking price, and the change in bid price compared with the previous day.

In OTC markets, dealers change their bid-ask quotes when they see market conditions changing. In an active dealer market, prices of OTC stocks can be revised upward or downward with the same swiftness as listed stocks. Many of the firms in OTC markets are not listed because they are not large enough or have not had a long enough financial history to meet the exchange's listing requirements. Many listed firms were formerly traded over the counter.

Look through the market pages of your *Journal* until you find a table labeled "Treasury Issues—Bonds, Notes, Bills." This table shows market information on U.S. bonds, notes, and bills. The largest part of the table is labeled "Treasury Bonds and Notes." It shows market information on all currently issued coupon-bearing U.S. Treasury debt. The first three entries in each line of the upper part of the table give the annual coupon rate, the year of maturity, and the month when the bond matures. These three items of information identify the bond. They are also frequently used by investors as the name of the bond. For example, if one of the lines in the table began "7 7/8s, 1993 Feb," the bond would ordinarily be referred to as "the seven-and-seven-eighths of February 1993."

Government bonds are traded over the counter. The remaining entries in each row of the table show the bid and asked prices for the bond, and the change in the bid price from the preceding day. The prices you see under the "bid" and "asked" columns are stated in decimals, but really mean the number of 32nds of a point. A value of 99.3 under the "asked" column means that each $100 of face value of the bond is being quoted by the dealer at a price of 99 and 3/32 of a dollar. This converts to a price in dollars of $99.0938. However, since Treasury bonds are sold in minimum lot sizes of $1,000, the actual asking price for a $1,000 bond is $990.94. Why quote prices in 32nds of a dollar? Why quote prices in terms of $100 of face value when $1,000 is the unit size? Tradition, dear reader, tradition. The last (right-hand side) number in the upper part of the table gives the yield to maturity on the bond.

The smaller section of the table at the bottom, labeled "U.S. Treasury Bills," gives information on the quoted prices for partially matured T-Bills. The first item of information in each row of this table is the date on which the bill matures. The next two numbers are the interest yield on the bill calculated respectively from the bid and asked prices of the bill, according to the Treasury's special method (see note 3 in chapter 5). The last number in each row gives the yield on the bill calculated from equation 5.1. You can see from this table that T-Bills may be bought with a wide variety of maturities, ranging from several days to about one year.

One last item of interest is a table entitled "Money Rates" that appears in various parts of the second section of the *Journal*. You will have to do some fishing around for this one. This table compiles current rates of interest on a wide variety of short-term financial assets. In it, you will find current prime rates, commercial-paper rates, T-Bill rates, eurodollar rates, and rates on money-market certificates and funds. It is a handy way to become instantly familiar with the current structure of short-term interest notes.

# PART II

# THE U.S. BANKING
# AND FINANCE INDUSTRY

## CHAPTER 6

# Banking Institutions —Past and Present

## CHAPTER OUTLINE

## IMPORTANT TERMS

dual charter
bank script
commercial banks
commercial loans
mutual savings banks
savings and loan associations
credit unions
thrift institutions
unit banks
branch banks
bank holding company
one-bank holding company
loan production offices

regulation Q
Automatic Transfer Service (ATS)
Negotiable Order of Withdrawal
  (NOW)
share-draft accounts
money-market certificates
all-savers certificates
depository institutions
nondepository institutions
insurance companies
pension funds
finance companies
mutual funds

---

## ✳MEMO

To:      All readers
From:    JWE

This chapter begins a section that deals with the banking and finance industry in the United States. The aim of this section is to familiarize you with how banking institutions evolved, how they are legally structured, what assets and liabilities they hold, and how they are managed. This first chapter is concerned with the evolution of banks and other financial institutions. The important aspects of how banks are organized in the United States are covered here. The chapter discusses the growth of savings and loan associations, mutual savings banks, and credit unions. The overlapping functions of these institutions are also dealt with. In this chapter, you can also learn something about how the sweeping changes made in the banking laws in 1980 affect the operation of banks and other banking institutions.

---

The design of the contemporary banking industry in the United States is in some ways similar to that of a new automobile. Neither was engineered "from the ground up" to be what it is today. Instead, both have evolved through time, with each year's current design retaining much from the past that has worked well, while adding new features intended to enhance the overall performance. The current structure of U.S. banking is a result of an evolutionary process dating back nearly to the start of the nation. We begin the chapter with a brief description of this evolution, as a way to better understand the "current model."

In your reading of this chapter, keep in mind that changes in banking structure are unfolding at a rapid if not dizzying pace. By the time you learn about the "current model" of U.S. banking, its congressional and White House architects may either have "recalled" parts of it, or made important changes. Thus, some of the information in this chapter may no longer be true by the time the book reaches your hands. However, in all likelihood, most of what you find here will be a correct description of the "current model" of U.S. banking.

## THE GROWTH OF COMMERCIAL BANKING IN THE UNITED STATES

Before the American Revolution, colonial loan offices in the American colonies were the forerunners of modern banks. These offices primarily made loans and issued their own paper money. In 1781, the Bank of North America was granted a federal charter to conduct banking operations with the public. This marked the introduction of banking in the fledgling United States of America.[1] Other banks quickly developed, gaining their charters (right to operate) mostly by special acts of the state government in which they intended to do business. By 1800, there were twenty-nine banks in the United States. In the late 1830s, Michigan and New York passed banking acts that allowed banks to be founded without special acts of law, but instead by meeting a set of legislative conditions. Other states followed this lead, thus greatly easing the administrative and political problems associated with forming new banks.

The Currency Act of 1863 and the National Bank Act of 1864 provided similar rules and conditions for the granting of bank charters by the federal government. The stated purpose of these national banks was (1) to issue uniform bank currency, (2) to strengthen the market for U.S. government securities, and (3) to help manage the financing of government debt.

With the side-by-side existence of federally chartered banks and those chartered by states, a *dual charter* banking system emerged in the United States that carries forth to the present. In chapter 7, the dual-charter system will be discussed more fully. At this point, it is only important to note that not too much time passed before both state and federally chartered banks were performing much the same banking functions. These included (1) making loans, (2) issuing bank currency or *bank script* as it is sometimes called, and (3) providing safe deposits for the savings of households.

These state and federally chartered banks were and still are referred to as *commercial banks.* The term *commercial* refers to the principal type of loans made by banks in the initial period of their existence. These loans, called *commercial loans,* were short-term, seasonal, and inventory-financing loans made to business firms. Since these loans aided commerce, they were called commercial loans and the lending institutions were called commercial banks.

## EMERGENCE OF THRIFT INSTITUTIONS

Since commercial banks focusing primarily on the needs of commerce and business, it is perhaps natural to expect other financial institutions to have developed with the needs of households primarily in mind. The first such development came quite early when in 1816, the first mutual savings bank was opened in Massachusetts. The word *mutual* indicates the form of legal ownership of these institutions. Their charter

---

1. A forerunner, the Pennsylvania Bank, was in operation in 1780, but primarily to finance the war effort rather than to perform banking functions.

authorizes their operation for the mutual benefit of the depositors. Depositors are the counterpart of stockholders in the corporate form of organization. Depositor-owners receive a distribution of the savings bank's earnings. Mutual savings banks can retain funds for contingencies, but are required by their charters to pay out to depositors all of the earnings produced by investing the depositors' funds.

Mutual savings banks were set up to be a safe and interest-earning repository for household savings. On the other hand, mutual savings banks were and still are chartered to provide mortgage loans to households to help facilitate home purchases. Indeed, for many years, mutual savings banks were legally bound to invest their depositors' funds in either home mortgages or government bonds. Recently, this restriction has been relaxed somewhat.

Mutual savings banks had their beginning on the eastern seaboard of the United States and have not expanded to any important degree beyond this geographic region. In most other parts of the nation, parallel household-oriented institutions called *savings and loan associations* developed, beginning in 1831. Savings and loan associations were set up both on a mutual basis and as stock corporations that could retain profits if they so desired. Their chartered purpose closely paralleled that of mutual savings banks. Mutual savings banks as well as savings and loan associations steadily grew into major factors in the home-mortgage market by the mid-twentieth century. During this period, they also established themselves as safe and interest-bearing repositories for household savings.

In 1909, still another type of financial institution began to appear. *Credit unions* were similar to savings banks in many ways, except that the right to make deposits in them and to borrow from them was limited to those who have a common bond of affiliation, such as with trade unions, religious groups, firms, or professions. Company credit unions in particular have grown rapidly in the last fifty years. Many have deposits automatically withheld from employee paychecks.

For the largest part of their existence, credit unions did not make mortgage loans. Instead, their lending activities were centered on making low-cost consumer loans to finance the purchase of automobiles and major appliances. In this way, the growth in credit unions filled a void only partially met by other financial institutions. However, in 1977, credit unions were authorized to make home mortgages, and have since entered this market.

Mutual savings banks, savings and loan associations, and credit unions are often called *thrift institutions,* a term that refers to their common goal of providing safe and interest-earning deposits that are primarily designed for household savers.

## UNIT AND BRANCH BANKING

Many banks operating in the United States have one office where all the bank's business is conducted. These are called *unit banks,* denoting

**TABLE 6.1**
**Breakdown of Branch and Unit Banking by State.**

| STATEWIDE BRANCH BANKING PREVALENT (16) | | LIMITED BRANCH BANKING PREVALENT (20) | | UNIT BANKING PREVALENT (14) | |
|---|---|---|---|---|---|
| Alaska | Nevada | Alabama | Mississippi | Colorado | Nebraska |
| Arizona | North Carolina | Arkansas | New Hampshire | Florida | North Dakota |
| California | Oregon | Georgia | New Jersey | Illinois | Oklahoma |
| Connecticut | Rhode Island | Indiana | New Mexico | Kansas | South Dakota |
| Delaware | South Carolina | Iowa | New York | Minnesota | Texas |
| Hawaii | Utah | Kentucky | Ohio | Missouri | West Virginia |
| Idaho | Vermont | Louisiana | Pennsylvania | Montana | Wyoming |
| Maryland | Washington | Maine | Tennessee | | |
| | | Massachusetts | Virginia | | |
| | | Michigan | Wisconsin | | |

Source: *Annual Statistical Digest of the Board of Governors of the Federal Reserve System, 1972–76*, p. 310.

that the bank is a single organizational unit. A *branch bank* is one that has multiple offices from which the bank's business is conducted. Branch banking is not permitted in all states, and in those where it is permitted, it is subject to varying limitations. For example, in Wisconsin, banks are allowed to establish new branches only within twenty-five miles of the home office. Other states permit branches to be formed anywhere in the state.

Table 6.1 shows which states fall into these categories. The table indicates that statewide branching is most common in the far western states, and limited branching is allowed in parts of the Midwest and East. The trend in recent years has been toward more branch banks and fewer unit banks. In 1950, there were 12,905 unit banks, and 1,241 branch banks with 4,721 total offices in the United States. By 1975, the number of unit banks had decreased to 9,111 and the number of branch banks had grown to 5,521 with 29,795 offices.

This steady movement toward dominance of banking by branch banks has not been unnoticed or unevaluated. Whether branch banking is or is not in the public's interest is an issue that has given rise to considerable debate in recent years. Some observers of the banking industry argue that branch banking introduces efficiencies in bank operations that benefit bank customers. Others counter that when all relevant factors are considered, this is not the case. One relatively clear result has been established by empirical research: a larger unit bank can usually operate at lower per-unit costs than a smaller unit bank.[2] In other words, there are economies of scale in unit banking. However, research also suggests that the added costs of operating several geographically separate offices of the same bank tend to offset scale economies, so that whether banking services are delivered more cheaply per unit by branch than by unit banking is far from clear.

2. An interesting analysis of the evidence in this area can be found in the Federal Reserve Bank of Chicago's *Midwest Banking in the Sixties*, March 1970, pp. 186–93. A more recent specific study of the issue can be found in William A. Longbrake and John A. Haslem, "Productive Efficiency in Commercial Banking," *Journal of Money, Credit and Banking*, August 1975, pp. 317–30.

A further argument concerning unit versus branch banking is that branch banking reduces the number of banks in a given banking area. One tabulation of the number of banks per metropolitan area shows that for unit-banking states, the average number of banks per area is about forty, whereas for states allowing limited branching, the average number is about twenty and for states allowing statewide branching, the average is about sixteen per metropolitan area. Branching thus tends to reduce the number of separate banks competing in a single geographic area. But does this mean that competition is reduced? And does it mean that the cost per unit of banking service available to the public is higher? There are not yet answers to these questions. As a result, the question of whether branch banking does or does not serve the public is still unresolved.

## BANK HOLDING COMPANIES

A *bank holding company* is a firm that owns one or more banks, which are the main business of the holding company. The phrase *holding company* can be thought of as referring to the holding of all the shares of one firm by another. Bank holding companies sometimes directly engage in business activities that earn profits. However, most derive the dominant portion of their income from the bank or banks they hold. Some holding companies hold several banks. Others hold only a single bank, and still others hold one or more banks along with other firms engaged in activities closely related to banking. An example of the latter would be a bank holding company that held two operating banks, a data-processing firm that specialized in servicing banks, and a real-estate investment firm.

The *one-bank holding company* is something of a curiosity. Although it may seem unusual for one firm to be set up principally for the purpose of holding another firm's shares, there are sound reasons why this arrangement is often attractive to bank managers. Holding companies can legally engage in forms of financing that are not available under the law to the banks they hold. The biggest case in point is commercial paper. Bank holding companies are allowed to issue commercial paper whereas the banks they hold are not. A bank holding company can thus issue commercial paper, and use the funds raised to buy certificates of deposit issued by the bank it holds. In this way, the bank held by a holding company has access to the commercial-paper market. In general, the motivation to create a holding-company structure on top of an operating bank is to allow more flexibility in raising funds.[3]

The growth in bank holding companies in the last three decades has been perhaps the largest change in the organization of U.S. bank-

3. States vary in their political attitude toward holding companies. In thirty-eight states, there are no restrictions on the formation of holding companies. The remaining twelve states prohibit holding-company formation in some ways.

ing. In 1957, there were 50 bank holding companies controlling a total of 417 banks. By 1977, the number of bank holding companies had reached 2,027, and the number of banks held was 3,903.

Many of the banks held by holding companies are branch banks. The growth in the number of branches owned by holding companies over the last thirty years is even more dramatic than the growth in the number of banking firms held. The total number of branches owned by holding companies was 851 in 1957. By 1977, this figure had grown to 21,223. Holding-company-owned banks accounted for about 7.5 percent of the total deposits in banks in 1957, and 72 percent of the total deposits in 1977. Clearly, as the decade of the 1980s progresses, banks that are not part of holding companies will be the exception rather than the rule.

Bank holding companies have also enabled banking activities to expand beyond the geographic limits imposed on a single bank. In 1927, the McFadden Act gave nationally chartered banks the right to open branches within the limits of the city, town, or village in which they were located if state laws did not forbid it. Legislation in the 1930s, most notably the Banking Act of 1933, further defined the concept of limited branching. However, expanding beyond these boundaries through the holding-company structure was not prohibited by this legislation. As a result, banks developed banking-related firms in distant states, and some holding companies, such as the First Bank System headquartered in Minneapolis–St. Paul, Minnesota, hold operating banks in several states. Thus, a form of interstate banking has grown from the holding-company structure.

In recent years, banks have found ways to expand their competitive turf beyond that associated with the holding-company structure. One such device is the *loan production office,* or LPO. A loan production office is a small facility set up to market and service loans, primarily commercial loans. Banks may set up LPOs in other cities or states without violating branching laws. Through these LPOs, banks can compete for loans beyond their chartered geographic area.

Banks are also achieving a form of interstate banking through the mail. At present, there are no specific restrictions preventing a bank in one city from soliciting the deposits of customers in another city or state through the mail. At present, mail-order banking is quite limited. But, if interstate banking by mail becomes widespread, then many large banks will begin to see all large banking markets throughout the country as potential arenas within which to compete for business.

## THE OVERLAPPING FUNCTIONS OF BANKS AND THRIFTS

Earlier, you read that the term *commercial banks* referred to these institutions' primary role in serving the needs of commerce and business. You also read that the organization and growth of thrift institutions were motivated by a central concern for the needs of household savers. The picture thus painted is one of separate institutions dealing with the banking needs of business firms and households. The reality is somewhat different.

To a degree, banks and thrifts have always had some overlap in the customers they serve and in the "products" they sell. Through time, the amount of this overlap varies, and the competitive edge of one or the other shifts in serving particular customer groups. An important job of government regulators is to adjust the laws applying to each, in order to maintain a competitive balance between banks and thrifts that best serves the public. This is not always easy. Regulations are slow to change, and banks and thrifts are quick to react. And, the job of regulating banks and thrifts is split between several government boards, as we shall see in later chapters. This complicates the job of coordinating the regulatory changes that apply to each type of institution.

The major reason the functions of banks and thrifts overlap is that both are concerned with maximizing profits. Thus, when an attractive financial service or market is recognized, each institution wants to participate in providing the service or serving the market. Some examples of this may help you to appreciate the nature of the competitive ebbs and flows that have more or less continually been at work to adjust the competitive balance between these two institutions.

As part of the sweeping changes made in the regulation of financial institutions in the 1930s, both banks and thrifts were restricted in the rate of interest they could pay on savings deposits. In *regulation Q*, the banking laws provided that thrifts could pay a somewhat higher rate of interest on savings than banks.[4] Also, banks were prevented from accepting business savings deposits. At the same time, banks were given the monopoly right to issue non-interest-bearing demand deposits. By these ground rules, separate functions were laid out for banks and thrifts. But, would the walls thus constructed hold up?

For a while, yes. But when the United States began to experience higher interest rates for extended periods of time in the 1970s, competitive pressures mounted on the part of banks and thrifts to each realize a bigger share of the income associated with those higher rates. In the mid-1970s, banks obtained regulatory approval to issue large certificates of deposit (over $100,000) at market rates of interest as opposed to regulation-Q ceiling rates. A similar charge was made in the regulations applying to large eurodollar accounts. This largely freed commercial banks from the regulation Q interest-rate constraints. With the growth of bank holding companies by this time providing a channel whereby banks could gain access to borrowed funds in the commercial-paper market, another avenue was thus opened

---

4.  At present, the interest-rate ceilings set up by regulation Q are being dismantled as a result of banking legislation passed in 1980. You can read about this legislation in chapter 10.

to obtain funds for lending and investment. When continued high interest rates increased the pressures on banks to pay interest on deposits held in checking accounts, the response was to begin to allow transfers via telephone from savings accounts to checking accounts. With this change, it became quite convenient for customers to hold the largest part of their checking balance in a savings account that earned interest, making a few phone calls a month to transfer funds into their checking account. In 1978, banks took the next logical step in this direction by providing for *Automatic Transfer Service* (ATS) accounts that did the same thing, only automatically. In an ATS account, when the checking account has a check drawn on it, funds are automatically transferred from an associated interest-bearing savings account into the checking account. With the ATS accounts, banks had essentially found a legal way to pay interest on checking balances, thus retaining and attracting funds into these types of accounts.

Thrifts did not sit idly by while these innovations in bank operations were taking place. For some time, thrifts had publicly expressed an interest in obtaining the authority to issue checking accounts for their household customers. Many people saw the role of thrifts as evolving into the household banking sector rather than the commercial banking sector. But, to be the household's banker, thrifts had to be able to issue checking accounts. The checkbook is the centerpiece of household financial accounts.

In 1972 in Massachusetts, and throughout New England by 1976, thrifts were issuing *Negotiable Order of Withdrawal (NOW)* accounts. These accounts are interest-bearing savings accounts upon which the holder can write an order of withdrawal of funds that can be transferred to a third party. These orders of withdrawal look almost like checks, but they are different in that they legally authorize the bearer to withdraw funds from the writer's savings account. Several court battles ensued over whether the NOW accounts were checking accounts. The results were mixed. But the pattern was clear. Thrifts were bent on finding ways to issue household checking accounts. The only question was whether their ingenuity would surpass that of their regulators.

Other mutually organized thrifts (predominantly credit unions) were issuing *share-draft accounts,* which are negotiable authorizations entitling the bearer to withdraw shares from a savings account held in a mutually owned thrift. Both NOW accounts and share-draft accounts gave thrifts the ability to offer household savers checking-type accounts that pay interest.

To respond to banks' access to funds through large CDs and commercial paper, thrifts obtained approval to issue *money-market certificates,* 6-month $10,000 notes carrying essentially market rates of interest tied to the 180-day U.S. Treasury Bill rate. The certificates gave thrifts access to household funds that otherwise would have been invested directly in short-term financial assets. More recently, the *all-savers certificate,* a federally tax-exempt one-year note whose interest rate is tied to a one-year Treasury Bill, provides thrifts with a way to attract and retain the savings of high-tax-bracket savers for whom tax-exempt investments yield high net rates of return.

## DEPOSITORY INSTITUTIONS IN THE 1980s

With the dramatic changes in the charters of banks and thrifts of the 1970s, each has moved substantially into the traditional "territory" of the other. The advent of NOW and share-draft accounts has provided thrifts with the license to issue the equivalent of interest-bearing checking accounts. In this environment, the need arises for a new classification of financial institutions and the regulations that apply to them.

A *depository institution* is a financial institution that holds checkable deposits. At the present time, depository institutions include commercial banks, savings and loan associations, mutual savings banks, and credit unions. A *nondepository institution* is a financial institution that does not hold checkable deposits, such as an insurance company or a security broker. Why build this distinction around checkable deposits? The simple reason is that checkable deposits are essentially money, and thus depository institutions help determine the supply of money by their expansion of deposits. Nondepository institutions are more nearly pure financial intermediaries, receiving inflows of funds for investment in primary securities.

In 1980, sweeping changes were made in federal banking laws in the United States that impact on the future growth of depository institutions for some time to come. In chapter 10, these changes will be discussed in detail. For now, it suffices to distill some of the main features of this legislation as it affects the growth of the financial institutions involved. A major philosophy embraced by the new law is that all depository institutions are treated in essentially the same way. Prior to the 1980 law, banks had one set of regulations and thrifts another. The 1980 law treats all depository institutions as a group. For example, prior to 1980, banks had specific reserve requirements set by the Federal Reserve Board and by state banking commissions. Thrifts did not. After the law, all depository institutions had to comply with reserve requirements established by the Federal Reserve.

The 1980 law in most respects gives thrifts the role they had sought during the 1970s—to become the complete household bank. In this respect, the change in law supports a trend toward more separation in the banking functions performed by banks and thrifts, with more emphasis being placed by commercial banks on serving the banking needs of business customers, and more emphasis being placed by thrifts on serving all the banking needs of households.

The infusion of computer technology into the banking industry has already begun to impact on this industry's way of doing business. And the trend that began in the late 1970s will continue to grow throughout the 1980s. Remote electronic tellers enable banking to take place at all hours and at locations other than the bank's office. With electronic tellers, customers can do nearly all their banking when and almost where they choose. The results of these transactions are fed back to the office for processing by mostly automatic computer operations. The next logical step beyond remote tellers is for depository institutions to tie in with home computers, so that customers could do remote banking operations in their homes. By early 1983, experiments along these lines were taking place in Florida and were being contemplated elsewhere.

## MODERN NONDEPOSITORY INSTITUTIONS

There are other important financial institutions that do not hold checkable deposits. They include life insurance companies, fire and casualty insurance companies, pension funds, finance companies, and mutual funds. These institutions regularly receive a portion of the income earned in the economy, as it flows into accounts by contractual agreements or by the discretionary deposits of income earners. These institutions then invest in the primary securities (stocks, bonds, and notes) of firms and in the bonds issued by state, local, and federal governments.

*Insurance companies* receive regular flows of premiums on policies and other contracts struck with their customers. They also have outflows associated with claims made by policyholders and with other contractual payments. But, at any point in time, insurance firms have a stock of accumulated funds to keep invested in earning assets. As a result, they become major factors in the market for corporate bonds and other types of primary securities.

*Pension funds* receive payments from workers over the lifetime of the workers' employment, then make payments to the pensioners upon their retirement. Accordingly, these institutions tend to have a stock of accumulated assets to be used for investment purposes. The payment commitments made by pension funds are based on earning projections on the accumulated funds held by them. Thus, these institutions have a strong motivation to keep funds invested at rates of interest consistent with their expected payments. Often, pension funds are interested in long-term investments where the earnings are predictable if not known with virtual certainty.

*Finance companies* make loans mostly to consumers for the purchase of durable goods such as automobiles, appliances, furniture, and televisions. These loans tend to be for relatively short maturities (four years or less) and are secured by the asset purchased. Finance companies thus produce a flow of monthly payments on outstanding loans, most of which is reinvested in new loans. A large portion of the funds advanced to consumers by finance companies are obtained in short-term financial markets through the issue of commercial paper.

*Mutual funds* are investment pools mutually owned by those who contribute money to them. They may consist of stocks, bonds, money-market instruments, gold, or any combination of these assets. Households invest in these funds on either a sporadic or planned basis; the funds then invest in securities consistent with the fund's objective. Mutual funds are divided into shares on the basis of the funds contributed. The value of each share is determined by the aggregate value of the securities held by the fund. Thus, savers share in any capital gains or losses the fund experiences. Accordingly, a mutual fund has a "price," which is the per-share value of the assets held by the fund, and which is quoted by security dealers and perhaps published in the *Wall Street Journal*.

## Important Ideas in This Chapter

**1.** Banking in the United States originated in the late 1700s with the primary purpose being to serve the needs of commerce and industry—thus the label, commercial banks.

**2.** In the early 1800s, thrift institutions emerged with the primary goal of serving the needs of household savers. These institutions include mutual savings banks, savings and loan associations, and credit unions.

**3.** Unit banking refers to the operation of one-office banking firms. Branch banking refers to multi-office banking firms. State laws vary in their attitude toward branch banking, and it is a controversial question whether branch banking is or is not in the public's interest.

**4.** A bank holding company is a firm set up primarily to own the shares in one or more banks. Bank holding companies give banks added flexibility in raising funds for investment, and have grown by leaps and bounds in the last several decades.

**5.** Over time, the markets served by banks and those served by thrifts have increasingly overlapped. Each institution has been successful in obtaining the license to provide widened banking services. By the late 1970s, a high degree of overlap had developed between the two institutions, with banks issuing the equivalent of interest-bearing checking accounts and with thrifts issuing the equivalent of checkable savings accounts.

**6.** The banking law of 1980 has delineated depository institutions as those which hold checkable deposits. Other financial institutions are called nondepository institutions. Depository institutions include commercial banks, savings and loan associations, mutual savings banks, and credit unions.

**7.** Nondepository institutions include insurance companies, pension funds, finance companies, and mutual funds. They are primarily concerned with using the funds flowing into their accounts to make investments in the primary securities of business and governments.

**Discussion Questions**

**1.** Is the state in which you live a unit-banking or a branch-banking state?

**2.** Learn as much as possible about the nature of bank holding companies in your state. How does the holding-company structure impact on the nature of banking in your state?

**3.** Has regulation Q been a good or bad thing for the public? Consider as many aspects of this question as possible.

**4.** Is the post-1980 role of thrifts in banking closer to or further from their initial role in banking in the early 1800s? Explain.

**5.** Distinguish between NOW accounts and ATS accounts.

**Suggested Readings**

For a more detailed analysis of the history of U.S. banking, see Bray Hammond, *Banks and Politics in America*, Princeton: Princeton University Press, 1957, chaps. 1 and 6. For more on the holding-company movement, see Gregory E. Boczar, "The Growth of Multibank Holding Companies: 1956–1973," *Federal Reserve Bulletin*, April 1976, pp. 300–301. The general subject of the growth of financial institutions is treated by Donald J. Jacobs, Loring C. Farwell, and Edwin Neave, *Financial Institutions*, Homewood, Ill.: Irwin, 1972. For a description of the changes in interest-rate ceilings and in the reserve requirements of banks and thrifts, see "The Depository Institutions Deregulation and Monetary Control Act of 1980," *Federal Reserve Bulletin*, June 1980, pp. 444–53.

## CHAPTER 7

# The Structure
# of Banking Institutions

## CHAPTER OUTLINE

## IMPORTANT TERMS

dual-charter system
bank script
legal tender
member bank

nonmember bank
FDIC
bank runs
correspondent bank

MEMO

To:        All readers
From:      JWE

Banking operations are conducted within a complex institutional structure in the United States. Before a bank opens its doors, it must obtain
a charter from some governmental body. It must build a relationship and
obtain the approval of banking authorities at several levels of government. And, if it is going to survive, it needs to develop working relationships with other banking firms.

This chapter is about some of the more important institutional factors
that form the structure of banking in this nation. The emphasis here is
not on the way the government regulates banking—that topic is reserved
for chapter 10 and beyond. In this chapter, you will read about the
differences between state and national banks, the differences between
banks that are members of the Federal Reserve system and those which
are not, and other related topics. The theme of this chapter is an overview
of the institutions that surround and shape U.S. banking operations.

A firm interested in becoming a bank cannot simply open its doors
and begin to accept deposits. It must obtain a governmental charter
that gives it the legal right to conduct banking operations. It must
form a relationship with the Federal Reserve system, and it will, in
all likelihood, need to form working relationships with other financial
institutions. The legal arrangements under which these steps are taken
form the institutional structure within which the banking system in
the United States functions. In this chapter, we will examine some
of the more important aspects of the institutional structure of U.S.
banking.

## STATE AND NATIONAL BANKS

Most communities have banks with "state" in their title as well as
banks with "national" in their title. Every bank is legally empowered,
or chartered, to operate either by the state in which it does business
or by the federal government. State and federally chartered banks
operate side by side under what is called a *dual-charter system*. When
a bank is newly formed, it has the option of applying for either a
state or federal charter. Similarly, an existing bank can make an application to change its charter from one type to the other. In practice,
such applications are routinely approved or disapproved depending
on the specifics of the case involved.

There are important differences between state and federally chartered banks. All federally chartered banks, that is, national banks, must be members of the Federal Reserve system. State-chartered banks have the option of joining or not joining the Federal Reserve system. National banks must comply with the banking regulations set up by the Federal Reserve. State banks are required to comply with some of the Federal Reserve regulations and some regulations established by their states. Before the banking act of 1980, states had a somewhat bigger say in the regulation of state-chartered banks than they now have. Part of the thrust of the 1980 law is to bring nearly all banking operations, regardless of bank charter, under the Federal Reserve's regulatory authority. (More on this in chapter 10.)

In the last twenty-five years, the number of state and national banks has remained in approximately the same proportion, with about one-third of the nearly 15,000 banks in the United States being national banks and the remaining two-thirds being state banks. However, although state banks are predominant in number, national banks are larger in terms of the number of deposits and total assets held. More than 55 percent of the total bank assets in the United States are held by federally chartered banks. That one-third of the banks control more than half of the total assets indicates that the larger banks tend to be national banks whereas smaller banks tend to be state banks.

The dual-charter system did not come into being as part of a grand banking design. Were the banking system in the United States designed all at once rather than over a period of two hundred years, it seems apparent that we would not have a dual-charter system. But that is not what happened. Instead, with the evolution of commercial banking in the early 1800s, banks were almost exclusively chartered by states, with federal charters being rare and requiring specific acts of Congress. By the time of the Civil War, the banking system essentially consisted of many thousands of small state-chartered banks. The Civil War created heavy demands on the banking system to accommodate wartime financing of the war effort. The diffused structure of banking then in place could not adequately accommodate the government's credit demands. This circumstance motivated the passage in 1863 of the National Currency Act.

The 1863 act stated that state-chartered banks could accept a national charter, and that newly formed banks could apply for a national charter rather than a state charter. Under this new national charter, banks could issue their share of a standardized form of bank currency. Prior to that time, banks issued their own currency, or *bank script*, which was backed by their own assets.

However, the 1863 act was flawed. It did not declare the new standardized currency to be *legal tender* (legal means to settle debts). Banks saw it as no different from their own script, except that since the currency was standardized, they could wind up being responsible for redeeming what amounted to another bank's script. No banks took up the new national charter until the next year when the law was revised.

The National Bank Act of 1864 designated the new bank currency as legal tender. By the end of 1864, more than six hundred newly formed banks were nationally chartered. No state banks joined the federal system until a year later, when Congress imposed a tax on state bank notes to further encourage growth of the federal system. This produced some switching of charters, and by the end of 1865, there were more than fifteen hundred national banks.

It is not clear whether it was the underlying intention of the legislative changes of 1863 through 1865 to eliminate state-chartered banks and replace them with federally chartered ones. In any case, it was not the effect. Although a large number of banks did switch, leading to the growth of a national banking system, the state-bank system did not fade away. Consequently, the dual-charter system evolved.

## MEMBER AND NONMEMBER BANKS

A *member bank* is one that belongs to the Federal Reserve system, whereas a *nonmember bank* does not. For state banks, membership is voluntary. For national banks, it is required by law. Thus, all national banks are member banks, whereas state banks are both members and nonmembers. Membership in the Federal Reserve system is obtained by applying for it and by meeting accounting and financial requirements set forth by the Federal Reserve Board.

The Federal Reserve system had no need for a membership drive when the main parts of the modern system were put in place in 1913. The Federal Reserve act of that year simply required that all federally chartered banks become members of the Federal Reserve. State banks were given the option of joining. Today, about 10 percent of the nation's nearly 10,000 state-chartered banks are members of the Federal Reserve system.

The advantages of belonging to the Federal Reserve have varied through time. Prior to 1980, member banks had the privilege of borrowing from the Federal Reserve discount window in addition to receiving Federal Reserve check clearing, fund transferring, and currency and coin services. However, member banks also were required to invest some funds in the low-yielding stock of the Federal Reserve. More important, member banks were required to hold their reserves with the Federal Reserve and earn no interest, while many state-chartered banks were allowed by state banking laws to hold their reserves in interest-bearing bonds. In this way, it was more costly to belong to the Federal Reserve than to be chartered by a state government.

The 1980 changes in the banking law dramatically changed the costs and benefits of belonging to the Federal Reserve system. Under the 1980 law, member and nonmember banks have nearly the same privileges of borrowing at the discount window and obtaining other services that only member banks formerly enjoyed. At the same time, the law imposes on all banks the same costs in terms of holding reserves with the Federal Reserve at zero interest. Thus, since the 1980 changes in the law, the distinction between member and non-member banks has for many operational purposes greatly diminished.

# THE FEDERAL DEPOSIT INSURANCE CORPORATION

The *Federal Deposit Insurance Corporation,* or FDIC, is a government-formed entity that insures the deposits of commercial banks. The FDIC is the result of an increasingly chronic problem in the 1920s and 1930s in the United States—that of bank failures. Over the period 1922–1925, an average of almost 600 banks failed per year in the United States. Over 1926–1929, the number of failing banks per year was more than 700. During the years of financial crisis and depression from 1930 to 1933, an average of 2,200 banks per year failed. By 1933, the public's confidence in banks had ebbed to a point where a growing number of people simply would not keep funds on deposit in any bank. Either direct experience with a failing bank or knowledge of other people who had lost money in a failure convinced more and more citizens that their savings were just not safe in a bank. Even those who maintained bank deposits were quick to withdraw them from any bank that gave the slightest indication of financial weakness. Since a rapid loss of deposits usually *produces* financial strains in a bank, the process was destructive. *Bank runs,* in which large numbers of depositors seek to withdraw funds over a short period of time, were all too frequent. By 1934, the banking system had approached a crisis point.

The FDIC was formed in 1934 amid this environment of crisis to provide assurances to the public that their funds were safe in banks. Initially, deposits were insured up to $2,500, an amount that was quickly raised to $5,000. In 1950, the maximum amount of insurance was raised to $10,000, and in 1966 to $15,000. Further increases followed. In 1969, the insurance limit was set at $20,000, in 1974 it was raised to $40,000, and in 1980 to $100,000.

The deposit insurance provided by the FDIC steadily restored the public's confidence in banks. The incidence of massive withdrawals of deposits from banks that were thought to be nearing insolvency became less and less. Consequently, the number of bank failures fell dramatically. In contrast to the 2,200-plus bank failures of the early 1930s, the average number of bank failures since World War II has been about six per year.

The most important aspect of the FDIC is its psychological impact rather than its financial resources. Because depositors have the government's promise to pay in case the bank cannot, they tend not to "panic" if the bank gets into financial trouble. Because a troubled bank does not lose its depositors, it has a much greater chance to work out its problems. Thus, because the government *promises* to pay, it seldom has to *actually* pay.

The success of the FDIC was perhaps a factor in the growth of companion agencies that insure deposits in thrift institutions. At present, deposits in any depository institution are insured either by the FDIC or a companion agency.[1]

## CORRESPONDENT BANKS

Small banks often find it useful to hold deposits in larger banks, generally in return for services provided by the larger bank. Two banks that have agreed on an exchange of services in return for deposits held have entered into a correspondent relationship. The bank that makes the deposit in another bank is usually called a *correspondent bank*. Generally, correspondent banks are smaller than those with which they correspond. They are often nonmember banks as well.

Typical of the services that might be provided to a correspondent bank in return for its deposit are investment advice and information services, the opportunity to share in loans developed by the larger bank, and access to interbank lending from the larger bank.

Prior to 1980, the correspondent relationship served another important function for the small bank. The demand deposit held by the correspondent bank at a corresponding member bank was an acceptable way for the smaller bank to hold its required reserve. The larger bank functioned as the Federal Reserve as far as the small bank's reserve position was concerned. Under the 1980 banking law, this aspect of correspondent banking is being phased out so that all banks will hold reserves at the Federal Reserve.

**Important Ideas in This Chapter**

1. Banks may be chartered either by the state in which they operate or by the federal government. In either case, the banks must comply with basic regulations of the Federal Reserve system, and if state chartered, they must comply with state regulations as well.

2. A member bank is one that belongs to the Federal Reserve. All national banks must be members of the Federal Reserve. State banks may be members if they choose. In the past, membership entitled the bank to services and privileges not available in the same way to other banks. However, with the recent changes in banking laws, all banks have approximately the same access to the services of the Federal

---

1. A separate agency, the Federal Savings and Loan Insurance Corporation (FSLIC) insures the deposits of savings and loan associations, and a third agency, the National Credit Union Share Insurance Fund (NCUSIF) insures the deposits of credit-union members. Deposits in mutual savings banks are covered by the FDIC.

Reserve system. Also, they now must comply with most of the requirements established by the Federal Reserve.

**3.** The Federal Deposit Insurance Corporation, or FDIC, was founded in the depression of the 1930s to insure deposits in banks, and thus to promote acceptance of banking services by an increasingly skeptical public. Since the FDIC has been in operation, the number of bank failures has fallen off dramatically.

**4.** A correspondent bank is usually a small bank that maintains a deposit in a larger bank in return for services provided by that larger bank. The services include investment advice and loan participation, and until recently, the holding of the correspondent's required reserve deposit.

**Discussion Questions**

**1.** If you were designing the U.S. banking system "from the ground up," would you have a single- or dual-charter system? Explain and defend your answer.

**2.** Do you think the changes in the banking laws of 1980 will cause more newly formed banks to seek federal or state charters? Explain.

**3.** Can you think of circumstances where banks could suffer "runs" by depositors in the modern-day United States? Explain.

**4.** Not all correspondent relationships are between smaller and larger banks. Why might two large banks enter into a correspondent relationship?

**5.** Do you see any relationship between correspondent banking and branch banking?

**Suggested Readings**

For much more detail on the regulatory structure governing financial institutions, see Samual B. Chase, Jr., "The Structure of Federal Regulation of Depository Institutions," in *Financial Institutions and the Nation's Economy: Compendium of Papers Prepared for the FINE Study*, Committee Print: Washington, D.C. USGPO, June 1976, pp. 157–170. For a history of the development of the FDIC, see Carter H. Golembe, "The Deposit Insurance Legislation of 1933," *Political Science Quarterly*, June 1960, pp. 181–200.

## CHAPTER 8

# Assets and Liabilities of Depository Institutions

## CHAPTER OUTLINE

MEMO—INTRODUCTION
COMMERCIAL-BANK ASSETS AND
  LIABILITIES
ASSETS AND LIABILITIES OF
  SAVINGS AND LOAN
  ASSOCIATIONS
ASSETS AND LIABILITIES OF
  MUTUAL SAVINGS BANKS

ASSETS AND LIABILITIES OF
  CREDIT UNIONS
TRENDS IN ASSETS AND
  LIABILITIES OF BANKS AND
  THRIFTS
IMPORTANT IDEAS IN THIS
  CHAPTER
DISCUSSION QUESTIONS
SUGGESTED READINGS

## IMPORTANT TERMS

commercial loans
mortgage loans
individual loans
borrowed liabilities
net worth
installment loans
share draft accounts

/MEMO

To:      All readers
From:    JWE

It is often said that the body is the ultimate accounting system. It faithfully records every calorie of food eaten and every bit of exercise undertaken, and displays the net result in the form of muscle and fat. It never loses track of a cookie, a pizza, or a five-mile run.

The balance sheets of financial institutions are a bit like the body. They faithfully record every deposit made, every loan made, every investment undertaken, and display the net result in annual and quarterly statements of assets and liabilities. We can learn something about the patterns of lending and investing in financial institutions and about the ways these institutions raise funds for investment, by reviewing their accumulated assets and liabilities.

This chapter is concerned with the present structure of assets and liabilities for commercial banks, savings and loan associations, mutual savings banks, and credit unions. The reasons for focusing on these institutions is that they are currently designated as depository institutions—those having the right to issue checkable deposits and thus contribute to the nation's money supply.

Financial institutions are fundamentally in the business of borrowing and lending. They incur costs to borrow so they can raise funds for investment and lending. Lending and investing produces revenues that are intended to pay borrowing and other costs, and in most cases earn a profit.

When financial institutions borrow, they incur liabilities that show up on the right-hand side of their balance sheets. Examples of liabilities incurred by borrowing are savings deposits in a mutual savings bank, and certificates of deposits in a commercial bank. In setting up a savings account, a financial institution is agreeing to borrow as much as the account holder wishes to deposit, at a rate of interest agreed on in advance. For a certificate of deposit, the amount of funds borrowed is also stipulated along with the interest rate.

When financial institutions invest or lend, they buy assets that show up on the left-hand side of their balance sheets. Examples of the assets in which financial institutions invest are loans to firms and U.S. government bonds. Both of these are promissory notes that entitle the holder to the payment of a stated amount of money at a future time, plus regular interest payments.

Because of this important connection between the borrowing and lending activities of financial institutions and their balance sheets, we can, by examining these balance sheets, learn something about how individual financial institutions lend and borrow. The cumulative effect of past borrowing and lending patterns is etched in accountant's ink in documents regularly prepared by financial institutions. The document may be called "Statement of Financial Condition" or "Assets and Liabilities" or just "Balance Sheet."

Depository institutions—commercial banks, savings and loan associations, mutual savings banks, and credit unions—are the most crucial to the study of money and banking because they hold checkable deposits which are a part of the nation's money supply. Thus, depository institutions are at the center of the process of creating, expanding, and contracting the supply of deposit-type money. It is important to see the types of deposits and other liabilities these institutions hold, and the types of assets in which the funds of depositors and others are invested.

## COMMERCIAL-BANK ASSETS AND LIABILITIES

Commercial banks were so-named a couple of centuries ago because of their primary function of serving the financial needs of commerce. Accordingly, it is logical to expect the principal assets of banks to be loans made to business firms. The same historical perspective also suggest the principal liabilities of commercial banks would be deposits made by households and firms. In other words, it is historically consistent to think of a commercial bank as an institution that provides a safe, interest-earning depository for household savings, and which makes these savings available primarily to meet the needs of commerce and industry. As in most matters of logic, there is much truth in this logical/historical view, but also some important exceptions.

Figure 8.1 shows the actual assets and liabilities for all commercial banks for the year 1981. From this chart, we can see that business loans are in fact the major earning asset of commercial banks. The sum of *commercial loans* (those made to firms), *mortgage loans* and other real-estate loans (mostly made to business), and other loans (virtually all made to business) is more than 45 percent of the total assets of commercial banks. *Individual loans* (made to households) add another 10 percent or so to this figure. Thus, more than half of the assets accumulated by commercial banks are in the form of loans. The other class of earning assets held by banks is investments in securities. U.S. Treasury securities plus U.S. agency debt and state and local and other securities account for almost 20 percent of the accumulated earning assets of commercial banks.

The category "Cash, Reserves, and Float" includes the funds held in vaults, the reserve accounts held at the Federal Reserve, and the cash items in process of collection. These items are assets that do not earn interest, but are required in conducting banking operations. As one might expect, much managerial effort is directed toward minimizing the amount of funds committed to these zero-earning assets in the profit-seeking financial institution, consistent with having adequate funds on hand and meeting legal reserve requirements. The remaining asset category, "Buildings and Other Assets," is mostly the value of the facilities in which banking operations take place.

Figure 8.1 also shows the structure of liabilities incurred by banks to raise the funds used to amass their holdings of assets. The structure of liabilities shows how the loans, investments, and buildings were financed. The largest type of liability is certificates of deposit. This category includes small-denomination household certificates of deposit and large-denomination marketable certificates of deposit, or negotiable CDs as they are called (see chapter 5). In recent years, the large-denomination CD has become an important source of funds for banks, and its share of the total time deposits held by banks has grown sharply.

The next most significant source of funds to banks is demand deposits and savings accounts, which together make up about 34 percent of the total liabilities of banks. In years past, commercial banks financed a large proportion of their loans and investments through demand deposits and savings accounts. In 1950, more than 85 percent of commercial-bank assets were financed this way. By 1965 the pro-

**FIGURE 8.1.**
**Commercial-Bank**
**Assets and Liabilities.**

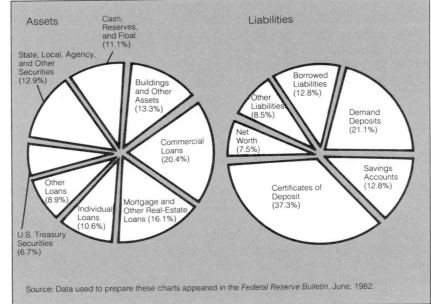

Source: Data used to prepare these charts appeared in the *Federal Reserve Bulletin*, June, 1982.

portion had fallen to 74 percent and by 1975 was less than 50 percent. Thus, commercial banks are relying less and less on traditional household-type accounts to finance their lending and investing.

The category labeled *borrowed liabilities* includes the funds that banks borrow from the Federal Reserve, from nonbank financial institutions, and from abroad. Borrowed liabilities are distinguished from deposits in that the bank goes into financial markets in search of the former while depositors bring the latter to the institution. It is a source of funds that has grown in importance in recent years as banks have found various types of borrowing to be a way to raise needed funds when required.

The final category in the liabilities chart, *net worth,* shows the accumulated earnings retained by commercial banks. It is the portion of commercial-bank assets financed by the ownership capital (or the equity funds) invested in banks by shareholders and retained in the firm by bank managers.

## ASSETS AND LIABILITIES OF SAVINGS AND LOAN ASSOCIATIONS

Savings and loan associations originally found their niche in the U.S. financial system by serving the financial needs of households. The aim of the early savings and loan association was to provide a safe and convenient way for households to earn interest on their savings while helping to finance the purchase of farmland and homes.

A look at the current structure of assets and liabilities of savings and loan associations shows that this original purpose is still dominant in the borrowing and lending in which these institutions engage. Figure 8.2 shows the composition of assets and liabilities of all reporting savings and loan associations for the year 1981. Almost 80 percent of the assets held by these institutions are mortgage loans, most of which are made to households to finance home or land purchases. Beyond this, a small part of the assets are held in the form of short-term securities such as U.S. Treasury Bills.

Inspection of the liabilities of savings and loan companies makes it clear that the savings accounts and certificates of deposit of households represent the main source of funds for these institutions' mortgage lending. About 80 percent of the liabilities of savings and loan associations are savings accounts, certificates of deposit, and money-market certificates and accounts. Nearly all these accounts are owned by households.

The accumulated assets and liabilities of savings and loan associations show that these institutions function primarily as conduits through which household savings are gathered and made available for those who want to borrow for the purpose of buying houses.

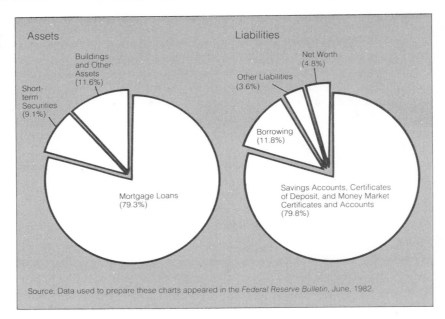

Source: Data used to prepare these charts appeared in the *Federal Reserve Bulletin*, June, 1982.

Thus, unlike commercial banks, savings and loan associations are quite specialized in their financial activities. Whereas commercial banks invest in a variety of commercial, industrial, residential, and individual loans, savings and loan companies direct most of their lending resources to housing.

This pattern is undergoing some changes at the present time. With the changes in banking laws in 1980, savings and loan associations and other thrifts have been given the license to serve more (if not all) household financial needs, including other types of loans and perhaps broader investment services. As savings and loan associations continue to evolve in response to the changes in the law, we may expect to see them move further into the position of the complete investment advisor of households, bringing directly to households a wider range of investment opportunities than the deposits and certificates now available.

## ASSETS AND LIABILITIES OF MUTUAL SAVINGS BANKS

The traditional function of the nation's mutual savings banks is similar to that of savings and loan associations. The accumulated assets and liabilities of these institutions have also evolved in a very similar way. Figure 8.3 shows these assets and liabilities. Mortgage loans are the largest asset category, while certificates of deposit and savings accounts are the dominant liabilities. In this respect, mutual savings banks have evolved in much the same way as savings and loan associations and broadly according to their original design.

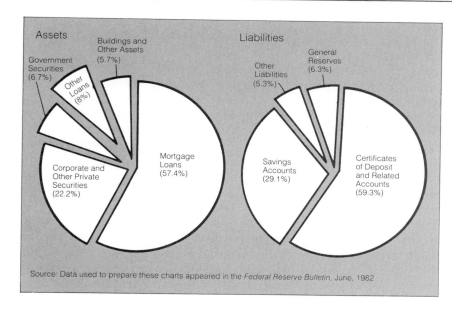

FIGURE 8.3.
Assets and Liabilities
of Mutual Savings
Banks.

Source: Data used to prepare these charts appeared in the *Federal Reserve Bulletin*, June, 1982.

One difference stands out in the composition of assets held by mutual savings banks. More than 20 percent of the assets held by these institutions are in the form of corporate and other private securities. The charters of savings and loan associations do not allow such investments. For savings and loan associations nonmortgage investments are more strictly limited in terms of both the proportion of assets and the type of security. (U.S. government securities are preferred, as a rule.) Mutual saving banks are permitted to invest a larger fraction of assets in a wider range of securities. Figure 8.3 shows that the degree to which this widened diversification has actually occurred has been significant.

## ASSETS AND LIABILITIES OF CREDIT UNIONS

A credit union is chartered to exclusively serve the members of some particular organization. The most common types of credit unions are those formed to serve the employees of a particular firm, trade union, religious or educational institution, or club or fraternal organization.

Credit unions serve their members by providing a convenient way to make regular deposits, maintaining a low administrative cost (presumably passing the saving on to members, and providing an easy avenue for members to arrange short-term loans. Until recently, virtually all the loans made by credit unions were *installment loans* involving periodic repayment and used to finance the purchase of automobiles or other durable goods. These loans are typically from one to four years in maturity. In the last few years, credit unions have been given the license to begin to make mortgage loans. With this emerging entry into long-term household lending, credit unions are placing an institutional foot on the traditional turf of savings and loan associations and mutual savings banks.

Credit unions are typically mutually owned by their member depositors. As such, they neither earn nor accumulate profits as an institution, but pay them out to members. Thus, deposits in credit unions are typically in the form of ownership of shares. To ''keep up'' with the emergence of checkable savings accounts in other thrifts, credit unions recently began issuing *share draft accounts* in which check-like drafts can be written by the account holder authorizing a third party to withdraw funds on demand. These share draft accounts have most of the features of a checking account, and have become an important enough account to cause credit unions to be classified as depository institutions.

Figure 8.4 shows the assets and liabilities of credit unions, in as much detail as allowed by the data these institutions provide to the Federal Reserve system. The asset and liability structure is quite simple. Almost 90 percent of the funds provided by credit unions come from member deposits, with the remaining 10 percent being mostly funds retained as contingency against future losses. About two-thirds of the assets of the institutions are loans made to members. The principal component of the remaining category of assets is investment in short-term securities. Thus, figure 8.4 does not contradict the view of credit unions being places where member savings are pooled and used to finance loans to members for automobiles and other consumer durable goods.

**FIGURE 8.4.
Assets and Liabilities
of Credit Unions.**

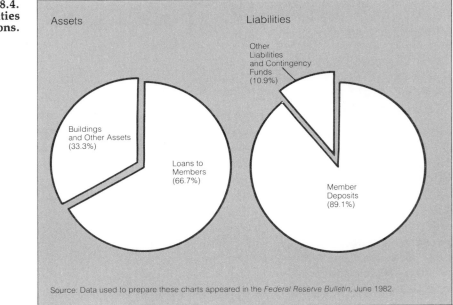

# TRENDS IN ASSETS AND LIABILITIES OF BANKS AND THRIFTS

Our discussion has so far focused on the composition of the assets and liabilities of commercial banks and thrifts individually. We have seen nothing about how these institutions compare in size. For financial institutions, total assets are a useful measure of size. Total assets show the sum total of all the institutions' investments, loans, and other assets. Because total assets equal total liabilities and net worth, total assets also show the sum of all deposits, accounts, and liabilities the financial institution has been able to accumulate through the years of its operation.

Table 8.1 shows the total assets of commercial banks, savings and loan associations, mutual savings banks, and credit unions. The main entries in the table are total assets of all institutions in billions of dollars. The numbers in parentheses are the percentage each institution's total assets make up of all depository institutions.

The data for 1945 show that commercial banks were the dominant financial institution among this group, with 86 percent of the total assets held by all such institutions. As years passed, commercial banks continued to control the largest share of the assets of all depository institutions, but the percentage of the total has fallen to about 66 percent.

On the other hand, savings and loan associations accounted for less than 5 percent of the total assets of depository institutions in 1945, and almost 25 percent of the assets in 1981. The relative importance of mutual savings banks fluctuated from about 9 percent in 1945 to under 7 percent in 1981. Credit unions have controlled a small but growing share of depository-institution assets throughout the period.

In interpreting the data of table 8.1, we must keep in mind that the roles of financial institutions have changed importantly over the period shown. Although the institutions listed are all classified as depository institutions, this has only recently been the case. Prior to the mid-1970s, the opportunity for thrifts to engage in traditional banking activities (and acquire the assets that go with these activities)

**TABLE 8.1.**
**Total Assets of Depository Institutions**

|  | 1945 | | 1970 | | 1981 | |
|---|---|---|---|---|---|---|
| Commercial Banks | 160.3 | (86.0%) | 576.2 | (67.8%) | 1,714.1 | (65.6%) |
| Savings and Loan Associations | 8.7 | (4.7%) | 176.2 | (20.7%) | 648.3 | (24.8%) |
| Mutual Savings Banks | 17.0 | (9.1%) | 79.0 | (9.3%) | 174.1 | (6.7%) |
| Credit Unions | 0.4 | (0.2%) | 18.0 | (2.2%) | 75.3 | (2.9%) |

Source: *Federal Reserve Bulletin* (Washington D.C.: Government Printing Office); and *Savings and Loan Fact Book* (Chicago: U.S. League of Savings Associations), various issues.

was limited. However, the combined effect of legal changes and managerial strategies has been to broaden the role of thrifts in the U.S. financial system. Savings and loan associations in particular are sharing more of the load of providing banking to the public, especially to households.

One important result of this trend is that the relationship between expansion of the money supply by financial institutions and bank reserves has broadened. In the analysis of deposit expansion and contraction in chapter 2, we discussed the expansion of commercial-bank demand deposits in response to new reserves. In the contemporary U.S. financial system, savings and loan associations, mutual savings banks, and credit unions all can issue checkable deposits, and all must maintain reserves against these deposits with the Federal Reserve system. And, in our official M1 definition of money, we collect together all the checkable deposits, whether held in commercial banks, savings and loan associations, mutual savings banks, or credit unions. Thus, all depository institutions now share in the process of money expansion and contraction that was illustrated in chapter 2 by reference to commercial banks. Accordingly, the stock of reserves available supports deposit expansion in all depository institutions combined. Whether the Federal Reserve's ability to control the growth in the money supply has been increased or decreased by these dramatic changes is a question that only time will resolve.

## Important Ideas in This Chapter

1. Financial institutions are fundamentally in the business of borrowing and lending. Borrowing creates liabilities, while the proceeds from borrowing enable assets to be acquired. Accordingly, an indication of the function of a financial institution can be obtained by reviewing its accumulated assets and liabilities.

2. Commercial banks maintain a diversified portfolio of loans to firms, to individuals, and for housing, as well as a substantial investment in securities, most of which are short-term.

3. The largest single liability of commercial banks is time deposits, many of which are large-denomination certificates that can be bought and sold in a secondary market. The traditional classes of bank liabilities, demand deposits and savings deposits, account for only about one-third of the total liabilities of commercial banks, a fraction that has been declining in recent years.

4. Savings and loan associations raise funds primarily through deposits made in savings and time accounts, and other certificates. The funds thus raised are mostly used to make mortgage loans to households for the purpose of financing purchases of homes and land.

5. The assets and liabilities of mutual savings banks are broadly similar to those of savings and loan associations, with the exception that mutual savings banks tend to make larger investments in private securities than savings and loan associations make.

**6.** Credit unions primarily lend their members' deposits to members who seek short-term loans to be used to finance the purchase of automobiles and other durables.

**7.** Banks are the dominant depository institution in terms of total assets. However, the relative size of banks compared with savings and loan associations and other thrifts is declining somewhat. Their share of the total assets of depository institutions has fallen from about 86 percent in 1945 to about 66 percent in 1981. The share of savings and loan associations has increased by the same number of percentage points over the same period.

**8.** With the recent changes in banking laws, depository institutions all contribute to expansion and contraction of the money supply (which is defined to include all checkable deposits), and all must hold reserves with the Federal Reserve system.

**Discussion Questions**

**1.** From data in the *Federal Reserve Bulletin,* you can construct pie charts similar to those in figure 8.1. Construct charts illustrating the assets and liabilities of commercial banks in 1970, and analyze the differences between your charts and those in figure 8.1.

**2.** With thrifts moving more squarely into the business of banking, what changes in the composition of their assets and liabilities might be expected? Explain.

**3.** If credit unions are given the authority to provide the same financial services to their members as banks or savings and loan associations, how might the structure and competitive balance of banking services change?

**4.** Life insurance companies are important financial intermediaries, but they are not depository institutions. Consult the *Federal Reserve Bulletin* to find the data required to prepare pie charts showing their assets and liabilities. Construct the charts and analyze your results.

**5.** Do the analysis called for in question 4, only for finance companies.

**Suggested Readings**

For a detailed overview of financial institutions, see Murray E. Polakoff, et al., *Financial Institutions and Markets,* Boston: Houghton-Mifflin, 1970. For a historical view of the growth of assets in financial institutions, see Herman E. Kroos and Martin R. Blyn, *A History of Financial Intermediaries,* New York: Random House, 1971.

# Managing Bank
# Assets and Liabilities

IMPORTANT TERMS

commercial-loan theory
shiftability theory
secondary reserves
primary reserves
anticipated income
liability management
federal funds
purchased funds

---

## MEMO

To:        All readers
From:      JWE

In the last chapter, we examined the assets and liabilities of depository institutions as a way of seeing how these institutions carry out their business of banking. The focus on assets and liabilities was not arbitrary. The individual banking firm's central management problem is to find the most profitable way to structure and deploy its assets and liabilities. The balance-sheet relationships discussed last chapter reveal how this has been done over the years.

The banking industry has always had some type of guidelines and philosophies concerning the structure of bank assets and liabilities. In many cases, these guidelines have come from the Federal Reserve system. In other cases, they have evolved from the banking industry itself. In this chapter, you will read about historical and contemporary approaches to bank asset and liability management; in this way, you will become more familiar with the nature of the problem of managing a banking institution.

---

Banks are usually corporations owned by shareholders who expect them to earn profits. Bank managers have a fundamental responsibility to earn profits for the bank's shareholders. But bank managers also have other responsibilities. One important one is to be able to pay a depositor who wants to withdraw funds from an account held at the bank. The bank has little control over withdrawal of funds from its depositor's accounts. Yet, it must have the funds available for this use if and when needed. Bank managers must also react to often unpredictable shifts in bank reserves by finding ways to keep enough funds in their bank's reserve deposit to meet legal requirements. Providing for the needs of depositors and for legal reserves means that the bank must maintain its assets in a form that enables ready access to funds when needed, that is, a degree of liquidity in the bank's assets is necessary. Providing profits for shareholders requires that the assets in which the bank invests yield a profitable return.

Liquidity and profits are usually in conflict. Funds held in a demand deposit are completely liquid but earn nothing. Funds held in short-term securities earn interest but are not as liquid. Funds committed to a business loan earn attractive income but are even less liquid. Thus, the continual bank-management trade-off is between liquidity on the one hand and profitability on the other.

In the history of U.S. banking, the trade-off has not always been resolved in the same way. In the early days of banking, the central theme was to specify particular types of earning assets in which banks should invest their funds in order to maintain an adequate level of liquidity. Later, more concern was given to the types of liabilities the bank holds, and their implications in terms of profitability and liquidity. One thing is certain. The profits-verus-liquidity problem has been with bankers since the beginning of banking in the United States. What has differed is the primary method of resolving it. We will first examine historical approaches to this problem, and then turn to contemporary banking approaches.

## THE COMMERCIAL-LOAN APPROACH TO BANK MANAGEMENT

From the beginning of banking in the United States to about the end of the Civil War, the *commercial-loan theory* provided bankers with clear guidelines concerning the types of assets in which bank funds could be invested. Under this theory, bank loans were to be short-term, self-liquidating, and "productive."

Short-term usually meant less than one year in duration. Self-liquidating meant that the borrowed funds were to be used for financing the kinds of temporary cash needs where borrowed funds flow back into company accounts quickly and more or less automatically. Seasonal financing is perhaps the classic example of a self-liquidating loan. A retail firm has a necessary inventory buildup at year's end to support Christmas sales, and an inventory reduction afterward. A self-liquidating inventory loan would be made in the late fall of the year, and would be repaid from the funds released by the subsequent inventory reduction. The more judgmental criterion, requiring that loans be "productive," was interpreted to mean loans should be made to support the production of goods by those engaged in commerce.

In short, the commercial-loan theory stipulated that banks were to invest in short-term business loans. Investment in either government bonds or the stocks and bonds of private firms did not fit the commercial-loan theory. Neither did investment in real estate or other tangible assets. The commercial-loan theory produced a structure of bank assets that had low risk of capital and that were more or less automatically liquidated on a short-term basis.

This type of asset structure had clear benefits. The short-term and low-risk nature of the bank's assets closely matched the short maturities of the bank's liabilities, which consisted mostly of deposits made by the bank's customers. A good portion of the typical bank's deposit liabilities could be withdrawn either on demand (checking deposits) or after a short waiting period (time deposits). Thus, a bank that kept its asset structure approximately as short-term as its liabilities was protected from sudden losses of liabilities that might occur in times of crisis when "runs" on banks were likely to take place.

Adherence to the commercial-loan theory had an important overall financial effect. It established banks as specialist financial institutions, primarily serving the credit needs of industry and commerce. Under the commercial-loan approach, the largest portion of household funds that were regularly placed on deposit at commercial banks flowed directly to commercial and industrial borrowers.

Figure 9.1 shows a hypothetical balance sheet for a commercial bank adhering to the commercial-loan approach. Besides funds used for facilities and to maintain required reserves, the dominant asset held to earn income is commercial loans, with other types of loans making up a small part of the investment portfolio.

The hypothetical commercial-loan bank's liabilities consist mostly of funds brought to the bank by its depositors, with modest contributions made by ownership funds (net worth) and other borrowings which consist of funds that the bank specifically raises through loans it negotiates. The dominance of deposits in the liability structure reveals one important operating property of a bank following the commercial-loan theory—growth in the bank's total assets is governed by growth in its deposits. Basically, the commercial-loan-theory bank only loans more to business if it has more funds placed on deposit in checking accounts and savings accounts.

## THE SHIFTABILITY APPROACH

Around the year 1900, a new philosophy governing the management of bank assets was emerging, called the *shiftability theory*. Under this theory, the important characteristic of a potential bank investment was whether it could be sold at little or no capital loss if the need arose to raise funds. The test of an acceptable bank asset became whether it could be "shifted" to another owner at no financial loss. Under this view, short-term securities such as U.S. Treasury Bills and call loans are acceptable assets for the prudent bank to hold in its portfolio. Indeed, the maturities on such short-term securities may be shorter than on business loans that meet the criterion of the commercial-loan theory. Moreover, the risk of default may be lower as well.

As a structure of dealers in government securities began to develop, a ready market for these assets emerged, which enhanced their shiftability and increased their attractiveness to banks guided by his philosophy.

Banks began to call their holdings of short-term readily marketable securities their *secondary reserves*, a term that implies these assets are close to *primary reserves* (cash and reserve account) in terms of their liquidity. Indeed, the liquidity position of a bank was gauged by the proportion of its assets invested in secondary reserves.

| ASSETS | | LIABILITIES AND NET WORTH | |
|---|---|---|---|
| Cash and reserves | 20 | Demand deposits | 80 |
| Loans—commercial | 130 | Savings accounts | 95 |
| Loans—other | 10 | Other borrowings | 10 |
| Buildings and equipment | 40 | Net worth | 15 |
| Total assets | 200 | Liabilities and net worth | 200 |

FIGURE 9.1.
Hypothetical Balance
Sheet of a Commercial
Bank in the
Commercial-Loan Era.

The shiftability approach had predictable problems whenever the financial system had a general need to raise cash. If too many individual banks are attempting to sell readily marketable securities, the market price falls as the interest rate is pushed up. This means that the securities are only "readily marketable" at a lower price than the bank paid for them. Banks needing liquidity in these circumstances will suffer a loss in converting their secondary reserves into regular or primary reserves. Generally, whenever market interest rates on short-term securities rise to any appreciable degree, the so-called secondary reserves of banks can only be liquidated at a loss to the bank. Fortunately for many U.S. banks, the periods where general liquidity problems and/or rising short-term interest rates occurred were not too frequent during the time when the shiftability approach held popular sway.

Figure 9.2 shows a hypothetical balance sheet for a commercial bank under the shiftability approach. The central difference we note between it and the balance sheet of the commercial-loan approach is that the composition of assets is altered in two ways. First, a proportion of assets is now held in short-term securities, or secondary reserves. Next, the proportion of loans made for other than commercial purposes is increased. These loans include mortgages, personal loans, and perhaps some longer-term loans to business. The thinking accompanying this asset shift is that the liquidity provided by the secondary reserves allows the bank to move some of its asset portfolio into less liquid loans that offer high rates of return but are outside of the commercial and industrial category.

The liability side of the hypothetical bank's balance sheet under the shiftability approach is no different from that of the commercial-loan approach. In both cases, the dominant liabilities are demand and

| ASSETS | | LIABILITIES AND NET WORTH | |
|---|---|---|---|
| Cash and reserves | 20 | Demand deposits | 80 |
| Short-term securities | 40 | Savings accounts | 95 |
| Loans—commercial | 50 | Other borrowings | 10 |
| Loans—other | 50 | Net worth | 15 |
| Buildings and equipment | 40 | Liabilities and net worth | 200 |
| Total assets | 200 | | |

FIGURE 9.2.
Hypothetical Balance
Sheet of a Commercial
Bank in the Era of the
Shiftability Doctrine.

savings accounts brought to the bank by its depositors. Thus, under the shiftability approach, the growth in bank lending is basically governed by the growth in deposits the bank holds.

The shiftability approach to asset management reduced the specialist role of banks by providing a rationale for banks to expand their lending beyond the commercial area into other areas where profitable investment opportunities could be found.

## THE ANTICIPATED-INCOME APPROACH

In the immediate post-World-War-II period, ideas and philosophies about bank asset management were broadened beyond that associated with the shiftability thesis. The *anticipated-income* approach to asset management embraces the view that the security of any loan is ultimately determined by the ability of the borrower to repay. The ability to repay is, in turn, a primary function of the borrower's income over the future period when repayment is due. Thus, the central question to be answered when a bank evaluates the addition of a new loan to its portfolio is the income the bank anticipates the borrower will generate during the life of the loan. With this focus, concern with whether the loan is productive in the commercial-loan-theory sense is distinctly secondary. Whether the asset is a loan or a short-term security is also secondary to the question of how the borrower's future income stream and repayment obligation compare.

Adherents of the anticipated-income approach argue that the most important test of the marketability of a financial asset is the stability of the future income stream of the borrower rather than the type of loan security involved. In other words, loans backed by secure and predictable cash flows are seen as easy to sell if the need arises to raise cash.

The hypothetical balance sheet of the bank following the anticipated-income approach would differ little from that shown in figure 9.2. Assets such as short-term U.S. government securities would continue to have an important place in the portfolio, since they would usually pass the anticipated-income test with flying colors. The biggest difference in such a hypothetical balance sheet is that the proportion of loans in the "commercial" category versus the "other" category would likely be subject to more variation over time than with the shiftability approach. Under the shiftability thesis, a bank might stipulate a target range for the proportion of loans in the commercial versus other category, whereas under the anticipated-income approach, a bank would determine the proportion by assessing how many individual loan opportunities in the two categories were attractive given the anticipated-income criterion.

# CONTEMPORARY BANKING: ASSET AND LIABILITY MANAGEMENT

The most important development in bank management philosophy in the last several decades involves the liability side of the balance sheet rather than the asset side. Until at least the late 1960s, the amount of funds available to a bank was thought to be generally fixed by the amount of deposits the bank held. The amount of deposit liabilities was seen increasingly as the governing constraint on the rate of growth of bank assets.

Basically, for a bank to double its total assets, it has to double its liabilities. However, the largest of these liabilities, demand and savings deposits, are accounts that are largely determined by the bank's customers. The total amount of such accounts is not within the control of the bank to any appreciable degree.

There are some things bank management can do to influence the level of its bank's deposits. A bank can pursue potential depositors more aggressively to try to obtain their accounts. Indeed, the late 1960s marks the time when many banks created marketing departments to more aggressively attract deposits. Within narrow limits, banks can improve the attractiveness of deposits when they wish to expand them. However, until the banking act of 1980, the maximum interest rates that could be paid on bank deposits were stipulated by law, and adhered to by most banks. Thus, banks have generally been prohibited from competing for deposits by offering higher rates of interest. The ability of banks to improve the attractiveness of deposits is limited to factors such as geographic convenience, attractiveness of facilities, check charges, minimum-deposit levels, and minor bookkeeping services. In practice, the "deal" offered to most depositors by most banks amounts to pretty much the same thing.

Contemporary banks have not been satisfied with limiting their growth to a rate prescribed by their depositors. Instead, they have pursued active strategies of acquiring other liabilities when attractive lending and investment opportunities arise. The term *liability management* refers to a strategy of raising funds for investment by actively seeking liabilities whenever attractive investment opportunities appear and market conditions permit.

Banks cannot raise funds through liability expansion without limits. But there are several types of liabilities they can and do regularly use to implement liability-management policy. One is the use of *federal funds*, the excess reserves of other banks. The excess reserves of some banks can usually be borrowed by other banks with deficient reserves in this market for periods of time ranging from overnight to several days. Since the 1950s, federal-funds markets have become an arena of increasing importance for banks to raise funds beyond those flowing from new or expanded deposits.

A second tool for liability management is the *large-denomination negotiable certificate of deposit* (see chapter 5). Since the mid-1960s, these liabilities have grown dramatically in importance as a way for banks to acquire the excess liquidity of nonfinancial business and state and local governments. From the bank's perspective, the key attribute of the large-denomination CDs is the ability to negotiate market interest rates on them, unlike small-denomination time deposits and savings deposits. Thus, as interest rates fluctuated in increasingly volatile patterns during the 1970s, the rates on large-denomination CDs could be maintained at competitive levels, thus keeping this avenue of borrowing from the nonfinancial business and public sector more or less continuously open.

A third avenue for implementation of liability management is the use of *eurodollar accounts* (again, see chapter 5). Rates on these deposits held in U.S. banks by foreigners can also be set at market levels, thus allowing banks to actively pursue available funds held by nondomestic firms or individuals.

With federal funds, large CDs, and eurodollar accounts, banks can engage in an active program of acquiring liabilities at their discretion rather than at that of their depositors. Liabilities such as these are often referred to as *purchased funds,* a term that reflects their key property—they can be bought (that is, borrowed) in the financial marketplace. Unlike deposit liabilities, purchased funds command the market rate of interest. Banks that want to expand their assets through the use of purchased funds must expect to pay the market's going rate for them. In turn, the task of bank management is to deploy these funds in investments that earn more than the cost of acquiring them.

Liability-management strategies are not inconsistent with the various approaches to asset management previously discussed. Instead, these strategies add a new and more flexible dimension to bank management. With banks following essentially the anticipated-income approach to asset acquisition and active liability management to acquire funds when opportunities arise, the types of lending and investment that banks can be expected to be engaged in are made even more flexible within the guidelines set forth by the Federal Reserve.

Figure 9.3 shows a hypothetical balance sheet for a bank following an active strategy of liability management. The central difference between this balance sheet and figures 9.1 and 9.2 is the much greater proportion of liabilities in the purchased-liability category. Instead of "other borrowings" being a minor source of funds, it now becomes a major source of funds to support lending and investing. The asset side of the hypothetical balance sheet shows the greater diversity in loans and investments, which corresponds to the anticipated-income approach.

Liability management shares one important property of the shiftability thesis. It is an avenue for a single bank to expand its lending, but is not a fundamental way in which the entire banking system can expand lending. Consider the CD tool. When banks offer firms an attractive interest rate on a low-risk bank-backed CD, firms can be

## Memorandum

To: All readers interested in the fed-funds market
From: JWE

The federal-funds market (called fed funds for short) is a source of borrowed funds and a lending opportunity that is unique to depository institutions. Specifically, fed funds are reserves that are on loan from one bank's reserve account at the Federal Reserve to another bank's reserve account. Thus, only depository institutions holding deposits with the Federal Reserve can participate in the fed-funds market. Many banks regularly and alternatively borrow and lend a portion of their reserve deposit in this way, usually as a way to make short-term adjustments in their reserve position.

The role of the Federal Reserve in the fed-funds market is mainly to act as a broker for the loans involved. The loans themselves are private deals between two banks, with the Federal Reserve having no liability. However, a Federal Reserve employee does arrange the deal, by calling potential borrowers and lenders, quoting bid and asked interest rates, and finally arranging the transfer of funds from one account to another.

The fed-funds rate is the current interest rate on fed funds. With the maturity of such loans ranging from overnight to about one week, the fed-funds rate tends to be the shortest interest rate commonly seen in the market. It is also quite sensitive to the specific amount of excess reserves available in the system. When reserves get scarce, the fed-funds rate quickly reflects this by rising. Movements of five percentage points in a single day in the fed-funds rate have occurred more than occasionally during recent periods of tightened reserves.

From time to time, banks find that lending via the fed-funds market can be more attractive than buying short-term securities. When the interest rate on fed funds rises above that of other alternative short-term loans, banks divert more funds to the fed-funds market. This switching of banks into and out of fed funds tends to cause patterns in other short-term rates to stay in line with the fed-funds rate over time.

expected to respond by trying to reduce their cash needs to a bare minimum. Thus, the existence of negotiable CDs can entice firms to work their cash harder and use their cash more efficiently. However, there are clear limits to how much extra cash can be generated in this

| ASSETS | | LIABILITIES AND NET WORTH | |
|---|---|---|---|
| Cash and reserves | 30 | Demand deposits | 80 |
| Short-term securities | 60 | Savings accounts | 95 |
| Loans—commercial | 120 | Other borrowings: | |
| Loans—other | 120 | Negotiable CDs | 100 |
| Buildings and equipment | 40 | Federal funds | 35 |
| Total assets | 370 | Eurodollar borrowing | 45 |
| | | Net worth | 15 |
| | | Total liabilities and net worth | 370 |

**FIGURE 9.3. Hypothetical Balance Sheet of a Commercial Bank in an Era of Active Liability Management.**

way. When maximum cash-efficiency levels have been reached, CDs will be harder to place, and interest rates that banks have to pay on them will rise. There is only so much liquidity available, and if individual banks want to hold more of it, they can do so only by enticing nonfinancial firms and other banks to hold less. Ultimately, the banking system will not be able to raise new funds by purchasing them via CDs.

The same limit applies to federal funds. If all or most banks want to borrow federal funds, there will be a scarcity of lenders and the interest rate will have to rise. After all, for every borrower of federal funds, there must be a corresponding lender.

The thrust of this discussion is that liability management may prove to be a frustrating experience for banks in an environment where there are less funds available than all banks together are seeking to acquire. In this case, the result will be higher interest rates on purchased funds, with the total amount of purchasable liabilities more or less fixed.

## PATTERNS OF BANK ASSET AND LIABILITY MANAGEMENT

In the last thirty or so years, the actual patterns of asset and liability management by banks correspond to several of the trends just discussed. Table 9.1 shows selected assets and liabilities for commercial banks over the period 1950–1981. The upper part of the table shows proportionate shares of total loans and investments for major loan and investment categories. The lower part of the table shows proportionate shares of total commercial-bank liabilities.

The composition of assets changed importantly over the years shown. Primary and secondary reserves (the cash and reserves plus government-securities categories) fell steadily from 66 percent of total loans and investments in 1950 to 35 percent of the total in 1981. This fall appears to indicate that banks in 1981 were considerably less liquid than they were thirty years ago. This may be true, but there are some important underlying trends which suggest that appearances may be deceiving.

The fall in cash and reserves relates to the fall in demand deposits and savings accounts shown in the liability portion of table 9.1. These accounts are the liabilities against which the biggest part of required reserves must be held. As demand deposits and savings accounts fell as a proportion of liabilities, reserves also fell. Keeping the minimum legally allowable amount of funds in reserves is just good bank management, and should not be interpreted as reflecting a weakened financial structure.

The steady fall in government securities as a proportion of total loans and investments is most probably explained by changes in the

**TABLE 9.1.**
**Selected Assets and Liabilities of Commercial Banks**

ASSETS (PERCENTAGE OF TOTAL LOANS AND INVESTMENTS)

|  | 1950 | 1955 | 1960 | 1965 | 1970 | 1975 | 1978 | 1981 |
|---|---|---|---|---|---|---|---|---|
| Cash and reserves | 24 | 23 | 20 | 16 | 17 | 15 | 15 | 12 |
| Government securities | 42 | 35 | 32 | 28 | 26 | 24 | 22 | 23 |
| Other securities | 2 | 2 | 1 | 0 | 1 | 1 | 1 | 1 |
| Commercial loans | 14 | 17 | 17 | 20 | 20 | 19 | 18 | 22 |
| Other loans | 18 | 23 | 30 | 36 | 36 | 41 | 44 | 42 |
| Total loans and investments | 100 | 100 | 100 | 100 | 100 | 100 | 100 | 100 |

LIABILITIES (PERCENTAGE OF TOTAL LIABILITIES)

|  | 1950 | 1955 | 1960 | 1965 | 1970 | 1975 | 1978 | 1981 |
|---|---|---|---|---|---|---|---|---|
| Demand deposits and savings accounts | 93 | 92 | 90 | 80 | 65 | 55 | 53 | 36 |
| Certificates of deposit | 5 | 7 | 8 | 12 | 20 | 33 | 25 | 41 |
| Other liabilities | 2 | 1 | 2 | 8 | 15 | 12 | 22 | 23 |
| Total liabilities | 100 | 100 | 100 | 100 | 100 | 100 | 100 | 100 |

Source: *Federal Reserve Bulletin* (Washington, D.C.: Government Printing Office), various issues. Data are end-of-year values.

markets for liabilities. As banks increasingly acquire purchased funds in markets that become more active and liquid, they evolve the attitude that uncontrollable outflows of deposits can be better offset by buying purchased funds rather than by liquidating secondary reserves. The need for secondary reserves thus falls. It is no accident that the fall in secondary reserves over the last thirty years is accompanied by a rise in the proportionate share of liabilities represented by purchased funds.

Table 9.1 also illustrates that the proportion of "other loans," including personal loans, mortgage loans, and other miscellaneous loans, has more than doubled in the last three decades. This means that commercial banks have continued to diversify their lending beyond the commercial area, and have increasingly broadened their role as a financial institution beyond that specified by the commercial-loan theory.

The various liabilities that appear in table 9.1 show important changes in proportion over the last thirty years as well. The most dramatic is the fall in demand deposits and savings accounts as a proportion of all liabilities. In 1950, 93 percent of all liabilities were demand deposits and savings accounts. In 1981, the comparable figure was 36 percent. Clearly, banks are relying less and less on the funds brought to them by their depositors. Instead, they are going out into the marketplace in search of the investment funds they require.

The "certificates of deposit" category in table 9.1 includes small, saver-type CDs as well as large negotiable CDs. The large growth in this type of liability from about 1965 onward is largely a result of growth in large negotiable CDs. Since 41 percent of all liabilities were certificates of deposit by 1981, the importance of the large CD to bank liability management is unmistakable. Table 9.1 shows comparable growth in the "other liabilities" category, which includes eurodollar borrowing and other purchased funds. By 1981, the sum of CDs and other liabilities accounted for more than 60 percent of all bank liabilities, compared with about 7 percent in 1950.

The overall picture emerging from the trends shown in table 9.1 is one of increasing diversity in the loans and investments that banks are undertaking, and much greater emphasis on buying and selling marketable liabilities such as CDs and eurodollar deposits as a way to maintain adequate liquidity and legal reserves.

## Important Ideas in This Chapter

1. The early period of banking in the United States was characterized by adherence to the commercial-loan theory, which defines appropriate bank loans to be short-term, self-liquidating, and productive in the sense they contribute to the production process in manufacturing and industry.

2. The shiftability theory followed the commercial-loan theory, and stipulated that the crucial criterion for an acceptable bank investment was whether it could be sold, or shifted, to another owner at little or no loss. This concept broadened the scope of bank investments to include short-term securities, which because of their perceived ease of marketability are often called secondary reserves.

3. The shiftability approach has problems when the financial system has a general need to raise cash. If most banks want to shift secondary reserves into the hands of others, they will push up interest rates.

4. The anticipated-income approach to bank asset management emphasizes the ability of borrowers to repay loans rather than the type of loan or investment made. It embraces the view that the ultimate security and liquidity of a loan is the borrower's ability to repay, which, in turn depends on the income the borrower will earn over the period of the loan.

5. Contemporary banking theory emphasizes the active management of bank liabilities as well as assets. In recent years, avenues have opened up whereby banks can increase liabilities at their own discretion rather than at that of their depositors.

6. Liability management is a term referring to strategies of buying so-called purchased funds (federal funds, large CDs, eurodollar accounts) when attractive investment opportunities arise and market conditions permit. Active liability management has become an important part of contemporary bank management.

7. In the United States, the proportion of loans and investments held in secondary and primary reserves has fallen sharply. At the same time, the proportion of noncommercial loans has risen sharply. Banks are financing their assets less and less by deposit liabilities and more and more by purchased funds, with demand and savings accounts supplying a little more than one-third of all liabilities in 1981 compared with more than 90 percent thirty years earlier.

**1.** Are the commercial-loan theory and shiftability approach incompatible? Explain as carefully as possible how they relate.

**2.** Why don't commercial banks make more long-term loans? Explain fully.

**3.** What are the most important implications of banks moving from a shiftability view to an anticipated income approach of asset management?

**4.** The movement toward more active liability management has occurred during a period when interest rates have been generally rising. Can you predict what will happen during an extended period of time when interest rates are falling?

**5.** If commercial banks hold less secondary reserves, which consist largely of U.S. government securities, who will pick up the slack as far as ownership of these securities is concerned? Will it be harder for the Treasury to finance the public debt?

For a discussion of banking theory up through the anticipated-income approach, see Herbert v. Prochnow, *Term Loans and Theories of Banking*, Englewood Cliffs, N.J.: Prentice-Hall, 1949. The Federal Reserve system maintains a table showing the various kinds of nondeposit funds raised by commercial banks, and the amount of funds in each category. See the table entitled "Major Nondeposit Funds of Commercial Banks" that appears in each issue of the *Federal Reserve Bulletin*.

# Accent on Managing Reserves

In the discussion of reserve requirements and the monetary multiplier in chapter 2, meeting reserves does not appear to be much of a management problem. Instead, it appears to be just something depository institutions are required to do in order to stay in business. Demand deposits either flow into the bank or are created by lending, requiring a fixed amount of funds to be set aside in the form of legal reserves.

In the contemporary world of banking in the United States, it is not so straightforward. Several kinds of liabilities have required reserves, with different ratios applying to each. The way of calculating required reserves has some distinct peculiarities. These two characteristics of bank reserve requirements

make meeting reserves a bank management problem of important dimensions. In this feature section, you can get acquainted with the general nature of the problem, and perhaps better appreciate how profit-seeking banks deal with the management of their reserve positions.

Table A.1 shows the current reserve requirements set by the Federal Reserve Board. There are six categories of liabilities against which reserves must be held. Besides demand deposits, reserves are required against other transactions accounts such as NOW, ATS, and share-draft accounts. Savings accounts and time deposits must be backed by required reserves as well. Different reserve requirements apply to so-called nonpersonal

**TABLE A.1.**
**Required Reserve Ratios as of July, 1982**

| | | | |
|---|---|---|---|
| **DEMAND DEPOSITS** | | **SAVINGS ACCOUNTS** | 3% |
| 0–2 million | 7% | **TIME DEPOSITS** | |
| 2–10 million | 9½% | 30–179 days | 6%[1] |
| 10–100 million | 11¾% | 180 days to 4 years | 2½% |
| 100–400 million | 12¾% | 4 years or more | 1% |
| over 400 million | 16¼% | **NONPERSONAL TIME DEPOSITS** | |
| **OTHER TRANSACTIONS ACCOUNTS** | | 0–4 years | 3% |
| 0–26 million | 3% | 4 years or more | 0% |
| over 26 million | 12% | **EURODOLLAR ACCOUNTS** | 3% |

*Source: Federal Reserve Bulletin*, July 1982.
[1]Except for the first 5 million, where the requirement is 3%.

time deposits, almost all of which are large-denomination negotiable CDs. Finally, reserves must be held against eurodollar accounts.

The required-reserve percentages vary widely among the various liability categories. Demand deposits have the highest reserve ratios whereas time deposits generally have the lowest. To the managers of a bank, all the liabilities listed in table A.1 are ways to raise funds for investment, each with a different type of cost. Some, such as nonpersonal time deposits, are costly in terms of interest that must be paid to depositors but relatively cheap in terms of reserves that must be held earning zero return, and costs to administer. Others, such as demand deposits, are cheap in terms of interest expense but expensive in terms of the reserves that must be held and the associated administrative costs. Bank managers continually seek to find the most efficient combination of liabilities considering the interest cost, reserve requirements, and administrative costs involved. (Keep in mind that if 10 percent of newly raised funds must be set aside for nonearning reserves, the effective return on the funds when invested is reduced by 10 percent.)

The reserve requirements shown in table A.1 are applied to all depository institutions as of 1980. Thus, commercial banks, savings and loan associations, mutual savings banks, and credit unions must maintain reserves whether they are members of the Federal Reserve system or not. Prior to 1980, only commercial banks that were Federal Reserve members held reserves with the system. With the 1980 law, a wider range of financial institutions now have the management problem of how best to structure their liabilities to manage reserves most profitably.

Reserve requirements are imposed against *net demand deposits*, which are derived by subtracting from actual (or gross) demand-deposit cash items in process of collection (float) and demand deposits due from domestic banks (interbank loans). Float is subtracted to avoid collecting reserves twice on the same deposits. When checks are written and deposited but have not cleared (the definition of float), the bank upon which they are written is not yet aware of them, so this bank shows the deposits on its books and holds reserves against them. At the same time, the bank in which they were newly

deposited shows them as a deposit and would also be required to hold reserves against them were it not for the new demand-deposit rule. The same type of double-counting would apply to interbank loans if these loans were not also subtracted in forming net demand deposits.

Two types of assets can be used to meet reserve requirements—cash held in bank vaults and reserve deposits held at regional Federal Reserve banks. Vault cash is relatively constant for most banks, so the primary asset involved in reserve management is the reserve deposit at the Federal Reserve.

A bank's reserve deposit fluctuates daily as checks are deposited in it and drawn against it. Reserves may be up to the legal amount on Monday but not on Tuesday. To deal with this problem, the Federal Reserve calculates reserves on hand for banks as the average of the reserves held each day of the week. However, weekends present a special problem. The funds in a bank's reserve account on Friday remain there until Monday, since no reserve transactions occur over the weekend. So, Friday's closing balance is also Saturday's and Sunday's balance. In other words, the Friday balance has special significance because it counts for three of the seven days used to compute the average balance.

In the Federal Reserve's method of calculating reserves, there are other wrinkles that affect bank management. Demand and other deposits held by a bank will vary daily in a way beyond the bank's control. It would be a tough timing problem for banks if they had to calculate their required reserves for today on the basis of today's deposits. To help make a bank's planning for reserves easier, the Federal Reserve has a time lag in the deposits that determine current reserve requirements. In this *lagged reserve accounting system*, the reserves required now are based on the average deposits for an earlier period. Banks thus know their reserve requirements somewhat in advance. Furthermore, the vault cash that is part of the reserve requirement is taken by the Federal Reserve to be the level held during the lagged period. For several years, the lag period used by the Federal Reserve was two weeks, and the deposits used to calculate reserves were the average daily values for a weekly period two weeks ago.

As of February 1984, the lagged reserve system will be replaced by what is called a *contemporaneous reserve accounting system.* Under this system, the average amount of deposits outstanding over a fourteen-day period ending every other Monday will fix the average reserves required as an average over the fourteen-day period ending two days later; that is, ending on alternative Wednesdays. Thus, a depository institution has only two days after its average deposits have been calculated to come up with the amount of reserves necessary to make average reserves correspond to legal requirements.

Table A.2 shows the deposits and reserves for a hypothetical bank over a two-week period. The "settlement day" is Wednesday of the second week, at which time legal reserve requirements must be met. To establish the average level of deposits against which reserves must be held, we calculate the arithmetic average for the fourteen days ending with the prior Monday. Thus, the deposits of 1,000 for Tuesday of Week One are the first to be included and the Monday, Week-Two deposits of 1,100 are the last to be included. The arithmetic average of these 14 deposit levels is 14,000 ÷ 14 = 1,000. Thus, 1,000 is the average level of deposits as of Monday to which reserves must correspond two days later. For simplicity, suppose the reserve requirement is a simple 10 percent.

The reserves required to "back" the average deposit level are thus 1,000 × .10 = 100. Under contemporaneous accounting, the average level of reserves over the 14-day period ending with *Wednesday* (as opposed to Monday) must be 100. For the data in table

A.2, the arithmetic sum of the reserves beginning with Thursday, Week One (80) and ending with the reserves as of Wednesday, Week Two (140) comes out to 1,400 ÷ 14 = 100, right at the legal requirement. Thus, this bank has its reserves at the legally required level.

As a practical matter, money-position managers at banks watch the deposit levels and reserve levels closely on a continuing basis, and make sure that enough reserves are placed on deposit to meet the average requirement on the average deposit level. This may involve some buildups near the end of the period, such as the rise to 140 on the last reserve day in our example.

An important dimension of reserve-position management by banks is dealing with Friday closing values. The values in table A.2 are end-of-day amounts. However, since Saturday and Sunday are not regular business days, the Friday closing amount applies to them as well. Thus, Friday's close "counts" three times each week in the calculations, or six out of the fourteen days. Accordingly, careful attention is paid to ending Friday with the lowest possible deposit levels and the highest possible reserve levels. Funds can be transferred among accounts, placed in overnight repos (see chapter 5) or other weekend accounts rather than in demand and/ or other checkable deposits.

The Federal Reserve's motivation for switching to a system of contemporaneous accounting for reserves is its belief that the new system will give the Federal Reserve a stronger degree of control over reserves. The two-week lag in the former system allowed

**TABLE A.2.**
**Bank A's Reserves and Deposits**

|       | WEEK ONE | | | WEEK TWO | | |
|-------|----------|----------|-------|----------|----------|
|       | Deposits | Reserves |       | Deposits | Reserves |
| Tue.  | 1,000    | na       | Tue.  | 1,400    | 110      |
| Wed.  | 800      | na       | Wed.  | 900      | 100      |
| Thur. | 1,300    | 80       | Thur. | 1,000    | 90       |
| Fri.  | 900      | 100      | Fri.  | 800      | 110      |
| Sat.  | 900      | 100      | Sat.  | 800      | 110      |
| Sun.  | 900      | 100      | Sun.  | 800      | 110      |
| Mon.  | 1,400    | 70       | Mon.  | 1,100    | 80       |
|       |          |          | Tue.  | na       | 100      |
|       |          |          | Wed.  | na       | 140      |

na = nonapplicable to the calculation.

banks to essentially expand deposits as market conditions suggested, that is, as opportunities to lend more funds appeared. Then, banks knew that they had two weeks to "come up" with the reserves necessary to back up the new deposits and loans. The pressures in the banking system were slow to develop, and the inclination of the Federal Reserve for many years was to provide added reserves when prior deposit growth placed reserves under heavy pressure.

With the two-day lag, banks have a much shorter time to produce reserves to back new deposits, a condition that adds a measure of discipline to deposit expansion that was not there under the two-week lag period. Some argue that under the new system, banks may have to actually consider their reserve position before expanding deposits, which seems to be what architects of the reserve accounting system had in mind all along.

Getting to know a bit more about the mechanics of meeting reserve requirements makes it clear that banks have several factors to consider in the management of their liabilities and their assets if they are to minimize the amount of bank assets tied up in zero-interest reserves. One such factor is the type of liability to hold, with demand deposits having the highest reserve requirements and other types of liabilities having lower requirements. With differing interest expense and different administrative costs on different liabilities, an important part of reserve management is evolving the most advantageous structure of reservable liabilities.

# PART III

# THE FEDERAL RESERVE SYSTEM

# Growth and Governance of the Federal Reserve System

## CHAPTER OUTLINE

MEMO—INTRODUCTION
ORGANIZATION OF THE FEDERAL
  RESERVE SYSTEM
LEGISLATIVE POWERS OF THE
  FEDERAL RESERVE
MANAGEMENT OF THE FEDERAL
  RESERVE
IMPORTANT IDEAS IN THIS
  CHAPTER
DISCUSSION QUESTIONS
SUGGESTED READINGS

## IMPORTANT TERMS

Board of Governors
Federal Open-Market Committee
  (FOMC)
Federal Advisory Council
Federal Reserve Act of 1913

banking acts of 1933 and 1935
disintermediation
Depository-Institution Deregulation
  and Monetary Control Act of 1980

## MEMO

To:        All readers
From:      JWE

The Federal Reserve system has a tough job. Those in charge of the system must ride herd on thousands of financial institutions that often may be interested in doing just what the Federal Reserve wants them not to do. If interest rates are high and the economy is booming, the Federal Reserve may be interested in holding down the growth in credit. But, high interest rates to a banker are like high prices of widgets to a widget producer. Bankers and widget makers want to expand production. The Federal Reserve also has the role of watchdog over the most sophisticated and rapidly changing financial system in the world. It is not an easy task to keep track of what is going on in it, let alone try to manage it in the interests of both the public and the owners of the private profit-seeking financial institutions that deliver the nation's financial services.

In this and the following two chapters, we will examine some of the important aspects of the Federal Reserve system to see how the system performs its job of policy-making and regulation. In this chapter, you will read about the organization of the system, its regulatory powers, and how the system is managed.

As with more than a few of our institutions, the current structure of the Federal Reserve system is the outgrowth of legislation, custom, and practice that has through the years responded to problems of the times. It is no accident that the three most significant legislative changes affecting the operation of the Federal Reserve occurred during or shortly after a period of crisis in financial markets. The financial panic of 1907 precipitated the Federal Reserve Act of 1913. The depression of the early 1930s brought forth the banking acts of 1933 and 1935, and the high interest rate and high inflation period of the 1970s provided the backdrop for the Depository-Institution Deregulation and Monetary Control Act of 1980.

In this chapter, the current organization of the Federal Reserve system (or Fed, as it is not disrespectively called) is discussed. The evolution of some of the important parts of the current system is traced. Finally, some thoughts are put forth on the contemporary management of the system.

## ORGANIZATION OF THE FEDERAL RESERVE SYSTEM

In the broadest respect, Congress is in charge of the Federal Reserve system in that it makes laws that set the structure of the system and stipulate how it shall be operated and governed. If Congress were to write legislation accordingly, it could take effective control of the activities of the system. But it has not done this. Instead, Congress has confined itself to passing not too frequent legislation that sets forth the ground rules within which the Federal Reserve system operates. Beyond this, the Fed has been left to carry out its functions quite independently.

Figure 10.1 summarizes the current structure of the system. Beyond Congress, the top decision-making body of the Fed is the seven-person *Board of Governors*. Each of the members is appointed by the president of the United States and confirmed by the Senate. Each serves a fourteen-year term, with one of the seven terms expiring every two years (in even-numbered years). This way of appointing the members of the Board of Governors makes them highly insulated from the political process. For example, a U.S. president cannot, during a term in office, measurably alter the composition of the board. The fourteen-year appointments virtually eliminate any political pressures that might exist with reappointments over shorter periods.

The chairperson of the Board of Governors is appointed by the U.S. president from among existing board members to serve a four-year term. The functions of the chairperson include bringing matters before the board, acting as a catalyst for policy review and changes, and acting as a communication link with Congress.

The Board of Governors sets reserve requirements within the ranges stipulated by Congress. It appoints directors of district Federal Reserve banks. It acts on applications for mergers, holding-company acquisitions, changes in charters, and other major organizational changes among member banks. The Board of Governors also has broad emergency powers to make sweeping changes in regulations affecting banks if conditions warrant declaration of an emergency. These powers include imposing various types of credit controls, requiring reserves against any type of depository-institution liability, and even requiring reserves against money-market mutual funds issued by private mutual funds.

*The Federal Open-Market Committee* (FOMC) is a twelve-person committee that oversees open-market operations. It consists of the seven members of the Board of Governors, plus five other people. These members are the president of the New York district Federal Reserve bank, plus the presidents of four of the other Federal Reserve district banks, who serve on a rotating basis. The New York Federal Reserve bank president serves as a permanent member presumably because the New York bank does the buying and selling of securities, which constitutes open-market operations.

**FIGURE 10.1.
Organization of the
Federal Reserve
System.**

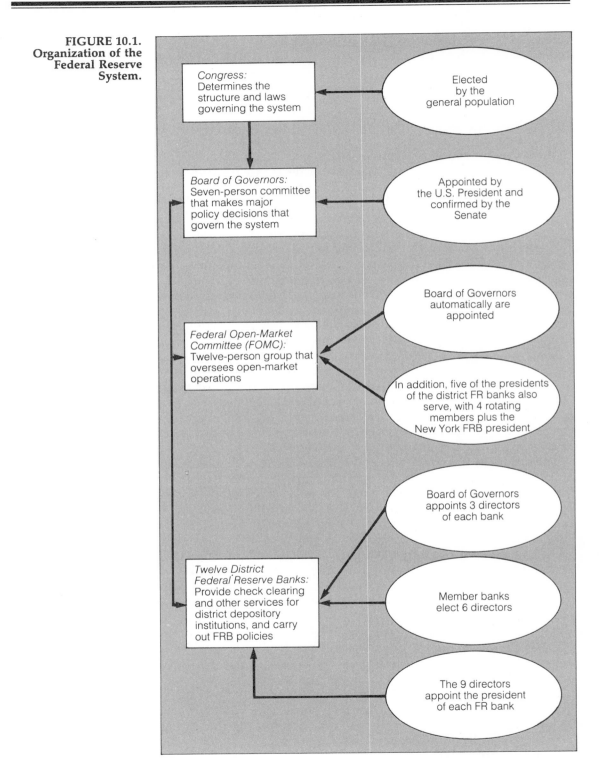

The FOMC determines open-market policy and oversees its administration. Like the Board of Governors, the FOMC does this primarily through regular meetings at which current and proposed policy is discussed in light of trends and developments in the economy.

The third major part of the Federal Reserve system is the structure of twelve district Federal Reserve banks. As figure 10.2 shows, the United States is geographically divided into twelve districts (denoted by the bold-face numbers), each of which has a Federal Reserve district bank. The districts correspond basically to population dispersion at the time they were established in 1913. Demographic changes since then make some of the districts quite a bit larger in scope than others.

The main duties of the district banks are (1) to provide check clearing and other related financial services for depository institutions in the district, (2) to carry out the policies of the Board of Governors, (3) to oversee and regulate member banks in the district in accordance with the policies and rules set forth by the Board of Governors, (4)

**FIGURE 10.2.**
**Geographic Structure of the Federal Reserve System.**

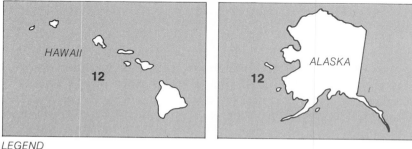

LEGEND

──────  Boundaries of Federal Reserve Districts

──────  Boundaries of Federal Reserve Branch Territories

●  Board of Governors of the Federal Reserve System

◉  Federal Reserve Bank Cities

•  Federal Reserve Branch Cities

·  Federal Reserve Bank Facility

Source: *Federal Reserve Bulletin*, June, 1982

to function as the banker for the U.S. Treasury, and (5) to set the district's discount rate with the approval of the Board of Governors. Each district Federal Reserve bank is managed by a president and a board of nine directors. The directors appoint the president of each district Federal Reserve bank. Six of the directors are elected by member banks in the district and three are appointed by the Board of Governors.

This system of election and appointment of key officials is quite diffused, with important contributions from banks, industry, the board, and the president of the U.S. It is virtually impossible for political leaders of any particular persuasion to "load" the federal system with like-minded leaders. The intended result of this process is to create in the Fed a highly independent agency that will tend to have "no axe to grind" concerning public policy, and will tend to function with little but the public interest in mind.

In addition to these major components of the Federal Reserve system, there is an additional organizational unit—the *Federal Advisory Council*. This is a twelve-person committee having one member from each Federal Reserve district. The Federal Advisory Council dates back to the original Federal Reserve Act of 1913. It has no authority, but gives advice on monetary policy in the form of resolutions, papers, and memoranda. In recent years, the Federal Advisory Council has not been an important influence on the conduct of monetary policy.

## LEGISLATIVE POWERS OF THE FEDERAL RESERVE

The modern Federal Reserve system dates back to the *Federal Reserve Act of 1913*. This act outlined in broad strokes the composition of the system. It laid out the twelve Federal Reserve districts, and designated a city within each district where a district Federal Reserve bank was to be located. The Federal Reserve Board was established primarily to coordinate the activities of the twelve district banks.

The act designated that every nationally chartered bank was required to belong to the system, and gave state-chartered banks the option of belonging. Each member bank was required to subscribe 6 percent of its equity (capital plus surplus) to the district Federal Reserve bank, thus providing the district bank with capital. In return, the district bank paid a dividend of 6 percent of the amount contributed per year to the member bank. The 1913 act also provided for the directorship of each district bank, stipulating that each bank would have nine directors, three elected by member banks to represent the interests of district bankers, three more elected by member banks to represent the interests of major customers of district banks, and three appointed by the Federal Reserve Board to represent the interests of the public. These parts of the 1913 act—dealing with membership, districting, and directorship of district banks—have survived essentially intact to the present time.

Other parts of the original act have been substantially altered by subsequent legislation. Among these, the 1913 act authorized each of the twelve district banks to issue, at its discretion, Federal Reserve Notes backed by a 40 percent reserve of gold and gold certificates. This authorization allowed the district banks to issue uniform liabilities that would be directly held by the public and used in trade as a medium of exchange. The Federal Reserve Notes were thought to be a necessary way to provide for the expanding monetary needs of a growing economy. To help circulate these notes, each district bank was allowed to *rediscount* commercial paper held by its member banks. Rediscounting means that the Federal Reserve district bank would buy the notes from member banks at a discount from the bank's cost. In selling the notes to the Fed at a discount, the member bank is in effect borrowing from the Fed at a rate of interest associated with the amount of discount. Since the member bank had already discounted the commercial paper in buying it from business firms, the rate of discount the Fed applied was called the rediscount rate. Later, as the Fed expanded the types of collateral (beyond commercial paper) against which it would loan funds to member banks, the interest rate charged on such loans became known as just the discount rate. Thus, the 1913 act created the forerunner of the modern discount window through which banks can borrow from the Federal Reserve.

Discounting and the issuance of Federal Reserve Notes meant that the expanding and contracting credit needs of commerce could be provided for more or less automatically. As firms expanded and had a greater need for short-term credit, they would borrow in the form of newly issued commercial paper, which banks would buy at a discount. Banks could rediscount this paper at the Fed, thus advancing funds to business. With this process, as the needs for funds expanded, the supply of both reserves and Federal Reserve Notes also expanded. Similarly, when business financial needs subsided, the maturing of existing rediscounted commercial paper caused reserves to flow back into the Federal Reserve, contracting the amount of reserves and Federal Reserve Notes outstanding.

Through the 1913 act, each district Federal Reserve bank was empowered to buy and sell government bonds. This meant that each district bank ran its own open-market operations according to its own policy. This open-market channel provided each district bank with another important way to add or contract the amount of reserves in its district.

The 1913 law laid out a system of highly diversified central banking. Each of the twelve Federal Reserve banks made its own open-market policy and determined the amount and rate of discounting to member banks. In short, each district bank operated in its district much the same as the present Board of Governors now operates in the entire nation. The role of the Federal Reserve Board in these operations was more of an overseer than a leader. It is pretty much agreed that for practical purposes, each district bank "ran its own show" in the years following the passage of the original Federal Reserve act.

In addition, the original Federal Reserve act initiated graduated reserve requirements depending on the size of the bank, established the Federal Advisory Council, and provided for development of a nationwide check-clearing system with the Federal Reserve banks having major responsibility.

The financial strains of the booming 1920s U.S. economy, followed by the disastrous financial crisis of the early 1930s, revealed a need for decisive leadership on the part of the nation's central banking system that seemingly could not be accommodated by the decentralized approach of the times. Credit expansion in the late 1920s was excessive, and fueled an expansion that could not last. Credit contraction in the early 1930s was equally excessive, and equally severe in its consequences. What was missing from the nation's central banking system was the reins of overall leadership that could steer a more even course through times such as the late 1920s and early 1930s. *The banking acts of 1933 and 1935* modified the Federal Reserve act in a way that provided that centralized leadership.

The 1933 and 1935 acts put in place much of the present structure of central governance of the Federal Reserve system. The seven-member and fourteen-year-term format of the Board of Governors was part of this legislation, as was the establishment of the centralized Federal Open-Market Committee. With the FOMC came the centralization of open-market policy, to be directed by one policy group and executed by the New York district bank.

In other sweeping changes, the 1930s legislation stipulated that the appointment of the president of each district bank required the approval of the Board of Governors. It provided that reserve requirements for all districts were to be set by the Board of Governors. Also, the discount rates set by each district bank were to be submitted to the Board of Governors for approval every two weeks.

In addition, the Board of Governors obtained authority via the 1930s acts to regulate the interest rates paid on time and savings deposits. This authority led to regulation Q, which formalized the interest-rate ceilings on deposits that were maintained from their initiation until their phasing out during the 1980s.

Clearly, the changes in the Federal Reserve system made in the 1930s were largely directed toward providing the system with central leadership via the Board of Governors. The board was given the tools to take charge of most of the important policy decisions available to the central bank. Similarly, the role of the district banks changed. Instead of functioning as twelve largely independent policy-making units, district banks now functioned as twelve parts of a single central-banking system.

The Federal Reserve system functioned in the post-World-War-II period until the early 1970s much as its architects had hoped. Banking in the United States progressed in a healthy fashion, and financial markets were remarkably stable. However, as the 1970s unfolded, several emerging patterns disturbed this stability. A rising inflation rate pushed interest rates to double-digit levels, a development that put great pressures on interest-rate ceilings. Savers were enticed to forgo putting their money in savings and time deposits, and instead make direct investments in Treasury Bills or other short-term notes where high market rates of interest were being paid. The term *disintermediation* was coined to describe the behavior of savers in bypassing financial intermediaries and going directly to primary financial markets. In this environment, the competition between banks and thrifts intensified, as each tried to stem the outflow of deposits associated with disintermediation. As a result, banks and thrifts found legal ways to encroach on each other's traditional turf.

During 1970s, savings and loan associations, mutual savings banks, and credit unions began issuing checkable-type accounts (the traditional monopoly of banks), while banks began aggressively seeking household savings through various types of high-interest certificates of deposit. From the perspective of the Federal Reserve, the most disturbing ingredient in this pattern of change was that the thrifts were behaving more and more like banks but were largely outside the structure of regulation applying to banks. Thus, an increasing volume of banking activities was taking place outside the scope of the Fed's regulatory powers.

The high interest rates of the 1970s also produced other changes in banking structure. They made it increasingly costly to hold reserves at the Fed, leading banks to more closely examine ways of minimizing their reserve obligations. One avenue that many seized upon was to change their charter from federal to state, thus complying with state rather than federal reserve requirements. Many states allow banks to hold reserves in the form of public bonds, and in some cases the amount of reserves required is noticeably less.

As the 1970s progressed, the Federal Reserve system faced a loss of membership of serious proportions. Between 1970 and 1979, the percentage of banks that were members of the Federal Reserve system fell from 42 percent to under 37 percent. The total deposits of member versus nonmember banks fell from about 80 percent of the total in 1970 to about 69 percent in 1979. A study done by the staff of the Board of Governors during the late 1970s further indicated that a number of rather large member banks were at that time actively studying the possibility of switching to state charters.

With the increasing role of thrifts in banking and the steady decline of Federal Reserve membership, the Board of Governors was faced with a growing loss of control over the nation's banking activities. It was again a time for major changes in the banking laws. The 1980 legislation represented such a change.

The *Depository-Institution Deregulation and Monetary Control Act of 1980* was the most significant change in U.S. banking laws since the legislation of the 1930s. It directly addressed the system's problem of loss of control in one sweeping change. Under the new law, all depository institutions—commercial banks, savings and loans associations, mutual savings banks, credit unions, and U.S. branches of foreign banks—are subject to the same reserve requirements on transaction-type (checkable) accounts and nonpersonal time deposits. No distinction is made between types of banks in this regard. The same reserve requirements are uniformly applied to all banks whether state or federally chartered, member or nonmember. Each now holds reserves with the system. Thrifts, which had increasingly been acting like banks, are now being treated like banks in terms of the reserves they must hold and the regulations with which they must comply.

The immediate reaction of state-chartered nonmember banks and thrifts might logically have been to wonder whether the Federal Reserve could legally absorb them within the system's regulatory structure. It quickly became clear that an act of Congress can indeed make such a change. With the 1980 law, the Federal Reserve system regained control of nonmember-bank deposits and gained control of the newly emerging transaction deposits of thrift institutions.

The law also contained other important changes. The Board of Governors was given the authority to impose a supplemental reserve requirement of up to 4 percent on transactions accounts of depository institutions as the board deems necessary. The board was given the authority to impose reserve requirements on eurodollar accounts at its discretion, and given the authority to impose reserve requirements on virtually any liability if the board determines its growth creates an emergency situation. This emergency power allows the board to respond quickly to any innovations in bank liabilities that may not be covered under existing law. (In recent years, banks and other depository institutions have displayed remarkable ingenuity in creating new types of liabilities over which reserve requirements have not been established.)

In the same law, all depository institutions were given the right to issue NOW accounts (see chapter 5), and all depository institutions were given the right to borrow from the Fed at the discount window. These changes represent a further legal step toward integrating banks and thrifts within the same regulatory structure.

Finally, the 1980 law provides for the phasing out of all interest-rate ceilings over a period of several years, as determined by a committee established under the law. Phasing out interest-rate ceilings is a response to the 1970s problem of disintermediation, and the innovations in financial instruments thus brought about. After ceilings are phased out, financial institutions will be able to adjust the amounts paid on passbook and other types of savings deposits as market conditions require. Disintermediation should become a thing of the past. However, with the elimination of an important source of funds that is now basically at a fixed rate, depository institutions will have to manage their assets more carefully to assure that they recover the more widely fluctuating cost of funds they will face in an era of no interest-rate ceilings.

## MANAGEMENT OF THE FEDERAL RESERVE

The legislative changes of the last several decades have greatly increased the power of the Board of Governors of the Federal Reserve system. At present, the Board of Governors makes the nation's monetary policy through the decisions it regularly makes on reserve requirements, open-market policy, and the discount rate. The board functions as a committee, with a chairperson at its head. Most of the business on policy matters is put to a committee vote. Thus, most of the board's authority is legally vested in the committee as a deliberative body. The chairperson has little in the way of formal power to act in policy matters.

Yet through the years, the chairperson of the Board of Governors has been highly influential in governing the nation's economic affairs. The chairperson's informal power has greatly exceeded any formal authority, most likely because this person is looked to for leadership and is a communication link with the committee. The chairperson is the principal spokesperson for the committee in the many appearances before Congress required during the course of a congressional session, bringing the board's view to Congress, and arguing the board's case. The chairperson is also the primary link with the press, regularly speaking to the public on behalf of the committee. Furthermore, the board chairperson is also the head of the FOMC, undoubtedly the second most influential body in making monetary policy. In all these roles, the chairperson typically exerts a quiet influence over the policies being pursued by the president and Congress, and to a degree influences other members of the Board of Governors as well.

Often as not, another person of more-than-meets-the-eye importance in Federal Reserve policy making is the president of the New York district Federal Reserve bank. This person's formal role in policy making is as a permanent member of the FOMC. Informally, the position as president of the largest of the twelve reserve banks allows for considerable influence in policy making. On more than one occasion in recent years, the New York Fed president has loomed as the second most important individual (next to the chairperson) associated with monetary policy making.

**Important Ideas in This Chapter**

1. The Federal Reserve system has as its head a Board of Governors. This board is vested with the primary job of policy making and regulation, with which the Federal Reserve is legally empowered.

2. The Federal Open-Market Committee, or FOMC, is charged with the responsibility of making and carrying out open-market policy.

3. The Board of Governors consists of seven members. Each member serves a fourteen-year term, and one of the seven terms expires every two years. The FOMC consists of all seven board members, plus five

other members who include the president of the New York Federal Reserve bank and four other Federal Reserve bank presidents drawn from the remaining district Federal Reserve banks on a rotating basis.

**4.** There are twelve district Federal Reserve banks, each of which has a president and nine directors. The president is chosen by the directors. Six of the directors are elected by member banks in the district, and three are appointed by the Board of Governors.

**5.** The Federal Reserve Act of 1913 formed the Federal Reserve system as a loose confederation of twelve district Federal Reserve banks, each of which had independent policy-making authority over monetary policy in the district. Individual banks were in charge of their own open-market operations and discount policy.

**6.** The banking legislation of 1933 and 1935 modified the original Federal Reserve act in the direction of centralizing authority at the Board of Governors, and forming the previous coalition of district banks into one central banking system with one policy-making board.

**7.** Open-market policy, discount rates, and reserve-requirement establishment were given to the Board of Governors as the main tools of monetary policy by the 1930s banking laws.

**8.** Through the combination of the movement of thrifts into banking and the loss of members through charter changes, the Federal Reserve system experienced a loss of control throughout the 1970s. The Depository-Institution Deregulation and Monetary Control Act of 1980 restored this control by requiring that all depository institutions maintain uniform reserves with the Fed against transaction and other accounts.

**9.** The 1980 act also provided for phasing out of interest-rate ceilings established by regulation Q, and gave the board authority to require reserves against broader classes of liabilities.

**Discussion Questions**

**1.** The 1930s banking laws provided for central leadership of the Federal Reserve system. Consider the nearly fifty years that have passed since then. Do you think centralized leadership of the Fed is more or less important now than in the 1930s? Explain.

**2.** What are the advantages and dangers of phasing out the interest ceilings? Think along as many dimensions of this question as possible.

**3.** Do you think it would be better for the nation if the chairperson of the Board of Governors was not also the chairperson of the FOMC? Explain.

**4.** In the 1980 banking law, securities brokers were not required to hold reserves. Yet, in recent years, some have begun to hold a variety of liabilities that look similar to those of banks. Find out what current liabilities are being held by large brokerages such as Merrill Lynch, and make a case either for or against these firms being required to hold reserves as with depository institutions.

**5.** What are some of the forms that competition is currently taking among thrifts and banks? Does it create regulatory problems as far as the Federal Reserve is concerned?

For a complete analysis of the 1980 banking law, see "The Depository Institution Deregulation and Monetary Control act of 1980," *Federal Reserve Bulletin*, Washington, D.C.: GPO, June 1980, pp. 444–53. For an interesting study of the management of the Federal Reserve, see Thomas Havrilesky, William P. Yohe, and David Schirm, "The Economic Affiliations of Directors of Federal Reserve District Banks," *Social Science Quarterly*, December 1973. A detailed description and analysis of the functions of the Federal Reserve system are found in *The Federal Reserve System, Purposes and Functions,* Washington, D.C.: Board of Governors of the Federal Reserve system, GPO, 1975.

**Suggested Readings**

## CHAPTER 11

# Factors Supplying and Absorbing Reserves

**To:**       All readers
**From:**     JWE

The amount of reserves held by depository institutions is a major if not *the* major object of the Federal Reserve Board's system of controls over the money supply. The extent to which Federal Reserve controls are effective in adjusting reserves (and the resulting money supply) to the levels consistent with the system's goals is to an important degree the test of how effective the Fed is as an agency of economic policy. The key role of reserves in the operations of the Federal Reserve makes it valuable for us to know something about what determines reserves beyond the basics we found in chapters 2 and 3.

In this chapter, reserves are dissected into nearly a dozen pieces. This allows isolation of the factors that contribute to the supply of reserves, and identification of the factors that absorb reserves. Thus, you can learn more about the important influences on this most important of policy aggregates—the reserve deposits of depository institutions.

In the last chapter, the level of depository-institution reserves was seen to be an important object of Federal Reserve regulatory efforts. Two of the Fed's major policy tools, open-market operations and setting reserve requirements, are directed toward either the amount of reserves or their legal encumbrance. The reason reserves play an important role in Fed policy is clear—they are the raw material from which depository institutions create most of the nation's money supply. Understanding how reserves are determined helps us judge the extent to which the Federal Reserve can control this monetary raw material.

To understand the factors that govern the amount of reserves present in the banking system, we must first become familiar with the balance sheet of the Federal Reserve system. Every asset and liability on the Fed's balance sheet contributes in some way to the level of reserves.

## THE FEDERAL RESERVE BALANCE SHEET

Figure 11.1 shows the consolidated statement of condition, or balance sheet, for the Federal Reserve system as of February 24, 1982. A comparable statement of condition can be found in any issue of the *Federal Reserve Bulletin*. Let us examine the assets and liabilities in the Fed's balance sheet, one at a time.

| ASSETS | (BILLIONS OF DOLLARS) |
|---|---|
| Gold certificates | 11.2 |
| SDR certificates | 3.6 |
| Coin | 0.4 |
| Loans to depository institutions[1] | 1.4 |
| U.S. government and agency securities | 135.3 |
| Cash items in process of collection | 8.0 |
| Other Federal Reserve assets | 8.9 |
| Total assets | 168.8 |
| **LIABILITIES** | |
| Federal Reserve Notes | 127.6 |
| Reserve deposits of depository institutions | 24.8 |
| Treasury, foreign, and other deposits | 5.9 |
| Deferred-availability cash items | 5.6 |
| Other Federal Reserve liabilities and capital | 4.9 |
| Total liabilities and capital | 168.8 |

**FIGURE 11.1.**
**Federal Reserve Balance Sheet as of February 24, 1982.**

Source: *Federal Reserve Bulletin*, March 1982.
[1]Includes a small amount of acceptances.

*Gold certificates* are legal claims held by the Federal Reserve on gold that is physically held by the U.S. Treasury. The Treasury sells gold to the Federal Reserve by issuing certificates against it. When the Federal Reserve receives these certificates, the Treasury's deposit (a liability on the Fed's balance sheet) is increased, and the holdings of gold certificates (an asset) is also increased. By issuing gold certificates, the Treasury can transfer the value of the gold it holds into a deposit held by the Federal Reserve, where the Treasury can then write checks on the deposit and thus spend it.

*Special Drawing Rights (SDR) certificates* are similar to gold certificates in that they are claims held by the Federal Reserve on SDRs held by the Treasury. In turn, SDRs are paper assets created by the International Monetary Fund (IMF) for allocation to and use by all affiliated nations instead of gold for settlement of international transactions. Thus, a nation can use SDRs to buy the currency of another nation when needed for international trade. SDRs are sometimes called international paper gold. When major trading nations in the western world agreed in 1970 to honor and use SDRs instead of gold for settlement of international accounts, it represented an important step by these countries in taking into their own hands control of the world's money supply.[1]

When the Treasury receives a new allocation of SDRs from the IMF, it may issue certificates against them, which are held by the Federal Reserve and which lead to an increase in the Treasury's de-

1. With the initiation of SDRs, major trading nations no longer had to rely on the mining of gold to bring about an increase in worldwide liquidity needed in international trade.

posit at the Fed. Upon receipt of an SDR certificate, the Fed increases its SDR-certificate account and increases the Treasury's deposit.

The Federal Reserve asset, *coin*, consists of the coin and other currency minted and/or issued by the Treasury but held by the Federal Reserve. A small amount of paper money is issued by the Treasury and may from time to time be held by the Federal Reserve as part of this account. However, most of the account consists of the coinage held in the vaults of Federal Reserve banks.

*Loans to depository institutions* are almost entirely the IOUs that depository institutions have negotiated with the Fed through the discount window. Lumped into this category are a small number of acceptances that depository institutions have discounted with the Fed. When a depository institution borrows from the Fed, this is the place on the Fed's balance sheet where the loan appears.

*U.S. government and agency securities* are the Fed's portfolio of federal government securities from which the FOMC buys and sells to implement open-market policy. As discussed in chapter 3, when the Fed writes a check to a private owner of government securities to buy securities for this portfolio, holdings of securities increase, and when the Fed's check clears, the reserve deposits of depository institutions rise.

*Cash items in process of collection* (an asset) and *deferred-availability cash items* (a liability) are best discussed together. These two categories are "holding tanks" for funds in transient from one bank's reserve account to another's. When the Federal Reserve gets a $100 check from the Chase Manhattan drawn on Manufacturers Hanover, the Fed does not immediately reduce the second bank's reserve account and increase the first bank's account. Instead, the Fed assumes the role of intermediary. It gives credit to Chase Manhattan after a preset waiting period of approximately two days (thus the "deferred" title) and also shows cash due from Manufacturers Hanover in the corresponding asset category. When the deferral period is over, the holding-tank accounts are cleared and the reserve accounts of the two banks are adjusted to show the shift of reserves.

The specific transactions in the following example may help you understand the two holding-tank categories on the Fed's books.

### FEDERAL RESERVE BANK

| ASSETS | | LIABILITIES AND NET WORTH | |
|---|---|---|---|
| (1) Cash items in process of collection: | | Deferred-availability cash items: | |
| Manufacturers Hanover | +100 | Chase Manhattan | +100 |
| (2) | | Deferred-availability cash items: | |
| | | Chase Manhattan | −100 |
| | | Reserve deposit: | |
| | | Chase Manhattan | +100 |
| (3) Cash items in process of collection: | | Reserve deposit: | |
| Manufacturers Hanover | −100 | Manufacturers Hanover | −100 |

In step (1), the Federal Reserve activates its middleman role by showing as *its asset* the funds due from Manufacturers Hanover and as *its liability* the funds owed to Chase Manhattan. Then in step (2) when the deferral period is up, the funds are transferred from the holding tank into Chase's reserve deposit. In step (3), the other side of the transaction is completed by reducing both "cash items in process of collection" and the reserve account of Manufacturers Hanover. The net result of these three sets of transactions is that reserves have been transferred from Manufacturers Hanover to Chase. However, a type of float is created in the process. Accordingly, we define *Federal Reserve float* as cash items in process of collection minus deferred-availability cash items. Thus, Federal Reserve float for the balance-sheet data of figure 11.1 is 8.0 − 5.6 = 2.4 billion.

*Other Federal Reserve assets* include the value of the buildings and equipment owned by the Fed, as well as miscellaneous assets not fitting into the other asset categories.

*Federal Reserve Notes* are the outstanding (that is, in circulation) ones, fives, tens, twenties, and so forth that constitute the nation's active supply of currency. Officially, they are IOUs issued by the Federal Reserves and backed by the assets of the system.

*Reserve deposits of depository institutions* are the combined reserve accounts of all depository institutions. The accounts contain the reserves held against all transaction accounts, and must legally be maintained at the levels prescribed by reserve requirements.

*Treasury, foreign, and other deposits* are U.S. Treasury and other official accounts held by governments with the Federal Reserve. The Treasury's account is of particular interest because it is through this account that the Treasury writes the checks to implement government-spending programs.

*Other Federal Reserve liabilities and capital* are miscellaneous liabilities, plus the paid-in-capital of Federal Reserve member banks, plus accumulated surplus.

We have reviewed the Fed's balance sheet item by item. Let us now look at it as a whole. Accounting practice insures that any changes made in the balance sheet will cause it to continue to balance in the sense that total assets will continually equal total liabilities. Thus, when the Fed increases an asset, it can only do so by reducing another asset (such as exchanging loans for securities), or by increasing a liability or capital account (such as increased borrowing and increased reserve deposits).

In thinking about the factors impacting upon reserves, we can group some of the asset and liability categories into a simple expression. Because total assets always equal total liabilities and capital:

**(11.1)**   Total Assets = Reserve Deposits + All Other Liabilities and Capital

or, by rearranging:

**(11.2)**   Reserve Deposits = Total Assets − All Other Liabilities and Capital

Thus, if other liabilities do not change, an increase in any Fed asset increases reserve deposits. Alternatively, if assets remain the same, a decrease in other liabilities or capital produces an increase in reserve deposits. Expression 11.2 is not hypothetical. It is the broad outline of the actual method used by the Federal Reserve to track patterns of change in the reserves of depository institutions. It is to this topic we now turn.

## THE DEPOSITORY-INSTITUTION RESERVE EQUATION

Figure 11.2 shows the factors supplying reserves to depository institutions, the factors absorbing reserves, and the amount of reserves present, as of the same time as the data in figure 11.1. The relationship shown in figure 11.2 is called the *depository-institution reserve equation*. The general correspondence of figure 11.2 and expression 11.2 is unmistakable. Indeed, with the exception of Treasury currency outstanding, all the factors supplying reserves are assets of the Federal Reserve System.[2] Similarly, with the exception of Treasury cash holdings, all the factors absorbing reserves are liabilities and capital of the Federal Reserve other than reserve deposits.

However, there are some new items in figure 11.2. *Treasury currency outstanding* consists mostly of coins minted and issued by the Treasury, plus a small amount (about 0.3 billion) of Treasury Notes. Figure 11.2 shows that the Treasury's issuance of coins supplements the reserves supplied by the Federal Reserve system.

The next new entry, *Treasury cash holdings*, is pretty much what the title suggests, the amount of currency held by the Treasury. To the extent that the Treasury holds currency, it is not available in bank vaults to help meet reserves—thus this entry appears on the list of factors absorbing reserves.

The category *currency and coin held by the nonbank public* is not the same as the category Federal Reserve Notes in figure 11.1. The figure 11.1 entry gave the total amount of currency issued by the Federal Reserve. In accounting for reserves, we must distinguish between currency held in the vaults of the Treasury, the Federal Reserve, and depository institutions, and currency held by the nonbank public. The currency held by the banking system is part of reserves, whereas that held by the public is a factor absorbing reserves, in other words, it is not available to satisfy reserve requirements.

2. To reconcile the factors supplying reserves with the total assets of the Federal Reserve system shown in figure 11.1, three corrections are required. First, subtract the 13.7 billion of Treasury currency outstanding, then add the 5.6 billion of deferred-availability cash items to get the 8.0 cash-items-in-process-of-collection entry instead of the float, and finally, add the 0.4 billion in coin held by the Fed, and you have the total assets of the Fed.

| FACTORS SUPPLYING RESERVES | (BILLIONS OF DOLLARS) |
|---|---|
| U.S. government and agency securities | 135.3 |
| Loans to depository institutions | 1.4 |
| Federal Reserve float | 2.4 |
| Other Federal Reserve assets | 8.9 |
| Gold certificates | 11.2 |
| SDR certificates | 3.6 |
| Treasury currency outstanding | 13.7 |
| Total | 176.5 |
| **LESS FACTORS ABSORBING RESERVES** | |
| Currency and coin held by the nonbank public[1] | 122.2 |
| Treasury cash holdings | 0.5 |
| Treasury, foreign, and other deposits | 5.9 |
| Other Federal Reserve liabilities and capital | 4.9 |
| Total | 133.5 |
| **EQUALS DEPOSITORY-INSTITUTION RESERVES** | |
| Reserve deposits of depository institutions | 24.8 |
| Currency in vaults of depository institutions | 18.2 |
| Total | 43.0 |

FIGURE 11.2.
Depository-Instutition Reserve Equation as of February 24, 1982.

Source: The *Federal Reserve Bulletin*, March 1982.
Note: This is a rearrangement of the reserve equation found in the *Federal Reserve Bulletin*, although it contains all the same ingredients.
[1]This is defined as total currency and coin outstanding less that held by the Federal Reserve, the U.S. Treasury, and depository institutions as vault cash.

Besides adjusting for bank-held currency, we must also account for Treasury-issued money, mostly coins. The 13.7 billion of Treasury-issued currency shown in figure 11.2 is interchangeable with the 127.6 billion of Federal Reserve Notes as far as supplying and absorbing reserves are concerned. Thus, to obtain the proper currency category for the reserve equation, we must make the following adjustments to the Federal Reserve Notes entry in figure 11.1:

|   |   |   |
|---|---|---|
| | Federal Reserve Notes issued | 127.6 |
| plus: | coins/notes issued by Treasury | +13.7 |
| less: | coin held by the Fed | −0.4 |
| less: | cash held by the Treasury | −0.5 |
| less: | vault cash of depository institutions | −18.2 |
| equals: | currency and coin held by the nonbank public | 122.2 |

One of the factors supplying reserves is the Federal Reserve float, earlier defined to be the difference between "cash items in process of collection" and "deferred-availability cash items." The Federal Reserve float represents reserves supplied by the Federal Reserve because of a net balance of checks in process of clearing against reserve accounts.

The depository-institution reserve equation shows all the factors that either supply or absorb reserves. U.S. government and agency securities are the most important and most variable source of reserves, as they are the mechanism by which open-market policy is implemented. As discussed earlier and in chapter 3, when the Federal Reserve buys securities for this portfolio, the check written in payment adds directly to reserve deposits.

When the Federal Reserve's holdings of either gold or SDR certificates increase, there is an impact on reserves. An illustration helps show how this impact occurs. Suppose that the U.S. Treasury buys 5 million of gold on the open market, paying by check. Three balance-sheet accounts are affected, as follows:

| U.S. TREASURY | | | FEDERAL RESERVE | |
|---|---|---|---|---|
| ASSETS | | LIABILITIES AND NET WORTH | ASSETS | LIABILITIES AND NET WORTH |
| Gold | +5 | | | Reserve deposit +5 |
| Fed deposit | −5 | | | Treasury deposit −5 |

| COMMERCIAL BANK | |
|---|---|
| ASSETS | LIABILITIES AND NET WORTH |
| Reserve deposit +5 | Demand deposit     +5 |

The first account shows the change in the Treasury's assets and liabilities. The Treasury now shows an increase in gold of 5 million but a decrease in its deposit with the Fed of 5 million when its check clears. For the Treasury, the transaction is an exchange of assets. For the Fed, it is an exchange of liabilities. The Treasury deposit falls by 5 million, while that of the commercial bank receiving the Treasury's check rises by 5 million. The commercial-bank account shows an increase in the asset, reserves, and an increase in the liability, demand deposits, when the check is deposited.

As a result of the Treasury's gold purchase, bank reserves are up, but the Treasury's account is down. Suppose the Treasury wants to recover the amount in its deposit at the Fed. It can do this by issuing to the Fed gold certificates against the newly purchased gold. The following entries occur:

| U.S. TREASURY | | |
|---|---|---|
| ASSETS | | LIABILITIES AND NET WORTH |
| Fed deposit | +5 | Gold certificates outstanding     +5 |

| FEDERAL RESERVE | | |
|---|---|---|
| ASSETS | | LIABILITIES AND NET WORTH |
| Gold certificates | +5 | Treasury deposit     +5 |

Thus, after the certificates are issued, the Federal Reserve shows the gold as an asset on its books, offset by the increased Treasury deposit. Accordingly, the Treasury shows its Fed deposit as an increased asset, offset by the gold certificates in which the Treasury has essentially "signed over" the new gold to the Fed. Although the Treasury has the same Fed deposit as before the transaction, the banking system has an increase in reserves as a result of the Treasury gold purchase.

Figure 11.2 indicates that reserves rise when a depository institution borrows from the discount window. Suppose Citibank borrows 5 million via the discount window. Here are the entries:

### FEDERAL RESERVE

| ASSETS | | LIABILITIES AND NET WORTH | |
|---|---|---|---|
| Loan | +5 | Reserve deposit—Citibank | +5 |

### CITIBANK

| ASSETS | | LIABILITIES AND NET WORTH | |
|---|---|---|---|
| Fed reserve deposit | +5 | Note Payable—Fed | +5 |

Thus, when the Fed makes the loan, it does so by making an entry in the reserve deposit of the borrowing bank, which is a Federal Reserve liability but Citibank's asset. Correspondingly, the Fed asset, "loan," is a liability to Citibank in the form of a note payable.

When the Federal Reserve issues more currency (that is, Federal Reserve Notes), bank reserves typically do not rise. Instead, depository institutions exchange currency for their reserve deposit or vice versa when their currency needs change. If a bank needs more vault cash, it writes a check to the Fed for the amount it wants. The Fed ships the currency to the bank, and the following entries result:

### FEDERAL RESERVE

| ASSETS | | LIABILITIES AND NET WORTH | |
|---|---|---|---|
| | | Federal Reserve Notes | +5 |
| | | Reserve deposit | −5 |

### COMMERCIAL BANK

| ASSETS | | LIABILITIES AND NET WORTH | |
|---|---|---|---|
| Vault cash | +5 | | |
| Reserve deposit | −5 | | |

There are legal limits on the amount of Federal Reserve Notes the Fed can supply to banks in this way, but experience shows that when these limits are approached, Congress increases them. This accommodating attitude should not be mistaken for a lack of concern or control. Since currency enters the financial system through depository institutions in exchange for existing reserves, the control over money growth still centers around the amount of reserves for which currency can be exchanged.[3]

## SOURCES OF GROWTH IN U.S. BANK RESERVES

The depository-institution reserve equation contains eleven categories that are involved in the determination of reserves. With this many ingredients, the reserve picture appears complicated. However, not all of these categories are active contributors to the actual change in reserves in the United States. For example, Treasury cash holdings are for all practical purposes constant over time. Although they are clearly a factor that absorbs reserves, the amount of reserves absorbed changes little through time. Thus, the account is of little policy concern. The net change in each factor supplying and absorbing reserves has been calculated for the years 1979–1981 (from year-end values). These calculations, which appear in figure 11.3, show the recent patterns of change in all the components in the reserve equation. The major factor supplying reserves over this period was increased holdings of government securities. The Federal Reserve float declined over the period, thus contributing negatively to the growth in reserves. Other factors supplying reserves showed small changes over the three-year period involved. The major factor absorbing reserves was an increase in currency and coin held by the public, with all other factors absorbing reserves little changed. This increase in currency held by the public is interesting, in that it suggests that over the period, the U.S. public made no important move toward becoming a cashless society. Instead, currency demand increased by almost 21 percent over the three-year period.[4]

The combined result of the changes in these factors is an increase in reserves of 3.3 billion, or about 8 percent over the period. Basically, figure 11.3 indicates that the public's need for more currency over the period was the dynamic factor absorbing reserves. This need was met by the Fed adding more reserves through open-market security purchases, which were then converted into currency by banks, and absorbed by the public through cashing checks and converting other transaction accounts into currency. It is a rather typical picture. Growth in currency in the hands of the public and growth in the Fed's portfolio

3. Currency could be used to expand the level of bank reserves if the Fed used Federal Reserve Notes to buy government securities for its portfolio instead of paying by check. In this case, the currency would become new bank reserves. However, this is not a practice to which the Fed subscribes.

4. Do you suppose the underground economy has anything to do with this pattern?

| NET CHANGE IN FACTORS SUPPLYING RESERVES | (BILLIONS OF DOLLARS) |
|---|---|
| U.S. government and agency securities | +21.7 |
| Loans to depository institutions | + 0.6 |
| Federal Reserve float | − 4.6 |
| Other Federal Reserve assets | + 4.1 |
| Gold and SDR certificates | + 1.5 |
| Treasury currency outstanding | + 2.7 |
| **Total new reserves supplied** | +26.0 |
| **LESS THE NET CHANGE IN FACTORS ABSORBING RESERVES** | |
| Currency and coin held by the nonbank public | +21.6 |
| Treasury cash holdings | + 0.2 |
| Treasury, foreign, and other Federal Reserve deposits | − 0.1 |
| Other Federal Reserve liabilities and capital | + 1.0 |
| **Total change in reserves absorbed** | +22.7 |
| **EQUALS THE NET CHANGE IN RESERVES** | |
| Reserve deposits plus vault cash | + 3.3 |

FIGURE 11.3.
Sources of Growth in
Bank Reserves,
December 31, 1978 to
December 31, 1981.

Source: *Federal Reserve Bulletin* for January 1979, and January 1982.

usually show a general correspondence. Clearly, the Fed's portfolio is the major category of Fed asset that "backs" the Federal Reserve Notes the system issues.

Reserves are the raw material of money. In this chapter, we have seen the factors that impact on reserves. How controllable are reserves? How controllable is the resulting money supply? Can the Federal Reserve regulate the amount of money in the nation by using the policy tools given it by Congress? These questions are the subject of the next chapter.

**1.** The assets of the Federal Reserve consist of claims on both gold and SDRs, coins, loans, government securities, float, and other assets. Of these, government securities account for about 80 percent of Federal Reserve assets.

**Important Ideas in This Chapter**

**2.** The liabilities of the Federal Reserve consist of currency (in the form of Federal Reserve Notes), reserve deposits, other deposits, deferred-availability items, and other liabilities and capital accounts. Of these, currency accounts for about 75 percent of the Fed's liabilities, and reserve deposits account for another 15 percent.

**3.** If other liabilities do not change, an increase in any Federal Reserve asset increases reserve deposits of depository institutions.

**4.** Alternatively, if assets remain the same, a decrease in other liabilities or capital produces an increase in reserve deposits.

**5.** The depository-institution reserve equation is a relationship between Federal Reserve and Treasury accounts that calculates reserves as the difference between all assets and other factors supplying reserves and all liabilities and other factors absorbing reserves.

6. Currency absorbs reserves when it is held by the nonbank public. In the reserve equation, the amount of currency and coin outstanding minus the amount held by the Treasury, the Federal Reserve, and the vaults of depository institutions, established the amount of currency that absorbs reserves.

7. When the Treasury buys gold or obtains SDRs, bank reserves go up. Borrowing by depository institutions at the Federal Reserve discount window increases reserves.

8. Issuance of currency by the Federal Reserve is usually accomplished by an exchange of reserves with a depository institution, leading to no net increase in reserves.

9. Although the depository-institution reserve equation contains eleven categories that contribute to the level of reserves, only a few are active ingredients in actual fluctuations in reserves in the United States. Currency in the hands of the public is the largest and most active factor absorbing reserves, whereas holdings of government securities is the most important factor supplying reserves.

**Discussion Questions**

1. Find a "statement of condition" for the Federal Reserve for the immediate post-World-War-II period. Calculate the change in each Fed asset and liability from this period to the period shown in figure 11.1. Analyze the growth in assets and liabilities over the period. How has the Fed been able to expand its assets, and in what areas?

2. Could the Federal Reserve float item in the depository-institution reserve equation be negative? Explain.

3. What would be the impact on reserves of a sharp decline in the public's demand for currency (say, caused by some type of payment innovation)? Explain.

4. Do an analysis of the factors supplying and absorbing reserves similar to figure 11.3 for the period 1977–1979. Contrast your results with those in figure 11.3.

5. Evaluate the statements: "The dollar is backed by government bonds, which are IOUs held by the public. Thus, we have one type of IOU (Federal Reserve Notes) backed by another."

**Suggested Readings**

For a detailed discussion of the Federal Reserve float, see A. Hoel, "A Primer on Federal Reserve Float," *Monthly Review of the Federal Reserve Bank of New York*, October 1975. For a detailed analysis of the Federal Reserve system's balance sheet and the factors supplying and absorbing reserves, see David H. Friedman, *Glossary, Weekly Federal Reserve Statements*, Federal Reserve Bank of New York, 1975. In addition, a good overview of the same process can be found in chapter 3 of *The Federal Reserve System: Purposes and Functions*, Board of Governors of the Federal Reserve System, 1974.

## CHAPTER 12

# Can the Federal Reserve Control the Money Supply?

IMPORTANT TERMS

monetary base
defensive operations
dynamic operations
open-market desk
money multiplier
nonborrowed reserves

---

## MEMO

To:        All readers
From:      JWE

Have you perhaps seen an article in a magazine or newspaper where the Federal Reserve Board is being criticized for either allowing money to grow too rapidly or restricting its growth too sharply? Such charges are not uncommon. However, they represent more than a clash of opinion on the proper rate of growth of money. They indicate above all else that the Federal Reserve (the Fed) can set the money supply at a level prescribed by its policy. How reasonable is it to suppose that the Federal Reserve can set the money supply according to the nation's dictates? After all, some 70 percent of the nation's money supply is issued by private depository institutions with objectives vastly different from those of the Federal Reserve.

This is the central question you can read about in this chapter. In it, we examine the ingredients in the money supply over which the Fed does and does not have control. In addition, we discuss the procedures by which the Federal Reserve implements its policy-making activities. The discussion allows you to decide for yourself how hard to come down on the policy makers at the Fed when the growth rate in money is not what you would like it to be.

---

Since its beginning in 1913, the Federal Reserve system has been structured and periodically restructured to enable it to control the nation's money supply. The authority to buy and sell government bonds from its portfolio and to lend to depository institutions at rates it sets, give the Board of Governors a strong measure of control over the amount of bank reserves in the financial system. The authority to adjust reserve requirements within ranges set by Congress gives the board the added ability to change the significance of the reserves present in the system. Through emergency powers and credit controls, the board has an array of other means available to bend the course of the money supply in the direction of that stipulated by Federal Reserve Board policy.

How effective are these tools in enabling the Fed to control the money supply? This often-debated question is important in helping us judge how potent the Fed is likely to be in carrying out a significant policy change regarding goals for money growth, or in reacting to unwanted fluctuations in the money supply. It is a question that logically splits into two parts: (1) how effectively can the Fed control bank reserves and currency, and (2) how predictably will depository institutions expand demand and other checkable deposits for each dollar of reserves in the banking system? In this chapter, we focus our attention on this two-part question. Then, we discuss how the Fed implements its part in the money-supply process, and the implications of these operating procedures for Federal Reserve control of money. However, before any of this, we discuss an important complication: the composition of the money the Fed seeks to control is changing importantly. Money is not what it was a decade ago, and its changing composition affects the Fed's efforts to regulate its growth.

## THE CHANGING COMPOSITION OF MONEY

Before bank checking deposits became widely used, money consisted of paper money and coin, that is, currency. Efforts by banking authorities to control money took the form of monitoring and regulating the amount of currency. With the emergence of demand deposits as the dominant vehicle for commercial transactions, the amount of demand deposits outstanding grew rapidly, and by the 1950s had reached better than four times the amount of currency. Money was officially defined by the Fed to be demand deposits plus currency, known as M1. This concept of money was the primary object of Federal Reserve efforts to regulate the money supply. The definition continued to be useful until the last half of the 1970s.

In the period between 1975 and 1980, a new type of deposit emerged in U.S. banking that made the former definition of money and the former policy focus no longer workable. Typified by NOW and ATS accounts (see chapter 5), this new type of deposit offered its owners the ability to write checks on funds held in interest-bearing accounts. These checkable deposits grew piecemeal in a legally contested environment during their initial years. In 1980, the depository-institution deregulation and Monetary Control Act authorized all depository institutions to issue NOW accounts. With this legal change, the checkable savings account had officially arrived on the U.S. banking scene.

Beginning in February 1980, and extending over the next two years, the statistical arm of the Federal Reserve reconciled its statistics with the 1980 banking act by redefining the basic definition of money to include "other checkable deposits," defined to be NOW, ATS, and share-draft accounts. Over the same period, the Fed also officially recognized traveler's checks as part of the statistical money supply. The result is a redefinition of the M1 money supply to include (1) currency, (2) traveler's checks, (3) demand deposits, and (4) other checkable deposits. The Fed also added a constellation of other measures of near-money financial aggregates, a discussion of which can be found in chapter 5. However, this array of new financial aggregates has not changed the focus of the Federal Reserve. Its primary attention continues to be focused on controlling the new M1 definition of money.

It is a concept of money that is changing rapidly. In table 12.1, the composition of the new M1 definition is shown at intervals over the period 1960–1982. The upper part of the table shows billions of dollars and the lower part shows proportions rounded to the nearest whole percent. The table shows the dramatic increase in other checkable deposits since 1975, with these accounts rising to 20 percent of the total money supply by 1982. Similarly, the shift of demand deposits into the new accounts is apparent by the fall in the proportion of demand deposits that accompanies the rise in other checkable deposits.

Table 12.1 also shows an increasing preference for currency among the U.S. public, with the currency proportion of M1 rising from 21 percent in 1960 to 28 percent in the 1980–1982 period. This trend in currency preference is interesting in that it occurs over a time when the use of credit cards has presumably reduced the public's need for cash balances to be used in everyday transactions. Some economists attribute the relative growth in currency demand to growth in the so-called underground economy (the economy in illegal products plus legal activities done "off the books" to evade taxes), most of which involves cash transactions.

These changes in the composition of money do not ease the Federal Reserve's task of monetary control. The amount of currency held by the public is hard for the Federal Reserve to control as a practical matter (more on this later). Basically, when people want to cash checks and hold more currency, depository institutions are obliged to respond. Moreover, the growth in NOW and ATS accounts in nonbank depository institutions has been and is likely to continue to be dramatic. The Fed's control over these institutions is still in the process of forming, as a result of the 1980 banking act. It was not until this act that thrifts were brought under the same regulatory structure

**TABLE 12.1**
**The Changing Composition of Money**

| | 1960 | 1965 | 1970 | 1975 | 1980 | 1981 | 1982 |
|---|---|---|---|---|---|---|---|
| | (billions of dollars) | | | | | | |
| Currency | 29.0 | 35.3 | 47.7 | 71.0 | 111.7 | 119.8 | 128.4 |
| Traveler's checks | 0.4 | 0.6 | 0.9 | 2.1 | 3.9 | 4.2 | 4.4 |
| Demand deposits | 112.0 | 129.2 | 162.4 | 211.1 | 263.9 | 239.9 | 234.9 |
| Other checkable deposits | 0.0 | 0.1 | 0.2 | 0.7 | 21.8 | 65.5 | 90.3 |
| Total M1 money supply | 141.4 | 165.2 | 211.2 | 284.9 | 401.3 | 429.4 | 458.0 |
| | (percentage of total) | | | | | | |
| | 1960 | 1965 | 1970 | 1975 | 1980 | 1981 | 1982 |
| Currency | 21 | 21 | 23 | 25 | 28 | 28 | 28 |
| Traveler's checks | 0 | 0 | 0 | 1 | 1 | 1 | 1 |
| Demand deposits | 79 | 79 | 77 | 74 | 66 | 56 | 51 |
| Other checkable deposits | 0 | 0 | 0 | 0 | 5 | 15 | 20 |
| Total | 100 | 100 | 100 | 100 | 100 | 100 | 100 |

Source: *Federal Reserve Bulletin*, various issues. Values are averages for the entire year.

regarding reserves as commercial banks. The Fed is not as familiar with regulating these institutions as with commercial banks. Finally, in recent years, depository institutions have set a dazzling pace of innovations in the types of financial instruments they originate. One can only wonder when a new near-money financial asset will emerge that will make the present definition of M1 as unworkable as the old definition became in the last half of the 1970s.

## CONTROLLING
## THE MONETARY BASE

The sum of demand deposits, other checkable deposits, and traveler's checks make up more than 70 percent of the money supply. They are issued by private depository institutions. The Federal Reserve Board exercises control over this portion of the money supply by changing either the legal ability or the incentive of depository institutions to issue this "bank money." In other words, the Fed's control over these deposits is indirect. By contrast, the Fed has a more direct control over reserves, which have been called the raw material of money. In addition, the Federal Reserve issues nearly all of the nation's currency, and thus directly controls this portion of the money supply.

Several years ago, the Federal Reserve Bank of St. Louis began tracking and reporting a financial aggregate that reflects the portion of the money-supply-generating process over which the Fed has a strong measure of direct control.[1] It called this measure the *monetary base*, a term suggesting that it is the foundation for the money supply. The monetary base consists of the level of bank reserves plus vault cash plus the currency in the hands of the nonbank public. The bank reserves used in calculating the monetary base are adjusted to reflect changes in reserve requirements. Thus, if reserve requirements rise by 10 billion while total reserves stay the same, the level of adjusted reserves will fall by 10 billion along with the monetary base. This fall in adjusted reserves and in the monetary base mirrors the reduced ability of depository institutions to expand the money supply given the higher reserve requirements.

According to some economists, the Federal Reserve cannot always be held accountable for movements in the money supply, since depository institutions issue more than 70 percent of it. However, the Fed can be assumed to be "in charge" of the monetary base, which over the long run governs the level of the money supply. This is an interesting view. But is it correct? Is the Federal Reserve really "in charge" of the monetary base? To answer this question, it is useful

1. In recent years, the Fed has followed the St. Louis bank in publishing its own measure of the monetary base, which is quite similar to (but not identical to) the St. Louis measure. Although the definitions of the two base measures are the same, there are differences in the method of calculating an adjustment factor.

to consider the two major parts of the monetary base separately. The question thus decomposes to (1) is the Federal Reserve in charge of the level of reserves and vault cash, and (2) is the Federal Reserve in charge of currency outstanding?

## Controlling Reserves

In the last chapter, the depository-institution reserve equation showed all the factors that either supply or absorb reserves. Briefly, the factors supplying reserves are (1) government securities, (2) loans to depository institutions, (3) Federal Reserve float, (4) gold certificates, (5) SDR certificates, (6) Treasury currency, and (7) other assets; the factors absorbing reserves are (8) currency and coin held by the nonbank public, (9) Treasury cash holdings, (10) Treasury, foreign, and other deposits, and (11) other liabilities and capital. As we saw in the last chapter, each of these eleven factors impacts on the level of reserves. The question of how well the Fed can control reserves is largely one of how effectively the Fed can offset changes in uncontrollable factors that supply or absorb reserves, by making changes in other controllable factors.

Let us examine the major uncontrollable factors in the reserve picture.[2] The Federal Reserve float is one such factor. Short-term unpredictable fluctuations in the float of several billion dollars have not been uncommon in recent years. Fluctuations in float are attributable to factors such as short-term bottlenecks in the logistical pipeline of checks flowing through the Federal Reserve system. Fluctuations in SDR certificates outstanding resulting from foreign capital or trade flows are a source of uncontrollable fluctuations in reserves that can reach more than a billion dollars in size on a short-term basis. Changes in the public's demand for currency occur more or less continuously, thus absorbing varying amounts of reserves. However, this factor is somewhat predictable, with changes in currency demand being strongly associated with seasonal reasons. The predictability of a substantial portion of the fluctuation in currency demand lessens the Federal Reserve's control problem as it relates to this variable. Finally, fluctuations in the "Treasury, foreign, and other deposits" category occur for a variety of complex reasons, and impart similar fluctuations in reserves.

To respond to the sum of these uncontrollable fluctuations in reserves, the Federal Open-Market Committee (FOMC) directs its operating officers to engage in what are called *defensive operations*. These operations attempt to buy and sell from the Fed's portfolio in such a way as to offset the effect of uncontrollable factors on reserves. In carrying out defensive operations, the Fed is not trying to change the

2. "Major" factors are those which fluctuate significantly over time and thus are important reasons for shifts in reserve position.

level of reserves, only to maintain the level in the face of changes in uncontrollable factors supplying or absorbing reserves. By contrast, *dynamic operations* are those aimed at either increasing or decreasing the level of reserves to carry out the Fed's policy directives. Both defensive and dynamic operations are carried out by the Federal Reserve Bank of New York at what is called the *open-market desk*.

In practice, it is difficult for an observer to discern between defensive and dynamic operations. Both involve open-market purchases or sales of bonds by the open-market desk. They differ only in that defensive operations are responding to changes in reserves that have already occurred or are about to occur, whereas dynamic operations are initiating changes in reserves. To separate the two, analysts of the Fed watch patterns of security purchases and sales that occur at the open-market desk. With experience, analysts will be able to break down these patterns into dynamic and defensive segments.

Defensive operations are not perfect. The Fed is not immediately aware of changes in uncontrollable factors, and these factors sometimes reverse themselves. Thus, fluctuations occur in reserves that the Fed does not want to occur, especially on a short-term (such as week-to-week) basis. Over longer periods, such as three to six month intervals, the Fed's defensive operations can erase most of the fluctuations in uncontrollable factors. Thus, we can assume that the level of reserves over longer intervals is fairly close to what Fed policy dictates it should be.

## Controlling Currency

The Fed's control over currency is a different story. People have come to assume that when they want to cash checks, they will always be able to do so. In other words, people expect depository institutions to keep enough currency in their vaults to satisfy the public's needs. Being able to freely exchange a demand or other checkable deposit for currency or vice versa is pretty much of a given in modern banking.[3] However, this "given" has important implications. It means that the following ratio:

$$c = \frac{\text{currency}}{\text{demand and other checkable deposits}}$$

is for practical purposes set by the public according to the public's inclination to hold currency. Thus, when the Fed increases the capacity of depository institutions to expand checkable deposits by increasing the level of reserves, it is also in effect authorizing more currency to be issued when the public so determines.

3. Of course, the Fed could legally refuse to issue more Federal Reserve Notes, causing depository institutions to be "short" of cash, but this is a completely unlikely scenario. From time to time, the Fed comes close to reaching the congressional limits on Federal Reserve Notes, at which time the limits are adjusted.

Through its control over bank reserves, the Fed has an ultimate control over all checkable deposits and thus the amount of currency outstanding. However, with $c$ in the area of .40 in recent years, the public has maintained a large reserve capacity to expand its holdings of currency. The value of $c$ is in practical terms beyond the immediate control of the Federal Reserve.

Increasing or decreasing $c$ is a quiet process. Suppose the public wishes to hold proportionately more currency. At depository institutions across the nation, more checks are cashed, and larger cash withdrawals are made from existing deposits. Then $c$ rises, and stocks of vault cash decline. To replenish these stocks, depository institutions order more currency from their district Federal Reserve banks, and with its shipment, the supply of currency rises.

When the public's changing demand alters the stock of currency, reserves are affected. Keep in mind that when a depository institution orders currency, it pays for it by having its reserve account reduced. As long as the newly ordered currency stays in the vaults of depository institutions, legal reserves are unaffected. But, when the currency flows into the hands of the public, legal reserves fall unless defensive moves are made by the Fed's open-market managers.

Experience shows that changes in the public's demand for currency occur slowly and usually predictably. Thus, open-market operations can usually react to changing currency demands by making offsetting changes in reserves. In this way, the Fed is able to exercise a good measure of control over the impact of currency on reserves without controlling the currency itself. To the policy makers at the Federal Reserve, the steadiness and predictability of changes in currency demanded and held by the public reduce the importance of fluctuations in this form of money. They can deal with a predicted rate of growth in currency as a given, and adjust the level of reserves to attempt to produce a growth in deposits sufficient to hit overall growth targets on the money supply.

## Recent Experience with the Monetary Base

In Fed efforts to achieve a certain growth role in the monetary base, the emphasis is squarely on controlling the growth rate of adjusted reserves while allowing for a predicted growth rate in currency. How well the Fed can succeed in adjusting the growth rate of the monetary base is largely governed by how well it can control reserves via defensive and dynamic operations.

In the United States, the record of the Fed has been varied in maintaining a steady course for the monetary base. A strong degree of control of the monetary base implies few ups and downs in the base over time. Rather, the base should track the Fed's policy course pretty much as a trend line, with defensive operations taking out the peaks and valleys. One measure of the smoothness of the course of the monetary base is the coefficient of variation, which is defined as the ratio of the standard deviation of the statistical series to the mean. The larger the coefficient of variation, the greater the variation in a statistical series compared with its mean value.

Over 1960–1969, the coefficient of variation for monthly changes in the adjusted reserves component of the monetary base was .129, and for changes in the entire monetary base it was .143. For 1970–1979, the coefficient of variation for the reserve component rose to .168, whereas for the monetary base it increased to .224. These statistics show three characteristics of the U.S. monetary base:

**1.** Most of the fluctuation in the base is caused by fluctuation in reserves, as indicated by the closeness of the values of the coefficients for reserves and the overall base.

**2.** The increase in the degree of variation during the 1970s compared with the 1960s shows that reserves and the monetary base were more volatile during the latter period than during the former. Whether this was caused by more fluctuation in uncontrollable factors supplying and/or absorbing reserves, or deliberate Fed policy is not clear.

**3.** The currency component of the monetary base is less predictable, as indicated by the widening gap in the latter period between the coefficients for reserves and total monetary base. In 1960–1969, the gap between the two was .014. In the 1970–1979 period, it rose to .056.

## CONTROLLING THE MONEY SUPPLY

To attain a smooth predetermined growth rate in the monetary base does not necessarily insure control of the money supply. More than 70 percent of the M1 money supply consists of deposits created by depository institutions. Although deposit creation is clearly constrained by reserves, the noose is at times slippery. Depository institutions have shown they can find many ways to loosen the Federal Reserve's grip. Just how much slippage occurs between the amount of reserves the Fed supplies and the amount of deposits the banking industry supplies? It is an important question. One way to examine it is to use the following expression:

M1 = Monetary Base × Money Multiplier

or

$$\text{Money Multiplier} = \frac{\text{M1}}{\text{Monetary Base}}$$

The *money multiplier* defined by this expression shows how much the money supply expands for each dollar of the monetary base. If the money multiplier is invariant over time, it means that control over the monetary base insures control over M1. The extent to which the money multiplier fluctuates widely is thus the extent to which depository institutions have slipped the Fed's noose on a regular basis.

An important reason for fluctuations in the money multiplier is that depository institutions do not use the reserves in the system as fully during some time periods as they do during others. At times, some institutions may have excess reserves that are not being advanced to borrowers via Fed funds. When lending conditions facing other banks warrant, they can seek to acquire these funds through interbank loans. As such pockets of excess reserves are emptied, the reserves in the system support more deposits. The motivation may also run the other way. Institutions with unused lending capacity and/or reserves may seek to make new loans with a varying degree of aggressiveness according to market conditions. The result is the same—an expansion or contraction in the amount of deposits for each dollar of reserves in the system.

Figure 12.1 shows actual movements in the U.S. money multiplier on an annual basis (the average value of M1 for a year divided by the average monetary base for the same year) over 1959–1981. Overall, the pattern is one of a fairly smooth downward trend in the value of the money multiplier. This downward trend is largely the result of

**FIGURE 12.1.
Annual Movements in
the Money Multiplier.**

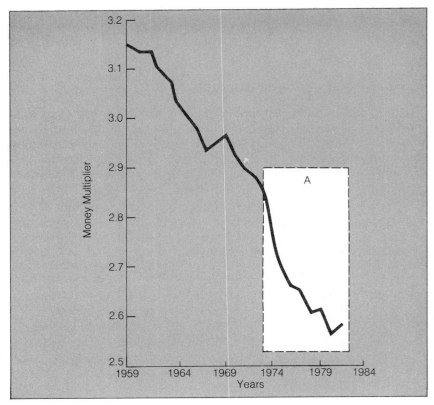

strong patterns of change in bank liability management, especially since about 1970. Over this period, banks have placed much greater emphasis on large-denomination CDs and other forms of purchased liabilities such as eurodollar accounts to raise funds. Many of these newer nondeposit liabilities nonetheless absorb required reserves, thus lowering the amount of deposits that each dollar of the monetary base will support.

For purposes of Fed control, the trend in the money multiplier is not as important as fluctuations around it. At least over shorter periods of time, the trend shown by the series can be projected forward. The fluctuations may come as surprises to policy makers. The pronounced fluctuations from trend are not frequent in figure 12.1. A significant upward fluctuation occurred during 1968–1969, which presumably had to do with the rapid pace of credit expansion that accompanied the booming economy of that period. Similarly, the money multiplier fell somewhat below its trend value during the recessionary years of 1974–1975. Beyond these two business-cycle-related movements, the money multiplier has shown a pattern of rather stable change with a downward trend.

Figure 12.1 shows movement from one annual average to the next. The money multiplier is not as stable if we look at it over shorter time intervals. Figure 12.2 shows the money multiplier plotted at quarterly intervals from the first quarter of 1973 to the first quarter of 1982. The

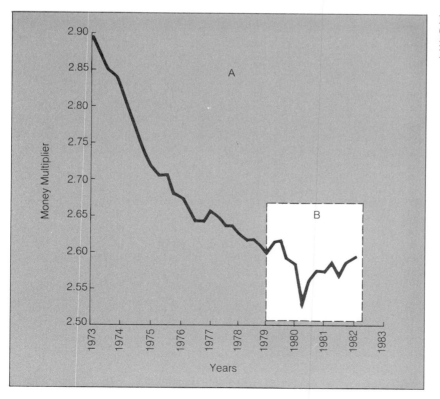

**FIGURE 12.2.**
**Quarterly Movements in the Money Multiplier.**

period of time shown in figure 12.2 corresponds to the portion of figure 12.1 contained in the box labeled A. It is much like a photographic enlargement of that period.

The fluctuations in figure 12.2 continue to show a reasonable degree of stability, especially for the period prior to 1979. An upward "blip" in the multiplier is now seen to occur on a quarterly basis during the latter part of 1976. This was the initial period of expansion following the recession of the prior two years. After 1979, the money multiplier becomes distinctly more volatile. The sharp downward spike in the multiplier during 1980 is more than the mild recession of that period would suggest. The most likely explanation for this recent volatility in the multiplier is the continued rapid pace of innovation in the financial instruments that substitute for traditional money, the most important of which is the checkable deposit such as the NOW and ATS accounts. Figure 12.2 suggests that the innovations of the period may have aggravated the Fed's problems of monetary control.

Figure 12.3 shows a monthly "blowup" of the period from January 1979 to March 1982. Thus, figure 12.3 covers the period in the box labeled B in figure 12.2. This monthly plot of the money multiplier shows more short-term perturbations in the series than either of the longer-range scans indicated. Many of the monthly fluctuations in the series smooth out over longer periods. Clearly, the money mul-

**FIGURE 12.3. Monthly Movements in the Money Multiplier.**

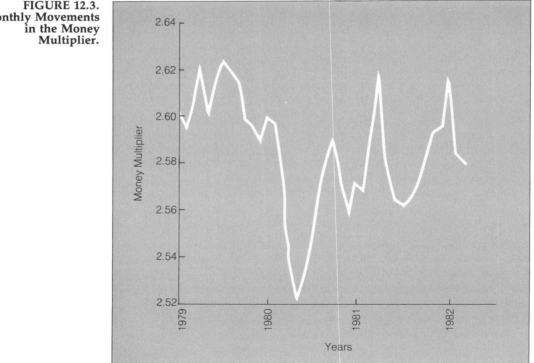

tiplier is more stable when considered over either annual or quarterly periods than over monthly periods.

Figures 12.1, 12.2, and 12.3 show that the money multiplier is less stable over shorter periods of time than over longer periods. Accordingly, the Fed's ability to control the money supply by controlling the monetary base is weaker over shorter periods than it is over longer periods. Some, even perhaps significant, fluctuations in the money supply on a month-to-month basis will occur for reasons that are beyond the Fed's control, even if the Fed is successful in maintaining reserves at levels consistent with Federal Reserve policy. Can the Fed control the money supply? Over longer periods, such as annual intervals, the answer is yes. Over periods as short as a month, the Fed's control is not as finely tuned as it would prefer.[4]

# FEDERAL RESERVE OPERATING PROCEDURES AND MONEY-SUPPLY CONTROL

To "run its shop" in an orderly fashion, the Fed has adopted procedures that are used to put into effect the adjustments in reserves that are indicated by the direction of current policy. Understanding these procedures helps us to see how well the Fed is likely to do in putting into effect a current policy change. These procedures and the specific policies toward which they are directed have not always been matters to which the public had access. Indeed, the Federal Reserve Board is somewhat like a teenager in that it has gone through various phases regarding how and what it wishes to communicate to those around it. For years, the Fed felt that it was in the public interest to make its major decisions, to issue its policy directives, and to formulate operating procedures largely in secret. Not until 1967 did the Fed allow the policy directives of the FOMC to be made public, and then only after a ninety-day delay. The thinking was that if the public knew too much about what the Fed was up to, its reaction might reduce the effectiveness of the policy.

However, gradually the Fed opened up. In 1975, the lag for making FOMC policy directives public was reduced to forty-five days. A year later, it was reduced to thirty days. During the same period, the Fed began articulating in various forms its intended policies for the upcoming year, and how it planned to implement these policies. Thus the Federal Reserve embarked on a path that students of modern management techniques typically embrace—it was stating goals and attempting to construct plans to carry out these goals.

4. This general conclusion is mirrored in an analysis of the same question by Anatol B. Balbach, "How Controllable Is Money Growth?" *Review, Federal Reserve Bank of St. Louis*, April 1981, pp. 3–12, and by Ralph C. Bryant, "Federal Reserve Control of the Money Stock," *Journal of Money, Credit, and Banking*, November 1982, pp. 597–625.

# Memorandum

To: All Readers interested in the analytical form of the deposit and money
    multipliers
From: JWE

In chapter 2, the deposit multiplier was defined to be the multiple by which demand deposits expanded when bank reserves increased. In its simplest form, it was derived from the following expression:

**(1)** $\Delta R = r_d \times \Delta D$

where $\Delta R$ is the change in bank reserves plus vault cash, $r_d$ is the required reserve ratio against demand and other checkable deposits, and $\Delta D$ is the change in demand and other checkable deposits. In light of current money definitions, it is easiest to consider demand and other checkable deposits to be a single entity. Rearranging expression (1) gives the deposit multiplier as:

**(2)** $\dfrac{\Delta D}{\Delta R} = \dfrac{1}{r_d}$

This form was described in chapter 2 as ignoring fluctuations in currency held by the public and reserves held against noncheckable deposits and other liabilities. Chapter 2 also dealt with the possibility that banks may hold excess reserves, which we ignore in this analysis. In the real world, these factors may contribute to fluctuations in the multiplier. Accordingly, it is useful in understanding the precise origins of such fluctuations to incorporate both currency effects and other required reserves into the multiplier expression.

We first deal with currency. Earlier in the chapter, the ratio of currency to demand and other checkable deposits was called $c$. That is:

**(3)** $c = \dfrac{C}{D}$

where $C$ is the amount of currency in the hands of the nonbank public. In discussing $c$, we pointed out some of the consequences of fluctuations in it. To incorporate currency fluctuations into the multiplier, let us assume that the main reason for fluctuations in $C$ is fluctuations in $D$, that is, suppose that the ratio, $c$, remains roughly stable over time. If so, then we can reliably express the *change in C* as:

**(4)** $\Delta C = c \times \Delta D$

In this chapter, as well as in the reserve equation in chapter 11, we have seen that when currency held by the public rises, reserves are absorbed, so that currency held by the public uses a portion of the reserves otherwise available in the banking system to support deposits. Accordingly, when currency is taken into account, expression (1) must be modified as follows:

**(5)** $\Delta R = r_d \times \Delta D + \Delta C$

Substituting (4) into (5) in place of the last term gives:

**(6)** $\Delta R = r_d \times \Delta D + c \times \Delta D$

or, equivalently:

**(7)** $\Delta R = \Delta D(r_d + c)$

which means that the deposit multiplier is:

**(8)** $\dfrac{\Delta D}{\Delta R} = \dfrac{1}{r_d + c}$

The second complication to be incorporated into the deposit multiplier is the holding of reserves on time, savings, and other deposits. Suppose the reserve requirements on these other deposits can be represented by the required reserve ratio $r_t$. If all other reservable deposits are denoted as $T$, the change in total reserves, $\Delta L$, to be held against them is thus:

**(9)** $\Delta L = r_t \times \Delta T$

A change in total reserves is now split into three components, one associated with demand and other checkable deposits, a second associated with currency in the hands of the nonbank public, and a third associated with time, savings, and other deposits, as follows:

**(10)** $\Delta R = r_d \times \Delta D + \Delta C + \Delta L$

To bring savings, time, and other deposits into our multiplier in the simplist way, we assume that fluctuations in them are largely determined by fluctuations in the level of demand and other checkable deposits. That is:

**(11)** $\Delta T = b \times \Delta D$

where $b$ denotes the ratio of a change in time and other deposits to a change in demand deposits. Incorporating (11) into (9) and inserting the result into (10) in place of $\Delta L$, as well as inserting (4) in place of $\Delta C$, gives:

**(12)** $\Delta R = r_d \times \Delta D + c \times \Delta D + r_t \times b \times \Delta D = \Delta D[r_d + c + (r_t \times b)]$

which now means that the deposit multiplier is:

**(13)** $\dfrac{\Delta D}{\Delta R} = \dfrac{1}{r_d + c + (r_t \times b)}$

Comparing this expanded multiplier with the simple version of expression (2) shows it to be smaller in value when currency effects and other liabilities are taken into account. Since at least some of these effects are bound to be present in the real world, we should accordingly expect the multiplier to be smaller than that implied by expression (2).

The money multiplier defined earlier in this chapter is not the same as this expanded deposit multiplier. Whereas the deposit multiplier in (13) shows the ratio of an expansion in deposits to an expansion in reserves, the money multiplier shows the ratio of an expansion in the M1 money supply to an expansion in the monetary base. That is, the money multiplier is:

**(14)** $\dfrac{\Delta M1}{\Delta B}$

where $\Delta M1$ is the change in the M1 money supply and $\Delta B$ is the change in the monetary base.

The deposit multiplier and the money multiplier are sufficiently related that we can derive the money multiplier from the deposit multiplier. A change in M1 can be written as follows:

**(15)** $\Delta M1 = \Delta D + \Delta C$

That is, any change in M1 is equal to a change in demand and other checkable deposits plus a change in currency held by the nonbank public. (For simplicity, we will ignore fluctuations in outstanding traveler's checks.) A change in the monetary base can be written as follows:

**(16)** $\Delta B = \Delta R + \Delta C$

That is, any change in the monetary base is equal to a change in bank reserves and vault cash plus a change in currency held by the nonbank public. Expanding (14) by using (15) and (16) gives:

**(17)** $\dfrac{\Delta M1}{\Delta B} = \dfrac{\Delta D + \Delta C}{\Delta R + \Delta C}$

Substituting expression (4) for $\Delta C$ and expression (12) for $\Delta R$ gives:

**(18)** $\dfrac{\Delta M1}{\Delta B} = \dfrac{\Delta D[1 + c]}{\Delta D[r_d + (r_t \times b) + c + c]}$

$$= \dfrac{1 + c}{r_d + (r_t \times b) + 2c}$$

Expression (18) shows that the money multiplier under discussion in this chapter can be expressed in terms of two key ratios and two types of reserve requirements. The ratio of a change in currency demanded to a change in deposits, c, impacts on the money multiplier as does the ratio of a change in

*(Memorandum continued on next page)*   **199**

time, savings, and other deposits to a change in demand and other checkable deposits, $b$. If, as we assumed earlier, these two ratios are constant over time, and the two required reserve ratios $r_d$ and $r_t$ are also constant, then the money multiplier will be entirely constant. If this were the case, a change in the monetary base would translate into a fixed change in the M1 money supply. However, our discussion earlier in this chapter of the actual multiplier in the United States shows that the money multiplier is not always constant. This analysis gives a fresh perspective as to the source of fluctuation in the money multiplier. The ratios $b$ and $c$ have varied, and the effective reserve requirements have varied some as well, the latter mostly a result of the changing composition of the deposits averaged together to get $T$ and $D$, and a result of more banks growing to the deposit thresholds where reserve requirements are higher.

The discussion in this chapter has further indicated that the effect of fluctuations in $b$, $c$, and the other ingredients of the money multiplier is more pronounced over shorter periods of time than over periods as long as one year. Presumably, the longer the time period over which we evaluate the money multiplier, the more nearly constant becomes the components of expression (18).

The immediate targets of the Fed's action plan have varied throughout the years. In particular, the focus of policy action prior to October 1979 differed measurably from that after this time. In the several years leading up to the period of late 1979, the Fed stated targets regarding both the federal-funds rate and the growth in the M1 money supply. These policy targets were not stated as specific numbers, but as ranges. A typical range for the M1 growth rate might be 4.5 percent to 7 percent, whereas for the federal-funds rate it might be 10 to 12 percent.

To implement these policy targets, the Federal Open-Market Committee instructed the open-market desk to maintain the federal-funds rate within a narrow tolerance range, usually one-half to one percentage point wide, within the wider target range. Within this band, the open-market desk was instructed to use open-market security purchases and sales to keep the day-to-day trading range for federal funds within a narrow trading range of about one-fourth of a percentage point. At the monthly meetings of the FOMC, fine tuning of the ½-to-1-percent tolerance range could be made without changing the wider federal-funds target range. By this means, the FOMC could loosen or tighten the federal-funds range gradually within the targeted range.

When the open-market desk found that reserves were tight enough to place upward pressures on the federal-funds rate, it more or less automatically bought securities, putting more reserves into the system and into the federal-funds market. It did the reverse when abundant reserves in the system placed downward pressures on the federal-funds rate. Thus, most of the day-to-day trading decisions made by the open-market desk were guided by the careful monitoring of the federal-funds rate.

Besides the tolerance and trading ranges for the federal-funds rate, the FOMC also gave the open-market desk instructions dealing with the desk's reaction to a situation where money growth was above or below the targeted range. Specifically, when money growth was above the target, the desk was authorized to move the federal-funds rate up without specific FOMC directive as long as it stayed within the target range.

Experience with this operating procedure eventually proved it to be unworkable as an effective means of monetary control. By the late 1970s, continued inflation had pushed interest rates up to levels considered "too high" by the Fed. By keeping the federal-funds-rate target below market rates, the Fed actively worked to keep short-term rates from rising. As the federal-funds rate approached the top of the target range, the open-market desk repeatedly responded by supplying more reserves, thus halting the rise in the federal-funds rate, and holding down short-term market rates. However, as the Fed supplied more reserves to meet its interest-rate target, it provided depository institutions with the means to expand money at a more rapid pace. As a result, the growth in the money supply dangerously exceeded its targeted growth rates. A dilemma was apparent. The Federal Reserve came to realize that it had to choose between targeting interest rates and targeting money growth. In periods of rising pressures on interest rates, stability could only be achieved by allowing excessive growth in reserves and thus money. Similarly, hitting money-supply targets during times of rising interest-rate pressures could only be achieved by allowing rapidly rising interest rates. In late 1979, the Federal Reserve made its choice.

In October 1979, the Fed announced that it would abandon its policy of targeting fed-funds rates and the operating procedures that accompanied this policy. Instead, the Federal Reserve Board chairperson, Paul Volker, said that its policy focus would henceforth be on the level of bank reserves, the monetary base, and on the money supply. The fed-funds rate was to be largely "cut loose" to find whatever level was consistent with market conditions. Similarly, the Federal Reserve said that it expected short-term interest rates to become more volatile, and perhaps reach new all-time highs. It warned banks to plan for this new era by getting their reserve-deposit ratios in order without expecting that rapid pressures on the fed-funds market would result in the Federal Reserve dutifully supplying more reserves.

After a period of grace, the Fed embarked on this new policy. It lowered the growth rate of reserves and money generally to within its targeted range, even though continued high inflation created a need for more funds. Fed-funds rates reached better than 30 percent at one point, with the prime rate rising to over 20 percent as well. However, the policy survived. Money growth remained relatively moderate through 1980 and 1981. By early 1982, the back of the inflation of the preceding ten years has been broken.

To implement this new policy, the Fed has revised its operating procedures. The FOMC announced it would no longer use the adjustable tolerance range for the federal-funds rate. The broader target range for this rate was widened, typically to five percent or more, and given less of a role in overall policy making. The variable that has replaced the federal-funds rate as the guide to day-to-day actions by the open-market desk is the level of *nonborrowed reserves* in the banking system. Nonborrowed reserves are total reserves less borrowings from the Federal Reserve system.

Under the new system, each week the FOMC estimates the average level of required reserves by analyzing the deposit condition of depository institutions. An estimate of the amount of excess reserves in the banking system is then added to arrive at the estimated level of total reserves for the week. From this total, the policy-determined level of borrowed reserves is subtracted to obtain the target for nonborrowed reserves.

To set this target, the FOMC first defines a money-supply growth target. An estimate is then made of the amount of total reserves that is thought to correspond to this money-supply target. Typically, the FOMC applies what it believes to be the money multiplier which will apply over the upcoming period, to get the monetary base and thus the level of reserves that is consistent with the money target. The policy-determined target amount of borrowing at the Fed discount window is then applied to arrive at the nonborrowed remainder. Then, nonborrowed reserves are managed on a day-to-day basis to hit this target.

By focusing on nonborrowed reserves and determining borrowed reserves largely by policy, the Fed obtains an important degree of control over total bank reserves. With a stable money multiplier, over longer periods, the Federal Reserve will obtain a similar degree of control over the money supply as well.

How important is it that the Fed control the money supply? Some say it is *the* crucial factor governing the economy. Others say it does not matter a great deal. Still others attach conditions to whether it does or does not matter. Thus, the question is debatable, primarily because it is a question of monetary and macroeconomic theory. To understand the importance of the money supply in the economy, you need to understand the economy's theoretical superstructure, and how money fits into it. That topic and others related to it occupy the next ten chapters of this book.

## Important Ideas in This Chapter

1. The money supply in the United States, composed of currency, demand and other checkable deposits, and traveler's checks, is changing in its composition. In recent years, currency has increased as a proportion of the total whereas demand deposits have decreased. Other checkable deposits have grown rapidly.

2. The changing composition of money complicates the Federal Reserve's task of controlling the money supply.

**3.** The monetary base consists of the level of bank reserves plus vault cash plus the currency in the hands of the nonbank public. It is often thought of as the raw material of money.

**4.** There are significant uncontrollable factors influencing bank reserves, as indicated by the depository-institution reserve equation. Among these, float, SDR certificates, and currency demand by the public are sometimes important sources of uncontrollable fluctuations in the level of reserves.

**5.** To react to and offset the impact of uncontrollable factors on reserves, the Fed engages in defensive operations designed to smooth fluctuations in reserves caused by uncontrollable factors.

**6.** Because checks are freely convertible into currency and vice versa, the public effectively controls the division of currency and demand and other deposits into its component parts. This means that the size of the currency component of the monetary base is largely determined by the public.

**7.** Because the public's currency demand is largely predictable, the lack of direct operational control over currency does not importantly detract from the Fed's ability to control the monetary base. The problem of control is largely one of controlling bank reserves.

**8.** In recent U.S. experience, most of the fluctuation in the monetary base has had to do with reserves, although currency has become more volatile in recent years. The overall variability in the monetary base increased in the 1970s, probably because of the effect of rapid innovation in the banking industry.

**9.** The money multiplier is defined to be the ratio of the M1 money supply to the monetary base. The stability of this ratio largely determines whether controlling the monetary base will result in controlling the money supply.

**10.** The money multiplier will fluctuate as the banking system uses reserves more or less efficiently in the creation of deposits. In recent years, the money multiplier has tended to rise and fall somewhat with fluctuations in general business conditions.

**11.** Over annual periods, the money multiplier has generally shown stable movement around a downward trend. Over quarterly periods, the pattern has been reasonably stable also. However, over monthly periods, the money multiplier has been quite volatile. The Fed's ability to control the money supply is accordingly much greater over longer periods than over shorter periods.

**Discussion Questions**

**1.** Suppose that in the next five years, the NOW/ATS checkable savings account almost entirely replaces the demand deposit. What are the implications of this pattern for monetary control?

**2.** Over the most recent years, which of the factors described as uncontrollable influences on reserves has shown the biggest variation? Can you suggest reasons for this?

**3.** Has the monetary base grown in a stable fashion over the last two years? Plot the growth in the monetary base and judge for yourself.

**4.** Plot the money multiplier on a quarterly basis over the last two years. Can you provide reasons for the variations you find? Do you think the major fluctuations in the money multiplier could have been predicted by the Federal Reserve?

**5.** Do you think that a broader definition of money, such as those described as M2, M3, or L in chapter 5, would lead to a more or less stable money multiplier? Explain your reasoning.

**Suggested Readings**

An interesting analysis of the long-run versus short-run ability of the Fed to control the money supply can be found in Jack L. Rutner, "The Federal Reserve's Impact on Several Reserve Aggregates," *Federal Reserve Bank of Kansas City Monthly Review*, May 1977, pp. 14–22. A discussion of Federal Reserve methods of implementing defensive operations can be found in *Open Market Policies and Operating Procedures*, Board of Governors of the Federal Reserve System, 1971, and in *Controlling Monetary Aggregates II: The Implementation*, Federal Reserve Bank of Boston, 1972. A theoretical and statistical analysis of the factors that determine the public's demand for currency versus demand deposits can be found in William E. Becker, Jr., "Determinants of the United States Currency–Demand Deposit Ratio," *Journal of Finance*, March 1975, pp. 57–74. An analysis of the post-1979 conduct of monetary policy that finds it to be little different from the pre-1979 period in its impact is found in William Poole's "Federal Reserve Operating Procedures: A Survey and Evaluation of the Historical Record since October 1979, *Journal of Money, Credit, and Banking*, November 1982, pp. 575–96.

# Accent on
# Interest-Rate Deregulation

Since the 1930s, the maximum interest rates that banks and thrifts can pay on most savings-type deposits have been set by law. This legislation, called regulation Q, was inspired by excesses in banking practices that took place mostly during the decade of the 1920s. During that period, banks were not prevented from investing in risky stocks or bonds. Moreover, they could even borrow to buy such securities, a practice called "margin buying."

Margin buying of securities magnifies the opportunity to make proportionately large profits or losses. For example, suppose the margin percentage (the maximum amount of a stock's value that can be borrowed) is 20 percent. Then, with a $2,000 investment, you can buy $10,000 worth of stock. If the stock rises in value to $12,000, you make a profit of $2,000 on your investment of $2,000 (less commissions and interest), for a rather healthy return. On the other hand, if the stock goes down in value from $10,000 to $8,000, your investment is gone. Before that time arrives, the lending agency, usually a broker, notifies you that the value of your stock is approaching $8,000, the amount of your margin loan, and that you must put up more money to "cover" your position, or the lending agency will simply sell your stock to recover its $8,000 principal.

In the 1930s, banks with margin positions in stocks came under heavy pressure when the prices of stocks collapsed. In desperation, some offered very high deposit rates to try to attract funds to help cover their margin positions and keep afloat. Many who deposited funds in these suspiciously-high-yielding accounts found they really were deals "too good to be true," when the bank failed. Regulation Q was designed to prevent such abuses of the public's trust in banks.

Under the banking act of 1980, provisions were established for the gradual phasing out of regulation Q interest-rate ceilings over a period of years extending into the late 1980s. What will happen? Will we return to the "shooting-from-the-hip" days of the late 1920s? The answer in all likelihood is no. In the 1980s, the Federal Reserve is watching what depository institutions are doing much more closely than during the 1920s. If a bank began offering depositors deals that were "too good to be true," (that is, out of line with market interest rates), the Federal Reserve would scrutinize the bank carefully, and probably introduce management changes in it and/or otherwise "step on" the problem bank.

Interest-rate deregulation probably will not cause our economy to return to the 1920s, rather, this deregulation is having and will continue to have different impacts on or economy. So that we can form some impressions about the likely impacts our deregulation on the 1980s economy, it is useful to consider the aftereffects of a change made on December 14, 1982. On this date, banks and thrifts were authorized to begin to

205

offer a new account generally called the Money Market Deposit Account, or MMDA (see chapter 5) that had no ceiling interest rate. Its interest rate could be set at whatever level the bank preferred. The thinking behind the authorization of the new account was that it would help stem the outflow of funds going from thrifts and banks and into the hands of the money-market mutual funds, a trend that had been occurring for several years.

The immediate results of the new deregulated account were startling. In the first three weeks of the accounts' life, more than 110 billion dollars poured into the accounts, according to a Federal Reserve estimate. Over the same period, an approximately 30-billion-dollar fall occurred in the total assets of money-market mutual funds. In the weeks and months that followed, the growth in the new account was less dramatic, but nonetheless substantial in nature, while the decline in the size of money-market-mutual-fund assets continued.

A shift in savings flows such as the one now described has important implications for lending conditions in specific sectors of the economy. Before the MMDA was introduced, a growing share of consumer savings was flowing into money-market funds. These funds invested it in such assets as T-Bills, commercial paper, banker's acceptances, commercial-bank CDs, and eurodollar deposits. Thus, a growing share of savings was moving largely into the hands of government, corporate, and other business borrowers that issue the financial instruments involved. As the new account diverts an increasing portion of these savings into banks and thrifts of all sizes, the picture changes. Specifically, small banks and thrifts experiencing large inflows of the new funds are now able to extend more loans to their customers, typically small business firms and household mortgage and other borrowers. Unlike their larger commercial-bank counterparts, small banks and thrifts are constrained significantly by growth in their deposits, in expanding their loans and other assets. (Purchased funds are not as available to the smaller banks and thrifts as they are to large institutions.)

The result of the specific deregulation of interest rates on the new MMDA-type deposits is thus a loosening up of lending conditions for small business borrowers and for households, which logic suggests leads to an increased level of lending to small business firms and households. This, in turn, results in more spending on capital goods by small business firms, more mortgage-financed construction spending by households, and possibly more spending on consumer durable goods typically bought on an installment basis, such as automobiles.

On the other hand, large commercial banks and direct business borrowers such as those firms issuing commercial paper, are confronted with less funds flowing through their usual borrowing channels. As the deregulation loosens small-business and consumer-financing conditions, it tightens large-business financing conditions. As this scenario plays fully out, interest rates on "big business IOUs" will realign with rates on the new deposits to produce the flow of funds into both type channels that is consistent with the needs (and thus willingness to pay) of the parties involved. And, at least potentially important changes will occur in spending patterns, jobs, and production levels in the housing, consumer durables, and other sectors of the economy—all because of a new deregulated-interest-rate account.

# PART IV

# WHAT DETERMINES THE GNP, INTEREST RATES, AND PRICES?

## CHAPTER 13

# Total Expenditures in the Economy

## CHAPTER OUTLINE

## IMPORTANT TERMS

# MEMO

To:      All readers
From:    JWE

This chapter is the first of several about macroeconomic theory. Theory in economics seeks to explain how our world works. It also can predict the economic consequences of political and other events. However, it cannot do so unequivocally. It cannot match the precision with which a chemist can predict the result of mixing together two substances. Economic theory cannot deliver predictions as accurate as those of a physicist. Why? Because our lab is not filled with the test tubes and controlled experiments of the chemist and physicist. Our lab is the real world, and it is full of changing influences and is often visited by one-time-only outside events. Thus, our measurements are imprecise. As a result, we profess our theories with some doubt, and we sometimes change our minds about what we think is right. Whereas the formula for sodium nitrate and the law of gravity are unchanging, theory in economics is subject to change. Thus, what you are going to read in the next few chapters is provisional. It is the best sense we can make of the world right now. But, our theories will change. You can count on that as surely as on the law of gravity.

The topic in this chapter is how and why consumers, firms, and others want to buy the goods and services produced in our factories and mills. It is about how the demand for the Gross National Product (GNP) is determined. From this chapter, you can get an appreciation of the main influences on consumer spending. You can also better understand the difference between the factors important in purchases of nondurable goods and those important in purchases of durable goods. You can build an understanding of why firms decide on new machinery and plant purchases. The government also contributes its part to total demand as it spends our tax dollars in the private economy. You will be able to better comprehend the role of government spending in this process as well.

In chapter 4, the GNP was defined as the total amount of current production of final goods and services. In this chapter, we are concerned with who buys the GNP and why. The "who" is easier to ascertain than the "why." We can discuss the "who" in the next few paragraphs. It will take the whole chapter to just scratch the surface about the "why."

Let us begin with the star of the show. Consumers are the principal players in the drama of U.S. aggregate demand. They account for upward of 60 percent of total spending. In their purchases of automobiles, appliances, furniture, clothing, food, and countless other goods and services, consumers spend more than all others combined.

The next biggest spender in the U.S. economy consists of the combination of the federal government, state governments, and the thousands of county, city, and other local governments. Government spending on goods and services accounts for better than 20 percent of total spending. Business firms account for most of the remainder of aggregate demand through their purchases of new plants and equipment, and their investment in inventories.

The GNP statistics give total business investment the distinguished-sounding name *Gross Private Domestic Investment.* However, part of the Gross Private Domestic Investment is the amount spent on new residential construction. New-home purchases and turret lathes may seem like strange bedfellows, but the thinking is that the purchase of a new house is more of an investment by households than it is a consumer expenditure. In reality, it is probably some of both. Thus, business investment, as officially defined, includes spending on plants and equipment, inventory additions, and new houses.

The smallest part of aggregate demand is net export demand. To arrive at net exports of goods and services, we subtract the amount of demand by U.S. residents for foreign products from the demand for U.S. goods by foreign residents. So much for the "who." Now on to the "why."

The collection of ideas about how demand for goods and services is determined is called a theory of aggregate demand. Aggregate demand and GNP are not the same thing. *Aggregate demand* is the total amount the public *wants* to buy. The GNP is the amount of current production that *actually took place.* Generally, the amount produced and the amount the public wants to buy are not the same. What happens when they differ? Inventories adjust and production might change. But that is getting ahead of ourselves. Right now the question is what determines demand. Let us look first at the consumer.

## CONSUMER SPENDING IN THE UNITED STATES

There are episodes in the lives of consumers that are totally beyond our economic theories. When Scott and Jane split up on a recent Saturday morning for separate shopping trips, she to pick up a new pair of hose at the department store and he to buy a new set of wiper blades at the car dealer, theory could not have predicted that she would come home with four dresses and two sweaters and he would drive home in a new car. In fact, neither of them could have predicted the actions of the other, or of themselves. Fortunately, when we think of economic theories about consumer spending and about the behavior of consumers, it is not our task to psyche out the behavior of each individual consumer.

Experience has shown that regularities in consumer behavior viewed in the aggregate far exceed those characterizing individuals. For every Scott who bought a new car on an unplanned basis, someone else who planned to buy one did not. Because we are on much more solid ground when talking about consumer behavior in the aggregate, this is the focus of our discussion.

What determines the level of consumer spending in the United States? The most important ingredient is the level of income consumers take home. Although many factors influence the amount consumers spend, there is little doubt that income is the basic ingredient driving consumer purchases. In other words, the family budget is constrained by the income brought home. Standards of living adjust to this budget constraint. How many cars, boats, and food processors we buy also is governed by the "bottom line" formed by the level of after-tax consumer incomes.

Do you need more persuasion on this point? If so, think about how you would react if you were given a checkbook by the president of Chase Manhattan Bank and told that you could write as many checks in it as you wished. The budget constraint formed by your former income level has just been relaxed, to put it mildly. Would you spend more? Would we ever see you again? Consumers in the aggregate tend to react the same general way. When the after-tax income of consumers rises, part of the income increase is regularly and predictably spent on new consumer purchases.

## Pure Consumption Goods and Assets

Economic research has sharpened our ideas about consumption in several ways. One of these has to do with what we mean by the term *consumption*. Apart from economics, the term refers to using up something. In economics, *pure consumption goods* are those which have no value as assets. They are used up upon (or very nearly upon) purchase. A ticket to a movie theater purchased today and reading "good for today only" is an example of pure consumption. A meal in a restaurant is another example, assuming no doggy bags. However, a pair of shoes is another matter. Although spending on shoes is officially called consumer spending, most if not all shoes are not used up upon purchase, but last for a period of time. The shoes are a *consumer asset* in that they give service in the present as well as in the future. A pure consumption good cannot be stored. Anything that is an asset can be stored. Consumers have an inventory of assets at any moment consisting of things such as automobiles, lamps, furniture, TV sets, clothing, and books (including this one). Why all this concern about the difference between pure consumption and assets? Economists have found that the theories that best explain pure consumption are different from those which explain why consumers buy assets.

## Permanent-Income Theory

Central to these theoretical differences is a concept that Professor Milton Friedman has called *permanent income*. Permanent income is a perception of a normal level of income consumers expect to earn over their working lives. Under this view, consumers continually assess the market value of their labor skills. This market value is called the value of *human capital*. From this, consumers develop an expectation about the long-run income that should flow from their human capital. At the same time, consumers assess the market value of their financial assets (things such as stocks and bonds). They maintain an expectation about the future earnings on these assets as well. Permanent income is defined as the expected earnings on both human capital and financial assets.

Permanent-income theory contends that household spending on pure-consumption goods is governed by permanent income rather than by actual income. Permanent income is an expectation that exists in the minds of consumers. Actual income is what consumers receive. It is in the wallet rather than in the mind. Permanent-income theory says that it is what is in the mind rather than what is in the wallet that governs what consumers will spend on pure consumption. Thus, as a labor union goes on strike in a major industry, workers in that industry may view their income loss as temporary and not influencing their expectation of the long-run earnings on their total capital. Under permanent-income theory, we should not expect spending on pure consumption goods by these industry workers to fall much. Most of the households affected by the strike would continue their spending on pure consumption goods, financing it by drawing on their savings or even by taking on added consumer debt.

Consumer purchases of assets are a different story. Recent research shows that the role of permanent income in the purchases of automobiles, furniture, and appliances is less important than it is for pure consumption.[1] What seems to be more important is the amount of nonpermanent or transitory income. *Transitory income* is defined as the difference between actual income and permanent income. Transitory income is unexpected. It is not part of the plans of consumers. When it is positive, it tends to stimulate spending on assets. (Some people go down and buy a new car.) When it is negative, it tends to discourage spending. (Some people decide to wait until next year to buy a new TV.) So the difference between permanent and actual income is an important influence on the amount of durable goods bought.

1. A number of studies using U.S. data have shown this to be true. Recent examples are articles by Michael Darby, "Postwar U.S. Consumption, Consumer Expenditures, and Saving," *American Economic Review*, May 1975, and J. W. Elliott, "Wealth and Wealth Proxies in a Permanent Income Model," *Quarterly Journal of Economics*, November 1980.

# Memorandum

To: Those interested in government policy and permanent-income theory
From: JWE

The U.S. government has not always accepted the permanent-income view, or at least so it would seem, judging from some of its actions. The classic examples are the various tax surcharges. The Johnson administration proposed a tax surcharge as a way of reducing a level of consumer demand considered excessive and inflationary. However, the surcharge brought about only a temporary reduction in the type of income that our theory calls transitory. The effect should have been to reduce consumer purchases of assets. Such purchases were not reduced, probably because some other flies were in the ointment. The Johnson surcharge was announced in a confusing way and was debated for more than a year before being enacted. During this year, consumers saved a little more than usual, as a precaution against whatever this new tax would do. When the surcharge was finally enacted, consumers found it to be smaller than anticipated, and responded by increasing rather than decreasing their rate of spending.

On the other hand, when consumers were offered tax rebates a few years later, the government sounded quite sympathetic to the theory in that it was suggesting that people should take their $100 tax rebate and use it to buy a new car. The government was suggesting what the theory predicted—that transitory income, such as a tax rebate, would be used to buy assets. Unfortunately, the amounts involved were apparently too small to create any changes in buying, even of assets, and the automobile industry was largely unaffected.

If the government were to take permanent-income theory seriously, it would believe that the only kind of tax changes that have a lasting impact on the consumer sector are those which change permanent income. Since such changes are not likely to be one-time surcharges or rebates, these tax tools would not be used as instruments of policy. Instead, more focus would be placed on changes in the basic tax rates and their structure.

## Consumption Patterns in the United States

What about the real-world relationship between income and consumption? Take a look at figure 13.1. It is called a *scatter diagram* because it displays the relationship between two variables as a scatter of points. Each point in a scatter diagram shows the value of one variable compared with the corresponding value of another. The less scattered the points, the stronger the relationship. Figure 13.1 compares the level of consumer income and the corresponding level of consumer spending (excluding durables) over the period 1950–1980.

Income is represented by a statistical series entitled *real Disposable Personal Income,* which is called real DPI. DPI measures the income and transfer payments received by households net of the taxes paid by them. Real DPI is computed by dividing DPI by an index of prices.

214

This corrects it for inflation and converts it into a measure of constant-dollar income. Accordingly, real DPI shows how much aftertax purchasing power is in the hands of households. Each point in figure 13.1 shows the amount of real DPI earned in a specific six-month period and the amount of real spending (excluding durables) in the same six-month period. For example, we can see that when real DPI was about $400 billion, consumer spending on nondurables and services was approximately $325 billion. The scatter diagram of figure 13.1 shows a strong relationship between income and consumption; not only do the two go up and down together, but the relationship is quite systematic.

Given the earlier discussion of the theoretical role of permanent income in consumer expenditures, why have we shown the relationship with actual income? Well, the problem is that permanent income is in the mind and is not observable. In research on the subject, economists have devised ways of approximating it. These approximations give reason to believe that when actual income is cumulated over longer and longer periods of time, the result converges upon permanent income. This is the approach taken in figure 13.1. Here we have averaged income over six-month periods, and compared it with spending averaged over the same six-month periods. This captures a good part of the permanent-income effect.

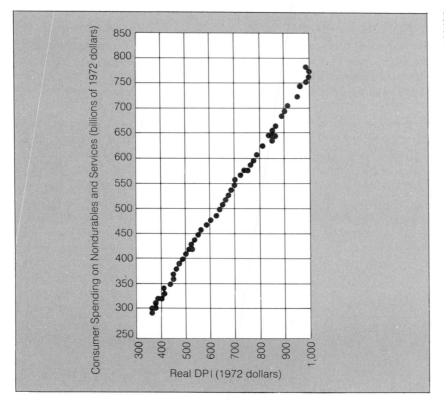

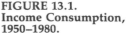

FIGURE 13.1.
Income Consumption,
1950–1980.

How about this measure of consumption? Permanent-income theory most strongly related permanent income to pure consumption. Here, the published statistical series that best corresponds to pure consumption has been used. The GNP series, nondurables and services, contains some goods that are assetlike, such as shoes and dress suits. They are not used up upon purchase. Thus, the category is too inclusive, but it still captures the major movements in pure consumption goods.

Figure 13.2 is a scatter diagram similar to figure 13.1, except that now the amount of real DPI is related to purchases of real consumer durables instead of nondurables and services. Figure 13.2 shows that the relationship beween the demand for durables and income is weaker than the relationship between nondurables/services and income. Although it is clear from this figure that income is related to durables purchases, the points are not as nicely grouped as in figure 13.1. To more fully explain durable goods demand, we must look beyond income levels. The major additional influence on durables spending is interest rates.

## SPENDING NOW OR SPENDING LATER— THE ROLE OF THE REAL RATE

In chapter 5, the real rate of interest was defined and discussed. It is the difference between the actual rate of interest and the expected rate of inflation. So, if one-year government bonds yield 12 percent today and you expect the inflation rate over the upcoming one-year period to be 10 percent, then the real return on the bond to you is 12 percent − 10 percent = 2 percent. If you buy it, you expect to have 2 percent more purchasing power next year than you have now. Although you earn 12 percent of the bond's price in interest, inflation reduces the purchasing power of the money you have invested by 10 percent. You expect to be able to buy 2 percent more goods in a year. The real rate is an expected increase in purchasing power.

There are reasons to believe consumer purchases are influenced by the real rate. The first thinking along these lines goes back to the work of Irving Fisher, an outstanding American economist who wrote in the early part of the twentieth century. Fisher saw the real rate as a reward for saving. If a household put off buying pure consumption goods now, it did so because of the lure of being able to buy more tomorrow. That is where the real rate comes in. The higher the real rate, the greater the incentive to spend less now and instead save for later (and larger) purchases. This means that the higher the real rate, the *lower* the current purchases of pure consumption goods.

Now, this is pretty solid thinking as far as it goes. However, the problem in applying it to the modern-day United States is that house-

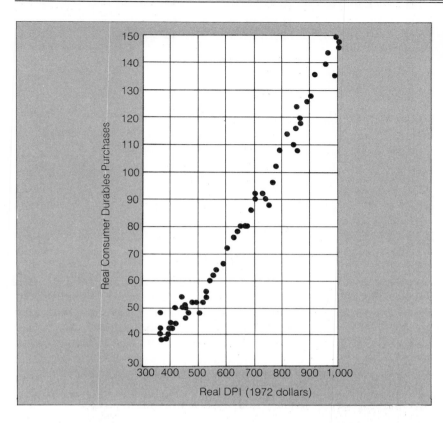

**FIGURE 13.2.**
**Income and Consumer**
**Durables Purchases.**

holds in our times hold a substantial amount of financial assets such as bonds, notes, and money-market funds on which they earn a real rate. When the real rate goes up, so does the income on some of these assets. So a rise in the real rate increases household incomes. This effect of real rates on incomes works in the opposite direction from the Fisherian effect we just talked about. Our household is torn by rising real rates. Fisher is whispering in one ear, "At these higher real rates, you should be saving more now, and postponing your consumer purchases until tomorrow." In the other ear comes the admonishment, "You just got a larger interest check on your savings certificates—do it—go out to a nice restaurant tonight." How do households in the United States actually respond to these cross-currents? With respect to nondurables and services, it is pretty much of a standoff. Research shows nondurables and services spending is largely independent of the real rate of interest. But durables purchases are another story.

## The Real Rate and Durables Purchases

Automobiles, boats, TVs, furniture, and some major appliances are all durable goods widely bought on credit. When the real interest rate

On January 14, 1981, the *Wall Street Journal* reported on the latest retail-sales figures. Retail sales were down for December 1980, after correction for the seasonal effects of Christmas. In explaining the weakness, the *Journal* reported that the consensus explanation of economists for the weakness was a continued strain on consumer spending power (in other words, real DPI was down), and rising interest rates. The rising interest rates were reported as having a particular impact on markets for automobiles and housing. In this thinking, the *Wall Street Journal* and our text agree.

goes up, this type of credit is available at less attractive terms. As a result, the effective price of the durable good rises. Consumers have reason to back off. Besides this, consumer assets compete to an appreciable degree with financial assets for the household's dollars. So, when real rates go up, there is a greater incentive for households to put more of their income into financial assets and less into new consumer assets. (Fisher is whispering again.) After all, households can always make do with the old car or TV for a while longer, especially when those money-market funds are yielding more. These two effects work in the same direction on the household.[2] When real rates rise, consumers are discouraged from buying assets by the higher credit-related effective price, and they are also induced to spend less on consumer assets so they can spend more on financial assets.

## Real Rates and Durables Spending in the United States

Higher real rates should mean less purchases of consumer durables. But do they? Look at figure 13.3. This scatter diagram shows the relationship between the real rate of interest on consumer savings certificates and the level of spending on real durable goods in the United States. Theoretically, the real rate in figure 13.3 should be the typical investor's expectation of the inflation-adjusted return on funds. But this expectation cannot be directly measured, so in its place is the real rate that investors actually obtained. It is called the *realized real rate*. It is calculated by taking a nominal interest rate, in this case

2. There is an increase in income in this case just as there was in the case of nondurables and services. And it works in the opposite direction from the other two effects just discussed. More interest-related income means more spending. However, this effect on durable goods has been found to be small. We can safely ignore it.

218

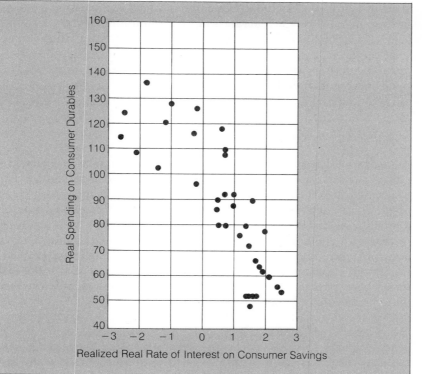

FIGURE 13.3.
Real Interest Rates
and Durables
Spending.

the rate on small-denomination certificates of deposit, and subtracting from it the inflation rate that actually existed over the average life of the certificate. For example, say the interest rate on the certificates was 10 percent on the average for the second half of 1975, for certificates having a maturity of three years. Then, the average annual inflation rate over the period from the second half of 1975 to the second half of 1978 is calculated and subtracted from the 10 percent. This difference is the realized real rate over this period. It shows the actual change in purchasing power that investors in such certificates realized over the 1975 to 1978 period.[3]

3. The way we interpret figure 13.3 depends on what we assume about the way the realized real rate and the expected real rate compare. The expected real rate is a forecast because it contains a forecast of inflation in the period ahead. If we suppose investors are pretty good forecasters, we would suppose that the difference between the expected and realized rates is small. Many economists are not willing to assume investors are accurate. However, many are willing to assume they are unbiased, a term that means they are not wrong on the average. The thinking is that if investors are wrong on the average, then they must not be learning from their mistakes, a rather illogical attribute to associate with investors. If we go along with this assumption that investors are unbiased, and we carry the logic one step further to assume that the forecasting errors investors make have no recognizable pattern (if they did, investors would use the pattern to improve their forecasts), then we can think of the realized real rate as equal to

What can we conclude about figure 13.3? The general picture is pretty clear. When the real rate is high, the amount spent on consumer durables is low, and vice versa. We can see a clear-cut pattern—rising real rates on consumer savings certificates are associated with decreased spending on durable goods and falling real rates are associated with increased spending on durable goods.

## CAPITAL-INVESTMENT SPENDING

A *capital good* is one that adds to the capital stock of business. The *capital stock* of business refers to the accumulation of factories, office buildings, machinery, and equipment used by business to produce its final products. Spending on capital goods is often viewed by economists as a key to the course of the economy. This is because fluctuations in capital-goods spending have contributed to most of the recessions in the history of the United States. Not that capital spending is the clear-cut cause of most recessions. But, like a pesky little brother or sister, capital-goods spending is almost always involved when economic trouble comes.

No wonder. When a firm buys a new plant or expands its operations into a new state, it is placing an important bet on the future. Capital goods such as new factories stand for decades, and it takes a good while for them to return to their owners the money put into them. Thus, their construction is a bet that the future will be promising. Predictions of the future are subject to sharp change and frequent revision by managers of large corporations. When corporate managers change their minds about how profitable it will be to produce goods and services in the future, then their demand for new capital goods changes. Predictions by managers of the profitability of new capital investment are revised frequently, sometimes by major amounts. The end result, spending on capital goods, is notoriously cyclical.

Capital goods are durable. In fact, for statistical purposes they are defined as equipment and facilities that last longer than a year. Many last much longer than that. Capital goods give services that are spaced out over time. In the process, they generate cash flows for their owners. That is why they are also called investment goods, and their purchase is referred to as capital investment.

### Investment Decisions by Firms

Basically, an *investment* is something for which you put some money down now in anticipation of a stream of returns later. When the

the expected real rate plus a random error. This random error will sometimes be positive, sometimes be negative, and will have an average value of zero. In this case, the major patterns we see in the realized rate in figure 13.3 are also present in the expected rate.

managers of a firm pay $50,000 for a new drill press, they anticipate earning a pattern of cash flows on the machine over the next several years. We usually can assume the firm's managers believe that the cash flows from the drill press will be at least as great as what they could earn by investing the money elsewhere in something of about equal risk as the drill press. But how should the profitability of a drill press or any capital good be determined? If we understand how the typical firm decides to go ahead on a capital investment or pass it up, we will be able to identify the major influences on capital spending. A drill press produces earnings far into the future. It can be sold to a scrap dealer when it wears out. Also, it costs money up front to buy it. How do these pieces fit together into a coherent business-investment decision?

The yield or *internal rate of return* fits the pieces of the capital-investment decision together nicely. In chapter 5, we defined the yield to maturity as the rate of discount that equated the present value of a stream of earnings from a bond to its market price. We can use the same idea to find the internal rate of return on a capital investment. Recall this equation from chapter 5 for the yield to maturity:

$$(13.1) \quad P_o = \frac{C_1}{(1 + r)} + \frac{C_2}{(1 + r)^2} + \cdots + \frac{C_n}{(1 + r)^n} + \frac{F_n}{(1 + r)^n}$$

To apply it to the return on a capital investment, all we need to do is define $C_1, C_2, \ldots C_n$ to be the cash flow produced by the capital good from year 1 to year $n$ in the future, $P_o$ to be the purchase price of the capital good, and $F_n$ to be scrap value of the capital good at the end of its life. The term $r$ in equation 13.1 is the rate of interest that makes the present value of the total cash flows from the capital investment just equal to its purchase price. Thus, if you deposited $P_o$ dollars in a bank account earning at a rate of interest $r$, you could withdraw $C_1$ after the first year, $C_2$ after the second, and so on up to $n$ years. When you withdrew the scrap value, $F_n$, at the end of $n$ years, you would have just depleted the bank account. The present value of the cash-flow stream is the size of the bank account you would need to exactly reproduce the earnings on the capital good, assuming you could earn at $r$ rate of interest. Thus, $r$ is the rate of interest that makes the cash flows from a capital good have a present value exactly equal to what the capital good costs.

For example, if you pay $63,831 for a drill press that lasts five years, has a scrap value of $10,000 at the end of that time, and produces cash flows of $20,000 a year over the five-year period, the yield to maturity comes out to exactly 20 percent per year. In other words, if we put these numbers in equation 13.1, a value of $r = .20$ would make the right-hand side equal to the left-hand side. Now, look what happens if you deposited the $63,831 in a bank account earning 20% annually. At the end of each of the five years, you withdraw $20,000. After the fifth year, you withdraw an additional $10,000. These withdrawals exactly reproduce the cash flows from the drill press.

| Year | Value at the start of year | Value at the end of year | Year-end withdrawal |
|------|----------------------------|--------------------------|---------------------|
| 1 | $63,831 | $76,597 | $20,000 |
| 2 | 56,597 | 67,917 | 20,000 |
| 3 | 47,917 | 57,500 | 20,000 |
| 4 | 37,500 | 45,000 | 20,000 |
| 5 | 25,000 | 30,000 | 20,000 + 10,000 scrap value |
| 6 | 0 | | |

These numbers show that you can exactly reproduce the flow of cash the machine makes if you deposit $63,831 at a 20 percent earning rate. To see how the numbers are calculated, let us review years 1 and 2. You start the account with $63,831. It earns $12,766 in interest the first year ($63,831 × .20 = $12,766), so it grows to $76,597 at year's end. The first year's $20,000 withdrawal reduces this amount to $56,597, which is the amount available at the start of the second year. The second year's 20 percent interest raises the amount by $11,319 to a year-end total of $67,917, and so forth.

In the U.S. economy, business managers know how much they must pay to buy a capital good. (They know $P_o$.) They can usually estimate the scrap value of a capital good. (They can estimate $F_n$.) They also can make an analysis of the expected cash flows from the machine over its useful life. (They hold an expectation about the $C_1$ through $C_n$.) So, they know all the information in equation 13.1 except the yield, $r$. Thus, equation 13.1 can be solved for the yield that makes the present value of the machine equal to its cost.

## The Cost of Capital and Investment Decisions

The yield on a new investment is the crucial measure of its profitability. Normally, if the yield on a new investment proposal is higher than the firm's minimum investment standard, the firm should proceed with the investment. If not, the proposal should be scrapped. This "minimum investment standard" is called the firm's *cost of capital*. The cost of capital is the combined rate of return that the firm's stockholders, bondholders, and other financiers expect the firm to earn on the money they have jointly invested in it. All investors in a corporation's securities have committed money because they expect to earn a real return that is at least as high as they could earn elsewhere for taking an equivalent risk.[4] We can safely assume that investors have a solid idea about the real return they expect to earn on their money. In other words, the cost of capital is known to them and to the firm's managers.

---

4. Some firms are riskier than others, because of either the business they are in or the financial condition they are in, and investors are notorious for requiring a high return for investing money in firms that they see as having high risk.

If the firm buys capital goods that are expected to produce a return lower than the cost of capital, then stockholders and other investors will be disappointed. Stockholders will quite likely react by selling their stock, driving its price down. This is not a pretty picture for managers of the firm. Even though managers of large corporations basically work for a salary, they have at least two reasons to be quite concerned about disappointed shareholders and falling stock prices. The first is that the salaries of many managers in modern U.S. corporations are tied to the price of their firm's stock through stock bonuses and options to buy stock. Thus, if the stock price goes down, so does the manager's compensation. The second reason is that when stockholders get too disgruntled, they sometimes rise up and give the offending manager the heave-ho. As the legal owners of the corporation, stockholders can do this through their voice on the board of directors. It happens often enough in the real world to be anything but hypothetical as a reason managers, when deciding on the purchase of new capital goods, would feel restricted by the best interests of stockholders. Thus, we may safely assume that managers care about meeting the expectations of their shareholders and other investors.

The cost of capital required by investors is related to present interest rates. Real interest rates on bonds, certificates, and other investments provide the environment against which all investors in securities evaluate the return on their investments. When real rates in general go up, so do the investors' minimum requirements concerning the return on new capital goods bought by corporations. Rising real rates mean that the cost of capital is rising. At higher cost of capital, corporations must be more choosy in making new investments if they are to satisfy the expectations of their shareholders. If real interest rates on bonds, notes, and certificates all rise by 2 percent, then stockholders will likely require a similar increase in the expected return on new investment projects. Managers will respond by excluding some capital-investment proposals that are of marginal profitability. The number of investment projects now promising a high enough return goes down, and with it the level of capital goods purchased. Thus, rising rates cause a reduction in the number of capital-investment projects acceptable to management. The bottom line: Capital investment and real interest rates are negatively related if everything else is held constant.

## Profit Expectations and Capital Investment

Earlier we said that the stream of expected future cash flows on a new capital good was required to calculate the rate of return on an investment project (the values of $C_1$ through $C_n$). In the real world, estimating those $C$'s is at best difficult. Why? Because they so completely embrace the future. Take the drill press we discussed earlier.

Suppose it will be used in the production of automobiles. This means that in order to estimate the cash flows from the drill press, we need to know the future level of production of automobiles upon which it will be used. Predicting future automobile sales is a goal that regularly eludes the best minds of Detroit. And no wonder. A prediction of future automobile sales requires assumptions about future gas prices, future import quotas, driving habits of future Americans, and demographic trends such as patterns of suburban living. Is this enough to give you the picture? Estimating the profitability of new investment projects is an uncertain business, and one that is in a state of continual revision. Rapidly changing estimates of the expected cash flows from new capital goods are an important reason for volatility in evaluating the return on new capital investments. The changing state of profit expectations ranks along with the real interest rate as a determinant of the level of spending on new capital goods.

## Capital Investment in the U.S.

So far, you have been reading and thinking about the logical case for why real interest rates and profit expectations determine the amount of new capital spending. How about the facts? Some evidence is shown in figure 13.4. In it, the capital investment is measured by the part of the GNP called *nonresidential fixed investment*.[5] It is shown as the solid line. The dotted line is the realized real rate of interest on corporate bonds.

The format of figure 13.4 is different from the previous three figures in this chapter. Rather than a scatter diagram, this is a chart that plots both variables over time. Why the switch? Because unlike the other relationships we considered earlier, there is likely to be a fairly long lag between changes in the variables influencing capital spending and changes in the rate of new capital outlays. It takes time for firms to translate changes in the attractiveness of investment into plans for new capital spending, more time to get these plans approved, still more time to get bids from builders of capital goods, and even more time to negotiate final contracts and get delivery of the goods. The lag between changes in the determining factors of capital spending and the actual spending has commonly been estimated to be in the range of one to three years.[6]

5.  The nonresidential-fixed-investment category includes most of the factories and equipment we have had at the center of our discussion. However, it also includes investment by not-for-profit organizations such as hospitals. Thus, it is a bit broader than our theoretical discussion calls for, but it is close enough to give us the impression we are after.

6.  See, for example, J. S. Duesenberry, G. Fromm, L. A. Klein, and E. Kuh, *The Brookings Quarterly Econometric Model of the U.S.*, Chicago: Rand McNally, 1954, pp. 690–91, and M. K. Evans, *Macroeconomic Activity: Theory, Forecasting, and Control*, New York: Harper and Row, 1969.

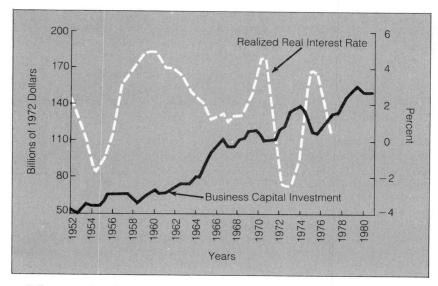

FIGURE 13.4.
Capital Investment
and the Real Rate of
Interest.

What we should be looking for in figure 13.4 is a pattern of change in realized real rates and later patterns of change in capital spending. Look at the period from 1960 to about 1966. A steady drop in the real rate occurred over this period, and it was marked by an above average rate of growth in capital spending, especially after 1964. The rising real rate that occurred over 1968–1970 seems to relate to a falloff in capital spending during 1969–1971. The sharp falloff in the real rate from about 1970 to 1973 was followed by an expansion in capital spending over 1971 to 1974. The equally sharp rise in the real rate from 1973 to 1975 was followed by a sharp drop in capital spending over 1974–1976. Then, as rates dropped after 1975, capital spending again picked up.[7] The association between the two is far from perfect, but it is clearly more than accidental.

Evidence on the impact of profit expectations on capital spending is not so easy to produce. The biggest problem is isolating profit expectations from other economic influences. We can get some clues as to the state of profit expectations by looking at stock prices. The movement of stock prices is not completely governed by changes in profit expectations. Clearly stock prices do change when profit expectations change. However, stock prices also change when the cost of capital changes, and when the riskiness of stock ownership changes. Although we cannot attribute all changes in stock prices to changes in profit expectations, we can at least get some crude information about the effects of profit expectations on capital investment by looking at how stock prices and capital investment relate over time. Figure 13.5 shows this relationship. Here stock prices are measured by the

7. The real rate stops at 1977 because this is as far as the series can be calculated as of 1980. Remember that this rate is the realized three-year real return to corporate bonds. To compute it, I had to use the actual inflation rate for the three-year period ahead. Thus, the 1977 rate used the inflation rate out to 1980.

**FIGURE 13.5.
Capital Investment
and Stock Prices.**

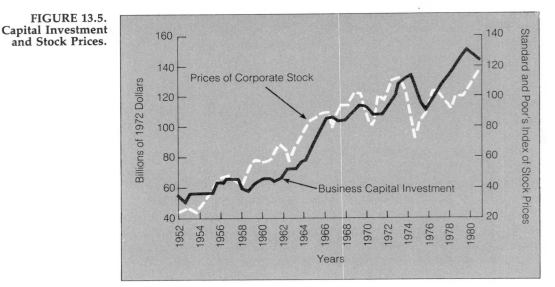

Standard and Poor's 500 Stock Index (see chapter 5) and capital spending is the same nonresidential-fixed-investment series used in figure 13.4. Although the relationship is not perfect, the general association here is hard to overlook.

The lag between the movement of stock prices and the movement of capital spending seems shorter than for real rates. This may be the result of other influences on stock prices, such as the cost of capital and risk changes. In addition, the stock market is notoriously whipped around by international events, domestic political events, and a host of other things that have only an indirect connection with profit expectations. Usually, we can logically explain most major stock market upheavals after they have happened. And, usually, these logical reasons can be connected with the expected profits from business capital, whether it be existing capital or new capital. But let us not kid ourselves. The stock market is sometimes more emotional than a mother at a wedding, and some short-term price changes are the result of this and little more.

We have identified two major influences on capital spending. The real rate of interest influences this spending as does the state of profit expectations by business. The first of these two is rooted in financial markets. The second is more elusive, susceptible to change, and volatile, and is the channel through which the plans of politicians and even the predictions of economists can have a bearing on the level of spending by firms in the economy.

## HOW GOVERNMENT
## SPENDING FITS IN

So far, we have been talking about the major influences on consumer and investment spending. Governments also spend money in the economy. (By governments we mean the federal government and the many state and local governments.) But unlike our analysis of consumer and investment spending, we have no theory to offer as to the determining factors for government spending. Instead, economic theory takes government spending as a given and deals with the effects of it rather than the determinants of it. Basically, government expenditures are a third type of spending that add to the sum of consumer and investment spending.

Have you ever wondered who spends more, the federal government or the state and local governments? Figure 13.6 plots the two in real or constant dollar amounts over time. Are you surprised to see that after 1968, state and local spending has been consistently and increasingly larger than federal spending? Perhaps this statement needs amplification. The figure shows that *purchases of goods and services* by governments relate that way. However, spending money directly in the economy is not all that governments do, as figure 13.7 illustrates. They also transfer it from one citizen to another. A *government transfer payment* is defined as an incomelike payment by the government that is made without the recipient rendering a service or selling a product in return. The main categories of transfer payments are social security and medicare payments made to the elderly and to widows, grants made by the federal government to states, and interest payments of the government debt. You will notice that when it comes to transfer payments, the federal government is a lot more active than state and local governments. In fact, the federal government transfers about three-fourths of the total taxes it collects and spends the other one-fourth directly in private markets. By contrast, state and local governments transfer only about one-twentieth of the taxes they collect.

What of these transfers? Do they have any impact on the economy, or can we view them as just affecting who will spend the available income rather than how much of it will be spent? It appears that

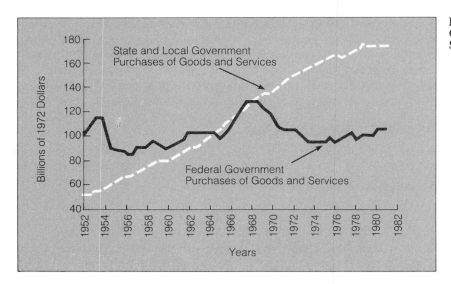

**FIGURE 13.6. Government Spending.**

**FIGURE 13.7.
Government
Transfers.**

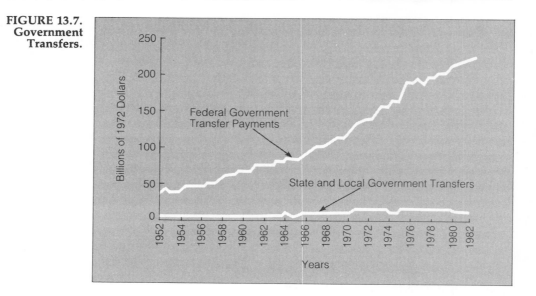

transfers are not economically neutral. The thinking is that those from who the taxes are collected would probably have spent about 90 percent of the transfer if they had kept it as income. On the other hand, transfer payments to the elderly are presumably almost all spent. The result is a somewhat higher fraction of total income spent across the whole economy than we otherwise would have. The massive flow of transfer payments made by the federal government probably leads to somewhat more spending than if it were not present.

Another major impact of the government occurs when taxes are collected. The basic impact of taxes is to reduce spendable income available to workers. They react by spending less on consumer goods than they would in the absence of taxes. In our analysis of consumer spending, we emphasized the role of aftertax income in consumer purchase decisions. When taxes are increased, the aftertax income of workers falls, and they buy fewer consumer goods. Thus, taxes are the other face of government activities. While rising government spending and increased transfers increase total spending in the economy, taxes reduce it.

## NET EXPORT DEMAND

Besides spending on U.S. production by consumers, firms, and governments, spending on domestic production takes place as a result of exports and imports. When a U.S. good is bought by a consumer in another nation, the effect on U.S. production is similar to the purchase of the same good by a U.S. consumer. Domestic income and production are affected. However, when a U.S. consumer buys an imported good, the effect on the U.S. economy is similar to the consumer having saved the money instead. In the import case, the money has gone for the purchase of the production of another nation. It has not contributed to production or incomes in the United States. As far as U.S. production goes, what matters most is whose *production* is being bought. What matters least is who is buying it. Because of this, when we are thinking about total demand in the U.S. economy, we *add* the amount of exports (because they are purchases of U.S. output) and *subtract* the amount of U.S. imports (because they are U.S. purchases of the production of other nations). The difference is called net exports, and is a component of aggregate demand. For now, we will work with net exports as if they are independent of the domestic economy, at least over short periods of time.

## A SUMMING UP: AGGREGATE DEMAND IN THE UNITED STATES

The term aggregate demand means demand for goods and services by everyone in the economy. All the component parts of a theoretical model of aggregate demand have been manufactured. It is now time for some assembly work. An automobile is assembled with wrenches and screwdrivers (not to mention robots). A theoretical model is assembled either with the tools of mathematics or with their more visual cousins, graphical methods. We will put ours together by graphs. Graphical models are easier to understand than mathematical models. And, they do most of the same things.

### Income-Consumption Effects

The first component is consumer demand. Demand for consumer goods depends on real DPI. In addition, demand for durable consumer goods depends on the real interest rate. Let us first focus on the income-spending relationship. Part (a) of figure 13.8 shows the income-spending relationship, identified as C. The vertical axis is real spending, and the horizontal axis is the real GNP. The relationship depicted by the C curve is called *consumption function.* The consumption function in figure 13.8(a) shows the amount of consumer spending that associates with each GNP level. For example, when total GNP is at 1,000, consumer spending is at 600, and when the GNP rises to 1,200, consumer spending rises to 740. Recall from our earlier discussion that consumer spending most directly relates to real DPI. However, figure 13.8 shows consumer spending related to the real GNP. Why? The real GNP consists of the total income earned by all parties involved in current production. (See chapter 4 for a refresher on this.) The real GNP includes all the real DPI earned by households. However, the real GNP reflects more than just household income. It is true enough that real DPI and real GNP usually rise and fall together. So we get basically the same picture in relating consumer spending to real GNP that we would get in relating it to real DPI. But, why this shift?

We have shifted to real GNP because we will soon add to this model the other parts of aggregate demand. When we add these parts, we will need a broader measure of total income than real DPI. To accommodate this, we use the less-precise relationship between consumer spending and real GNP depicted in figure 13.8.

The translation from real DPI to real GNP is not without costs. It hides from view an important aspect of the economy: the effect of taxes on spending. If income taxes rise, any specific real GNP level now produces a smaller amount of real DPI. The smaller real DPI leads to less consumer spending. For example, if real GNP is 1,000 and real DPI is 700, a 10 billion increase in income taxes does not change real GNP but reduces DPI to 690 billion. Accordingly, the new amount of consumer spending that corresponds to 1,000 of real GNP is less than before the tax change.

Graphically, the relationship between consumer spending and real GNP shifts when taxes are changed. To see this, start at position $C_1$ in part (b) of figure 13.8. At a real GNP of 1,000, consumer spending is at 600. Now, suppose we have a 50 billion increase in income taxes. The first effect is that real DPI falls by 50 billion. Suppose that this income drop leads to a decrease in consumer spending of 40 billion. Real GNP is unchanged. Thus, the 1,000 in real GNP now produces 540 in consumer spending instead of 600. Consumer spending is similarly lower at all levels of the GNP. The consumption function shifts down from position $C_1$ to position $C_2$.

### Real-Interest-Rate Effects

Earlier, we talked about how the real rate of interest influences consumer spending by affecting spending on consumer durables. The

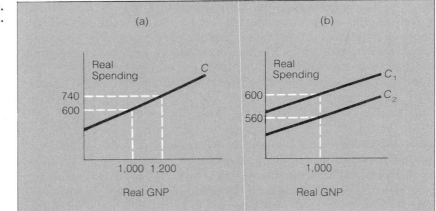

FIGURE 13.8.
Consumer Demand.

## CHAPTER 14

# How Much
# Will Be Produced
# —The Simplest Case

## CHAPTER OUTLINE

## IMPORTANT TERMS

labor-force capacity
plant capacity
$y = E$
product market equilibrium
inventory–sales ratio
intended inventory changes

income—expenditure multiplier
autonomous spending
induced spending
$1/(1 - b)$
production function

## MEMO

To:        All readers
From:      JWE

The aggregate-demand model of the last chapter is an important part of the contemporary macroeconomic model. But demand is only part of the process that determines the level of real GNP that will be produced. As we continue to develop the full explanation of how production, employment, prices, and interest rates are determined, experience shows it is preferable to do things one step at a time. This chapter takes the first of several steps toward the complete picture. In it, an explanation of how the GNP is determined is developed under the assumptions that (1) interest rates do not change because of other changes occurring in the economy, and (2) prices do not change because of other changes occurring in the economy. Neither of these assumptions holds in the real world. So why make them? Because they lead to an easy starting point in formulating a model that explains rather than assumes both the level of interest rates and the level of prices.

There are times when changes in the economy have little impact on either interest rates or prices. In these times, a simple macroeconomic model such as the one described in this chapter will be useful in structuring your thinking about how the economy works. However, such times are not normal. Rather, they tend to develop when serious depression occurs. The model you will consider in this chapter has two uses: the first is as a vehicle to analyze economic behavior during times of depression, and the second is as a stepping stone to a model that applies to normal times.

---

The amount of products and services coming from the factories, mills, and shops in the United States is always changing. Why? We make a start in answering this question in this chapter.

"Demand calls the tune" is a phrase summarizing the idea that the main reason production rises or falls is that aggregate demand rises or falls. According to this view, firms that find sales outpacing production respond primarily by increasing production. Not that firms are always playing catch-up. Firms forecast the demand for their products. Many are willing to adjust their production up or down on the basis of these forecasts of market demand. Firms may expect demand to change as a result of observing demand actually changing, or they may be persuaded by forecasts that it will shortly change. In either case, it is the expectation of changing demand that leads to production changes in an aggregate-demand-governed economy.

There are limits to which demand governs production. These limits are established by the productive capacity of the economy. There is only so much factory space and so many labor hours available for use. When the labor force (see chapter 4) is basically fully employed, the economy is operating at its *labor-force capacity*. When plants and other work places are being fully utilized, the economy is at its *plant capacity*. Either of these capacities constrains the economy from translating changes in demand into changes in production. In pursuing the logic behind "demand calls the tune," we are assuming that capacity permits all changes to take place, we are assuming that excess capacity is present in terms of both workers and plants.

## AGGREGATE DEMAND AND PRODUCTION

Aggregate demand establishes the level of the GNP. This statement means we can use the aggregate-demand framework of chapter 13 to explain fluctuations in production. Figure 14.1 shows how. In it, the vertical axis shows real aggregate demand, which we denote by $E$. The horizontal axis is the real GNP, which we call $y$. Aggregate demand is the sum of consumer spending, $C$, investment spending, $I$, government spending, $G$, and net-export spending, $X$ (in symbols, $E = C + I + G + X$). Because $C$ rises with the real GNP, so does aggregate demand. Thus, $E$ is shown as an upward sloping function of $y$, just as in the last chapter. We also know from chapter 13 that the $E$ curve is positioned by the real interest rate, the tax level, the level of government spending, net exports, and the state of profit expectations.

Something new has been added beyond what we saw in the previous chapter. It is a dotted line, rising at a 45-degree angle. Along the 45-degree line, values of $E$ and values of $y$ are the same. As a reminder of this, the line is labeled $y = E$. To become familiar with this, take any value of GNP along the $y$ axis and project it up to the 45-degree line, then over to the $E$ axis. It will give the same value on the $E$ axis that you started with on the $y$ axis.

Let us look at some specific points in figure 14.1. Suppose firms expect aggregate demand to be 1,200. By following their forecasts, they will produce the same amount of real GNP. Thus, the real GNP is at 1,200. But at a real GNP of 1,200, aggregate demand, $E$, is only 1,100, as shown in figure 14.1. The expectations of firms have been too optimistic. Firms have overestimated market demand by 100. Accordingly, production will be cut back, as firms realign production levels with a lowered expectation of market demand. If firms cut back production by 100, yielding 1,100 instead of 1,200, spending falls also. At the lower real GNP, aggregate demand is less than 1,100. The imbalance is only partially corrected. Why? By cutting back produc-

FIGURE 14.1.
Aggregate Demand
and Production.

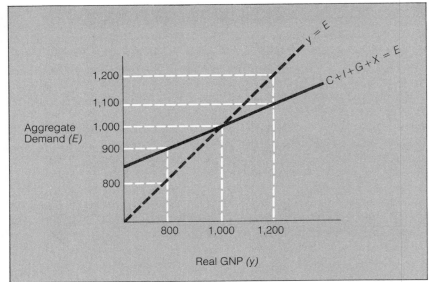

tion, firms pay out less income to workers and others. It is this cutback in income that lowers the demand below its former level of 1,100. The problem is not solved. What next? Cut back some more, until the real GNP falls to 1,000. At this level, producers' expectations are no longer incorrect. Aggregate demand is at 1,000 when production is at 1,000. If firms produce 1,000 of real GNP and pay out 1,000 in total incomes, enough demand will materialize to buy exactly the amount produced, not more and not less. $E$ equals $y$. If real GNP is less than 1,000, say 800, then demand exceeds the amount produced. At a real GNP of 800, total demand in figure 14.1 is 900. Spending exceeds production to the tune of $900 - 800 = 100$. Shelves in stores are depleted, orders flow to firms for replenishment, and production tends to rise. If firms increase production by the 100 shortfall, they will find it is still not enough, because higher income causes demand to increase. Only at 1,000 are the production and demand sides of the market in balance.

## PRODUCT MARKET EQUILIBRIUM AND INVENTORIES

The point where aggregate demand $(C+I+G+X)$ equals production is defined as *product market equilbrium*. Graphically, product market equilibrium occurs where the dashed line and the solid line in figure 14.1 cross. Equilibrium is where $E = C + I + G + X = y$.

Do you see how inventories fit into this picture? Whenever producers overestimate demand, they produce more than is being purchased. Inventories mount. When inventories of unsold goods become excessive, production is cut back. Inventories are brought back into line. On the other hand, when producers' expectations are too conservative, firms do not produce as much as is demanded. Inventories become depleted. Production is increased. Inventories are rebuilt. Thus when inventories fall below normal levels, it is a signal that pressures are mounting for an increase in production.

Figure 14.2 contains U.S. data that illustrate this point. The solid line is the quarterly change in production of durable and semidurable goods. It is calculated by subtracting from real GNP the following: (1) real government purchases, (2) real consumer services, and (3) real net exports. The remainder reflects the part of real GNP where inventories are maintained. The dashed line is the *inventory-sales ratio* in manufacturing and trade. Why ratio? Because when sales go up, firms intentionally make some additions in inventories. These *intended inventory changes* stand in sharp contrast to the unintended changes just discussed.

Intended inventory changes include additions of materials and components to be used to increase production. Work-in-process inventories (partially completed products) go up automatically when production is increased. Also, when more production and sales are anticipated, firms want to hold larger inventories of finished products. These intended inventory changes either occur as a by-product of changes in production and sales, or are changes firms want to make to respond to changes in sales. These changes do not indicate inventory imbalances.

Intended inventory changes tend to be closely related to sales. Thus, when we divide inventory levels by sales as in figure 14.2, we produce a measure of inventory position that takes into account most intended changes. For example, if inventories rise by 10 percent but sales also rise by 10 percent, it is quite likely that most of the inventory increase is because of the sales increase and is intended. In this case, the ratio of inventories to sales is unchanged. We receive no "warning

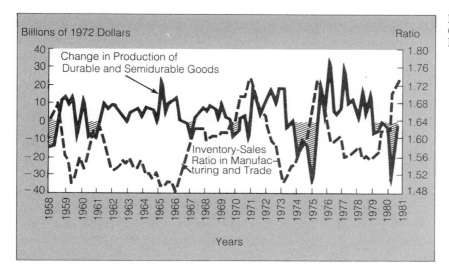

**FIGURE 14.2. Output annd Inventories.**

lights." However, when the inventory-sales ratio goes up or down to any significant degree, we can interpret the pattern as being mostly unintended. It is a warning light that firms' production levels and the economy's demand are inconsistent.

With this understanding of the inventory-sales ratio and of inventories output, you can see that figure 14.2 pretty much bears out our discussion of the role of inventories. When output falls, as in 1960, 1966, 1969–70, 1973–75, and 1979–80 (indicated by the cross-hatched areas), a rise occurs in the inventory-sales ratio. In other words, when unwanted inventories pile up, production falls. On the other hand, when production is going up, the inventory-sales ratio is usually going down. The years 1975–76 are good examples of this. The indication is that inventories are dropping below their intended levels in such cases.

We do not see much of a lead-lag pattern in figure 14.2. Most of the time when output falls, the associated rise in the inventory-sales ratio is concurrent with it rather than in advance of it. The same is true of the patterns of rising output and falling inventory-sales ratios. Thus, it is appropriate to view movements in inventory-sales ratios as symptoms of evolving changes in the production of inventories goods rather than as indicators of upcoming changes in production.

## THE MULTIPLIER EFFECT

Earlier in this chapter you read:

> At a real GNP of 800, total demand in figure 14.1 is 900. Spending exceeds production to the tune of $900 - 800 = 100$. Shelves in stores are depleted, orders flow to firms for replenishment, and production tends to rise. If firms increase production by the 100 shortfall, they will find it is still not enough, because higher income causes demand to increase. Only at 1,000 are the production and demand sides of the market in balance.

This passage is about the *income-expenditure multiplier*, often shortened to *the multiplier*. The multiplier has to do with the association between new spending in the economy, production, and the resulting induced demand. More production creates more income which leads to more spending.

The type of "new spending" is important. Spending that initiates multiplier effects is *autonomous spending* in that it is independent of current economic activity. It is not spending that takes place because people have more income. That would be *induced spending*. Autonomous spending affects the economy but is not affected by it.

Suppose capital investment spending (autonomous) rises by 100. Production goes up by this same amount, as does total new income. This 100 in new income does not all go to consumers. In the United States, about 70 of the 100 increase would typically be in the form of real DPI, and real DPI is what counts in consumer spending. The other 30 would be in the form of taxes and corporate/personal profits. The increase of 70 in real DPI tends, on the average, to stimulate consumer spending by about .9 of the increase, or .9 × 70 = 63. Thus, the 100 in new real GNP winds up increasing consumer spending by about 63. The ratio of induced consumer spending to new real GNP is 63 ÷ 100 = .63.

However, this is not the end of the multiplier story. The 63 in induced consumer spending stimulates a further increase in production and income. Suppose production is increased by 63 to match the increase in demand. This increase in production/income leads to a further rise in induced consumer spending of .63 × 63 = 39.6. This spending increase leads to another increase in production, and the multiplier process goes on, with the amount of increases at each step becoming smaller. (Each increase is 63 percent of the last increase.) Finally, the effect fades out. But by the time it does this, it has produced an amount of total production that is a multiple of the original autonomous spending. *The ratio of the total real GNP produced by an autonomous-spending change to the autonomous-spending change itself is the multiplier.* The whole process is called the multiplier process.

This example is carried out further in table 14.1. The initial autonomous spending of 100 finally leads to 270 in total production before

**TABLE 14.1**
**Multiplier Effects**

| Step | New Autonomous Spending | New Production and Income | Induced Consumer Spending |
|------|------------------------|---------------------------|---------------------------|
| 1 | 100 ⟶ | 100 ⟶ | 63 |
| 2 | | 63 ⟵ | 39.6 |
| 3 | | 39.6 ⟵ | 24.9 |
| 4 | | 24.9 ⟵ | 15.7 |
| 5 | | 15.7 ⟵ | 9.9 |
| 6 | | 9.9 ⟵ | 6.2 |
| 7 | | 6.2 ⟵ | 3.9 |
| 8 | | 3.9 ⟵ | 2.5 |
| 9 | | 2.5 ⟵ | 1.6 |
| 10 | | 1.6 ⟵ | 1.0 |
| • | • | • • | • |
| • | • | • • | • |
| • | • | • • | • |
| Total | 100 | 270 | 170 |

it runs its course. The multiplier is $270 \div 100 = 2.7$. It also leads to an increase in consumer spending of $.63 \times 270 = 170$. The 270 in total new real GNP consists of the initial 100 of new spending plus another 170 of induced consumer spending.

How did I know that the 100 in new spending in table 14.1 would lead to 270 of new GNP? An algebraic formulation of the multiplier helps show how. The total amount of new spending can be broken into an initial autonomous part and an induced part. Call the new autonomous spending $dE_a$. (The $d$ means the change in the variable, $E$ stands for expenditure, and the subscript $a$ refers to autonomous.) Call the new induced consumer spending $dE_i$ ($i$ stands for induced). Call the total change in spending $dE$. The change in total spending equals:

**(14.1)**   $dE = dE_a + dE_i$

According to our model, when expenditures rise, production also rises. If the economy starts at equilibrium and then spending changes, equilibrium is not restored until production (real GNP) changes by an equal amount. Thus, as a condition for equilibrium:

**(14.2)**   $dy = dE$

where $dy$ means the change ($d$) in real GNP ($y$). Replacing the right-hand side of expression 14.2 by its parts gives:

**(14.3)**   $dy = dE_a + dE_i$

Expression 14.3 shows that in equilibrium, total production changes by the sum of the change in autonomous spending and induced spending.

Induced consumer spending rises with real DPI, which rises with the real GNP. In other words, $dE_i$ is a function of $dy$. In our earlier example, $dE_i$ was .63 of $dy$. Call this fraction of induced spending $b$. What we have just said is:

**(14.4)**   $dE_i = b \times dy$

Put that into expression 14.3 in place of the last term and you have:

**(14.5)**   $dy = dE_a + b \times dy$

Now, collect the $dy$'s on the left-hand side and you have:

$$dy - b \times dy = dE_a \qquad \text{or}$$
$$dy(1 - b) = dE_a \qquad \text{or}$$
**(14.6)**   $dy = 1/(1 - b) \times dE_a \qquad \text{or}$
**(14.7)**   $dy/dE_a = 1/(1 - b)$

Earlier, we defined the multiplier as the ratio of the total real GNP produced by an autonomous-spending change to the change itself. That is exactly the left-hand side of expression 14.7. Thus, the multiplier is equal to $1/(1 - b)$. In our example where $b = .63$, the mul-

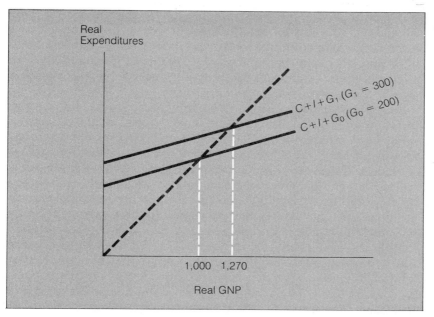

FIGURE 14.3.
Multiplier Effects.

tiplier is $1/(1 - .63) = 2.7$. The total effect of the 100 in the new autonomous spending is $2.7 \times 100 = 270$, according to expression 14.6.

To relate the multiplier to the graphical model, look at figure 14.3. For simplification, we will for now exclude net exports from the picture. If the initial position of the aggregate-demand curve is at $C + I + G_0$ where $G_0 = 200$, then in equilibrium, real GNP is 1,000. If the (autonomous) level of government spending rises by 100 to a new value of 300, the aggregate-demand curve shifts up by 100 to $C + I + G_1$. But, equilibrium real GNP rises not by 100 but by 270 to a new value of 1,270. The ratio of the added real GNP to the change in autonomous expenditure is 2.7[1]. The effect would be the same for any autonomous-spending change that would shift the aggregate demand curve upward. Examples are an increase in capital investment and a change in attitude by households.

## PRODUCTION AND EMPLOYMENT—
## HOW DO THEY RELATE?

Economic policies are often discussed and judged on the basis of their consequences for employment and unemployment. "What can/should /will the government do about the unemployment problem?" is a group of questions you hear a lot. There is much more public concern

1. The slope of the aftertax aggregate-demand function is $b$. It shows how much additional spending will occur for each dollar of additional real GNP. If $b$ is larger, the multiplier will be larger, and the aggregate-demand function steeper.

and debate about employment than there is concerning "What can /should /will the government do about the real GNP?" And, for good reason. Employment problems are about people and paychecks. Real GNP problems sound more abstract. But are they? How do the two relate? Is there an entirely different set of ideas to explain employment?

In the United States and in most other advanced economic systems, total employment and the real GNP are closely related. The technical bridge between the two is called the *production function*. The economy's production function is the broad relationship between our total use of labor, physical capital, materials, and technology and the resulting real GNP. Labor, capital, materials, and technology are called inputs to the production function. The real GNP is the output. Thus, the economy's production function is a broad summary of the relationship between the inputs to production and the output of production.[2] Output changes when we change any of the inputs to the production function. If we increased only physical capital (plants and machinery) by, say, 10 percent, we could produce more real GNP. But that takes time. In the immediate time period (this quarter), firms cannot change their output to any significant degree by designing, building, and starting up brand-new plants. The lag in bringing new capital on stream is from one to three years (see chapter 13). In the immediate future, the main way firms change output is by changing the amount of labor they use. So, when we are analyzing economic behavior in the short-run, that is, this quarter, we can expect labor changes to be the main reason for output changes.[3]

How close is the actual connection between labor use and real GNP? Figure 14.4 is a scatter diagram showing the relationship between real GNP and the amount of total hours worked over six-month periods from 1950 to 1980. Like a well-worn clutch, the connection between labor use and real GNP is not without its slippages. People can work harder or not so hard. Energy can be conserved by using more labor in its place. The way we produce can be systematically changed when it is economical to do so. However, it is an impressive relationship. Employment and production do indeed rise and fall together. As a practical matter, we can talk about economic effects on real GNP and economic effects on employment almost interchangeably.[4] The im-

---

2. It is a summary because production does not take place at the level of the whole economy, but within factories and mills. Each of the many thousands of individual production processes in the nation has its own production function.

3. In other words, the main way firms have to change the amount they produce in the short-run is by hiring or laying off people. Over longer periods, they can either build new plants or sell the ones they have. But in the immediate future, layoffs and production cutbacks go together and production increases and hiring programs go together.

4. Or, you can treat the two as absolutely interchangeable if you want to be almost right.

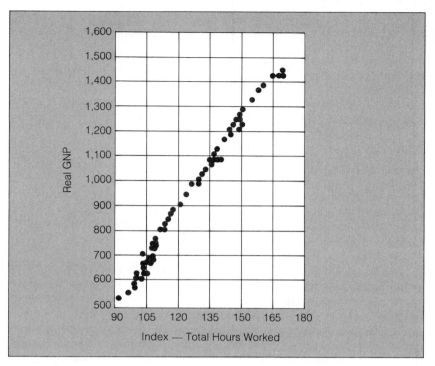

**FIGURE 14.4.**
**Output and**
**Employment in the**
**United States.**

plication in terms of our model is that changes in demand largely govern changes in both the real GNP and the amount of labor employed. In talking about multiplier effects on real GNP, we also are implicitly talking about the same effects on employment.

The multiplier effect has an important impact on the way government spending influences the economy. Our model (as shown in figure 14.3) now illustrates that when government spending rises, the aggregate-demand curve shifts and the real GNP goes up by a multiple of the government-spending increase. Employment goes up with the rising real GNP. Therefore, government spending has a clearcut effect on jobs. So do tax changes. When income taxes are reduced, the amount of real DPI increases for each and every level of the real GNP. The figure-14.3 model accounts for this effect by a shift in the aggregate-demand function. For a tax cut, the aggregate-demand curve shifts upward. As this happens, the equilibrium real GNP rises, and actual output is increased to the new equilibrium point. Jobs increase.

## SOME MISSING INGREDIENTS, AND THE TASK AHEAD

The conclusions about how government spending and taxing impact on real GNP and employment emerge clearly and simply from the model now constructed. Therein is a cause for suspicion. Some very important ingredients in any "economic stew" are missing from the model of the economy shown in figure 14.3. These missing ingredients may be affecting the conclusions just reached on the role of government in the economy. Three particular missing ingredients stand out: the level of prices and the inflation rate; the level of interest rates; and the amount of money in the economy.

We have not talked about any role for prices in our model. Instead, we have proceeded as if prices could be counted on to remain constant while aggregate demand shifts and production changes. Since in reality prices do not remain constant, we must at some point add them to the picture. We shall do so in the chapters to follow. We have also proceeded as if shifts in the aggregate-demand curve will not affect interest rates. But observation of financial markets suggests this may not be the case in the United States. Thus, interest rates need to be considered also. Finally, in our description of equilibrium real GNP and employment, we have made no reference to how much money is circulating through the economy's financial markets, and is in the wallets and accounts of the public. This means that so far we have not considered how changes in the stock of money influence economic activity.

In the following two chapters, we shall interweave the roles of prices, interest rates, and the money supply into our economic model. It will complicate matters somewhat. However, it will be worth it, because it will produce a more refined and more nearly correct approach to evaluating questions such as the role of government spending and taxing in the economy.

In the next chapter, we will take up the related questions of the role of interest rates and the supply of money in the macroeconomy. We will continue to ignore prices in this discussion, in order to take things one step at a time. In the chapter to follow, the impact of prices on our economic model will be the center of attention.

## Important Ideas in This Chapter

**1.** The main assumption about the relationship between aggregate demand and the amount produced is that "demand calls the tune." In other words, fluctuations in aggregate demand are the primary reason for fluctuations in the amount produced.

**2.** The equilibrium value of total production is where $y = E$, that is, where the level of real GNP produced is the same as the level of aggregate demand.

**3.** Inventories are the buffer between changes in demand and changes in production. When demand rises faster than production, inventories fall below intended levels. When demand lags behind production, inventories mount beyond intended levels.

**4.** Because consumer spending rises with real DPI and the GNP, new autonomous spending in the economy has a multiplier effect on total real GNP produced. As more is produced, more spending occurs, leading to more production. The income-expenditure multiplier is the ratio of the total real GNP produced by an autonomous-spending change to the autonomous-spending change itself.

**5.** The amount of real GNP produced and the amount of labor hours employed are closely related in the United States. The relationship is summarized by the production function, which is the association between inputs to production and the amount of production. Therefore, explanations of how real GNP is set are also explanations of how employment is set and vice versa.

**1.** Will the inventory-sales ratio always, usually, or seldom rise during a recession? Explain.

**2.** Does an inventory buildup predict a recession or is it a symptom of a recession? What does the figure in the text indicate along these lines?

**3.** Is the multiplier affected when income-tax rates are changed? Explain your answer fully.

**4.** Does a change in government spending lead to a change in the multiplier? Explain.

**5.** How do changes in profit expectations impact on the macroeconomic model of this chapter? Show the effect graphically.

**Discussion Questions**

The original presentation of the ideas on economic equilibrium and the multiplier process is John M. Keynes, *The General Theory of Employment, Interest, and Money*, New York: Harcourt, Brace, 1936. However, this is tough reading for the noncommitted. More readable versions of this discussion can be found in most macroeconomic texts, such as that of Robert J. Gordon, *Macroeconomics*, second edition. Boston: Little, Brown and Company, 1981.

**Suggested Readings**

# Money and Interest Rates

## CHAPTER OUTLINE

## IMPORTANT TERMS

## MEMO

To:     All readers
From:   JWE

In the last chapter, we talked about how the real GNP was determined without reference to the supply of money available to the public to be used to buy and sell the goods and services that make up the real GNP. We also assumed that interest rates and prices did not change as a result of shifts in demand. We saw a role for interest rates in our model—they determine in part the level of capital spending—but interest rates were viewed as being set independently of the real GNP.

In this chapter, we develop our macroeconomic thinking further by developing the roles of interest rates and the money supply in the macroeconomy. We essentially view interest rates as being the result of comparing the public's demand to hold its financial wealth in the form of money with the amount of money available in the economy. From this perspective, we can place the role of money and the role of interest rates squarely into our emerging macroeconomic framework.

Demand calls the tune. $C + I + G + X = E$. The multiplier. $y = E$. These are all parts of the macroeconomic collage you have seen in the last two chapters. But where does money fit in? Answer: It fits into an important slot right in the middle of the macroeconomic scenario. To begin to see how money fits in, we first define money to be currency plus all checkable deposits. At each moment, there is a certain amount of money held in people's wallets and in the checkable deposits of individuals and firms. The amount of money actually held in this way is called the *stock of money*, or the *money supply*. All of the stock of money is held by somebody all of the time, and none of it is issued but unclaimed. However, occasions arise when the amount of money being held by people and firms is different from the amount they wish to hold. What if there is more money in circulation than people want in their wallets and checkbooks? How will they react? What determines how much money people will want to hold? These are the questions. Now, on to the answers.

## THE DEMAND TO HOLD MONEY

What influences the amount of money people and firms want to hold? In other words, what determines the public's *demand for money*? Before we answer this, one important distinction needs to be made. Money is not the same as income. Income is purchasing power earned through production. Money is the purchasing power you are holding in your wallet and in your checkable deposits. We can safely assume your demand for income is infinite. You would always prefer more to less. But this is not true concerning your demand for money. There are definite limits on the proportion of your financial resources you want to have in your wallet and in your checkbook. Exploring what determines this limited demand for money is our present concern.

## Transactions and the Demand for Money

An economic transaction occurs when you buy or sell a good or service. The amount of money that people and firms want to hold rises and falls with the number of transactions they make. As people buy more consumer goods and services, they find it convenient to hold more cash and bigger checking accounts. As the volume of business transacted by firms increases, the firms increase their demand to hold money.

To see the reasoning behind this, let us look at the spending habits of two men. One buys $3,000 worth of goods and services per month. The other buys $1,500 worth. Suppose they both have $300 of money on hand in their wallets and in their checkbooks at the start of a typical month. To make the example simple, let us assume that both spend evenly during the month. The month has thirty days. The big spender spends $3,000 ÷ 30 = $100 per day. The small spender spends $1,500 ÷ 30 = $50 per day. After three days, the big spender has spent all of his money holdings, and has to go to his broker and to the bank for more. How does he get more? He sells some of his holdings of bonds, notes, and savings certificates and puts the money into his checking account. The small spender can go six days before his money is exhausted. Then he has to do the same thing. To keep money balances at or below $300, the big spender will have to go to the bank to sell notes ten times within the month (every three days means ten times a month). The small spender will have to go to the bank five times. This means that the big spender experiences more inconvenience and spends more time in keeping his money balances as low as the small spender's balances. Most big spenders say who needs it? The tendency in the real world is for those making more transactions to avoid the extra time and inconvenience by holding larger money balances than those buying less. Firms behave the same way. Firms doing a large volume of business normally carry larger balances of money than smaller firms.

## Real or Nominal Values?

*Real money demand* means the demand to hold an inventory of purchasing power. Purchasing power is the ability to buy goods and services. If prices go up, people's money holdings have to rise just so the same purchasing power is maintained. For example, if prices rise by ten percent, people need ten percent more money holdings to keep their nest egg of purchasing power constant.

In our discussion of the effect of transactions on the demand for money, we mean the demand for real money holdings. Here is the thinking. The demand to hold money rises with the volume of transactions made. Money is a buffer between earning purchasing power and spending it. If higher prices require that people have more dollars to make the same volume of transactions (that is, to buy the same goods), then the amount of money people want to hold rises in proportion, so that the amount of goods that can be bought with the money held stays the same. For example, if prices doubled, our earlier $3,000 spender would now require $6,000 to make the same transactions. If he kept his money holdings at $300, while buying $6,000 worth of goods and services, he would have to go to the bank to shift assets around every one or one-and-a-half days instead of every three days. After the price rise, the big spender holds only one to one-and-a-half days worth of purchasing power. Clearly, the demand for money by the big spender would rise until he was content with the amount of purchasing power being held as money. Thus, money demand is a demand for real money balances.

Similarly, the stock of money relevant to our analysis is the *real money supply*, found by dividing the actual money supply by the general price level. Thus, if the actual supply of money increased from 200 billion to 400 billion over a certain period of time, but the price level also doubled (from an index value of 2.00 to an index value of 4.00), then the real money supply remained constant at 100 over the time period. It would take 400 billion actual dollars to buy the same goods and services at the end of the period that 200 billion would have bought at the start of the period.

## Money Demand and the Real GNP

When we think about the total real demand for money by all concerned in the economy, we need a similarly broad measure to reflect the effects of transactions on money demand. The real GNP is by now a friendly term. It is commonly used to measure the effect of transactions on the total real demand for money.[1]

The influence of the volume of transactions on the demand for money is called the *transactions demand for money*. What we have said so far can be summarized like this: The transactions demand for money is an upward-sloping (positive) function of the real GNP. The higher

1. The GNP does not measure all transactions. Financial dealings, transfers, and trading in used goods are examples of transactions omitted from the GNP. However, trends in GNP transactions probably reflect most of the patterns in these omitted transactions. Thus, the GNP can be viewed as an index of a more complex measure of transactions.

the real GNP, the more money will be demanded by those making the larger transactions. A falling real GNP reduces the amount of money demanded, since firms are doing less business and consumers are buying less.

## Interest Rates and Money Demand

We talked earlier about convenience and trips to the bank as reasons why people who make more transactions hold more money. But why not hold all your financial assets in the form of money? Then there would be no inconvenience at all! The answer is that deposits that can be used as money do not earn as high a rate of interest as other financial assets. Thus, holding your whole bundle of purchasing power as money will cost you income.

For our purpose, a *money deposit* is defined as any type of checkable account that can be directly used for transactions. Examples are checking accounts, checkable savings accounts, share-draft accounts, and money-market funds. All these except traditional checking accounts pay interest. Thus, money deposits in general pay interest. However, the rate of interest on money deposits will always be lower than depositors could earn elsewhere. Why? Because money deposits do not just provide interest income to their holders. They also provide the transactions services of money. In other words, they can be used to pay bills. Financial assets such as short-term notes, savings certificates, and commercial paper provide interest income but do not offer transactions services. Thus, the short-term financial assets have to provide more interest income than the money deposits to be equally attractive to money holders.

Are you convinced that short-term notes tend to have a higher interest rate than money deposits? If not, put yourself in this spot. Suppose you have $1,000 that you plan to spend during the next month in more or less a steady stream. Two options are available. The first is to put the $1,000 into a checkable savings account earning 6 percent. Then you write checks on it as the month progresses. The second is to lend it out in the form of a series of short-term notes that can be redeemed as you need them. All you need to do is visit the bank and sign a redemption form. Then you take the money (from the redemption of the note) and put it into your regular checking account and write checks on it. If the interest you could earn on the notes was the same 6 percent you get on the checkable savings, which would you choose? Most people would choose the checkable savings account every time. The rate is the same on both but the checkable savings account also gives direct transactions services—no need to go to the bank.

If money deposits and short-term notes both actually yielded 6 percent, short-term notes would go the way of the dinosaur. This analysis is reason enough to argue that the two rates will not be the same. Various depository institutions set the rate on most money deposits. Investors in the credit market set the rate on short-term notes. Supply and demand will prevail. The rate on short-term notes will rise enough above the rate on money deposits to make the two comparable in the eyes of investors. Suppose the rate on short-term notes is stable at 8 percent when the rate on checkable savings is at 6 percent. This tells us that 2 percent is enough of a difference in interest rates to compensate holders of short-term notes for the loss of money services they incur.[2]

The point of all this is very general. *Short-term financial assets that do not offer money services will generally have higher interest rates than money deposits.* Understanding this point paves the way for understanding how and why interest rates impact on the demand to hold money.

When interest rates on short-term financial assets rise compared with money-deposit rates, the relative attractiveness of the two alternatives is altered. Financial assets now look more appealing to holders of money deposits. If the interest-rate difference between checkable savings and short-term notes was 2 percent and now has gone up to 4 percent, some holders of the checkable deposits decide to switch funds out of money deposits and into financial assets. As they switch, the demand for money falls.

The same idea can be expressed this way: with higher interest rates on short-term financial assets compared with money deposits, there is simply more of a reward to depositors for putting up with the added inconvenience and maybe the added brokerage and other transactions costs of the financial assets. Thus, a rising interest-rate difference convinces a steady stream of holders of money deposits to switch. The demand for money falls as the short-term interest rate rises compared with the rate on money deposits.

There is a tendency among depository institutions in the United States not to change the rate of interest on money deposits very often. For a simple, yet reasonably accurate, picture of money demand in the United States, we can assume the rate of interest on money deposits is an autonomous variable. Then, short-term fluctuations in the difference between rates on financial assets and rates on money deposits are mostly a result of fluctuations in the rate of interest on financial assets. We will not make much of an error in assuming that when the rate of interest on short-term financial assets changes, the demand for money changes in the opposite direction.

## Real Rates or Nominal Rates?

Earlier in this chapter, we talked about real money demand. Still earlier, in chapter 5 and beyond, we distinguished between real in-

2. As financial institutions make assets such as CDs and repo's (see chapter 5) more easily convertible into money deposits, the cost of money services goes down, and the interest-rate difference between such assets and money deposits gets smaller.

terest rates and nominal rates. These distinctions raise a question: Is it real or nominal interest rates that influence the demand for real money balances? The answer is that it is nominal rates.

Let us pursue the reasoning. You get the real rate by subtracting from the nominal rate the expected rate of inflation. Suppose that money deposits pay no interest. The options are to hold either zero-interest money or interest-bearing financial assets. Suppose the nominal interest rate on the assets is ten percent and the inflationary expectation is ten percent. The real rate is zero. If the real rate is what motivates the money holder, then shouldn't the financial asset be seen as giving no return, while money deposits provide transactions services? Does this mean there is zero demand for the financial assets? The answer is no, because the money deposits do even worse—they provide a negative real return. If money earns a zero rate of interest while prices go up by the expected ten percent, then money held now will buy ten percent less later—money's real return is $-10$ percent.[3]

This example shows that the relevant interest-rate comparison between money and financial assets involves the expectation of inflation in both of the interest rates concerned. We can compare the nominal return on financial assets against the nominal return on money, or equivalently, the real return on financial assets against the real return on money. It comes to the same thing. The gap between the return on financial assets and the return on money is the same whether we think in nominal or real terms.[4] Since nominal interest rates are observable whereas real rates can only be approximated, the weight of logic and reason comes down on the side of the nominal rate as the better of the two. Thus, the interest rate that influences the demand for money is a nominal one.

So far, we have reasoned that the demand for money rises, as the real GNP rises and falls, as the nominal interest rate rises. In figure 15.1, these two influences on money demand are assembled into a graphical money-demand function. The interest rate is on the vertical axis and the demand for real money is on the horizontal axis. When real GNP equals some specific level $y_0$, the money-demand function is in the left-hand position labeled $y_0$ on the graph. With real GNP at $y_0$, the demand for money decreases as the interest rate rises, and vice versa. At an interest rate of 6 percent, the demand for money is 340 when $y = y_0$. If the interest rate goes up to 8 percent, the demand for money falls to 332, again assuming $y = y_0$.

If the real GNP increases, the money-demand function in figure 15.1 shifts. If the real GNP goes up from $y_0$ to $y_1$, more money is demanded at all interest rates. For example, when the interest rate is

3. Why would depositors hold money or any other asset on which they expect to earn a negative real return? Because, in the case of money, people receive transactions services that are valuable enough to make up the negative difference and make money as attractive as other assets.

4. In our example, the score is either 10 to 0, or 0 to $-10$.

To: Money—demand skeptics
From: JWE

Do you think all this about managing money balances is a bit hypothetical? People worrying about how much interest they are losing out on and shifting their balances around to capture every last fraction of a percent—is it so much Alice-in-Wonderland stuff? No—if anything, it may be getting more nitty gritty than our discussion suggests. I know of several U.S. corporations that have diversified manufacturing divisions which manage their cash position centrally. And, do they. Each evening the division zeros out its checking account, wiring the funds to the central office in New York. The next morning, the central office is advised of how much cash the division needs for the day. That amount is wired back to them. Under this system, firms can keep the absolute-minimum total cash balances, and in addition, lend them out overnight from New York.

Even households have been getting in on the act. Since money-market mutual funds "went public" in late 1975, the amount of household savings going into them increased from zero to more than 200 billion dollars in 1982. That is one of the biggest shifts in household assets in history. It did not happen because of any fad—it was a straightforward attempt to get more interest income. Overnight repurchase agreements (chapter 5) are another example of close management of cash by firms.

6 percent, the demand for money rises from 340 at $y_0$ to 360 at $y_1$. Graphically, the money-demand function shifts to the right, from position $y_0$ to position $y_1$. If income rises further, from $y_1$ to $y_2$, the demand for money at 6 percent increases further, from 360 to 375. The curve shifts into the position labeled $y_2$. Thus, in figure 15.1 *we represent the income effect on money demand by a shift in the function, and the interest-rate effect on money demand by a movement along the function.*

## MONETARY EQUILIBRIUM

*Monetary equilibrium* occurs when the real demand for money equals the real amount of money outstanding. In equilibrium, the real GNP and interest rate are at levels that cause people and firms to be happy with their money holdings. Figure 15.2 helps us understand equilibrium by depicting it graphically. In figure 15.2, the money-demand function is in the position labeled $y_0$. The real supply of money is 340 billion. We assume the money supply is a fixed amount, established as a result of Federal Reserve policy. It is not influenced by interest rates. Thus, the money supply enters figure 15.2 as a vertical line positioned at 340 billion dollars. When the real GNP is $y_0$ and the

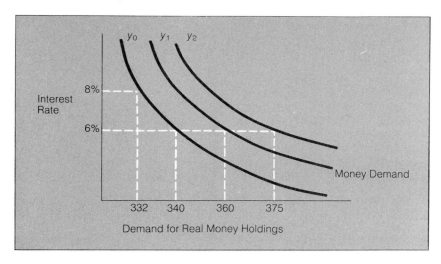

FIGURE 15.1.
Money Demand.

interest rate is 6 percent, the demand for money equals the money supply, and equilibrium occurs.

Adjustments occur when the supply of money differs from the amount people and firms want to hold. Suppose the economy is in monetary equilibrium and the Federal Reserve adds new bank reserves through open-market policy. Banks quickly convert these new reserves into loans and checkable deposits. Since checkable deposits are part of the money supply, these actions by banks increase the money supply. Let us say the result is a 5-billion-dollar increase in the money supply. Figure 15.3 shows the change graphically. Before the money-supply increase, monetary equilibrium occurred at 6 percent and $y_0$ when the demand for money was 340 billion. But the money supply shifts to the new level of 345, and now exceeds the demand. People and firms respond by attempting to shift the extra

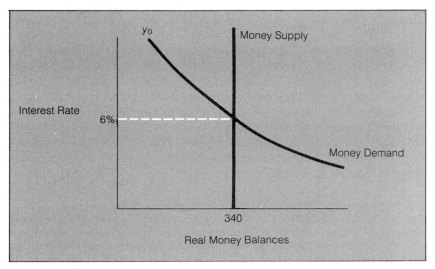

FIGURE 15.2.
Monetary
Equilibrium.

**FIGURE 15.3.
An Increase in the
Money Supply.**

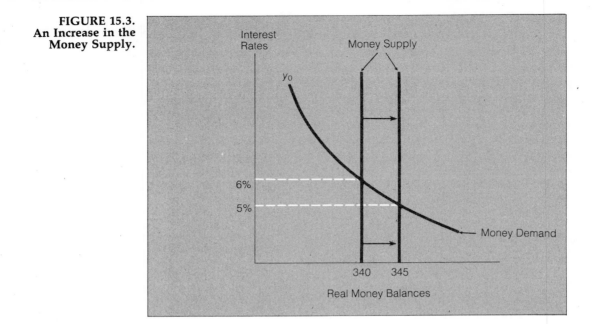

5 billion dollars in their accounts into financial assets. This increased
demand for financial assets drives up their prices, thus lowering their
yield. In other words, the response of money holders to the excess 5
billion dollars lowers interest rates.[5] Figure 15.3 shows that if the
interest rate falls to 5 percent, then monetary equilibrium is reestablished for the 345-billion-dollar money supply. The drop in the interest
rate from 6 percent to 5 percent has persuaded holders of money to
hold an additional 5 billion dollars.

　　Figure 15.3 shows that an increase in the money supply lowers the
interest rate if the real GNP stays the same. But does this actually
happen? In chapter 13 we found that if interest rates are lower, more
capital investment takes place. This added capital investment shifts
up the $C + I + G + X$ curve and increases the real GNP. Thus, when
the money supply increases, the resulting fall in interest rates leads
to a rise in $y$. Figure 15.4 shows this secondary effect. The figure is
identical to figure 15.3 except for the shift in the money-demand
function to the dashed position labeled $y_1$. Monetary equilibrium is
initially at 6 percent and $y_0$ when the money supply is 340 billion.
The addition of 5 billion dollars lowers the interest rate, which causes
$y$ to increase. When $y$ reaches $y_1$ and the interest rate falls to 5.5
percent, monetary equilibrium is reestablished.

5.  However, everyone does not succeed in reducing their money holdings. If you
feel you have more money in your checking account than you need, you may
respond by buying a savings certificate, and paying by check. Now, *someone else*
(the savings and loan association) has the excess cash balance. On it goes, stopping
only after the fall in the interest rates changes the minds of money holders.

At this point, we cannot say which is larger, the interest-rate effect or the real-GNP effect of a money-supply change. That will have to wait. However, our model of monetary equilibrium does indicate that when the money supply rises, interest rates fall and the real GNP rises.

## The LM Curve

Monetary equilibrium does not occur in isolation. It is related to aggregate demand in the market for goods and services. Specifically, if government spending, capital investment, or consumer demand shifts, monetary equilibrium changes. Let us examine this more closely. Suppose the $C + I + G + X$ curve (aggregate demand) goes up. Given our present model, so does real GNP. As the real GNP rises, the transactions demand for money increases. This makes the demand for money greater than the supply. For monetary equilibrium to be restored, interest rates must rise. Why? When there is no change in the money supply but an increase in the transactions demand, people attempt to increase their money holdings by selling financial assets. Prices of these financial assets fall. Interest rates rise.

Figure 15.5 illustrates this discussion graphically. In part (a), monetary equilibrium is shown for three successively larger real GNP values, denoted as $y_0$, $y_1$, and $y_2$. The real money supply is assumed to be set at 360 billion. So when the real GNP is $y_0$, monetary equi-

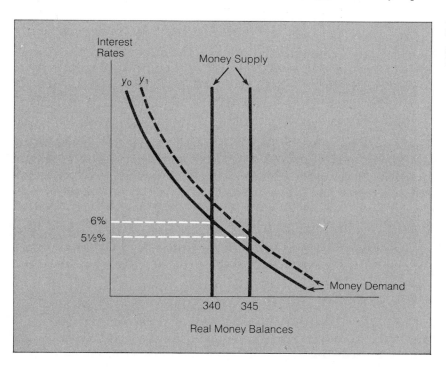

**FIGURE 15.4.
The Effect on GNP of an Increase in the Money Supply.**

**FIGURE 15.5.**
**Money Demand**
**and Supply.**

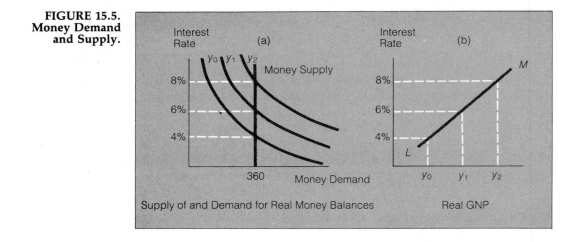

librium occurs at an interest rate of 4 percent. Now if the real GNP rises to $y_1$, the money-demand function shifts into the position labeled $y_1$. With the money supply still at 360 billion, the interest rate must rise to 6 percent to restore equilibrium. If the real GNP rises further, to $y_2$, an interest rate of 8 percent is required to establish monetary equilibrium. Figure 15.5 shows us that with a constant money supply, higher interest rates are required as the real GNP rises, if money demand and supply are to be kept in balance.

Part (b) of figure 15.5 shows how the interest rate and the real GNP relate when monetary equilibrium occurs. It is derived from the money demand and supply curve in part (a). On the vertical axis is the interest rate. On the horizontal axis is the real GNP. Part (b) plots the three monetary equilibrium combinations that are shown in part (a), and fills in all the ones in between by connecting the three points with a line.

The curve in part (b) is called the *LM curve* (because that is what its inventor, Sir John Hicks, named it). *The LM curve shows all the combinations of interest rates and real GNP levels that produce monetary equilibrium when the real money supply is unchanged.* The LM curve slopes upward. Why? Because as long as the real money supply is unchanged, meeting the transactions needs of higher real GNP levels requires higher and higher interest rates.

## CHICKENS, EGGS, AND ECONOMIC EQUILIBRIUM

The LM curve suggests that we need to know the real GNP in order to know where interest rates will stabilize. The LM curve is, after all, a functional relationship between interest rates and the real GNP under conditions of monetary equilibrium. But the reverse is also true. We need to know the interest rate in order to know the real

GNP, because (1) the interest rate has an important influence on capital spending, (2) capital spending is part of aggregate demand, and (3) real GNP adjusts to aggregate demand. Thus, we cannot possibly know where real GNP will stabilize without knowing the interest rate. Is there a chicken and egg problem here? You bet there is. In the model we are talking about, product market equilibrium and monetary equilibrium are jointly established. We cannot know each without the other. The interest rate and the real GNP are simultaneously determined.

Finding this simultaneous solution for the real GNP and the interest rate raises some complications. However, they are not severe. And we already have half of the tools for the solution in the form of the LM curve.

The LM curve shows the relationship between interest rates and the real GNP under conditions where real money demand and supply are equal. To complete the solution, we need a comparable relationship showing how the interest rate and the real GNP compare when aggregate demand equals production (that is, when $y = E$). With this relationship, we could see if there is a *particular* interest rate and real GNP that satisfies money holders and also equates aggregate demand with the real GNP.

## The IS Curve

We already have all the theory we need to construct a relationship showing how the real interest rate and the real GNP compare when $y = E$. In figure 15.6, part (a), the economy's aggregate-demand curve is shown in three positions. The reason for the different positions of the curve is changing real interest rates. When real interest rates are 5 percent, the aggregate-demand curve is in the lower position labeled

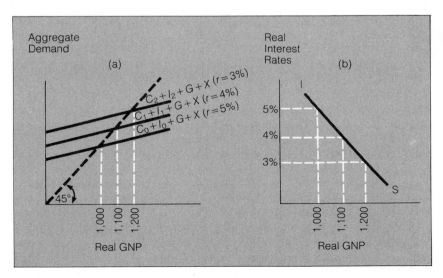

**FIGURE 15.6.**
**Aggregate Demand, the Real GNP, and the IS Curve.**

$r = 5$ percent. If the rate falls to 4 percent, the curve shifts up to the middle position, and if the rate is 3 percent, the curve rises to the upper position labeled $r = 3\%$.

The curve shifts when real interest rates change, because the demand for capital investment and for consumer durables are negative functions of real interest rates. Higher real rates curtail spending on consumer durables, housing, and capital goods. This is denoted in figure 15.6, part (a) by different values of $C$ and $I$ for each interest rate. $C_0$ is smaller than $C_1$, $I_0$ is smaller than $I_1$, and so forth.

In figure 15.6, part (a), an interest rate of 5 percent leads to an equilibrium real GNP of 1,000. A rate of 4 percent leads to an increase in the equilibrium real GNP to 1,100, and a 3 percent rate produces an equilibrium real GNP of 1,200.

In part (b) of the figure, the interest rates and corresponding real GNP values from part (a) are plotted one against the other. The points are then connected by a line. This is the missing curve. We call it the IS curve (again, because Sir John Hicks, its inventor, called it such). *The IS curve shows all the combinations of interest rates and real GNP levels that equate aggregate demand with the amount of real GNP produced.* The IS curve slopes downward. The downward slope is the result of our earlier theory about what determines spending on capital goods and on consumer durables. Lower interest rates lead to more of this type of demand. More demand leads to more GNP. For aggregate demand to be 1,200, the real interest rate must be 3 percent. If the real rate is 5 percent, aggregate demand will be 1,000.

The IS curve shows all interest rate-real GNP combinations that lead to product market equilibrium. The LM curve shows all interest rate-real GNP combinations that lead to monetary equilibrium. Is there a single interest rate and real GNP that satisfies both conditions? Yes, it is where the two curves cross. Where they cross is a single and unique interest rate-real GNP combination that is on both curves. Finding out where two curves cross is usually an easy matter—just put them on the same graph and look. However, there is one hitch that has to be resolved before we can correctly put these particular two curves on the same graph.

## Inflationary Expectations and the IS Curve

The hitch has to do with real and nominal interest rates. The interest rates influencing monetary equilibrium (the rates in the LM curve) are *nominal*. Those influencing product market equilibrium (the rates in the IS curve) are *real*. To put the IS and LM curves together, we must have the same kind of interest rate on the vertical axes of both curves.

The easy way out of this fix is to convert the IS curve's real rate into a nominal rate. The nominal rate equals the real rate plus the expected inflation rate. Thus, to convert the IS curve's real rate into a nominal rate, we have to add the economy's inflationary expectation to it. Are you wondering how this inflationary expectation is determined? People and firms determine it as they make decisions about spending, investing, and saving. They build and continually revise forecasts of the future inflation rate. The economy's inflationary expectation is the typical view of upcoming inflation held by people and firms that are making spending and saving decisions.

In the real world, people and firms use their expectation of inflation to translate the nominal rates they see in financial markets into the real rates that influence their spending decisions. We can do the same thing graphically. Look at figure 15.7. It is an IS curve, but now the interest rate on the vertical axis is a nominal rate. The real GNP is on the horizontal axis as before. Let us call this modification the *nominal IS curve*. Suppose for a moment that the expectation of inflation in the economy is zero—that is, people and firms are expecting *no* inflation ahead. In this case, the nominal rate and the real rate are the same. Suppose the IS curve is in position $I_0S_0$ initially. With the IS curve in this position, a real GNP of 1,000 and an interest rate of 3 percent produce product market equilibrium. Now, suppose the inflationary expectation goes up from zero to 5 percent. (People and firms have revised their forecasts of inflation from zero to 5 percent for the period ahead.) A nominal rate of 3% + 5% = 8% is now required to give a 3 percent real return. An 8 percent interest rate now produces the same spending and saving decisions as a 3 percent rate did when the inflationary expectation was zero. In figure 15.7, the same product market equilibrium that formerly occurred at a real GNP of 1,000 and an interest rate of 3 percent now occurs at a real GNP of 1,000 and an interest rate of 8 percent. In other words, the

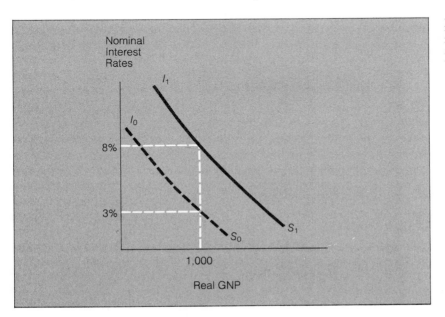

**FIGURE 15.7.
Inflationary
Expectations and the
IS Curve.**

IS curve has shifted into the position $I_1S_1$ as a result of the 5 percent inflationary expectation.

If inflationary expectations increase above 5 percent, the nominal IS curve shifts further to the right. If inflationary expectations decrease below 5 percent, the nominal IS curve shifts to the left. The bottom line: resolving the problem of real and nominal rates only requires remembering that when we use nominal rates in the IS curve, inflationary expectations help position this curve. When inflationary expectations change, the nominal IS curve shifts. If inflationary expectations go up, so does the nominal IS curve. If expectations go down, so does the nominal IS curve.

## PRODUCT AND MONEY MARKETS COMBINED

Interest rates and the real GNP: the two are jointly determined. Interrelating the IS and LM curves shows how. In figure 15.8, a nominal IS curve and an LM curve have been put on the same graph. Nominal interest rates are on the vertical axis and the real GNP on the horizontal. The two curves together make up the *IS–LM model.* Let us see how it works. At a rate of 6 percent and a real GNP of 1,200, equilibrium jointly occurs in both money and product markets. This point is where the two curves cross. It is the only combination of interest rates and real GNP that is common to both curves. We define *joint product market and monetary equilibrium* as the point where the IS and LM curves intersect.

In figure 15.8, no interest rate and real GNP other than 6 percent and 1,200 will last. Why? Because one of the two markets is out of equilibrium at any other combination. Take the combination 8 percent

**FIGURE 15.8.
The IS–LM Model.**

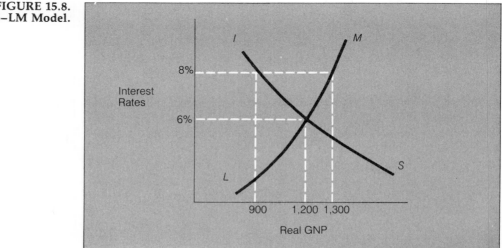

and 900. This produces equilibrium as far as product markets are concerned. It is a point on the IS curve. But it is not also a point on the LM curve. When the interest rate is 8 percent, monetary equilibrium occurs at a real GNP of 1,300. If the real GNP is actually only 900, then more money is being held in money balances than is demanded. The result is that interest rates will fall, until the excess money is all absorbed. However, as interest rates fall, movement along the IS curve occurs. Finally, at 6 percent and 1,200, everybody is happy. The amount produced and the amount demanded are the same, and the demand for money equals its supply. The message is that if any interest rate and real GNP combination occurs other than 6 percent and 1,200, adjustment takes place to move back to this point.

## Government Spending and the IS-LM

To illustrate how to use the IS-LM model, we return to our earlier example of an increase in government spending. In part (a) of figure 15.9, we show the simple aggregate-demand function. When $G = G_0$, the aggregate-demand curve is in the lower position and equilibrium real GNP is 1,000. Suppose that government spending goes up by 100 billion to $G_1$, thereby shifting the aggregate-demand curve to the higher position. Assume the multiplier is 2.7. Real GNP rises by

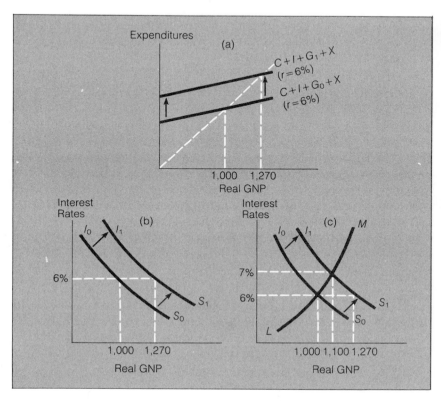

**FIGURE 15.9.
Impact of Government
Spending on the
IS–LM Model.**

# Memorandum

To: New owners of the IS–LM model
From: The factory representative

## OFFICIAL IS–LM OWNER'S MANUAL

Congratulations. You are now the owner of a quality product, the IS–LM model. Used wisely, it will give you years of economic understanding. This manual shows how to operate your new model and gives tips for its trouble-free use.

## ASSEMBLY AND ADJUSTMENTS

To set up your model, you need first to determine where to position the IS and LM curves. To position the IS curve, you need to know (1) the government spending level, (2) tax rates, (3) profit expectations, (4) net exports, and (5) inflationary expectations. With these, you can determine where to put the IS curve on the graph included with your model. Note: When any of these five variables change, you must reposition your IS curve to take the change into account. The following handy reference table may be cut out and kept beside your model to help in repositioning your IS curve when necessary.

| When this variable rises | Move the IS this way |
| --- | --- |
| government spending | to the right |
| tax rates | to the left |
| profit expectations | to the right |
| net exports | to the right |
| inflationary expectations | to the right |

*Note:* When any of these variables falls, the IS curve must be shifted in the opposite direction from that shown above.

To properly place your LM function on your graph, you first take the money-demand function from its shipping container, then carefully set it equal to the real money supply which was shipped to you separately from the Federal Reserve. Now you can position your LM curve. Keep in mind, if the demand for money increases, your LM curve will shift back to the left. Don't be alarmed. This is normal. If more money is shipped from the Federal Reserve, your LM curve must be shifted to the right. Otherwise, monetary equilibrium is disturbed and the model will malfunction.

## OPERATING INSTRUCTIONS

With your IS and LM curves positioned, the solution of your model is where the two cross. This gives the level of real GNP and the interest rate that jointly produces product market and monetary equilibrium. As long as the IS and LM curves are positioned as you have them, no changes will occur in the real

$2.7 \times 100 = 270$ to a new value of 1,270. The interest rate is 6 percent before and after the shift in government spending. The increase in government spending shifts the IS curve. Part (b) of figure 15.9 shows what happens. Before the shift, a 6 percent interest rate associated with 1,000 in real GNP. The IS curve was in position $I_0S_0$. Now, the 6 percent rate associates with 1,270. The IS curve has shifted to $I_1S_1$.

So far, we could have said as much without the IS-LM model. The shift to a new equilibrium at 1,270 is the same result we saw in chapter 14. But the LM curve adds a new dimension, as shown in

GNP or in interest rates. If changes occur in government spending, taxes, profit expectations, net exports, inflationary expectations, the public's preference to hold money, or the real supply of money, then either your IS or LM curve or both will shift. Then the real GNP and interest rates will change. The model will have moved to a new equilibrium. When the real GNP and/or interest rates change, other changes also take place in your model. To fully understand how your model works, you should be aware of these secondary changes. They are:

*When real GNP increases:*
- real DPI rises
- real consumer spending rises
- employment goes up
- the unemployment rate falls

*When interest rates rise:*
- capital spending falls
- consumer durables spending falls

MAINTENANCE AND SERVICING
Your model requires a minimum of servicing. However, you should be aware of predictable changes that will occur in it as time passes. First, as the population grows, as general living standards rise, and as new factories are brought on stream, your IS curve will shift slowly out to the right. This is normal and should not be a cause for worry. Similarly, you can expect the Federal Reserve to continually expand the money supply as time passes. You may also observe a steady decrease in the demand for money as time passes. People and firms are finding ever more efficient ways to use their money, and as they do this the demand-for-money function shifts to the left and the LM to the right. This problem is becoming more severe. As a result, the factory is considering a total recall of the money-demand function so safety changes can be made to eliminate the possibility that the function will fall off the right-hand side of the graph.

These slow rightward shifts in the IS and LM mean that it is normal for you to observe steady growth in the equilibrium real GNP produced by your model. However, various recent owners have advised the factory of other abnormal shifts as well. Occasionally, sharp changes in consumer attitudes cause the bottom to fall out of the automobile market. When this happens, your IS curve shifts sharply to the left and becomes quite unstable. The factory takes no responsibility for such a shift or the decline in real GNP that goes along with it. Similarly, unpredictable upswings and downswings occur in housing markets, and in markets for capital goods, both of which lead to sharp vibrations in the IS as well. These shifts occasionally cause a red "recession" light to come on. When this occurs, push the reset button and wait for a few months, and the light will go off. On rare occasions, the IS becomes so unstable that it falls off the graph entirely. If this happens, call your local factory representative immediately for servicing.

part (c) of figure 15.9. The original and shifted IS curves from (b) are redrawn, but now the LM curve is added. We can see that the original equilibrium of 6 percent and 1,000 no longer holds. The new equilibrium is at 7 percent and 1,100. Why didn't real GNP rise to 1,270? After all, isn't the multiplier 2.7? Part (c) shows that considering monetary equilibrium as well as product market equilibrium reduces the net expansionary effect of government spending. When the government demands 100 billion more goods, additional money is required to enable the new transactions to take place. However, the money supply has not changed. The needed money is lured out of the balances of money holders by a higher interest rate. The higher rate produces a cutback in investment and durable-goods spending. This spending is cut back by 170 billion (1,270 − 1,100) as a result of the interest rate rising from 6 percent to 7 percent.[6] When the government spends more, the monetary side effect is a cutback in private spending. The depressing effect of increased government spending on private spending is called the *crowding out* effect. There is still a net expansionary effect of the 100 billion in government spending. But the effect of the government spending is reduced by the crowding out effect.

## How Much Crowding Out?

The amount of crowding out that will occur depends on how steeply the LM curve rises. Look at part (c) of figure 15.9 and try to visualize this. If the LM curve is nearly vertical, then the monetary side effect will almost completely offset the government-spending increase. The net effect of the spending on the real GNP will be almost nil. On the other hand, if the LM curve is almost horizontal, there will be very little monetary side effect. Real GNP will rise almost to its maximum value of 1,270. Thus, how serious crowding out is depends on the steepness of the LM curve.

But, on what does the steepness of the LM curve depend? The LM curve gets its shape from the demand-for-money curve. Because the demand for money falls with the interest rate, the LM curve rises with it. If you are not convinced of that, go back to figure 15.5 and redraw the three money-demand curves in part (a) so that they fall more steeply. In doing this, you are making the demand for money *less sensitive* to the interest rate. (If it is steeper, money demand does not fluctuate as much when interest rates change.) Now, derive the LM curve in part (b) with your steeper money-demand curves. You should come up with this result: when the demand for money becomes less sensitive to the interest rate, the LM curve becomes more nearly vertical. Thus, the degree of crowding out in our model depends on how sensitive the demand for money is to the interest rate. If the demand for money is quite insensitive, then a lot of crowding out occurs. If the demand for money is quite sensitive to the interest rate, then very little crowding out occurs.

There is a logical reason why the degree of crowding out depends on the sensitivity of the demand for money to the interest rate. If the

6. If you do not see why 1,100 is subtracted from 1,270 here, notice that in part (c), when the IS curve is in the position $I_1S_1$, a 6 percent interest rate results in a real GNP of 1,270 whereas a 7 percent rate results in a real GNP of 1,100. So, the pure effect of the interest-rate increase is to reduce private spending by 1,270 − 1,100 = 170. The government-spending increase is a separate question, and the reason for the shift in the IS curve.

demand for money is completely insensitive to the interest rate, then the entire stock of money is held only for transactions. Accordingly, in monetary equilibrium, the whole stock of money is being used for transactions. No money can be made available for more transactions by pushing up the interest rate. As a result, the total number of transactions and the total GNP possible are *fixed* by the supply of money. Therefore, if the government wants to make more transactions, all other parties combined must make less.

On the other hand, if the demand for money is quite sensitive to the interest rate, then a small rise in the interest rate greatly decreases the desired money holdings, and enables a larger volume of transactions to take place. In this case, some parties can make more transactions without others making fewer transactions.

The monetary dimension added by IS-LM analysis shows that the simple conclusions reached in chapter 14 on the economic impact of government spending may be almost totally correct, partially correct, or almost totally incorrect, depending on the shape of the LM curve.

## Increasing the Money Supply

We have spent much of this chapter seeing how money fits into the macroeconomy. What does our model say will happen if the Federal Reserve puts more money into the economy? Suppose 10 billion is added to the money supply as a result of Federal Reserve open-policy actions. What happens? Figure 15.10 shows the impact on monetary equilibrium that occurs when the supply of money is changed.

Part (a) of figure 15.10 shows the economy's money-demand function for three real GNP values $y_0$, $y_1$, and $y_2$. The initial money supply is 360 billion. Monetary equilibrium occurs at interest rates of 4, 5, and 6 percent when the real GNP is $y_0$, $y_1$, and $y_2$, respectively. The resulting LM curve is shown in part (b) and labeled $L_0M_0$. When the 10 billion of new money is added, monetary equilibrium is disturbed.

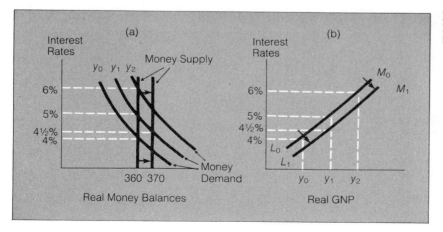

**FIGURE 15.10.
Increasing the Money Supply.**

# Memorandum

To: Those interested in seeing the theory expressed in quantitative terms
From: JWE

In this memo, the superstructure of the theory that has been discussed in this and the previous chapter is expressed in algebraic terms. What you read here lays bare the logical relationships in the models. Furthermore, it does so in a precise yet simple form. Nonetheless, this memo is no substitute for the words and ideas in this and the last chapter. Rather, it is a kind of algebraic shorthand that can help solidify what you have learned to this point. Our procedure is to form the basic relationships involved in the macroeconomic model, and then to assemble these relationships into a quantitative statement of equilibrium, first for the assumptions of chapters 13 and 14 and then for the assumptions of this chapter.

In chapter 13, the consumption function was defined as the relationship between consumer spending and consumer aftertax (or disposable) income. Denoting $C$ as consumer spending, $Y$ as gross income (the same as the GNP), and $T$ as all taxes paid, the consumption function can be written as:

**(1)** $C = \underline{C} + b[Y - T]$

where $b$ is a coefficient that shows how much C changes when a change occurs in $[Y - T]$, and $\underline{C}$ refers to the amount of consumer spending that is exogenous, that is, independent of current aftertax income. In what follows, underlined variables always refer to exogenous amounts and lowercased letters always refer to coefficients that have positive values.

In the discussion of aggregate expenditures in chapter 13, the level of business investment was taken as an exogenous variable, as was the level of government spending and net exports. Thus:

**(2)** $I = \underline{I}$

and

**(3)** $G + X = \underline{G}$

Taxes are assumed to be partly exogenous (such as property taxes) and partly determined by the level of gross income. Thus:

**(4)** $T = \underline{T} + cY$

In chapter 14, equilibrium was described as the condition where total expenditures equals the amount of income currently produced. Thus:

**(5)** $Y = C + I + G + X$

Substituting (1), (2), and (3), into (5) gives:

**(6)** $Y = \underline{C} + b[Y - T] + \underline{I} + \underline{G}$

Replacing $T$ in expression (6) by expression (4) produces:

**(7)** $Y = \underline{C} + bY - b[\underline{T} + cY] + \underline{I} + \underline{G}$

If we solve expression (7) for $Y$, the result is:

**(8)** $Y = \{1/[1 - b(1 - c)]\}\,[\underline{C} - b\underline{T} + \underline{I} + \underline{G}]$

Expression (8) shows that the equilibrium position of $Y$ is the result of a multiplier (the terms in the left-hand outer brackets) and a multiplicand, which consists of the values of all exogenous expenditures upon the economy, $\underline{C}$, $\underline{I}$, and $\underline{G}$, less the expenditure impact of exogenous taxes, $b\underline{T}$. (Recall from chapter 14 that a tax increase is not generally expected to reduce spending by the amount of the tax increase, but by the fraction of it that consumers normally spend.)

If all taxes are autonomous, then c is zero and the multiplier shown in expression (8) simplifies to $1/[1 - b]$, which is the same as that developed in chapter 14. When c is assumed to be nonzero, the term $(1 - c)$ can be seen to reduce the effective value of $b$ in the multiplier expression and thus reduce the multiplier effect. (Consider the extreme case where the tax rate, $c$, approaches 1. In this case, $b$ approaches 0 and the multiplier approaches 1. Gulp!)

This chapter incorporates into the earlier model the role of interest rates and the role of the money supply. To augment expression (8) to reflect these changes requires the addition of several new functions. The first of these functions deals with capital investment. Capital investment was earlier taken to be exogenous; now it is assumed to partly exogenous and partly a function of the real interest rate. Expression (9) shows this relationship:

(9) $I = \underline{I} - d[R - \underline{P}]$

where $R$ is the nominal rate of interest and $\underline{P}$ is the prevailing inflationary expectation. Notice that for this purpose we assume the inflationary expectation is exogenous. Although this may not be strictly true, it simplifies our present model building without introducing serious distortions. Notice also the minus sign preceding the $d$ coefficient. This indicates that the impact of the real rate on $I$ is negative.

To complete this expanded model, we must add the role of the demand for and supply of money. The demand for money, $L$, is assumed to be a positive function of the level of income and a negative function of the nominal interest rate. Since chapter 15 holds the level of prices constant, we will take advantage of this simplification by not even bringing the subject up. Rather than dealing with real money balances and real income, just keep in mind that movements in real and nominal variables are the same thing when prices are invariant. Thus, money demand is given by:

(10) $L = eY - fR$

The supply of money is assumed to be exogenous, that is,

(11) $M = \underline{M}$

Equilibrium in money markets is described as the condition where the supply of money equals the demand, as follows:

(12) $M = L$

or

(13) $\underline{M} = eY - fR$

Expression (13) can be solved for $R$ as follows:

(14) $R = [e/f]Y - \underline{M}/f$

Expression (14) is one way to state the LM curve algebraically. It could also be done by solving (13) for $Y$. A parallel representation of the IS curve results from inserting expression (9) into (8) in place of the value of $I$ which we previously assumed to be exogenous. Doing this gives:

(15) $Y = \{1/[1 - b(1 - c)]\} [\underline{C} - b\underline{T} + \underline{I} - d(R - \underline{P}) + \underline{G}]$

If we incorporate the LM curve of expression (14) into the IS curve of expression (15), the result is the algebraic equivalent of the position where the IS and LM curves cross—the joint product and money market equilibrium position. This is given by expression (16):

(16) $Y = \{1/[1 - b(1 - c) + de/f]\} [\underline{C} - b\underline{T} + \underline{I} + (d/f)\,\underline{M} + d\,\underline{P} + \underline{G}]$

Among the conclusions we reach from expression (16) are these:

**1.** Exogenous components of consumption and investment demand impact on the economy via a multiplier process, as do government spending and net exports.

**2.** The money supply impacts positively on the level of $Y$. The higher the money supply the larger the equilibrium $Y$.

**3.** The multiplier is affected by the coefficients in the money-demand function. The larger the value of the income effect on money demand, $e$, the smaller the multiplier. The larger the value of the interest-rate effect

(Memorandum continued on next page)

on money demand, *f*, the larger the multiplier.

**4.** The multiplier is also affected by the impact the interest rate has on investment spending. The larger the value of the interest-rate coefficient, *d*, the smaller the multiplier.

**5.** An increase in inflationary expectations produces a higher equilibrium *Y*, by lowering the real interest rate and stimulating investment.

Expression (16) gives the value of *Y* in equilibrium. A companion statement can be derived for the associated equilibrium value of *R*, since the two are jointly determined by the IS–LM framework. To derive this statement, we first solve (13) for *Y*:

**(17)** $Y = [f/e]R + M/e$

Since both (17) and (16) now give the value of *Y* in equilibrium, they can be set equal to each other and the resulting expression can be solved for *R*. Doing this gives:

**(18)** $R = \{1/[f(1 - b(1 - c)) + de]\} \{e \underline{C} - be \underline{T} + e \underline{I} + de \underline{P} + e \underline{G} - \underline{M} [1 - b(1 - c)]\}$

Here are some of the implications that result from expression (18):

**1.** Exogenous increases in consumer or investment spending will increase interest rates, as will rising government spending.

**2.** Tax increases will lower interest rates.

**3.** Interest rates will rise if inflationary expectations increase, that is, a positive relationship exists between the two.

**4.** Increases in the money supply will lower interest rates, since the $\underline{M}$ term enters the equilibrium expression with a negative sign. However, if an increase in the money supply leads to an increase in inflationary expectations, then the negative impact may be in part or all undone or even converted into a net positive impact.

The algebraic version of the IS–LM models has led to no new conclusions beyond those reached by shifting key curves in the graphical models studied in this and the previous two chapters. But it has provided a concise quantitative expression of some of the main ideas. If you want to explore some further implications of the equilibrium expressions (16) and (18), examine how equilibrium is affected if the interest-rate effect on money demand, *f*, is quite small, and if the interest-rate effect on investment spending, *d*, is quite small. Think about how the economy behaves differently in the two cases.

With the old money supply (360), a real GNP of $y_1$ and an interest rate of 5 percent equated the demand for money with the supply. But with a 10-billion-dollar larger money supply, 5 percent and $y_1$ are no longer equilibrium values. Part (a) shows that 4.5 percent and $y_1$ now produce monetary equilibrium. In other words, with more money, the same real GNP now associates with a lower interest rate in equilibrium. This means that adding more money shifts the LM curve to the right. Part (b) shows this shift. After the increase in the money supply, monetary equilibrium is at 4.5 percent and $y_1$, indicating that the LM curve has shifted to the dashed position labeled $L_1M_1$. So now we know that the LM curve shifts to the right when the money supply increases. We can deduce that it shifts to the left when the money supply is reduced.

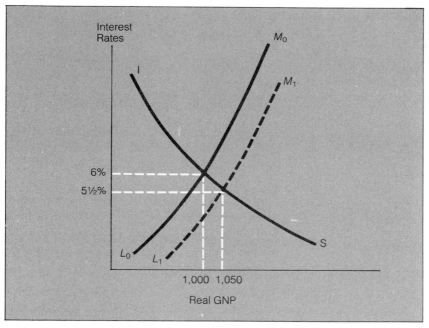

FIGURE 15.11.
Full Effects of an
Increase in the Money
Supply.

Figure 15.11 shows the total impact of an increase in the money supply. When the LM curve is in initial position $L_0M_0$, joint equilibrium occurs at 6 percent and a real GNP of 1,000. The 10 billion of new money shifts the LM curve to $L_1M_1$. The equilibrium real GNP goes up to 1,050 and the interest rate falls to 5.5 percent. The 10 billion increase in the money supply expands the real GNP and lowers interest rates. The larger real GNP generates more jobs and more real DPI, leading to an increase in consumer spending. The lower interest rates lead to more durable-goods and capital spending.

Adding the role of interest rates and the supply of money has increased both the complexity and the realism of our economic model. It has also altered some of the conclusions we reached in chapter 14 about how the economy works. Government is now seen to at least partially crowd out private spending when its own spending is increased. Changing the money supply is found to have effects on both interest rates and the real GNP.

But the model is still not complete. Throughout this chapter, we have reasoned from the assumption that the level of prices stayed constant while all the other changes were taking place. In the United States, that is not the case. Prices are an important part of the process by which the economy adjusts to changes in government spending, the money supply, and other autonomous variables. In the next chapter, we will examine how prices fit into our economic model.

**1.** Two major influences determine the demand for money: income and the rate of interest.

**Important Ideas in This Chapter**

**2.** Income influences the demand to hold money because more money is wanted by persons and firms when they make more transactions, and they make more transactions when income rises.

**3.** When we talk of money demand, we are talking about the demand to hold real money balances. Real money balances are nominal balances deflated by an index of general prices.

**4.** Short-term financial assets that do not offer the services of money will generally have higher interest rates than the rate on money deposits. The difference between the two in part measures the value of money services.

**5.** The rate of interest that counts in the demand for real money is a nominal rate, since nominal rates take into account the expected loss of purchasing power caused by inflation.

**6.** Monetary equilibrium occurs when the real demand for money equals the real amount outstanding. At this point, holders of money are content holding the stock of money in circulation.

**7.** When the demand for money does not equal the supply, both income and interest rates adjust until the demand for money is brought into line with the supply.

**8.** The LM curve shows all the combinations of interest rates and real GNP that produce monetary equilibrium when the real money supply is unchanged. The LM curve slopes upward, because meeting the transactions needs of higher real GNP levels requires higher and higher interest rates in order to keep monetary equilibrium.

**9.** The IS curve shows all the combinations of interest rates and real GNP levels that equate aggregate demand with the amount of real GNP produced. The IS curve slopes downward because higher real GNP levels require lower interest rates if the higher real GNP levels are to be sustained by higher aggregate demand.

**10.** The nominal IS curve relates nominal interest rates and the real GNP under conditions where product market equilibrium occurs. When inflationary expectations change, the nominal IS curve shifts.

**11.** The IS–LM model is the combination of the IS and LM curves. The IS–LM model specifies a unique interest rate and real GNP combination that produces joint equilibrium in monetary and product markets.

**12.** Addition of the LM dimension to our model shows that some crowding out occurs when government spending increases. When government spending increases, the IS curve shifts to the right. The amount of the crowding out depends on the shape of the LM curve. When the LM is nearly horizontal, little crowding out happens. When the LM is nearly vertical, almost complete crowding out occurs.

**13.** When the money supply is increased, the LM curve shifts to the right. In our model, the real GNP rises and the interest rate falls. Consumer spending goes up. Employment rises. Capital spending increases.

**1.** Can you think of any conditions where a negative nominal interest rate could be found in financial markets? Before answering, explain in your own words the meaning of a negative nominal interest rate.

**2.** How has the appearance of checkable deposits that pay interest influenced the demand for money? Could the interest rate on checkable deposits ever exceed that on commercial paper? Explain.

**3.** Assume that inflationary expectations are sharply revised upward as a result of the appointment of a new chairman of the Federal Reserve Board. How would this revision in expectations impact on the real GNP, interest rates, consumer spending, and jobs?

**4.** How will increasing the supply of money impact on real GNP, interest rates, and capital spending when the LM curve is (a) close to horizontal, (b) close to vertical? Show each effect graphically.

**5.** Use the IS–LM model to show how a collapse in the demand for automobiles impacts on the real GNP, interest rates, jobs, and consumer spending.

A fairly complete and yet readable book on both the theory and the evidence regarding the demand for money is D. Laidler's *The Demand for Money: Theories and Evidence, 2nd ed.* Regarding the IS–LM model, there is still no substitute for the original work by J. Hicks, "Mr. Keynes and the Classics: A Suggested Interpretation," *Econometrica* 5, April 1937, pp. 147–59. However, a more detailed development of the IS–LM model can be found in any contemporary macroeconomics text. See, for example, Robert J. Gordon, *Macroeconomics*, 2nd ed., Boston: Little, Brown, 1981.

## CHAPTER 16

# The Effect of Prices
# on Aggregate Demand
# and the Amount Produced

## CHAPTER OUTLINE

## IMPORTANT TERMS

price-demand curve
marginal product of labor (MPL)
real wage
MPL = W/P
demand-for-labor curve
supply-of-labor curve
downwardly rigid wages
aggregate-supply function

## *MEMO*

To:        All readers
From:      JWE

When the IS-LM model of the previous chapter is solved, the result is the equilibrium interest rate and the associated amount of real GNP to be produced. We have assumed in its development that prices are constant. It is now time to drop that assumption and examine what happens if prices change.

In this chapter we first examine how the level of aggregate demand is influenced by prices. Then we deal with the question of how the price level influences the amount of products and services that firms will be willing to supply to their markets. The role of prices in both aggregate demand and aggregate supply leads to an explanation of the level of prices that will be consistent with both demand and supply in the economy.

The amount of products that firms are willing to supply is importantly influenced by both prices and the cost of labor. It is unreasonable to suppose that firms will happily deliver to markets products on which they are making less profits than they could make by delivering either more or less. Prices and the cost of labor are important links in our analysis of the firm's supply decision. In developing this link, we must split our thinking into two parts. The first case is one in which wages are assumed to adjust efficiently to changes in labor-market conditions. The second case is where wages are assumed to be downwardly rigid. There are important implications associated with whichever of these cases is more nearly the case for the real world. In this and in later chapters, we develop these implications.

Prices. You cannot understand the full workings of the economy without understanding the role played by changes in the prices of products and services. Prices influence the position of the IS-LM curve, and by doing so influence the total amount of aggregate demand in the economy. Prices also affect the amount of production that firms find it profitable to supply to the nation's marketplaces. It is now time to examine how prices influence the economy.

## PRICES AND AGGREGATE DEMAND

In the last chapter, the LM curve was defined to be a graphical plot of all values of the real GNP and interest rates that balance the demand for real money balances with the real money supply. It is through the real money supply that prices have a direct impact on the LM curve and on IS-LM analysis. Since the real money supply is defined as the nominal stock of money, $M$, divided by an index of general prices, $P$, it is clear that if $M$ remains constant, an increase in $P$ reduces $M/P$. In other words, rising prices erode the purchasing power of the money supply, reducing its real value.

Figures 16.1 and 16.2 show the actual importance of this price effect on the $M_1$ money supply in the United States in recent years. In figure 16.1, the growth in the nominal or unadjusted money supply is shown. It has risen steadily over the entire period shown in the graph. In figure 16.2, this money supply is divided by the price level as measured by the GNP deflator. This shows that some substantial changes have occurred in the resulting real money supply, and that the real money supply has not always grown. In fact, notice that prices began rising at a clearly higher rate at about 1973, and this coincides with a sharp fall in the real money supply. It is no accident. Prices have tended to change more rapidly and in a more volatile way than the money supply. So, to a large degree, significant movements in the price level in the United States tend to become translated into opposite movements in the real money supply.

The effect of prices on the real money supply is important for IS-LM analysis, because when the real money supply changes, the LM curve shifts. In the last chapter, we saw that an increase in the real money supply shifts the LM curve to the right, whereas a decrease in the real money supply shifts the LM curve to the left. As the LM curve shifts, so does the interest rate and real GNP combination that

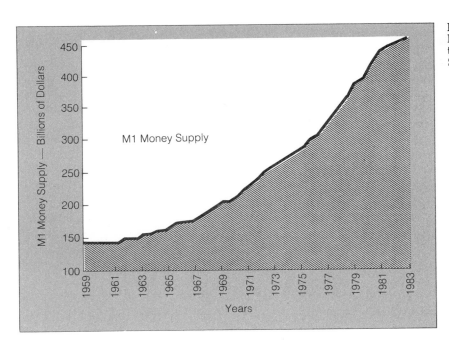

**FIGURE 16.1.
Pattern of Growth in
the M1 Money
Supply.**

**FIGURE 16.2.
The Real M1 Money
Supply and the
Price Level.**

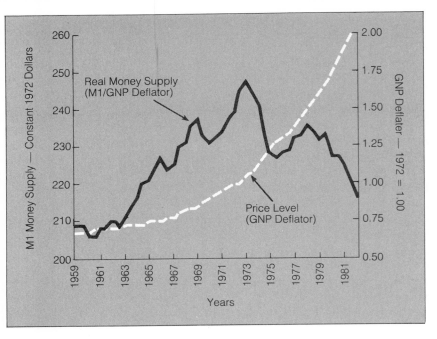

associates with IS-LM balance. Thus when prices change, the solution to the IS-LM model changes with it.

Figure 16.3 shows this situation graphically. With the nominal supply of money set at $M_0$, a price level of $P_0$ produces a real money supply of $M_0/P_0$ which positions the LM curve at the point where equilibrium real GNP is at $y_0$. If prices rise to $P_1$, the real money supply is reduced to $M_0/P_1$ and the LM curve shifts back to the left to the point corresponding with $y_1$. A further increase in prices to $P_2$ leads to a further shift of the LM curve and to a further reduction in the IS-LM solution point to $y_2$. Thus, rising prices reduce the IS-LM equilibrium value.

To understand why this effect occurs, focus on what is happening to interest rates during periods of rising prices. When prices rise from $P_0$ to $P_1$, the primary impact of the resulting erosion in real money balances is that pressures for funds are placed on financial markets. These pressures result in interest rates being driven up from $r_0$ to $r_1$. This rise in interest rates reduces expenditures on capital goods, housing, and consumer durables, and results in a decline in the total demand for the real GNP.

Figure 16.4 shows the net effect of rising prices on the real GNP. It is a plot of the three price levels used in figure 16.3 and the resulting values of $y$. We refer to this relationship as the *price-demand curve*. The price-demand curve summarizes the conclusion drawn from figure 16.3: rising prices reduce the level of aggregate demand.

Changes (other than price changes) that shift the IS or LM curve also shift the price-demand curve. For example, if government spend-

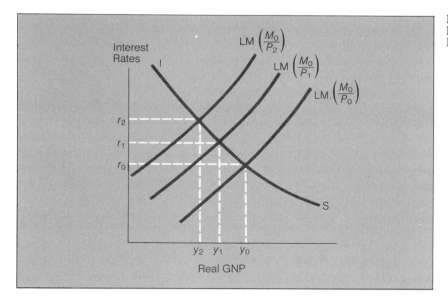

FIGURE 16.3.
Price Changes and the
IS–LM Intersection.

ing is increased, the IS curve shifts to the right. The value of $y$ that associates with all price levels goes up. Figure 16.5 shows this effect. The initial position is where the IS curve is at $I_0S_0$ and real GNP is at $y_0$. An increase in government spending shifts the IS curve out to the new position of $I_1S_1$ and a new real GNP of $y_1$. The price-demand curve shown in the lower part of the figure was positioned initially at a location where $y_0$ and $P_0$ were on the curve. After the government spending increase, the same price level, $P_0$, associates with a higher real GNP, $y_1$. Thus, the price-demand curve shifts from the position labeled $D_0$ to the position labeled $D_1$.

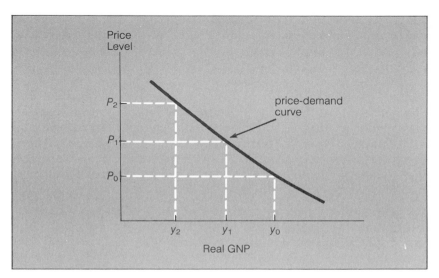

FIGURE 16.4.
Prices and Aggregate
Demand.

FIGURE 16.5.
Shifts in the Price–
Demand Curve.

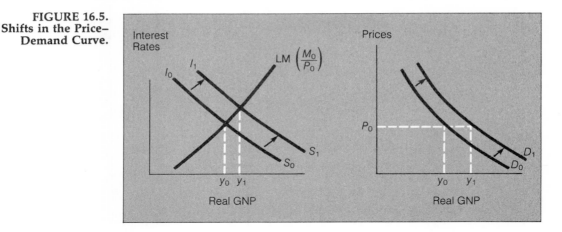

## PRICES AND THE AMOUNT PRODUCED

In chapter 14, the question of how much production firms are willing to supply to the nation's product markets was answered simply by the assumption that the amount produced will be adjusted to equal the amount demanded. In other words, we set $y = E$. In the last chapter, we continued with $y = E$ in placing money and interest rates into the macroeconomic model. This was a useful simplification because it allowed us to focus quickly and fully on the factors determining aggregate demand and the intersection of the IS-LM. However, as a reflection of the actual behavior of producers, the simple assertion that $y$ adjusts to $E$ is seriously lacking. One of the primary reasons $y = E$ is just too simple is that it has no role for changes in prices in determining the amount that will be produced. It thus supposes that the level of output producers will supply to product markets is independent of the prices they will receive. This is not logical, and it also is not even an approximation of the actual pattern of behavior of U.S. firms. The breakdown in logic associated with $y = E$ is principally that it makes no provision for whether the production is profitable. It is logical to expect that firms always produce the amounts of products that gives them the highest possible profits. But who is to say that the amount of products that maximizes business profits will equal the amount demanded? After all, total demand, $E$, is the combined spending of consumers, firms, governments, and net foreigners. It has little coordination with the profit-oriented plans of firms. There is obviously a need for much more detail about how production is determined than $y = E$.

### Production Decisions and the Demand for Labor

To arrive at the answer to these questions, we need to look in more detail at the typical firm's decision on how much output to produce.

You saw earlier that when firms change the amount they produce, they do so almost entirely (in the short-run) by changing the amount of labor they use. Selecting the amount of output to produce and the amount of labor to use are essentially the same decision looked at in two different ways. When a firm's managers find the level of production that maximizes profits, they also find the profit-maximizing amount of labor to use.

How do firms find this profit-maximizing amount of labor use? How do firms decide how many people to hire and how many hours to work? Economic theory does not deal with *how* managers find this answer. Managers probably have their own pet systems for doing it. But economic theory can state, without question, the *conditions that must be met* for the profit-maximizing amount of labor to be employed. Thus, if we are ready to assume that firms typically use the amount of labor that maximizes their profits, we can describe the conditions to which firms' hiring decisions correspond, even though we cannot describe how firms actually make the calculations and adjustments.

One key ingredient is the *marginal product of labor,* or MPL, defined as the additional production that an additional labor hour produces when other inputs to production are fixed.[1] "Marginal" here does not carry the everyday meaning of "being barely tolerable." It means "at the margin," which is the same thing as additional or incremental. If the marginal product of labor is four units, it means that if an additional hour of labor is used, the incremental or marginal addition to production is four units. The amount of production generated by an hour of labor varies with the amount of labor used. As more and more labor is used in a plant of a fixed size, its marginal contribution falls. Whereas the two-thousandth labor hour might add five units to production, the four-thousandth labor hour normally adds less. With the plant size fixed, as more people are hired, equipment and machinery are used less efficiently as are the skills and resources of the work force.

A falling MPL is a shorthand way of saying that each additional person hired to work in a plant of a fixed size results in a smaller addition to total production. This growing inefficiency associated with adding people and increasing production reaches a point where hiring more people is not worth it. This point is where the marginal product of an hour of labor falls below the real cost of that hour. The MPL is measured in units of product. To compare this with the cost of labor, we need to convert the wage rate (the dollar cost of an hour of labor) into the cost measured in terms of the firm's product. For an individual firm, we can do this by dividing the wage rate per hour by the price of the firm's product. The result is the *real wage.*[2] It measures the cost

---

1. Itinerant mathematicians may recognize the MPL as the first derivative of the production function.

2. We are dividing dollars/hour by dollars/unit. The result is measured in terms of unit/hour. The dollars cancel out.

of an hour of labor in units of the firm's output rather than in dollars. Look at an example. If the wage rate a firm pays is $10 per hour and the firm's product sells for $5 per unit, then the cost of an hour of labor to the firm, *measured in terms of its own output,* is two units ($10/ $5 = 2). The firm has to give up 2 units of its output to hire an hour of labor.

On to the bottomline. The profit-maximizing firm adds labor hours as long as the marginal product of labor is greater than the real wage. To help see why, look at table 16.1. It shows production, employment, MPL, and real-wage data for a hypothetical firm. The first two columns show various production levels and the hours of labor required to produce the corresponding units. The marginal product of labor in the third column is calculated by dividing each 100-unit increase in production by the corresponding increase in the hours of labor required to produce it.[3] For example, it takes 303.3 − 276.3 = 27 hours of added labor to increase production from 1,000 to 1,100. The MPL over this range is (1,100 − 1,000)/(303.3 − 276.3) = 3.7 units/ hour. Notice that it takes more and more labor hours to continue to increase production by increments of 100 units. At 1,600 units of production, it takes a whopping 500 labor hours to squeeze out another 100 units of production. We may assume from these data that the absolute capacity of the plant is not much greater than 1,700 units regardless of how much labor is used. The last column shows the real wage, which we assume is constant at 2.0 units of output, and which is the result of dividing a $10 wage rate by a $5 price per unit of product.

If production is at 1,100 units, an hour of labor adds about 3.7 units of output and costs 2.0 units of output. In this range, labor is a good deal for the owners of the firm. The difference between the 3.7 units added to production by each labor hour used and the 2.0 units of labor cost added by each hour is an addition to profits. The profit-maximizing firm would want to hire the 27 hours of labor necessary to expand output from 1,000 to 1,100[4]. But why stop there? Even more profits can be gained by expanding production further. At 1,400 units, 35.7 hours are required to increase production by 100 units. The MPL is now down to 2.8 units. But with the real wage at 2.0, labor still more than pays its way. Sure, the contribution to profits is smaller than at 1,100 units of production. At 1,100 units, each new hour of labor adds 3.7 − 2.0 = 1.7 units of product to the firm's profits. At 1,400 units, each hour adds 2.8 − 2.0 = 0.8 units. That is less of an addition. However, hiring the added labor still adds *something* to

---

3. It is an approximation because it is averaged out over a range. In strict terms, the MPL is calculated over an imperceptibly small region of change.

4. If you are skeptical about this way of looking at it, try a dollars-and-cents approach. The 27 labor hours cost the firm $10 each for a total of $270. The 100 units of product provided sell for $500. We are not assuming any other costs, so profits go up by $230.

**TABLE 16.1**
**The Marginal Product and the Real Wage**

| Units of Production | Hours of Employment | Marginal Product of Labor (approx.) | Real Wage |
|---|---|---|---|
| 1,000 units | 276.3 hours | 3.8 units/hour | 2.0 units/hour |
| 1,100 | 303.3 | 3.7 | 2.0 |
| 1,200 | 331.1 | 3.6 | 2.0 |
| 1,300 | 360.5 | 3.4 | 2.0 |
| 1,400 | 396.2 | 2.8 | 2.0 |
| 1,500 | 446.2 | 2.0 | 2.0 |
| 1,600 | 546.2 | 1.0 | 2.0 |
| 1,700 | 1,046.2 | 0.2 | 2.0 |

profits. As long as continued hiring adds some increment of profits, total profits keep getting larger. Profits are maximized at the output where the MPL has just fallen to the level of the real wage. This occurs at an output of 1,500, where the MPL is reduced to 2.0. Here, the cost of labor is just offset by the added production the labor generates. Profits can go no higher. They are maximized.[5] All profitable labor has been hired at 1,500 units. If more labor is hired, it will cost the firm more than it will add to production, and profits will fall. For example, increasing production from 1,500 to 1,600 units takes 100 hours of labor. The MPL is 1.0 while the cost is 2.0. The firm would pay out more than it takes in to increase production to 1,600 units. A profit-maximizing firm would stop short of this point.

If labor is hired up to the point where the falling MPL is equal to the real wage, then profits are maximized. In other words, the condition a firm must meet for maximizing profits is:

$$MPL = W/P$$

where $W$ is the hourly wage rate and $P$ is the price per unit of the firm's product.

We have just seen a precise model for the amount of labor hired by a profit-maximizing firm and the amount of output produced as a result. For this model to be a useful guide to our thinking, it is not required that firms in the real world follow it exactly. Many may not know their MPL schedule or knowingly go through the type of thinking process we just did. But if a firm manages to maximize its profits, then it will meet this profit-maximizing condition whether it knows it or not.

Our main concern in all of this is not with the firm but with the economy. At the level of the entire economy, the real wage takes on a somewhat different meaning. The $W$ now means the average wage

5. For you dollar-and-cents types, the cost of the 50 additional labor hours required to expand production by 100 units at this level is $50 \times \$10 = \$500$ while the revenue from selling the 100 units is $100 \times \$5 = \$500$. Revenues and costs both rise by the same amount. Profits are unchanged.

rate. The $P$ now means a general index of all consumer prices. Thus, $W/P$ is the same as a wage rate measured in constant dollars. The MPL schedule is the sum of all the MPLs (of the type shown in table 16.1) in the economy. We can represent it as a smooth curve such as the one in figure 16.6. This curve shows that as more labor is employed in facilities fixed in size, the aggregate MPL falls. For example, when the employment of labor is 100 million people, the MPL is at 7.4 units of real GNP per hour of labor. If profit-maximizing conditions hold across the whole economy, firms will together demand the quantity of labor where the MPL equals the aggregate $W/P$. And, they will adjust their labor demands to respond to changes in the real wage. Figure 16.7 shows this effect. When the real wage is at $(W/P)_1 = 8.0$ aggregate production units, business profits are maximized by employing 95 million workers. If the real wage rises to $(W/P)_0 = 8.5$ aggregate units, firms cut back their labor demand to 85 million workers, where they again maximize profits at the higher real wage. Thus, in the U.S. economy and others like it, where firms typically maximize profits, *the demand for labor is a downward-sloping function of the real wage.*

## Labor Supply

Firms demand labor. But workers supply it. In understanding employment, we must consider the objectives of workers as well as those of firms. Theoretically, workers continually trade off between working less and playing more, and working more and playing less. The crucial economic variable in this decision is the real wage. From a worker's viewpoint, the real wage is the amount of purchasing power that goes

**FIGURE 16.6. Aggregate Labor Demand.**

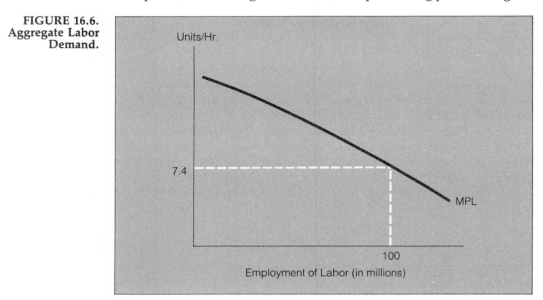

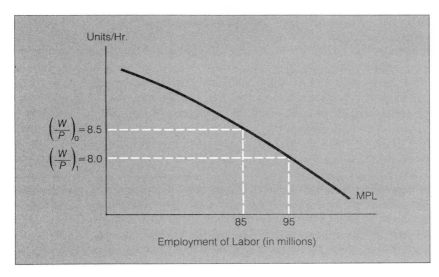

FIGURE 16.7.
The Marginal Product
of Labor and the
Real Wage.

along with working. Focusing on the real wage as the main measure of the reward for working embodies the view that workers understand that a 10 percent increase in wages accompanied by a ten percent increase in prices leaves them right where they were before the wage increase. Thus, the assumption is that workers are not fooled by what is happening to their money wages. They have their eye on what really counts—their real wage.

The basic theory of the supply of labor is simple. If the real wage is higher, more workers will come forth and offer their labor services. If the real wage goes down, leisure will look better. Less labor will be offered in labor markets. Of course, this is not true of all workers. Some classic breadwinners with a lot of bread to win are locked in to a life of work, and their offer of employment is immune to fluctuations in the real wage. But, others have a choice. They can decide how much to work, or even whether to work at all. These are the workers that make the size of the pool of potential workers sensitive to the real wage. When the real wage is rising, more workers decide to participate in the work force, and the participation rate goes up. A declining real wage discourages some from participating, and the pool of potential workers becomes smaller. The result of this behavior is that *the supply of labor is an upward-sloping function of the real wage.*

When we put the supply of labor and the demand for labor functions on the same graph, the result is the aggregate labor-market model. This is shown in figure 16.8. The demand for labor hours is given by the MPL curve. The supply of labor hours is an upward-sloping function of the real wage. Where the two curves cross is a particular real wage that jointly satisfies both sides of the labor market. We denote the number of people employed by the letter $N$. When the real wage is at $(W/P)_0$, the amount of labor demanded by firms is equal to the amount supplied by the pool of potential workers. The rate $(W/P)_0$ is the equilibrium real wage. Employment at $(W/P)_0$ is stable at $N_0$.

What if the real wage is not at equilibrium? Suppose it is higher. If the real wage in figure 16.8 is at $(W/P)_1$, the demand for labor is less than at $(W/P)_0$. It falls to $N_d$. On the other hand, a higher real wage increases the incentive to work, and so the supply of labor rises to $N_s$. After this rise, the pool of available workers at $(W/P)_1$ is larger than the demand by firms for labor. Firms hire the smaller amount, $N_d$. By hiring $N_d$ workers, firms are using labor up to the point where the marginal product of labor equals the real wage. Thus, they are maximizing profits. However, unemployment is present, equal to the difference between $N_s$ and $N_d$. (There are $N_s$ workers but only $N_d$ jobs.) This unemployment problem leads to downward pressures on the real wage. In a labor market where wages and prices fully adjust to changing conditions, $(W/P)_1$ cannot persist. It falls. During times of inflation, the existence of unemployed workers dampens the pace of wage increase compared with the pace at which prices are rising. Wages tend to rise less rapidly than prices, so that the real wage falls. During noninflationary times, the actual wage rate may fall when there is an unemployment problem. In any event, in a labor market that responds to changing conditions of supply and demand, the real wage goes back to the equilibrium value of $(W/P)_0$ through some combination of wage and price adjustments. The unemployment disappears. The opposite adjustment occurs in the case where the real wage is lower than equilibrium. In this case, the demand for labor exceeds the supply and a labor shortage is present. The real wage rises in response to this shortage. The rising real wage reduces the demand for labor and increases the supply. Balance is regained at $N_0$, the full-employment point.

When the labor market is in equilibrium, the real wage rate equates $N_d$ with $N_s$. Firms are maximizing profits because the MPL also equals

**FIGURE 16.8. The Aggregate Labor Market.**

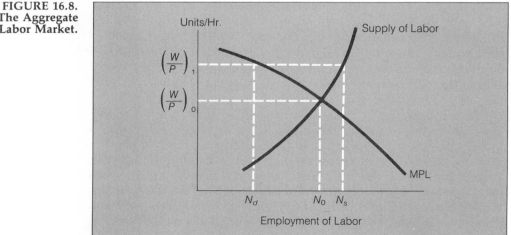

the real wage. This profit-maximizing level of employment corresponds to a point on the labor-supply function, so that all active job seekers at the equilibrium real wage are employed, except where there are frictional and structural employment problems as discussed in chapter 4.

Earlier, we found that in the short-run, the primary way firms change their level of production is to change the amount of labor they employ. Thus, as employment goes up and down, so will the amount of real GNP produced. The implication is clear: *In deciding on the profit-maximizing number of workers to employ, firms are also jointly deciding the amount of real GNP they will produce and supply.*

## THE AGGREGATE-SUPPLY CURVE

This discussion of the labor market began with the objective of providing a more detailed view of the production decision so that we could see specifically how the level of prices fits into this decision. We are now fully equipped to define how prices influence the amount of production that will take place. However, we do not have a single conclusion to draw. There are two important variations of the price-production relationship, depending on what we assume about the adjustment of wages in the labor market.

### Case One: Wages Are Rigid Downward

Some observers of U.S. labor markets contend that wages do not generally respond to downward market pressures as theory suggests they should. Specifically, when the real wage is higher than equilibrium, the supply of labor is greater than the demand. Unemployment is present, and the wage rate should fall. But does it? Some economists say that the answer is no.

In this section, we pursue the implications of such *downwardly rigid wages* for the price-production relationship. Consider the situation where wages and prices are at levels producing labor-market equilibrium. The situation is depicted in figure 16.9 by the real wages $W_0/P_0$, where the employment level is $N_0$ and the supply of labor equals the demand. From this starting point, suppose that demand for products and services weakens, leading to a drop in prices. The price level falls to $P_1$, which raises the real wage to $W_0/P_1$. The higher real wage motivates more workers to join the labor force, which raises the labor supply to $N_s$. Firms react to the higher real wage by cutting employment back to $N_1$, where they again maximize profits. (The MPL equals the real wage.) Unemployment appears equal to the distances between $N_s$ and $N_1$. Because wages do not adjust to the pressures of unemployment, the labor market stabilizes at $N_1$ where a level of production, $y_1$, takes place (shown in the right-hand graph).

Figure 16.9 shows that when wages do not change in response to changing prices, then lower prices lead to less production. We can follow the same reasoning to see why higher prices lead to more production—but only within limits. If we now start at the real wage $W_0/P_1$ in figure 16.9, with the economy operating *below* equilibrium and consider the effects of a price *increase*, we can see that the result will be a lower real wage, a higher profit-maximizing level of employment, and an increase in the real GNP produced from $y_1$ towards $y_0$. However, this situation exists only until the real wage returns to $W_0/P_0$. At this point, prices have risen enough to lower the real wage to the level that produces equilibrium in the labor market. If prices continue to increase, the real wage will fall below its equilibrium value, producing a labor shortage. Most economists who assert that wages are downwardly rigid assume the wages are flexible upward. In other words, the wage rate is assumed to rise in response to a shortage of labor. Upwardly flexible wages continually push the real wage back to its equilibrium value when labor shortages threaten.

This adjustment is illustrated in figure 16.9. Suppose that we start at equilibrium at $N_0$, and that increases in demand push up prices beyond $P_0$ to the higher level $P_2$. The real wage is temporarily reduced below equilibrium to $W_0/P_2$. At this lower real wage, the supply of labor is reduced to $N_f$ while the demand is stimulated to $N_2$. A shortage of labor appears, equal to the distance between these two points. This shortage places pressures on the real wage, which rises. When the wage rate has risen to $W_2$, equilibrium is again restored. The new real wage, $W_2/P_2$, is the same as $W_0/P_0$, and no lasting change in employment occurs.

Figure 16.9 has shown that for the case of downwardly rigid wages, higher prices lead to more production, up to the point where full employment of the labor force occurs. From this analysis, we can derive the net relationship between prices and the amount produced. The relationship between prices and production is called the *aggregate-supply function*, so named because it shows the amount producers will supply at various price levels.

**FIGURE 16.9.**
**Prices and Production**
**When Wages**
**Are Rigid.**

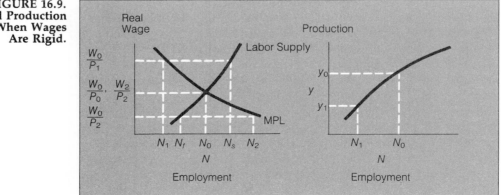

Figure 16.10 shows how an aggregate-supply function is derived from the analysis of figure 16.9. The three price levels, $P_0$, $P_1$, and $P_2$, are shown with the corresponding real GNP values from figure 16.9. The curve drawn through the points shows that the aggregate-supply function slopes upward until the full-employment level of real GNP is reached, where it then becomes perfectly inelastic to prices.

## Case Two: Wages Are Flexible

A number of economists feel that in the United States, wages are flexible enough to keep the real wage at or close to equilibrium most of the time. According to this view, periods of unemployment and labor shortages will tend to be systematically corrected by changes in the prevailing real wage rate. A clearly different aggregate-supply function results in the case of flexible wages, as shown in figure 16.11. When the real wage is at $W_0/P_0$, equilibrium in the labor market occurs at an employment level of $N_0$ and a production level of $y_0$. If the price level goes up to $P_1$, the real wage temporarily falls to $W_0/P_1$. For this real wage, profit-maximizing firms are induced to hire additional laborers to bring the work force up to $N_t$. However, this lower real wage will not last. As firms seek to add workers, a labor shortage appears, resulting in the wage rate rising to $W_1$. Balance in the labor market is restored when the real wage returns back to its original level, as in the upwardly flexible case just examined. Also, as with the earlier case, the higher level of employment, $N_t$, never materializes. Instead, employment settles at the same level as before. The adjustments in wages resulting from the labor shortage in the labor market have wiped out the incentive to expand output and employment in the face of higher prices.

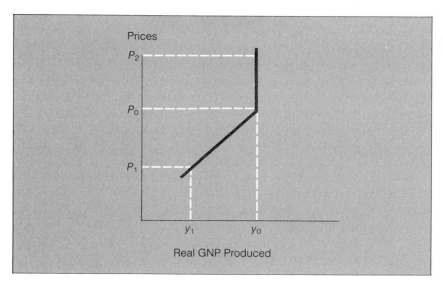

FIGURE 16.10.
An Aggregate-Supply
Curve for Rigid
Wages.

# Memorandum

To: Readers skeptical of profit—maximizing behavior and aggregate supply
From: JWE

In this chapter, we have defined the way that prices affect both aggregate demand and the amount of production that firms are willing to supply. In constructing an aggregate-supply curve, we examined two important cases. The first is that of rigid wages. When wages are downwardly rigid, we found an upward-sloping aggregate-demand schedule. When wages are flexible, we saw that a perfectly vertical aggregate-supply curve results.

When aggregate demand and aggregate supply are considered together, they form a comprehensive picture of how prices, real GNP, and interest rates are determined. In the next chapter, we will examine the interaction of aggregate demand and supply.

The United States got a solid lesson in aggregate supply during the 1971–73 period of wage and price controls. The controls were applied strictly to selected critical areas of the economy. One good example was building materials. With the prices of new houses skyrocketing, this was a crucial area and a focal point of control. Tough restrictions were put on granting price increases on many building products, including the venerable two-by-four. But the building-materials firms had more options than the wage-price board had members. The control prices of certain products, including two-by-fours, were set at levels that gave producers less profits than they would receive if they did something else with their trees. Producers responded by expanding foreign sales (over which few controls existed) and producing more pulp and other products that were more profitable. Generally, the firms did just what you would have wanted them to do if you owned stock in them. They abandoned markets where controlled prices resulted in substandard profits. They expanded markets where profits were best.

One result was a shortage of two-by-fours and selected other "controlled" wood products. No matter that demand was heavy for these wood products. When demand increased, nothing at all happened to supply. The equilibrium value of $y$ was not responding to changes in $E$. Americans began hearing that the trees were all used up. Save-a-tree programs flourished. A totally plastic world was envisioned. Those who checked carefully were puzzled to find that we had more trees than ever in the Pacific Northwest. In fact, more were being planted than were being harvested. In the process of being puzzled, we rediscovered one of the basics of free-enterprise economics— producers are not inclined to furnish products on markets where profits are inadequate.

The opposite adjustment occurs if prices weaken. Suppose the starting real wage is $W_0/P_0$, and prices fall to $P_2$. The real wage goes up to $W_0/P_2$, and unemployment appears, equal to $N_s$ minus $N_d$. However, this unemployment does not last, because the wage rate falls as a result of it. When the wage rate has fallen back to $W_2$, the real wage $W_2/P_2$ is restored to its equilibrium value, and wages stop falling.

Only one level of employment and real GNP is sustainable when wages are flexible—it is the full-employment level. This is not to say that according to this view, the level of employment is constant over time. Each month, quarter, and year, both the labor-supply and labor-demand functions are in different positions. Accordingly, the equilibrium level of employment differs through time. The position of $N_0$ may even be quite volatile. However, when wages are flexible, employment and real GNP produced are not affected by changes in prices because of the offsetting adjustments in wages that take place.

The lower right-hand graph in figure 16.11 shows the aggregate-supply curve that results from the flexible-wage case. As before, it is a plot of the price level and the resulting real GNP. The equilibrium real GNP is seen in this graph to be perfectly inelastic to prices for all levels of prices. Thus, when wages are flexible, the aggregate-supply curve is vertical.

**1.** Prices reduce the purchasing power of the money supply. In the United States, the real money supply has followed a pattern substantially different from that of the nominal money supply.

**2.** When the real money supply changes, the LM curve shifts. This is the primary way that the level of prices affects the IS–LM model.

**3.** Price increases decrease the equilibrium real GNP established by the IS–LM intersection. This leads to a negative relationship between aggregate demand and the level of prices.

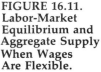

**Important Ideas In This Chapter**

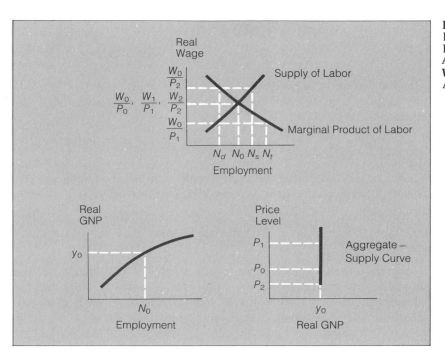

**FIGURE 16.11. Labor-Market Equilibrium and Aggregate Supply When Wages Are Flexible.**

**4.** Understanding a firm's motives for supplying goods and services requires understanding the firm's criteria for profit-maximization.

**5.** The firm's profit-maximizing amount of production and profit-maximizing level of employment are established by equating the marginal product of labor with the real wage rate.

**6.** Maximizing profits establishes the demand-for-labor function. The demand for labor is a downward-sloping function of the real wage.

**7.** People's decision to supply labor is conditioned by the real wage. The supply-of-labor function is an upward-sloping function of the real wage.

**8.** Equilibrium in the labor market occurs when the real wage rate has adjusted to that unique point where the demand for labor just equals the supply. At this level, the labor force is fully employed except for frictional and structural problems.

**9.** If wages are downwardly rigid, they will not respond to labor-market pressures that would otherwise reduce them. The result of downwardly rigid wages is that price changes lead to changes in the real wage in the opposite direction. Accordingly, price changes lead to changes in the amount of employment and production.

**10.** If wages are flexible, they do respond to demand and supply pressures in the labor market. Thus, when prices change, the resulting change in the real wage leads to an imbalance between labor supply and demand. This imbalance in turn causes wages to change until the imbalance is eliminated. Thus, the labor market remains in equilibrium, and price changes have no lasting effect on the real GNP.

**Discussion Questions**

**1.** What happens to the price-aggregate-demand relationship when the supply of money is changed? Be sure you understand why the effect takes place.

**2.** How does a tax cut impact on the position of the price-aggregate-demand curve? Explain.

**3.** Does a pattern of increasing automation of factories have any impact on the aggregate-supply curve? Explain this fully.

**4.** Have the conclusions of this chapter altered the prior assumption that in equilibrium, $y = E$, and that changes in $E$ are the primary changes in $y$?

**5.** Suppose that wages are not totally rigid, but just sticky, so that they adjust to changing market conditions, but slowly, such that the labor market is not fully adjusted most of the time. How does this affect the shape of the aggregate-supply curve?

Short and readable articles about the statistical evidence regarding the degree to which the labor market is fully adjusted appear occasionally in the monthly *Review of the Federal Reserve Bank of St. Louis.* The aggregate demand and aggregate supply framework is found in some macroeconomics texts, a good example of which is Robert Gordon's *Macroeconomics, 2nd ed.*, Boston: Little, Brown, 1981. The old master on the subject is Alfred Marshall, who covered much of this ground in 1924 in his classic *Money, Credit, and Commerce*, London: Macmillan.

**Suggested Readings**

## CHAPTER 17

# How Prices
# Are Determined

IMPORTANT TERMS

aggregate demand and supply
  analysis
seller's market
equilibrium price

buyer's market
perfectly inelastic aggregate-supply
  curve
zero multiplier effect

```
╔═══════════════════════════════════════════════════════╗
║                                                       ║
║   ⁄⁄EMO ══════════════════════════════════════         ║
║                ═══════════════════════════════         ║
║                                                       ║
║   To:        All readers                              ║
║   From:      JWE                                      ║
║                                                       ║
║                                                       ║
║   When prices rise, the purchasing power of the na-   ║
║   tion's money supply is reduced. This kind of        ║
║   inflation-induced money squeeze leads to higher     ║
║   interest rates as the LM curve shifts back. The     ║
║   result is a lower real GNP, and a negative          ║
║   relationship between the amount of real GNP         ║
║   demanded and the level of prices. On the other      ║
║   hand, when prices rise, the real wage may be cut    ║
║   if some unemployed labor is present. A cut in the   ║
║   real wage leads to more production and thus to a     ║
║   positive relationship be-tween the amount of        ║
║   goods supplied and the price level. But, if wages   ║
║   adjust flexibly to keep the labor market more or    ║
║   less in equilibrium, then price increases only      ║
║   translate into similar wage increases, leading to   ║
║   no change in the real wage and accordingly no       ║
║   incentive to increase the supply of goods and       ║
║   services.                                           ║
║                                                       ║
║   This is the picture that emerged from the last      ║
║   chapter. In this chapter, we put the pieces to-     ║
║   gether to form an explanation of how prices are     ║
║   set, considering the different motives of buyers     ║
║   and sellers of the real GNP. Once this is done, we  ║
║   reexamine what has happened to our multiplier       ║
║   as the roles of interest rates, the money supply,   ║
║   and prices have been added to the macroeconomic     ║
║   model. To give you a hint, let us say that the      ║
║   multiplier has not come away undamaged. And,        ║
║   that is the under-statement of the book.            ║
║                                                       ║
╚═══════════════════════════════════════════════════════╝
```

In the last chapter, we examined the way prices affect aggregate demand for goods and services. We also saw how prices influence the amount of goods and services that firms are willing to produce. But, we did not see how prices themselves are determined. That is the business of this chapter. In it, we bring together the concepts of the price-demand relationship and the price-production relationship to form a model of the economy that allows us to examine the way prices, interest rates, real GNP, employment, and other variables change. The first and central task in this endeavor is to consider how prices are determined.

## DEMAND, SUPPLY, AND THE PRICE LEVEL

On the surface, it is quite simple. From the standpoint of the whole economy, the amount demanded and the amount supplied determine the price level. This approach to determining prices is called *aggregate demand and supply analysis*. We have developed the component parts of this approach. What is required is assembly of the finished product.

Figure 17.1 shows this assembly. The price-demand relationship is labeled $D$ and the price-production relationship is called $S$. For now, the aggregate-supply curve corresponding to last chapter's rigid wages (case one) is used for this discussion. Suppose the price level is at $P_1$. The aggregate-supply curve shows that, at this price, firms maximize profits by supplying a real GNP of $y_S$. (At $P_1$, the real wage equals the MPL when enough workers are hired to produce $y_S$ units of output.) The price-demand curve shows that at $P_1$, the IS and LM curves intersect at a level of total demand equal to $y_D$. The gap between $y_D$ and $y_S$ is the amount by which demand for goods and services exceeds the supply. In general, the situation is one of a *seller's market*, where the amount of purchasing power exceeds the products for sale.

With such excess demand, the price level is pushed up. As prices rise, the gap between demand and supply narrows, and it disappears when the price level has risen to $P_0$. The price level $P_0$ is an *equilibrium price* in that it produces an amount of profit-maximizing production that is just equal to the amount of aggregate demand given by the intersection of the IS and LM curves. There is no excess demand or supply, and prices are stable. If the price level is above $P_0$, the profit-maximizing level of supply exceeds the amount of aggregate demand, a glut of products exists, and a *buyer's market* appears where the amount of purchasing power falls short of the amount of goods being sold. Prices fall back toward $P_0$ in this case, where again no excess demand or supply occurs.

## SHIFTING DEMAND AND THE PRICE LEVEL

The aggregate supply-demand framework shown in figure 17.1 is a simple and correct way to summarize the influences that determine the price level in the U.S. economy. However, it can be tricky to properly use as a guide to your thinking in that it may summarize too much. Most of the interesting questions regarding matters such as the price level have to do with how government spending affects prices, how tax changes figure in, how changes in the money supply impact on prices, or how changing labor-force patterns affect prices. To answer these kinds of questions, we must be able to translate shifts in IS, LM, or labor-demand–supply curves into the resulting impact on the price-supply and price-demand curves.

Let us examine an example of this by tracing through the full impact of an increase in government spending. Figure 17.2 shows the process. In part (a) of the figure, assume the economy's IS curve is in the position $IS_0$ and the LM curve is in the position $LM(P = P_0)$. The

FIGURE 17.1.
Determining Prices.

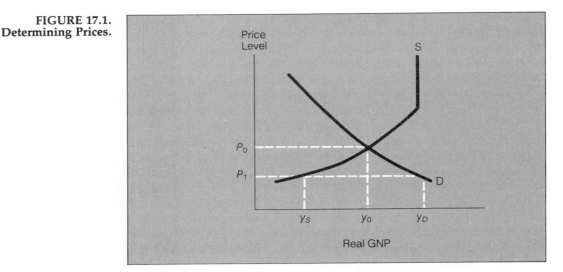

equilibrium level of aggregate demand is at a real GNP of $y_0$ and an interest rate of $r_0$. From this starting point, suppose that government spending rises. This increase shifts the IS curve upward to a new level denoted by $IS_1$. Now, *if there were no change in prices*, the new equilibrium real GNP would be at $y_1$, where the shifted IS curve intersects the (solid) LM curve.

Part (b) of figure 17.2 shows, however, that there *will* be a change in prices as a result of this shift in the IS curve. Let us examine how this occurs. With the price-demand curve in the initial position $D_0$, the equilibrium price level is at $P_0$ where the real GNP is at $y_0$. This real GNP is the same as that which equates the IS and LM curves in the upper graph. How do we know?—because in the last chapter we derived the price-demand relationship by varying the price level and finding the value of $y$ that equated the IS and LM curves. In defining the $D_0$ curve, we thus constrained every point on the D curve to correspond to an intersection of IS and LM. After the IS curve shifts to $IS_1$, the initial price level of $P_0$ now corresponds to a higher equilibrium $y$ ($y_1$ instead of $y_0$). In part (b) of figure 17.2, the result is a rightward shift in the D curve to $D_1$. To see why this shift occurs, notice that at the price level of $P_0$, the amount of equilibrium aggregate demand is now $y_1$ rather than $y_0$. So, after the shift, the point labeled A in part (b) corresponds to price level $P_0$ and its corresponding level of aggregate demand, $y_1$.

With the price-demand relationship shifted by the increase in government spending, a new higher price level must evolve. When equilibrium is restored, the price level is at $P_1$ and the level of aggregate demand is at $y_2$. In part (a) of figure 17.2, the increase in prices from $P_0$ to $P_1$ contracts the real money supply which shifts the LM curve backward to the position shown by the dashed line and labeled $LM(P = P_1)$. At this position, aggregate demand and supply are in balance at the new price level. The net effect of the increase in government

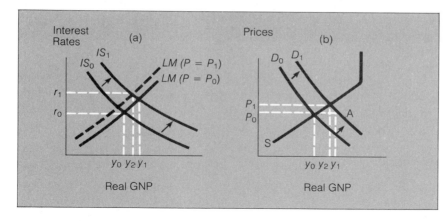

**FIGURE 17.2.
Government Spending
and Prices.**

spending thus is (1) a higher real GNP, (2) higher prices, and (3)
higher interest rates, which have gone up to a new equilibrium value
of $r_1$. Notice that if prices had not risen as a result of the spending
increase, the effect on real GNP would have been greater. Real GNP
would have risen to $y_1$ if prices had stayed the same. But the rising
prices lowered the real money supply which partially offset the expansionary effect of the government-spending increase, causing the
real GNP to rise only to $y_2$.

The example we have just considered assumes that wages are
downwardly rigid so that the aggregate-supply curve is upwardly
sloping. If we instead assume that wages are sufficiently flexible that
the labor market is in equilibrium most of the time, the results of an
increase in government spending are quite different. Figure 17.3 shows
the way the analysis changes. We start in part (a) at equilibrium with
the IS curve is $IS_0$ and the LM curve is $LM(P = P_0)$. The government-
spending increase shifts the IS to $IS_1$ just as in the previous case. The
shift in the IS produces a similar shift in the price-demand curve,
from position $D_0$ to position $D_1$. But *no additional real GNP is produced*
as a result of this shift. The aggregate supply is perfectly inelastic to
prices, because firms find that price increases are met with similar
wage increases, so that the real wage does not fall and additional
production is not profitable. So, production stays at $y_0$ and prices
absorb all the increase in demand by rising to $P_1$. When prices have
risen to this new level, the real money supply has been reduced
enough to shift the LM curve to the dashed position labeled $LM(P = P_1)$. Equilibrium between IS and LM now occurs at the same real GNP
as before, but at the higher interest rate, $r_1$.

Thus, when wages are flexible, an increase in government spending
causes (1) no increase in real GNP or in jobs, (2) higher prices, and
(3) higher interest rates. In this case, the higher prices resulting from
an increase in government spending completely choke the expansionary effect of the spending increase.

There are several other important reasons for the price-demand
relationship to shift besides changes in government spending. Why

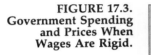

**FIGURE 17.3.**
**Government Spending**
**and Prices When**
**Wages Are Rigid.**

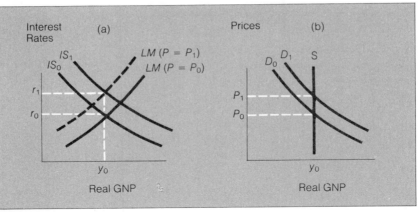

not test yourself on these ideas by seeing whether you can trace through the effect of each of the following changes in IS–LM equilibrium, on the price-demand curve, and on prices. (I will sketch out the correct answers in footnotes.)

**1.** Inflationary expectations rise.[1]

**2.** The supply of money is increased.[2]

**3.** The demand for automobiles declines sharply.[3]

## CHANGES IN SUPPLY AND PRICE LEVEL

Changes in demand are not the only influences on the price level. When conditions affecting aggregate supply change, the price level adjusts. To examine how this process works, let us consider the impact of an important shift in the machine methods used by firms. Consider the ongoing pattern of using increasing numbers of industrial robots to do repetitive production-line tasks. We can safely as-

1. A rise in inflationary expectations shifts the IS curve to the right and up (see chapter 15). This shifts the D curve to the right. Prices rise, interest rates rise, and real GNP increases when there are rigid wages. When wages are flexible, real GNP is not changed.

2. An increase in the supply of money shifts the LM curve to the right. This shift produces a rightward shift in the D curve, leading to higher prices, lower interest rates, and an increase in real GNP when wages are rigid.

3. If the demand for any consumption good decreases, the IS curve shifts to the left. This can be visualized by thinking of the simple $C + I + G + X$ curve shifting down, which causes the derived IS curve to move left. The price-demand curve also shifts left, and prices fall, as do interest rates. Real GNP declines if wages are downwardly rigid. If not, real GNP is unaffected.

sume that adoption of industrial robots increases the marginal product
of labor. The thinking is that the additional machines per worker
make each additional hour of labor able to produce more additional
output than would be the case if more "by hand" methods of production were used.

Figure 17.4 shows the effect graphically. At this point, we assume
that wages are flexible so that the labor market remains at equilibrium.
In part (a), the labor-market model is shown, with the labor-supply
curve labeled $LS$ and the initial labor-demand curve labeled $MPL_0$.
The initial equilibrium level of employment is $N_0$ at a real wage of
$W_0/P_0$. The productivity-enhancing shift in production methods toward robots affects the model by shifting the marginal product of
labor from its initial position of $MPL_0$ to the right to $MPL_1$. With each
added hour of labor now more productive, and the real wage unchanged, (initially) firms find they can increase profits by expanding
employment. If employment reaches $N_1$ when the real wage is $W_0/P_0$,
firms are again on their demand labor curves and profits are maximized. However, this will not happen. The initial labor shortage represented by $N_1 - N_0$ will lead to an increase in the real wage. When
the real wage has risen to $W_1/P_1$, the shifted labor-demand curve is
in equilibrium with labor supply. Employment stabilizes at $N_2$.

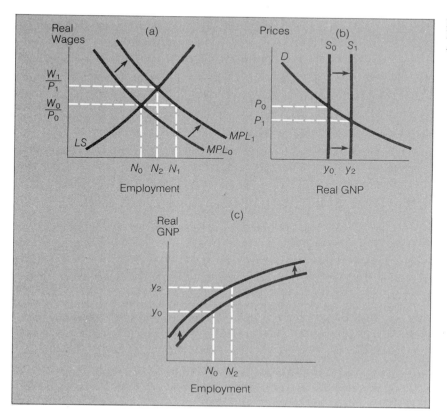

**FIGURE 17.4.
Industrial Robots and
Aggregate Prices.**

Part (c) of figure 17.4 shows the employment-output relationship. When employment is $N_0$, the resulting real GNP is $y_0$. After the shift in productivity, this relationship mirrors the shift by shifting up as well. (More output now associates with the same production.) Thus, the new equilibrium employment of $N_2$ increases the real GNP to $y_2$. With wages flexibile, the aggregate-supply curve shown in part (b) of figure 17.4 is perfectly inelastic. It is shown in the initial position of $S_0$ where real GNP is at $y_0$. (This is the same $y_0$ that in the employment-output graph corresponds to $N_0$, i.e., the level of employment that clears the labor market.) As the productivity shift increases equilibrium output to $y_2$, the vertical aggregate-supply curve also shifts to that position. This outward shift in the aggregate-supply curve that follows from the initial shift in the labor-demand function thus lowers the price level from its initial value of $P_0$ to a new value of $P_1$. So, the net result of a robot-induced (or any other) increase in the marginal product of labor is an increase in the real GNP and employment, a reduction in the price level, and an increase in the real wage.[4]

Let us consider another shift affecting the aggregate-supply curve. Suppose that the participation rate of the overall U.S. work force (the fraction of the working population seeking jobs) increases for reasons unrelated to the real wage. This type of change has in fact been occurring in the United States for several years. Although a slight decline in the participation rate among males has occurred over recent decades, the participation rate among females has increased dramatically, causing the total to rise by a substantial amount. Most economists attribute this increasing participation rate not to rising real wages (a movement along the labor-supply curve), but to sociological factors relating to the changing role of women in the U.S. work force.

Figure 17.5 shows the impact on prices and the real GNP of an increase in the labor-force-participation rate. In part (a), the supply-of-labor curve is in the initial position labeled $S_0$. With the demand-for-labor curve constant, equilibrium in the labor market occurs at a real wage of $W_0/P_0$, where employment is at $N_0$. A positive shift in the participation rate means that more workers are willing to offer labor services at the same real wage as before. Thus, the labor-supply curve shifts to the right to the new position labeled $S_1$. At first, the supply of labor now exceeds the demand with the real wage at $W_0/P_0$. Labor supply increases to $N_s$, while labor demand is unchanged at $N_0$. This condition of excess labor services leads to a downward adjustment in the real wage. When the real wage has fallen to $W_1/P_1$,

4. If wages are downwardly rigid, the results are close to the same. Suppose you start with a real wage of $W_1/P_1$ in figure 17.4 but with the labor-demand curve in the initial position of $MPL_0$. Unemployment would be present. A shift in the labor-demand curve to $MPL_1$ reduces the unemployment and increases real GNP. The aggregate-supply curves $S_0$ and $S_1$ both slope upward, but a shift still occurs, increasing output. To be sure you understand this, redraw figure 17.4 with the assumptions of (1) downwardly rigid wages and some unemployment, and (2) upward-sloping aggregate-supply functions.

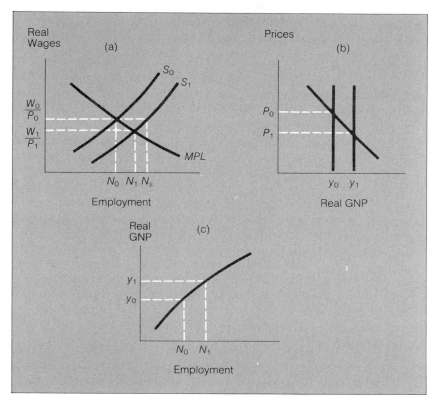

**FIGURE 17.5.
Changing Labor-Force-
Participation Rates
and Prices.**

the labor market is again cleared, and the excess work force has been
fully absorbed. The result is a higher profit-maximizing level of employment and a lower real wage.

Part (c) of figure 17.5 shows that the increase in employment translates into an increase in the equilibrium real GNP from $y_0$ to $y_1$. In
part (b), the effect on the vertical aggregate-supply curve is to shift
it outward from its initial position corresponding to $y_0$ to a new position corresponding to $y_1$. This shift in turn leads to a fall in the price
level, from the initial level $P_0$ to the new level $P_1$. Thus, an increase
in the work-force-participation rate leads to lower prices by lowering
the real wage which stimulates more employment and greater production. With the price-demand relationship remaining unchanged,
this added production leads to a reduction in the general price level.

## THE MULTIPLIER, INTEREST RATES,
## AND PRICES

The multiplier was introduced a few chapters back as we developed
the simplest form of our macroeconomic model, the $C + I + G + X$
model. When the roles of interest rates and the money supply were
added to this model to form the IS–LM model, there was no further

discussion of the multiplier. When the role of prices was also added to the IS–LM model to form the aggregate-supply-and-demand model, there was again no discussion of the multiplier. Nonetheless, the multiplier has been changing as more and more influences have been brought into our macroeconomic framework. In this section, we examine how the multiplier changes when the roles of interest rates and prices are added to the model.

To examine the multiplier in these new contexts, we first assume that an autonomous expenditure change takes place, initiating the multiplier effect. In the following example, an increase in government spending is assumed. The same multiplier effects would occur for any autonomous increase in aggregate demand. However, using government spending is of special interest because understanding the impact of the government sector on the economy is a topic of great importance.

In figure 17.6, the multiplier process is shown graphically for (1) the simple model where interest rates and prices are assumed constant—the $C + I + G + X$ model, (2) the model where the role of interest rates is incorporated, but where prices are assumed to remain constant—the IS–LM model, and (3) the model that incorporates the role of both interest rates and prices—the aggregate-supply-and-demand model.

In part (a), the $C + I + G$ approach is shown. Exports, $X$, have been left off to simplify the figure a bit. The economy is in the initial

**FIGURE 17.6. The Multiplier, Interest Rates, and Prices.**

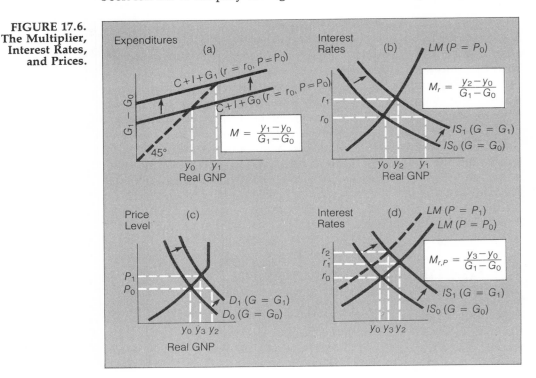

position shown by the aggregate-demand curve labeled $C + I + G_0$ ($r = r_0$, $P = P_0$). Government spending increases from its initial level of $G_0$ to a new higher level of $G_1$. This shifts the aggregate-demand curve up to the position labeled $C + I + G_1$ ($r = r_0$, $P = P_0$). Both interest rates and prices are assumed to remain the same after the shift (at $r_0$ and $P_0$), as denoted by the labels on the aggregate-demand curve. The equilibrium real GNP under these conditions rises from $y_0$ to $y_1$. The multiplier is shown in the box beside the graph, and is denoted as $M$.

When the demand and supply of money was added to this picture, the conclusion was that interest rates would not in general remain the same faced with an increase in aggregate demand. The IS–LM model does away with the assumption that interest rates are constant, and instead offers an explanation of *how* interest rates *will* change when a shift in aggregate-demand occurs.

Part (b) of figure 17.6 shows this added dimension. From the simplest model, we already know that the shift in demand would increase the real GNP from $y_0$ to $y_1$, if interest rates were to stay constant at $r_0$. This indicates that the IS curve shifts from the position labeled $IS_0$ ($G = G_0$) to the position labeled $IS_1$ ($G = G_1$). Why? Because we know that the increase in government spending increases the real GNP to $y_1$ if interest rates remain unchanged. But, the added dimension of the LM shows us that interest rates will change as a result of the government-spending change. In equilibrium, they will rise to $r_1$, where the real GNP is $y_2$. This new real GNP is smaller than that corresponding to the simple model, reflecting the depressing effects of the higher interest rates on the amount of capital spending in the economy. Accordingly, the multiplier is given by the expression labeled $M_r$. Clearly, $M_r$ is smaller than $M$, since the numerator is less. In this analysis, prices are assumed to remain unchanged when aggregate demand shifts. However, we know that this assumption is also not wholly realistic.

Parts (c) and (d) of figure 17.6 show how the multiplier process is further modified when we figure in the role of prices. In part (d), we begin with an initial equilibrium position of the IS curve at $IS_0$ ($G = G_0$) and the LM curve at $LM$ ($P = P_0$). This produces the same equilibrium as in part (b), at $y_0$ and $r_0$. The increase in government spending shifts the IS to $IS_1$ ($G = G_1$). *With prices unchanged,* equilibrium changes to $r_1$ and $y_2$, also the same as in part (b). But, adding the aggregate-supply-and-demand dimension shows that the shift also shifts the price-demand relationship. By how much? We already know from the IS–LM framework that if prices stay constant, while interest rates rise to $r_1$, real GNP rises to $y_2$. Part (c) of figure 17.6 shows that the price-demand curve shifts rightward by the amount $y_2 - y_0$, from its initial position of $D_0$ ($G = G_0$) to the new position $D_1$ ($G = G_1$). In other words, with prices constant at $P_0$, the demand shift would increase $y$ from $y_0$ to $y_2$. But prices do not stay constant. The demand shift causes them to rise, and this reduces the equilibrium real GNP to $y_3$. In the IS–LM graph in part (d) of figure 17.6, the price increase shifts the LM curve from the position labeled $LM$ ($P = P_0$) to the new position labeled $LM$ ($P = P_1$), producing the new equilibrium of $y_3$.

When the role of prices is added, the multiplier is further reduced, since $y_3$ is less than $y_2$. The resulting multiplier is shown as $M_{r,p}$, and it is less than $M_r$ and $M$. Clearly, adding the role of interest rates and prices to the simplest model whittles away at the size of the economic response to an increase in government spending. However, in adding the role of prices, we have assumed that wages were rigid, so that the aggregate-supply curve is upward-sloping. If we instead assume that the labor market is in equilibrium most of the time, the multiplier process is brought to a complete halt.

Figure 17.7 shows this situation. In part (a), the IS–LM curve is shown as it was in figure 17.6. The government-spending increase has shifted the IS from $IS$ ($G = G_0$) to $IS$ ($G = G_1$). If prices were constant, the real GNP would rise to $y_2$. Here is where the difference arises. With the flexibility of the real wage, the labor market translates every increase in prices into an increase in the money wage. Employment and the real GNP thus are independent of the price level, and the aggregate-supply curve is vertical. This case is one of a *perfectly inelastic aggregate supply curve.* This is shown in part (b) of figure 17.7. The shift in the price-demand curve in part (b), from its initial position of $D_0$ ($G = G_0$) to $D_1$ ($G = G_1$), does not lead to any higher equilibrium real GNP, but only to higher prices. The price level rises to $P_2$, absorbing all of the demand shift by higher prices. In part (a) of figure 17.7, the higher price level shifts the LM curve back to the dashed position labeled LM ($P = P_2$). When prices have risen to $P_2$, the LM has shifted enough that demand again equals $y_0$ (the initial value), and full equilibrium is restored. A *zero multiplier effect* occurs in this case, since no change has occurred in the equilibrium value of the real GNP as a result of the government-spending increase.

**FIGURE 17.7.
The Multiplier When
the Labor Market
Is in Equilibrium.**

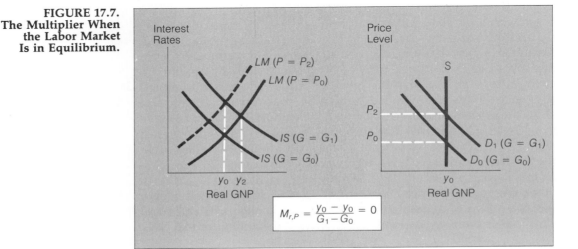

Figures 17.6 and 17.7 have shown that the nature of the multiplier process is greatly reduced when applied to an economy such as that of the United States where prices, interest rates, and wages are active parts of the economic adjustment process. Indeed, if the labor market is fully adjusted, the multiplier process is nil.

Perhaps by now you have decided that whether the labor market is fully adjusted or not is a question of substantial importance in deciding how an economy like ours behaves. Whether the level of government spending has any impact on the real GNP hinges on this question. So does the influence of any other kind of shift in aggregate demand on the level of production. In fact, the main theoretical debate in the last ten or so years among economists has concerned the degree to which the labor market is or is not fully adjusted most of the time. In subsequent chapters, we will examine this question and the debate it sparks. In the process, we shall develop the essential differences between economists known as "monetarists" and those known as "Keynesians."

**1.** In terms of the whole economy, the amount demanded and the amount supplied together determine the price level.

**Important Ideas in This Chapter**

**2.** The equilibrium price level in the economy occurs when the profit-maximizing level of production just equals the amount of aggregate demand at that price.

**3.** If the amount of demand shifts, the price-demand curve also shifts and the price level changes. A shift in the price-demand curve corresponds either to a shift in the IS curve or to a shift in the LM curve.

**4.** When a shift occurs in the marginal product of labor, the resulting change in the labor-demand curve leads to a shift in the economy's aggregate-supply curve.

**5.** Shifting sociological factors can lead to changing patterns in the labor-force-participation rate. When this occurs, the labor-supply curve shifts, producing a similar shift in the economy's aggregate-supply curve.

**6.** When the aggregate-supply curve shifts, prices in the economy change, falling when the curve shifts positively and rising when the curve shifts negatively.

**7.** When we compare the progressively more complete forms of the macroeconomic model, we find that the multiplier is reduced as the macroeconomic model is made more complete.

**8.** When interest rates and the money supply are incorporated into the model, the multiplier is reduced by the effect of interest rates on the model.

**9.** When prices are incorporated into the analysis, the multiplier is reduced further if the aggregate-supply curve is not vertical, and is eliminated if the aggregate-supply curve is vertical.

**Discussion
Questions**

**1.** Trace through fully the effects on the economy of a general tax cut on personal incomes. Deal with how interest rates, prices, and the real GNP change as a result of this tax cut.

**2.** Can you think of circumstances where we could dispense with the more complicated IS–LM and aggregate supply-demand models, and realistically develop our economic reasoning from the simple $C + I + G + X$ model?

**3.** Think of three things that could shift the aggregate-demand curve. Now come up with three things that could shift the aggregate-supply curve. Be sure to indicate which way each would shift the curve.

**4.** For the case of an inelastic aggregate-supply curve, the analysis of this chapter shows that an increase in government spending leads to no increase in the real GNP. But government spending is part of the real GNP. How is this possible?

**5.** Can you think of a situation where the aggregate-supply curve is likely to be highly elastic, that is, almost flat? Explain.

**Suggested
Readings**

For a further discussion of the adjustment of the economy to changing levels of demand and supply when prices are seen as determined by aggregate demand and supply, a book by Martin J. Bailey entitled *National Income and the Price Level*, 2nd ed., New York: McGraw-Hill, 1969, remains a clear and concise explanation.

## CHAPTER 18

# Is the Economy Self-Correcting?

## IMPORTANT TERMS

natural-rate hypothesis
natural rate of unemployment
deficient demand
Say's law of markets
credit market
loanable-funds theory
demand for loanable funds
supply of loanable funds
household saving
credit market equilibrium
crowding out
liquidity trap

# 𝄞MEMO

To:   All readers
From:  JWE

In the last two chapters, we learned that some important aspects of the economy—multipliers, prices, interest rates—depend on whether or not the labor market is approximately fully adjusted most of the time. If it is, the economy has important self-correcting features. If left alone, it will tend toward full employment of the labor force to the limits of barriers associated with skill, frictional factors, and labor mobility. If the labor market is typically out of adjustment, then the implications for prices, interest rates, and employment are much different.

Thus, it is extremely important whether the economy is or is not at a position of approximately full employment most of the time, and thus whether it has important self-correcting features most of the time. This chapter examines the issues associated with this question. They are thorny issues, and they separate thinking in economics into "camps" that campaign for one or the other of the opposing viewpoints involved. At the heart of the matter is how the credit market works, a topic to which considerable time is devoted in this chapter.

Chapter 17 concluded that the behavior of the economy is importantly influenced by whether the labor market is or is not fully adjusted most of the time. A fully adjusted labor market leads to a vertical aggregate-supply curve. A labor market where wages are downwardly rigid and where some unemployment exists as the normal case leads to an upward-sloping aggregate-supply curve. The economy behaves quite differently under these two scenarios. In this chapter, we pursue the implications of this difference, and examine the case for and against the proposition that the labor market is adjusted fully most of the time.

## THE NATURAL RATE OF UNEMPLOYMENT

The *natural-rate hypothesis* is the contention that the labor market is in fact approximately fully adjusted most of the time, so that the amount of employment and the rate of unemployment are usually at their equilibrium or "natural" levels. It allows for departures from full adjustment, but only on a transitional basis. In terms of the natural-rate view, when the supply and demand of labor are not the same, adjustments in the real wage faithfully occur to bring them back together. Accordingly, the amount of unemployed workers in the economy at each period of time is due entirely to those who lack marketable skills, those who are "between jobs," those who are unemployed because of geographic immobility (that is, they will not change their location to take an open job), and those who are unemployed because of seasonal reasons. Workers who are willing to work at the going wage rate and who have the skills and the mobility to fill available jobs are all at work. The *natural rate of unemployment* is the unemployment rate (see chapter 4) corresponding to a fully adjusted labor market. Thus, it measures those who are unemployed as a result of skill barriers, seasonal factors, frictional factors, and geographic immobility.

If the natural-rate hypothesis is true, the implications for the economy are profound. Employment is inherently stable. When the unemployment rate rises above the natural rate, the real wage adjusts downward, eliminating it. No need for government jobs programs, wage and price controls, or other forms of public assistance. The economy's labor markets are self-correcting according to the natural-rate view.

But is the natural-rate hypothesis true? After all, we do observe substantial fluctuations in the actual unemployment rate, as figure 18.1 shows. Over the period 1967–1982, the quarterly unemployment rate fluctuated from below 3.5 percent to above 6 percent, then down below 5 percent, then up sharply to almost 9 percent, then back down to under 6 percent again, then back up to the 9 percent region.

Adherents of the natural-rate hypothesis explain the data in figure 18.1 in two primary ways. First, they assert that the unemployment statistics are not gathered in a way to allow correct measurement of the degree to which the labor market is fully adjusted. The problem

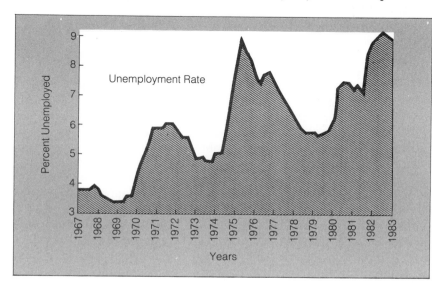

**FIGURE 18.1.
Patterns in the
Unemployment Rate.**

is with the questions asked by field workers who gather the sample data on which unemployment estimates are based. One of the questions on the form is "Are you seeking work?", and it is used to classify those sampled as either job seekers or non–job seekers. Natural-rate theorists assert that this form of data collection does not distinguish between those who are seeking work at the current wage and those who are seeking work, but only at a higher real wage than the market provides. This latter group in fact represents the upper half of the labor-supply curve, to the right of the equilibrium point. They are unemployed by their own choice, rather than by market conditions. This "voluntarily unemployed" group is certainly of concern to statisticians and policy makers. Natural-rate theorists argue that this group is inappropriately included in the unemployment-rate data that are used for purposes of deciding whether the economy is at its natural rate of unemployment.

Natural-rate theorists' second response to the data in figure One is that the figure does not show how much of the fluctuation in the actual unemployment rate is a result of fluctuations in the natural rate. The natural rate corresponds to the equilibrium level of employment. This equilibrium level is determined by the intersection of the demand and supply curves of labor. As these curves shift, the equilibrium changes, and with it the natural rate of unemployment. Natural-rate theorists assert that the fluctuation in the natural rate of unemployment over time may account for a large part of the fluctuation in the actual rate of unemployment.

For these reasons, most natural-rate adherents prefer not to focus on the unemployment-rate data in judging the condition of the labor market. An alternative is to use data on total employment, which measures the number of people at work. Questions concerning who is seeking jobs and at what wage rate are not involved in calculating the level of employment. The number of employed people is a direct measure of the equilibrium level of employment referred to in the labor-market model.

Figure 18.2 shows the quarterly pattern in total employment in the United States over 1966–1981. The chart shows that employment grew steadily until 1970, where it flattened in the mild recession of 1970, grew steadily again from the middle of 1971 to 1974, fell by about 2 million workers during the recession of 1974, rose steadily until late 1979, and fell again in the 1980 recession. In all, the employment picture looks considerably more stable than the unemployment rate. Natural-rate theorists say this is because the employment data are not contaminated as are the unemployment-rate data, and that the employment data give a direct reflection of the economy's labor-market equilibrium position.

The picture painted by the natural-rate hypothesis is one where firms decide on their employment and the amount they will produce by maximizing profits through equating the marginal product of labor with the real wage rate. This rule governs the amount of products to

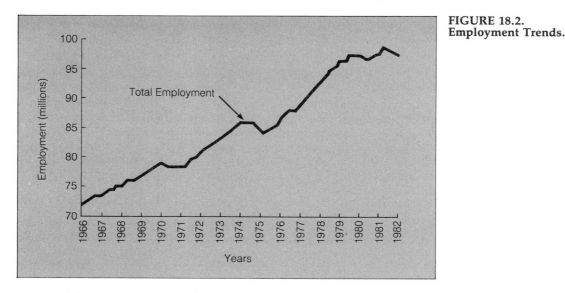

FIGURE 18.2.
Employment Trends.

be supplied to markets. Some opponents of the natural-rate theory point out that this view ignores market realities in that it gives no attention to the possibility that demand will not be sufficient to buy all the profit-maximizing output. Suppose the profit-maximizing rule stipulates that firms supply a real GNP of 1,000. What guaranty is there that consumers and others will want to buy this amount? After all, they have no concern with the firms' profit-maximizing rule. What if only 900 in goods and services is demanded by consumers, firms, governments, and net foreigners?

This *deficient demand* argument is a frontal attack on the natural-rate hypothesis. It is accordingly also an attack on the proposition that labor markets remain in equilibrium most of the time. For the natural-rate hypothesis to remain viable, a logical response must be made to the deficient-demand argument. The response offered by natural-rate theorists involves (1) Say's law of markets, and (2) a more detailed examination of how credit markets work.

## SAY'S LAW OF MARKETS

Simply stated, *Say's law of markets* (named after J. B. Say, a nineteenth century French economist) is that producing a real GNP of a certain size creates a level of aggregate demand equal to the real GNP produced.[1] If 1,000 is produced, the amount of aggregate demand will

1. Laws in economics are different from laws in politics and government. Economic laws are not passed by legislatures. They are tendencies that are believed to be so strong that they have the force of a law in the physical sciences. They are more closely related to laws in physics than to laws on the books of a state or city.

be 1,000. If 900 is produced, then demand will be 900, and so forth. The logic behind this proposition is all-important. It is understanding the logic of Say's law that helps us to judge whether it is a law that applies to our world. Here is the logical progression that produces Say's law:

1. Producing a real GNP of, say, $1,500 creates both $1,500 worth of products and $1,500 worth of incomes paid to all parties. Remember from chapter 4 that we cannot count something as part of the GNP unless it creates an equal amount of current income. Thus, producing a real GNP of $1,500 generates $1,500 in total incomes. This pool of income is an amount of purchasing power created in the process of production, which is by definition equal to the production itself.

2. Production generates an equal amount of purchasing power. The purchasing power created by production can be disposed of in two basic ways. It can be spent by those receiving it to buy current production or it can be saved. The portion of current income saved can be put into financial accounts, hoarded, or transferred abroad. Let us at this point suppose that the proportion of the saving flow in the economy that is hoarded or transferred abroad (net of dishoarding or transfers from abroad) is small enough to be disregarded for practical purposes. Thus, unspent current income is nearly all allocated to financial accounts in banks and other financial intermediaries, or invested directly.

3. All or nearly all of the amount of savings flowing into financial accounts will be loaned to business and other borrowers by banks and other financial intermediaries. Financial institutions that are paying interest on the financial accounts of savers will in general put all these funds to work earning interest by loaning them to primary borrowers such as business and government.

4. All the money borrowed (by business and others) from financial institutions will be spent by those who borrow it. The basic reason for borrowing is to enable purchases to take place in advance of income earned. Business borrowers typically are borrowing to finance new capital spending. Governments borrow to finance spending that exceeds taxes collected. It is assumed that no significant amount of borrowing takes place just to enable the funds to sit idly in a checking account.

5. As a result of the credit market, all the currently produced purchasing power will be used to buy products—demand will equal production.

Sometimes a picture is worth a thousand words. Other times not quite that much. But, for whatever it's worth, Figure 18.3 is a flow diagram that shows the operation of Say's law in pictures. It starts with the assumption that producers have found that producing $1,500 worth of goods and services maximizes their profits. The rest of the actions flow from this production decision. The picture illustrates that the flow of production generates purchasing power, which is allocated to spending or saving. The saving in turn flows through credit markets into the hands of spenders. Thus, the connection between production

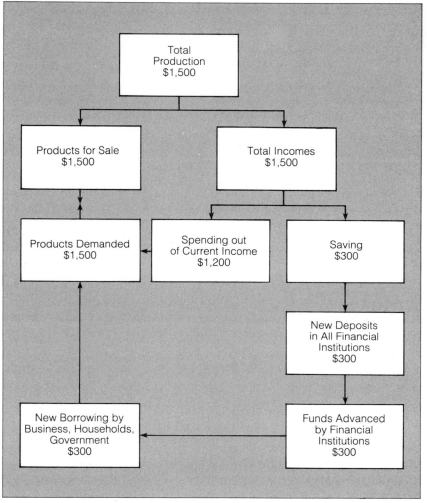

**FIGURE 18.3.
Production,
Purchasing Power,
and Production.**

and the derived expenditures is a "closed loop." However, as with our verbal description of this process, no account is taken of the international sector or of hoarding. If U.S. consumers either hoard or buy more from producers abroad thus foreign consumers buy from U.S. producers, a siphoning off of part of the purchasing power from U.S. production occurs. In this case, the loop is no longer closed.

Suppose producers now find that it maximizes their profits to increase production up to 1,700. An additional 200 in incomes are now being generated in the economy. The portion of this additional income not being spent on current production by those earning it goes "up for sale" to the highest bidder in credit markets. When the sale is done, all the new saving will have been borrowed. Borrowers will spend it, and thus, all the 200 of added income will again show up as demand. Supply will have created its own demand.

To: Readers who remember Yoda and the moneyless economy from chapter 1
From: JWE

The discussion of Say's law has something to do with Yoda's moneyless economy (chapter 1). Part of the thinking in Say's law has to do with the fund of purchasing power generated by production. Say's law argues that those earning income will not want to waste it. What they do not consume of their current income they will lend out to someone who wants to spend it. Now, let us rephrase this to apply to a world with no money. People would be paid in units of products instead of in money. It would not be necessary to tell you that the amount of products determine the amount of purchasing power—in the case of barter, the amount of products *are* the purchasing power. And, with products as purchasing power, earning more than you spend means having goods sitting around in your backyard. In the case of the Yoda example, the goods are sitting around in your Iowa computer account. In either case, there is an incentive to lend any excess product at interest. And, what about the interest? Well, it is measured in terms of product in a barter system. You get credit for so many units of some product when you lend out your "saving" of excess production. Exercise your understanding of this. Go back and read the text discussion of Say's law and rethink how it would read in the case of Yoda's moneyless economy.

In summary, the answer provided by natural-rate theorists to the question "What if people don't want to buy the profit-maximizing level of real GNP"? is "They will want to buy it, because producing it creates enough purchasing power for its entire purchase, and the credit market sees to it that none of this power goes unused."

For Say's law to hold, credit markets must work smoothly to provide a borrower for every dollar of saving. For, if some savers cannot find a borrower for their excess income, then the closed loop of Say's law is broken. In this case, frustrated savers will by default become hoarders.

So far, our macroeconomic theory has not had much to say about the workings of credit markets. We have talked about how interest rates are determined, but only in the context of the amount of *money balances* that people and firms want to hold. The implication of our earlier analysis is that the excess holdings of money will be allocated to borrowers in credit markets, and this is what makes the interest rate change. But, clearly, our concern so far with the credit market has been quite indirect. We now take a direct look at how credit markets work.

# CREDIT MARKETS AND THE THEORY OF LOANABLE FUNDS

The *credit market* is the national financial arena where lenders and borrowers square off. Each day, they haggle, negotiate, and cajole. And each day most, if not all, of the funds brought to the market by the lenders end up in the hands of the borrowers. The interest rate is the focal point of the haggling between lenders and borrowers. When more funds are available in the nation's credit market than borrowers want, borrowers prevail and the interest rate drops. Financial pros describe it as a borrower's market. When funds are scarce, lenders prevail and the rate of interest goes up. It is then a lender's market. The rate of interest reaches equilibrium when borrowers and lenders are both happy with the amount of funds borrowed and lent. Who are the borrowers? Who are the lenders? Why do they increase or decrease the funds in the credit market? The answers to these questions make up the essentials of what is called *loanable-funds theory*.

## The Demand for Loanable Funds

In the United States business firms almost always are borrowers. New spending by business on capital goods usually exceeds the amount of retained profits and depreciation write-offs of business. The difference must be financed. Firms issue stocks and place public and private notes in order to finance their capital investment plans. When the federal government incurs a deficit in its budget, it also becomes a borrower. Over the decade of the 1970s, government was a persistent borrower in the nation's money markets. In fact, on occasion the government has been a bigger borrower than business. A third group of borrowers consists of consumers and borrowing in order to finance the purchase of automobiles and other durable goods.[2]

The sum of business, government, and consumer borrowing plans is called the *demand for loanable funds*. For business, the demand for new capital goods is closely related to the demand for funds to finance the purchase of the goods. Thus, we can expect the demand for loanable funds by business to be a downward-sloping function of the real rate of interest because capital spending is a downward-sloping function of the real rate. The higher the real rate, the lower the demand for both capital goods and the funds to finance their purchase. The lower the real rate, the higher the demand for capital goods and the funds to finance them.

---

2. Consumers also borrow in the form of mortgage loans made to finance home purchases. When they do this, they are acting as business and are purchasing what officially is a capital good (residential construction). In our discussion, we assume mortgage borrowers are part of general business borrowers.

In chapter 13, we saw that consumer-durables spending is also sensitive to the real interest rate. The demand for consumer durable goods and the demand for funds to finance their purchase also go hand in hand. To make things simple, we can combine the two ideas. *The demand for loanable funds to finance both business capital goods and consumer durable goods can be thought of as primarily a downward-sloping function of the real rate of interest.*

The government is not influenced to any important degree by the real rate of interest (or by any other variable in our model for that matter). The government budget position is an autonomous variable. Not that it doesn't change. It changes plenty. But it changes for reasons unrelated to the economic determinants of the supply and demand for funds.

What we have said so far about the classical credit market is summarized graphically in 18.4, 18.5, and 18.6. In figure 18.4, an illustrative private (capital investment plus consumer durable) demand-for-funds curve is depicted and labeled *P*. It is a downward-sloping function of the real interest rate. For example, at a real rate of 3 percent, the amount of funds demanded by business and consumers is 50 billion. If the real rate falls to 2 percent, the demand for private funds rises to 60 billion.

The government borrows in the same credit market in which private borrowers seek funds. Whenever the government spends more than it receives in taxes, it runs a deficit in its budget. A budget deficit can be financed in one of two ways. First, the government could print up new money and use it to pay its bills. (Are you envisioning a Treasury official peeling off a wad of 100-dollar bills newly printed

**FIGURE 18.4.
The Demand for
Loanable Funds.**

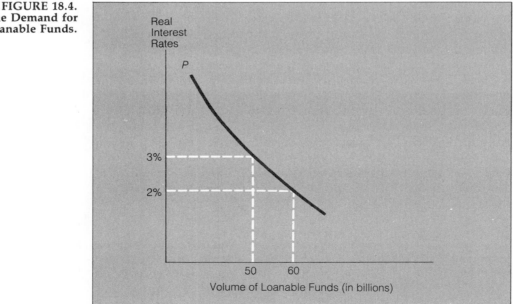

to pay for a new 2-million-dollar jet?) In the United States, this way of handling a budget deficit is not used. Instead, when the U.S. government runs one of its frequent budget deficits, it routinely finances it by borrowing in credit markets. The connection between budget deficits and government borrowing is good enough that we can think of the government's budget deficit and the government's demand for funds in credit markets as being of the same magnitude.

Figures 18.5 and 18.6 show how the government demand for funds fits into the classical credit market. Figure 18.5 illustrates a government budget deficit. At a real rate of 3 percent, the private demand for funds is 50 billion, as before. (The *P* curve is in the same position as in figure 18.4.) Suppose the government is financing a 20-billion deficit. The size of this deficit is the result of government programs and tax rates and is unrelated to the real rate. At all real rates, the total demand for funds is 20 billion higher than the private demand. The *P* + *D* curve illustrates this graphically (*D* stands for deficit financing). The *P* + *D* curve is the total demand for funds when the private demand is given by the *P* curve. If the deficit widens, the *P* + *D* curve shifts to the right in a parallel fashion. A cut in the deficit shifts the *P* + *D* curve to the left.

When the government runs a surplus, it does not reissue all of its bonds as they mature. If the Treasury has 5 billion of maturing bonds and only reissues 3 billion, it in effect buys back some of its own

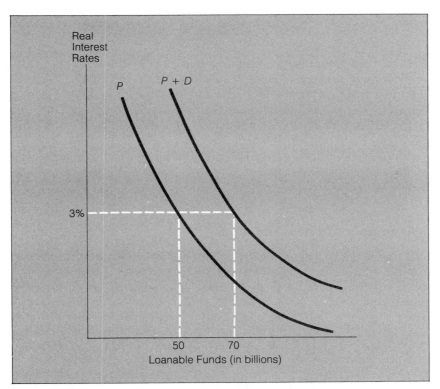

**FIGURE 18.5.**
**The Demand for**
**Credit with**
**Government Deficits.**

FIGURE 18.6.
Credit Demand with
Government
Surpluses.

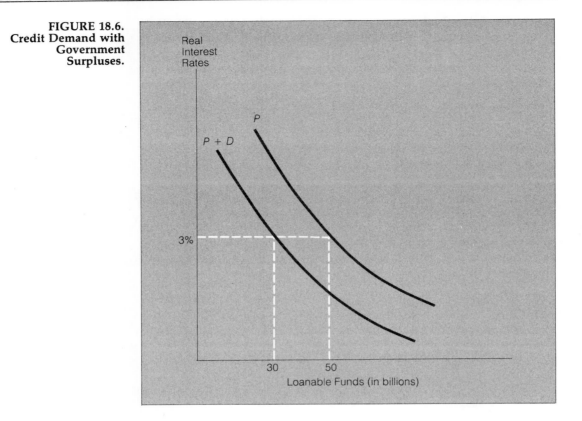

bonds. This amounts to a negative demand for funds.[3] Figure 18.6 shows the case of a government surplus. With private credit demand given by the $P$ curve, the total demand lies to the left, at the position $P + D$. Assume the government runs a 20-billion budget surplus. Then, at a real rate of 3 percent, private demand for funds is 50 billion and total demand is 30 billion.

Finally, if the government budget is perfectly balanced, there is no demand or supply of loanable funds by government, and the $P$ curve is also the *total*-demand-for-funds curve.

## The Supply of Loanable Funds

So far, we have talked exclusively about the demand for loanable funds, ignoring the source of the funds that business and government borrow? This source, called the *supply of loanable funds,* is basically household savings. *Household saving* is defined as DPI minus personal-consumption expenditures. So, household saving is a flow of funds earned by households but not currently spent by them on consumer goods. Some household saving goes directly into credit markets. When households buy stocks and corporate bonds, they become direct sup-

3. In other words, the government becomes a supplier of funds to the credit market when a surplus is present.

pliers of funds to credit markets. However, household saving mostly flows into banks, savings and loan associations, credit unions, mutual savings banks, insurance companies, and other financial institutions.

Financial intermediaries do not sit on these funds. After all, they are, in most cases, paying good money to acquire the saving of households. Accordingly, financial intermediaries lend funds to business at as high a rate of interest as the market allows. Financial intermediaries advance most of the funds in credit markets. But, they cannot lend what they do not have—they cannot make funds appear from a magician's hat.[4]

In a broad sense, financial intermediaries are limited in how much they can lend to business by the amount of consumer saving flowing through their tellers' windows and across their desks. This is not to say the two must go exactly together.[5] Banks regularly lend either somewhat more or somewhat less than this inflow by using a variety of asset-management techniques. But, fundamentally, a financial intermediary is just what the term says—a go between—when it comes to the question of how the loanable funds in credit markets got there. Households basically supply the funds through saving.

In looking at what determines the amount of funds households want to supply, we can use what we already know. In chapter 13 we saw that when income rises, households tend to spend a fraction of it and save the rest. The part saved increases the supply of funds to credit markets. In other words, the amount of funds being made available to credit markets is a positive function of the amount of consumer income.

The other thing we already know is that when the real rate of interest goes up, the amount households spend to buy consumer goods falls. This means that household saving rises when the real interest rate rises. Remember, saving is defined as income minus consumption. Thus, with income constant, whenever consumption falls, saving rises.

The relationship between the real rate and consumer saving is the key relationship for our analysis of credit supply. Earlier we saw that the demand for credit falls with a rising real rate. We now see that the supply of credit rises with an increasing real rate. The real rate is the key to adjusting the two sides of the market.

## Equilibrium in the Credit Market

We now have the whole picture of the credit market, and can see how it works. *Credit market equilibrium* is the particular interest rate

4. The ability of banks to advance funds is discussed in chapters 2 and 8.

5. Banks and other intermediaries also regularly tap the short-term excess cash of nonfinancial business in the form of certificates of deposit and in other similar ways. The easiest way to incorporate this idea into our credit-market framework is to view this process as business lending to itself via the intermediary of a bank.

and volume of loanable funds where no net pressures are brought about to change either the interest rate or the volume of loanable funds. Credit market equilibrium is shown in figure 18.7. The demand for funds is the curve labeled $P + D$. This is the same curve we saw in figures 18.5 and 18.6. The supply-of-funds is the positively sloped curve labeled $S$. Equilibrium occurs at a real rate of 2 percent. At 2 percent, the supply of funds equals the demand. Suppliers and demanders of funds are both happy at this rate. A volume of 55 billion of loanable funds changes hands from lender to borrower. There are no lenders left with money to lend. Borrowers obtain all the loans they want at the 2 percent rate. The market is cleared.

What if the real rate is higher than 2 percent? If the rate is 4 percent, more funds will be supplied because consumer-durables purchases fall and saving rises. Deposits in financial institutions rise. In figure 18.7, the result is that financial institutions are willing to supply 60 billion to credit markets when the real rate is 4 percent. But, at 4 percent, the demand for funds is down. The higher associated cost of capital discourages purchases of capital goods and consumer durables. Demand for funds is 45 billion. There are 15 billion of excess funds in the credit market. Competition among financial institutions to buy the bonds, stocks, and notes of firms and other borrowers is

**FIGURE 18.7.
Classical Credit
Market.**

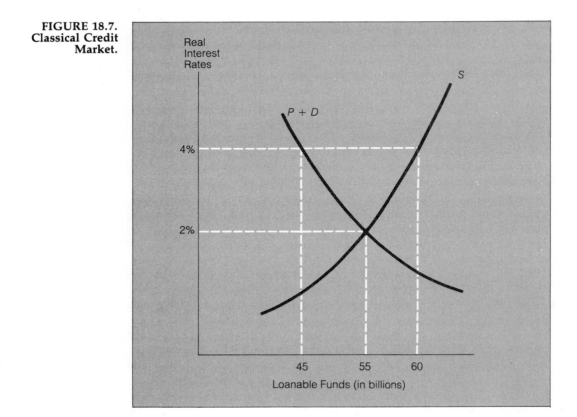

keen. The value of the securities is pushed up. Interest rates must fall in such a borrower's market. How far? Down to 2 percent, where the gap between the supply and demand has been eliminated.

If the real rate is lower than 2 percent, the demand for funds is greater than the supply. A shortage of funds exists. It is a lender's market. The real rate is pushed up. The pressure continues until the rate has risen to 2 percent.

In equilibrium, the real rate that evolves in the credit market is one that equates the amount of saving with the amount of borrowing. As long as this equilibrium occurs, all the income earned in current production but not spent by those who earned it will flow into the hands of borrowers who will spend it. When the credit market is cleared, Say's law is at work.

## DEFICIT SPENDING AND THE CREDIT MARKET

One of the striking implications of the natural-rate hypothesis is that government spending has a zero multiplier because of the resulting vertical aggregate-supply curve. Our loanable-funds model can be applied to the question of how government spending impacts on the economy as well. However, to do so, we must make some assumptions about how the government spending is financed. If no new taxes are levied, and the money supply is not increased, any new government spending either creates a reduced surplus in the budget, or increases the deficit. In our earlier analysis of the impact of government spending when the aggregate-supply curve is vertical, we did not assume taxes and/or the money supply were simultaneously changed; thus, we were implicitly assuming that government spending was financed by increasing the deficit. But, deficits are borrowed in the credit market. Our present model of the credit market enables this aspect of an increase in government spending to be examined carefully.

Let us trace through our model the effects of an increase in government spending that is financed by expanding the budget deficit. In figure 18.8, suppose that initially the demand-for-funds curve is in the position $P + D_0$. The equilibrium real rate is 2 percent. The steady-state volume of funds flowing from lenders to borrowers is 55 billion. Suppose also that $D_0$ is 10 billion, meaning that a 10-billion government budget deficit is being financed. The private demand for funds is $55 - 10 = 45$ billion. So, at a 2 percent real rate, private borrowers are seeking 45 billion of loanable funds. Now, the government decides to spend an additional 10 billion and finance it by increasing the deficit from 10 billion to 20 billion. Then $D$ rises by 10 billion, shifting the demand-for-funds curve to $P + D_1$. Under the pressure of this increased demand for funds, the equilibrium real rate rises to 3 percent.

To: Readers curious about government–business competition for funds
From: JWE

The two main parties involved in acquiring the savings of households in credit markets are government and business. Like brother and sister going after a limited supply of cookies, these two parties often are engaged in a competition to see who acquires the limited amount of funds available in credit markets. *Crowding out* is a term used to denote that one of the two parties is squeezed out of the credit market, and thus cannot spend what it could not borrow. A question that may arise about this crowding-out process is who crowds out whom?

There is good reason to believe that all the crowding out is by government of private demand. U.S. Treasury debt is almost all sold on a sealed-bid basis. The government announces it has 5 billion (or some other predetermined amount) of new bills and bonds for sale, and accepts bids on them on a certain date. As the date approaches, the bids come in. They are offers by lenders to buy so many bonds at a proposed price. The Treasury opens them at the prescribed hour and ranks them according to the highest proposed price. Keep in mind that the higher the price on a bill or bond, the lower the interest cost to the Treasury. (If necessary, review the discussion of this in chapter 5.) The Treasury then works down this ranking until it has sold all of the 5 billion. And, it always sells all the debts it seeks to sell. Price is no object. The Treasury will take whatever price is required in order to sell all of its new debt. Period. End of thought.

Not so with private borrowers. Firms wait anxiously and up to the last minute, assessing market conditions, probable interest costs, and competing offerings, before they decide to sell securities. When a heavy calendar of offered securities by the government and others confronts corporate borrowers, many withdraw their issues.

The difference between the two types of borrowers is pretty clear. The government always ends up successfully borrowing the funds it seeks. Private offerings are frequently postponed, reduced, or canceled because of market conditions. When crowding out occurs, can there be any doubt who crowds out whom?

Look at the points labeled A and B. They help us understand what is going on behind the scenes when the equilibrium real rate moves from 2 percent to 3 percent. Point A shows that the total demand for funds at a 3 percent real rate *would have been* 48 billion at the *old* government deficit of 10 billion. At 3 percent, private demand for funds is 38 and public demand is 10. Now, at the new larger government deficit, and the new 3 percent equilibrium real rate, the total demand for funds is 58, composed of the 38 billion of private demand (that we just saw would materialize at 3 percent) plus 20 billion of public demand.

At the new 3 percent equilibrium rate, consumers are persuaded to save 3 billion more and accordingly to spend 3 billion less on durable goods. This is shown by a move *along* the supply-of-funds curve from 2 percent, 55 billion to 3 percent, 58 billion.

How do these shifts fit together? How has economic activity changed as a result of the increase in government deficit financing? First, the government will definitely succeed in raising the additional 10 billion it needs to finance its new spending. (For more on this, see the last memo.) So, government spending rises by 10 billion. Consumers have been induced to save 3 billion more (58 − 55) out of their unchanged incomes, so we can infer that consumer spending must be down by 3 billion. What about investment spending? At 2 percent, 45 billion was being borrowed for private investment spending. At the new equilibrium of 3 percent, this demand drops to 38 billion. So, investment spending is down by 45 − 38 = 7 billion.

But, wait. Government spending up by 10 billion. Consumer spending down by 3 billion. Investment spending down by 7 billion. There is no net increase in spending! The increased government spending has just caused an offsetting decline in spending in private markets. With no net increase in spending, production does not increase. But the composition of production does change. Less consumer durables and less capital goods are being produced, while more government goods are being produced. However, no more total production occurs. The credit-market model we have now developed backs up what we said earlier about the natural-rate view of the effects of an increase in government spending. According to this view, government spending has a zero multiplier. No increase in real GNP. No

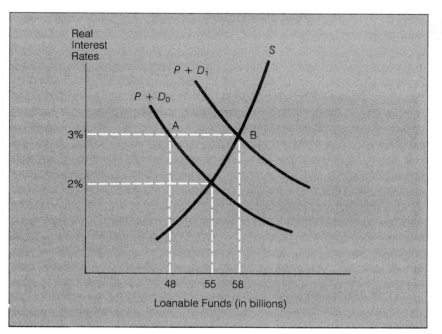

**FIGURE 18.8.**
**A Change in the**
**Demand for Funds.**

# Memorandum

You have been reading about the credit market from a theoretical viewpoint. It is a mistake to conclude from this that the credit market is a very abstract topic. To the contrary, it is written about in the newspapers every day, particularly in the *Wall Street Journal*. And what the *Journal* says is usually consistent with the credit-market model you have just been reading about. However, this consistency is not always plain to see. Let us make it so. Here are some quotes from the *Journal*.

> A 19½ prime rate became widespread yesterday as most major banks cut from 20% their base interest charge on corporate loans.
>
> The move . . . reflected declining loan demand coupled with a reduction in the bank's own cost for gathering funds for lending.

This statement follows nicely from the loanable-funds model. "Declining loan demand" means that the demand-for-funds curve in the credit-market model has shifted to the left. Draw yourself a picture of a shift like this and you will see that the result is a drop in the equilibrium interest rate. The part of the *Journal*'s statement about "a reduction in the . . . cost for gathering funds" means that banks are having to pay less for funds to advance in credit markets. Accordingly, they are willing to advance more funds for a given flow of consumer saving. The supply-of-funds curve in the credit-market model shifts to the right as a result of this change. This shift also leads to lower rates, as you can easily verify. So, the *Journal* and the credit-market model are definitely in agreement here.

> But, other interest rates rose yesterday as the nation's money and capital markets labored under the heavy supply of U.S. Treasury securities being auctioned this week

This statement follows from the credit-market model also. All you have to do is translate the part about a "heavy supply of U.S. Treasury securities" to mean that the government is demanding more funds in credit markets. When the government or corporations demand more funds, they do so by supplying more bonds and other securities in exchange. To supply a bond is to demand funds. So, the heavy Treasury-

net new jobs. The government spending crowds out an equal amount of private spending.[6]

## REALLOCATING PURCHASING POWER THROUGH THE CREDIT MARKET

The last example of an increase in government spending illustrated the condition called *crowding out*, which occurs when the demand for

6. If the government cuts its deficit by reducing spending, the process works in reverse. A reduction in the government-spending deficit shifts the demand-for-funds curve to the left. The real rate falls. Consumer saving falls and spending on consumer durables picks up. Capital spending rises in response to the decline in the real rate. The decline in deficit-financed government spending is offset by an increase in consumer and capital investment spending.

bond supply shifts the demand-for-funds curve to the right. Interest rates rise.

This second quote came from the same article as the first. So, on the same day that the prime rate was being cut by banks, rates on bonds and Treasury Bills increased. This illustrates something about the credit market that has so far escaped our analysis. Banks and other intermediaries that pass household savings through to borrowers do so in a number of distinct markets. In chapter 5 you saw that the prime rate was a short-term rate that applies largely to credit lines of business. Bill rates are also short-term, but are for discounted securities. Bond rates are longer term than the other two. A credit market exists for each type of security, and for all other types available as well. Interest rates on the various securities generally follow each other systematically, but it is not too surprising to see one type of rate fall while another rises. A divergent pattern reflects differences in the specific supply and demand conditions in each individual market. More light is shed on what prompted this particular situation in a later part of the same article.

Much of the drop in loans, moreover, represented a switching of borrowings by companies from banks to the market for commercial paper, or corporate IOUs. Rates in that market have been sharply below the prime fee, with many businesses being able to raise funds at less than 17%.

Firms are reacting to the situation where the commercial-paper rate is less than the prime rate in a very businesslike manner. Instead of borrowing from banks for their short-term working capital needs, some firms are selling short-term IOUs (commercial paper) in return for the excess short-term cash of others. Why not, with the interest rate on commercial paper 2.5 percent below the prime rate? But the result of this switching is that the prime rate falls while the commercial-paper rate (and the other rates to which it is closely related) rises. Eventually, the two rates tend to get back into their usual alignment. But in the meantime, the two rates move in opposite directions. In the United States, buyers of commercial paper and Treasury bills are often the same people and institutions. So, if the U.S. Treasury is increasing its financing via new T-bills at the same time that shifting patterns of business financing are increasing the flow of new commercial paper, then rising rates in these markets are the result. Do not forget the demand-for-funds curve. So, our credit-market model nicely accounts for the varying interest-rate patterns reported by the *Wall Street Journal*.

credit by both government and business exceeds the supply. The credit market resolves this problem by allocating credit to the highest bidder.

Can we see any evidence of this crowding out? Take a look at figure 18.9. It shows the level of federal government borrowing in private credit markets (the solid line) and the total private borrowing by business (the dashed line). The data prior to 1974 show clearly enough that rising government borrowing does seem to associate with falling private borrowing and vice versa. However, it is the 1974–77 period that is of key interest in this chart. As the economy slipped into the recession of 1973–75, employment fell and the government collected less taxes. The result was a skyrocketing deficit in the federal government budget. Treasury borrowing similarly skyrocketed from 1975–77. Look what happened to private borrowing over the same period. It fell to a low of just over 5 billion dollars for the first six months of

1975, compared with better than 40 billion a year earlier. Then, as public borrowing fell, private borrowing picked up. Beginning in late 1979, the rise in public borrowing was again accompanied by a fall in private borrowing.

Figure 18.9 does not prove that government spending and borrowing crowd out private spending and borrowing. It does establish that when public borrowing goes up, private borrowing goes down and vice versa. In a courtroom, that would be called circumstantial evidence. There is no eyewitness to the crime. However, figure 18.9 does place the suspect on the scene with a smoking revolver in hand.

We may profitably view this crowding-out effect in a broader way. When the real GNP is produced, a pool of purchasing power is created. This purchasing power cannot be enlarged without more production. So, if the government wants to purchase more, it will have to first acquire a bigger part of this pool of purchasing power from the private sector of the economy. If the government gets more, the private sector gets less. *Reallocating purchasing power is what the credit market is all about.* When the government wants more, it enters credit markets. Consumers and firms are induced by rising interest rates to

**FIGURE 18.9.
Government and
Private Borrowing.**

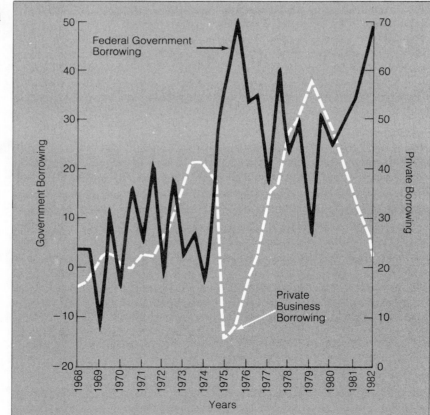

loan their purchasing power to the government in exchange for interest income. With reduced purchasing power, consumers and firms buy less as the government buys more. Fundmentally, the government does not add new purchasing power to the economy when it increases its spending. It only reallocates the purchasing power already there. More purchasing power comes about only by producing more goods and services.

## THE CREDIT MARKET AND THE REAL GNP

In our discussion of the credit market, we have assumed that the real GNP (and therefore total purchasing power in) the economy is determined independently of the credit market. Is this reasonable? Natural-rate theory says yes. Here is why. The real GNP is set by the profit-maximizing decisions of firms. The credit market's main variable, the interest rate, does not enter into these profit-maximizing calculations in any important way. Even though interest rates are a cost of production, they do not vary with production. Thus, the profit-maximizing decisions of firms regarding how much real GNP to produce is independent of what is happening in the credit market. Because the two are not related, the real GNP can be assumed to be autonomous as far as the working of the credit market is concerned.[7]

However, when changes do independently occur in the real GNP, credit markets are affected. If the real GNP goes up, total purchasing power increases, and consumer spending and saving rise. The supply-of-saving curve responds by shifting to the right. With more total income, more saving takes place at any and all real interest rates. Figure 18.10 shows the overall effect on the credit market. With the demand for funds given by $P + D$, assume the initial supply of funds is given by the curve labeled $S_0$. If the real GNP rises, the supply-of-funds curve shifts right to $S_1$. The real rate falls in response to the increased flow of funds. More capital spending takes place, as the equilibrium volume of loanable funds rises from 50 billion to 55 billion.

How about the demand-for-funds curve? Are you wondering whether it shifts when the real GNP rises? The business demand for funds is related to future profit expectations, not current production. The government demand is given by the budget deficit or surplus. If government increases its spending in proportion to a rise in the real GNP, while taxes collected also rise in proportion to the real GNP, then the size of the deficit is independent of the current real GNP.

7. However, the credit market does *allocate* the independently determined production, among consumers, firms, and the government. Firms will have to adjust the kind of output they produce in response to credit-market-induced changes in the composition of the real GNP. But, the dealings in the credit market do not impact upon the level of total production. Say's law provides that total purchasing power continues to equal total products produced.

**FIGURE 18.10.
Impact of a Changing
Real GNP.**

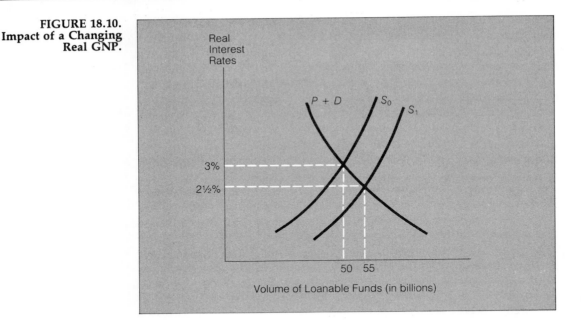

Accordingly, the demand-for-funds curve would not systematically rise and fall because of similar changes in the current real GNP.[8]


## WHAT ABOUT RECESSIONS?

The natural-rate hypothesis envisions a fully adjusted labor market that corrects its own imbalances by changes in the real wage rate. The labor market is at or nearly at full employment most of the time in the sense that the supply of labor equals the demand. The credit market rechannels all currently earned but unspent income into the hands of borrowers-spenders. Demand in general cannot be deficient. In recessions, inventories of unsold products pile up.

But, what about recessions? For example, there are repetitive cycles in the automobile industry where there is an obvious oversupply of newly produced cars. Natural-rate theorists believe that recessions and gluts such as those periodically seen in the automobile industry are the result of the wrong products being produced, and will correct themselves. When the automobile industry produces nine million cars, enough purchasing power is created to buy all nine million. But, if the public wants other products instead, cars may go unsold while shortages of other products crop up. When such disruptions are severe, they can add up to a recession, because adjustments to such

8. However, current production could reasonably be argued to condition future profit expectations, in which case this effect could shift the funds-demand curve when real GNP rises. We ignore this possibility in the interest of simplicity.

imbalances take time to occur. For example, when automobile inventories mount, a signal is sent to automobile makers to cut back the level of production or change the product being produced. Also, a signal that production should be increased is sent to the areas of the economy where demand is greater than production. In time, the imbalances disappear. But, production cutbacks in one sector of the economy may precede buildups in areas to which the demand is shifting. If this occurs on a large enough scale, a recession is produced, according to natural-rate theory.

The depression of the 1930s in the United States was an exception to the pattern envisioned by natural-rate theorists. In the early part of that decade, the demand for funds contracted severely as qualified firms sought no new funds for expansion.[9] In 1933, new investment fell short of depreciation of old capital for the only time on record. Interest rates on short-term notes fell to well below 1 percent. Yet, demand for funds did not pick up. More funds were available than were sought by qualified borrowers in credit markets. An inconsistency developed in the demand and supply of funds. Financial institutions preferred to "sit on" their funds rather than supply them to credit markets at almost zero interest rates. In this situation, the credit market lost its ability to rechannel savings into the hands of spenders. The purchasing power flowing into banks was essentially hoarded, sitting idly in bank reserve accounts. The funds were described as falling into a *liquidity trap*. A general deficiency in demand followed the massive cutbacks in production and employment. Say's law was temporarily suspended.

Depressions are not normal times. The depression years were perhaps the only experience in the United States where credit markets did not function adequately to enforce Say's law. Natural-rate theorists are willing to concede that in such extraordinary times, the labor market will not clear, demand will not adjust to supply, and most of the propositions associated with the natural-rate hypothesis do not hold.

This chapter has completed the model of the economy that associates with contemporary macroeconomic theory. This model can be used to structure and organize your thinking about how the economy behaves. In the next two chapters, we use the model now developed as a guide for thinking about some important questions related to how the economy behaves. The first of these—the subject of the next chapter—is what causes inflation. There has not been a more important question than this for the U.S. economy of the decade of the 1970s. The next group of questions, to be taken up in chapter 20, deals with the impact of government fiscal and monetary policies on the behavior of the economy.

9. Firms going bankrupt were interested in acquiring funds, to be sure. But, financially troubled borrowers are not seen by lenders as good risks. Therefore, they drop out of the demand-supply picture as far as interest-rate determination is concerned.

**Important Ideas in This Chapter**

**1.** The natural-rate hypothesis is the contention that the labor market is approximately adjusted most of the time, such that the amount of employment and the rate of unemployment are usually at their equilibrium or "natural" levels.

**2.** Under the natural-rate view, the unemployed consists of those who are (1) voluntarily unemployed because they are seeking higher wages than the market wage for their skills, (2) untrained for available jobs, (3) seasonally unemployed, or (4) between jobs.

**3.** Natural-rate theorists contend that current unemployment data are not informative as to whether the labor market is or is not in equilibrium. This is due to the way the data are collected. They also point out that the natural rate itself may be shifting. Thus, to correctly measure whether the labor market is in equilibrium or not requires separating shifts in the equilibrium level of unemployment from situations where the supply of and demand for labor diverge.

**4.** An important critique of the natural-rate hypothesis is that demand is often deficient relative to the amount supplied, leading firms to produce according to the level demanded. The natural-rate theorists' response to this is to invoke the logic of Say's law.

**5.** Say's law is the proposition that producing a real GNP of a given size creates a level of aggregate demand equal to the real GNP produced. With the credit market acting to recycle unused purchasing power via arranging contracts between savers and borrowers-spenders, a general deficiency in demand should not be expected.

**6.** The credit market is the national financial arena where lenders and borrowers engage in trades of financial instruments. Together, they determine the interest rate.

**7.** The theory of how credit markets operate is called loanable-funds theory. It examines the demand for and supply of credit, and deals with how the real interest rate is set.

**8.** Equilibrium in credit markets occurs at the specific real rate of interest where the supply of funds flowing into these markets equals the demand for funds. If the two are not equal, then the real rate changes.

**9.** Crowding out occurs in credit markets when one or more demanders of funds increases the demand for credit at all interest rates. This increase causes the real rate to rise, which reduces the demand for credit by other parties. Thus, the available credit is reallocated among demanders.

**10.** Reallocating purchasing power is a major function of credit markets. For example, if the government wants more purchasing power than it has via taxes collected, it enters credit markets and borrows. The purchasing power the government acquires will not be acquired by private borrowers, so the result is a reduction in private purchases in line with the increase in government purchases.

**11.** Saving flows are the major source of the supply of credit. When the real GNP rises, the supply of saving can be expected to rise, thus shifting the supply-of-funds curve.

**12.** Natural-rate theorists feel that recessions are periods where specific product lines (such as automobiles or housing) are produced in quantities that exceed the demand for them. In such times, the total amount of purchasing power still is adequate to buy all the aggregate output—however, the mix of products in demand is not the same as that being produced. The shortfall in demand for some products must, according to Say's law, translate into an excess demand for other products. It takes a period of adjustment for the economy to absorb important shifts in demand from one industry to another. Recessions occur when such shifts are significant.

**13.** The depression of the 1930s is a different matter. In that period, the credit market apparently did not function adequately to allocate all purchasing power to current expenditures, and a general breakdown in demand occurred.

**1.** Assume that the natural-rate thesis is on trial for its life. Put yourself in the position of the attorney for the prosecution. Construct the best possible case against this hypothesis. Use any sources you wish. Now, be the attorney for the defense. Do the same from this point of view.

**Discussion Questions**

**2.** Does the idea of a credit market applied to a barter economy make any sense? Explain, describing how such a market in a barter system would or would not work.

**3.** How is the credit market affected if a substantial number of households use their savings to buy diamonds and gold from U.S. dealers? What if they buy diamonds and gold from European dealers?

**4.** Suppose that a taste-related (independent of current income) increase in the demand for automobiles occurs. Households go on a spending spree and buy 25 percent more automobiles than last year, even though real DPI is about the same. Is the credit market affected by this change? How? Will real GNP go up? Explain.

**5.** What do crowding out and the size of the multiplier have to do with each other? Explain as carefully as possible.

Crowding out is a subject that has been of interest to the research staff of the St. Louis Federal Reserve Bank for more than a decade. To read about evidence and studies regarding crowding-out effects,

**Suggested Readings**

check recent issues of the monthly *Review of the Federal Reserve Bank of St. Louis.* For a statistical analysis of the impact of the credit market on the U.S. economy, see Gary Fromm and Lawrence Klein, ''The NBER/NSF Model Comparison Seminar: An Analysis of Results,'' *Annals of Economic and Social Measurement,* Winder 1976.

## CHAPTER 19

# What Causes Inflation?

///EMO

To:        All readers
From:      JWE


Inflation is like living through a flu epidemic. If you have a case of it, you worry about how to get rid of it while you suffer. If you don't have it, you worry about how to keep from getting it. There has not been a more headline-grabbing topic in economics in recent years than inflation. In this chapter, we look the subject straight in the eye, from the vantage point of now having covered enough theory to examine it in a systematic way.

First, we consider how shifts in demand impact on the price level. Then, we examine the role of productivity in inflation. We deal with the meaning and causes of stagflation—the twin occurrence of inflation and recession. Then, the central role of the money supply in inflation is discussed, leading to an analysis of the noninflationary growth rate in the money supply. The monetary conditions associated with continual inflation are the final topic in this chapter.

In the United States and most western European nations, inflation was the most serious economic problem of the decade of the 1970s. For most of these nations, the problem continues into the 1980s. The question "What causes such an inflation?" is fundamentally one involving macroeconomic theory. We have now pursued enough of this theory to systematically examine the problem of inflation.

Recall from chapter 4 that *inflation* occurs when prices are rising at a more or less continuous and significant pace. In terms of the macroeconomic model we have now developed, inflation occurs when prices are adjusting from one equilibrium position to a newer and higher equilibrium position. Basically, anything that significantly raises the equilibrium price level in the economy leads to a period of inflation as prices adjust upward to the new position. For inflation to continue for long periods, the equilibrium level of prices must be moving up fast enough that actual price adjustments cannot close the gap. The inflation of the 1970s in the United States was of this type. Prices were continually adjusting upward toward continually changing equilibrium positions.

In the discussion that follows, we examine the impact on equilibrium prices of various underlying changes in the economy. We then talk of inflationary periods that occur as actual prices adjust to these equilibrium positions. It should be understood that the processes we describe could evolve into *continual inflation* if one or more underlying influences on equilibrium prices is steadily changing in a way to repeatedly push up the equilibrium price level.

One set of conclusions about inflation emerges if the economy is operating at a level of employment below the natural rate. Another set of conclusions emerges when the economy is at the natural rate. We first examine the below-natural-rate case.

# INFLATION WHEN WAGES ARE RIGID AND UNEMPLOYMENT EXISTS

The main reason the economy could be expected to operate below the natural rate is that wages are rigid and will not go down when market conditions indicate they should. In this case, an increase in demand for products and services generally leads to some combination of an increase in the real GNP and inflation until higher prices are reached. We now trace through our macroeconomic model the specific consequences for inflation of a shift in demand.

## Changes in Demand and Inflation When Wages Are Rigid

Some basics of this case are depicted in figure 19.1. In part (a), the IS curve is initially at $IS_0$ and the LM curve is at $LM(P = P_0)$. The equilibrium aggregate demand occurs when the real GNP is at $y_0$ and the interest rate is at $r_0$. In part (b) of figure 19.1, the price-demand curve is initially in the position $D_0$ corresponding to a real GNP of $y_0$ and a price level of $P_0$. If the natural rate of employment occurs, a real GNP of $y_f$ is produced, as is denoted in part (a) of the figure. This $y_f$ level of real GNP corresponds to the vertical part of the aggregate-supply curve, $S$, in part (b). The initial equilibrium in figure 19.1 is below this $y_f$ level, indicating that employment is less than the natural rate. Thus, some involuntary unemployment exists and the economy is operating at less than its labor-force capacity.

If some component of aggregate demand increases (such as government spending, capital outlays, consumer spending, or net exports), the IS curve shifts outward similar to the shift from $IS_0$ to $IS_1$ shown in part (a) of figure 19.1. This shift in demand also produces a shift in the derived price-demand curve, which moves out to the position labeled $D_1$. Prices now rise, because of the increase in demand, from $P_0$ to $P_1$. This shift in turn decreases the real money supply, shifting the LM curve in part (a) of figure 19.1 back to the position labeled $LM(P = P_1)$. At this point, the economy stabilizes at $y_1$ and $r_1$, with the price level stabilizing at $P_1$.

A period of inflation occurs as the economy adjusts from price level $P_0$ to price level $P_1$. But, it is not an endless process. If no further

**FIGURE 19.1.
Changes in Demand
and Inflation.**

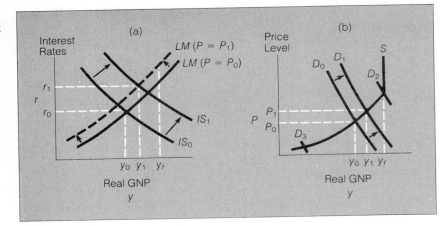

shifts occurred, the economy would experience a period of *intermittent
inflation* that would last only as long as prices took to reach the new
equilibrium level $P_1$.

With the price-demand curve starting from the initial position $D_0$,
any increase in demand (positive shift in the IS curve) produces both
an increase in the real GNP and a period of intermittent inflation that
ends at the higher but stable price level $P_1$. But, if the price-demand
curve starts from the position $D_2$ (where the economy is at the natural
rate), the result of an increase in demand is *only* an increase in prices,
as the $D_2$ curve shifts up along the vertical aggregate-supply curve.
On the other hand, if the price-demand curve is in the initial position
$D_3$, the result of an increase in demand is primarily an increase in the
real GNP, with little increase in prices, as the $D_3$ curve moves along
a nearly horizontal aggregate-supply curve.

## Changes in Productivity and
## Inflation When Wages Are Rigid

Changing demand is not the exclusive catalyst for price increases.
Changes that affect the aggregate-supply curve also affect the equilibrium price level, and can be a cause of inflation. One important
supply-related influence is the pattern of labor productivity. Recall
from our earlier discussion of the labor market that the demand-for-
labor curve is given by the marginal-product-of-labor schedule, which
is the amount by which output increases when the amount of labor
is increased. Many factors affect the position of the marginal-product-
of-labor curve. Among them are (1) the skills and training of the labor
force, (2) the amount of machinery and equipment the labor force has
to work with (generally the more machinery and equipment per worker,
the more output per hour), and (3) the fullness of production.

In the case of the third factor, experience shows that when recessions occur, workers are initially not laid off in proportion to the

decline in production taking place. A 10 percent decline in production might produce a 2 to 4 percent decline in the amount of labor hours employed. There are several reasons for this pattern. The existing work force has increasing amounts of company-specific training, which makes such personnel costly to replace. Clerical and managerial personnel have been molded into an organization that would be costly to re-establish after a period of significant layoffs. And, management does not know whether an initial decline in demand for the firm's products is temporary or lasting, and thus is reluctant to begin layoffs until the situation is clarified.

For all these reasons, the tendency in the United States is for recessions to lower the productivity of the labor force. The ratio of output to hours worked generally falls in recessions in the United States. We may assume that the marginal product of labor also falls.

Figure 19.2 examines the consequences for prices of a decline in the marginal product of labor, which could be occurring for any of the three reasons just listed. First, consider part (a) of the figure. Initially, the demand-for-labor curve is in the position labeled $MPL_0$. With the supply of labor at $SL$, the equilibrium level of employment corresponding to the natural rate is $N_{f,0}$. But, because of the rigid wages we are assuming, the real wage is at $W_0/P_0$, when the amount of profit-maximizing labor is $N_0$. Unemployment is equal to $N_s$ minus $N_0$. In part (b) of figure 19.2, the production function is shown in the initial position $Q_0$. When $N_0$ labor is employed, the real GNP produced is $y_0$. In part (c) of figure 19.2, when $y_0$ is produced, aggregate supply and demand are in balance, leading to the stable price level $P_0$. (Also note that the natural level of employment, $N_{f,0}$, leads to a real GNP of $y_{f,0}$, which corresponds to the vertical part of the aggregate-supply curve in part (c) of the figure.)

The assumed shift in productivity moves the labor-demand curve from $MPL_0$ to $MPL_1$. Two important related changes occur. First, the equilibrium level of employment falls to $N_{f,1}$. Second, the production function moves down to the position labeled $Q_1$. To visualize why the production function moves down, draw a vertical line through the new and old production functions. It shows that a given amount of labor associates with less production after the fall in labor productivity. The fall in the production function in turn decreases the equilibrium real GNP from $y_{f,0}$ to $y_{f,1}$. Accordingly, the aggregate-supply curve shifts upward and backward from the initial position $S_0$ to the new position $S_1$. To see the reasoning behind this shift, go back to part (a) of the figure and look at the horizontal line corresponding to the real wage $W_0/P_0$. At the initial price level $P_0$ (and thus at $W_0/i0/P_0$), employment was at $N_0$. After the fall in productivity, the same price level and real wage correspond to a smaller employment level. A smaller $N$ translates into a smaller real GNP. Now, go to part (c) of the figure and look at the horizontal line corresponding to $P_0$. It shows that a smaller real GNP occurs at $P_0$ after the change.

**FIGURE 19.2.**
**Changes in**
**Productivity and**
**Inflation.**

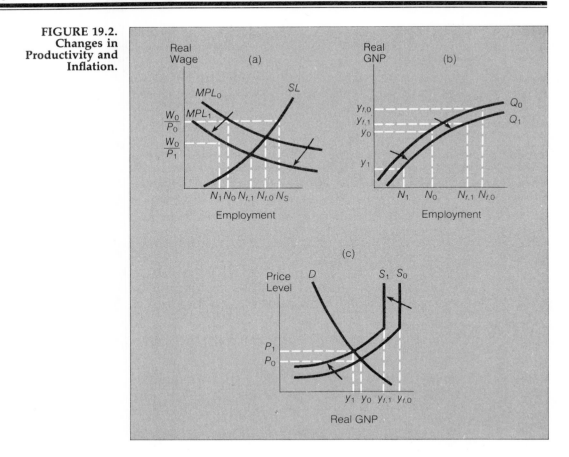

**FIGURE 19.2. Changes in Productivity and Inflation.**

When equilibrium is restored, the decrease in labor productivity leads to (1) a rise in prices to $P_1$, (2) a fall in employment to $N_1$, (3) a reduction in the real wage of labor to $W_0/P_1$, and (4) a decline in the real GNP to $y_1$. None of these is an attractive change in the economy. Indeed, the scenario just developed provides sound reasoning for the contention that productivity *growth* is a key to achieving price stability, rising employment, rising real wages, and a rising real GNP.

## INFLATION UNDER THE NATURAL-RATE HYPOTHESIS

If labor markets are in equilibrium most of the time as the natural-rate hypothesis contends, the impact on prices of demand shifts is not the same as we have seen for the rigid-wage case. We now trace through the same changes examined in figures 19.1 and 19.2, only now for the case of the natural-rate hypothesis.

## Demand and Inflation
## Under the Natural-Rate Hypothesis

When the natural-rate hypothesis holds, the aggregate-supply curve is vertical. The amount of goods and services supplied by firms becomes insensitive to prices, because all price changes are met by similar changes in wages, thus leaving the real wage unchanged. Figure 19.3 shows the results of a change in demand under this condition. In part (a), the IS and LM curves intersect initially at the natural level of real GNP, $y_f$. The IS curve is in the position $IS_0$ while the LM curve is in the position $LM(P = P_0)$. A shift in demand occurs, shifting the IS curve to $IS_1$. If the price level stayed at its initial level of $P_0$, aggregate demand would rise to $y_1$, the new intersection of the shifted IS curve with the initial LM curve. Part (b) of figure 19.3 shows that this increase in demand shifts the price-demand curve from its initial position of $D_0$ to $D_1$, which now shows that aggregate demand is at $y_1$ when the price level is $P_0$. But, the excess of aggregate demand over supply causes prices to rise. Inflation occurs, until the price level reaches $P_1$, where aggregate demand and supply are again in balance. At that price level, the LM curve has shifted back to the position $LM(P = P_1)$, where aggregate demand equals $y_f$ and markets are all in balance.

The net result of a shift in demand under the natural-rate hypothesis is a period of inflation leading to a higher equilibrium price level. The real GNP does not change as it would generally be expected to do under rigid wages. Interest rates are pushed up by the added pressures of the higher price level on the real money supply.

## Productivity and Inflation
## Under the Natural-Rate View

Figure 19.4 shows the situation of a decrease in the marginal product of labor under the natural-rate view. The labor-demand curve starts

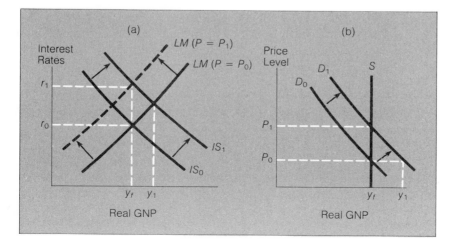

**FIGURE 19.3.
Demand and Inflation
Under the Natural-
Rate View.**

in the position $MPL_0$ with the real wage at $W_0/P_0$ and the level of employment in equilibrium at $N_{f,0}$. The production function is at $Q_0$, the equilibrium real GNP is $y_{f,0}$, and the price level is $P_0$ as determined by the intersection of the price-demand curve $D$ with the initial aggregate-supply curve $S_0$. Assume now that productivity drops, shifting the labor-demand curve to $MPL_1$. The equilibrium employment level declines to $N_{f,1}$, and the actual employment level quickly adjusts to this new position. The drop in the marginal product of labor shifts the production function down to $Q_1$. The new equilibrium real GNP is reduced to $y_{f,1}$, which shifts the aggregate-supply curve to the position labeled $S_1$, and causes prices to rise to $P_1$.

The net effect of the decline in productivity is a rise in prices to $P_1$, a fall in employment, a fall in the real wage to its new equilibrium level of $W_1/P_1$, and a decline in the real GNP. These conclusions are the same as those of the case of rigid wages. For productivity changes, the rigid wage and natural-rate models coincide, which means that our assessment of how changing labor productivity affects the economy is independent of whether we adopt the natural-rate or rigid-wage view.

## INFLATIONARY RECESSIONS

In the 1970s in the United States, recessions led to increased rather than reduced inflationary pressures. In the recession of 1974–1975, the inflation during the recession was almost twice as severe as before the recession began. The same pattern was repeated in the recession of 1980. Some writers coined the term *stagflation* to describe the twin occurrence of recession and inflation.

The examples we have worked through in figures 19.2 and 19.4 show how stagflation can occur given either the rigid-wage or the natural-wage hypothesis. During recessions, the demand for products and services falls, causing the IS curve to shift to the left. The leftward shift in the IS curve produces a leftward movement in the price-demand (D) curve in figures 19.2 and 19.4.[1] However, as discussed earlier, recession also causes a decline in productivity. The productivity decline causes the aggregate-supply function to move in the directions shown in figures 19.2 and 19.4. If the aggregate-supply curve shifts back faster than the D curve shifts back, *then a net leftward shift in the aggregate-supply curve will occur*, and the result will be just as it is shown in either figure 19.2 or figure 19.4.

1. In both 1974–1975 and 1980, the Federal Reserve system offset some of this leftward movement in the D curve by increasing the growth rate of the money supply during the recession. The effect of an increase in the money supply is to move the LM curve to the right, which offsets the effect of the falling IS curve on the price-demand schedule.

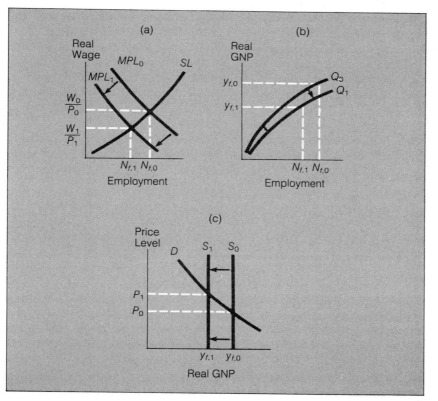

**FIGURE 19.4.**
**Changes in Productivity and Inflation Under the National-Rate View.**

Table 19.1 contains data for recent expansionary and recessionary periods in the United States. Annualized growth rates for all the primary variables in our analysis are shown. The values correspond quite well to the theoretical analyses presented in figures 19.2 and 19.4. Notice first the pattern of change in productivity. Average productivity, as measured by the ratio of real GNP to hours worked, rose during the two expansionary periods shown and declined during both recessions. From this we can assume that the two recessions were accompanied by leftward shifts in the aggregate MPL function. This corresponds to the shifts examined in figures 19.2 and 19.4. Table

**TABLE 19.1**
**Performance of the U.S. Economy during Expansion and Recession**

| ANNUAL RATE OF CHANGE IN: | EXPANSION 1971.1–1973.4 | RECESSION 1973.4–1975.1 | EXPANSION 1975.1–1980.1 | RECESSION 1980.1–1980.4 |
|---|---|---|---|---|
| Inflation | +5.5% | +10.3% | 7.9% | 9.8% |
| Employment | +3.5% | − 2.4% | +3.5% | −1.3% |
| Real wage | +1.5% | − 3.3% | −0.7% | −1.8% |
| Real GNP | +5.1% | − 3.8% | +4.9% | −1.4% |
| Real GNP per employee | +1.5% | − 1.5% | +1.2% | −0.2% |

19.1 shows that prices, employment, the real wage, and the real GNP responded according to the script provided by these figures.[2]

For the 1971–1973 period when expansion occurred in the United States, a moderate inflation rate was accompanied by growth in employment, the real wage, and the real GNP. During the 1973.4–1975.1 recession, inflation nearly doubled from the prior period. Employment fell. The real wage fell. The results for the next expansion-recession are nearly the same, with the exception being that the growth rate in the real wage did not become positive during the expansion. The rate of decline during the prior recession was reduced, but wages did not rise enough over the expansion to offset the effect on real wages of the rising overall pattern of inflation.

## INFLATION AND MONEY GROWTH WHEN WAGES ARE RIGID

So far, changes in demand for products and services and changes affecting the aggregate-supply curve have been examined for their consequences regarding inflation and changes in the price level. How about the money supply and inflation? In chapter 1, the example of the barter economy illustrated the impossibility of inflation in a moneyless system. From that it was concluded that the problem of inflation is inherently one involving money. In this section we examine how that linkage works for the case of rigid wages and some unemployment. Figure 19.5 shows the situation.

In part (a) of figure 19.5, the economy is in an initial equilibrium position with the money supply at a level $M_0$. The price level is $P_0$, given by the intersection of the aggregate-supply curve $S$ and the aggregate-demand curve $D_0$. With the money supply at $M_0$ and prices at $P_0$, the LM curve is in the initial position denoted by $LM(P = P_0, M = M_0)$. This produces an equilibrium real GNP of $y_0$ and an interest rate of $r_0$. Since $y_0$ is less than the full-employment level, $y_f$, some unemployment exists.

Suppose now that the Federal Reserve increases the money supply by injecting new reserves into the economy via open-market policy. The money supply rises to $M_1$. This rise in the money supply shifts the LM curve to the new position labeled $LM(P = P_0, M = M_1)$. The added money increases demand at the price level $P_0$, so the price-demand curve shifts to the right, from its initial position, $D_0$, to the new position $D_1$, as shown in part (b) of figure 19.5. Prices rise as a result of the shift in demand, causing the LM curve to move back

2. Even so, other contributing factors were at work (besides those shown in the figures), particularly in the early 1970s when the OPEC oil cartel produced an important exogenous upward pressure on prices. Various agricultural perturbations also contributed to the situation, as did inflationary expectations in the latter part of the decade.

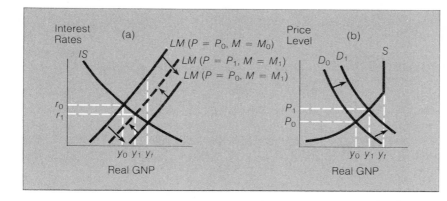

**FIGURE 19.5.
Inflation and Money
Growth When Wages
Are Rigid.**

toward its initial position. When the price level has risen to $P_1$, aggregate demand equals supply. The LM curve has moved to the position labeled $LM(P = P_1, M = M_1)$ where the IS and LM are in balance, and where the economy stabilizes.

The result of the increase in the money supply, given rigid wages and some unemployment is to (1) increase prices, (2) increase the real GNP, and (3) lower interest rates. The length and severity of the inflation depend on how much the supply of money is increased relative to the economy's need for it.

## INFLATION AND MONEY GROWTH
## UNDER THE NATURAL-RATE VIEW

Under the natural-rate hypothesis, money has some differing effects on the economy than under the rigid-wage case. Figure 19.6 shows the natural-rate case. The IS and LM curve intersect initially to produce the equilibrium $y_f$ and $r_0$ with the price level stable at $P_0$. The money supply is again increased to $M_1$, which shifts the LM curve to the position labeled $LM(P = P_0, M = M_1)$ and also shifts the price-demand curve to the position labeled $D_1$. Prices begin to increase, and continue until the price level has risen to the new equilibrium level $P_1$. At this level, the LM curve has shifted completely back to its initial position. (That is, the curve is in the same position when $P = P_0$ and $M = M_0$ as it is when $P = P_1$ and $M = M_1$.) We know that the curve goes back to its initial position because if it remained to the right of the original point, the amount of demand would still exceed the amount produced. And, as long as this condition exists, prices keep rising.

When the economy stabilizes, the rise in prices is exactly in proportion to the increase in the money supply, while real GNP has not increased. The new real money supply, $M_1/P_1$, is the same as the old real money supply, $M_0/P_0$. The introduction of the new money by the Federal Reserve has added to the purchasing power of the economy,

**FIGURE 19.6.**
**Inflation and Money**
**Growth—The Natural-**
**Rate View.**

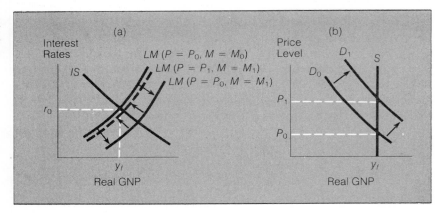

but not to the goods available for sale. As a result, the price of goods is bid up until all the new purchasing power is exhausted.

Under either the rigid-wage or natural-rate view, expanding the money supply leads to inflation until a new higher equilibrium price level is attained. The main difference between the natural-rate conclusions and the rigid-wage conclusions is in what happens to real output when money is expanded. Under the rigid-wage case, the expansion of money leads to an increase in production and to more employment, while it lowers the interest rate. But under the natural-rate view, no additional production takes place and interest rates return to their initial level. One important implication of the natural-rate view is that the *supply of money has no significant connection with the production of goods and services* in the economy or with the amount of employment that will take place.

The reason for these differences can be put simply. Under the rigid-wage view, the inflation that results from money growth lowers the real wage, and the lower real wage induces firms to increase production and employment.

## MONEY GROWTH AND CONTINUAL INFLATION

The last two sections have shown that if the economy is in an equilibrium position and the supply of money is increased, the result is inflation until a higher equilibrium price level is attained. The connection between money and inflation holds whether the natural-rate or rigid-wage assumption is made. But, this does not mean that any and every expansion of the money supply leads to inflation and raises prices. As the economy's equilibrium real GNP rises, the economy needs more money for transactions. If the supply of money is growing over time at just the rate at which the real GNP grows, then no inflation will occur as a result of the money growth.[3]

3. Notice that this is the same conclusion as in the rigid-wage case discussed earlier.

Let us pursue the logic behind this last statement by first considering some of the main reasons why the equilibrium real GNP might be changing over time. We shall focus on the natural-rate case, but the main conclusions are the same for the rigid-wage view. Fundamentally, the equilibrium real GNP is produced as a result of firms hiring the profit-maximizing amount of labor. In turn, the profit-maximizing amount of labor is determined by the intersection of the labor-supply curve with the aggregate marginal product of labor. From year to year, the work-age population normally grows. As this occurs, the supply curve of labor shifts to the right.

At the same time, new firms are formed and existing firms are enlarged. This added capacity increases the total demand for labor by all firms at each real wage. In addition, changes in technology regularly make existing labor more productive. For these reasons, the demand-for-labor schedule (the MPL curve) can be expected to regularly shift to the right from year to year.

Visualize both the labor-supply curve and the labor-demand curve regularly shifting to the right and you will see a picture of a normally growing natural level of employment. The word *normally* is important. There are no guarantees that the natural rate of employment will grow through time. But, as long as population grows, the number of firms producing increases, the size of existing firms increases, and technology increases the productivity of labor, then the natural employment level will rise.

Growth in the natural employment level does not occur in isolation. At the same time, growth both in population and in the income from a growing natural employment level can be expected to lead to a pattern of growth in the demand for goods and services. This growing demand causes the IS curve to continually move to the right.

Figure 19.7 shows this growth process. In part (a), the IS and LM curves are in the initial position shown by $IS_0$ and $LM_0$. They intersect at the natural level of real GNP denoted by $y_{f,0}$. Part (b) of figure 19.7 shows the aggregate-supply curve initially at $S_0$ and the price-demand curve at $D_0$. Thus, the price level is $P_0$. With the passage of time, say a year, the growth in the natural level of employment shifts the associated natural level of the real GNP to $y_{f,1}$. The aggregate-supply curve reflects this shift by moving to $S_1$. Concurrently, the growth in demand shifts the IS curve to $IS_1$. As long as there are no shifts in the demand for money, the growth in the money supply will determine how far the LM curve moves during the same time period.

Suppose that no increase in the money supply occurs. The LM curve thus remains in the position $LM_0$ while the IS curve shifts to $IS_1$ and the natural level of the real GNP moves to $y_{f,1}$. Equilibrium in product and money markets occurs at point C. As a result, the price-demand curve moves to the position $D_c$ while the aggregate-supply curve has moved to $S_1$. At a price level of $P_0$, demand falls short of aggregate supply, and prices must drop. If prices were fully flexible, deflation would occur until the price level had dropped to $P_c$. This drop in prices would increase the real money supply, which would shift the LM curve in part (a) of figure 19.7 to point $a$. At this point (when prices reach $P_c$), demand equals supply and the price level stabilizes.

If prices were either slow to fall or rigid in the downward direction, the situation just described would have another ending. Instead of prices falling to restore equilibrium, the deficiency in demand represented by the horizontal distance between point $y_{f,o}$ and $y_{f,1}$ would lead to a cutback in the real GNP produced. This cutback would continue until the gap between aggregate supply and demand was eliminated. Thus, with downwardly sticky prices, a policy of not increasing the money supply in a situation of a growing real GNP and growing demand leads to a thwarting of economic growth. Since downwardly sticky prices are a reasonable assumption to make for the United States, the most relevant question is not whether or not the money supply should be increased in a growing economy, but by how much.

Suppose the money supply is increased by an amount that shifts the LM curve to the right enough to intersect the $IS_1$ curve at point $b$. With the IS and LM curves intersecting at point $b$, the price-demand curve is in the position $D_b$. Aggregate demand exceeds supply at price level $P_0$, and inflation proceeds until prices reach $P_b$. Thus, a rate of money growth that moves the LM curve to point $b$ is inflationary.

Money growth that shifts the LM curve to point $a$ is noninflationary. If this rate of money expansion occurs, the price-demand curve in part (b) of figure 19.7 moves to the position labeled $D_a$ where it intersects the aggregate-supply curve at the initial price level $P_0$. The rate of money growth that moves the LM curve to point $a$ provides just the money needed by the economy for the increased transactions associated with producing the real GNP $y_{f,1}$ rather than $y_{f,0}$.

If the IS curve continues to shift over time to the position labeled $IS_2$ while the natural real GNP moves to $y_{f,2}$, additional money growth is warranted. If the objective of the Federal Reserve system is to foster stable prices, can you see whether the proper rate of money growth

**FIGURE 19.7.
Money Growth and
Inflation.**

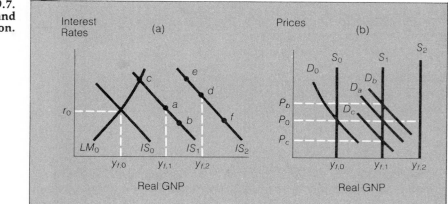

corresponds to the LM curve shifting to point $e$, point $d$, or point $f$? The answer is point $d$. If the LM curve moves to this position, demand just equals aggregate supply, and the price level remains stable at $P_0$. Point $e$ leads to deflation or more likely a reduction in economic growth. Point $f$ leads to another round of inflation as prices adjust upward in view of the excess demand.

Continual inflation occurs if the rate of money growth is persistently greater than that required by growth in the natural level of the real GNP. Thus, points $a$ and $d$, where the natural real GNP intersects the IS curve, set the noninflationary rate of money growth each period. If money is expanded beyond these points, say to the level associated with points $b$ and $f$, then inflation can continue indefinitely.

The last three sections of this chapter have examined how the supply of money in the economy impacts on the price level. We have defined a growth rate in money through time that leads to stable prices. One observation is crucial: money growth is a key to inflation. That conclusion can be established by using a perspective different from the IS–LM and aggregate supply-demand model of this chapter. The thesis involved is called the quantity theory. The results for the role of money in the economy are much the same, but the reasoning process differs. In the next chapter, the quantity theory and its associated reasoning process will be presented.

**Important Ideas in This Chapter**

**1.** Shifts in the IS curve lead to periods of rising prices if no changes occur in aggregate supply. If wages are rigid and some unemployment exists, shifts in demand also lead to an increase in the real GNP.

**2.** Declining productivity can also lead to rising prices, by shifting the demand-for-labor function. This process works the same regardless of whether we adopt the natural-rate or rigid-wage view.

**3.** In the two recent recessions in the United States, productivity declined significantly. This has led to an increase in prices, a decline in the real wage, and to falling employment.

**4.** The twin occurrence of inflation and recession is sometimes called stagflation. Stagflation is importantly related to the emerging cyclical pattern of productivity.

**5.** Regardless of whether we adopt the natural-rate or rigid-wage view, money growth beyond the needs of the economy leads to rising prices.

**6.** When wages are rigid, money growth also produces growth in the real GNP to the extent that unemployment exists. Under the natural-rate view, money growth does not lead to growth in the real GNP, only to rising prices.

**7.** If money growth is just sufficient to provide for the added transactions associated with normal growth in the real GNP, then price stability will occur in the absence of other changes. However, if the rate of money growth is chronically greater than the growth in the natural real GNP, continual inflation will occur, as prices adjust upward toward a continually rising equilibrium.

**Discussion Questions**

1. Trace through the model of this chapter the impact of a general tax cut on prices. Will it be inflationary?

2. Suppose that the changing role of women in society leads to a rightward shift in the supply-of-labor function. Trace this through the model in order to find out whether it will or will not have an effect on the price level.

3. From data in the *Survey of Current Business* or the *Federal Reserve Bulletin*, examine the latest recession to see if it corresponds to the patterns shown in table 19.1. Account for any differences you find.

4. Suppose a recession occurs. Should the rate of money growth be increased or decreased, according to the analysis in this chapter?

5. Can you see reasons why the Federal Reserve Board might find that it did not want to increase the money supply by exactly the amount associated with growth in the natural real GNP, but by either a lesser or greater amount?

**Suggested Readings**

Two articles by Nobel laureate James Tobin are of interest to those wishing to pursue the ideas in this chapter further. The first is "Inflation and Unemployment," *American Economic Review,* March 1972, 1–18. The second is "Keynesian Models of Recession and Depression," *American Economic Review,* May 1975, 195–202. An interesting discussion of the different behavior of actual prices in various types of market structures is presented by Arthur Okun, "Inflation: Its Mechanics and Welfare Costs," *Brookings Papers on Economic Activity,* 1975:2, Washington, D.C.: The Brookings Institution. A comprehensive treatise on the inflation process is contained in Robert J. Gordon's "Output Fluctuations and Gradual Price Adjustments," *Journal of Economic Literature,* June 1981, 493–530.

## CHAPTER 20

# More on Inflation: The Quantity Theory

## CHAPTER OUTLINE

## IMPORTANT TERMS

identity
theoretical statement
equation of exchange
income velocity of money
quantity theory

inflation rate
money growth
velocity growth
real growth rate
noninflationary money growth rate

*MEMO*

To:        All readers
From:      JWE

In the last chapter, you saw how changes in the money supply affect prices. You saw that, under the natural-rate hypothesis, changes in supply of money that are beyond the needs of the economy for transactions lead to inflation. Those conclusions were reached by reasoning through the IS–LM model and the aggregate supply-demand framework.

Under the natural-rate hypothesis, an alternative reasoning process called the quantity theory leads to almost all the same conclusions. It is a very different-looking model that concludes the same things about the relationship between money and prices as the IS–LM framework, but from a different logical route.

Theoretically, it is even possible to derive one approach from the other. We will not do that here. Instead, the quantity theory is presented as an important way to think about and analyze the money-price relationship in addition to the IS–LM/aggregate supply-demand approach.

Back in chapter 1, we talked about the use of cigarettes as prison money. We talked about the case of an approximately constant supply of goods in prisons. With the supply of goods fixed, more cigarettes meant higher prices for the available prison goods. With more packs of purchasing power in their pockets, the prisoners were willing to pay more for each good they wanted. Keep that example in mind. Also, keep in mind a related fact from the real world's history book. There has never been a period of runaway inflation in any civilized nation that was not accompanied by a similar runaway rate of growth in the supply of money. With these two thoughts, you are in the right frame of mind to think seriously about the quantity theory.

## THE EQUATION OF EXCHANGE

The quantity theory of money is developed from an accounting identity. An *identity* is a mathematical statement that is true by definition. For example, it is an identity that $3 \times 4 = 6 \times 2$. It is not refutable by either evidence or arguments of logic. A *theoretical statement* in economics pertains to the behavior of people or firms. Theoretical economic statements are not true by definition. They can be right or wrong. They are refutable. The consumption function is an example. It proposes that:

$$\frac{\text{consumer}}{\text{spending}} = f \text{ (real DPI, real interest rate)}$$

where $f$ means "some function of." Many economists think this theoretical statement correctly represents household behavior. But, we could be wrong. The consumption function is a refutable statement. Nonetheless, the consumption function has an equal sign in it, as does the identity. This is a source of confusion, because the equal signs do not mean the same thing in the two cases. For the identity, logic absolutely requires that the equal sign holds for all conditions. For the theory, the equal sign holds only if our theory is correct. To minimize this kind of confusion, we will use an extra line on equal signs used in identities. So, the identity just shown is written $3 \times 4 \equiv 6 \times 2$.

The *equation of exchange* is an accounting identity that defines the nominal GNP in two different ways. Here is the first way:

**(20.1)**   $GNP \equiv P \times y$

where $P$ is an index of general prices for GNP goods (the GNP deflator) and $y$ is the real GNP. Notice the three-part equal sign. Expression (20.1) is true by definition.

The second way of defining the nominal GNP is:

**(20.2)**   $GNP \equiv M \times V$

where $M$ is the money supply and $V$ is the ratio of the GNP to the money supply—$V$ is called the *income velocity of money*. The value of $V$ indicates how rapidly money is flowing from buyers to sellers in the process of producing the GNP and exchanging it for income. Because $V$ is defined as the ratio of GNP to $M$, expression (20.2) is also true by definition.

In the U.S. National Income Accounting system, the GNP and $P$ are estimated statistically. They are then used to derive $y$, the real GNP. So, (20.1) always holds for U.S. data. In (20.2), the stock of money, $M$, and the GNP are what we estimate statistically. Then $V$ is derived as the ratio of GNP/$M$. So, (20.2) also always holds for U.S. data.

Since (20.1) and (20.2) both equal the GNP, they also equal each other. In other words, it is also an identity that:

**(20.3)**   $M \times V \equiv P \times y$

But, this is not just *an* identity. This is *the* identity at the base of the classical theory. Expression (20.3) is the equation of exchange. It shows how the supply of money, the income velocity, the price level, and the real GNP relate in an accounting sense.

## THE QUANTITY THEORY

We transform the equation of exchange into the strongest and simplest form of *quantity theory* by forming a hypothesis about the behavior of the velocity of money, and by invoking the natural-rate view.[1] Here is the hypothesis: *The income velocity of money varies independently of the supply of money and the price level.* Let us think about what this does and does not say. It does *not* hypothesize that the velocity of money is constant from year to year. The value of $V$ can change over time under the quantity theory. However, it *does* hypothesize that the reasons for changes in $V$ are unrelated to changes in $M$ and $P$. In other words, we can look at $V$ as an exogenous variable in the equation of exchange.

How logical is it to suppose that $V$ is exogenous with respect to $M$ and $P$? Consider the price level first. The hypothesis is that when the price level rises (or falls), it will have no significant impact on velocity. Is this reasonable? After all, when prices rise rapidly, there is logic to support the idea that people and firms will seek to reduce their money holdings. Money depreciates in value as prices rise. Money holders can thus be expected to shift some of their purchasing power into other assets that are more inflation-proof. But, if people and firms are buying and selling the same real GNP but seeking to hold less real money, then in equilibrium the ratio of the GNP to money will tend to rise. Since $V$ is defined to be this ratio, it sounds as if $V$ is not completely exogenous with respect to $P$.

On this point, quantity theorists back off a little and agree in a guarded way. Most agree that instances of severe inflation (say, greater than 50 percent per year) produce a significant increase in velocity. For severe inflations, most quantity theorists see people behaving the way we have just supposed. But, for inflations of lesser magnitudes such as that in the United States, quantity theorists assert that velocity is pretty much unaffected. What are we to make of this? Well, it is clear that we need to add a qualification to the first hypothesis: $V$ will be exogenous only if the inflation rate is small enough to avoid a stampede by money holders into inflation-sheltered alternatives.

The second aspect of the velocity hypothesis is how the supply of money and velocity relate. Does money turn over slower when we increase the supply of it and faster when we reduce it? On this point, quantity theorists rely on statistics to show that the velocity of money is unrelated to how many dollars are in circulation.[2] In other words, the quantity theory takes it as a statistical matter that $V$ does not vary as $M$ varies.

1. A somewhat more complicated version of the quantity theory presumes that a temporary increase in the real GNP follows an increase in the money supply. This version thus employs a modification of the natural-rate approach. In this discussion we stick to the simple form.

2. A number of quantity theorists add the qualification that, to assume $V$ is independent of $P$, we must exclude the possibility that the supply of money is increased or decreased by an abnormal amount. In the event of a very large expansion in the money supply, for example, quantity theorists expect velocity to slow down.

## What Influences Velocity?

If $M$ or $P$ do not associate with changes in $V$, what does? Quantity theorists see a number of influences on $V$. One is how often people are paid, which relates to how much money they want to keep in their billfolds. The less in the billfolds, the greater the velocity. Another influence is the way the banking industry does its business, especially how quickly checks are processed. Another is the acceptance of credit by firms. The more customary credit becomes, the greater the velocity, since a fixed money supply can support more transactions when credit is more readily available. The use of credit cards is an example of a growing form of short-term consumer credit that increases the velocity of money. Other influences on velocity are depressions, wars, and economic panics. In such times of crisis, people are not likely to maintain their usual habits in the use of money. Depressions may lead to hoarding, panics may lead to a flee from money, and a war may have either effect. Velocity can be expected to change in such abnormal economic times.

The net effect of these influences on velocity is twofold. (1) They are reasons for velocity to have a trend over time. (2) They are reasons for velocity to occasionally stray from this trend in response to depression, war, panics, and so forth. The quantity-theory view is one where velocity is determined by economic habits, banking laws, business practices, and outside events.

## Real GNP and the Quantity Theory

To complete the quantity theory, we need to remember that under the natural-rate view, the real GNP, $y$, is determined by firms when they make employment decisions. The level of $y$ is a product of the labor market. *Accordingly, $y$ is independent of both the supply of money and the price level.* Let us pursue this contention further.

The supply of labor is governed by the real wage. The demand for labor is the aggregate marginal product of labor. When profits are maximized, the marginal product equals the real wage. Where the labor supply equals the demand, employment and $y$ are set. The supply of money has no role here. A change in the money supply is not a cause for either the supply- or demand-for-labor curves to shift. If they do not shift, the equilibrium level of employment does not change, and neither does the real GNP.

Understanding why the price level and $y$ are independent under classical theory requires some thinking about how the labor market adjusts to price changes. Suppose prices go up by 5 percent. Since prices are in the denominator of the real wage ($W/P$), the real wage falls. The lower real wage would stimulate more employment and a large $y$ if it would last. But, it will not. The reduced real wage is not a happy event for workers. Their purchasing power has been cut by the price increase. The supply of labor drops as marginal members of the work force are unimpressed by the now lower real wage, and drop out. The increased demand for labor and the reduced supply create a labor shortage. As a result of the shortage, the money wage is driven up, thus offsetting the effect of the price increase on the real wage. Equilibrium is restored at the same real wage, employment, and $y$ levels as before, except now at higher prices and wages.

At present, the crucial aspect of this adjustment process is that the changes in price did not change $y$. Price changes only produced offsetting changes in wages. So, even though prices appear as the denominator of the real wage in the classical labor-market model, the level of $y$ and the level of prices are independent. Accordingly, $y$ is determined independently of both the money supply and the price level, under the natural-rate view.

## The Quantity Theory in Motion

We have now reasoned our way to an important point in understanding the quantity theory. The velocity of money and the real GNP can both be taken as exogenous with respect to the money supply and prices. So, two of the four variables in the equation of exchange are exogenous. A third, the supply of money, is largely governed by the policies of the Federal Reserve system. With three of the four variables in the equation of exchange either exogenous or determined by government policy, the fourth variable, the price level, will be determined *as a result of the other three*. Prices are what is determined by the quantity theory.

Here is the way the quantity theory works. The Federal Reserve sets the supply of money. Banking laws, business customs, and outside events combine to fix the velocity of money. So, $M \times V$ is determined. The real GNP, $y$, is the supply of goods. It is determined by the supply and demand for labor, and is independent of the price level and the money supply. So, if the Federal Reserve increases the supply of money, the supply of goods will remain the same. But, a larger money supply means more purchasing power. With more purchasing power and the supply of goods unchanged, prices rise. The quantity theory sees the real world working much the same way as the prison economy of chapter 1. More purchasing power and a fixed supply of goods for sale mean higher prices in both cases. This close connection between money and prices is the main result of the quantity theory.

## A Short Side Trip for a
## Scenic View of the Quantity Theory

To better understand what the quantity theory is saying, we will find it useful to reconstruct it and the equation of exchange in terms of the percentage changes in the variables involved. There is a good reason for this. We just saw that the quantity theory explains the level of prices. But, there is much more concern with understanding and explaining the inflation rate than the price level. The inflation rate is the percentage change in the price level. By taking a short symbolic side trip, we can transform the equation of exchange and the resulting quantity theory so they are expressed in percentage changes. In this form, the quantity theory explains the inflation rate.

First notice that (20.3) actually holds only for some specific period of time, such as a year, a quarter, or a six-month period. For example, the real GNP produced *over 1981* multiplied by the average price level *for 1981* is what equals the average money supply *for 1981* multiplied by the average income velocity *for 1981*. A more specific way to write (20.3) which illustrates this idea is:

**(20.4)**   $M_t \times V_t \equiv P_t \times y_t$

where the $t$ subscripts refer to the values of the variables for some specific time period $t$. Now, there is a not-so-famous old saying that goes, "identities that hold for $t$ also hold for all other time periods" (such as $t - 1$, $t + 1$, $t - 5$, and so on). We can reason from this that if the equation of exchange holds for time period $t$, it also holds for $t - 1$. So, we can deduce (20.5):

**(20.5)**   $M_{t-1} \times V_{t-1} \equiv P_{t-1} \times y_{t-1}$

Now, take the natural log of both these expressions:

**(20.6)**   $\log M_t + \log V_t \equiv \log P_t + \log y_t$

**(20.7)**   $\log M_{t-1} + \log V_{t-1} \equiv \log P_{t-1} + \log y_{t-1}$

(Taking logs of both sides of an identity does not destroy the identity. If $x \equiv y$, then $\log x \equiv \log y$.) Now, subtract (20.7) from (20.6) by subtracting each term in (20.7) from its corresponding term in (20.6). Here is what results:[3]

**(20.8)**   $\Delta \log M + \Delta \log V \equiv \Delta \log P + \Delta \log y$

where the symbol $\Delta$ refers to the *change* in the variable from time period $t - 1$ to time period $t$. For example, $\Delta \log M = \log M_t - \log M_{t-1}$.

Now, it is a mathematical truism that the change in the log of a variable is approximately equal to the percentage change in the variable itself. This means that the change in the log of the money supply, ($\Delta \log M$) approximately equals the percentage change in the money supply. If we denote the *percentage change* in a variable by putting a dot over it, what we are now saying is: $\dot{M} \cong \Delta \log M$, $\dot{V} \cong \Delta \log V$, $\dot{P} \cong \Delta \log P$, and $\dot{y} \cong \Delta \log y$, where the wiggly line over the equal signs

---

3. Subtracting one identity from another preserves the result as an identity. Thus, we have not lost the three-pronged equal sign by expressing the equation of exchange as (20.8).

To: Those interested in Professor Friedman's approach
From: JWE

Professor Milton Friedman is a brilliant economist, a Nobel laureate, and probably the most well-known quantity theorist of our time. Friedman's specific approach to the quantity theory leads to the same conclusions as the one you are reading about in this chapter. But, it gets there differently. Friedman stresses that the quantity theory is really a theory of the demand for money—and one that follows the broad outlines of the theory you read about in the last chapter. However, there is one important difference between the money-demand theory of the last chapter and the quantity theory of Friedman. It has to do with the role of the interest rate in influencing money demand.

To see Friedman's approach, think about the last chapter for a minute. It concluded that real money demand is a positive function of the real GNP and a negative function of the interest rate. In theory, Friedman largely agrees with this money-demand theory. However, as a statistical matter, Friedman argues that the impact of interest rates on money demand is so small that it can be ignored for practical purposes. Accordingly, the Friedman demand for money becomes a function of only the real GNP. (Actually, he would also replace real GNP with "permanent aggregate income," defined the same way as permanent consumer income was defined in chapter 13.)

Friedman's money-demand function winds up being the quantity theory. To see how, we must use symbols. The simplest way is:

$$\frac{M_d}{P} = k \times y$$

where $M_d$ is the demand for money, $k$ is

means "approximately equal to." Putting these percentage changes into (20.8) in place of their log terms gives:

**(20.9)** $\quad \dot{M} + \dot{V} \cong \dot{P} + \dot{Y}$

Expression (20.9) now has an "approximately equal to" sign instead of the identity sign because the substitutions we made are only approximately correct.[4]

This version of the equation of exchange shows that *money growth* (the percentage change in the supply of money) plus *velocity growth* (the percentage change in the velocity of money) approximately equals *the inflation rate* (the percentage change in prices) plus the *real growth rate* (the percentage of change in the real GNP). Suppose we now impose on (20.9) the quantity-theory hypothesis that velocity growth is independent of money growth and inflation. Also, let us again use the natural-rate thesis to reason that the real growth rate is set in-

4. The approximation we are talking about here is quite good when the percentage change is under about 10 percent. Most of the data we will work with in the framework of (20.9) are in this range.

constant and positive (reflecting the relationship between real money demanded and real income), and $P$ and $y$ are the price level and the real GNP, respectively. Thus, $M_d/P$ is real money demand. The expression says that real money demanded is proportional to real GNP. Multiply both sides of this expression by $P$ and you get:

$$M_d = k \times P \times y$$

Now, Friedman assumes that the money market is generally in equilibrium where the demand for money equals the supply. The money supply is denoted as $M$, which means that $M_d = M$. Imposing this condition on the Friedman money-demand function gives:

$$M = k \times P \times y$$

or

$$M \times \left(\frac{1}{k}\right) = P \times y$$

Does this look familiar? It is the same as the equation of exchange, (20.3), except $V$ is replaced by $1/k$. In the quantity theory you read about, the hypothesis was that $V$ was exogenous. Friedman argues that the value of $k$ is stable over time and also is exogenous.

So, the money-demand model of the last chapter becomes the quantity theory when the role of the interest rate is eliminated. Do you recall the discussion at the end of the last chapter about the shape of the LM curve and the resulting degree of crowding out? It said the steeper the LM, the more nearly complete the crowding out. When crowding out occurs, more money is required to allow the GNP to go up. Increases in demand not accompanied by more money will not cause output to rise. That sounds like the quantity theory. If the demand for money is completely insensitive to the interest rate, as Friedman supposes, the LM curve is vertical. A vertical LM curve means that $y$ cannot increase without an increase in the money supply—demand no longer determines $y$. Have you read enough to get the impression that a lot hinges on how sensitive the demand for money is to fluctuations in interest rates?

dependently of the other terms in (20.9). Gathering these two exogenous terms together in parentheses, and rearranging algebraically, we have:

**(20.10)**   $\dot{P} = \dot{M} + (\dot{V} - \dot{y})$

Expression (20.10) shows that the inflation rate, $\dot{P}$, is equal to the money growth rate $\dot{M}$, plus the difference between velocity growth and real growth, $(\dot{V} - \dot{y})$. Let us think further about each of the parts of the last term. If velocity grows, then people are using the supply of money more efficiently since the ratio of GNP to the money supply is rising. Expression (20.10) shows that this has the same impact on inflation as it would if more money were added to the economy. A 5 percent growth in the money supply accompanied by a 1 percent growth in velocity has the same impact on inflation as a 1 percent growth in money accompanied by a 5 percent growth in velocity. In other words, the effect on inflation is the same whether we have more money or use what we have more efficiently. However, the two are not completely interchangeable. Under the quantity theory, the growth in money is under the control of the Federal Reserve and can be adjusted by policy actions. The growth in velocity is an exogenous influence on the economy and not the subject of policy actions by the government. The real GNP growth term, $\dot{y}$, has a negative relation to the inflation rate. As the economy grows, more money is absorbed for transactions. Less is available to create inflation.

Now for the scenic view of the quantity theory which (20.10) provides. As each year routinely fades into the next, outside influences, laws, and customs combine to establish how the velocity of money will change over the emerging year. Thus, $\dot{V}$ is formed in advance. At the same time, the labor force is pretty well set for the oncoming year. The factories, mills, and equipment that will be used to produce the year's real GNP are in place, as is the technology to be used in production. Producers are in the final stages of setting the year's production plans consistent with maximizing their profits. So, real growth, $\dot{y}$ is pretty well determined also. Therefore, as the curtain rises on a new year, $(\dot{V} - \dot{y})$ is on the books. What remains is for the Federal Reserve to implement policies that will determine the final growth rate in the money supply. From the combined influences of money growth, velocity growth, and real GNP growth, the inflation rate for the year evolves.

Consider an example. Suppose velocity growth shapes up to be 3 percent. All the economic indicators and forecasts show that real GNP growth promises to be 4 percent. With these inputs, the inflation rate depends on what the Federal Reserve does with the money supply. Putting $\dot{v} = 3\%$ and $\dot{y} = 4\%$ into (20.10), we can calculate the relationship between money growth and inflation as follows:

$$\dot{P} = \dot{M} + (3\% - 4\%)$$

or

$$\dot{P} = \dot{M} - 1\%$$

So, if the money supply is expanded by 1 percent, no inflation will result. If money grows by 5 percent, the inflation rate will be 4 percent and so forth.

Under the quantity theory, the key things are that $\dot{V}$ and $\dot{y}$ are predetermined. They influence prices but are not influenced by prices. With $\dot{M}$ the result of government policy, the inflation rate is the final result.

The quantity theory offers the Federal Reserve a guideline as to the rate at which money can be expanded without contributing to inflation. To obtain the guideline, all you have to do is set the inflation rate equal to zero in (20.10) and then solve for the rate of money growth. Doing this gives the *non-inflationary money growth rate* as:

**(20.11)**   $\dot{M} = \dot{y} - \dot{V}$

which says that under the quantity theory, the noninflationary rate of money growth is equal to the growth rate in the real GNP less the percentage change in the efficiency of money.

# THE QUANTITY
# THEORY AND THE REAL WORLD

How well does the quantity theory fit the realities of life in the United States? Let us look at some recent data on the subject to find out. The quantity theory's central thesis is that changes in the velocity of money are independent of changes in (1) the inflation rate, and (2) the money supply. We can gain some impressions about the realism of each part of this thesis by examining a couple of scatter diagrams.

To construct them, we define money as demand deposits, currency, traveler's checks, and other checkable deposits, that is, M1. The real GNP is $y$, and the GNP price deflator is $P$. For all variables, the percentage changes are from one year to the next, and the time period is 1960–1980. Figure 20.1 shows the scatter of points depicting the relationship between percentage changes in velocity, $\dot{V}$, and corresponding changes in the inflation rate, $\dot{P}$. If the inflation rate and velocity are systematically related, we expect to see the scatter of points lined up and tracing out some type of a function, just as the consumption-income scatter was in chapter 13. We do not. Instead, these points are scattered randomly about. From figure 20.1, we can conclude that there is no obvious or dominant association between velocity and the inflation rate. In figure 20.1, the quantity theory gets high marks.

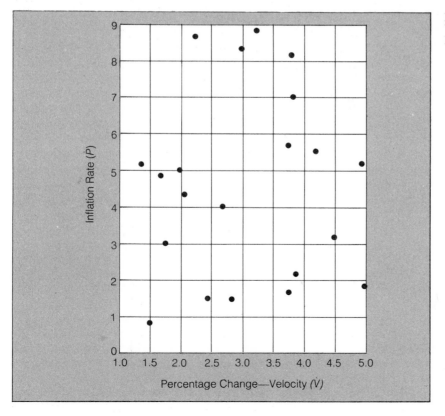

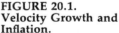

FIGURE 20.1.
Velocity Growth and Inflation.

The other part of the quantity theory is that velocity growth is independent of money-supply growth. Figure 20.2 shows the scatter diagram for these two variables. As with the first scatter, the points in figure 20.2 look as if they got there by accident. The only nonrandom thing we see in figure 20.2 is a grouping of the points toward the right-hand half of the figure. However, that is only because the growth in money has usually been in the 4 to 8 percent range rather than in the 0 to 4 percent range. The crucial aspect of figure 20.2 is whether movements in money growth systematically associate with movements in velocity growth and vice versa. They do not. Thus, figure 20.2 provides more support for the quantity theory.

Figures 20.1 and 20.2 together give us no cause to doubt the quantity theory's contention that velocity is independent of both inflation and the money supply. On the other hand, these figures do not prove that theory. In fact, they give only a basic impression about the truth of it. More refined methods of data analysis could refine these impressions. But, keep one thing in mind. If the quantity theory's central thesis was badly out of touch with the real world, then it would have shown up in figures 20.1 or 20.2.

The quantity theory requires growth in $\dot{V}$ to be independent of both inflation and money growth. But that is not all. For the quantity theory to work the way we have described, changes in the real GNP, $\dot{y}$, must also be independent of the inflation rate and the growth rate in money. If this is also true, then money growth translates directly

**FIGURE 20.2.
Velocity Growth and
Money Growth.**

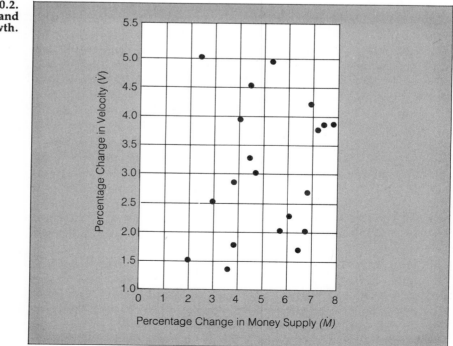

into inflation. Figures 20.3 and 20.4 are the relevant scatter diagrams for this question.

Figure 20.3 shows the scatter of points for the relationship between growth in the real GNP and the inflation rate. There is no easily discernible trend displayed by these points, except that they are grouped in the right-hand side of the figure. As before, this is only because of the predominance of real GNP growth rates in the 2 to 6 percent range. Figure 20.3 does not contradict the notion that the real GNP is in fact largely independent of the inflation rate.

In Figure 20.4, the relationship is shown between the growth in money and the growth in the real GNP. In this scatter diagram, the points are more clustered in the upper right-hand quadrant of the figure. This means that most of the actual data over 1960–1980 fell in the upper ranges of both $\dot{M}$ and $\dot{y}$. Do you see a weak positive relationship in the scatter? Perhaps so. The scatter suggests a slight tendency for larger growth rates in money to associate with larger growth rates in the real GNP. But, the association is vague. Figure 20.4 does not support the argument that the growth in money is a dominant influence on the growth in real GNP. As a result, the scatter in figure 20.4 does not conflict with the quantity theory's contention that $\dot{M}$ and $\dot{y}$ are largely independent. But, figure 20.4 raises suspicion about that contention.

If the quantity theory applies to the United States, then the four scatter diagrams we have seen should not show any significant relationships between the variables plotted. With one questionable ex-

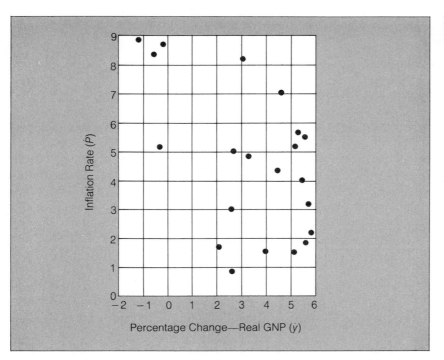

FIGURE 20.3.
Real GNP Growth and Inflation.

To: Readers who like to think in terms of graphs
From: JWE

You can formulate the "percentage change" version of the quantity theory on a graph pretty easily. So, if you like to think in terms of graphs, this is the memo for you. Just start out with the quantity-theory expression:

**(20.10)** $\dot{P} = \dot{M} + (\dot{V} - \dot{y})$

and notice that the inflation rate, $\dot{P}$, is the dependent or y variable, so it goes on the vertical axis. Also, the controllable or x variable is the rate of money growth, $\dot{M}$. So, it goes on the horizontal axis. Now, expression (20.10) is a simple linear equation with the slope being one (it is a 45-degree line) and the intercept being $(\dot{V} - \dot{y})$. It looks like this:

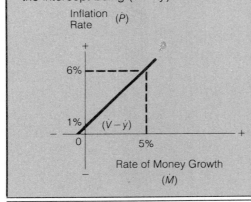

For the curve plotted, real GNP growth is 3 percent and velocity growth is 4 percent. So, $(\dot{V} - \dot{y})$ is 1 percent. Accordingly, the curve crosses the axis at 1 percent. Notice that if real GNP growth exceeded velocity growth, the curve would cross the vertical axis below the zero point. It would have a negative intercept. For the curve positioned as shown, an illustrative 5 percent rate of money growth translates into a 6 percent inflation rate. However, notice that when real GNP growth *increases*, the curve shifts *down*, and when velocity growth *increases*, the curve shifts *up*.

ception, they do not. The conclusion is that quantity theorists need not cower in the face of the charge that their theory is a relic from the past that bears no resemblance to the contemporary world. We have not seen proof that the quantity theory is clearly right. But, we have seen enough to suggest it is not clearly wrong!

That being the case, let us consider some illustrative episodes in U.S. economic policy as seen through the eyes of a quantity theorist. Take the year 1961. Velocity growth in M1B was 1.5 percent. Growth in the real GNP was 2.6 percent. So, money became 1.5 percent more efficient, but the economy needed 2.5 percent more of it to produce the larger real GNP. Expression (20.11) tells a quantity theorist that the money supply could have increased by $(\dot{y} - \dot{V}) = 2.6\% - 1.5\%$

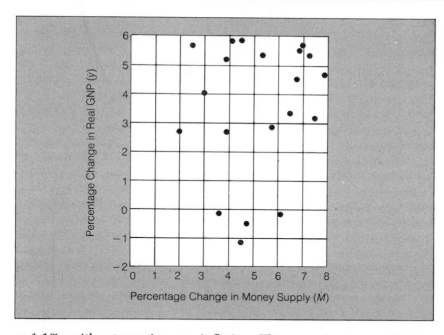

**FIGURE 20.4.**
**Real GNP Growth and Growth In the Money Supply.**

= 1.1%, without creating any inflation. This growth rate would just provide for the needs of the larger GNP without adding any excess purchasing power to the economy. The money supply actually increased by 2.0 percent over the year. Prices went up by 0.9 percent. All in all, it was a pretty good year.

The year 1980 was not so good. Velocity increased by 2.3 percent in that year. Real GNP fell by 0.1 percent from the previous year. A falling real GNP means that less money is required for transactions. We can still apply expression (20.11) to find the noninflationary growth in money, but in doing so we must remember the negative sign. Noninflationary money growth for 1980 under the quantity theory is $(-0.1\% - 2.3\%) = -2.4\%$. A quantity theorist reasons that 2.3 percent less money was needed in the 1980 economy because of the increase in the efficiency of the money already there, and another 0.1 percent less money was needed because of the smaller real GNP produced. It was a year when a zero inflation rate required the money supply to decrease by 2.4 percent. The money supply actually increased by 6.2 percent. The annual inflation rate was 8.6 percent.

## HOW DIFFERENT IS THE QUANTITY THEORY?

In the last chapter, we examined how growth in the supply of money influences prices under the natural-rate hypothesis. We saw that the noninflationary growth rate in money depends on how fast the natural real GNP is growing. The quantity theory makes this idea more specific—the noninflationary rate of money growth can be increased by 1 percent for every percent increase in the real GNP growth rate, $\dot{y}$.

But, the quantity theory adds a dimension not considered in our earlier analysis—that of velocity growth. Velocity growth reduces the noninflationary rate of money growth on a one-to-one basis. In our IS–LM and aggregate supply-demand analysis of the last chapter, we assumed that the demand-for-money function did not shift while changes were occurring in the money supply and in the real GNP. This means we supposed that the amount of money required to support each dollar of the real GNP remained constant except for the effects of changing interest rates. But, if velocity increases, less money is required to support each dollar of the real GNP. In the words of the last several chapters, the demand-for-money function shifts to the left when velocity increases, which shifts the LM curve to the right. (It may be useful to work through the money-demand function to derive the LM curve and verify this for yourself.)

Because an increase in velocity shifts the LM curve to the right, it has the same effect on our analysis as an increase in the money supply. Thus, if velocity increases, the LM curve shifts even though no money is added, and the noninflationary growth rate of the money supply is reduced. When we add this dimension to the analysis of the last chapter, the conclusions of the quantity theory and the conclusions reached in the natural-rate case in the last chapter are nearly identical.

Questions of policy, such as how fast the money supply should grow, are the wedge that drives economists and political leaders into "camps." Policy issues are questions of what we should or should not do as a nation. So far in the last several chapters, we have not dealt with such questions. Instead, we have pursued the logic of macroeconomic theory, and dwelt on how the resulting model works. The next chapter is about policy, and about the camps into which policy issues divide economists.

## Important Ideas in This Chapter

1. An identity is a statement true by definition whereas a theoretical statement is refutable and subject to change. The quantity theory evolves from an identity to a theoretical statement because of a key hypothesis made about velocity of money.

2. The equation of exchange is an identity relating the price level, the real GNP, the money supply, and the velocity of money in an accounting sense.

3. The central hypothesis of the quantity theory is that the velocity of money varies independently of the supply of money and the price level.

4. Under the quantity theory, the velocity of money is a function of economic habits, banking laws, business practices, and events outside the economy. Velocity can be assumed to be exogenous in the equation of exchange.

5. The natural-rate hypothesis is important to the quantity theory. It insures that the real GNP will also be an exogenous variable in the equation of exchange. Employment and the real GNP are set by profit-maximizing decisions in the labor market, and the adjustment of wages to price changes insulates the employment and real GNP levels from fluctuations in the general price level.

6. With the velocity of money and the real GNP exogenous, the money supply determines the price level, under quantity theory.

7. The quantity theory is easily transformed to one that explains the inflation rate instead of the price level. Upon transformation of the theory, the growth in money plus the growth in velocity is approximately equal to the growth in the real GNP plus the inflation rate.

8. The quantity theory offers a guideline for noninflationary money growth. If money grows by the difference between the growth in the real GNP and the growth in velocity, then no inflation will result.

9. Simple scatter diagrams plotted over 1960–1980 for U.S. data show little correspondence between the growth in velocity and the growth in money, or between velocity growth and inflation. They do not contradict the main premise of the quantity theory.

10. Scatter diagrams also show that the growth in the real GNP has little systematic relationship with either the inflation rate or the growth in money. However, the scatter diagram raises suspicions about the latter relationship.

11. In general, we cannot show from the graphs that the quantity theory is correct. But, we can say from the evidence we have seen that it is not clearly wrong.

**Discussion Questions**

1. Can you think of a good logical reason why the velocity of money would not be independent of the supply of money? Hint: think about the IS–LM model.

2. Can you think of any reasons why the real GNP would not be independent of the money supply? Hint: look at the last hint.

3. If the noninflationary rate of money growth in the United States for 1980 was −2.4 percent, what basis is there for the Federal Reserve actually expanding money by 6.2 percent.

4. Over the twenty-one years from 1960 to 1980, the growth in M1B velocity has averaged slightly more than 3 percent per year. How can you account for this steady upward movement in velocity?

5. Overheard in the restroom: "The faster the real GNP grows, the lower will be the inflation rate." Does this statement have any theoretical backing, or is it best left where it was overheard?

**Suggested Readings**

Milton Friedman's version of the quantity theory is among the classics available to readers today. One of his writings on the subject is *Studies in the Quantity Theory of Money*, Chicago: University of Chicago Press, 1956. A good review by Friedman and Anna Schwartz of the empirical evidence on behalf of the quantity theory is contained in an article entitled "Money and Business Cycles" in the *Review of Economics and Statistics*, 45, February 1963, supplement, 32–64. Also, a good statement of Friedman's version of quantity theory along with criticisms and a reply by Friedman is found in a book edited by Robert J. Gordon entitled *Friedman's Monetary Theory*, Chicago: Aldine Publishing Company, 1974.

## CHAPTER 21

# Economic Policy

## CHAPTER OUTLINE

## IMPORTANT TERMS

economic policy
discretionary monetary policy
rules policy
Phillips curve
demand-management policies
supply-side economics

tax-wedge theory
aftertax real wage
bracket creep
Laffer curve
rational expectations

---

# MEMO

To:      All readers
From:     JWE

Normally unflappable economists sometimes get red-faced when questions of economic policy are discussed. Policy in economics deals with what is right and what is wrong—what we should be doing and what we should not. Economic policy breeds advocates. The subject of this chapter is economic policy. In it, you can read about several important and continuing policy questions in economics.

One of these questions has to do with the role of the Federal Reserve in regulating the growth rate of the money supply. The proper policy role the Board of Governors should play is a question that has been the subject of considerable debate over the last several years in economics. A second such issue is the question of how inflation and unemployment relate in the economy. Can we jointly fight these twin evils, or must we live with one to avoid the other?

Another question of policy you can read about in this chapter is whether the focus of government attention should be on managing the level of aggregate demand, or alternatively, on providing improved incentives to produce and supply the nation's goods and services. Whether we should focus on demand- or supply-side economics is one of the most provocative questions of policy of the last half-decade.

Finally, this chapter covers the implications for policy of a public that alertly uses all available information to form its expectations. The perhaps innocent-sounding idea of a rational public has some important ramifications for the effectiveness of economic policy in the United States.

---

Policy refers to guidelines, rules, dos and don'ts, and shoulds and shouldn'ts. *Economic policy* means the guidelines, rules, and general dos and don'ts that apply to the economy. In the United States presidential administrations usually articulate economic policies toward which they work. Many times, political debates between incumbents and challengers importantly revolve around the wisdom of the economic policies followed by the incumbent, or the wisdom of the policies being proposed by the challenger.

Here are some examples of economic policies: (1) create a deficit in the federal budget whenever the economy goes into a recession, (2) expand the rate of money growth when the economy is weak, (3) tax high-income earners proportionately more than low-income earners, (4) tax heaviest those economic activities which the government wants to discourage, and subsidize the activities the government wants to stimulate. Each of these examples of policy is a guideline for the specific programs and laws that political leaders might seek and support.

Economic policies usually follow from applying theory. Consider the first case of a policy of deficit spending as a response to recession. If the policy maker reasoned from the rigid-wage model of the economy, it follows logically that to increase spending without increasing taxes during a recession produces a net rightward shift in the IS curve. This shift is a positive stimulus to the real GNP and to jobs. Thus, the policy would envision the government taking an active counter-cyclical role in managing the economy during times of recession.

Economic policies are rarely without their critics. In the case of the first illustrative policy, those who feel the natural-rate hypothesis correctly depicts the economy find such a policy misguided. They see the result of deficit spending during a recession to be high interest rates and crowding out of private spending, with no net effect on either real GNP or jobs. For every bit the deficit spending shifts the IS curve outward, the crowding out shifts it back. Since the resulting high interest rates cause less capital investment, natural-rate theorists see no gain and some loss from pursuing the first policy.

Policy differences such as the one just outlined occur primarily because economists follow differing theoretical models to their logical conclusion. It is a disagreement about which specific theories best fit the economy that creates major policy debates among economists. If economists could agree on the theory that best explains behavior in the real world, their policy differences would be greatly narrowed.

# MONETARY POLICY-RULES VERSUS DISCRETION

How should the Federal Reserve Board respond to a weakening economy? Suppose that the Federal Reserve is convinced from the economic indicators it reads about that a recession is in the process of starting. It is time for a policy to be invoked. The major alternatives available to the Federal Reserve are (1) to expand the level of bank reserves when the economy weakens, thus enabling banking institutions to expand the money supply, or (2) to take no extraordinary action when the economy weakens, but instead to continue to expand bank reserves at a predetermined rate, set by the noninflationary rule described in chapter 20. The first alternative is called a *discretionary monetary policy*, and the second is called a *rules policy*.

Advocates of the discretionary policy embrace the notion that more rapid money expansion will shift the LM curve to the right, lower interest rates, increase the equilibrium level of aggregate demand, and lessen the impact of it if not totally head off the recession. They also argue that the rules approach is irresponsible because it ignores the problem, and allows important governmental antirecessionary machinery to go unused.

Advocates of the rules alternative generally follow either the natural-rate hypothesis or the quantity theory. They see a declining need for money balances because of the recession, and feel that if the money growth rate is speeded up, the result will be only more inflation. Any impact of more rapid money growth on output and jobs that may occur will be transitory. To these advocates, speeding up money growth will do nothing to offset the recession, but will instead contribute to more inflation.

Professor Milton Friedman, who advocates the rules view, would add a second type of argument to that now presented. He contends that a recession which is clearly signaled by available economic indicators may in fact be nine to twelve months away, it may be only one to three months away, or it may not occur at all. (Someone once remarked that the stock market, a leading indicator, had correctly predicted nine of the last five recessions.) So, the indicators are only a rough guide to action.

But, this problem is not the end of Professor Friedman's critique. He has also argued that it takes time for changes in monetary policy to be put into place once the need for them is recognized. And, beyond this lag, the in-place policies take time to work on the economy.

Friedman's essential point is that the total lag between the recognition of a need for a policy change and the impact of the implemented change on the economy is generally long and highly variable. As a result, he suggests that by the time a policy is put into place, the need for it may have changed. And, of course, Friedman would highlight the quite ripe possibility that it may do no good (the natural-rate view) even in the unlikely case that it is timely.

These observations, along with adherence to the natural-rate hypothesis, have led a number of economists to advocate a monetary policy built around rules rather than one based on the discretion of the Federal Reserve. The policy guideline put forth by main advocates of a rules approach to monetary policy follows directly from the quantity theory. The rules policy sets a fixed rate of money growth that corresponds to the long-term growth in the real GNP less the long-term growth in the velocity of money. This fixed-money-growth rate is essentially the capacity rate of growth in the economy corrected for the general pattern of increasing efficiency in the use of money.

The fixed-money-growth rule avoids the need to forecast by not altering the rate of money growth during either recessions or inflation. Adherents of the natural-rate hypothesis find the fixed-growth rule particularly attractive since they feel that expanding money more rapidly during recessions does no good anyway. Others argue that because recessions require less money, keeping the money growth rate constant during them adds some stimulus to the economy without running the risk of overdoing it.

To: Readers who drive
From: JWE

Some advocates of the fixed-growth-rate rule contend that trying to change the growth rate in money to fit short-term economic conditions is like trying to drive a car under the following conditions: (1) after you turn the steering wheel, a totally unpredictable and varying amount of time (between five and fifty seconds) elapses before the front wheels turn, (2) once in a while, when the wheel is turned to the right, the car goes to the left, and (3) the windshield is painted black, meaning the only way you can see the route is to look through the side and rear windows. Thus, it is necessary to judge where you are going exclusively by looking at where you are (the side windows) and where you have been (the rear window).

Does this sound like a fun drive? Fixed-growth-rate advocates argue that the long and variable lags between money and the economy create conditions (1) and (2), and the necessity of using economic indicators that give present and past economic conditions creates condition (3). So, instead, they would devise a driverless car that automatically goes in a direction that corresponds to the average direction of the road. Thus, when the road takes a short-run bend, the fixed-growth-rate car would go off, plow through the weeds, and eventually return to the road when the bend evened out.

The issue between the rules and discretion advocates is whether the first car can be steered in a way that avoids fewer weeds than the second car is sure to encounter.

Adherents of a policy of discretion by the Federal Reserve argue that the fixed-growth rule does not make use of the most powerful governmental antirecessionary weapon, the supply of money. Thus, they contend that the fixed-growth rule constitutes bad money management.

## THE PHILLIPS CURVE

In the late 1950s, Professor A. W. Phillips, a British economist, published a study of wage rates and unemployment rates in the United Kingdom that showed them to be importantly negatively related. By the early 1960s, many American economists had followed Phillips's lead, and had begun to study an Americanized version of Phillips's curve that related the inflation rate to the unemployment rate. U.S. data over the 1950s and mid-1960s were reported as showing a negative relationship between inflation and unemployment. Thus, the higher the unemployment rate, the lower the inflation rate, and the lower the unemployment rate, the higher the inflation rate. The general relationship between inflation and the unemployment rate came to be called the *Phillips curve*, and became the subject of much debate during the decade of the 1970s.

Part of the reason for debate and interest in the Phillips curve is the continuing series of policy statements adopted by the U.S. government beginning with the Employment Act of 1946. That act committed the government to pursue *both* full-employment policies and policies of price stability. Clearly, the implication of the Phillips curve is that the government cannot have it both ways. It must sacrifice some inflation to vigorously pursue full-employment policies, and some unemployment to vigorously pursue anti-inflationary policies. Which direction government policy should be pushed—whether toward full employment with inflation or toward no inflation and high unemployment—became a highly politically charged issue that appeared to many to boil down to a question of individual values.

The question of how the Phillips curve relates to macroeconomic theory came up increasingly in the 1960s and the early 1970s. For those who adopt the rigid-wage view, Phillips curves are a direct product of applying the IS–LM, aggregate supply-demand model. Figure 21.1 shows the key relationships involved. Parts (a) and (b) show the situation for case 1, which concerns rigid wages. In this case, the aggregate-supply curve, denoted as $S$ in part (a), is upward-sloping, becoming vertical at the full-employment level of real GNP, $y_f$. With the price-demand curve in the position $D$, the equilibrium price level is $P_0$ while the real GNP is $y_0$. Now, suppose the rate of government spending increases. The resulting shift in the IS curve to the right shifts the $D$ curve to the right. This shift in the $D$ curve causes prices to rise toward the new equilibrium. Thus, inflation either begins or increases (depending on whether prices were initially changing from period to period) while prices adjust toward the new equilibrium. At the same time, the unemployment rate is reduced. The economy has thus moved to a position of higher inflation and reduced unemployment. The greater the rightward shift in the $D$ curve, the higher the equilibrium price level, the smaller the unemployment rate, and the greater the price inflation required to reach the higher equilibrium price level.

As a consequence of the relationship now described between price movements and movements in the unemployment rate, the Phillips-curve relationship shown in part (b) of figure 21.1 emerges. For the example just given, the upward movement in the inflation rate and downward movement in the unemployment rate constitute a move upward by this Phillips curve in the direction of the arrow. Note that the Phillips curve becomes a vertical line when the unemployment rate reaches the full employment level, $U_f$.

Case 2, the flexible-wage or natural-rate case, is shown in parts (c) and (d) of figure 21.1. Notice the sharp contrast with what we have just seen. With the vertical aggregate-supply curve, $S$, that characterizes this case, the price level is $P_e$ while the equilibrium real GNP is at $y_n$. If government spending is increased as in the former case, the $D$ curve shifts to the right, and the equilibrium price level shifts up. Inflation increases as prices adjust toward this new equilibrium. But, no changes occur in the equilibrium real GNP or in the unemployment rate, both of which remain at their natural levels, $y_n$ and $U_n$.

The Phillips curve for the natural-rate case is the vertical line shown in part (d) of the figure. It illustrates that for the natural-rate case, the unemployment rate and the inflation rate are completely independent. Essentially, the unemployment rate is the result of the interaction of the labor supply and demand functions, while the price level is the result of the operation of the quantity-theory mechanism. Thus, for natural-rate theorists, the government can simultaneously pursue its seemingly conflicting objectives of full employment and price stability.

The statistical evidence during the 1960s gave some support for nonvertical Phillips curves in the United States. However, as the 1970s progressed, less and less statistical support could be found for the presence of a systematic Phillips curve. In particular, the recession of 1970 saw a rise in both the inflation and unemployment rates. The recession of 1974–1975 confirmed this more strongly, with inflation doubling while the unemployment rate rose to more than 10 percent at one point. And, when the economy emerged from each of these two periods of high unemployment, the inflation rate fell. The experience led some to suggest that not only had the Phillips curve

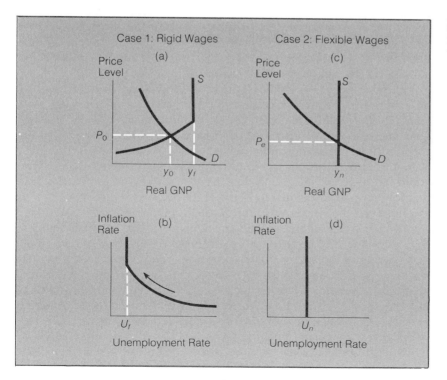

**FIGURE 21.1.**
**Phillips-Curve Relationships.**

disintegrated, but a new upward-sloping trade-off had emerged between inflation and unemployment. Indeed, in the case of the natural-rate hypothesis, the analysis of inflationary recessions in chapter 19 showed a logical case for an upward-sloping inflation–unemployment trade-off.

Those who continue to support the notion of the Phillips curve explain the experience of the 1970s by arguing that falling patterns of productivity and other factors combined to cause the Phillips curve to shift to the right. Thus, the upward-sloping appearance of the recent curve is, in reality, a downward-sloping curve that is shifting. In any event, the experience of the 1970s greatly reduced the practical importance of the Phillips curve trade-off and quieted the debate over whether more inflation and lower unemployment is better or worse than less inflation and higher unemployment.

## THE DEMAND-SIDE APPROACH TO POLICY

One of the more current and fundamental issues in economic policy in recent years is whether the focus of government policymaking should be on components of aggregate demand at all. The traditional tools of fiscal policy which include taxes, government spending, and government transfers, each impact on the economy its effect on aggregate demand. In other words, traditional fiscal policy works by shifting the IS curve and accordingly shifting the price-demand relationship. The response of production and jobs to demand shifts depends on whether the economy is or is not at the natural rate. Generally, the assumption has been that it is not.

Policies that seek to manage the level of total demand in the economy by adjusting the government's part of it in such a way as to stabilize the total are referred to as *demand-management policies*. Demand-management policies reached their greatest visibility during the Kennedy administration, where some government economists argued that with proper use of fiscal policy, the level of total demand could be greatly stabilized. With demand stabilized, production and employment would similarly stabilize to prevent recessions.

Those who believe in the natural-rate hypothesis are not persuaded that demand-management policies offer any such answer. Instead, they visualize any increase in government demand as requiring the prior commandeering of purchasing power generated in the private sector. Thus, to natural-rate theorists, an increase in government spending does not occur in isolation. It represents the exercise of purchasing power that has to be raised from the private sector, either by increasing taxes or by borrowing and deficit-financing of the expenditure. (Increasing the money supply is still another route by which additional demand can be financed, but in focusing on fiscal policy we shall ignore it at this point.) Either way merely reallocates purchasing power without changing its total when the economy is at its natural rate.

A key result of embracing the natural-rate hypothesis is the conclusion that demand-management policies will not be effective in stabilizing the economy. Instead, natural-rate theorists are led by this theory to prefer a passive fiscal policy where the levels of government spending and taxing are set at socially required levels, not at levels directed toward economic stabilization goals. On the other hand, a key result of embracing the rigid-wage view of the economy is the conclusion that demand-management policies hold the key to an active and important role for the government in stabilizing the economy.

## THE SUPPLY-SIDE
## APPROACH TO POLICY

The newest approach to government policy, associated with the presidential administration of Ronald Reagan, is to direct the central focus of governmental resources away from demand management and toward the supply side of the nation's markets. *Supply-side economics* means a policy orientation toward the aggregate-supply function, viewing it as the key to growth in the economy. Supply-side thinking emphasizes *incentives*—to produce, invest, and save. In the supply-side view, people and firms are seen as responding importantly to prices, wages, interest rates, and other incentives that affect the costs and benefits of their economic activities.

In the supply-side view, people work primarily because of the wage rate, not just because the job is available. Business firms invest primarily because of the rate of return. People save primarily because of the interest rate they are paid. This all sounds pretty obvious, but it has some important implications.

One such implication is that the government discourages work by taxing the income earned by doing it. Thus, when income taxes are raised, work becomes a less attractive alternative to leisure, under a strict "incentives" view. At some point, the disincentive effect of rising income taxes will cut deeply into the size of the work force, and prohibit the economy from being able to supply a growing pool of both products and purchasing power.

A second implication is that taxes on corporate profits and capital gains are disincentives to capital investment and financial investment in corporate equities, respectively. Firms are less inspired to take the risk associated with a new capital investment if they know that a good share of the profits will be handed over to Uncle Sam. Similarly, financial investors are reluctant to risk their funds if they have to share profits with the government. Thus, in the supply-side view, the process of investment and growth in business capital is inhibited importantly by rising taxes on corporate profits and capital gains.

With work made increasingly unattractive by rising tax rates, more workers are led to drop out, or perhaps go underground by working "off the books" to evade tax liabilities. With the profitability of investing in financial assets reduced by capital-gains taxes and taxes on dividends, those with capital to supply instead choose to buy tax shelters such as international investments in old masters, diamonds, or gold, or to invest "off the books."

In the view of supply-side policy makers, the tax system has little effect on total demand (it is viewed as reallocating purchasing power), but may have a powerful effect on incentives to work and invest, and thus on the amount of both labor and capital made available to the production process.

Such are the general concerns of supply-side theorists. One specific articulation of supply-side philosophy is the *tax-wedge theory* associated with the work of Professor Robert Mundell, Arthur Laffer, and others. The crux of the tax-wedge model is the notion that because of taxes and other deductions, the proceeds to the worker from working are less than the cost to the firm for the worker's services. In the language of the labor-market model used in earlier chapters, the real wage that determines labor demand is different from (higher than) the real wage that determines how much labor workers will supply.

Figure 21.2 shows how this situation graphically produces a wedge. Supply- and demand-for-labor curves are shown, similar to previous labor-market models. However, there are important differences in this model's curves. The supply of labor is now assumed to be a function of the worker's *aftertax real wage.* In our earlier model, taxes were not considered. Similarly, the demand for labor is now assumed to be a function of the total cost (including taxes imposed on the firm)

FIGURE 21.2.
The Tax Wedge.

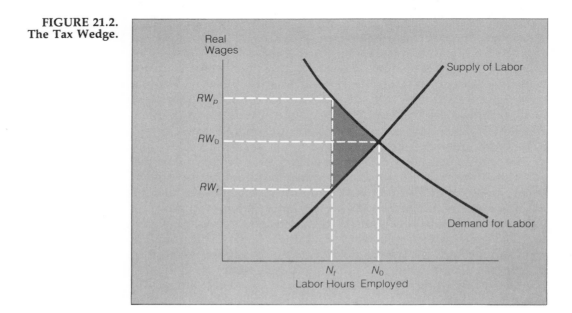

of employing labor. Given these assumptions, a real labor cost to firms of $RW_p$ generates a demand to employ $N_t$ worker hours, while an aftertax real wage of $RW_r$ generates an equal amount of labor hours supplied. Thus, the labor market is in equilibrium.

The points $N_0$ and $RW_0$ are the employment levels and the real wage that would put the labor market in equilibrium if no taxes were involved. When we recognize income taxes and assume they are taken into account by both workers and firms, the equilibrium employment level is lower, the wage cost to firms is higher, and the real take-home pay of workers is lower. The shaded area is the tax wedge that gives this theory its name.

If taxes on labor rise, the tax wedge widens and the equilibrium level of employment is reduced. Figure 21.3 illustrates the point. In this graph, the labor market is initially in equilibrium with employment at $N_0$, where the real-wage cost to firms is $RW_p$ and the aftertax real wage of workers is $RW_r$. Now, assume income taxes are raised by an amount that immediately lowers the aftertax real wage of workers from $RW_r$ to $RW_t$. As a result of this fall in the rate of real take-home pay, work incentives and the supply of labor are reduced to the amount $N_s$. The real cost of labor for firms remains unchanged. Thus, the demand for labor stays at $N_0$. As a result, a labor shortage develops, shown graphically as the distance $N_0 - N_s$. The labor shortage drives up the nominal wage rate, as firms are forced to bid aggressively for the shrinking labor pool. This rising nominal wage increases both the real cost of labor to firms and the aftertax real wage of workers. When the cost to firms has risen to $RW_q$ and the aftertax real wage has risen to $RW_f$, the labor shortage disappears and the

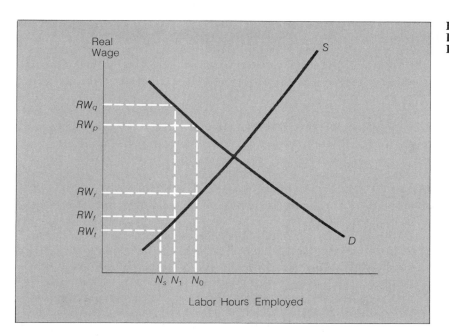

**FIGURE 21.3.
Effects of Rising Tax
Rates on Employment.**

**TABLE 21.1**
**Tax Wedge Accounting: Illustrative Real Labor Costs as Viewed from Two Perspectives**

| THE WORKER | | THE FIRM | |
|---|---|---|---|
| Change in hourly pay plus fringes | +8.5% | Change in hourly labor cost plus fringes | +8.5% |
| *Less:* inflation | 8.9% | *Less:* inflation | 8.9% |
| *Equals:* the change in real wages | −0.4% | *Equals:* the change in real wages | −0.4% |
| *Less:* the increase in social-security rates | 1.0% | *Plus:* increased costs of complying with government occupational safety and health rules | 1.5% |
| *Less:* the increase in income-tax rates | 1.5% | *Plus:* the increase in employer social-security rates | 1.0% |
| *Equals:* the net change in aftertax take-home pay | −2.9% | *Equals:* the change in aftertax labor costs | +2.1% |

labor market is again in equilibrium. *But, the level of employment has fallen as a result of the tax increase.* The tax wedge has increased.

More on the specific components in the tax wedge as it applies to the United States is shown in table 21.1. This table shows percentage changes in a number of taxlike variables with the values being illustrative of the period 1976–1980 in the United States. However, some of the estimates are crude, so that the table should be seen as more illustrative than definitive. The left-hand column shows the components leading to the aftertax real wage as seen from the perspective of the worker. The right-hand column shows the ingredients in the net real cost of labor to the firm. The first three rows for each perspective are the same. They show the growth rate in nominal hourly pay plus fringes, less the inflation rate, which equals the change in the real wage uncorrected for taxes. For the data shown, this declined slightly, because inflation was higher than the nominal wage increase.

From the worker's perspective, the road is all downhill from here. Rising social-security rates applied to higher maximum amounts of income earned has caused the effective social-security rate to rise by about 1 percent. *Bracket creep,* the increasing income-tax rate that goes along with rising nominal but not real wage rates, has increased the percentage of income taxes paid by about 1.5 percent. These two categories mean that the representative worker in the table has experienced a fall in aftertax take-home pay by some 2.9 percent.

On the other side of the ledger, the firm's picture is quite different. The decline in the inflation-adjusted wage of 0.4 percent by itself lowers the firm's cost of labor. But, increased costs associated with complying with increasingly rigorous government occupational safety and health regulations raise costs by about 1.5 percent. The employer's contribution to social security rises at the same rate as the worker's contribution: thus this cost to the firm is up by about 1.0 percent. The result of these additional costs is that the total cost to firms of an hour of labor has increased by more than 2 percent.

For the data in table 21.1, the real take-home pay of workers has fallen, while the real cost of labor to firms has risen. It is the worst of both worlds to supply-side theorists. The rising labor costs are a disincentive for firms to hire workers, while the falling aftertax real wage is a disincentive for workers to supply labor. The tax wedge has widened over the time period covered by table 21.1.

The disincentive effect of income taxes and other taxlike transfers has an important further implication for supply-side policy makers. In the tax-wedge model, higher tax rates lower the equilibrium amount of employment. With lower employment, fewer workers are paying the higher tax rates. This means a 5 percent increase in income-tax rates will generate *less* than a 5 percent gain in revenues. It is approximately correct (to a log approximation) that if the tax rate goes up by 5 percent and as a result the equilibrium level of employment falls by 3 percent, then tax revenues will rise by 5 − 3 = 2%. One can envision a situation where rising tax rates could reduce the equilibrium level of employment by a large enough amount that less, not more, revenues would be collected. This is the thinking behind the *Laffer curve,* so-named after Professor Laffer, who brought the relationship to the attention of the public and his fellow economists in the middle and late 1970s. Figure 21.4 shows a Laffer curve, which relates the income-tax rate to the amount of total tax revenues collected.

The horizontal axis in figure 21.4 shows income-tax rates running from 0 to 100 percent. The vertical axis shows the total tax revenues

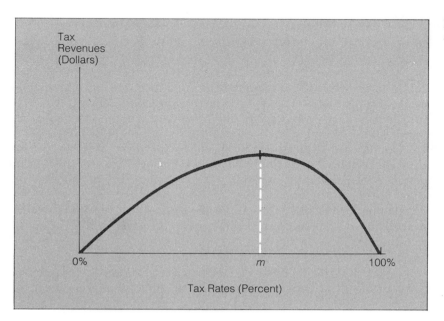

**FIGURE 21.4.**
**A Laffer Curve.**

that result from these rates. The curve shows the likely shape of the relationship. At both zero and 100 percent rates, no taxes are collected. (For the zero rate, there is no bill to pay, whereas for the 100 percent rate, the presumption is that work would cease.) For tax rates ranging from zero to $m$, an increase in the tax rate reduces the level of employment by proportionately less than the increase; thus tax revenue rises. Beyond $m$, further increases in taxes reduce equilibrium employment by proportionately more than the increase, causing total tax revenues to fall.

Some advocates of the supply-side policy contend that income taxes in the United States have reached the so-called prohibitive range beyond $m$. Thus, if income taxes are cut, the equilibrium level of employment will rise by enough to cause more instead of less revenues to be collected. This belief is part of the reasoning process that led the Reagan administration to propose a three-year tax cut of 10 percent per year. It was argued that the effect on equilibrium employment and on work incentives in general of such a prolonged and substantial cut in tax rates would lead to more revenues being collected at the lower tax rates. In other words, the thinking was that income-tax rates in the United States were by 1980 in Laffer's prohibitive range.

## RATIONAL EXPECTATIONS

Professors John Muth, Robert Lucas, Thomas Sargent, and Neil Wallace are among a group of economists whose work during the period 1972–1980 constituted a new attack on the ability of economic policy to work positive effects on the economy. These economists have criticized much of economic theory on the grounds that the theory assumes the public either is ill-informed or does not use the information they possess in a rational way. According to proponents of rational expectations the result is models of expectations that assume people are wrong on the average. The *rational expectations* view is that the public takes all relevant information into account in the most efficient manner when forming their expectations. According to Muth, if an expectation is formed rationally, it will use the best available theory to structure all the relevant information into a prediction of the future course of the economy. Although the expectation may not be correct, it will not on the average be wrong if it is rational.

Assuming expectations are rationally formed has some potentially important implications for economic policy. Consider the program of investment tax credits devised in the United States during the 1960s. Under this program, new capital investments made while the credit was in effect entitled firms to a substantial saving on their tax bills. The purpose of the program was to give the policy maker the latitude to put the credit into effect when capital spending needed a boost,

## Memorandum

To: Underground readers
From: JWE

One of the implications of the tax-wedge model is that if taxes get too high, more and more people are motivated to work in other ways to earn a living. Some of these ways are illegal, others are legal but done on a "cash" basis that is unreported as income. In other words, one plausible result of a growing tax wedge is the growth in the so-called underground economy. Recent estimates, such as those reported in *Business Week*, April 5, 1982, indicate that underground economic activities in the United States are reaching important proportions. They include the following activities and estimated amounts for 1981:

| unreported income from legal activities | |
|---|---|
| from self-employment | $115 billion |
| interest income | 20 billion |
| corporate profits | 18 billion |
| rents and royalties | 15 billion |
| wages and salaries | 80 billion |
| total | $255 billion |

| unreported income from illegal activities | |
|---|---|
| drugs | $ 45 billion |
| bribery and fraud | 25 billion |
| prostitution or pornography | 21 billion |
| gambling, loan sharking, et cetera | 14 billion |
| stolen goods | 20 billion |
| total | $125 billion |
| Total legal and illegal unreported income | $380 billion |

These estimates are obtainable only indirectly, and only by our making some assumptions that may or may not be true. However, several separate estimates of the size of the underground economy put the total within 60 billion of the amount shown here.

We can safely conclude that the underground economy is doing a pretty good business in any event. And, most of it is in cash, or so one would expect. Many economists attribute the rather strange figures on cash holdings to the effects of the underground economy. If the stock of currency is divided by the total population, it shows that cash holdings in 1981 in the United States amounted to $541 on average for every man, woman, and child in the country, a figure that is up from $187 in 1965. Are you holding that much in your wallet right now? Do you know any ten people that together are holding that much? Clearly, there must be a lot of attaché cases checked into lockers at bus stations!

thus helping to avoid the often-violent cyclical swings in capital spending. But, firms that know of this purpose (and it is a matter of public record) rationally respond by building into their investment strategies the way they expect the government to behave. Thus, if they see the economy beginning to weaken, they would delay capital investment in anticipation of the investment tax credit being imposed. So, the weakening in the economy would be fueled by the reaction of firms to the policy they expect the government to apply. Then, when a more seriously weakening economy does lead to the tax credit being imposed, the delayed spending takes place, leading to a boom. It is an example of the expectation of the anticyclical policy causing the cyclical problem to become worse.

As a second example, consider the Federal Reserve's policy on the growth rate in the money supply. Suppose the public studied the pattern of behavior of the Board of Governors, and discovered that when the real GNP rate falls for two successive quarters, the growth rate in money is speeded up. Under rational expectations, this information will not be wasted. When the public sees real GNP falling, they will factor an increase in the growth rate of money into their expectations of the future course of the economy. Interest-rate expectations will respond accordingly as will actual interest rates. In fact, the economy will adjust to the *effects* of an expected growth in money even before it occurs.

This adjustment to expectations handcuffs the Board of Governors. If it now increases the growth rate of money by an amount consistent with its past behavior, it will find that no economic effects occur. The economic effects of its anticipated action have already occurred, when the public built them into their structure of expectations. This creates quite a problem. With the public behaving rationally, the only way the Board of Governors can have an impact on the economy is to implement a policy that is not expected by the public—that is, to deal in a policy of surprises.

The overall implication of assuming the public form their expectations rationally is that much government policy becomes ineffective in producing economic changes to the extent the policy is systematic and thus predictable by the public. Since much public policy is in fact systematic and predictable, the rational-expectations critique suggests that many of the government's policy tools may not work in the way that the government believes they will. As a result of this thinking, most economists who feel that expectations are in fact rational tend to support a rules approach to monetary policy, and also tend to feel that a passive approach to demand-management policy is best advised.

**Important Ideas in This Chapter**

1. Economic policy refers to the guidelines, rules, and general dos and don'ts that apply to the economy.

2. Major policy differences occur because advocates follow differing theories to their logical conclusions. Theoretical differences create policy differences.

3. An important controversy in the application of economic policy is whether policy should be adjusted according to the predictions and the discretion of the Board of Governors, or whether instead it should follow a predetermined set of rules that corresponds to noninflationary growth of the economy.

4. Professor Friedman advocates a rules policy, by invoking the natural-rate hypothesis and the quantity theory, and by arguing that the lags between the recognition of a need for changing monetary

policy and the change in the economy that results from it are too long and too variable to allow effective discretionary policy making.

**5.** The Phillips curve is the relationship between the inflation rate and the unemployment rate, which is presumed to be negative, and which creates a trade-off between anti-inflationary and full-employment policies.

**6.** Data during the 1970s in the United States have not been supportive of the Phillips curve trade-off. At best, they illustrate a rapidly shifting and unstable relationship. At worst, they indicate the relationship during the 1970s may be positive.

**7.** Demand-management policies are guidelines that lead the government to adjust its part of aggregate demand in such a way as to offset fluctuations in the private sector and thus stabilize the growth rate in total demand.

**8.** Demand-managment policies were popular parts of U.S. government administrations during the 1960s and early 1970s.

**9.** The supply-side approach to policy emphasizes the government's role in influencing incentives to produce, invest, and save. In the supply-side view, people and firms are seen as responding importantly to prices, wages, interest rates, and other incentives that affect the costs and benefits of their economic activities.

**10.** When the role of income taxes is placed into the labor-market model, a tax wedge is formed that causes the equilibrium level of output to be less than it would be in the absence of taxes. The higher the income-tax rate, the greater the tax wedge, and the less the equilibrium level of output.

**11.** The effect of income taxes on equilibrium output means that increases in tax rates will not increase tax revenues by the same proportion. Instead, an increase in the tax rate will produce an increase in revenue that is less, perhaps much less, than that suggested by the tax increase itself. The opposite is true for tax cuts. The effect on revenue may be much less than the tax cut would suggest.

**12.** The rational-expectations view is that the public takes all relevant information into account in the most efficient way when forming their expectations. If expectations are rational, then the public will tend to predict the systematic aspects of policy making by the government, and will adjust to the expectations that these policies will continue. As a result, if the government acts systematically and predictably in setting its polilcy, then its policy actions will have already been anticipated by the public and will have little effect on the economy when they occur.

**Discussion Questions**

**1.** Prepare a scorecard comparing a discretionary monetary policy with a rules policy. Add up the pluses and minuses, and see where each policy stands.

**2.** Plot some data at both quarterly and annual intervals over the period 1970 to present on the Phillips curve. What do your plots show?

**3.** Does the supply-side approach to economics conflict with demand-management policies, or is it complementary to such policies?

**4.** Consider as many recent changes in the federal laws as you can find that relate one way or the other to the size of the tax wedge.

**5.** "If expectations are rational, the government can have an impact on the economy only by dealing in surprises and deception. This is not exactly the way to run governmental policy." Comment on the correctness of these statements.

**Suggested Readings**

There are two good readings on the role of discretionary policy versus rules policy. See Franco Modigliani "The Monetarist Controversy, or Should We Forsake Stabilization Policy?", *American Economic Review*, March 1977, pp. 1–19; and Milton Friedman, "The Role of Monetary Policy," *American Economic Review*, 58, (March, 1968) pp. 1–17. More on tax-wedge theory can be found in an article by Arthur Laffer, "Supply-Side Economics," *The Financial Analysts Journal*, September 1981. A comprehensive survey of the Phillips-curve literature can be found in A. M. Santomero and J. J. Seater, "The Inflation-Unemployment Tradeoff: A Critique of the Literature," *Journal of Economic Literature*, June 1978, pp. 499–544.

## CHAPTER 22

# The Ongoing Economic Policy Debate

## IMPORTANT TERMS

Keynesian
neoclassicist
monetarist
perceived price level

```
MEMO ═══════════════════════════

To:        All readers
From:      JWE


It is when economists become advocates of one type of policy or another
that they get classified, sorted, and grouped into "camps." The groupings
are then usually provided with an overall title. Currently, there are three
such groupings in economic policy making. They are the Keynesians,
the monetarists, and the neoclassicists.

In this chapter, you first read about the differences between these three
groups in terms of the theories each accepts as most relevant to the
world in which we live. Then, you examine five important questions on
which the ongoing debate and disagreement among these groups re-
volve. These questions involve the effect of fiscal and monetary policy
on the economy, the proper target of policy, the policy trade-offs that
must be made, the root causes of inflation, and the role of the Federal
Reserve in setting interest rates. Finding answers to the controversial
questions asked in this chapter is among the most important tasks for
economic research during the next several years.
```

There is no serious disagreement among economists about the goals
they would like to see the economy attain. All else the same, stable
prices are preferred to inflation, low unemployment preferred to high
unemployment, and low interest rates to high interest rates. The
issues that divide economists and make them advocates of one kind
of policy or another are generally questions of (1) whether specific
economic goals such as price stability and full employment *can* be
jointly attained, and (2) what the government can do to promote
attainment of such goals.

Over the decade of the 1970s, the policy positions commonly held
by economists tended to follow from variations of two broad and
contrasting patterns of thinking. Not surprisingly, these contrasting
patterns of thinking evolve from similarly contrasting theoretical
viewpoints. Differences in the theories that economists believe best
explain how the real world works are the main reason for differences
in the policies that economists advocate.

## KEYNESIANS, MONETARISTS, AND NEOCLASSICISTS

A *Keynesian* is so-named because of a general adherence to the economic theory of John Maynard Keynes, the world-famous British

economist whose 1936 book, *The General Theory of Employment, Interest, and Money,* redirected the main stream of thinking in economics away from the motives of suppliers and producers and toward the role of aggregate demand in setting the level of production. Most Keynesians believe that wages are sufficiently downwardly rigid that the labor market is usually operating at below-equilibrium levels, with some unemployment beyond the frictional/structural/seasonal level. Keynesians do not accept the natural-rate hypothesis.

With the belief that some slack exists in the labor market most of the time, Keynesians can generally follow the IS–LM model to derive the economic consequences of their policy prescriptions. Keynesians think in terms of multiplier effects, fiscal policy, and an active role for government in managing aggregate demand. In turn, management of aggregate demand is seen as the key to managing the course of the economy. Keynesians make up one main intellectual camp in the continuing debate over economic policy.

In the other intellectual camp are monetarists and neoclassicists. A *neoclassicist* is so-named because of a general adherence to the classical system of economic thought that preceded Keynes. The prefix *neo* indicates that the pre-Keynesian ideas held by this group have undergone modifications and modernizations, but have not been fundamentally changed. Neoclassicists believe that the natural-rate hypothesis is a good approximation of the way the world works. Therefore, they feel the labor market is in equilibrium most of the time. This leads to the conclusion that multiplier effects of fiscal policy are zero, that crowding out is the main effect of government spending, and that the role of the government vis-à-vis the economy is to inhibit as little as possible the incentives to work, produce, invest, and save. Neoclassicists see aggregate demand as being derived from levels of production rather than being the cause of changes in production. Generally, neoclassicists accept the flexible-wage/natural-rate version of the aggregate supply/demand model for chapter 17.

*Monetarists* are so-named because of the central role they attribute to fluctuations in the money supply in the economy. A monetarist is guided most strongly by the quantity theory. Many monetarists do not fully accept the natural-rate hypothesis in the short-run, although they do in the long-run. Over short-run periods, monetarists believe that changes in the money supply can produce changes in production and employment. Over the long-run, changes in the money supply lead to no lasting changes in production or employment, but only to price changes. Fiscal policy is thought to have only a temporary effect on jobs and production to the extent that it creates inflation. Later in the chapter, we further discuss how the monetarist's logic works to produce these conclusions. For now, it suffices to recognize that the monetarist's position is somewhat intermediate between the neoclassical acceptance of the natural-rate hypothesis and the Keynesian belief in continual slack in the labor market. We now examine a number of important policy questions on which there is solid disagreement among Keynesians, neoclassicists, and monetarists.

## CAN FISCAL AND
## MONETARY POLICIES CREATE JOBS?

Because Gordon is up almost every day at 5:30 A.M., people call him an early riser. Because he is noisy in the morning, his wife, Kathy, is also an early riser. She endures by listening to the radio. Radio programming at 5:30 A.M. involves horoscopes, hog-market reports, and not-for-prime-time news stories. On one particular morning, the programming included a taped speech by a local representative delivered the day before in the U.S. House of Representatives. A (fictitious) part of it went as follows:

> My esteemed colleagues, this bill marks an important step in the pathway to full employment. With its passage, we will have created 100,000 new jobs. Yes, my friends, because of what we do here today, 100,000 Americans who are now unemployed will be on the job again, working at useful public employment. Streets will be cleaner, libraries better staffed, road work done more quickly, and above all, people will be earning paychecks again that can be spent in the economy. And it's not just in the economy we are talking about here, my friends. It is in the stores and shops that are in your very own home districts. Can there be any doubt that the spending of these paychecks will add to still further employment, as the demand for goods by the new workers leads to a need for higher production? Employment in the economy—yea, in your own districts—will expand. Ultimately, the citizens will be happier. Can you discharge your responsibility as a public servant more effectively? Vote with me for this landmark full-employment bill.

Let us tune in for a minute to Gordon and Kathy's reaction to this speech.

*Kathy:* That sounds pretty good to me, Gordo. What do you think?

*Gordon:* Mistaken giveaway mentality. Politicians get elected by creating the impression that they are responsible for whatever prosperity occurs in their voting district. And, on occasion, they feel a need to do something like this jobs bill so they can take a little extra credit for events over which they had no actual influence.

*Kathy:* But, the government bill can certainly create 100,000 public jobs. That will be 100,000 more jobs than existed before. And the paychecks from those jobs will certainly lead to more spending, which will lead to even more jobs. Don't forget the multiplier from your old econ class. It sounds like a solid way for the government to do something to increase employment and stimulate economic growth.

*Gordon:* Kathy, you are only seeing part of the picture. How do you think the government is going to pay for these 100,000 jobs? The same economics class you are talking about should have taught you that paying for the jobs undoes all the good economic effects you have listed. The net effect of it is zero.

*Kathy:* How can that be? I don't get it.

*Gordon:* (fumbling through his bookcase and taking out a book): Here, read chapter 18 of Elliott's money and banking book when you get home from work. It's all in there. We'll talk about it at dinner tonight.

## The Keynesian Position on Fiscal-Policy Effects

The difference in viewpoints you just read about illustrates a central conflict between Keynesian and neoclassical perspectives. This conflict involves the effectiveness of fiscal policy in stimulating output and employment. The example of the government jobs program is as good as any to illustrate the conflict. When a new government job is created, the salary paid for the job officially becomes a part of government spending. When the government pays the salaries of 100,000 new workers, the $G$ part of $C + I + G$ goes up.

Suppose the average annual salary for these 100,000 new jobs is $20,000 per job. The new annual government outlay then is 100,000 × $20,000 = 2 billion dollars. Figure 22.1 illustrates the effect on the economy of this increase of two billion dollars in government spending, by using the IS–LM and aggregate supply/demand model with rigid wages and operating at less than full employment. Assume that before the jobs program begins, aggregate demand and production are in balance at a real GNP of 1,200 and an interest rate of 8 percent. Government spending is at $G = 250$ billion. The price level is at 100. The net multiplier, considering both interest rates and prices, is 2.7. When the jobs program is put into effect, government spending rises by two billion to $G = 252$. As a result of this increase in government spending, both the IS curve and the price-demand curve shift to the right. Thus, prices rise to 103—see part (b) of figure 22.1—while interest rates rise to 9 percent. The new equilibrium real GNP rises

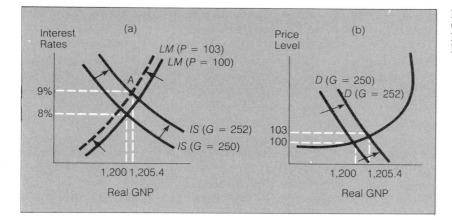

**FIGURE 22.1.
Government Jobs
Programs—A
Keynesian View.**

by $2.7 \times 2.0 = 5.4$ to 1,205.4, which corresponds to point $A$ in the IS–LM graph. Not only has the government directly added 100,000 new jobs and 2 billion dollars in real GNP, the multiplier effects of it have induced another 3.4 billion dollars in real GNP and still more new jobs in the private sector to produce this 3.4 billion of induced output. The costs for this gain are moderately higher prices and interest rates as the economy moves upward on the Phillips curve.

What's more, suppose that the average private and public wage earner pays 25 percent of his/her income in taxes. The 5.4-billion total increase in real GNP then results in $5.4 \times 125 = 1.35$ billion paid in new taxes. Thus, the two billion of government spending only results in a net government outflow of $2.00 - 1.35 = 0.65$ billion. Keynesian analysis not only backs up Kathy's and the politician's thinking—it goes them one better.

## The Neoclassical and Monetarist Position on Fiscal-Policy Effects

Both neoclassical economists and monetarists assume the natural-rate hypothesis and thus assume a vertical aggregate-supply curve. Under this view, the impact of the creation of 100,000 new government jobs is quite different.

With a vertical aggregate-supply curve, the shift in the IS and price-demand curves produced by the two billion of new government spending only causes higher prices and interest rates. Real GNP and total employment stay the same. But, how can 100,000 new jobs result in no increase in total jobs? The financing of the two billion of new government spending is the answer. Suppose the two billion is raised by allowing a deficit to appear in the federal budget. If the government was spending 250 billion and taking in 250 billion in taxes before the program started, spending now rises to 252 billion and a deficit in the federal budget of 2 billion appears. This deficit is financed by borrowing in private credit markets. Instead of the Treasury raising 5 billion at its weekly T-Bill auction to replace maturing debt, it will now raise an additional sum to cover the emerging deficit. (See chapter 5 for more on the T-Bill market.)

*The additional 2 billion the government borrows is 2 billion that private borrowers cannot borrow.* If private borrowers are turned away from the credit market empty-handed, they do not spend the money they had planned to spend. We can safely assume that all who sought to borrow wanted to spend the borrowed money. so, if private borrowing/spending goes down by 2 billion because government borrowing/spending goes up by 2 billion, then total spending does not change at all. While the 100,000 jobs are quite visibly added in the public sector, they are invisibly lost in the private sector, casualties of capital-investment cutbacks occurring because of high interest rates.

Thus, in neoclassical thinking, there is a crucial offsetting side effect, crowding out, that goes along with creating the 100,000 new government jobs. As a result, a fiscal stimulus such as this jobs program cannot produce gains in employment or production.

## The Keynesian Position on Monetary Policy

Gordon and Kathy's conflicting view of the impact of fiscal policy on the economy applies in large part to the impact of monetary policy as well. Under Keynesian thinking (with some unemployment in the labor market), an increase in money (1) shifts the LM curve to the right, (2) lowers interest rates, (3) increases the real GNP and employment, (4) increases jobs, and (5) increases prices. The main reason for the increase in jobs and output is the stimulus of the lower interest rates on capital-investment spending. Thus, monetary policy to a Keynesian is a method by which the government can implement demand-management economic policies. Concerning the rules versus discretion discussion in the previous chapter, Keynesians tend to advocate a policy of discretionary use of the money supply to stabilize aggregate demand.

## The Neoclassical
## Monetarist Position on Monetary Policy

For both monetarists and neoclassicists, either the quantity theory or the flexible-wage IS–LM model adequately describes the expected final result of increases in the money supply that exceed the needs of the economy. If the economy is in equilibrium and the supply of money is increased, the result is ultimately higher prices with no change in the real GNP or employment.

For neoclassicists, this result is to be expected both in the short-run and in the long-run. Over the short-run, increases in the money supply shift the LM curve to the right. The price-demand schedule also shifts to the right, sliding up along a vertical aggregate-supply curve. Prices rise, reducing the real money supply, and causing the LM curve to retreat to its initial position. When stability is restored, the price level has risen by the same proportion as the nominal money supply, so that the real money supply remains unchanged. Thus, the result of the increase in the money supply is a proportionate increase in prices—just as in the quantity theory.

For monetarists such as Professor Friedman, the final result is the same, but the route the economy takes over the short-run to arrive at this destination differs. Monetarists have a slightly different view of the labor-market adjustment process than neoclassicists. Monetarists contend that it is the *perceived price level* rather than the actual price level that governs the behavior of workers and firms in making decisions to supply and demand labor. Since firms generally set prices, they are in a better position to know when prices are in the process of changing. Workers tend to wait until price changes actually occur at the retail level for the products they buy before changing their perceptions of the price level. As a result of this timing difference in the way price changes are perceived by firms and workers, monetarists feel that changes in money can have an influence on the labor market, and thus have an influence on the level of employment.

Here is how the monetarist process works. When money is expanded, firms are quicker than workers to realize that the added purchasing power represented by the new money will increase prices. So, they perceive that the real wage is about to fall. Accordingly, they are willing to hire more workers at the present real wage than before the money expansion. They accomplish this by increasing the money wage rate, but by less than the expected fall in prices, so that the real cost of labor is seen as falling. Workers see the increase in wages but are slow to perceive the more-than-offsetting increase in prices. Thus, they are willing to supply more labor services. Employment temporarily increases and more output is produced.

However, the process is short-lived. When prices begin to actually rise on the products workers buy, the workers' perceptions of the price level and the real wage converge on those of the firm, and the labor market returns to its former equilibrium level through wage adjustments. Output falls back to its former level, and the only lasting effect of the increase in money is a proportionate increase in prices.

Thus, both neoclassicists and monetarists find no role for monetary policy in creating lasting changes in real output and jobs, and the temporary role that some monetarists do find is only a result of worker expectations that are not consistent with those of firms.

## SHOULD GOVERNMENT POLICY BE DIRECTED TOWARD DEMAND OR SUPPLY?

Using the IS–LM aggregate supply/demand framework, Keynesians quite logically find a crucial role for active demand-management policies. Fluctuations in demand are seen in the IS–LM model (with unemployment) as being an important source, if not *the* source, of fluctuations in the real GNP and in jobs. Since the government can increase or decrease its demand and that of the private economy by fiscal and monetary policy, it is easy to see why policy makers who reason from the Keynesian framework advocate government demand-management policies.

When we recognize that neoclassicists and monetarists both accept the natural-rate hypothesis, we can see why they tend to dismiss demand-management policies as ineffective in doing anything but producing inflation and high interest rates. For neoclassicists in particular, increases in government demand only crowd out private demand. Since demand is derived from the process of production (Say's law), the key to getting more production and jobs is not to try fruit-lessly to create more demand out of thin air but to increase the in-centives of firms and workers to work and produce more. With more production will come more demand.

Thus, neoclassicists and monetarists tend to align with supply-side economic policies whereas Keynesians tend logically to align with demand-mangement policies. This is not to say that Keynesians can-not be found who also support an active government role in increasing supply-side incentives. The two types of policies are not mutually exclusive. But, the dominant theme in Keynesian policy making is not to stimulate the incentives to supply, but to control and manage the level of aggregate demand.

## IS THERE A PHILLIPS CURVE?

The discussion of the Phillips curve in the previous chapter should help you to draw your own conclusion as to where Keynesians and monetarists/neoclassicists stand on this question. Keynesians, with their perception of the underemployed economy as the usual case, need only shift the level of demand in the IS–LM model to see a Phillips-curve relationship appear. As demand (the IS–LM intersec-tion point) increases, the price-demand curve shifts upward along the aggregate-supply curve. Inflation picks up as the economy moves toward full employment. A negative relationship is present between the inflation rate and the unemployment rate.

For Keynesians, the experience of the 1970s was one in which Phillips curves were shifting, not one where these curves vaporized. As principal reasons for the perceived violent shifts in the Phillips curves over the 1970s, Keynesians point to the supply shocks asso-ciated with the OPEC oil crisis of the period. Keynesians contend that the inflation resulting from the cartel's price increases could not be explained by the usual macroeconomic relationships; thus, OPEC caused a violent shifting of the curve. In addition, Keynesians argue that the great increase in production costs in the 1970s that were associated with cleaning up pollution problems and improving industrial safety and health standards were similar "outside" influences that shifted the Phillips curve.

On the other hand, neoclassicists need only evaluate the effects of a demand shift in their model to conclude that no Phillips-curve re-lationship is present. When demand increases, nothing happens to the natural rate of employment. Thus, output stays the same. The demand increase results only in higher prices. The neoclassical vertical aggregate-supply curve produces a vertical Phillips curve. Neoclas-sicists see no trade-off between the "twin evils" of inflation and un-employment. Instead, inflation and unemployment are viewed as variables set by two independent sets of influences.

For monetarists, an intermediate position is taken. Because monetarists see money expansion as able to produce short-run effects on employment and the real GNP, they typically believe that short-run Phillips-curve relationships are possible, insofar as such relationships are produced by money expansion. During the period when expectations are adjusting to an increase in money, employment rises. Thus, unemployment will go down as prices are going up. A short-run Phillips-curve relationship appears. But, to monetarists, it is more illusionary than real. As soon as expectations of workers and firms align, the employment effect of money expansion disappears, and so does the Phillips-curve relationship. And, the quicker the alignment of expectations, the less significant this short-run Phillips curve becomes.

## WHAT IS THE UNDERLYING CAUSE OF INFLATION?

The answer to this question is more complicated to a Keynesian than to either a monetarist or a neoclassicist. To a Keynesian, much depends on where the economy is operating compared with its capacity level. Consider first the impact of an increase in aggregate demand on inflation. If the economy is at a high rate of unemployment with much excess plant capacity, then aggregate demand can increase with little or no inflation. For, in this case, the aggregate-supply curve is assumed to be nearly horizontal. Thus, when aggregate demand and the price-demand curve shift to the right, the real GNP rises with little or no accompanying rise in prices. On the other hand, if aggregate demand increases when the economy is operating in the upward-sloping region of the aggregate-supply curve, inflation will result. Accordingly, to a Keynesian, an increase in aggregate demand may or may not be inflationary, depending on how close the economy is to its capacity.

The same is true for the inflationary effects of money expansion. Expanding money shifts the LM curve out and increases the level of equilibrium aggregate demand in the economy. If the economy has considerable excess capacity and is operating on the close-to-flat part of the aggregate-supply curve, money can thus be expanded with little effect on prices. So, the Keynesian position is that increasing money beyond that needed for transactions may or may not be inflationary depending on the amount of unused capacity in the economy.

For both neoclassicists and monetarists, the question of what causes inflation is less iffy. Either would agree with Keynesians that an increase in aggregate demand would lead to price increases. But, since the economy is seen as gravitating toward full utilization, the result of demand shifts is primarily inflation. With a vertical aggregate-supply curve, real output does not adjust to excess aggregate demand. Prices go up instead.

Monetarists and neoclassicists are specific about what can cause an increase in aggregate demand and what cannot. First, a shift in the demand by any particular group (consumers, firms, government) will *not* cause an increase in aggregate demand, according to neoclassical analysis. If consumers independently want to spend more, they do so by supplying less savings to credit markets. (They spend more of their income.) With less loanable funds available, firms borrow less and are thus forced to reduce their capital-investment spending.

If firms independently want to spend more, they must raise the purchasing power in financial markets. When firms bid for the available funds, the real rate is driven up, thus inducing more consumer savings. Consumers respond to the higher real rates by saving more and spending less.

When the government increases its purchases, it does so either by bidding purchasing power away from firms in credit markets, or by taking purchasing power from consumers in the form of taxes. In the first case, the borrowing/spending of firms falls as the government spending rises, and in the second case, purchases of consumers fall as that of the government rises.

Accordingly, it is the neoclassical/monetarist view that aggregate demand will not rise because some component of it independently rises. Say's law dictates that the total amount of purchasing power available in the economy (that is, aggregate demand) is dictated by the amount produced. One group in the economy can buy more only by borrowing or otherwise acquiring some of the purchasing power of other groups.

In the neoclassical/monetarist view, *the only source of a general increase in aggregate demand other than an increase in production is an increase in the money supply.* When the money supply is increased, the price-demand curve shifts to the right, up along the economy's vertical aggregate-supply curve, and inflation occurs while the economy adjusts to the new higher equilibrium position. So, in the neoclassical/monetarists view, money is the only source of aggregate-demand increases, besides that generated by increasing production, and money is an unequivocal source of increases in prices.

One point concerning inflation on which little disagreement exists between Keynesians and monetarists is that when changes occur in productivity or in other supply variables, the resulting shift in the aggregate-supply curve will have an impact on the equilibrium price level and the inflation rate. For example, if productivity goes up, the aggregate-supply curve shifts to the right, reducing the equilibrium price level and the inflation rate.

# CAN THE FEDERAL RESERVE BRING DOWN INTEREST RATES?

Public policy makers are frequently heard admonishing the Federal Reserve to do something about high interest rates. To Keynesians, this is a reasonable call for action, because they believe that actions taken by the Board of Governors to change the money supply will result in changes in interest rates. Specifically, if the supply of money is increased, the interest rate will fall. Thus, if interest rates are too high, it is because the growth in money has been too small.

Monetarists and neoclassicists argue that the Federal Reserve has very little control over market interest rates. (The Federal Reserve does set the discount rate, but it is not a market rate of interest, and in any event, it is usually set in a way to be consistent with market interest rates, such as the Treasury Bill rate.) To see how each group arrives at their conclusions, consider the graphs shown in figure 22.2.

Parts (a) and (b) show the Keynesian case. With the IS and LM curves in the initial positions shown by $IS_0$ and $LM(P = P_0, M = M_0)$, the equilibrium interest rate is $r_0$. If the supply of money is increased to $M_1$, the LM curve shifts to the position shown as $LM(P = P_0, M = M_1)$. This shift in the LM causes a shift in the price-demand

**FIGURE 22.2.**
**The Interest Rate and Money under Neoclassical Monetarist and Keynesian Theories.**

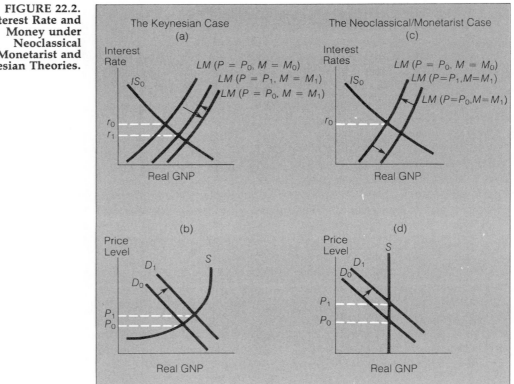

curve in part (b) from its initial position of $D_0$ to the new position $D_1$. The equilibrium price level rises to $P_1$ from its initial value of $P_0$. This price rise reduces the real money supply which shifts the LM curve back to its new equilibrium position of $LM(P = P_1, M = M_1)$. At this point, prices are at a level that equates aggregate supply and demand, and equilibrium is regained. The interest rate is at the new lower value of $r_1$. So, for the Keynesian case, increasing the money supply has indeed brought down interest rates. Moreover, as long as excess capacity exists, further increases in the money supply will continue to bring down rates. The Federal Reserve is in fact in charge of interest rates, given the Keynesian framework.

The monetarist/neoclassical case is shown in parts (c) and (d) of figure 22.2. With the economy initially in equilibrium at $IS_0$ and $LM(P = P_0, M = M_0)$ with interest rate $r_0$ and price level $P_0$, assume again that the money supply is increased to $M_1$. This shifts the LM curve to the dotted position labeled $LM(P = P_0, M = M_1)$ and also shifts the price-demand curve from $D_0$ to $D_1$. This causes prices to rise, which again begins to cause the LM to shift back to the left toward the original position. But, with the vertical aggregate-supply curve of this model, prices keep rising as long as aggregate demand exceeds the unchanged level of supply. Accordingly, prices continue to rise until the amount of aggregate demand is reduced to its former level, where it again equals supply. This means that prices keep on rising until the LM shifts back to its original position. Thus, the curve $LM(P = P_1, M = M_1)$ lies exactly on top of the original curve. Demand has been reduced to the original level of supply, and interest rates stabilize at their former level, $r_0$. Although some temporary drop in interest rates may have taken place during this adjustment period, no lasting interest-rate effects of the money expansion have occurred. What has instead happened is that the inflationary effects of the additional money have reduced the purchasing power of the larger money supply to that of its former level. With no more real money in the economy, interest rates do not fall. This reasoning leads monetarists and noeclassicists to argue that despite any adjustments the Board of Governors may make in the supply of money, has little control over the interest rates in financial markets.

Some monetarists, notably Professor Friedman, argue that when the Federal Reserve expands money, it usually leads to *higher*, not lower, interest rates, and when the Federal Reserve tightens money, the result is usually lower, not higher, interest rates. This view leads to the idea that the Board of Governors can do something about high interest rates, by not increasing the supply of money. Instead, to bring down interest rates, the Federal Reserve should reduce the money supply!

Figure 22.3 shows the reasoning behind this conclusion. In part (a), the IS curve is in the position labeled $IS(P_e = P_{e,0})$—the $P_e$ variable stands for the economy's inflationary expectation—while the LM curve is in the position $LM(P = P_0, M = M_0)$. Thus, the initial interest rate

FIGURE 22.3.
Money and Interest
Rates Under
Monetarism.

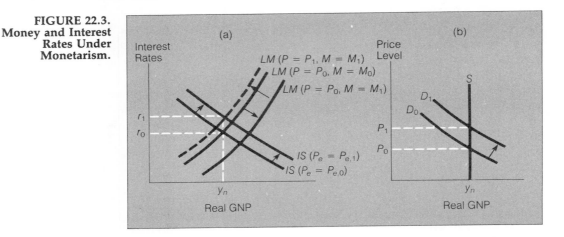

FIGURE 22.3.
Money and Interest
Rates Under
Monetarism.

is $r_0$ while the price level is $P_0$. When the money supply is increased
to $M_1$, the initial response of the economy is as before. The LM curve
shifts to the dotted position $LM(P = P_0, M = M_1)$ and the price-
demand curve shifts to $D_1$, as shown in part (b) of the figure. However,
in Friedman's view, the public will in all likelihood be quick to expect
that the increase in the money supply to $M_1$ will lead to inflation and
higher equilibrium prices. Thus, inflationary expectations rise from
their initial level of $P_{e,0}$ to a new higher level of $P_{e,1}$. This shifts the IS
curve from its initial position to the new position labeled $IS(P_e = P_{e,1})$.
(If you need to recall the logic behind this, see the section on Chickens,
Eggs, and Economic Equilibrium in chapter 15.)

As before, prices keep rising as long as aggregate demand exceeds
the unchanged level of supply. This requires an increase in prices to
$P_1$ sufficient to shift the LM curve to the position $LM(P = P_1, M = M_1)$. At this equilibrium position, demand equals supply, and equilibrium interest rates have risen to $r_1$. The money expansion has led
to higher equilibrium interest rates.

Monetarists who hold the view illustrated in figure 22.3 accept the
view that the Federal Reserve can do something about high interest
rates, but the medicine is exactly opposite from the Keynesian cure.

## Important Ideas in This Chapter

The main ideas in this chapter can be conveniently summarized in a
table that contrasts and compares the Keynesian, neoclassical, and
monetarist positions. Table 22.1 gives this summary.

## Discussion Questions

1. How do you think a Keynesian would respond to the neoclassical/
monetarist analysis of the result of a 100,000 government jobs program?

2. Express in your own words the argument that leads to the conclusion that the only way that aggregate demand can be increased
besides increasing production is to increase the money supply.

**TABLE 22.1**
**Summary of Important Ideas**

| | KEYNESIANS | NEOCLASSICISTS | MONETARISTS |
|---|---|---|---|
| Does the natural-rate hypothesis hold? | No | Yes | Basically, but not for short-run periods |
| What is the shape of the aggregate-supply curve? | Upward-sloping | Vertical | Temporarily upward-sloping, but ultimately vertical |
| Is the quantity theory accepted? | No | Yes | Yes |
| Can fiscal and monetary policy create jobs? | Yes | No | No—fiscal No—monetary (except temporarily) |
| Should government policy be directed toward demand or supply? | Demand | Supply | Supply |
| Is there a Phillips curve? | Yes | No | Only for temporary periods |
| What is the underlying cause of inflation? | Demand shifts | Money | Money |
| Can the Federal Reserve bring down interest rates? | Yes | No | No, except perhaps in reverse |

**3.** Outline the main points in the economic policies of the current U.S. presidential administration. Are the policies Keynesian, monetarist, or neoclassical?

**4.** Does the record show that periods of rapid money growth in the United States have led to rising, falling, or independently changing interest-rate patterns?

**5.** Suppose we were to move to a barter economy (Yoda's world of chapter 1). Which theoretical conclusions would be most affected by this change—Keynesian, monetarist, or neoclassical?

An article by James Toben, "Inflation and Unemployment," *American Economic Review*, March 1972, pp. 1–18, chronicles the thinking over time on a number of the issues of economic policy discussed in this chapter. A paper by A. Santomero and J. J. Seater, "The Inflation-Unemployment Tradeoff: A Critique of the Literature," *Journal of Economic Literature*, June 1978, pp. 499–544, gives a comprehensive review of the Phillips-curve debate over the last twenty years. A useful analysis of inflation theory is contained in a paper by Robert Gordon, "Recent Developments in the Theory of Inflation and Unemployment" *Journal of Monetary Economics*, 2, (April, 1976) pp. 185–219 and a statement of the neoclassical approach is contained in an article by F. E. Hagen, "The Classical Theory of the Level of Output and Employment," in M. G. Mueller, ed., *Readings in Macroeconomics*, 2nd ed.

**Suggested Readings**

# A Night Out at the Theater

You have now pursued macroeconomic theory in some detail. In the last chapter, you examined the controversy over economic policy separating monetarists and Keynesians. You are pretty well armed with facts on the question. But, who is right? If you are not quite sure, maybe a break will help. Why not take in a play. I've got just the one for you. It unfolds in the next several pages.

Let me tell you a little about it. It is a three-act drama involving two economists. One is a Keynesian and the other is a monetarist. Both economists are trying to persuade an uncommitted person that they are correct in their views on several important economic questions. You and the rest of the audience are peeking in on this one-on-one confrontation. With what you know, you can intelligently criticize and evaluate the arguments of these two adversaries.

Don't go too fast through the script. Do some thinking as you read. A thoughtful reading of this play can help you synthesize some of the things you've been reading. It is time for you to decide where you stand on the issues involved.

Oh, I almost forgot. Before the play starts, here is one long-stemmed rose. When the play ends, you will want to toss it at the feet of the actor who is most nearly right in his views of the economy. To your seats now, please.

## Cast of Characters

**Samuelson Smith** *is an economist in the tradition of John Maynard Keynes. The phrase "in the tradition of" means that Smith shares many of Keynes's central beliefs on how the economy works. Yet, Smith does not share all the thinking of Keynes. Smith's views on the economy represent those of a significant fraction of economists in the United States today. They are called neo-Keynesians (neo meaning modified and changed through the years).*

*Friedman Jones is an economist whose thinking is rooted in the work of economists before Keynes. Specifically, the work of Irving Fisher, Alfred Marshall, Leon Walras, and Frank Knight form the basis of the thinking of Jones. In the 1950s, Jones's theory was thought of as a relic from an earlier age. But, as years passed, this theory appeared more relevant to modern times. Today, the thinking of Jones represents that of a significant fraction of economists in the United States. They are called monetarists or classical economists.*

*Mac Peterson is not an economist. He is a college student with an as-yet-uncommitted major. In his spare time and during the summer, he drives a truck to help pay his way through school. He belongs to a union and is active in local union affairs and politics. He enjoys keeping up on current events, and prides himself on being well informed.*

Oh, I have a small walk-on part also. I had hoped for a bigger role, but I flunked the screen test. In any event, sit back and enjoy your night out at the theater. But, remember to stop and think along the way.

## Act 1—Inflation and Money

SCENE: A downtown Milwaukee restaurant. Samuelson Smith, Friedman Jones, and Mac Peterson are seated around a small table. On the table are half-empty glasses, some change, several graphs and figures, some scratch paper, and Mac's elbows.

*Mac:* OK hotshots, when I was complaining earlier about the rising cost of living and my pinched wallet, you said we'd talk about it later. Well, it's later. I want to know why prices are going up and what can be done about it.

*Friedman:* I can explain it to you without a lot of economic gobbledygook, because you are concerned with one of the most basic points in economics. Suppose you go to an auction and are given monopoly money as you enter. The monopoly money is of no value outside the room. But, it can be used to buy the goods sold at the auction. Any money not used becomes useless when the auction is over. Under these circumstances, would you keep any of your monopoly money aside at this auction, or would you spend it all?

*Mac:* Well, quite obviously, I would spend it all. So would everyone else. But what is the point?

*Friedman:* Just hold on. Now, if 100 items are going to be sold at the auction and I give out $1,000 at the door, all of it will be spent and the average price per item sold will be $1,000/100 = $10. This price per item is a miniature version of the CPI for the auction. Now, if instead of $1,000 I give out $1,500, do you suppose people will now bid more for the items?

*Mac:* Sure, now they will spend a total of $1,500 instead of $1,000, and the average price will rise to $1,500/100 = $15 per item.

*Friedman:* Yep. So the 50 percent by which I increased the supply of money at the auction has directly resulted in an increase of 50

percent in the average price. Do you receive any messages here?

*Mac:* About the economics of auctions with monopoly money, yes. About the economics of the world I live in, I am not so sure. If I don't spend all my money, it will not be taken from me at the end of the month.

*Friedman:* The comparison is closer than you think. Suppose that for the income you earn, you want to hold about $400 in your checkbook and in your wallet all the time. Since cash and checking accounts are the government's official way of defining money, this is your holding of money. Economists call it your demand for money. Now, suppose that for whatever reason, you have $500 of money holdings. What do you do?

*Mac:* Well, I'd transfer the extra $100 into a savings certificate.

*Friedman:* OK—then the savings and loan association would take your $100 and lend it out to someone wanting to borrow for the purpose of buying a house. It would have contributed to someone else making an economic transaction. The person who sold the house in turn would have extra cash balances now, and would convert them into some form of financial asset just like you did. As a result, more economic activity and spending would take place. Well, the bottom line on all of this is that whenever the amount of money in the economy is more than people and firms want to hold, the excess money will be either loaned out or spent. If the money is loaned out, the borrower will spend it, since people usually don't borrow money unless they want to buy something with it. So, in either event, excess money holdings will result in additional spending.

Now, come back to the auction idea. If money is added to the economy beyond the amount people and firms want to hold, and the result is more spending, it is like giving out more monopoly money at the door. Added dollars in the economy result in additional dollars of spending. If no more goods and services are available to buy than before, the result will be higher prices, just like at the auction.

*Mac:* Well, it sounds reasonable.

*Friedman:* It's more than reasonable. It is the cornerstone of economics. Look at figure A.1

**FIGURE A.1.**
**Money and Prices in**
**the United States.**

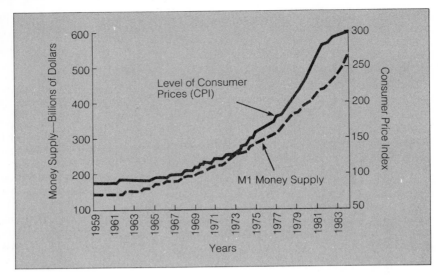

if you need further convincing. This is a plot of the level of consumer prices compared with the total stock of money. Can there be any doubt that the general patterns of change in the two are similar? In fact, notice that the gap between the two series narrows from about 1971 to 1973. This is because money grew faster than prices over this period. But, then prices take off and restore the same relationship that existed earlier.

*Mac:* But, 1971 to 1973 was the period of price controls in the United States.

*Friedman:* Right, and the chart is showing you that since the growth of money continued over this period, all it did was to delay the increase of prices until after the controls were over. What do you suppose would have happened if the growth in money over the period 1968 to 1980 had been about the same as it had been over 1948–1967?

*Mac:* Well, I suppose that prices would have risen by a much smaller amount according to everything you are saying and from what I see in figure A.1.

*Friedman:* Congratulations, Mac. You have just discovered one of the eternal truths.

*Samuelson:* Mac, you've just been sold a bundle of phony goods. Friedman means well, but he is just plain wrong about the closeness of the connection between money and prices. Let's go back to the part of the

conversation where he was asking you what you would do with 100 extra dollars in your checking account. You said that you would transfer it to a savings certificate. This is where the problem starts. The savings and loan association now has more money to lend out. The effect of this is to push down interest rates both on the mortgages such savings and loan associations originate *and* on the savings certificates you and others buy from them. Here is the effect that Friedman forgot about. With falling rates of earnings on savings certificates, you will probably decide to hold more money in your cash account. It just isn't worth it to put it into savings at lower interest rates. So, spending won't go up by the entire $100 but by a smaller amount. In fact, if interest rates are already low, you may just leave the entire extra $100 in your checking account and spend none of it. Where is Friedman's connection between money and prices in this case?

*Mac:* Well, interest rates would have to be pretty low for me to let extra money sit around as cash.

*Samuelson:* But, would you keep larger cash holdings at a 4 percent interest rate than you would at a 10 percent interest rate? That is the question.

*Mac:* I'm not sure, but I may not play it quite so close if rates were 4 percent. At 10 percent rates, I would have my cash down to a minimum.

*Samuelson:* So, the point is, if expanding the supply of money lowers interest rates, then people and firms will want to hold more money. In other words, the demand for it will rise. Much of Friedman's extra spending will not take place. So, the added money in his example will not be as inflationary as he suggests. And, what's more, the effect of added money will be that more goods and services are added to the economy for purchase. Here's what will happen. When interest rates on mortgages and corporate bonds fall, both the construction industry and the machinery and equipment producers will find their business improved. Lower mortgage rates will stimulate more spending on new houses, so more new houses will be available for people to buy with the added money. Also, the newly produced plant and equipment resulting from the lower bond rates will absorb some of the added money. It is as if giving out Friedman's monopoly money resulted in more items being added to his auction. Whether the overall price level will rise or not is a good question.

*Mac:* Well, Samuelson, what does cause the price level to rise if not additional money?

*Samuelson:* Basically, it has to do with how close the economy is to full capacity, and with the never-ending battle between unions and management. Whenever excess plant space is available, most firms will respond to an increase in demand for their products by supplying more products. However, when their plants are being operated at close to capacity, they will probably raise prices. That is why a recession is generally good medicine for an inflation. When the economy is growing too rapidly and is close to capacity production, inflationary pressures mount. A recession is a significant decline in production that opens up some excess capacity. Producers then respond to increases in product demand by increasing the amount produced rather than increasing prices. But, another factor in recent U.S. recessions is the inherent inflationary pressure created by the emerging strategies of both large labor unions and large corporations.

*Mac:* Samuelson, for God's sake, you are starting to sound like a textbook. Could you please speak English?

*Samuelson:* Thanks, Mac, I needed that. What I'm trying to say is that prices in the economy are tending more and more to go up by the difference between the rate of increase in wages and the rate of increase in productivity of labor. I'm still not doing too well, am I Mac? Let's try it this way. If you get an increase in your hourly wage of 5 percent and at the same time begin producing 5 percent more output per hour, do you know what happens to your company's unit labor cost?

*Mac:* I don't know and I don't care. That's the company's problem.

*Samuelson:* Not really, as I'll show you soon. What happens to your firm's per unit cost of your labor in my example is that it stays constant. So does the profit margin per unit, and so would the price, the way firms are pricing their products these days. You see, if an hour of your labor costs the firm 5 percent more, but also produces 5 percent more of the firm's product, the cost for each product stays constant even though the firm is paying you 5 percent more. We call the ratio of units of output to the number of labor hours used the productivity of labor. Experience shows us that when a firm's unit labor cost stays the same or rises, prices of its output tend to do the same. The association is not perfect, but it's very good.

*Mac:* What are you getting at?

*Samuelson:* A very important concept. The underlying inflation rate in the economy is the difference between the rate of increase in wages and the rate of increase in productivity. In 1980, the general rate of increase in hourly compensation in the private sector was about 9.5 percent while the increase in productivity was only about 0.5 percent. The result is that unit labor costs across the entire private sector of the economy went up by 9.5% − 0.5% = 9.0%. This upward move in unit labor costs motivated producers to pass it through to their customers by increasing prices by an approximately similar percentage.

*Mac:* So, you are telling me that the solution to inflation involves either reducing the increase in hourly wages or increasing the rate of gain in productivity, so that this underlying inflation rate will come down.

*Samuelson:* Yes, that's a realistic appraisal of the problem. And, what a problem. The rate of wage increase does not fall easily, and the rate of productivity gain does not rise easily. What we need to do is increase the 0.5

percent and reduce the 9.5 percent so that the two meet somewhere in the middle. If the rate of change in hourly wages and the rate of change in productivity were exactly the same, unit labor costs would be unchanged, there would be a zero underlying inflation rate, and the level of prices would be about stable.

*Mac:* Aren't you being a little bit unrealistic? Have we *ever* had a time in the United States when the rate of wage gain and the rate of productivity increase were the same?

*Samuelson:* Indeed, and they were our best times. Look at my figure A.2. I have plotted these two statistical series for you. The solid line is the growth in hourly wages and the dotted line is the growth in productivity. Notice the period from about 1959 to about the end of 1966. It is the longest noninflationary period in U.S. history. It's no accident that productivity and wages were generally in line with each other during that period. Since then, productivity has fallen while wages have risen. The result is a growing underlying inflation rate (the difference between the two lines) and growing actual inflation.

*Mac:* Umm, well, I . . .

*Samuelson:* Sorry to interrupt, but as long as we are looking at graphs, I have another one

that shows something basic about the role of productivity. Look at figure A.3. In it, I've plotted the real hourly wage as the dotted line. The real wage you earn is your actual wage adjusted to account for rising prices. It shows how much of an increase in actual purchasing power you have from year to year. Notice that it has been negative in some recent periods.

*Mac:* What exactly does a negative growth in the real wage mean?

*Samuelson:* It means that although your wages went up, the prices of consumer goods went up more, so that your higher wages actually buy less. The solid line in figure A.3 is the change in productivity. Do you notice anything interesting about the two?

*Mac:* Well, they do track well together.

*Samuelson:* Please, Mac, a little more excitement. This is one of the strongest relationships you'll find in economic data. And one of the more potent in its implications. It is showing you that the rate by which the purchasing power of an hour of labor changes over time is closely related to the change in the productivity of that labor, and has little to do with the rate by which hourly dollar-valued wages are changing. To illustrate this, let's consider the last five years

**FIGURE A.2.
Wages and
Productivity.**

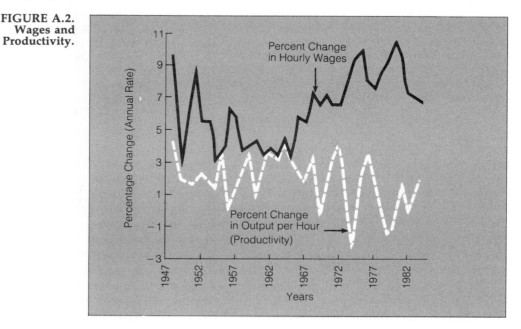

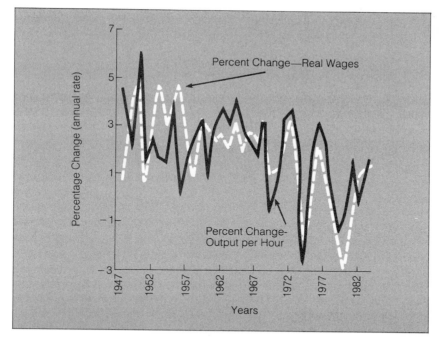

**FIGURE A.3.
Real Wages and
Productivity.**

or so. Dollar wage gains have been in the range of 8 to 10 percent. Yet, the rate of change in the purchasing power of an hour of labor has been below its long-run trend, *as has productivity.* The best sustained period for growth in the purchasing power of labor hours was from 1959 to 1966 when both productivity and wages were growing in the range of 3.5 to 4.0 percent. In both cases, the governing variable was the accompanying trend in productivity.

*Mac:* Why does it work that way?

*Samuelson:* Well, basically, when firms pay out wage increases that exceed productivity, their costs go up and they simply raise prices to compensate for it. Workers are also consumers, and they feel the bite when they spend their artificially enlarged paychecks. If wages rise by 12 percent and productivity by 2 percent, our arithmetic says that prices will be increased by the difference of 10 percent. Then real wages will go up not by 12 percent, but by only 12% − 10% = 2%.

*Mac:* Where is the role of Friedman's money in all this?

*Samuelson:* Basically, it's way out in the cheap seats.

*Friedman:* Mac, he made a wrong turn way back that has been a problem throughout his analysis. He told you that more money would cause interest rates to fall. That led to more construction and more capital goods and so on. But it doesn't work that way. When more money comes into the economy, interest rates don't fall to any noticeable extent. In fact, they may even rise, because of the public's inflationary expectations. So, Samuelson's good things that follow do not really follow. Any added money becomes inflationary just like I said. Your gut reaction was right. Your demand to hold money is basically independent of the rate of interest on savings or other securities.

*Mac:* Friedman, how do you respond to this stuff about the underlying inflation rate?

*Friedman:* Well, he has described the tail of the dog as being the dog itself. It is the existence of excess money in the economy that motivates firms and workers to agree on wage bargains that are greatly in excess of productivity. Notice that wages and productivity began getting seriously out of line at about the time the growth of money picked up. If money was not expanding excessively, wages would not be going up beyond the limits of productivity, and the underlying inflation rate would be nonexistent.

*Samuelson:* Mac, Friedman is the one who has it turned around. The growth in money in the United States since 1967 has been forced by the needs of an economy in which inflation has been taking hold. If the money supply hadn't been expanded, interest rates would be intolerably high.

*Friedman:* Have you looked at them lately?

*Mac:* Waiter, waiter, could you get over here? I need a diversion.

### Act 2—Inflation and Unemployment

SCENE: A Milwaukee area tennis club. Mac, Samuelson, and Friedman are sitting at courtside waiting for Elliott to arrive for a game of doubles.

*Mac:* Have either of you two played tennis with Elliott?

*Friedman:* Yea, a couple of times. He's pretty good, but he has no serve and his backhand is erratic.

*Mac:* I'll remember that. Say, speaking of remembering, do you remember our discussion the other day at the restaurant about the way that recessions take the pressure off of prices? I want to hear some more about that. Samuelson, it was your thing. Do you have anything else to say about it?

*Samuelson:* Well, Mac, it's a very important part of the history of U.S. economic policy. President Kennedy was the first president to conduct economic policy based on the idea that the proper public response to an inflationary situation is to reduce total spending, either by reducing government spending or by increasing taxes.

*Mac:* By "total spending" you mean . . . ?

*Samuelson:* I mean the total amount spent on goods and services by consumers, firms, and the government. The government can affect total spending directly, by changing its own outlays. It can also impact on total spending indirectly, by changing taxes. Consumers then react to tax changes by changing their spending. The so-called new economics of the

Kennedy era was all about the government taking an active role in the regulation of total spending. Economists call this aggregate-demand management.

*Mac:* Why do you people invent names like *aggregate-demand management* for an otherwise perfectly understandable idea?

*Samuelson:* For the same reason that your union doesn't allow anyone to come along and drive a truck. If you want to be a truck driver you have to learn the ropes and join the union. In economics, our union card is a language barrier. Besides, it's a kind of verbal shorthand.

*Mac* (half to himself): Oh brother, I'm sorry I asked.

*Samuelson:* Well, anyway, the idea of a demand-management policy is that weakening patterns in the private sector of the economy can be offset by increases in government demand, by spending more and taxing less. Booms in the private sector can be stabilized by the reverse. The government is usually partially offsetting what is happening in the private sector by its demand-management policy.

*Mac:* Well, it sounds reasonable that the government could produce enough weakness in total spending in the economy to either cause or contribute to a recession. The question in my mind is, will that stop an inflation? It sounds almost too simple.

*Friedman:* The fact is, it used to work somewhat that way in the United States but it doesn't anymore. Look at this chart. [Friedman whips figure A.4 out of his tennis bag.] This is a plot of the inflation rate in consumer prices, and it also shows the periods officially defined as recessions. Look at the recessions of 1954 and 1958. In the first one, prices actually fell over the course of the recession, making a negative inflation rate. In the 1958 experience, the inflation rate was reduced from about 3 percent at the start of the recession to only about .5 percent at the end of it. But, since then, the effect of recessions on inflation has not been nearly so good. In the 1970 recession, for example, the inflation rate going in was about 6 percent and coming out about 4.5 percent. In the big recession of 1973–1975, the inflation rate going in was 8.25 percent, and coming out it was

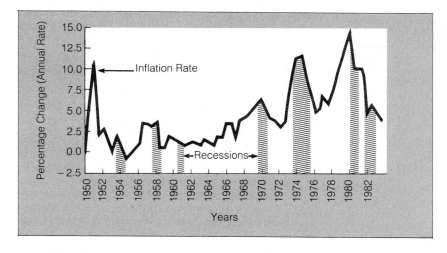

**FIGURE A.4.
Inflation and
Recession in the
United States.**

8.5 percent. And, it rose dramatically *during* the recession. The short recession of 1980 appears to be a duplicate of this experience.

*Samuelson:* The reason for this recent experience goes back to something we were talking about at the restaurant, Mac. Do you remember the discussion about the role of productivity and wage increases, and the underlying inflation rate?

*Mac:* Yep. The higher the growth rate in productivity, the smaller the upward pressure on unit labor costs and the lower the inflation rate, all else held constant.

*Friedman and Samuelson* (in unison): My God, we're creating a monster here!

*Samuelson:* Well, during recessions, productivity falls rapidly in the initial stage because business does not tend to lay off workers and managers in proportion to the decline in production that is occurring. When the amount produced is falling by 10 percent, but the number of people employed is falling by only 3 to 4 percent, the result is that output per hour (productivity) falls. What is happening is that the work force is used with some slack during this period.

*Mac:* So, when productivity falls, unit costs rise, and firms raise their prices even more, even though it's a recession.

*Samuelson:* Exactly.

*Friedman:* Now, Samuelson, with these realities in mind, explain again why it is that recessions are good medicine for inflations.

*Mac:* Yes, it sounds as if recessions just make inflations worse.

*Samuelson:* Where is Elliott? I want to get this game started.

*Mac:* No, really. I want an answer to this.

*Samuelson:* Well, my view is that recent recessions have not been severe enough to alter this emerging pattern. Business managers are willing to minimize their layoffs and work-force reductions in response to output declines because they don't feel the government will allow the recession to become severe enough to really make this strategy a problem. And union leaders don't seem swayed by the idea that their productivity is falling during slack recessionary periods. They ask for even larger wage increases. Firms give in and pass along the costs to us customers. The only real drawback to this strategy is the loss of market to foreign competition. But, many U.S. industries haven't really had to worry about that in recent years because of the already chronic balance-of-payments problem associated with the OPEC era.

*Mac:* This is a very nasty situation.

*Friedman:* One thing should be cleared up. Samuelson's main argument just put forward rested on the idea that recent recessions have not been severe enough to discipline firms and unions into behaving differently. But, the 1973–1975 recession was the worst since the Great Depression. Unemployment reached almost 10 percent, and the decline in output was severe. How much more of a recession is required? Are we supposed to believe the government would sit by and watch a more serious recession without intervening?

*Samuelson:* I think duration is the key. It has to last longer and create a real scare in the private sector.

*Mac:* How about just putting a bloody horse head in the beds of the presidents of the five hundred largest corporations if you want to produce a scare? That worked in *The Godfather.*

*Friedman:* As long as we're on this subject, Samuelson, tell Mac about your Phillips curves, and the trade-offs implied by them. And, Mac, you should know up front that Samuelson and I almost totally disagree about this concept.

*Samuelson:* Right. Phillips was an English economist who made a name for himself by his analysis of the relationship between the rate of unemployment and the rate of wage increase in his country. Basically, the idea is that as unemployment rises, unions will not bargain as hard for wage gains, and management will resist more strongly. The result is a negative association between wage change and unemployment. When the idea was examined in the United States, we made the jump from wage gains to the inflation rate, so that the U.S. Phillips curve is a relationship between the inflation rate and the unemployment rate. The same reasoning suggests that because high unemployment takes pressures off of wages, it also takes the pressure off of prices. Thus, the higher the unemployment rate, the lower the inflation rate. The Phillips curve implies a trade-off between inflation and jobs. The more jobs you are willing to give up as a society, the more price stability you have.

*Mac:* But, doesn't the rate of unemployment go up during a recession?

*Samuelson:* Yes, it does. We officially define a recession as a period where *production* declines, but it is always the case that employment declines as well. Recently, the employment declines have occurred a little later than the production declines, as our discussion of the idea of falling productivity during the onset of a recession suggested.

*Mac:* But, the point is, if inflation is made worse by recessions as we were saying earlier,

and recessions are a time when the unemployment rate rises, then where is your Phillips curve trade-off? It sounds instead like a recession gives us the worst of both ends of the trade-off—more inflation and *also* more unemployment.

*Samuelson:* Well, I can explain that . . .

*Friedman:* Sure, sure. Why not look at some evidence? Here [figure A.5] is a plot of U.S. Phillips-curve data over the period 1950–1966, which is roughly before the current inflationary probem began. I have somewhat skeptically drawn a dotted line through the points in a way that tries to capture the approximate pattern illustrated by the points.

*Mac:* Wait a minute. This is a different type of chart than you two showed me before. Rather than looking at an economic variable as it changes over time, I'm now looking at a plot of one variable compared with another.

*Samuelson:* Right. Each point is the inflation rate over a six-month period and the corresponding unemployment rate over the same period. It shows how well they relate. I don't think this relationship is all that bad. You can see that the general tendency is for higher unemployment rates to associate with lower inflation rates and vice versa.

*Friedman:* Mac, let me put it this way. If the dotted line in figure A.5 were the target and the actual points were the bullet holes from your deer rifle, do you think you'd get your kill in the Wisconsin north woods?

*Mac:* Well, . . .

*Samuelson:* I think Friedman is a little grouchy today. Elliott is late. I wonder if we shouldn't warm up a little.

*Friedman:* Not so fast, Mr. Phillips curver. Why not take a look at the Phillips curve over the period of the current inflation, roughly from 1967–1981? [He pulls out figure A.6.] I haven't drawn any kind of a line through it because I can't figure out if it would be downward sloping or upward sloping or what. The best way to characterize these points is that they represent no systematic relationship at all.

*Mac:* What about this, Samuelson?

*Samuelson:* What has been happening here is that the Phillips curve has been shifting out in

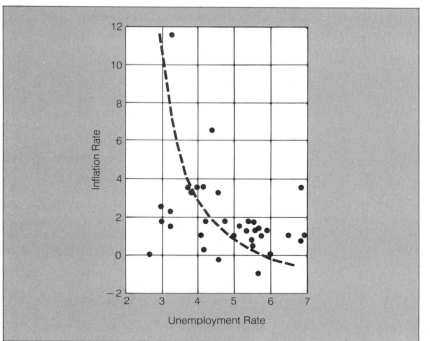

**FIGURE A.5.
The U.S. Phillips
Curve, 1950–1966.**

recent years. If you look carefully at the
figure, you'll see maybe three separate sets of
Phillips-curve points, each one sloping down
but shifted up and to the right of the other.
The changes in the economy of the type we
were discussing earlier have caused these
shifts, and it should be an important objective
of public policy to shift the Phillips curve back
toward the left.

*Friedman:* Samuelson, you are showing your
soft theoretical underbelly when you have to
resort to phrases like "sloping down but
shifted up" to try to describe what obviously
isn't there. The fact is, Mac, that there
probably never has been much of a Phillips
curve, even in the earlier period, and for good
reasons. Inflation is caused by more money in
the economy than individuals and firms want
to hold. Unemployment is determined by
different economic influences. The two are
largely independent, as the latest figure
vividly illustrates. Therefore, when we talk
about shifting the curve or moving along the
curve or trading jobs for price stability, we are
misleading ourselves. The world just doesn't
work that way.

*Mac:* Friedman, you explained earlier how you
can see prices being determined by the

quantity of money. But what you just said
about unemployment raises some new
questions. You said that unemployment is
determined "by different economic
influences." What are these?

*Friedman:* The key thing about it for our
discussion is that the supply of money does
not enter into it. Firms look at a variety of
factors when they decide on their production
level, but the supply of money is not one
such thing. So, since prices respond to the
supply of money on a nearly one-to-one basis,
there is no way in which inflation and
unemployment are importantly related.

*Mac:* I gather that you two don't exactly see
eye to eye on this. I believe I need another
opinion. Didn't you tell me Elliott was an
economist, Friedman?

*Friedman:* Yes, I did. Oh, here he comes now.
Walt Elliott, I'd like you to meet Mac
Peterson. I believe you know Samuelson.

*Elliott:* Hi Samuelson. Nice to meet you, Mac.

*Mac:* Walt, we were just discussing the
Phillips curve. Do you think there is a Phillips
curve trade-off between inflation and
unemployment, or do you think the two are
largely independent?

**FIGURE A.6.**
**Unemployment and**
**Inflation, 1967–1980.**

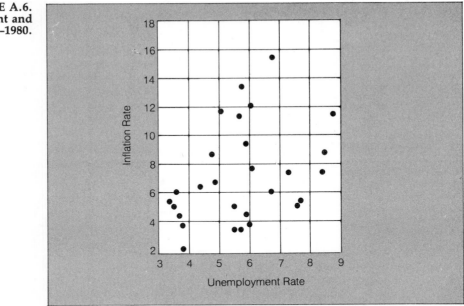

*Elliott:* I think you are talking about a changing world. In the 1950s and through to about 1966 or so, I think you can see signs of a Phillips curve, and perhaps strong enough signs for it to be a guide to public policy. But, this inflation has changed all that. In the present-day United States there is no evidence for a Phillips curve. Inflation and the rate of unemployment are largely independent these days if not positively related. But, the economic relationships in the world change from time to time. We may yet return to a world of Phillips curves. But we are not there now.

*Mac:* Thanks. (To himself: Jeeze, this one's as bad as the other two.)

*Elliott:* Speaking of change, wait until you see my new serve, Friedman. It is a real cannon.

### Act 3—Inflation and Government Deficits

SCENE: Restaurant on the University of Wisconsin, Milwaukee, campus. Mac, Friedman, and Samuelson have just ordered lunch.

*Mac:* Are you two up for a little more economics? I hear talk of the deficit coming down. I am trying to search into what you two have been saying about inflation to discover if lowering the deficit should help inflation. Put another way, I am trying to sort out whether a deficit adds to the inflation.

*Samuelson:* I'll be happy to give you my views, and I'm sure we won't be able to prevent Friedman from giving his. Whether a deficit is inflationary is not clear until we know what shape the economy is in when the deficit occurs. First of all, the "deficit" you read about in the newspapers refers to the situation where the total outlays of the federal government exceed the total federal tax revenues. In other words, a deficit exists when the federal government is spending more than it is taking in through taxes.

*Mac (to himself):* I like his "in other words" better than the first way he explained it.

*Samuelson (continuing):* Now, if the federal budget starts out in balance with a zero deficit or surplus, and the government moves to a deficit, it does so either by increasing its spending or by reducing taxes. Either one of these ways, or some combination of them, stimulates aggregate demand. If we have slack in the economy, production will go up as a result, and jobs will increase. So, if there is slack in the economy, the emergence of a deficit can be a positive thing in that it contributes to increasing employment. On the other hand, if the economy is operating with little or no slack, the added demand for goods and services associated with the deficit will not increase production or jobs, but will cause prices to go higher. It will in this case be inflationary. So, it depends on the amount of slack in the economy as to the impact of moving to a deficit. Now, if we have a deficit and we move to a balance, the situation is reversed. Moving to a balance is accomplished by the government reducing the total level of demand. This should create more slack in the economy, reduce the level of production and employment, and dampen inflation.

*Friedman* (with eyes bulging): Samuelson, I thought we . . .

*Mac* (interrupting): Please, you two. I don't want to talk about that Phillips-curve stuff.

*Friedman:* OK, OK. Here's the other side of the story. What Samuelson is forgetting about is the way a deficit is paid. When the government spends more than it takes in, it makes up the difference by borrowing from the private sector. It accomplishes this by issuing bonds. When the government sells a bond, it entices a private citizen to loan his or her money. The government then uses this money to pay its bills. This is a vital point in understanding the total impact of government spending. When the government increases its spending and finances it by a deficit, look closely at what is happening. Government spending goes up. But private spending goes down *by the same amount.* Why? Because the money that the government borrowed would otherwise have been borrowed by someone in the private sector. And, the borrower in the private sector would have spent the amount borrowed, just like the government spent the amount it borrowed. There is only so much money available by lenders in each month or quarter. The available pool of loanable funds is split up by private borrowers and by the government, depending on who is willing to pay the most for it. And, we can rest assured that all the money in the pool of loanable funds will get loaned out. So, all of it will get spent by the borrowers.

*Mac:* What if there is more money to loan out than there are potential borrowers?

*Friedman:* In that event, the interest rate falls. This discourages lenders and perks the interest of borrowers, and the two balance out. The opposite happens if demand for

funds outpaces supply. The interest rate goes up. But, the essential point is that the government doesn't increase total aggregate demand by a deficit-financed increase in spending. It just increases its spending and reduces the spending of potential borrowers in the private sector.

*Mac:* But, you seem to be saying that deficit-financed government spending doesn't add anything to total spending, but only displaces private spending. This seems to imply that deficit-financed government spending will not help employment. Is that right?

*Friedman:* Yes.

*Mac:* Well, just hold on now. Suppose government undertakes a one-billion-dollar jobs program that creates 100,000 jobs. How can you say that will not add to jobs?

*Friedman:* It would not add a single net new job. Raising the one billion dollars to pay the salaries of the 100,000 new government workers would drain away from the credit market that same amount of money. Firms that wanted to borrow money for the purpose of new capital additions or new construction would find the market tight and the interest rate rising, and so would not get the funds. (If the government gets a bigger share of the pool of loanable funds, then the private sector must get a smaller share.) So, spending on new facilities and business equipment would weaken, resulting in work-force reductions in those industries producing equipment and facilities. The 100,000 jobs would quietly be lost in the private sector as they were loudly being added to the public sector. We call this the "crowding out" effect of government spending.

*Mac:* Then, it sounds like what you are saying is that government deficit financing is not really inflationary because it does not create extra demand for goods and services, but instead crowds demand out of the private sector. Isn't that a bit ironic?

*Friedman:* Maybe. But, that's the way it works.

*Mac:* Samuelson, do you agree with any of this?

*Samuelson:* Only partially. I believe that when government spending goes up, the financial pressures lead to an increase in interest rates, and this in turn leads to a reduction in the

FIGURE A.7.
Money and Deficits in
the United States.

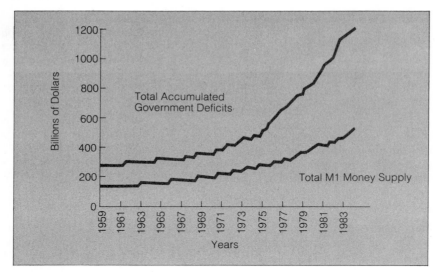

amount spent on new facilities and machinery. You could call this partial crowding out. But, I don't think it is a quantitatively important factor . . .

*Mac (interrupting):* But, Friedman, what if the government met the deficit by printing new money? We hear a lot of talk about running the printing presses and about printing-press money. That sounds to me as if it defuses the crowding-out argument.

*Friedman:* You have just hit on a common misconception about the process of money creation. The truth of the matter is that the U.S. government doesn't pay any of its bills with money it has printed up. For it to do this would require the government to pay its bills with cash. The government pays all its bills by checks. Besides, the Federal Reserve prints currency whereas the Treasury Department pays the nation's bills. They are separate agencies.

*Mac:* But, don't these government checks add to the money supply?

*Friedman:* No. Here's what happens. When the U.S. Treasury issues a bond to deficit-finance an expenditure, it receives a check written by someone in the private sector. When it then initiates its own check to pay a bill, it effectively cancels out one check with the other. It is as if the Treasury has just signed over the check to its creditors.

*Mac:* Well, then, when does the government print up more money? When does it turn to the printing press?

*Friedman:* Actually, Congress sets limits as to how much currency can be issued. The government prints up all the money the banks request, as long as the amount stays below the limit set by Congress. In turn, banks request more currency when their vault cash gets low.

*Mac:* Why would their vault cash get low?

*Friedman:* It's a function of how much cash the public wants to hold. When the public want to hold more cash, they just transfer money from their checking account into cash. When vault cash falls, banks order more through the Federal Reserve much like you and I cash checks when currency runs out. When a bank gets more cash, its reserves are reduced. So, it doesn't get the currency "free" but has to transfer another of its assets into currency.

*Mac:* It doesn't sound as if the influence of the government's printing press is very great in the real world.

*Friedman:* That's right. However, the term has some historical significance. In almost all the classic hyperinflations in history, such as those in Germany, and Poland in the early part of the twentieth century, the government did eventually get into the business of printing up money capriciously and using it to keep the government financially afloat. But, to apply that term to the United States misses the boat.

*Mac:* So, there isn't much of an association between the government deficit and the growth in the money supply.

*Friedman:* No. In fact, look at figure A.7. The solid line shows the total accumulated federal deficit over the years. Each year's deficit adds to the total. Of course, when the government runs a surplus, it would subtract from the total. The dotted line shows the total accumulated supply of money in the economy. The sharp period of growth in the

accumulated deficit since 1974 was in no way accompanied by a similar growth in the stock of money.

*Mac:* Boy, the things you learn at lunch.


THE END

CURTAIN CALL

*Elliott:* (comes back on stage to address the audience): In a moment, Friedman Jones and Samuelson Smith will be coming back on stage to take their bows. Remember that rose I gave you? Well, it's time to decide to whom you will give it. Shh, here they come now.

# PART V

# FINANCIAL FLOWS AND SECURITY MARKETS

## CHAPTER 23

# Flow-of-Funds Analysis

IMPORTANT TERMS

real assets
financial assets
net worth
flow-of-funds matrix
sources of funds
uses of funds

> # /MEMO
>
> To:       All readers
> From:     JWE
>
> Credit and security markets are not entirely different from markets for live cattle. In the latter case, when more animals are brought to market for sale, the price goes down unless demand also rises. If we were interested in understanding the price of beef, it would be valuable to learn as much as possible about what determines the number of animals brought to the market.
>
> In credit markets, the number of dollars brought to the market is an important determinant of how much interest a dollar will bring. In chapter 18, the general importance of the supply of loanable funds to credit markets was developed in the context of a theory that explains interest rates.
>
> This chapter takes a close-up look at the determinants of the supply of loanable funds to credit markets. In recent years, the Federal Reserve Board has developed data on flow of funds that enable the sources of loanable funds to be pinpointed. This chapter's analysis is oriented along the lines of these data, and provides a basis for better understanding the system of data called the flow-of-funds accounts.

In chapter 18, credit markets were analyzed to help us understand how interest rates are determined. In that chapter, interest rates in U.S. credit markets were shown to stabilize when the flow of loanable funds into the market is equal to the demand for these funds by borrowers. If the flow of funds increases while the demand for funds remains constant, the interest rate falls. A decrease in the flow of loanable funds leads to rising interest rates.

This credit-market perspective makes clear the importance of flows of loanable funds in understanding why interest rates change. In this chapter, we examine funds flow in some detail, using a simplified flow-of-funds model of the U.S. economy. The objective is to see how the financial flows of households, firms, and banks evolve and interrelate to produce the cash that investors seek in financial markets.

## BALANCE SHEETS IN THE PRIVATE SECTOR

In the discussion of credit markets in chapter 18, the supply of funds flowing into the market was largely attributed to households, which funnel their savings through financial intermediaries to the credit market. As a broad picture, this is quite correct. However, it is not complete. One complication is that households are not the only economic agents that save. Business firms also generate a type of savings. In addition, financial institutions can decide to supply to credit markets either somewhat more or less funds than they receive in new deposits.

To take these and other complications into account, we will first construct the balance sheets of the main sectors involved in the flow-of-funds process. They are households, nonfinancial firms, and financial institutions, the latter of which we shall simply refer to as banks. From the combination of these balance sheets, we can build a model of the funds-flow process that takes all the important factors into account.

Figure 23.1 shows simplified balance sheets for the three sectors. Actual balance sheets are more complex than these, with assets and liabilities subdivided into many more categories. Many of such details get in the way of (rather than contribute to) a clear understanding of the main points of the flow-of-funds analysis. Thus, the balance sheets in figure 23.1 have been streamlined.

For all three sectors, assets are of two types, real and financial. *Real assets* are physical in nature and last longer than a single accounting period. Their durability means they remain on the books of their owners for more than a single accounting period. Most real assets depreciate in value as they wear out (land is an exception). In addition, many real assets increase or decrease in market value as a result of changing prices. *Financial assets* are either money or claims on money. Financial assets include checking accounts, savings accounts, bonds, stocks, and so forth. These assets do not physically depreciate, but many do change in value over time when interest rates change. In the simplified analysis of figure 23.1, we assume all real assets are net of depreciation, and that the values shown on the balance sheets (book values) correctly represent the actual values of financial assets and liabilities.

There are several important interrelationships among the three sectors. In the household sector, financial assets include accounts held in all types of financial institutions, which for present purposes are simply called "bank deposits," as well as stocks and bonds of nonfinancial business. These household assets are liabilities to other sectors. Bank deposits are claims held by households against banks. Thus, in the banking sector, these deposits, labeled "personal deposits" are shown as liabilities. Accordingly, they must have the same asset value to households (200) as they have liability value to banks. The correspondence in this case (and all other categories where a similar relationship exists) is denoted by a number in parentheses after the asset and liability. For bank deposits, the number (1) denotes the correspondence. Bonds and stocks are further examples of the same type of asset/liability relationship. These financial instruments

FIGURE 23.1.
Balance Sheets of
Household, Banking,
and Business.

**HOUSEHOLDS**

| ASSETS | | LIABILITIES AND NET WORTH | |
|---|---|---|---|
| *Real* | | Bank loans outstanding (4) | 500 |
| Land, houses, durables | 700 | Accounts payable to | |
| | | business firms (5) | 100 |
| *Financial* | | Net worth | 1,000 |
| Bank deposits (1) | 200 | | |
| Corporate bonds (2) | 300 | Total | 1,600 |
| Corporate stocks (3) | 400 | | |
| Total | 1,600 | | |

**NONFINANCIAL BUSINESS**

| ASSETS | | LIABILITIES AND NET WORTH | |
|---|---|---|---|
| *Real* | | Bank loans outstanding (7) | 1,500 |
| Land, plant, equipment, | | Corporate bonds (2) | 300 |
| and inventories | 2,000 | Corporate stocks (3) | 400 |
| | | Net worth | 1,400 |
| *Financial* | | | |
| Accounts receivable from | | Total | 3,600 |
| households (5) | 100 | | |
| Bank deposits and notes (6) | 1,500 | | |
| Total | 3,600 | | |

**BANKS**

| ASSETS | | LIABILITIES AND NET WORTH | |
|---|---|---|---|
| *Real* | | Personal deposits (1) | 200 |
| Land, offices, equipment | 400 | Business deposits and | |
| | | notes (6) | 1,500 |
| *Financial* | | Net worth | 700 |
| Business loans | | | |
| outstanding (7) | 1,500 | Total | 2,400 |
| Personal loans | | | |
| outstanding (4) | 500 | | |
| Total | 2,400 | | |

are assets to households and liabilities/net worth to the nonfinancial firms that issued them.

In a similar fashion, the household liability called "accounts payable to business firms" and labeled (5) appears on the books of nonfinancial business as an asset, "accounts receivable from households." As before, the 100 that households owe to business is the same amount that business shows as receivable from households. The other group of household liabilities, "bank loans outstanding," shows up in the banking sector as an asset labeled "personal loans outstanding."

The category *"net worth"* in the household sector shows the total accumulated excess of assets over liabilities. Each year, households add to net worth to the extent that they earn income that they do not spend on current consumption. This unspent current income (or saving) is allocated over some combination of real and financial assets. As this occurs, the value of assets and net worth rises by the same amount. Similarly, in the nonfinancial business and banking sectors, net worth is the result of accumulated past profits that are retained by the firms involved.

In the nonfinancial business sector, assets include "bank deposits and notes" which translate into the banking sector's liability, "business deposits and notes." The business liability "bank loans outstanding" similarly becomes the banking asset "business loans outstanding."

These balance sheets are a starting point in our funds-flow analysis. They show the holdings of assets and liabilities of the three sectors *at a point in time*. A balance sheet can be compared to a snapshot. Both show a picture of "what is" but neither shows movement to the current position. Yet, in flow-of-funds analysis, it is the movement from one balance-sheet position to another that is important, for this movement produces a flow of funds.

## FROM BALANCE SHEETS TO FLOW OF FUNDS

To see how changes in balance sheets lead to flows of funds, suppose that the balance sheets in figure 23.1 are for the end of the last full year, and that we also have available the year-end balance sheets for one year earlier. From these two reference points, we can draw up a statement of the net change in the balance sheets from year to year. Figure 23.2 shows this net change for a hypothetical year-to-year comparison.

The titles of the categories and numerical codes in figure 23.2 are the same as in figure 23.1 However, the entries throughout figure 23.2 show the change in the asset or liability from the previous period. For example, the +100 for household real assets shows that the holdings of these assets rose by 100 over the year.

For the household sector, the yearly changes show that household total assets expanded by 200, financed partly (10 + 30 = 40) by expansion of debt, and partly (160) through growth in net worth. In other words, the purchase of 200 of additional assets by households was paid for partly by borrowing and partly by allocating current income to asset purchases rather than to consumption—that is, by saving. Earlier, net worth was defined as the accumulation of past saving. Accordingly, the change in net worth can be equated with the flow of current saving.

FIGURE 23.2.
Changes in Sector Bal-
ance Sheets Year-to-
Year.

**HOUSEHOLDS**

| ASSETS | | LIABILITIES AND NET WORTH | |
|---|---|---|---|
| *Real* | | Bank loans outstanding (4) | + 10 |
| Land, houses, durables | +100 | Accounts payable to | |
| | | business firms (5) | + 30 |
| *Financial* | | Net worth (saving | +160 |
| Bank deposits (1) | + 80 | Total change | +200 |
| Corporate bonds (2) | + 10 | | |
| Corporate stocks (3) | + 10 | | |
| Total change | +200 | | |

**NONFINANCIAL BUSINESS**

| ASSETS | | LIABILITIES AND NET WORTH | |
|---|---|---|---|
| *Real* | | Bank loans outstanding (7) | +110 |
| Land, plant, equipment, | | Corporate bonds (2) | + 10 |
| and inventories | +120 | Corporate stocks (3) | + 10 |
| | | Net worth (profits retained) | + 60 |
| *Financial* | | Total change | +190 |
| Accounts receivable from | | | |
| households (5) | + 30 | | |
| Bank deposits and notes (6) | + 40 | | |
| Total change | +190 | | |

**BANKS**

| ASSETS | | LIABILITIES AND NET WORTH | |
|---|---|---|---|
| *Real* | | Personal deposits (1) | + 80 |
| Land, offices, equipment | + 5 | Business deposits and notes (6) | |
| | | | + 40 |
| *Financial* | | Net worth (profits retained) | + 5 |
| Business loans | | Total change | +125 |
| outstanding (7) | +110 | | |
| Personal loans | | | |
| outstanding (4) | + 10 | | |
| Total Change | +125 | | |

The changes shown for the nonfinancial business and the banking sectors have a similar interpretation. The asset changes show how funds were deployed, whereas the liability and net worth changes show how the change in assets was financed. For example, in the nonfinancial business sector, the major change in assets was an expansion of 120 in real assets. The accompanying liabilities show that the primary way this was financed was through an expansion in bank loans.

From the changes in assets and liabilities for the various sectors, we can construct a statement of the funds supplied to financial markets. Notice that nonfinancial business increased its assets "bank deposits and notes" by 40 over the period. In enlarging these deposits, the nonfinancial-business sector supplied 40 in new funds to the banking sector. Similarly, households supplied an additional 80 to the banking sector by expanding their asset "bank deposits" by this amount over the period.

Figure 23.3 shows how all these changes in assets and liabilities fit together into a picture of the funds available in financial markets. Numbers in parentheses are keyed to the corresponding categories in figures 23.1 and 23.2. In part A, the total funds supplied to the banking sector are compiled. In our simplified example, these consist of funds supplied by households and nonfinancial business firms. In the actual U.S. economy, governments, foreign depositors, and others complicate this picture. For our illustrative data, both households and nonfinancial firms added to their bank deposits, thus supplying funds to the banking sector. If either sector had reduced its deposits, it would have made a negative contribution to this flow of funds into the banking sector.

Part B of figure 23.3 shows the funds advanced to final borrowers by all lenders. The banking sector advanced 120 to financial markets by increasing business loans by 110 and personal loans by 10. In this example, the 120 advanced to borrowers by banks is exactly the same amount by which business and personal bank deposits increased.

This is not necessarily the case in the real world. Generally, the banking sector is limited in expanding the sum of all of its assets by the amount its liabilities and net worth expand. Let us go back to

| | |
|---|---|
| **A.** Funds Supplied to Banks | |
| By households, increasing bank deposits (1) | + 80 |
| By nonfinancial busness, increasing bank deposits and notes (6) | + 40 |
| Total funds supplied to banks | + 120 |
| | |
| **B.** Funds Advanced to Final Borrowers | |
| By banks | |
| Increasing personal loans (4) | + 10 |
| Increasing business loans (7) | + 110 |
| Total funds advanced by banks | + 120 |
| | |
| By households | |
| Increasing business bonds held (2) | + 10 |
| Increasing business stock held (3) | + 10 |
| Total funds advanced by households | + 20 |
| | |
| Total funds advanced by banks and households | + 140 |
| | |
| **C.** Funds Raised by Final Borrowers | |
| By firms (bonds, stocks, and bank loans) | + 130 |
| By households (personal loans) | + 10 |
| Total funds raised by final borrowers | + 140 |

FIGURE 23.3.
**Funds Supplied to Financial Markets.**

figure 23.2 briefly. In our example, the banking sector's assets consist of real assets, business loans, and personal loans. Its liabilities consist of personal deposits, business deposits, and net worth. Thus, the total amount by which loans *plus* real assets can be expanded is limited to the amount of expansion in total deposits *and* net worth. Since real assets and net worth expanded by the same amount, 5, this means that the amount of expansion in the sum of personal and business loans is exactly equal to the sum of new business and personal deposits. But, if net worth had expanded by more than real assets, then the banking sector could have used the excess to expand loans by more than deposits rose.

Now back to figure 23.3. In addition to banks, households directly advanced funds to final borrowers by purchasing newly issued corporate stocks and bonds.[1] By directly buying the securities of business, households bypassed financial intermediaries to become direct suppliers of funds to financial markets. For our illustrative data, the total amount of funds advanced by banks and households is 140.

In part C of figure 23.3, an accounting is made for the funds raised in financial markets by final borrowers. Firms issued new securities and made new bank loans totaling 130 (10 stocks, 10 bonds, and 110 bank loans). In addition, households borrowed 10 in new personal loans. Thus, the 140 in total funds advanced equals the total funds raised by final borrowers. No loanable funds have been "left on the table" and gone unborrowed.

Figure 23.3 shows how the data in figure 23.2 (giving changes in balance-sheet positions) can be assembled into a statement of the flow of funds into financial markets. Thus, when balance sheets change, funds flow into and/or out of financial markets. The data in figure 23.2 can be assembled in a different way to show explicitly how balance-sheet changes in household, business, and financial sectors interrelate. The result is called the flow-of-funds matrix.

## BUILDING A FLOW-OF-FUNDS MATRIX

A *flow-of-funds matrix* shows the sources and uses of funds for each major sector of the economy, and for the economy as a whole. A *source of funds* for any sector of the economy is produced by increasing a liability, increasing net worth, or decreasing an asset. Increasing a

---

1. In our simplified model, households are the only holders of stocks and bonds. In this case, all purchases and sales of existing stocks and bonds among households net to zero, since one household is a buyer while another is a seller. Thus, the only way for the household sector to increase its holdings of stocks and bonds is to buy the newly issued securities of business. In the United States, this is still basically the case, but the existence of nonhousehold holders of stocks and bonds complicates the issue somewhat.

liability is borrowing. Increasing net worth is saving. Decreasing an asset is selling something you own. All three are ways of raising funds. *Uses of funds* are to expand assets or to reduce liabilities. Thus, buying a new durable good and paying off existing debt are uses of funds.

From the statement of changes in balance sheets given in figure 23.2, we can construct the flow-of-funds matrix showing sources and uses of funds for each sector of our simplified model of the economy. Figure 23.4 shows this flow-of-funds matrix. Looking back at figure 23.2 helps us see how it is constructed. For the household sector, both net worth and financial liabilities increased over the period. These are the sources of funds to the household sector. Households used these funds to expand real assets and financial assets. (All changes in financial assets have been grouped together for the purpose of this matrix.) Similarly, the changes in assets and liabilities have been listed as either sources or uses of funds for the other two sectors. Then, the total values for all three sectors have been computed. For example, net worth increased for the household sector by 160, for the business sector by 60, and for the banking sector by 5. The sum of these three, 225, shows the total increase in net worth for all sectors.

The flow-of-funds matrix shows some important attributes of the economy's financial flows. Notice that total financial assets increased by the same amount as total financial liabilities. The arrow connecting the two illustrates this equality. This is necessarily the case. The financial liabilities of some sectors of the economy are the financial assets of other sectors. Thus, the change in total financial assets always equals the change in total financial liabilities. Also, total sources and uses of funds for all sectors are necessarily equal. Thus, if financial assets and liabilities are equal, it must be the case that net worth always changes by the same amount as real assets. This is also illustrated by an arrow which connects the two.

**FIGURE 23.4.
The Flow-Of-Funds
Matrix.**

| | HOUSE-HOLDS | | BUSINESS | | BANKS | | TOTAL | |
|---|---|---|---|---|---|---|---|---|
| | Uses | Sources | Uses | Sources | Uses | Sources | Uses | Sources |
| NET WORTH (SAVINGS) | | 160 | | 60 | | 5 | | 225 |
| REAL ASSETS | 100 | | 120 | | 5 | | 225 | |
| FINANCIAL ASSETS | 100 | | 70 | | 120 | | 290 | |
| FINANCIAL LIABILITIES | | 40 | | 130 | | 120 | | 290 |
| TOTAL SOURCES AND USES | 200 | 200 | 190 | 190 | 125 | 125 | 515 | 515 |

NONFINANCIAL

The equality between growth in net worth and growth in real assets has a logical explanation. Earlier, the change in net worth was described as the amount of current income that is not being used for current consumption or expenses. A sector does not necessarily accumulate real assets in just the amount of its increase in savings (net worth), it may also increase financial assets or reduce financial liabilities. But, since some sector's financial assets are another sector's financial liabilities, the accumulation of financial assets nets to zero, leaving real-asset accumulation as the only possible overall result of an increase in net worth.

The flow-of-funds matrix shows how the total savings currently generated in the economy is being distributed. For the data shown, households generated 160 in savings, but only accumulated 100 in new real assets. The remaining 60 is the net amount by which households increased their financial assets. (Actually, households increased their financial assets by 100, but they also increased financial liabilities by 40. Thus, a net increase of 60 occurred.)

For the nonfinancial-business sector, saving was 60 whereas real-asset expansion was 120. This was accommodated by a net increase of 60 in financial liabilities. In the banking sector, net worth and real assets both expanded by 5, so that this sector had exactly offsetting increases in financial assets and liabilities.

The business sector was able to expand real assets by 60 more than its increase in net worth, by enticing the household sector to increase its net holdings of financial assets by 60. In increasing its holdings of financial assets, the household sector allocated a portion of its current saving that otherwise would have gone toward real-asset purchases. Through the medium of financial instruments, mostly issued by the banking sector, business thus acquired the use of a portion of household savings. The flow-of-funds matrix helps show these relationships clearly.

## FLOW OF FUNDS RELATIONSHIPS IN THE UNITED STATES

The analysis of this chapter has been of a simplified model of funds-flow relationships. The actual flow-of-funds data for the U.S. economy are somewhat more complicated, but not significantly different. The major difference is the addition of a number of sectors not included in this chapter's example. Figure 23.5 shows the main flow-of-funds table for the United States presented by the Federal Reserve in the monthly *Federal Reserve Bulletin*.[2]

Of the categories in figure 23.5, the first three are those included in our simplified model. However, in the Federal Reserve data, our

2. Besides this table, the *Bulletin* also presents data on the funds advanced in credit markets.

| FUNDS RAISED by: | 1976 | 1978 | 1980 | 1982 |
|---|---|---|---|---|
| Households | 89.5 | 169.3 | 117.5 | 89.7 |
| Nonfinancial business | | | | |
|    Corporate | 54.5 | 79.3 | 95.7 | 101.8 |
|    Noncorporate nonfarm | 15.4 | 32.4 | 33.8 | 30.4 |
|    Farm | 10.2 | 14.6 | 14.4 | 8.4 |
| Banks and nonbank finance | 22.5 | 77.5 | 68.5 | 107.9 |
| Governments | | | | |
|    Federal government | 69.0 | 53.7 | 79.2 | 98.1 |
|    State and local governments | 15.2 | 19.1 | 27.3 | 36.3 |
| Foreign | 19.6 | 33.2 | 29.3 | 16.0 |
| Total funds raised | 296.0 | 479.2 | 465.6 | 488.6 |

FIGURE 23.5.
Flow of the Funds in the United States.

Source: *Federal Reserve Bulletin*, December 1982, table A44.
Note: Data for 1982 are for the first half of the year only.

category "nonfinancial business" has been broken down into three subcategories, as shown. The two new categories that appear in figure 23.5 are funds raised by governments (federal, state, and local) and those raised by foreign borrowers. An inspection of the magnitudes of these new categories shows the federal government to be among the largest of all borrowers, typically borrowing as much or more than business in private capital markets.

It is not possible to go from the type of flow-of-funds data shown in figure 23.5 to a complete statement of balance sheets, because of the special accounting methods of the federal government. The federal government does not do its official accounting in terms of assets and liabilities. Instead, every dollar the U.S. government spends is treated as an expense rather than an asset purchase. Thus, there is no official governmental net worth. Nonetheless, the flow-of-funds statisticians do construct some asset, liability, and net worth figures for the federal government, which include changes in outstanding government bonds as an important ingredient.

The additions associated with the actual U.S. flow-of-funds system do not obliterate the basic relationships we have discussed. Financial assets still equal financial liabilities. Thus, the change in net worth equals the total accumulation of real assets. And, the excess of savings over real assets in all sectors sums to zero. Just as in the simplified model, financial markets in the United States are arenas where the business sector typically seeks to acquire a portion of the savings generated in other sectors of the economy so that it can expand business real assets by more than business net worth expands.

Although you may be finding it interesting to know something about the U.S. flow-of-funds system, you also may be applying the "so-what?" test. Who uses these data, and for what purpose? One important user is the Federal Reserve system, which uses the data to help monitor financial market conditions. The flow-of-funds data help the Board of Governors see where major borrowing needs are emerging, and allow the board to better gauge how tight or easy credit conditions are likely to be in specific financial markets.

A second group of users of the data are private forecasters concerned with building a prediction of the path of interest rates over the near-term. The flow-of-funds data allow a prediction to be made of the overall volume of funds available in financial markets compared with the projected demand for them. This framework can be a useful guide to sizing up the financial market and interest-rate outlook.

**Important Ideas in This Chapter**

1. Flow-of-funds analysis is concerned with the supply of loanable funds to the nation's financial markets. Although households are an important component in the supply of loanable funds, they are not the only influence on this flow of funds.

2. The balance sheets of the household, nonfinancial business, and banking sectors are interrelated. Financial assets held by households are liabilities for other sectors.

3. Net worth shows the excess of assets over liabilities in each sector. Net worth rises when current income exceeds current consumption.

4. When balance sheets change over time, fund flows are created. Expanding either liabilities or net worth produces funds that can be used to expand assets or reduce other liabilities.

5. A flow-of-funds matrix shows the sources and uses of funds for each major sector of the economy, and for the economy as a whole.

6. Total financial assets and total financial liabilities must change by the same amount over time, and must always be equal in total. This equality means that for the whole economy, the change in real assets and the change in net worth are also necessarily the same.

7. If one sector of the economy wishes to expand real assets by a larger amount than the change in its net worth, it must acquire a portion of the savings of another sector. Typically, in the United States, households are net suppliers of a portion of their net worth to financial markets, and nonfinancial business firms are net acquirers of funds.

**Discussion Questions**

1. Comment on the following statements: "Buying a real asset is purchasing something that was produced as a part of the nation's output, and which created income for its producer. Buying a financial asset is only buying a piece of paper. It is only right that the real asset contributes to net worth while the financial asset does not."

2. Under what conditions can the banking sector be a net supplier of funds to financial markets, as opposed to a medium through which the savings of others pass to final borrowers?

3. Suppose the household sector had a net decline in its holdings of real assets. Would this category be a source or a use of funds?

**4.** Suppose the business sector reduced its financial liabilities by 10 billion in a particular year. Is this a source or a use of funds?

A fully developed analysis of the U.S. flow-of-funds system is presented in Raymond W. Goldsmith, *Capital Market Analysis and the Financial Accounts of the Nation*, Morristown, New Jersey General Learning Press, 1972. An interesting analysis of the development of the flow-of-funds approach is given by J. Cohen, "Copeland's Money-flows after Twenty-Five Years: A Survey," *Journal of Economic Literature*, March 1972, pp. 1–25. A good source on the mechanics of the U.S. system can be found in *Introduction to Flow of Funds*, Board of Governors of the Federal Reserve System, February 1975.

**Suggested Readings**

## CHAPTER 24

# Financial Markets in the United States

## CHAPTER OUTLINE

## IMPORTANT TERMS

financial markets
New York Stock Exchange (NYSE)
American Stock Exchange (Amex)
regional exchanges
Pacific Exchange
Boston Exchange
Philadelphia Exchange
Midwest Exchange
specialists
individual investors
institutional investors
pension-fund managers
mutual-fund managers
trust-fund managers
insurance-company investors
New York Exchange (bonds)

American Exchange (bonds)
over-the-counter
bid price
asking price
bid-ask spread
capital markets
money markets
primary market
secondary market
futures markets
futures contract
hedging
call option
put option
striking price
efficient market

## MEMO

To:       All readers
From:     JWE

Funds flow from lenders to borrowers through the medium of the financial marketplace. References to these markets in the popular press are frequent, and usually highly general. The stock market, the bond market, and money markets are often-heard terms. But what images do they provoke? Are they shorthand references to a more detailed picture? Or are the phrases themselves the picture? In this chapter you can read enough about the stock, bond, and money markets to get a good idea of what these financial arenas are like in the United States.

New financial markets are growing in size and importance on the American financial scene. Financial futures markets and options markets are the two most important newcomers. In this chapter you can read about these two markets as well.

The subject of how efficiently financial markets work is both provocative and highly important in building a perspective of how financial markets actually function. The final topic considered in this chapter is market efficiency. Theoreticians and market analysts alike are concerned with the degree of completeness with which financial markets absorb new information into the prices of financial assets.

All *financial markets* share a common function. They are an arena where lenders and borrowers make deals for the funds that lenders want to lend and borrowers want to borrow. Financial markets are the economically vital device that makes the unspent current income of one group in the economy available to another group wishing to spend more than current income will allow. As the last chapter showed, ultimate lenders are primarily households, while financial institutions armed with household deposits are actually in the "trenches" of the financial marketplace. Borrowers are usually business firms, the federal government, and home buyers. If it were not for well-functioning financial markets, these borrowers would not be able to obtain the funds needed for industrial growth, housing, and public programs; and households and financial institutions would be frustrated in their attempts to lend out excess funds at interest. Fortunately for all those involved, financial markets in the United States work efficiently most of the time.

## U.S. SECURITY MARKETS

In reality, the stock market in large part consists of a group of organized exchanges where common stocks of private corporations are traded. The largest of this group is the *New York Stock Exchange* (NYSE) located on Wall Street in New York City. The second largest stock exchange is the *American Stock Exchange* (Amex), also in New York City. Are you wondering why there are two stock exchanges in the same city? The answer requires some background explanation. A corporation wanting to "list" its stock on an organized exchange must satisfy the officials of the exchange that it is sufficiently stable financially, and that its stock is worthy of serving as an appropriate investment vehicle for those who trade on the exchange. Broadly speaking, the exchange puts its stamp of approval on the stocks it lists for trading. The listing requirements of the NYSE are more demanding than those for the Amex, particularly in terms of size and financial stability. Accordingly, newer and/or smaller firms that have not established a sufficiently extensive financial track record to obtain a NYSE listing may be able to list on the Amex. Investors trading Amex stock are aware of such differences, and are willing to shoulder the added risk because of the higher return they logically expect. Thus, New York has two stock exchanges to accommodate listing a wide variety of small and large corporations. Firms may not be listed on both exchanges at the same time.

Besides the NYSE and the Amex, there are four other organized stock exchanges in the United States, which are frequently called *regional exchanges*. They are the *Pacific Exchange* (in San Francisco), the *Boston Exchange*, the *Philadelphia Exchange*, and the *Midwest Exchange* (in Chicago). These exchanges are much smaller than the NYSE and the Amex. They list both stocks that are usually too small for Amex listing and are not listed elsewhere, and stocks that are also listed on either the Amex or the NYSE. The dual listing of some stocks, both on one of the two major exchanges and on one of the four regional exchanges, for years meant that a stock could (and sometimes did) sell for differing prices on different exchanges. However, in recent years the reporting and accounting for transactions in such dual-listed stocks have been consolidated on one of the two major exchanges, even though the physical trading of the stocks may take place on the regional exchange.

Stocks are traded on exchanges by *specialists* who are professional market makers. Each stock has a specialist who keeps a working book on it showing all existing offers to buy and sell by prospective traders. These buy and sell orders flow into the market more or less continuously. Specialists try to match buy and sell orders as much as possible by adjusting the market price of the stock continually. However, often specialists will buy and/or sell for their own accounts in order to provide for an orderly market. For example, suppose the lowest sell order (standing offer to sell) for a particular stock is to sell 100 shares at $56 per share, while the highest buy order (standing offer to buy) is to buy 100 shares at $55 per share. Also suppose that the latest transaction in the stock was a trade made at $55⅛. This is considered the price of the stock. If an investor places an order to buy 100 shares "at the market," he or she is authorizing the specialist to fill the order at the lowest price the market will allow. Since the lowest sell order is at $56, it is conceivable that the specialist would match the order to buy at market with the order to sell at $56. If so, the quoted price of the stock would rise to $56 from $55⅛. In practice, most specialists would not allow the price of a stock to jump this much in a single transaction. Instead, to the person placing the market order, the specialist would sell 100 shares from his or her own account at an intermediate price of $55½. Thus, the market price that would be quoted to all prospective traders would move up from $55⅛ to $55½. If another order came to the specialist to buy at the market, the specialist might then fill the market order with the standing sell order at $56, thus moving the market price up to this amount. In this fashion, the market price of stocks is driven up or down according to whether there is a preponderance of buyers or sellers of the stock.

The buyers and sellers of stocks basically fall into two categories: individuals and institutions. *Individual investors* buy and sell stocks for their own account, using their own accumulated savings. They are sometimes called "the public" by Wall Street insiders. *Institutional investors* are professionals who manage someone else's money. Among the more important institutional investors are: (1) *pension-fund managers* who invest funds contributed for retirement by employees in private and public organizations; (2) *mutual-fund managers* who invest funds made available by individuals who buy shares in mutual funds as a way of participating in the stock market without the experience or confidence to do so by directly buying stocks; (3) *trust-fund managers* who invest funds placed in trust accounts by individuals for the purpose of being professionally managed; and (4) *insurance-company investors* who invest insurance reserves amassed by these firms over the years.

Figure 24.1 shows how these investors make their buying and selling intentions known. Both groups deal with brokers, who are the basic information link. Investors obtain quotes, information, and advice from brokers. When a broker receives a buy or sell offer, it is transmitted to the broker's representative on the floor of the stock exchange. To be able to trade shares, brokers must have representatives who are members of the stock exchange, which legally empowers them to conduct transactions on the floor of the exchange. As figure 24.1 suggests, the main flow of information between a broker and the floor representative is customer offers to buy and sell. The floor representative then deals with the specialist for the security involved, placing with the specialist actual orders to buy and sell stock. The specialist usually deals with several brokers' representatives, who are grouped around the specialist's trading post on the exchange floor, each with buy or sell orders. The various floor rep-

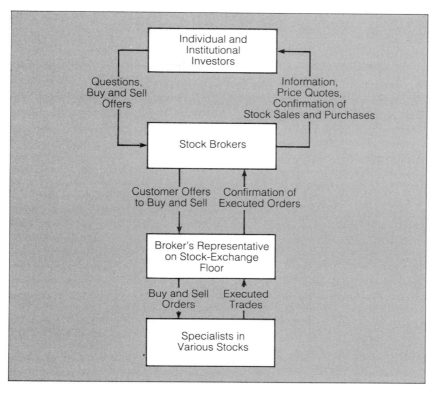

**FIGURE 24.1.**
**Flow of Investment**
**Information.**

resentatives communicate their orders to each other through the specialist, and the specialist officially executes trades among them.

Then information on executed trades is transmitted from the broker's representative to the broker, and relayed from the broker to the individual or institutional investor. In this way, offers to buy and sell by individuals and institutions are continually entering the exchange floor and impacting on the price of stocks.

The bond market is quite similar to the stock market in that it consists largely of a group of organized exchanges where bonds are traded. The counterparts of the NYSE and the Amex are the *New York Exchange* and the *American Exchange.* These exchanges list bonds issued by the same type of corporations that would be listed on the parallel stock exchange. In addition, the four regional exchanges list bonds of smaller firms and provide markets in these bonds. Prices of bonds are set in much the same way as stocks, with marketmakers matching buy and sell orders, and with the price of bonds continually adjusting to clear these orders.

## Trading Over-the-Counter
## versus Trading on Exchanges

Not all stocks and bonds are traded on organized exchanges. The securities of many firms are instead traded *over-the-counter*, which means that they are bought and sold from the inventory of a security broker or dealer at prices quoted by the dealer, much as a consumer good would be purchased over a store counter at retail.

An over-the-counter dealer works with a continually changing bid and asked price for each security traded. The dealer's *bid price* is an offer to purchase shares of a stock at that price. The dealer's *asking price* is an offer to sell shares. The asking price is maintained higher than the bid price, with the difference compensating the dealer for the funds tied up in carrying an inventory of the stock, plus the costs of conducting transactions. For example, for a particular stock, the present asking price might be 16, while the bid price is 15¼. Thus, the dealer is announcing that at this moment, he is willing to pay 15¼ for shares of stock and is willing to sell shares at 16. The ¾ of a point difference is called the *bid-ask spread*.

Unlike the organized stock and bond exchanges, there is no single geographic marketplace where traders can meet face to face to deal in over-the-counter securities. Instead, many hundreds of dealers and brokers participate in making markets in individual securities. Investors access this market over the telephone, usually through their security broker. To tie the diverse pieces of the marketplace together, a group called the National Association of Security Dealers has established a communication network that gives brokers across the country current information on the bid-ask quotes of dealers in all major over-the-counter securities. Using this computer-based information system, investors can thus obtain price information on over-the-counter securities, which is comparable to that produced by the prices quoted on securities listed on the major organized exchanges.

## Money Markets and Capital Markets

Markets where stocks, bonds, and other long-term securities are traded are often called *capital markets*, a term that refers to the notion that borrowers in these markets are seeking long-term business financing of the type that supports the purchase of plant, equipment, and other real capital goods.

Financial markets where short-term notes are traded are called *money markets*, even though it is not money that is bought and sold in them. Securities traded in money markets include Treasury Bills, commercial paper, banker's acceptances, large certificates of deposit, Eurodollar Deposits, and repurchase agreements (see chapter 5 for a description of these financial instruments). The label *money market* refers to the nearness of these short-term financial instruments to money itself. Following the same thinking, professional portfolio managers often refer to their holdings of "money" or "cash" as the total of all short-term financial instruments held. Similarly, money-market funds consist entirely of these instruments.

Unlike stock and bond exchanges, money markets have no visible geographic arena. They are over-the-phone markets, involving more than forty money-center banks located in New York, Chicago, San Francisco, and other financial centers; more than thirty-five dealers in U.S. government securities; and a few specialists who deal in commercial paper and/or banker's acceptances.

Quotes of current prices and rates for money-market instruments are obtained by traders via telephone contact with the dealers and/or banks that buy, sell, and broker the sale of these instruments. This makes money markets more of a private "for professionals only" arena than markets for stocks or bonds. However, the *Wall Street Journal* gives daily quotes on most major money-market instruments.

## Primary and Secondary Markets

A *primary market* in a security is the market for newly issued securities. In a primary market the seller of the security is also the issuer of the security, and is seeking to raise funds for investment purposes. A *secondary market* is the market for existing securities. In these markets, the security is sold by someone other than the issuer. In primary markets, a flow of funds occurs from lender to ultimate borrower. By contrast, no new funds flow to ultimate borrowers as a result of secondary market trading in securities.

In U.S. security markets, primary and secondary market activity goes on side by side. Newly issued shares of a stock are routinely sold at the same time trading of existing shares takes place. In bond markets, new issues of ten-year corporate bonds do not substantially disrupt trading in existing comparable corporate bonds. However, most of the activity in both bond and stock markets is secondary-market activity. The volume of trading on organized exchanges is *all* secondary market in nature, since newly issued stocks are not put through the exchange. Instead, new issues of stocks and bonds are sold directly to investors by brokers and dealers on behalf of the issuing firm.

In contrast to stock and bond markets, in money markets most of the market activity is primary in nature. Secondary markets do exist for Treasury Bills, commercial paper, large CDs, and banker's acceptances. However, the volume of trading in these secondary markets is overshadowed by the impact of sales and purchases of newly issued securities on the market. With maturities of a few weeks to less than a year, money-market securities are often bought to be held to maturity (unlike long-term bonds). A ready supply of newly issued money-market securities is available to replace maturing notes. Thus, the primary market becomes the major market for such financial instruments.

# FUTURES MARKETS

The financial instruments that trade in money and capital markets share a common attribute—they are vehicles for funds to pass from lenders to borrowers. *Futures markets* serve a different fundamental purpose. In futures markets, contracts are originated and traded that give the holder the right to buy something in the future at a price specified by the contract. A *futures contract* entitles the holder to buy a fixed quantity of either a commodity or a financial instrument at a price stated in the contract at a time in the future specified by the contract. The contract obligates its originator to deliver or sell the stated quantity of commodities or financial instruments at the contract price on the future date. Once originated, futures contracts then trade, often actively, until the contract delivery date has been reached.

Futures contracts have a market value that fluctuates with the current price of the underlying commodity. To see why, consider this example. Suppose you were the owner of a futures contract purchased a few months ago committing you to buy ten ounces of gold at a price of $300 per ounce four months from now. Suppose also that the present price of gold is $280 per ounce. If the price of gold does not change, you will have to buy at $20 above the market price to make good on the deal. Now, make the assumption that the price of gold rises over the next four months to $400 per ounce at about the date specified on the contract. At this point, a contract that entitles you to buy what is selling for $400 at a price of $300 is quite valuable, being worth at least $(400 - 300) \times 10$ ounces = $1,000. As the owner of the contract, you can realize your profit either by taking delivery of the ten ounces of gold for the contract price of $3,000, then selling the gold for the market price of $4,000; or by selling the contract prior to the delivery date and realizing the profit on the value of the contract itself.

Generally, as the price of a futures-market commodity rises or falls, so does the market value of the futures contract. In this example, if gold had risen to $500 after one month, then fallen to $200 after the second month, and risen again to $400 at the end of the contract period, it is likely that various traders in these contracts would have had both profits and losses by buying and selling the contracts at similarly fluctuating market prices.

Futures contracts are bought and sold for two reasons. First, they are bought and sold for *hedging*. Suppose you are a manager negotiating a contract for production and delivery of copper wiring, and work is to commence six months into the future. To be assured of the cost of copper to you, you may buy a futures contract that sets a price now for delivery of copper to you after six months, thus hedging your costs. Or, suppose you are a dealer in corporate bonds and have just purchased a large quantity of newly issued bonds from the issuing firm. You expect to resell these bonds in small lots at a profit over the next month. But, if interest rates rise in the next month, the market value of these bonds will go down, and you might suffer a sizable loss. To protect against this, you can sell futures contracts for similar bonds even though you do not own the specific bonds involved. If interest rates do indeed rise, and the price of bonds falls, the futures contract you sold earlier goes down in value. As the delivery date approaches, you can buy futures contracts for the same bonds to cover those you earlier sold, only now at greatly reduced prices. Since you sold the futures contracts for a greater price than you now are paying for offsetting contracts, you make a profit on the transaction. The gain made on this transaction offsets the loss taken by holding the bonds during the period when interest rates increased, and your position in the bonds is hedged.

Besides hedging, futures contracts are bought and sold for purely speculative reasons. The price movements in future contracts can be dizzying, and large profits and losses can occur over short periods of time. Thus, those investors with a large appetite for risk can find a veritable Thanksgiving feast in futures markets.

In the United States, futures markets exist for commodities, including coffee, cotton, orange juice, potatoes, sugar, corn, oats, soybeans, wheat, barley, flaxseed, rapeseed, and rye. In addition, futures markets exist for cattle, hogs, pork bellies, lumber, plywood, copper, gold, heating oil, platinum, and silver. Newer futures markets have recently been operating in major currencies, in U.S. Treasury bonds and Treasury Bills, in GNMA certificates (government-backed mortgage-based bonds), and in bank-issued CDs. More recently, stock-index futures have been originated that fluctuate in value with the Standard and Poor's 500 stock index and with the NYSE composite stock index (see feature section 1 for a description). These contracts are unique in that there is no deliverable commodity at the expiration of the contract period. Thus, any hedging or speculation done with these stock-index futures encompasses the contract price only.


## OPTIONS MARKETS

A stock option is a contract giving the owner the right to either buy or sell a fixed number of shares of a stock (usually 100) at any time before an expiration date at a price specified in the option. A *call option* is a contract that gives the owner the right to buy shares at a preset price for a specified period of time, and a *put option* gives the owner the right to sell shares at a preset price for a specified period.

Options are traded on four organized exchanges: the Chicago Board Option Exchange, the American Option Exchange, the Philadelphia Option Exchange, and the Pacific Option Exchange. Not all stocks listed on the major exchanges have corresponding options. Instead, option trading is confined to the larger and more actively traded stocks. For each stock option traded, several contracts are available. They vary because of the contract price, called the *striking price,* and because of the length of time over which the option can be exercised.

Table 24.1 illustrates one firm's stock options in terms of various striking prices and varying expiration dates. Focus first on call contracts. Notice that twelve different contracts are potentially available

**TABLE 24.1**
**Contracts Available for IBM Options as of August 20, 1982**

| STRIKING PRICE | CALL CONTRACTS | | | PUT CONTRACTS | | |
|---|---|---|---|---|---|---|
| | EXPIRATION DATES | | | EXPIRATION DATES | | |
| | OCT. 82 | JAN. 83 | APR. 83 | OCT. 82 | JAN. 83 | APR. 83 |
| $55 | 12 | 12½ | — | ¼ | $^{15}/_{16}$ | — |
| $60 | 7¼ | 9 | 10¼ | $^{15}/_{16}$ | 1⅞ | 2¾ |
| $65 | 3¾ | 5¾ | 7 | 2⅜ | 3½ | 4 |
| $70 | 1$^{5}/_{16}$ | 2¾ | 4⅛ | 4¾ | 5⅜ | 6⅛ |

with increasing striking prices and longer maturities. The table shows the prices of the various contracts, expressed in the form quoted by the *Wall Street Journal*. Each entry in the table is the price *per share* of the corresponding option contract. However, since option contracts can be traded only in 100-share lots, each price must be multiplied by 100 to arrive at the price of the actual contract sold.

For example, the $55 call contract expiring in October, 1982 is quoted at $1,200. For this price, a buyer of the contract is entitled to purchase 100 shares of IBM at $55 per share any time between August 20, 1982 and the contract's expiration in October of that year. On August 20, IBM stock closed at $66 per share. Thus, if the contract were exercised, the owner would realize a gain of $1,100 by buying the 100 shares under the option at $55 and selling them at $66. But paying the $1,200 option price to earn $1,100 means a net loss of $100. From this, we can assume that investors will not be buying this contract and exercising their call option. Instead, investors are paying $1,200 for this contract rather than $1,100 because they expect IBM stock to rise above $66 per share sometime before October. If this occurs, they can either sell their contract at a profit, or exercise it. For example, if IBM stock rose to $72 per share, the $55 call contract would be worth the "exercise value" of ($72 − $55) × 100 = $1,700 plus a premium based on the investors' expectations of a further rise.

Notice how the call-contract price goes down as the striking price goes up from $55 to $70. The $70 contract expiring in January 1983 is quoted at 2¾ or $275 per contract. Investors in this case feel that the right to purchase IBM at $70 − $66 = $4 per share above the current market price at any time before January is worth $2.75 per share. Apparently, there is an expectation prevalent in the market that IBM will rise above $70 by several points before January.

Notice also that the call-contract prices rise as the contract period is lengthened. Investors apparently realize that stock prices inherently fluctuate, so that the longer the option period, the greater the chance that the stock will reach or exceed the striking price. This perception translates into higher contract prices for more distant contracts.

Notice the price of put options rises with the striking prices for the example shown. This is the reverse of the pattern for call contracts, and quite logically so. In the case of the call option, the market is willing to pay less for the $70 call contract than for the $55 call contract because of the expectation that an increasingly higher price for IBM has a decreasing probability. In the case of the put contract, this same expectation means higher contract prices for higher striking prices. The put contract gives the owner the right to sell at the striking price, so the farther the actual price is below the striking price, the more value that attaches to the contract. If IBM should fall to $50, the $70 contracts would be worth ($70 − $50) × 100 shares = $2,000 plus a premium based on the market's expectation of further declines.

Also, the general tendency for stocks to fluctuate more widely over longer periods of time translates into higher put-contract prices as the contract period is lengthened. Thus, for both puts and calls, "buying more time" in a contract comes only at a higher contract price.

Put and call options can be used for both hedging and speculative reasons. For example, investors can hedge an investment position with options in order to lock in a short-term profit, carrying it into a period where it can be taken as a long-term gain and taxed at a much lower rate. Suppose an investor in IBM bought 500 shares early in 1982 at a price of $54 per share. The stock then rose to its August 20th price of $66. The investor has a profit of ($66 − $54) × 500 = $6,000, but if it is realized immediately, the gain will be taxed as regular income. If the gain can be carried on the investor's books for a longer time, it can be taxed at greatly reduced capital-gain rates. If the investor continues to hold the stock, its price may go down, destroying the gain. To lock in the present profit, the investor can buy five 100-share put contracts on IBM. Suppose the investor needs to lock in the gain until April 1983, and chooses the $65 put contract for this purpose. This requires an outlay of $400 per contract times five contracts, or $2,000.

If IBM stock continues to rise between August and April, say to $75, the investor's put contract becomes worthless, but an additional profit of ($75 − $66) × 500 = $4,500 accrues on the investment. So an additional net gain of $4,500 − $2,000 = $2,500 occurs in this case. However, suppose instead that the price of IBM stock falls, returning to the original purchase price of $54 per share. Now the $6,000 profit on the shares is gone. But, the options have gone up in value. Note that in August, the right to sell at $65 when the market was $66 was worth $4 per share. This is a "premium" over the exercise price of $66 + $4 − $65 = $5 per share. If the stock drops to $54, and the same premium applies, then the contract would be worth $65 − $54 + $5 = $16 per share. That is, the right to sell at $65 when the market price is $54 would be valued at about $16 per share (with the extra $5 premium reflecting the market's assessment of the possibility of a further fall). If our investor now sells the five contracts at $1,600 apiece, a net profit on the put contracts of $1,600 × 5 = $8,000 − $2,000 (purchase price) = $6,000 occurs. The profit has been locked in and the investor's position hedged.

The speculative uses of options are more straightforward. Clearly, buying call options requires a much smaller outlay than buying the corresponding shares, and yet the option holder is entitled to a large portion of the profits accruing from movements in the shares. Doubling or tripling one's investment capital in options markets is easy to visualize given volatile markets. However, the risk in options is an order of magnitude higher than in the corresponding stock. Unlike a stock, an option has a definite life. When the expiration date arrives, the option must be exercised, sold, or put into the trash can. If you hold a $70 expiring call contract to buy IBM and the stock is selling at $68, the trash can is the only workable option. Your contract would have a zero market value, and exercising it would *cost* you $200 per contract. This example illustrates that in options markets, it is possible to lose all of one's investment capital in a rather short period of time.

## EFFICIENCY OF FINANCIAL MARKETS

How quickly do prices of stocks and bonds adjust to changing market conditions? Are there times when stocks are undervalued? Are there good stocks that investors in general are overlooking? These questions are part of a general issue called market efficiency, which has been at the forefront of controversy and discussion concerning financial markets for better than a decade and a half.

An *efficient market* in stocks or bonds is defined as one where the prices of all securities remain continuously adjusted to changing information affecting their value. In an efficient stock market, the price of each stock fully reflects all the information publicly known about the firm, its current sales and profit outlook, and most important, its future outlook. As new information impacting a firm's prospects surfaces, the price of the firm's stock quickly takes it into account, rising or falling to the degree that the information affects the firm's profit outlook.

Nothing escapes the eye of an efficient marketplace. Suppose a drug company announces the invention of a new drug that prevents baldness. Prior to the announcement, the firm's stock is selling at $16 per share, while the firm is earning $1.60 per share in net profits. Its price-earning or PE ratio is $16 ÷ $1.60 = 10. (For more on PE ratios, see feature section 1.) In an efficient market, investors will be quick to translate the news of the new product into the amount of sales and profits it will mean to the firm over the foreseeable future. This will quickly affect the firm's stock price. Suppose that investors typically expect the product innovation to add an average of $0.60 per share to profits over the next decade. If the same PE ratio applies, this translates into an increase in share price of $0.60 × 10 = $6 per share. Thus, as a result of the newly announced information on the firm's product line, the well-informed investor has reason to believe that the increased expected profitability of the firm should lend to its stock price rising from \$16 to \$22 per share. In an efficient market, this rise in price occurs in a very short period of time, say in one to three days.

Efficient markets act on expectations. When the best available information leads the well-informed investor to expect prices to change in the future, speculation causes the prices to change in the present. To see why, return to the example of the drug firm. If investors come to expect that the stock is worth \$22 and is selling for \$16, there will be a rush to buy, and a reluctance to sell on the part of those who own the stock. Prices will rise quickly until they begin to approximate the level of the market's expectations. When the price reaches about \$22, investors in an efficient market see the stock as correctly reflecting the new information on the firm, and the price stabilizes—until some new development occurs.

The type of information that can impact on a stock's expected and actual price is quite varied. Whenever a firm reports earnings or sales, investors revise their expectations of future prospects. When an influential investment analyst or brokerage house publishes an opinion on a stock, its price usually responds. World events that impact on the prospect of war and/or peace affect the prices of all stocks. News on the inflation rate, the pattern of interest rates, and Federal Reserve policy usually have an impact on the expected and actual prices of many if not all stocks.

Thus, efficient markets do not indicate that prices of securities are necssarily stable, changing only infrequently. Rather, market efficiency implies that investors are able to translate the hundreds of pieces of information that surface each business week into the best estimate of how each should affect the prices of stocks and bonds. The markets engage in a continual process of bidding the actual prices of securities to these expected levels.

An important implication of efficient markets is that investors as a rule do not overlook any securities in this process. There are no securities whose prospects justify a higher (or lower) price than the market is currently setting. In other words, in an efficient market, there are no undervalued (or overvalued) stocks. To an adherent of efficient-market theory, there is always a reason a firm's stock is either expensive-looking or cheap-looking. Consequently, an investor cannot expect to earn more than the normal return on stocks of similar risk when making a new investment in a particular stock. If prices of stocks have adjusted fully to the available information, then no investor can reasonably expect to buy a stock and see it double or triple in price over a short period of time. If reason existed for the stock to double or triple in price, the market would already have bid the stock's price up to a much higher level.

This is not saying that stocks never double and triple in price over short periods. History shows that this does on occasion happen. But, to an efficient-market adherent, such price movements occur because

To: Those interested in market efficiency
From: JWE

Here is a reportedly true story about a bank that conducted a study of market efficiency in the mid-1970s. This bank's trust-funds operation regularly invests millions of dollars in the stock market for clients. To see how efficient the market really was, the bank conducted an experiment. It reasoned that in an efficient market, stocks chosen at random should produce the same average return as those selected by the bank's professional analysts as long as the riskiness of the two sets of stocks was equalized. (The riskier the stock, the greater the positive return in a "good" market, and the greater the negative return in a "negative" market.) Furthermore, the bank's managers reasoned that if stocks could be bought at random, but under "sales" conditions, the return to the randomly selected group might be even better. Thus, the plan was formed to go back over the previous several years, and suppose that the bank's trust operations would have bought whatever stocks were being sold by the "big block" trader of a large Wall Street brokerage and underwriting firm.

A big-block trader arranges for the purchase or sale of unusually large blocks of stocks that would disrupt the market were they handled in the usual way. The trader contacts potential buyers, informs them of the availability of the stock in question, and negotiates a price for trading the block, which may be sold in pieces to several buyers. Generally, selling an unusually large block of stock depresses the price of the stock, at least temporarily. Under efficient-market theory, any such big-block effect should be temporary, lasting only a few days at most. Thus, by buying stocks being sold in big blocks, the buyers get a somewhat favorable price. This should lead to a somewhat higher rate of return than usual.

Thus, in the bank's hypothetical experiment, stocks were bought from a specific big-block trader at random. Adjustments were made in the portfolio to equalize the riskiness of the randomly selected stocks with that of the stocks actually selected by the bank's trust-fund officers over the same period of time. Then, the return on the risk-adjusted random portfolio was compared with the actual performance. Under efficient-market theory, the random-portfolio return should be somewhat higher because of the big-block effect. This is the way the experiment turned out. Can you suppose that the trust-fund officers took smaller-than-normal raises after the results of that study were made known?

of new information that could not have been known or predicted when the stock's price was lower. So, efficient-market adherents agree that it is possible to make either very large gains or very large losses in security investments, but it is unreasonable to suggest that any such gains could have been *expected* by investors using all the information available at the time investment decisions were made.

Evidence has been accumulating for some time on the efficiency of financial markets in the United States. The general message contained in this evidence at the present time is that U.S. financial markets are highly, if not perfectly, efficient. The flood of new financial and economic information entering financial markets is indeed quickly and fully built into investors' expectations of future security returns, and present prices are bid to levels consistent with these expectations. A well-informed investor may make a fortune in security markets, but that investor cannot reasonably expect to earn more than the normal return on securities. Over the long-run, for every investor who makes a windfall gain is another who makes a crushing loss.

**1.** The New York Stock Exchange and the American Exchange are the two most important organized exchanges where common stocks are traded at what are essentially auction market prices.

**2.** Stocks and bonds not traded on organized exchanges are traded over-the-counter, a term that refers to the practice of dealers making markets in these stocks by offering to both buy and sell them at prices they quote. A national system of over-the-counter markets has developed in the United States.

**3.** Markets where short-term financial instruments are traded are called money markets, referring to the nearness of these instruments to money itself. Markets in longer-term securities are called capital markets.

**4.** A primary market is one for a newly issued security. A secondary market is one for an existing security. Stock and bond exchanges are for secondary-market trading, whereas brokers and dealers handle primary-market sales and purchases.

**5.** Futures contracts are agreements to buy and sell a quantity of a commodity or financial instrument at a fixed price at a set time in the future. They are useful in hedging and are an object of speculation as well.

**6.** Call options are contracts entitling the holder to buy a set number of shares (usually 100) of a stock at a fixed price anytime until an expiration date.

**7.** Put options are contracts entitling the holder to sell a set number of shares (usually 100) of a stock at a fixed price anytime until an expiration date.

**8.** Put and call options are useful in both hedging and speculation, and can be a way of locking in profits or taking a high-risk investment position.

**9.** The question of efficiency in financial markets is concerned with how fast financial markets adjust to changing market conditions. In an efficient market, prices of securities are continuously maintained in adjustment with the state of information affecting the future prospects of the security.

**Important Ideas in This Chapter**

**10.** Efficient markets act on expectations. Whenever the majority of investors expect a price to change, it changes quickly. Thus, in an efficient market, actual prices reflect the market's best expectation as to what prices should be in the future.

**11.** Evidence accumulated over the last fifteen or so years in the United States suggests that financial markets are highly, if not perfectly, efficient. It is a better premise to assume efficiency than to ignore it.

**12.** An important implication of efficient markets is that a well-informed investor cannot expect to make a greater-than-normal return. When such returns occur, it is a result of the unforeseen development of new influences on share prices.

**Discussion Questions**

**1.** Find out as much as you can about the way the specialist on the NYSE and Amex works. Can you see any way that the exchanges could function without the specialist?

**2.** List as many different uses of futures contracts as you can think of, consulting someone in the securities industry if necessary to help complete your list.

**3.** Can you think of any reason for buying both a put and a call contract on the same security for the same expiration date at the same striking price?

**4.** Suppose markets are efficient and you are able to group stocks into equally risky categories. Is it true that within each category you should be able to pick stocks to invest in, just by throwing darts at a list of stocks? What is the thinking involved in your answer?

**5.** If security markets are efficient, how can we account for those individuals who have made fortunes in the market? (They usually write books about it.)

**Suggested Readings**

A good overview of the operation of the U.S. money market is provided by Wesley Lindow, *Inside the Money Market*, New York: Random House, 1973. A good and highly readable account of the history and theory of stock-market investment that combines the theoretical with the pragmatic is B. Malkiel's *A Random Walk down Wall Street*, 2nd ed., New York: Norton, 1981. An irreverent but engaging treatise on the practical side of investing is contained in Adam Smith's *The Money Game*, New York: Random House, 1967. Finally, a review of the development of the efficient-market literature and its testing is found in Eugene Fama, "Efficient Capital Markets: A Review of Theory and Empirical Work," *Journal of Finance*, papers and proceedings, May 1970, pp. 383–417.

## CHAPTER 25

# The Structure of U.S. Interest Rates

IMPORTANT TERMS

Yield curve
term structure of interest rates
expectations theory
preferred habitats
segmented market

## MEMO

To:     All readers
From:   JWE

There are times in financial markets when short-term interest rates rise while long-term interest rates fall, and vice versa. There are other times when short-term and long-term interest rates rise and fall together. A close observer of financial markets might also detect patterns of rising or falling rates on U.S. government bonds, while corporate bonds remain unchanged.

Why do these changing patterns occur? It is the main topic of this chapter. You will learn that interest-rate movements do not occur in isolation, but as parts of regular patterns that unfold for understandable reasons. Although the chapter may not be of help in predicting future interest-rate movements, it may lead to a better understanding of why interest rates change the way they do.

Pick up the *Wall Street Journal* sometime and count the number of different interest rates you can find quoted there. After you get to a hundred or so, the message of the exercise will surely come through. The U.S. financial marketplace generates a large number of interest rates, each of which varies every business day. This array of interest rates raises provocative questions. Are there systematic relationships among these rates? Are market interest rates similar to hundreds of fish swimming independently in a pond, or are they instead more similar to schools of fish that stick together? Why are some rates higher than others? These questions are pertinent to this chapter's analysis.

Table 25.1 shows many of the "fish" in the financial "pond." In part A, the major money-market instruments in the United States are arranged in rows according to their maturities, with longer maturities going to the right. The entries in the table are the market interest rates for each type of financial instrument as of a date arbitrarily chosen, August 27, 1982. Going down the table, the money-market instruments are listed in order of increasing interest rates, with the highest rates at the bottom of the table. Part B contains interest rates for government and private bonds, arranged the same way.

Examine the "90 days to maturity" column in part A. Why do you suppose anyone with money to invest for 90 days would choose the 7.75 percent return on Treasury Bills rather than the 9.70 percent return on CDs? What accounts for this nearly 2 percent difference in yields?

The answer is risk. Treasury Bills are backed by the federal government, and have never defaulted on payment of interest or prin-

**TABLE 25.1**
**Selected Interest Rates**

**A. MONEY MARKET**

| INSTRUMENT | MATURITY | | | | | |
|---|---|---|---|---|---|---|
| | 30 Days | 60 DAYS | 90 DAYS | 120 DAYS | 150 DAYS | 180 DAYS |
| U.S. Treasury Bills | — | — | 7.75 | — | — | 8.99 |
| Commercial Paper | 8.00 | 8.38 | 8.50 | 8.85 | 9.00 | 9.40 |
| Banker's Acceptances | 9.10 | 9.30 | 9.45 | 9.85 | 10.35 | 10.30 |
| Certificates of Deposit | 9.40 | 9.50 | 9.70 | — | — | 10.62 |

**B. CAPITAL MARKET**

| INSTRUMENT | MATURITY | | |
|---|---|---|---|
| | 1 YEAR | 5 YEARS | 10 YEARS |
| U.S. Government Bonds | 10.55 | 12.32 | 12.54 |
| High-grade Industrial Bonds | 11.50 | 12.87 | 13.20 |

Source: All rates are taken from quotes published in the *Wall Street Journal*, August 27 1982.

cipal. Commercial paper is backed by the general assets of the firm that issues it. There are a number of times when issuers of commercial paper have defaulted on payment of principal at maturity. Generally, the track record of issuers of commercial paper is excellent. But, it is not perfect. The difference in yields between T-Bills and commercial paper shows that investors feel a measurable difference exists in the risk of default between the two.

The same reasoning applies to the difference in yields between commercial paper and banker's acceptances, and between banker's acceptances and CDs. Banker's acceptances are sometimes originated by firms with financial track records that do not warrant issuing commercial paper—thus the need for backing by a bank. The marketplace displays the belief that banker's acceptances are not as safe as commercial paper by creating almost a full percentage-point difference in interest rates between the two. Large CDs are seen to be even riskier, most likely because of the preponderance of them being issued by banks, which typically are highly leveraged in terms of their relationships of liabilities to net worth. Of course, one can debate the issue of whether CDs are really riskier than banker's acceptances, or whether commercial paper is really more risky than T-Bills. But, in the plainest way possible, investors in the financial marketplace have spoken their mind on the matter by bidding interest rates to the configuration shown in table 25.1 We may draw from these data the general rule that interest rates on financial instruments of equal maturity will differ because of the market's perception of differences in the safety of the financial instruments.

Another clear-cut pattern in the "fishpool" of short-term rates appears when we look across the rows of part A of table 25.1. In each of the four cases shown, the rates rise as the time to maturity is lengthened. Although this is the case for the data of late August 1982, interest rates do not always rise with lengthened maturities. On other occasions, longer maturities may associate with lower interest rates. We examine the reasons for this relationship later in the chapter. For now, it sufficies to observe that time to maturity definitely affects interest rates.

Part B of table 25.1 shows that the same two basic effects on interest rates apply for longer-term rates. Investors perceive U.S. government bonds as less risky than bonds issued by firms in the private sector, and create an interest-rate differential between government and private bonds of equal maturity on this account.

As the time to maturity is lengthened for either government or corporate bonds, the interest rate rises. As with money-market rates, this rising pattern is not always present in bond markets. But a systematic relationship generally exists between the time to maturity and the interest rate on these longer-term capital-market instruments.[1]

## THE ROLE OF RISK

The relationships in table 25.1 have a strong logical foundation. To see it, put yourself in the position of an investor. If you feel that holding the IOU of a firm entails more risk of default than holding the IOU of the government, you will not be indifferent in your selection. If the interest rates are the same, you will pick the government's IOU every time, given this perception of risk. Because of this, the interest rate on the two *cannot be the same*. For, if they were, the private firm's IOU would find no investors. Thus, the private IOU must offer an interest rate that is enough higher than the government's IOU to entice investors to bear the added risk. The interest-rate difference you observe in table 25.1 between U.S. Treasury Bills and commercial paper is a direct measure of the market's assessment of this risk difference.

The market's risk assessment is not the same at different points in time. This is illustrated by figure 25.1, which shows how the interest rates on 180-day (six-month) commercial paper and 180-day Treasury Bills have varied over the last several years. Notice that the gap between the two interest rates varies considerably through time. In the recession of 1970, the gap was nearly 1.25 percent. As the economy expanded in 1971–1973, the gap narrowed to less than .5 percent. Then, with the severe recession of late 1973 to early 1975, the gap widened to more than 2.5 percent, its largest value in recent years. As expansion took over and the economy grew, the gap narrowed sharply, only to widen again as the general economic weakness of the early 1980s developed.

1. Municipal bonds (those issued by state and local governments) are a special case, because their interest payments are exempt from federal taxes. This makes their yield uniformly lower than corporate bonds, with most of the difference accounted for by this special tax status.

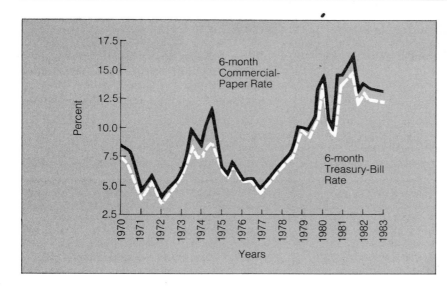

**FIGURE 25.1.**
**Interest Rates on**
**Commercial Paper and**
**U.S. Treasury Bills.**

This figure contains an important message: when the private sector of the economy is experiencing economic difficulty, investors react by requiring a higher interest rate for holding the IOUs of the private sector compared with that of the government. The figure illustrates that the relationship is a predictable one. It is likely to be repeated for most recessions and expansions. Some financial analysts explain the behavior of investors in creating these differing interest-rate gaps as "hiding out in T-Bills" when economic difficulty occurs.

## THE ROLE OF TIME TO MATURITY

Table 25.1 showed that the interest rates on both short-term and long-term financial instruments varies systematically with the length of the contract. The yield curve formalizes this relationship. A *yield curve* shows the complete structure of yields (that is, interest rates) for bonds that are identical in every respect except for the time to maturity. Figure 25.2 shows the yield curve for U.S. government securities as of the end of May 1980. At this time, more than a hundred different issues of government bonds were outstanding in the market. These bond issues are all very similar if not identical in terms of their legal and financial characteristics. In terms of riskiness, all issues are identically backed by the federal government. The various issues differ because of the time to maturity and because of the size of the semiannual interest payment, or coupon, that each carries.

The reason government bonds have differing coupons is largely because of the Treasury's modus operandi. Recall from chapter 5 that when a bond carries a coupon higher than the market interest rate, its price will be bid down below par so that it yields the market rate.

# Memorandum

A vivid example of rapidly changing assessment of risk by investors was provided by a crisis in the Mexican economy that occurred in late August of 1982. Prior to the crisis, selected short-term rates were:

| | |
|---|---|
| 90-day large CDs | 10.20% |
| 90-day Treasury Bills | 9.40% |
| T-Bills with one week to maturity (secondary-market yield) | 8.15% |

where the latter rate is that quoted by bond dealers for 90-day T-Bills having seven days to go until maturity.

A short period of high inflation and domestic and international turbulence had placed severe pressures on the Mexican banking system, which resulted in several Mexican banks either defaulting on their maturity debt obligations, or indicating that they would be defaulting on them. Many of these obligations were held by U.S. banks. On hearing of the problem, investors quickly reassessed upward the riskiness of loans made to Mexican banks. Many investors sought to sell CDs issued by U.S. banks, fearing that U.S. bank loans made to Mexican banks were in trouble; then U.S.–bank CDs would be placed in a perilous position as well. A panic-type shifting of short-term investment funds out of CDs thus occurred.

Investors reasoned that shifting funds into T-Bills was prudent, at least until the situation became clearer and more stable. Within a couple of trading days, the same selected interest rates were now:

| | |
|---|---|
| 90-day large CDs | 10.68% |
| 90-day T-Bills | 7.88% |
| T-Bills with one week to maturity (secondary-market yield) | 5.01% |

The "risk premium" for CDs over 90-day T-Bills, formerly 10.20% − 9.40% = 0.80%, now stood at a whopping 10.68% − 7.88% = 2.80%, while the gap between T-Bills with approximately 90 days to maturity and those with one week to maturity had been pushed by liquidity-conscious investors from 1.35% to 2.87%. Clearly, investors had reacted to the crisis and the uncertainty associated with it by "hiding out" in T-Bills.

---

The opposite occurs if the coupon is above the market rate. The Treasury customarily sets the coupon rate on newly issued bonds at about the market interest rate at the time the bonds are issued. This enables the bonds to be issued at about their redemption or par value. Since interest rates vary over time, so do coupon rates on newly issued bonds. As a result of this practice, wide differences in the coupon level are present among the government bonds shown in figure 25.2. Experience with yields shows that the size of the coupon on government bonds cannot be ignored in a precise analysis of yield-curve relationships. However, quantitatively, the effect of different coupons on yield-curve relationships is small, and can be ignored for our purpose.

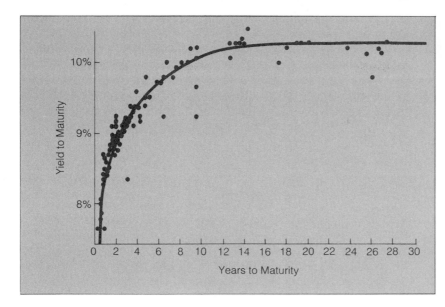

**FIGURE 25.2.**
**Yield Curve for U.S.**
**Government Bonds,**
**May 1980.**

Thus, the major factor determining the yield on U.S. government bonds is the time to maturity. Each of the $x$'s in figure 25.2 corresponds to the time to maturity and yield for an issue of government bonds. Clearly the $x$'s form a systematic, although imperfect, relationship between yield and time to maturity. A curve has been drawn through the $x$'s to represent this relationship. This smoothed curve is the yield curve. As of May 1980, the yield curve was positively sloped, rising sharply over the shorter maturities and then flattening out over longer maturities.

But, yield curves do not always look this way. Figure 25.3 shows the yield curve for U.S. government bonds one year later. By this time, the yield curve had "flipped over"—that is, the shorter-maturity bonds had higher yields than the longer-maturity bonds.

For the yield curve in figure 25.2, investors were willing to forfeit interest return to hold short-term bonds instead of long-term bonds. In fact, the yield of about 8 percent on three-month bonds was a full 2 percent lower than the yield on ten-year bonds. But, a year later, the situation was reversed. Investors were willing to forfeit interest to hold long-term bonds instead of short-term bonds. Here, the three-month yield of about 13 percent is more than 2 percent higher than the yield on ten-year bonds. An important shift in interest-rate relationships had obviously occurred over this year.

Figure 25.4 shows how often such shifts have occurred in recent years. In this figure, the yield on five-year U.S. government bonds is shown along with the yield on six-month Treasury Bills. When the five-year rate is above the six-month rate, the yield curve is upward-sloping, as in May 1980. But, when the six-month rate is above the five-year rate, the yield curve is downward-sloping, as in May 1981. Figure 25.4 shows that the yield curve was continuously upward-

FIGURE 25.3.
U.S. Government
Bonds, May 1981.

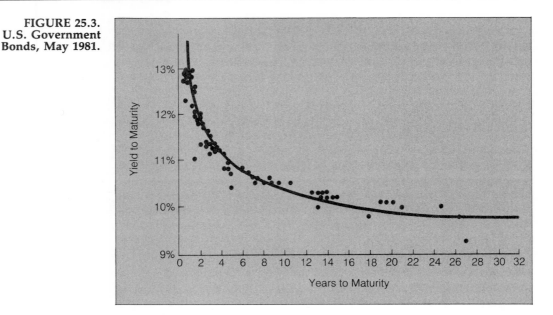

sloping from 1970 to mid–1973, when it flipped over. It remained
downward-sloping until mid–1974, when it became positive. The curve
remained positive until late 1978, when it again inverted. From this
point on, several shifts occurred in the curve as the financial environment in the United States became increasingly turbulent. Thus,
most of the time, the yield curve for U.S. government securities has
been upward-sloping, but the exceptions have been notable and are
becoming more frequent. Why do these dramatic changes occur? These
questions require an appreciation of the theory of the term structure
of interest rates.

## The Expectations
## Theory of the Term Structure

The *term structure of interest rates* is the structure of yields that make
up the yield curve. The *expectations theory* of the term structure offers
an explanation of the shape of the yield curve. To see the thinking
associated with the expectations theory, consider this example. Suppose you have $1,000 that you can invest for two years. In looking
around financial markets, you see two options. The first is to buy a
two-year bond that yields 10 percent per year. The second is to buy
a one-year bond yielding 8 percent, and reinvest in another one-year
bond at the end of the first year. (To keep things simple, we will
ignore any transactions/brokerage costs.) Which do you choose? Don't
be too quick to choose the two-year bond. For, if the yield on one-
year bonds rises to 14 percent one year from now, then the option
of buying the one-year bond and reinvesting the proceeds after a year

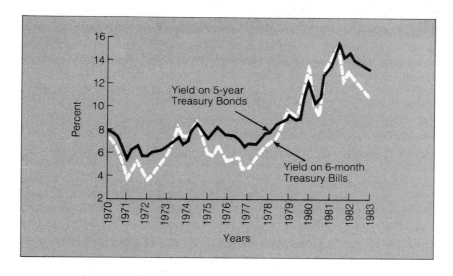

**FIGURE 25.4.
Yield-Curve
Relationships.**

offers the best deal. This route would yield a total return over two years of 8% + 14% = 22%, while the two-year bond would yield a total two-year return of 10% + 10% = 20%. (We will ignore compounding, assuming instead that the return earned in each year will be spent on consumer goods. In this case, we can simply add together the yearly yields to get a two-year yield.) On the other hand, if the yield on one-year bonds next year stays at its present value of 8 percent, then the total return from buying the one-year bond and reinvesting after one year would be 8% + 8% = 16%—a distinctly inferior alternative to the two-year bond.

Figure 25.5 illustrates this investment problem graphically. Clearly, the preferred alternative depends on rates on one-year bonds one year from now. Of course, investors cannot know these future rates. But, in order to choose between alternatives such as we have considered, investors must act on an expectation of future rates. Expectations theorists argue that if the one-year and two-year rates in the market are 8 percent and 10 percent respectively, it is precisely because investors expect the one-year rate a year into the future to be 12 percent. A 12 percent expected one-year rate makes the one-year and two-year alternatives give the same total return over a two-year period.

According to expectations theory, any structure of one- and two-year yields other than that shown in figure 25.5 could not persist, given the 12 percent expectation. Suppose the one-year rate was 7 percent and the two-year rate was 11 percent. Given the expectation that the one-year rate a year into the future would be 12 percent, the return on investing in the one-year-and-reinvest alternative is 7% + 12% = 19%, while the return from buying and holding the two-year bond is 11% + 11% = 22%. Investors would overwhelmingly prefer the two-year bond to the one-year bond. Those holding the one-year bond would see an advantage in selling it and buying the two-year bond instead. Demand for the two-year bond would rise and demand

**FIGURE 25.5.
Yield-Curve
Relationships.**

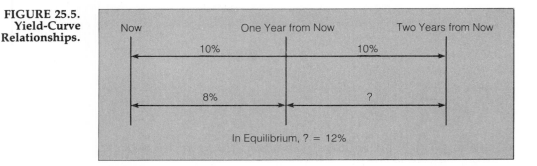

for the one-year bond would fall. The price of the two-year bond would accordingly rise, lowering its yield. Similarly, the price of the one-year bond would fall, raising its yield. These adjustments would continue until the total return from holding the two-year bond is the same as the total return from buying the one-year bond and reinvesting. Rates would continue adjusting until the one-year rate was 5 percent and the two-year rate was 10 percent. Thus, under the expectations theory, it is the expectation of future interest rates that is the principal factor determining the term structure of current interest rates contained in the yield curve.

For a 12 percent expectation, the resulting yield curve slopes upward, as shown in part (a) of figure 25.6. But, if expectations change, the yield curve shifts. Part (b) illustrates this for a change in the expected one-year rate to 9 percent. This change in expectations can be expected to bring about adjustments in both the one- and two-year rates. However, for the purpose of keeping this example simple, we will work through examples assuming that the total adjustment is in the two-year rate. (The added complication of having both rates adjust would add nothing to our analysis.) Thus, the one-year rate is assumed to remain constant at 8 percent. If expectations drop to 9 percent, the two-year return on the one-year-and-reinvest alternative is 8% + 9% = 17%. The two rates are now out of balance. Equilibrium is restored when the yield on the two-year bond falls to 8.5 percent, where 8.5% + 8.5% = 17% also. Accordingly, the effect of the drop in the expected one-year rate one year into the future from 12 percent to 9 percent is to flatten out the yield curve, as shown in part (b).

If the expected one-year yield falls further to 7 percent, the yield curve adjusts more, as shown in part (c). In this case, the two-year yield must fall to 7.5 percent to equate the two-year return to the one-year-and-reinvest return. Note that this additional decline in the expected rate not only flattens out the yield curve more, but also causes it to become downward-sloping.

It is no accident that in figure 25.6, the yield curve slopes *upward* whenever the expected one-year return one year into the future is *above* the present one-year return—parts (a) and (b)—and slopes *downward* when the expected one-year return is *below* the current one-year

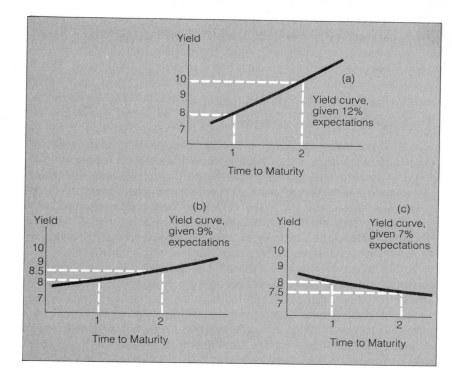

**FIGURE 25.6.**
**Changing Expectations and Shifting Yield Curves.**

return—part (c). Indeed, suppose the expected one-year-ahead return was 8 percent, the same as the current one-year return. Then, the equilibrium two-year rate is also 8 percent (so that both options give a two-year return of 16 percent) and the yield curve is perfectly horizontal.

These observations lead us to an important general principle: under the expectations theory, rising yield curves indicate the market's expectation that future short-term rates will be higher than current short-term rates; falling yield curves display the market's expectation that future short-term rates will be lower than current short-term rates; and flat yield curves indicate an expectation that future short-term rates will be the same as present short-term rates.

Under the expectations theory, expectations on future interest rates not only establish the relationship between one- and two-year yields, but they also govern the entire structure of short-term and long-term interest rates. For example, the relationship between the six-month T-Bill rate and the twelve-month T-Bill rate is determined by the expected six-month yield six months into the future. The relationship between the two-year bond rate and the five-year bond rate is governed similarly by the expected interest rate on three-year bonds that will prevail two years into the future. And, on it goes for all interest rates in the market. Expectations theorists argue that this must be so for all interest rates, for if it were not, some securities would dominate others in the market because they would offer a distinctly better deal. Experience suggests that such "better deals" are disposed of shortly by adjustments in prices caused by the buying and selling activity of profit-oriented investors.

## Variations of the Expectations Theory

Not all theorists accept the expectations theory in the form just discussed. Some argue that it is unreasonable to expect investors to bid to equality the yields on contracts that are not the same in terms of risk. Our one-year-and-reinvest versus two-year-buy-and-hold example illustrates this problem. The two-year contract involves no uncertainty. But, the one-year-and-reinvest option involves reinvesting in the future at an interest rate that is not known. Thus, assuming that certainty is always preferred to uncertainty, then if the two-year return on the two-year bond was the same as the expected two-year return on the one-year-and-reinvest option, a market of investors with a negative appetite for risk would always prefer the two-year option. In this case, the one-year-and-reinvest option must offer an unexpected two-year return which is higher than that of the two-year contract. For example, with a 12 percent expectation of next year's one-year rate, and a current one-year rate of 8 percent, a current two-year rate of 9 percent might be equilibrium. In this case, the certain two-year return of 9% + 9% = 18% is comparable to the uncertain return of 8% + 12% = 20%.

Making allowances for differences in the certainty of market returns alters the term-structure picture somewhat. But, it does not fundamentally change it. According to this view, the structure of current long- and short-term rates is still determined by the market's expectation of future rates, with only the quantitative impact affected. Under this variation of the expectations theory, we can still reason that major movements in the yield curve occur because of changes in the investors' expectations about future interest rates, with expectations of rising rates increasing the slope of the yield curve and with expectations of falling rates flattening the yield curve's slope.

Besides making allowances for uncertainty in the expectations theory, other theorists have argued that major financial markets where a term structure of interest rates occurs are not really single markets, but clusters of markets that are only weakly connected. According to this view, they become clusters of markets because of the differing objectives and constraints of investors who work in them, with many investors having what has been described as *preferred habitats* along the yield curve.

To illustrate this preferred-habitat theory, we will consider the term structure of the yields of U.S. government bonds. Banks are regular and often heavy investors in government bonds. However, they seldom buy bonds having maturities of more than three to five years.

Insurance companies are also frequent investors in Government bonds, but often as not they will be interested primarily in bonds with maturities of fifteen to twenty years. Banks are motivated to keep their investments short-term by a need to stay relatively liquid in the assets they hold, so as to avoid the potential risk of capital that could be involved should they need to liquidate a position in a bond prior to its maturity. On the other hand, insurance companies have objectives of locking in income on a long-term basis to meet other goals. Thus, these two institutions are led by their own goals to prefer different regions on the curve. According to adherents of this view, the result is a *segmented market* where little interaction and/or overlap exists among the segments. However, within each segment we may be able to draw the conclusions of the expectations theory about the behavior of yields. But, according to market-segmentation theorists, we would be led astray by drawing these conclusions about the overall behavior of yields.

Much of the statistical evidence that has been generated concerning term-structure theory supports the basic premises of the expectations theory. In addition, the weight of current evidence suggests that investors do not take differences in certainty/uncertainty into account. The evidence concerning whether preferred habitats and market segmentation actually occur in U.S. financial markets is much more confusing. Although some evidence has been presented suggesting that the long-term regions of U.S.-government-bond yield curves are segmented, the same cannot be said of the region of the curve encompassing maturities from about zero to seven years. Over this region, the actions of speculators is apparently sufficient to obliterate any and all preferred habitats that might otherwise be present.

**Important Ideas in This Chapter**

**1.** A look at interest rates in the U.S. financial marketplace shows that two important reasons for differences in interest rates are differences in risk of default and differences in time to maturity.

**2.** The higher the default risk, the higher the interest rate, if all else remains the same. The default-risk factor in interest rates increases during recessions, and declines during expansions.

**3.** Generally, the longer the maturity, the higher the interest rate, all else the same. However, an increasing number of exceptions to this rule have appeared in recent times.

**4.** The yield curve is the relationship between yields on bonds that are the same in every respect except maturity. This curve shows how the market yield on a bond is affected by the maturity of the bond.

**5.** The expectations theory of the term structure argues that the basic determinant of the structure of current yields is the expected future yield on bonds of short and long maturities.

**6.** Under the basic expectations theory, the yield curve slopes upward when the expectation of future short-term rates lies above the current level of short-term rates. An expectation of falling short-term rates leads to a downward-sloping yield curve. A flat yield curve indicates the expectation that future rates will be the same as current rates.

7. Some term-structure theorists argue that investors will not be indifferent to alternative financial contracts that differ in the certainty with which each delivers a return. Thus, a certain two-year contract will be preferred to a one-year-and-reinvest option unless the latter offers a higher expected return than the former. The difference in expected returns between two such contracts measures the degree to which the market has a negative appetite for risk.

8. Other theorists argue that divergent institutional goals and constraints cause actual financial markets to become segmented, as far as the operation of the expectations theory is concerned. For example, according to this view, there arises a short-term government-bond market and a long-term government-bond market, each of which might show different behavior in response to changing financial market conditions.

9. A reasonable degree of statistical support has been found for the main propositions of the expectations theory, and for the variation that suggests the market has a negative appetite for risk. However, evidence that markets are effectively segmented is limited, and confined to the long-term region of the government-bond yield curve.

**Discussion Questions**

1. Use a recent *Wall Street Journal* to reconstruct table 25.1 for the current period. Analyze the result, comparing it with the interest rates in table 25.1. Comment on the similarities and differences.

2. What is the present shape of the yield curve for U.S. government (that is, Treasury) bonds? What yield are investors expecting on one-year bonds one year from now?

3. Suppose investors have never taken the question of uncertainty into account in their investment decisions, and have followed the expectations theory in equating the returns on all combinations of financial contracts. Now, they begin to take such differences into account. How does the yield curve change?

4. Considering one-year intervals only, what are all the combinations of contracts that are possible for an investor with a four-year time horizon? For example, one possibility is to invest in a three-year bond and reinvest for one year after the third year. Another is to buy a series of four one-year bonds.

5. Does or does not the expectations theory argue that the expected four-year return on all the combinations you found in question 4 will be bid into equality by investors?

An excellent and more detailed treatise on term-structure theory is presented in James C. Van Horne's *Financial Market Rates and Flows,* Englewood Cliffs, N.J.: Prentice-Hall, 1978. An excellent study of the general cyclical properties of interest rates can be found in Joseph W. Conard's *The Behavior of Interest Rates,* New York: National Bureau of Economic Research, 1966. A survey of the different branches of term-structure theory can be found in Charles R. Nelson's *The Term Structure of Interest Rates,* New York: Basic Books, 1972.

**Suggested Readings**

# Accent on Famous Speculative Roller Coaster Rides

John M. Keynes once described investing in the stock market as being analogous to entering a beauty-judging contest where the best judge is declared to be the contestant whose rankings best correspond to the average ranking of all contestants. Thus, the problem is not to pick the truly most beautiful person, but to pick the beauty that the average judge would perceive to be Number 1. Keynes's point is that in selecting stocks, the keen investor picks those which he or she feels will be seen by the average investor as producing the best expected return for the risk involved.

Whether the business prospects of such favorably viewed firms actually materialize is beside the point. Rather, the crucial concern is how the future profitability of the firm is viewed by other investors. Fundamentally, a stock or any other asset is worth what another person will pay for it.

A famous example illustrating this point took place in Holland in the early 1600s. At that time, the tulip was introduced to the Dutch, having been brought there from Turkey. The bulbs were immediately popular although quite expensive because of their limited supply and foreign origin. At the height of the upsurge in popularity of the new tulip bulbs, a nonfatal plant disease spread among Dutch gardens that produced "stripes" of differing colors among the tulips. These infected bulbs were called "bizarres" and were prized highly by Dutch flower growers. Their market value rose rapidly.

Before long, the bizarre bulbs became an object of speculation among Dutch investors. At first, some proprietors of garden shops bought large supplies of the bizarres, planning to sell some to their customers and the rest to other merchants at higher prices. Handsome profits were reaped on this type of inventory speculation. Before long, the general Dutch population was engaged in the wildest type of speculation in tulip bulbs. Prices of the bulbs doubled, then tripled, then fell back, only to rise again to new highs. Talk of the likely future direction of tulip bulb prices dominated all else in Dutch financial circles. Those whose common sense told them that bulb prices were three or four times higher than reason would support sat by and watched their friends and neighbors make profits as prices went still higher. Many of the common-sense doubters eventually capitulated, finally reasoning that there was simply no end to how high tulip-bulb prices could go. Worry about tulip bulbs being recklessly overpriced vanished. Even an options market in the bulbs (see chapter 25) developed to serve the speculative needs of the Dutch public. simply no end to how high tulip-bulb prices could go. Worry about tulip bulbs being recklessly overpriced vanished. Even an options market in the bulbs (see chapter 25) developed to serve the speculative needs of the Dutch public.

Of course, the wild uphill ride in the speculative tulip-bulb bandwagon became an equally wild downhill ride. Prices began to weaken, then tumbled, then fell by half, then half again, and so on. Dealers in bulbs refused to honor commitments. The government intervened to attempt to restore stability. Recently won fortunes quickly vaporized. When the speculative bubble in tulip bulbs finally burst, the shock waves were so severe that they threw the Dutch economy into a severe and prolonged depression.

Versions of the Dutch tulip-bulb craze visit groups of U.S. stocks regularly and have even characterized the entire stock market. In early March 1928, RCA stock sold for about $90 per share. Six months later, its price had risen to more than $500 per share. Had the company's outlook improved enough over this six-month period to warrant this appreciation in value? The answer is clearly no. Rather, the appreciation in this and hundreds of other stocks is based on a version of the tulip-bulb craze. Investors became completely unconcerned about the underlying business prospects of RCA and other firms. Speculators were simply focusing on the meteoric rise in the price of stocks and becoming increasingly convinced that there was no reason for this rise to end.

Of course it did end, and abruptly so in the market crash beginning in late 1929. From its value of over $500 per share in late 1928, RCA reached about $12 at its low point in 1932 (adjusted for stock splits). Hundreds of other stocks fell from hyperinflated values as rapidly as balloons stuck with pins. Like Holland, the United States was visited by a long and deep depression during the several years after the collapse of the speculative craze in stocks.

A miniature version of the tulip-bulb craze reappeared in the U.S. stock market in the 1960s. In 1959–1961, a "growth stock" craze pushed prices of many stocks of firms located in new building industries to unbelievable levels. The simple logic was that these budding firms would be tomorrow's giants and were worth a growth bonus. A then-relatively-small emerging firm called Microwave Associates went from a price in the low teens to over 60 in 1961. At its 1961 high, Microwave Associates sold at a price-earnings multiple of 85 compared with about 17 or 18 for the overall market (see feature section 1 for a description of price-earnings multiples). Other "growth darling" stocks,

such as IBM and Fairchild Camera, carried 1961 price-earnings multiples of over 80.

Among professional investors, the attitude in 1961 was that the growth darlings were outrageously overpriced at price-earnings multiples of 25. Yet, as many rose easily and quickly to multiples of 30 and 35, the tulip-bulb mentality took hold. The term "overpriced" was discarded. The question was only when to jump in. When price-earning multiples reached 50 and beyond, even they ceased to have much meaning. Growth stocks were floating untethered in the financial stratosphere.

In 1962, profit-taking overtook the growth darlings, turning their prices lower. A sell-off followed. Investors found that prices fell as easily and quickly as they had risen. Those who had persisted in arguing the craziness of the situation now held sway. From its value of over 60 in 1961, Microwave Associates sold off to a low of 8 in 1962, at which point its price-earnings multiple had dropped from above 80 to about 13. The price of IBM stock was cut in half over the same period, along with scores of other growth darlings.

The growth-darling mentality was reincarnated a few years later in a sweeping speculative interest in new issues of stock. After observing that new issues were doing well, investors began seizing upon new issues and driving up their prices beyond all reasonable levels. Each new stock issue became a potentially explosive speculative "play" in the "New-issues game." Of course, the run up in new-issues prices typically was followed by a sell-off, as new-issue money moved to the next play.

Another variation on the tulip-bulb craze both accompanied and followed the new-issues wave. This involved so-called story stocks—stocks of firms that are in a special market or financial situation which has intriguing possibilities for future profits. For example, a typical "story" might go as follows: This firm has a patent on a device that you attach onto the carburetor of a car, and it increases gas mileage by ten miles per gallon. The firm has not actually started producing it yet, but the market potential is incredible—not to mention the possibility that the devices will be bought out at a high price by a Detroit automaker. Of course, they are making no profits now, but the future is fantastic.

Most story stocks were of this type—making no profit now but an incredible although fuzzy future ahead. The more complicated the story, the higher the price. Generally speaking, story stocks went the way of the growth darlings, with the heady uphill ride followed by the sickening fall from favor.

As the 1970s began, trading on the U.S. stock market became increasingly dominated by institutional investors such as trust-, pension-, and mutual-fund managers. Unlike household investors, institutional investors must answer for and defend logically their investment decisions. At regular meetings with their client, institutional money managers must explain why they bought and sold the stocks shifted into and out of the client's portfolio. As institutional investors played a growing role in the stock market, a group of "institutional darling" stocks emerged that were ideally suited to the needs of portfolio managers. These institutional favorites had several properties in common: (1) each had many million shares outstanding, so that it could accommodate the large-block trading that characterizes institutions, without disruptive movements in prices; (2) each was a well-established stable firm with a strong market position and strong financial characteristics; and (3) each had been a good solid investment over the period of the late 1960s and early 1970s, and thus had a good track record as a performance stock.

The group of stocks having these characteristics numbered no more than fifty or so. (They were sometimes called the nifty fifty.) Included were the stocks of such firms as IBM, Xerox, Avon Products, Procter and Gamble, General Electric, McDonald's, Disney, and Polaroid. The attractiveness of these stocks to money managers was clear. They were proven performers, not fly-by-night story stocks, growth darlings, or unproven new issues. A fund manager's prudence was above question when holding such stocks. In their meetings with clients fund managers could explain price declines in these stocks as nothing to worry about. By simply holding the stocks confidently through ups and downs in the market, people would steadily gain long-run returns.

As the "institutional darling" thinking expanded, more fund managers steadily bought and steadfastly held the shares. With a steady flow of demand and little selling, share prices of the institutional darlings moved steadily upward. A so-called two-tier market emerged, with patterns in the prices of the institutional favorites moving separately from price patterns for the general market of stocks. Generally, the difference in patterns between the two tiers was clear. The general market went up and down, while the institutional darlings went up.

The institutional darlings increasingly took on tulip-bulb characteristics. Insightful money managers could see that if most institutions steadily bought and held these stocks, this persistent demand would lead to prices rising indefinitely. Other speculators could also see the pattern, and many decided to climb on this institutional bandwagon themselves. By 1972, price-earnings multiples for the group were typically in the 60–80 range, compared with 15–18 for the remainder of the market. Some market pros argued that the underlying demand by institutions insured permanently rising prices for the group—investing in these stocks was seen as a sure thing.

The period from 1973 to 1980 saw a slow shake-out of the institutional firms. As one firm after another experienced product, marketing, and financial difficulties in this turbulent environment, money managers dumped their shares in favor of other institutional darlings. But, finally, the list of favored stocks dwindled to the point where the two-tier market picture crumbled away. By 1978, the typical price-earnings multiple for the institutional darlings had fallen from a 1972 range of 60–80 to the same 10–12 range as the rest of the market. In the process, severe losses were posted in professional managed portfolios. As with previous speculative episodes in the market, the losses were abrupt, staggering, and sobering.

Where will the tulip-bulb thinking pop up in the future? Only time will tell. But three things are certain: (1) We will have more speculative episodes in the U.S. stock market. (2) When they occur, they will involve a dizzying ride of some prices to unbelievable levels that will tempt even the most conservative investor to get on board. This temptation will be fueled by the stories that will abound of the overnight fortunes made. (3) When prices weaken, they will fall so quickly and steeply that rational thinking will suggest it cannot continue. But, history suggests it will, wiping out fortunes overnight and sending investors into other lines of business.

# PART VI

# INTERNATIONAL
# FINANCE

# International Banking and Financial Markets

## IMPORTANT TERMS

foreign correspondent banks
foreign branches
Edge Act corporations
International Banking Act of 1978
foreign affiliate
International Banking Facilities
  (IBFs)
letter of credit
import letter
export letter

bill of exchange
sight draft
time draft
banker's acceptance
eurodollar market
eurobond market
spot market in foreign exchange
forward market in foreign exchange
arbitrage

```
┌─────────────────────────────────────────────────────┐
│  ╱╲╱╲EMO ═══════════════════════════════════════     │
│                                                       │
│   To:        All readers                              │
│   From:      JWE                                      │
│                                                       │
│   The last decade has been one of rapid growth in     │
│   international trade. With this growth has come       │
│   attendant growth in international financial and     │
│   banking needs. Not surprisingly, the institutions   │
│   set up to accommodate international banking          │
│   business have also grown in size and changed in     │
│   nature; so have the instruments of international     │
│   finance.                                            │
│                                                       │
│   In this chapter, you can read about international    │
│   banking institutions— how they are organized and    │
│   how they operate. You can also read about the        │
│   nature of important international money and bond      │
│   markets. Finally, the foreign exchange market is     │
│   discussed, and some important terms associated       │
│   with this market defined.                            │
│                                                       │
└─────────────────────────────────────────────────────┘
```

During the decade of the 1970s, the dollar value of foreign purchases and business dealings by people in the United States exploded. In the first quarter of 1970, Americans were importing goods and services at a rate of 38.3 billion dollars per year. By the second quarter of 1981, that figure had risen to 263.3 billion dollars. From a nation with comparatively moderate international business transactions, the United States had become involved in the international marketplace in a major way. Figure 26.1 shows the pathway taken by both imports and exports during the 1970s and early 1980s. This figure shows that both imports and exports have grown rapidly, but that imports have consistently outpaced exports by a significant margin since about 1976.

There are several reasons for the growth in international business portrayed in figure 26.1. One reason is simply the inflation that took place over the period. Inflation continually increased the dollar value of international transactions, apart from increases in the volume of goods and services bought and sold. Inflation in foreign-oil prices alone was staggering. Beginning in 1973, Middle Eastern nations formed an oil-producing cartel that agreed to fix the price and quantity of Middle Eastern oil produced. Then the Middle East oil cartel began a series of mind-boggling increases in the price of oil produced in that region. As a result of the combination of price and quantity increases, the dollar value of imported oil soared, from a rate of under 3 billion dollars per year in early 1970 to over 83 billion dollars per year in mid-1981. One side effect of this trend was to shift the U.S. car buyer's preferences away from larger, "gas guzzler" type cars to smaller, more fuel-efficient cars. Many of the most popular of these

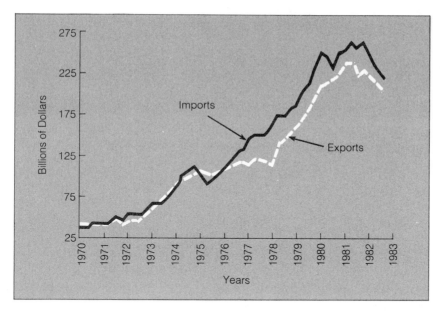

**FIGURE 26.1.
Exports and Imports.**

cars were imports from Japan and elsewhere. As a result, the dollar volume of imported cars increased from a rate of 5 billion per year in 1970 to over 36 billion in mid-1982.

Figure 26.2 shows the combined dollar volume of imported oil and imported autos from 1970 to 1982. The two most noticeable periods of rapid escalation in the dollar value of oil imports are in late 1973–early 1974, and during 1979. Both periods corresponded to rapid increases in the price per barrel of imported Middle Eastern oil. The falloff in the dollar value of imported oil during 1981 is the result of

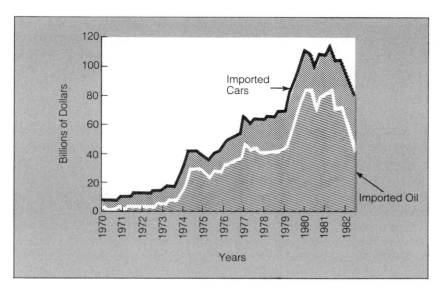

**FIGURE 26.2.
Imports of Oil and
Autos.**

cutbacks in the per-barrel price of oil made by the oil-cartel nations, coupled with a reduction in the total usage of oil by U.S. drivers. However, the dollar volume of imported cars continued to rise during this period, as it has since about 1974, when concern for fuel efficiency greatly increased.

Although the rapid escalation of imports over the 1970s has pushed the United States into the center of the international business stage, the trend has not occurred in isolation. After the 1973 oil crisis, many underdeveloped and developing nations began to borrow in the international financial marketplace to help finance growing oil imports. By 1982, Brazil and Mexico had accumulated international debts of 87 billion and 81 billion, respectively, while Venezuela, South Korea, Poland, and Indonesia had international debts of between 20 and 35 billion each. To accommodate this growth in international financial transactions, the banking institutions that serve international business needs have had to grow and change.

## STRUCTURE OF INTERNATIONAL BANKING INSTITUTIONS

One of the older arrangements to accommodate international banking business is the *foreign correspondent* banking relationship. This is a contractual arrangement whereby a U.S. and a foreign bank exchange banking services and deposits to the mutual advantage of both parties. Thus, U.S. banks channel international dealings through their correspondents in other nations as much as possible, in return for the same consideration by these foreign banks.

International correspondent banking relationships are complicated by differences in the laws, customs, and banking practices in various nations. A U.S. bank may want to carry out a routine U.S. banking operation through a correspondent in France, only to find out that such an operation is expressly prohibited in that nation. Differences in laws can lead to a number of international banking services that are "one-way-streets," a problem that places strains on such correspondent relationships. Correspondent relationships also can inhibit U.S. banks in finding the most competitive way to do their international banking.

U.S. banks are finding it increasingly advantageous to establish *foreign branches,* judging from the growth in these branches during the 1970s. By the early 1980s, the number of foreign branches of U.S. banks had grown from a handful a decade earlier to more than 800. Basically, these foreign branches are required to comply with U.S. banking laws regarding required reserves, types of deposits, and types of assets held. They are also subject to the same scrutiny by Federal Reserve bank examiners as domestic branches. However, the Federal Reserve recognizes differences in banking laws and practices among nations, and gives foreign branches leeway to allow them to be competitive in these foreign markets. Thus, in practice, branches of U.S. banks operating in other nations may follow very different practices in their loan policy, in the types of deposits they hold, and in the way they raise funds for investment.

One specific form taken by foreign branches is the *Edge Act corporation*. An Edge Act corporation is a domestic bank subsidiary that must be engaged in strictly international operations. The name follows from the Edge Act of 1919 (Senator Walter Edge of New Jersey being the principal legislator). Although Edge Act corporations are located in the United States, they are exempt from many domestic banking regulations, most notably the prohibition against interstate branching. Thus, a bank can have Edge Act subsidiaries in several different states. However, keep in mind that such subsidiaries are not doing domestic banking, but are each competing in the international marketplace.

U.S. banks have generally found that foreign branches give them a valuable presence in foreign financial markets. This presence allows foreign investment opportunities to be appraised more quickly and prudently, it broadens the scope of money-market activities of the domestic bank to include foreign money markets, and it allows the bank's customers to be served in a more complete and sophisticated way. Indeed, the rapid development of foreign branching among U.S. banks and the attendant increased use of foreign money markets are binding money markets in different nations together into an emerging worldwide financial marketplace.

The growth of foreign branches of U.S. banks has been accompanied by a smaller but substantial trend toward branching by foreign banks in the United States. Banks in many other nations have recognized that the same advantages that accrue to U.S. banks through foreign branching can be realized by setting up branches of their own in the United States. Before 1978, foreign banks were allowed to operate in the United States with few regulations. However, under the *International Banking Act of 1978*, foreign banks were required to comply with U.S. banking laws with only minor exceptions. Thus, foreign branches now must operate under the same "rules of the game" as the U.S. banks with which they increasingly compete.

An international banking structure of increasing importance is the *foreign affiliate* of a U.S. bank. A foreign affiliate is a bank that is chartered and operated in a foreign country, but is owned by a U.S. bank holding company. Generally, a foreign affiliate must comply with all the laws of the nation in which it operates. It is not under the regulation of the Federal Reserve and need not comply with its regulations. In addition, such institutions may not be doing only banking functions, in terms of the U.S. definition of that term. Rather, some may be hybrids of stock brokerage firms, security dealers, even real-estate concerns.

Because foreign affiliates are not under the umbrella of U.S. banking regulation, they provide U.S. banks with a more flexible way to do foreign banking than branches provide. Perhaps as a result, the

# Memorandum

To: Those interested in offshore banking
From: JWE

As of the latter part of 1981, the total assets of foreign branches of U.S. banks had reached over $460 billion—a considerable sum of money by any standard. Of this total, about $160 billion were in London branches. However, over $150 billion were in branches located in the Bahamas and the Cayman Islands in the Caribbean. It may come as a surprise that the size of the international banking operation in a tourist paradise such as the Caribbean islands is nearly as large as in London, whose credentials as an international banking center go back to the beginning of international trade.

The reason for this growth is that the governments of the Bahamas and the Caymans have constructed laws that have set their nations up as tax shelters for banking operations. U.S. banks learned that funds transferred to Caribbean branches were more profitable because of lower taxes on the earnings, and that regulations concerning asset and liability management were more liberal. Branches began to spring up faster than coconuts grow. However, these Caribbean branches have typically been more on paper than in the flesh. Important lending and fund-raising decisions involving such offshore facilities are generally made "back home" with the Caribbean branch functioning as an accounting entity.

In late 1981, the Federal Reserve dealt with the offshore problem by passing legislation defining and giving license to what are called *International Banking Facilities*, or IBFs. An IBF is either a foreign bank or a foreign branch of a domestic bank (such as many of the Caribbean operations) that operates in the United States. Under the 1981 legislation, IBFs can do banking within the United States but be regulated largely as though they were located abroad. Their transactions are considered to be the same as offshore transactions, free from many of the regulations that apply to domestic banks.

A bank need not even open up a separate office to form an IBF. As with the Caribbean operations, IBFs are largely bookkeeping creatures. A bank initiating an IBF need only inform the Federal Reserve and then segregate a portion of its assets, liabilities, and transactions as belonging to the IBF.

If you are wondering why banks do not convert all their assets to IBF status, the answer is that the services of IBFs are not available to domestic residents. An IBF can only transact international business. It is restricted to accepting deposits and making loans to foreigners or foreign branches of U.S. firms. Generally, funds cannot be raised in domestic capital markets. These restrictions have not dulled the popularity of IBFs. Since their inception, IBFs have grown dramatically, and have diverted much of the flow of offshore funds.

growth in foreign affiliates has been rapid in recent years. Equally rapid has been the increase in transactions with affiliates, including asset/liability transfers between foreign affiliates and domestic banks.

To a degree, domestic banks can adjust their portfolio (mostly for purposes of Federal Reserve examination) by shifts in assets and/or liabilities to or from foreign affiliates. It is easy to anticipate that the future will see further growth in foreign affiliates accompanied by some form of Federal Reserve control over the activities of domestic banks and their foreign affiliates, most likely aimed at creating more independence between the two.

## INTERNATIONAL BANKING ACTIVITIES AND FINANCIAL INSTRUMENTS

As international banking has grown, so have the banking facilities and organization concerned with this activity. Most larger banks now have international departments that perform all the functions of a domestic bank, but on an international basis. Growth in international banking also has been accompanied by growth in specialized financial instruments designed to facilitate trade in the somewhat riskier environment of banking across national boundaries.

A *letter of credit* is an important instrument in facilitating trade between nations. It is a document issued by a domestic bank on behalf of a person or firm in the United States that wants to buy imported goods. The letter of credit guarantees payment to the foreign seller by the issuing bank, in the event of default by the buyer. Such a guarantee is important in international transactions between private parties, because a business firm in one nation has no legal recourse in the event of a default in payment by a person or firm in another nation. In other words, a seller in one nation cannot "take to court" a buyer in another nation. Both domestic and foreign business firms have come to accept the letter of credit as a sufficient guarantee of payment, and international transactions have grown rapidly with its use.

There are two types of letters of credit. An *import letter* guarantees payment in the importer's currency, and an *export letter* guarantees payment in the exporter's currency. The difference between the two involves which party bears the risk of fluctuations in the exchange rate. To illustrate the role of a letter of credit and the risk involved, let us suppose that a U.S. firm is selling a computer to a British company. The price of the computer could be agreed to either in U.S. dollars or in British pounds. In this case, the price is negotiated in dollars, with the amount being set at one million dollars due on delivery of the computer in six months. From the standpoint of the British firm, the computer is an import, and thus payment is in the importer's currency. To protect its position, the U.S. firm stipulates that it wants a letter of credit guaranteeing payment in dollars before shipping the computer.

In agreeing to this deal, the British firm assumes the risk that dollars may become more costly to obtain in six months when payment is due. Suppose that at present, a pound can be exchanged for 1.75 dollars. This means that at present, the British firm would need $1,000,000 \div 1.75 = 571,428$ pounds to close the deal, which it would exchange for the needed dollars. If, during the next six months, the pound-dollar exchange rate falls to 1.65 dollars per pound, the effective cost of the computer to the British buyer has gone up to $1,000,000 ÷ 1.65 = 606,061 pounds. Had the U.S. firm agreed to take payment for the computer in pounds, setting the price at the equivalent of one million dollars at an exchange rate of 1.75, then the U.S. firm would bear the exchange-rate loss, since the 571,428 pounds it would receive would translate into only $942,857 at the reduced exchange rate of 1.65.

This exchange-rate risk is not all negative. Exchange rates both rise and fall, leading to the possibility of unanticipated profits as well as losses. In our example, if the pound-dollar exchange rate increased from 1.75 to 1.85, the British firm would be able to buy the computer for an effectively lower price ($1,000,000 ÷ 1.85 = 540,541 pounds). Thus, by fixing the price of the transaction in the currency of one or the other nation's currency, letters of credit impose the risk of fluctuating exchange rates on one of the two parties.

International transactions are often completed by the drawing up of a *bill of exchange*, which documents the transfer of goods and/or services in exchange for financial payment, and officially closes an international transaction. The bill of exchange is sent to the importer's bank, complete with all appropriate records of the transaction, and upon its receipt, the bank effects payment. A bill of exchange may be a *sight draft*, which is payable upon receipt and verification, or a *time draft*, which specifies payment on a future date.

A time draft has special significance. When a bank accepts the obligation on behalf of the buyer of the goods to make a future payment for goods received now, it is in effect borrowing money from the bank or firm in the foreign nation from which the goods came. The time draft becomes an IOU held against the bank by the international party. It is called a *banker's acceptance*, a financial instrument discussed in chapter 5. In recent years, a secondary market has arisen in banker's acceptances which allows any international party not wishing to hold the IOU to sell it at a discount. In turn, these acceptances become attractive money-market instruments for managers of short-term institutional portfolios such as money-market funds (also discussed in chapter 5). In many international transactions financed by time drafts, the acceptance is immediately sold by the international party at discount to investors in U.S. money-market instruments, thus transferring financing of the transaction back into the domestic money market.

## INTERNATIONAL MONEY AND CAPITAL MARKETS

In recent years, banks in many nations have become accustomed to making loans and accepting deposits that are denominated in currencies of other nations. As this practice has increased, the markets for both short-term credit and long-term debt have become more closely linked. As dollar-denominated IOUs are more frequently being traded between French and West German banks, and West-German-mark-denominated IOUs are more frequently being traded between financiers in other nations, the world's financial markets are forming an international money and capital market. At present, dollar-denominated deposits dominate this international marketplace, forming what have been labeled the eurodollar and eurobond markets.

## The Eurodollar Market

The term *eurodollar market* refers to the market for dollar-denominated deposits and loans held by and/or originated by mostly European financiers. It is basically a dollar-denominated credit market in Europe and elsewhere. Let us consider an example. A French businessman who has taken payment for wine sold to a U.S. firm in dollars may become the owner of a dollar deposit in a checking account in a U.S. bank as a result of the transaction. There are several ways the French-man can earn interest on these funds. One is to use them to buy a dollar-CD in the same U.S. bank. By doing this, the Frenchman can earn interest at short-term U.S. CD rates. However, if short-term rates in the French market are better, or if the Frenchman is suspicious of U.S. financial institutions, the U.S. bank deposit can be moved to a French bank that accepts eurodollar deposits. Effectively, the French-man "signs over" ownership of the dollar/demand deposit to the French bank in return for a CD or other deposit denominated in francs. From the standpoint of the U.S. bank, only the ownership of the demand deposit has changed— it is now owned to a French bank instead of a French businessman. But, the French businessman can now earn French rates of interest on the account. The French bank is interested in this transaction because it can now make a dollar-denominated loan using the dollar demand deposit now acquired. Rates of interest on such loans are often quite attractive to foreign bankers.

The most important group of borrowers in eurodollar markets are business firms that want to combine the exchange of currency with financing for a transaction. For example, a French firm wanting to buy a U.S. good and also obtain local financing may decide to borrow the funds in dollars rather than francs. Of course, this fixes the French firm's obligation to repay in dollars, thus placing the exchange-rate risk on the borrower. Besides business firms, eurodollar borrowers include central banks of nations with short-term credit needs, and U.S. banks that from time to time have found borrowing dollars in Europe to be a way of producing extra reserves during times of liquidity crunches.

## The Eurobond Market

The *eurobond market* is the international market for long-term debt capital involving currencies of other nations. A eurobond might be denominated in dollars, but issued by a West German firm and bought by a French investor. Eurobonds are a reflection of the increasing internationalization of capital markets. The motivation for a West German firm to issue debt in dollars could be some specific use of the dollars, such as financing the construction of a plant in the United States. But, likely as not, the reason is that denominating its bond issue in dollars gave it appeal to specific investors, which enabled the issue to be placed at a lower interest cost to the firm. In short, many decisions to deal in eurobonds are made because this type of financial instrument offers the best deal possible for a given set of circumstances.

Another motivation for a foreign firm in need of capital in dollars to borrow these dollars outside the United States is the disclosure rules of the U.S. Securities and Exchange Commission. If a French firm wants to issue dollar bonds in the U.S. bond market, it must meet all the U.S. rules on disclosure, including a prospectus and other public documents. Firms that are reluctant to meet these requirements naturally seek to borrow long-term dollars from investors in other nations via the eurobond market.

## THE FOREIGN-EXCHANGE MARKET

The eurodollar and eurobond markets are a way for business firms in one nation to acquire borrowed funds in another nation's currency without exchanging their own currency. In international transactions, this is the exception rather than the rule. In most transactions between firms of two nations, one party must exchange domestic currency for that of the other nation. So that this exchange is accommodated, a structure of foreign-exchange markets exists in major cities throughout the world, most notably in London, Paris, Zurich, New York, and Tokyo. In these exchange markets, traders can arrange to buy other currencies for immediate delivery or at a specified future point in time. The market for immediate delivery is called the *spot market in foreign exchange,* and the market for later delivery is called the *forward market in foreign exchange.*

### The Spot Market in Foreign Exchange

Most foreign-exchange transactions are handled by major banks. These banks quote current exchange rates to parties wanting to exchange currencies of all denominations. Each bank monitors the exchange rates of other banks and communicates with them regarding market conditions. In practice, what is exchanged in these markets is not actually currency (except for small amounts used for tourism and the like). Instead, traders exchange bank deposits denominated in one currency for deposits denominated in another. Thus, a West German firm wanting to trade German marks for dollars would exchange ownership of mark-denominated deposit in a West German bank for a dollar-denominated deposit in a U.S. bank.

Individual banks with surpluses of one type of currency will seek to exchange that currency for another in short supply. Thus, banks dealing in foreign exchange in a particular nation trade among themselves to an important degree to smooth out individual bank differences in the inflow and outflow of different currencies. When general shortages of currencies exist among banks in a specific country, banks deal with their counterparts in other nations to arrange for international currency exchanges.

With so many banks involved in foreign-exchange trading in different nations, each quoting exchange rates, it is logical to expect differing rates for banks in a particular nation and across nations. Although some differences do exist, they are kept small by the actions of currency speculators. Currency speculators are ever-watchful of the exchange rates for various currencies, and the opportunities they might present for *arbitrage*. An arbitrage opportunity arises when exchange rates allow a speculator to exchange one currency for a second, then exchange the second for a third and so forth, eventually winding up with more of the original currency than initially was exchanged. To illustrate an arbitrage opportunity, let us consider the following exchange rates:

| | |
|---|---|
| Greek drachmas per U.S. dollar | 72.40 |
| French francs per drachma | 0.10 |
| British pounds per franc | 0.09 |
| U.S. dollars per pound | 1.69 |

A currency speculator could initially exchange $10,000 for 724,000 Greek drachmas. Then these drachmas could be exchanged for 72,400 French francs. In turn, the francs could be exchanged for 6,516 British pounds. Finally, these pounds could be exchanged for $11,012, for a profit of $1,012. Since such exchanges could be arranged in a short period of time over the phone, it is a lucrative opportunity for the light-footed quick-acting currency speculator.

When arbitrage opportunities arise, quite logically, speculators seize them. However, as a result, pressures are brought to bear on the currencies and the exchange rates involved. In our example, if many traders are seeking to exchange dollars for drachmas, a shortage of drachmas emerges, and the number of drachmas a dollar can be exchanged for falls. Similar pressures are brought to bear on the franc-drachma, pound-franc, and dollar-pound exchange rates. Soon, the opportunity for arbitrage profits vanishes. Thus, because of the active role of speculators, exchange rates remain adjusted with each other most of the time, such that no arbitrage profits are possible.

## The Forward Market in Foreign Exchange

The same group of banks and related institutions that deal in present, or spot, currency exchanges also maintain a market for future delivery of currencies. The market where future currency exchanges are arranged is called the forward market in foreign exchange. In the forward market, a trader can contract for delivery of any foreign currency (actually bank deposits) in exchange for his/her own at a specified time in the future.

An important use of forward markets is to hedge against future changes in exchange rates. In our earlier discussion of import and export letters of credit, we discussed the question of which party in an international transaction bears the risk of fluctuations in the exchange rate between the time a bargain is struck and the time payment is made. Forward markets are a way for the party bearing the exchange-rate risk to shift it to another party. This can be done by buying the necessary currency for forward delivery at the time of settlement. For example, a British firm that buys a U.S. computer and agrees to pay one million dollars in six months could buy a forward contract guaranteeing delivery of one million dollars in six months in exchange for a set number of British pounds. If the British firm does this, it is no longer just concerned with fluctuations in the dollar-pound exchange rate over the six-month period, but it also wants to protect itself from the added outlay required if exchange rates move unfavorably. These risks have been shifted to the seller of the forward contract who now bears both the risk of loss and the potential for profit associated with exchange-rate fluctuations over the next six months.

Speculators are also active in forward-exchange markets. A speculator who thinks that the exchange rate is going to rise or fall for a particular currency exchange can invest in that prediction by buying a forward contract. If a ninety-day forward contract for 1,000 British pounds is bought at an exchange rate of $1.68 per pound, the speculator could use $1,680 to exercise the forward contract, purchasing 1,000 pounds. In the spot market, the 1,000 pounds now can be exchanged for $1,800 (the exchange rate is $1.80). Forward markets also present the same type of arbitrage opportunities that were discussed in conjunction with the spot market.

**Important Ideas in this Chapter**

1. The growth of international business transactions in the United States was rapid during the decade of the 1970s, spurred by the large growth in the dollar value of imported oil, and the growth in auto imports.

2. To accommodate foreign banking business, domestic banks establish foreign correspondents, with whom they trade services; and foreign banches, which operate much the same way as domestic branches except that they are permitted greater latitude by the Federal Reserve to respond to competitive conditions in the foreign market.

**3.** Foreign affiliates are owned by U.S. bank holding companies, but are chartered and operated in a foreign country. They are not regulated by the Federal Reserve, but are instead governed by the laws of the country in which they operate. They have been popular in that they have maximum latitude for operation according to the competitive conditions in the foreign marketplace.

**4.** Growth in international banking has also been accompanied by growth in specialized financial instruments designed to facilitate trade across national boundaries.

**5.** Letters of credit, both import and export, are important vehicles that facilitate international trade, as they guarantee payment by a bank of the buyer's obligation. Import letters fix the obligation in the importer's currency, and export letters fix the obligation in the exporter's currency.

**6.** Bills of exchange document the transfer of goods and/or services in exchange for financial payment. They may be in the form of a sight draft, which is immediately payable, or a time draft, which is payable after a period of time.

**7.** Time drafts are called banker's acceptances, and have become liquid in recent years because of the development of a secondary market in them. Thus, a foreign bank holding a time draft can sell it at present at a discount rather than wait for future payment.

**8.** The eurodollar market refers to the market for dollar-denominated deposits and loans held by and/or originated by mostly European financiers.

**9.** The most important group of borrowers in eurodollar markets are business firms that want to combine the exchange of currency with financing an international transaction. Others in this market are central banks of nations with short-term credit needs, and U.S. banks, which from time to time use it as a way to borrow needed reserves.

**10.** The eurobond market is the international market for long-term debt capital involving currencies of other nations. It is pursued by those seeking long-term capital denominated in the currencies of other nations, such as financiers of plant and equipment to be built in other nations, and also by those simply seeking the best available financial deal.

**11.** Foreign-exchange markets are made by banks in all major trading nations. These banks quote exchange rates for all currencies involved in international trade.

**12.** The spot market for foreign exchange is the market for immediate delivery of the currency of another nation. The forward market is the market for future delivery of the currency of another nation.

**13.** Arbitrage is the process of taking advantage of inconsistencies in the overall structure of exchange rates so that one could make multiple currency swaps and end up with a profit. The active role of speculators in foreign-exchange markets makes the opportunity of arbitrage profits short-lived, and keeps the structure of exchange rates generally consistent.

**14.** The forward market in foreign exchange allows those transacting international business to protect themselves against the risk of fluctuating exchange rates. When forward foreign currencies are bought, the price of an international purchase can be fixed in the buyer's currency, even though the deal may be specified in the seller's currency.

**Discussion Questions**

**1.** Why is there a need for specialized instruments for international trade and finance? Why not just do business internationally the way it is done domestically?

**2.** Find out whether eurodollar deposit rates are higher or lower than rates on comparable deposits in the United States. Can you find an explanation for the differences you found?

**3.** Evaluate this statement as to whether it is true or false, and explain your answer. "The forward exchange rate represents the best prediction of what the actual exchange rate will be in the future."

**4.** Construct a specific example of how arbitrage could produce profits in the forward exchange market.

**5.** Are there situations where it would be wise for a business to assume the exchange-rate risk of an international transaction rather than hedging or insisting on payment in its own currency? Explain.

**Suggested Readings**

For a complete description of the institutional structure of foreign-exchange markets in the United States, see Roger Kubarych, *The New York Foreign Exchange Market*, New York: Federal Reserve Bank, 1979. For a business-oriented and in-depth treatise on the implications and risks associated with exchange-rate movements, see Robert Z. Aliber, *Exchange Risk and Corporate International Finance*, New York: Halsted Press, 1979. Also, various issues of the *Annual Report of the International Monetary Fund*, Washington, D.C., contain analyses of contemporary developments in international finance and foreign-exchange markets.

## CHAPTER 27

# International Dollar
# Flows and Exchange Rates

IMPORTANT TERMS

dollar inflow
dollar outflow
balance on current account
merchandise trade balance
capital flow
Special Drawing Rights (SDRs)

capital account
capital-account balance
exchange rate
currency speculation
relative price effect

---

## MEMO

To:      All readers
From:    JWE

In the last chapter you read about the institutions, instruments, and types of markets where international business and finance takes place. This chapter puts those institutions, instruments, and markets in motion. In this chapter, we discuss the way we measure flows of dollars into and out of the United States. The balance on international accounts is examined.

Then, attention focuses on how exchange rates are actually set in foreign-exchange markets. With this perspective, we examine how a nation's exports and imports are affected by fluctuations in its exchange rate. This leads to exchange rates being the centerpiece of a self-correcting mechanism that reduces both surpluses and deficits in currency positions of most nations involved. The implications of this self-correcting mechanism are discussed.

---

In poker, if you do not win a hand occasionally, you run out of chips. If you keep buying chips from other players, you run out of money in your wallet. If you keep writing IOUs to obtain more chips, you will be viewed with increasing suspicion by the other players, and eventually your IOU will no longer be accepted. Financing international trade is not too different. A nation cannot continually buy more from other nations than it sells to them, because doing so will ultimately involve the creation of more IOUs than other countries will accept.

Fortunately, in recent years, the world has begun the construction of a system of international payments that, within limits, prevents this from happening. It does so by having built-in regulators that tend to keep the system on an even keel. In this chapter, we examine the present system of payments, beginning with a look at how international financial flows are measured, and then dealing with how exchange rates are set, and the consequences of exchange-rate fluctuations.

## MEASURING DOLLAR FLOWS TO AND FROM ABROAD

A *dollar inflow* is a reduction in the net dollar-denominated claims held by foreigners. The term *net* in this case refers to the dollar claims held by foreigners in either foreign or U.S. banks, plus foreign deposits held in U.S. banks, minus the *sum* of dollar deposits held by U.S. depositors abroad, *plus* foreign deposits held by U.S. depositors either in U.S. banks or abroad. When a U.S. seller sells a product to a foreign buyer, an inflow of dollars occurs. Whether payment is in dollars or in foreign currency does not matter, as one type of deposit can be exchanged for the other.

Selling products to foreign buyers is not the only transaction that produces a dollar inflow. Airlines, other firms, and individuals also perform services for international customers for which they receive payments. Thus, exports of services are a second source of dollar inflows.

A third source of dollar inflows is the earnings on U.S. investments abroad. Especially in the years since World War II, U.S. firms have established extensive industrial and commercial operations outside the nation. The profits from these operations are a source of dollar inflows. In addition, a dollar inflow is produced by the earnings on foreign securities held by U.S. investors.

Table 27.1 shows these three inflows and the amounts corresponding to each for 1981. The category "Earnings on Foreign Investments" is denoted as "net" to indicate that it is the earnings on foreign financial and business investments *net* of earnings on U.S. investments held by foreign investors. The same is true of the exports of services—they are stated net of services rendered to U.S. buyers by foreigners.

A *dollar outflow* is the opposite of a dollar inflow. A dollar outflow is an increase in net dollar claims held by foreigners. Table 27.1 shows that the largest producer of dollar outflows is imported merchandise, that is, purchases of foreign goods by U.S. buyers. However, another contributor to dollar outflows is military transactions, which result in transfers of funds abroad. Another source of dollar outflows is private transfers to agencies such as the Red Cross and other charitable groups. Finally, dollar outflows occur as a result of government transfers when grants, and gifts of food, clothing, and equipment are given to other nations, as well as other types of foreign aid.

The difference between total dollar inflows resulting from exports and earnings and total outflows caused by imports, military, and other transfers is called the *balance on current account.* The current-account balance shows the overall effect of current business transactions and current transfer flows. The 1981 value of 4.5 billion means that the net dollar-related claims held by foreigners were reduced by 4.5 billion over the year because of current business transactions and transfers. On a current basis, there was a net inflow of dollars.

Figure 27.1 shows the current-account balance over the last decade or so. Clearly, the dollar inflow of 1981 is not always the case. The large drop from the 1975 level of over 18 billion to the 1977–1978 levels of −15 billion or more is a graphic portrayal of the effects of larger imports of Middle Eastern oil that was rising in price at a dizzying

**TABLE 27.1**
**The U.S. Current-Account Balance for 1981**

|  | BILLIONS OF CURRENT DOLLARS |
|---|---|
| Inflow of dollars from: |  |
| Exporting merchandise | 236.3 |
| Net exports of services | 7.4 |
| Earnings on foreign investments, net | 33.0 |
| Total current inflow | 276.7 |
| *Less:* Outflow of dollars from: |  |
| Importing merchandise | 264.1 |
| Military transactions | 1.5 |
| Private transfers, net | 2.1 |
| Government transfers, net | 4.5 |
| Total current outflow | 272.5 |
| *Equals:* Balance on current account | 4.5 |

Source: *Federal Reserve Bulletin*, July 1982.

pace. Thus, over the 1977–1978 period, dollar balances held by foreigners increased as a result of current business transactions and transfers.

News reports of the U.S. international position sometimes refer only to merchandise bought and sold internationally, ignoring the effects of services and transfers. The differences between merchandise exports and merchandise imports is called the *merchandise trade balance*. In 1981, this balance was 236.3 − 264.1 = −27.8 billion dollars.

**FIGURE 27.1.**
**Current-Account**
**Balance.**

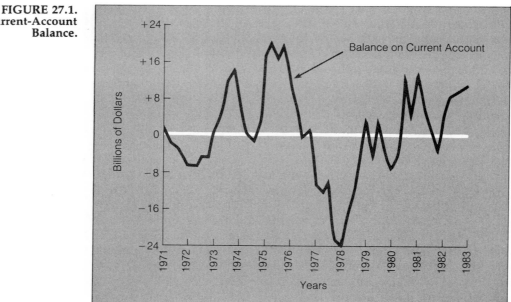

Presumably, the attention often directed toward the merchandise balance is based on the belief that a nation's fundamental trade position rests on the amount of actual goods moving back and forth from its shores. However, in an increasingly service-oriented world, excluding net exports of services seems arbitrary in any attempt to uncover the underlying trade position of a nation. In addition, in an era where the multinational corporation is the norm rather than the exception, ignoring profits on international business and financial operations does not seem to move in the direction of producing a clearer picture of the international position. These factors indicate that the current-account balance is preferred to any narrower measure as a gauge of the fundamental international position of a nation resulting from business activities and transfers.

The current-account balance is not intended to take all financial flows into account. The most important omission is a *capital flow* which occurs when a business investor in one nation invests in a new plant in another, or when a financial investor in one nation buys a security issued in another nation. Payment for the plant or the security entails a dollar flow. Besides capital flows, shifts occur in the official balances of foreign nations, and in the U.S. balances held abroad. When these accounts rise or fall, a change in dollar flow occurs.

Finally, major western nations have evolved a system of "worldwide checking" that allows nations to pay for currency exchanges by an international form of paper money called *Special Drawing Rights*, or SDRs (you can read more about this topic in the next chapter). An international agency called the International Monetary Fund periodically issues SDRs to participating nations as a way of increasing the overall pool of money that can be used for international transactions. When the United States receives more SDRs, a situation equivalent to an inflow of dollars occurs because it represents balances that can be used in trade.

These capital flows are assembled in table 27.2 into a statement of the noncurrent financial flows called the *capital account*. The table shows data for 1981. Capital inflows occur as a result of new private investments made in the United States by foreigners, increases in the official accounts of foreign governments, and new allocations of SDRs. Capital outflows are produced by new private investments made by U.S. investors in foreign assets, and increases in U.S. government accounts abroad.

The difference between capital inflows and capital outflows is called the *capital-account balance*. For 1981, this balance was −30.3 billion, largely because the amount of new U.S. investment abroad substantially exceeded the foreign investment in the United States.

Capital flows are often regarded as less fundamental to a nation's international position than current-account flows, because of their great instability. Figure 27.2 shows the capital-account balance for the last decade or so, and vividly illustrates this instability. A large part of the reason for the pattern observed is the movement of investment

**TABLE 27.2**
**U.S. Capital-Account Balance for 1981**

|  | BILLIONS OF CURRENT DOLLARS |
|---|---|
| Capital inflows produced by: |  |
| New private investments from abroad | 73.1 |
| Increases in accounts of foreign governments | 4.8 |
| Allocation of SDRs | 1.1 |
| Total capital inflows | 79.0 |
| *Less:* Capital outflows produced by: |  |
| New U.S. private investments made abroad | 99.0 |
| Increases in U.S. government accounts abroad | 10.3 |
|  | 109.3 |
| *Equals:* Capital-account balance | −30.3 |

Source: *Federal Reserve Bulletin*, July 1982.

funds among world security markets. When conditions in U.S. money and/or capital markets are attractive relative to those in other nations, an inflow of investment funds occurs. An outflow of capital occurs when foreign money and/or capital markets are relatively more attractive to investors in the United States and around the world. But, when changes occur in the relative attractiveness of financial markets, rapid and sometimes large changes in flows of financial capital follow. Needless to say, financial markets in the United States and elsewhere have an inherent tendency to go up and down quickly and sharply.

**FIGURE 27.2.**
**Capital-Account**
**Balance.**

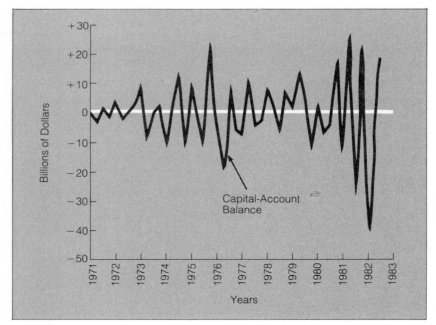

With these upswings and downswings goes the capital-account balance.

Volatile or not, capital flows produce the same changes in dollar claims that current-account flows produce. In a year such as 1981 when the United States ran a 30.3-billion deficit on its capital account, and a 4.5-billion surplus on its current account, net dollar claims held by foreigners went up by 30.3 − 4.5 = 25.8 billion dollars. If foreigners hold dollar claims that rise above their needs for conducting business in dollars, they will quite logically be interested in either switching some of their dollar balances into balances of other currencies, or investing in financial assets. Either way, when the size of foreign dollar holdings exceeds the need for them in transactions, foreigners will generally seek to exchange dollar deposits for deposits denominated in other currencies. When this happens, the exchange rate changes. We now examine how this occurs.

## CURRENCY SUPPLY AND DEMAND AND EXCHANGE RATES

An *exchange rate* is the price of one nation's currency relative to that of another nation's currency. Accordingly, an exchange rate shows the number of units of one currency required to buy a unit of the other currency. For example, the dollar-pound exchange rate gives the number of dollars required to buy one British pound; if it is $1.80, then $1.80 is required to purchase one British pound.

An exchange rate is like a stock price in that it rises and falls with market pressures of supply and demand. If the United States persistently runs combined deficits in its current and capital accounts, then the resulting persistent increase in foreign-held dollar deposits leads to their being exchanged for deposits denominated in other currencies. If the number of depositors trying to exchange dollar deposits for deposits in other currencies becomes large relative to those seeking to exchange other currencies for dollars, the exchange value of the dollar falls.

A simple supply-demand diagram aptly illustrates the process for the spot market in dollar-yen exchange. The forward market (see the previous chapter) works the same way for largely the same reasons, and will not be separately discussed. In figure 27.3, the spot exchange market between U.S. dollars and Japanese yen is depicted. On the vertical axis is the exchange rate, measured in the number of yen per dollar. The horizontal axis shows the quantity of dollars being exchanged for yen in any period of time. The downward-sloping curve labeled D is the demand schedule for dollar deposits from the standpoint of those holding yen deposits. To understand the negative slope of this curve, first keep in mind that a rise in the number of yen a dollar will bring (that is, a movement up the curve) is the same as a fall in the number of dollars a yen will bring. Thus, as the yen-dollar exchange rate rises, the yen-deposit owner can exchange his or her holdings for fewer and fewer dollars, and thus would demand less and less dollars in exchange for yen.

The curve labeled $S$ in figure 27.3 is the supply curve for dollars by those seeking yen in exchange. As the exchange rate rises and a dollar brings more and more yen in exchange, it becomes increasingly attractive for holders of dollar deposits to exchange them for yen deposits. Thus, the supply curve slopes upward in a positive direction.

When the supply and demand curves are in the positions labeled $D$ and $S$, exchange rate $E_0$ will evolve as the only sustainable exchange rate. An exchange rate such as $E_h$ will create more supply of dollar deposits than demand for dollar deposits. With more offers to exchange dollars for yen than to exchange yen for dollars, exchange dealers will find it necessary to lower the exchange rate. When the rate comes down to $E_0$, the imbalance has been eliminated, and the exchange rate stabilizes. Similarly, an exchange rate lower than $E_0$ will generate a shortage of dollars, leading the exchange rate to rise toward $E_0$.

If the United States runs persistent deficits in its international account, then holders of dollar deposits will want to shift their portfolios

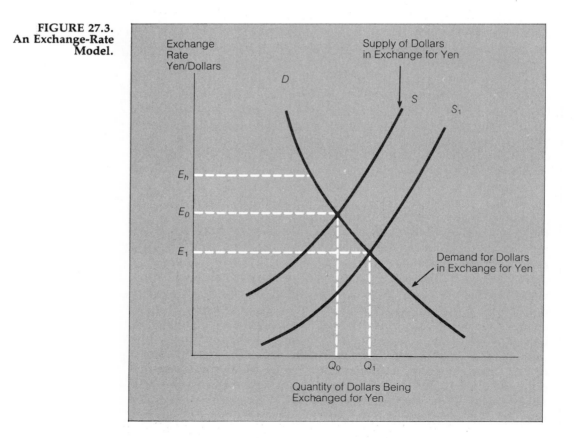

FIGURE 27.3.
An Exchange-Rate
Model.

of dollars versus other currencies. The supply curve of dollars thus shifts to the right, to a position illustrated by $S_1$. Exchange rate $E_0$ is no longer sustainable but must adjust downward to $E_1$, where equilibrium is again restored. If deficits persist, then continual shifts in portfolio positions occur, the supply curve of dollars continually shifts to the right, and the yen/dollar exchange rate continues to fall. In this situation, holders of yen deposits are only willing to exchange them if they receive more and more dollars per yen, while holders of dollar deposits are forced by market conditions to accept fewer and fewer yen per dollar. How do the parties to such an exchange know when the deal is "good enough" to pursue? What factors determine the position of the demand and supply curves depicted in figure 27.3? They are questions to which we now turn.

## THE INTERACTION OF EXCHANGE RATES AND FOREIGN TRADE

Part of the reason for currency demand and/or supply is *currency speculation*. Currency speculators may feel that the exchange rate is low and is going to rise. If so, they can make profits by buying foreign exchange in the spot market (see the previous chapter) now and selling later. Suppose a holder of a deposit of 1,000 West German marks is convinced that the mark/dollar exchange rate of 2.222 marks per dollar is going to rise. The speculator acts on this conviction by exchanging the 1,000 marks for $1,000 \div 2.222 = \$450$. In a month, the speculator's prediction turns out to be correct, and the mark/dollar exchange rate has risen to 2.50. At this point, the speculator converts the $450 deposit back into marks, receiving a deposit in the amount $\$450 \times 2.5 = 1,125$ marks. The speculator has turned a profit of 125 marks on the deal, less any commissions that must be paid.

Alternatively, a currency speculator with the conviction that the mark/dollar exchange will rise could buy a contract for forward delivery of dollars in exchange for marks one month hence. To examine this, assume the forward exchange rate is equal to the current rate of 2.222. Then, if the exchange rate rose to 2.5 after one month, the speculator could take delivery of the dollar deposit ($450 for 1,000 marks) and immediately exchange the dollar deposit of $450 for 1,125 marks. On the other hand, the speculator could just sell the forward contract for a profit, since this right to exchange at a rate below the market exchange rate would now have a market value.

Although currency speculators are factors in both the spot and forward markets for currency exchange, more fundamental factors are at work to position the supply and demand curves in these markets. These fundamental factors have to do with the impact of exchange rates on the relative prices of goods and services in the two nations involved. Basically, when the mark/dollar exchange rate rises,

West German products become relatively cheaper to U.S. buyers, while U.S. products become relatively more expensive to West German buyers. That is, when exchange rates change, relative prices of products in the two nations are altered.

Table 27.3 helps illustrate this relative price effect by using an example of two automobiles, one produced in the United States and the other produced in West Germany. Each can be bought in either West Germany or in the United States. The West German car sells for 25,000 marks, and the U.S. car sells for $10,000. Suppose they are highly comparable in terms of performance and styling. If the exchange rate is 2.5 marks/dollar, a U.S. buyer finds that the West German car costs the same as the U.S. car, since $10,000 will be required to purchase the 25,000 marks needed to buy the West German car.

At the same 2.5 marks/dollar exchange rate, the West German buyer finds this also to be true. It takes 25,000 marks to buy the $10,000 needed to purchase the U.S. car. Thus, from the standpoint of both West German and U.S. car buyers, the outlays are the same for either car.

If the exchange rate changes, this equivalence no longer holds. The table illustrates this by presenting a range of exchange rates on either side of 2.50. Suppose the mark/dollar exchange rate rises to 2.86. From the standpoint of the U.S. buyer, the West German car is now a good deal. It takes only $8,750 to buy the 25,000 marks required for the West German car, which makes the West German car a bargain compared with its U.S. counterpart. On the other hand, the West German buyer now requires 28,571 marks to buy the U.S. car, which is overpriced compared with the comparable West German car. The fluctuation in exchange rates has changed relative prices. The expected result of this increase in the mark/dollar exchange rate and corresponding change in relative prices is an increase in the imports of

**TABLE 27.3**
**Relative Price Effects of Fluctuating Exchange Rates**

| PRICE TO A U.S. BUYER | | EXCHANGE RATE | PRICE TO A WEST GERMAN BUYER | |
|---|---|---|---|---|
| U.S. CAR | WEST GERMAN CAR | MARKS/DOLLAR | U.S. CAR | WEST GERMAN CAR |
| $10,000 | $ 8,750 | 2.86 | 28,571 DM | 25,000 DM |
| $10,000 | $ 9,000 | 2.78 | 27,778 DM | 25,000 DM |
| $10,000 | $ 9,250 | 2.70 | 27.027 DM | 25,000 DM |
| $10,000 | $ 9,500 | 2.63 | 26.316 DM | 25,000 DM |
| $10,000 | $ 9,750 | 2.56 | 25,641 DM | 25,000 DM |
| $10,000 | $10,000 | 2.50 | 25,000 DM | 25,000 DM |
| $10,000 | $10,250 | 2.44 | 24,390 DM | 25,000 DM |
| $10,000 | $10,500 | 2.38 | 23,810 DM | 25,000 DM |
| $10,000 | $10,750 | 2.33 | 23,256 DM | 25,000 DM |
| $10,000 | $11,000 | 2.27 | 22,727 DM | 25,000 DM |
| $10,000 | $11,250 | 2.22 | 22,222 DM | 25,000 DM |

To: Those curious about the stock market and exchange rates
From: JWE

On November 5, 1982, the *Wall Street Journal* ran an article entitled "Dollar Follows Stock Market to High Levels." Perhaps you are wondering why the dollar's exchange rate would follow the stock market? This memo examines the relationship. First, the U.S. stock market had moved up like a rocket during the month of October 1982, with the Dow Jones average rising from a low of about 780 to 1,050 on the day of the article. That move in stock prices had not been accompanied by similar moves in stock prices on other exchanges around the world. By November 1, it appeared to many international-securities traders that the U.S. stock market was "where the action is." Thus, currencies from all over the world were being exchanged for dollars in order to be sunk into the U.S. stock market. The demand for dollar deposits soared, and along with it the exchange rate of the dollar compared with most other currencies. From a value of just under 2.42 marks/dollar four months earlier, the mark/dollar exchange rate soared to 2.582 marks/dollar. The yen/dollar exchange rate went up to 277.1 yen/dollar from 251.2 four months earlier. Other exchange rates made similar moves.

According to the *Wall Street Journal* article, analysts expected speculators to drive the rates still higher. Some thought that the lowering of the discount rate by the Federal Reserve in the next several weeks would spur the U.S. stock market further, and thus draw in more foreign capital, raising exchange rates higher. These speculators were frantically building positions in dollars to take advantage of the trend.

Thus, the stock market, Federal Reserve policy regarding domestic interest rates, and the money supply all impact on foreign exchange rates.

West German cars by U.S. buyers, and a decrease in the exports of U.S. cars to West Germany.

If the mark/dollar exchange rate moves in the other direction, the import-export effect is reversed. A fall in the mark/dollar exchange rate to 2.22 makes the West German car more expensive to U.S. buyers than its U.S. counterpart, while making the U.S. car relatively cheap to West German buyers. Thus, the expected result of a falling mark/dollar exchange rate is higher exports of U.S. cars to West Germany coupled with a decrease in the number of West German cars imported to the United States.

The effect of exchange rates on relative prices is not confined to cars. All West German products become cheaper to U.S. buyers when the mark/dollar exchange rate rises, while all U.S. products become more expensive to West German buyers. When the mark/dollar exchange rate falls, West German products cost U.S. buyers more, while U.S. products cost West German buyers less. Accordingly, exports and imports of all products between the United States and West Germany are affected by shifts in the mark/dollar exchange rate.

# A SELF-ADJUSTING SYSTEM OF INTERNATIONAL PAYMENTS

The *relative price effect* of exchange-rate fluctuations has important implications for the international payments position of the nations involved. The relative price effect is the crucial link in producing a self-adjusting system of international payments. To see this self-adjusting process, we will consider the West Germany–United States example further. Suppose that for some time the exchange rate between the two nations remained in the vicinity of 2.5 marks/dollar, and that at this level the two nations ran an approximate zero balance on the current accounts of each nation. Now, suppose that U.S. firms engage in large industrial expansions in West Germany, leading to net U.S. capital outflows, and an overall continuing deficit on the U.S. international account. Dollar balances held by foreigners build, leading eventually to an increased amount of dollars being brought to foreign-exchange markets to be exchanged for marks. The supply curve of dollars shifts to the right, and the mark/dollar exchange rate falls to accommodate this increased supply. Suppose the rate falls from 2.50 to 2.22.

Relative prices change because of the fall in the exchange rate. Exports of U.S. goods to West Germany are stimulated while imports of West German products to the United States are cut. Before long, the U.S. current account shows a growing surplus. Eventually, the surplus on the current account is enough to offset the capital outflow, and the U.S. overall payments position is in balance. When this happens, dollar balances no longer increase, and the downward pressure on the mark/dollar exchange rate disappears. With a stable exchange rate, relative prices are stable, and the overall balance between the payments positions of the United States and West Germany is restored.

In this example, the appearance of a deficit in the international position of one nation set into play forces that led to its disappearance. The deficit caused exchange rates to fall, which stimulated exports and discouraged imports, which reduced the deficit in the international payments position.

Exchange-rate movements are not the only factor that can change relative prices in two nations. When inflation rates in two nations differ, changes occur in relative prices that are independent of exchange-rate fluctuations. In fact, the change in relative prices that results from differing inflation rates in two nations alters the attractiveness of imports versus exports, and leads to the same type of adjustments as if the relative prices had been changed by exchange-rate fluctuations.

In the real world, exchange rates respond to the kinds of influences illustrated by the supply-demand model discussed earlier. Relative prices are changed when this occurs. Deficit and/or surplus positions do adjust just as in our example. But, not perfectly so. What we have

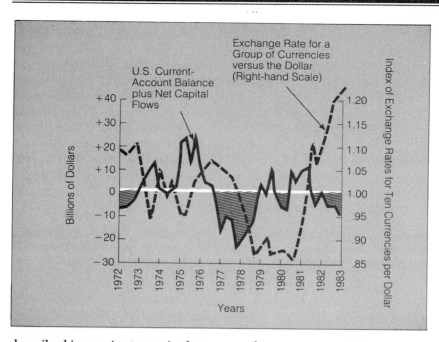

FIGURE 27.4.
Exchange Rates and
the U.S. International
Position.

described in precise terms in these pages happens generally but somewhat slowly in the real world.

Still, the self-correcting aspect of the present international monetary system stands out as its most dominant feature. Figure 27.4
illustrates this point in the case of the United States. In this figure,
the U.S. current-account balance is combined with the balance on the
capital account to arrive at the overall international payments position,
shown as the solid line. The shaded areas are periods in which deficits
appeared on this combined account, and the unshaded areas represent surpluses. The dashed line is the exchange rate for a group of
ten prominent world currencies versus the dollar, where each currency's exchange rate is weighted by the volume of trade with the
United States during recent years.

The pattern suggested by our discussion is present in figure 27.4,
but with a time lag. First, notice that the period from the beginning
of 1973 to the middle of 1974 was one of steady surpluses in the
overall U.S. international account. The surpluses over this period
associate with the rise in the exchange rate from the middle of 1973
to the beginning of 1974. In turn, the rising exchange rate associates
with a fall in the U.S. surplus during the first part of 1974. The
continuing payments surpluses from late 1974 until mid-1976 associate
with a rising exchange rate beginning in early 1975 and ending in
early 1976. With higher exchange rates, the payments position moved
sharply into deficit, spurred by increasing oil imports. As this deficit
progressed, exchange rates fell, and continued to fall until the payments position moved into a solid surplus in mid-1980. At this point,
a sharp rise in the exchange rate occurred, more so than would be

warranted by the surplus position. At least some of this movement appears to be the result of the work of speculators, who created something of a "bull market" in the dollar during this period.

Figure 27.4 is a picture of an international payments system that has clear self-adjustment tendencies, even if it is not always fully adjusted. But, self-adjustment is only one feature of our contemporary international monetary system. In the next chapter, more features of this system are discussed.

## Important Ideas in This Chapter

**1.** When the level of net dollar-denominated deposits held by foreigners falls, a dollar inflow occurs. Important sources of dollar inflow are exports in excess of imports, and profit flows on international investments.

**2.** The current-account balance shows the net effect of current business transactions and current transfer flows on the net dollar deposits held abroad.

**3.** The merchandise trade balance is the difference between exports and imports of merchandise. It is a narrow measure of international activity, but one that is often reported as indicating a nation's international position.

**4.** The current account does not take into consideration the flow of capital among nations. A capital flow occurs when direct financial or real investments are made in other nations.

**5.** The capital account takes into consideration these capital flows, and assembles them into a statement of the balance on the capital account.

**6.** Capital flows are often regarded as less fundamental to a nation's international position than current-account flows, simply because of the inherent volatility of the financial flows involved. Investment funds move rapidly and unpredictably across national borders in search of the highest available return.

**7.** In the present international monetary system, the exchange rate for various currencies is set on the basis of supply and demand, with exchange rates rising and falling much like stock prices do on a major exchange.

**8.** One factor in foreign-exchange markets is currency speculation, which causes exchange rates to periodically rise and fall. However, a more fundamental factor is the demand for and supply of foreign exchange produced by the needs of international business.

**9.** When the exchange rate of the dollar rises, other nations' products become relatively cheaper to U.S. buyers, while U.S. products become more expensive to foreign buyers. This is called the relative price effect of exchange-rate fluctuations.

**10.** The relative price effect creates a self-adjusting system of international payments. When a nation experiences a deficit in its international position, its currency exchange rate falls. This fall stimulates exports and discourages imports, leading to an elimination of the deficit. The tendency is for exchange-rate fluctuations to maintain an approximate balance in the international payments among all nations.

**1.** Suppose a wealthy U.S. citizen give one million dollars to a European orphanage. Does this impact on the U.S. international payments position? Explain.

**2.** In what way are international capital flows less "fundamental" than current-account flows? Which do you think is more important, and why?

**3.** Suppose you firmly believe that the yen/dollar exchange rate will fall by 10 percent over the next six months. What actions can you take to make some money if your belief is correct?

**4.** What factors besides the exchange rate impact on relative prices in two nations?

**5.** Describe in your own words how the self-adjusting mechanism operates in the case of a nation that is running a large surplus in its overall international payments balance.

**Discussion Questions**

For a number of interesting essays dealing with the movement of exchange rates in recent years, see the Federal Reserve Bank of Boston, *Managed Exchange Rate Flexibility: The Recent Experience*, Boston: Federal Reserve Bank, 1978. For a sparkling discussion of the self-adjusting feature of a system of freely floating exchange rates, see Milton Friedman, "The Case for Fluctuating Exchange Rates," in his *Essays in Positive Economics*, Chicago: University of Chicago Press, 1953.

**Suggested Readings**

## CHAPTER 28

# The International Monetary System

---

## CHAPTER OUTLINE

## IMPORTANT TERMS

international monetary system
gold standard
pegging
fixed exchange rates
bill of exchange
gold-exchange standard
floating exchange rate
Gold Reserve Act

gold-bullion standard
World Bank
International Monetary Fund (IMF)
Special Drawing Rights (SDR)
Smithsonian agreements
two-tier system
European Monetary System

# /MEMO

To:        All readers
From:      JWE

A great person (most likely a historian) once said, "a little history doesn't hurt anyone." Abe Lincoln often professed that understanding why the past unfolded the way it did was an important prerequisite to being able to assess the present and predict the future. Lincoln's comment is sage advice in terms of understanding how the present system of international payments works. Understanding our present system is greatly facilitated by following a quick historical pathway from the days of frigate ships to the days where the main thing floating is exchange rates.

That is what happens in this chapter. From the gold-standard era in the nineteenth and early twentieth centuries, the development of the system of international payments is traced forward. The importance of the post-World War II reformulations in monetary institutions is discussed, as is the period of crisis from 1971–1973 out of which was born the present system of international payments and exchange rates.

For decades, the realities of international trade and finance have made it necessary for nations to sit down together and formulate working rules for conducting international business. The structure of such rules, and the institutions evolved by nations to police them, is called the *international monetary system*. The term *system* implies order, rules of operation, and interlocking parts. The present international monetary system has these attributes. Many of the features of the present system were inherited from the past. Others were born out of the ashes of past failures.

In this chapter, the central concern is with understanding how the present international monetary system works to facilitate trade and finance among nations. However, it is impossible to understand and appreciate the present system without important references to the past. Thus, the first task of this chapter is to examine the evolution of the present system over time.

## THE PATHWAY TO THE PRESENT INTERNATIONAL MONETARY SYSTEM

For many years, most notably encompassing the seventeenth, eighteenth, and nineteenth centuries, the international means of payment for goods received from other nations was gold. There was simply no substitute for it. Most major trading nations used gold for domestic currency, and recognized gold as having a known and certain value. Stipulating that international transactions were to be settled by payment in gold seemed the only workable alternative. Importers regularly shipped gold bullion to exporters in other nations, in the holds of sailing ships often as not. International money *was* gold, in the first phase of the evolution of our monetary system.

As time passed, the role of gold was gradually reduced, and finally eliminated. At present, international money is not connected in any substantive way with gold, but is a combination of paper assets not unlike domestic money in the United States. How did gold evolve from being the star of the international show to not even being in the cast? To answer this, we will first examine the international monetary system as it existed at the time gold played its most important role.

## The Gold-Standard Era

A *gold standard* is a system of international payments in which a nation guarantees the free exchange of gold and paper money at a set price. Going "on" the gold standard means putting such a guarantee into force, and going "off" the gold standard means abandoning such a guarantee. The United States had been on and off the gold standard in the decades prior to 1879. In that year, the United States joined most other major trading nations in adopting the gold standard. The gold-standard era was thus born, and lasted until 1913.

The way a gold-standard nation guarantees a set price of gold is by offering to either buy or sell it at a set price, plus or minus small handling charges. Thus, if the United States agrees to buy and/or sell gold at $20 per ounce, then the market price cannot stray from this amount. (No one buying could find a seller who would sell for less, since the gold could always be sold to the government at $20, and no seller could find a buyer willing to pay more than $20, with the government ready to sell at $20.) The guarantee to buy and/or sell at a fixed price is called *pegging* the value of a currency. Because other nations know that the dollar can be exchanged for a set amount of gold, the value of the dollar for international transactions is also fixed in terms of gold.

If two nations peg the value of their currencies relative to gold, then they also fix the exchange rate between the two currencies. To see why, consider a situation where the Bank of England has set the value of the British pound at 4 pounds per ounce of pure gold, while the U.S. Treasury has set the value of the U.S. dollar at $20 per ounce of pure gold. Then, an exchange rate of $20 \div 4 = 5$ dollars per pound between the two currencies is fixed. With both currencies tied to gold in a fixed way, they are necessarily tied together.

During the gold-standard era, all major trading nations pegged their currencies to gold.[1] Exchange rates among major trading currencies were defined by the combination of these pegged values, thus constituting a system of *fixed exchange rates*.

Under the fixed-exchange-rate system in place between 1879 and 1913, it was frequently the case that excess supplies of some currencies appeared on foreign-exchange markets, at the same time that demand exceeded supply for others. Indeed, whenever a nation imported more than it exported for longer than a year or two, an excess supply of its currency would inevitably appear on foreign-exchange markets. When such an excess supply appeared, the central bank of the nation involved had to intervene, buying up the excess supply of its own currency, paying primarily with gold and secondarily with other currencies. Only by intervention could the government make good on its guarantee to fix the currency vis-à-vis gold, for otherwise the exchange rate would fall to clear the market, exactly as in the exchange rate supply-demand model discussed in the preceding chapter. When excess demand for a currency appeared, as in the case of a nation running a surplus in international payments, the surplus nation's central bank had to intervene to keep the exchange rate from rising, by selling its currency in return for gold and other currencies.

Thus, under the 1879–1913 gold-standard system, when a nation ran a deficit in its international payments balance, the result was an outflow of official holdings of gold, so that the exchange rate would be stabilized. A nation running a surplus in its international payments experienced an inflow of gold as it supplied more of its currency on exchange markets to prevent the exchange rate from rising.

Besides gold flows occurring as a result of the intervention of central banks, gold flows among nations also resulted from trading between exporters and importers. However, often as not, private gold flows also caused additions or subtractions in official holdings, as people receiving gold sold it to their central bank for their own currency.

In any event, the shipment of gold among nations proved to be costly in terms of time, storage costs, and losses caused by theft. As a result, businesses in various nations cautiously began using forms of paper money instead.

The bill of exchange is an example of this. A *bill of exchange* is the guarantee of a bank to pay a fixed sum of money in a specified currency after a fixed period of time. Importers and exporters began to buy and sell existing unmatured bills of exchange in what amounted to a secondary market. This meant gold shipments could be avoided.

To see how this works, suppose a British importer has a payment in dollars to make to a U.S. exporter. Rather than shipping gold, the British importer could use British pounds to buy a dollar-denominated bill of exchange (belonging to a British exporter who had sold a prod-

1. Some also pegged their currencies to silver, forming a dual or bimetallic standard.

uct to a U.S. buyer and received the bill of exchange in payment). Because the bill of exchange is a claim on dollars, the British importer can use it to pay the bill for the U.S. products being imported to Great Britain.

Used this way, bills of exchange became a form of international paper money. Their successful use to finance international transactions depended entirely on how much faith exporters and importers had in their ability to carry value from one nation to another. As the twentieth century progressed, international traders came more and more to accept the bill of exchange and documents like it as a kind of makeshift form of international money.

## The Gold-Exchange Standard

World War I brought with it a fragmentation of the gold-standard system, as several important trading nations were no longer willing to buy and sell gold at fixed prices during the war. When the war ended, higher world prices coupled with an increased level of international trade by most major trading nations created a need for an international monetary system with more liquidity and greater flexibility than the gold-standard system. What evolved was called the *gold-exchange standard.* With this modification of the gold standard, nations agreed to make payments of international debts in one of several prominent currencies rather than in gold. Most notably, the U.S. dollar and the British pound were designated as key currencies to be used for this purpose.

Rather than holding gold as international reserves, nations using the gold-exchange standard instead held short-term securities such as Treasury Bills, banker's acceptances, and bank deposits denominated mostly in dollars. The advantages were clear. Storage was no longer a problem. Transfer of ownership and of the reserve assets themselves was no longer cumbersome, but could be handled through the mail. Moreover, interest could be earned on the securities held. Also, the dollar-denominated securities could be exchanged for gold at the U.S. Treasury at the option of the security holder for a fixed price. Since the United States stood firmly behind its commitment to buy and sell gold for dollars at a set price per ounce, the securities held in international reserve accounts were "as good as gold."

The worldwide depression of the early 1930s crippled the U.S. domestic banking and financial system. It also threatened the stability of the U.S. international position, since many U.S. citizens joined foreign dollar holders in seeking to exchange paper dollars for gold. This "run" on the paper dollar was a product of deep fears of U.S. financial collapse held by the public during those times. Paper-money holders all over the world believed that gold had lasting value in the United States and elsewhere, but they questioned the value of the dollar and other paper currencies.

As a result of these problems, in April 1933, gold coins were called in by the U.S. Treasury along with all outstanding gold certificates. The Treasury temporarily discontinued sales and purchases of gold to all parties, including U.S. citizens. The dollar then had a *floating exchange rate* in that the rate was no longer fixed by the standing offer of the Treasury to buy and sell gold at a set price per ounce.

In 1934, the *Gold Reserve Act* further altered the U.S. international monetary system by creating a *gold-bullion standard*. Under this standard, U.S. citizens were prohibited from buying or selling gold to or from the Treasury, but the government was committed to buying and selling bullion at a fixed price per ounce internationally. Thus, the dollar no longer floated, but was again fixed by the Treasury's commitment.

## The Bretton Woods System

Discussions had taken place among allied nations during World War II about the needed changes in the international monetary system following the war. These discussions culminated in a series of agreements reached by major trading nations that met after the conflict at Bretton Woods, a resort in New Hampshire. The Bretton Woods system set up new institutions to govern the further development of the international monetary system in the postwar period. The overall philosophy of the Bretton Woods agreement was that the development and growth of international trade required more than the occasional meetings among nations that had characterized the prior system. Instead, international agencies were to be formed that would have as their mission the continual monitoring and governance of the entire system.

Two such institutions that originated in the Bretton Woods agreements have survived to the present time. One of these is the *World Bank,* an institution initially set up to facilitate the economic recovery of Western Europe after the devastation of the war. Nations could approach the World Bank for loans to finance this rebuilding process. The United States contributed heavily to the supply of loanable funds available to the World Bank. Once wartime reconstruction was complete, the World Bank turned its attention to providing capital for developing nations to use in their industrial development. This is the main function of the contemporary World Bank.

Perhaps the most important institution created by the Bretton Woods agreements is the *International Monetary Fund,* or IMF. The IMF has evolved as the monitoring and governing agency envisioned by the Bretton Woods philosophy. It sets up and deals with changes in the rules governing foreign-exchange markets, and controls exchange rates in selected cases where exchange rates are fixed. The IMF initially acquired a pool of currencies contributed by member nations. Individual members nations can apply to the IMF to borrow from this pool to help finance balance-of-payments deficits. Through the years, most member nations have borrowed from the IMF, and additional contributions have been obtained to facilitate the steady increase in borrowing that has accompanied growth in international trade and finance.

Even though there were increases in the funds contributed by member nations through the years, by the late 1960s the borrowing needs of member nations were putting strains on the lending capacity of the IMF. The need was clear for some form of internationally accepted credit that could be used to expand the pool of available credit beyond the contributed funds of members. The *Special Drawing Right,* or SDR, came into existence in the late 1960s to meet this need. The SDR is similar to an IMF check in that its holder can exchange it for foreign currencies to be used to finance international payments. SDRs can be signed over from one nation to another in return for currencies, and can pass into the hands of a third party, much as a private check in the U.S. banking system. From time to time, the IMF issues an additional quantity of SDRs to member nations, thus expanding the size of the pool of international currency. With the smooth transition to the use of SDRs, the international monetary system had come a long way toward reducing the role of gold in international transactions. There is no doubt that SDRs are a direct embodiment of paper money on the international basis.

In the years following World War II, the international monetary system that evolved via the Bretton Woods agreements essentially continued the gold-bullion standard of the prewar period. Most major exchange rates were fixed by the commitments of nations to freely exchange gold (or in some cases, silver) for currencies.

During the 1950s and early 1960s, the dollar was increasingly used as a reserve currency throughout Western Europe. Its value was secure, as the United States ran continual surpluses on its international accounts, thus producing a continual inflow of dollars. As dollars became scarce in Europe, gold was sold to the U.S. Treasury in exchange for dollars. Thus, the inflow of dollars translated into an inflow of gold. Gold reserves in the United States mounted steadily, thus deepening the "backing" of the dollar.

In the mid-1960s this situation began to turn around. A number of reasons combined to produce overall deficits in the U.S. payments position. Dollar deposits held abroad began to rise. From 1969 to 1971, the cumulative U.S. payments deficit was more than 40 billion dollars. This brought increasing exchanges for dollars held by foreigners for gold held by the U.S. Treasury. The gold outflow increased from a trickle to a stream. In the early 1970s, the dollar deposits held abroad exceeded the U.S. gold reserves by nearly three to one. Clearly, if even one-third of those holding dollar deposits sought to exchange them for gold at the U.S. Treasury, the U.S. supply of gold would be deleted. There could be no doubt that a major crisis was brewing as a result of this situation.

Speculators brought it to a head. When it became clear that the United States was nearly unable to honor its commitment to buy and sell gold at a fixed number of dollars per ounce, speculators saw that profits could be made if the exchange rate of the dollar were changed by any important degree. Since there was a glut of dollars on foreign-exchange markets, the direction of the required movement was clear. The price of gold had to be increased from $35 to $40 or $50, or perhaps more. Speculators holding dollar deposits sold them in exchange for other more stable currencies, or for gold. And, why not? If today $35 will buy an ounce of gold, and in a month that ounce can be exchanged for $50, the opportunity for profits is clear.

The speculative selling of dollars hastened the crisis along by adding greatly to the already existing glut of dollars on foreign-exchange markets. As a stop-gap measure, the United States increased the price of gold from $35 to $38. Far from solving the problem, this only whetted the appetite of the speculators, who had realized tangible profits from their dollar sales. They saw no fundamental change in the U.S. payments position or gold supply, and began selling in even larger numbers. The crisis deepened.

In August 1971, the United States negotiated the *Smithsonian agreement*, which suspended the commitment of the United States to buy and sell gold to private foreign buyers or sellers, but retained this commitment for gold purchases and sales to and from foreign governments. Thus, a *two-tier system* came into effect where the price of gold to foreign governments was fixed but where the price to private buyers and sellers was not fixed. Instead, the private price was free to fluctuate on world gold markets according to supply and demand. Because the official price remained fixed, exchange rates remained fixed.

The immediate result of the two-tier system was that the private price of gold soared to more than $100 per ounce while the official price remained at $38. Speculators again made large profits, but the stability of the dollar's exchange rate was not affected. Under the two-tier system, the rate of exchange of currency and gold fluctuated daily on gold markets while the rate of exchange of one currency with another remained fixed by the setting of official settlement prices for each currency vis-à-vis gold.

As the market price of gold departed farther and farther from the official price, the two-tier system became increasingly fragile. Many began asking questions such as "how can the United States continue to make official transactions in its gold account at prices that are less than one-third of the market price?", or "how long will other nations be willing to hold dollar-denominated reserves in lieu of gold when the market price of gold is three times higher than the official gold value of their reserves?" To the last question, the answer was not long in coming. France led the way first by expressing skepticism about the U.S. position, and then by buying gold from the United States to hold as official reserves in place of dollar-denominated securities. Because dollar-denominated reserves were being replaced by gold, the value of reserves increased by three times its original amount. To the French, the dollar was no longer "as good as gold." Other nations followed France's example in moderation. The dwindling U.S. gold supply now made it apparent that further changes were necessary beyond the two-tier system.

As a band-aid measure, the United States in February 1973 raised the official price of gold from $38 to $42.22 per ounce. Although this increased the dollar value of the U.S. gold stock by 11.5 percent, it did nothing to resolve the long-run problem of insufficient gold relative to growing dollar-denominated deposits abroad.

## The Floating-Rate System

One month after the 11.5 percent devaluation, the battered and broken gold-bullion standard finally suffered a killing blow. After the February announcement, further speculation sent the market price of gold soaring, and made it apparent to all nations that the two-tier system was doomed. In March 1973, major trading nations met in an emergency meeting in Brussels and agreed to abandon fixed exchange rates. For its part in this agreement, the United States suspended indefinitely all purchases and sales of gold to any parties. There was no longer an official price and a market price of gold.

At the same time, currency exchange rates were "cut loose" from the gold-related fixed parties of the past decades, and allowed to evolve to whatever levels cleared foreign-exchange markets. From the time of the meeting in Brussels onward, the international monetary system has been characterized by floating exchange rates. The arrangements informally agreed to in Brussels were formalized and officially adopted by IMF member nations at meetings held in January 1976 at Kingston, Jamaica. At those meetings, the fixed-exchange-rate structure established out of the Bretton Woods accords was formally abolished and replaced with a market-determined system of flexible exchange rates.

What about the role of gold in this new structure of flexible exchange rates? The dismantling of the fixed-exchange-rate system brought with it the abolishment of gold as a component of the international monetary system. Nations can still choose to hold reserves in gold in the present system, buying and selling it in return for the currencies they need to conduct international business. But, to do so involves trading in a highly fluctuating market. A nation would be just as well off to hold its reserves in copper, wheat, or hog bellies as in gold. Gold is a commodity in the present system, not a form of international money.

If gold is no longer our international money, what has replaced it? If we define international money specifically to mean a commonly accepted form of international payment, that is, an international me-

**TABLE 28.1.**
**The Changing Nature of International Money**

| ERA | INTERNATIONAL MONEY |
| --- | --- |
| Gold standard | Gold coin, certificates, and bullion, with a minor role for bills of exchange |
| Gold-exchange standard | Dollar-denominated securities, with some role for gold coin, certificates, and bullion |
| Gold-bullion standard | Dollar-denominated securities, with some role for gold bullion and a growing role for SDRs |
| Floating exchange rates | Securities denominated in many currencies, and SDRs |

dium of exchange, the answer is that international money has evolved over the years. Table 28.1 shows how international money has changed from the gold-standard era to the present time. In the gold-standard era, gold formed the centerpiece of the supply of international money. But, as the table shows, as we moved into the gold-exchange and gold-bullion eras, gold was joined by more and more paper assets, thus reducing the system's dependence on gold in international transactions.

As nations moved into the floating-exchange-rate era, the use of paper forms of international money had become sufficiently entrenched that gold could be eliminated altogether as a component of this money without noticeable effects on the liquidity of the international monetary system. Rather than crashing to the ground, gold silently slithered out of the system during the currency crisis of early 1973.

## THE PRESENT INTERNATIONAL MONETARY SYSTEM

In the years since gold was done away with and exchange rates were set loose to find their own levels, the present system has evolved some. But, so far, the changes from the Brussels agreements have been minor. Prior to the Brussels meetings, the dollar was a key reserve currency in that it was tied to gold via the U.S. commitment to buy and/or sell. After such commitments by all major trading nations were abandoned, there was no longer any particular reasons for nations to hold dollar-denominated reserves as opposed to any other currency. But, in selecting a reserve currency, a nation is interested in liquidity in being able to exchange its reserve assets for those denominated in other currencies. Thus, one important criterion is that a well-developed financial market exist in the nation whose currency is being held as reserves. Liquidity also requires that securities can be found in such markets in which there is regularly a large volume of trading—such that the transactions of a foreign official government would not greatly disturb the market. The dollar has

To: Those who watch the stock market and oil prices
From: JWE

The stock market is thought by some Wall Street pros to be the final arbitrator of whether a world event is good or bad. This memo describes a curious illustration of the point. In early 1983, the OPEC oil ministers ended a multiday series of meetings in near-disarray. From statements issued by several of the participants, the OPEC cartel was on the verge of collapse. Oil prices appeared headed downward by several dollars a barrel. When the news reached Wall Street, a widespread selloff occurred. To the uninitiated, this was a mystery. The prospect of lower oil prices seemed to translate into lower gasoline prices, and lower prices for everything produced from petroleum. The likelihood of a clearly lower inflation rate seemed to follow. So, why did investors greet the news of the crumbling cartel with such a lack of enthusiasm?

Something else was on their collective mind. From about 1974 onward, U.S. banks had been making increasingly large loans to non–OPEC oil-producing nations such as (and most notably) Mexico and Venezuela. Generally, these loans were not made by a single bank, but by groups of banks, each taking a percentage of the loan. The loans typically were made at very attractive interest rates, and soon became an asset highly pursued by larger U.S. banks.

When oil prices continued to weaken in late 1982, signs began to appear that some of the borrowing nations may have trouble repaying. The repayment plans of the oil-producing nations were premised on prevailing oil prices, and depended in no small way on future flows of oil revenues. Analysts who began to add up what this meant for U.S. banks found out that in some cases, the total participation in loans made to such oil-producing nations exceeded the net worth of specific banks.

Thus, when the news broke that oil prices may be headed downward still further, the positive anti-inflationary side of the story was swamped by the fear that loan defaults by non–OPEC oil producers may lead to the collapse of one or more large U.S. banks. The nightmare that followed this scenario involved the general collapse of the banking system, panic, and depression.

However, the stock market quickly stabilized when the IMF raised its colors. This organization began to take a more active role in the situation, including marshaling a large fund of money that could be made available to back up problem loans. Thus, the market's immediate fears were overcome. But, the situation illustrates the growing interdependence of nations in an era of widespread international banking.

proved to be an ideal currency in this respect. As a result, the dollar accounts for upward of 80 percent of the western world's reserves. Thus, the dollar still remains a key reserve currency, but now because of the large, liquid, short-term financial markets in the United States, rather than because of the government's commitment to buy and sell gold. Rather than being "as good as gold," the dollar held as a reserve currency is "as good as the T-Bill market."

In the Brussels accords and more formally at the Jamaica meetings, the European nations developed a modified version of the floating-rate system that solves communication and clerical problems. If all European currencies floated against all other currencies, a large and fluctuating matrix of exchange rates would have to be continually maintained throughout Europe. Although this would be a delight for currency arbitragers, it would create administrative headaches for both foreign-exchange dealers and governments. Thus, from the beginning of the floating-rate era, some European exchange rates have been fixed against each other, but allowed to jointly float against the dollar. This makes the European currencies perform as a single currency when compared with the dollar. In 1979, all major European countries agreed to formalize this arrangement into the *European Monetary System*, a structure that fixes European exchange rates against each other, but jointly floats this array of rates against the dollar. When currency imbalances develop among European currencies, the fixed rates are changed to correct the condition.

The experience with floating exchange rates has generally been positive. Since their introduction, no major currency crises have occurred, even though the OPEC oil embargo and massive price increases in oil have thrown payments balances into large deficits in many oil-importing nations. The floating-exchange-rate system has led to exchange rates adjusting, often rapidly and significantly, in response to events such as OPEC. But, there have been no runs on currencies, no closing down of exchange markets as in the crises of the early 1970s. Instead, the markets in foreign exchange have quietly adjusted away imbalances between supply and demand by changing exchange rates. Moreover, the self-adjusting feature of the floating-rate system, discussed in the previous chapter, has worked, albeit not perfectly.

In the years since Brussels, the use of SDRs has been more frequent and sophisticated. They are indeed evolving as the IMF's check. To illustrate the use of SDRs in the contemporary system, let us suppose that West Germany is in need of francs. It indicates to the IMF that it wants to turn in a quantity of SDRs it holds to obtain francs. The IMF responds by examining the positions of various members to find one that can comfortably accept the SDRs in return for some other currency—that is, a nation with surplus holdings of some major currency. Suppose that the IMF determines that Japan has large-enough dollar balances that it can participate in the exchange. The IMF has the authority to designate Japan as the recipient of West Germany's SDRs in return for dollar balances that Japan is holding as a result of a Japanese trade surplus with the United States. Thus, Japan gets SDRs in return for dollars. West Germany gets these dollars in return for SDRs, which it then exchanges for the francs it needs on the foreign-exchange market. In this and most international transactions involving SDRs, the IMF plays the role of broker, arranging trades of assets among member nations.

**1.** A gold standard is a system of international payments in which a nation guarantees the free exchange of gold and paper money at a set price. The government makes good on this guarantee by honoring a standing commitment to buy and sell gold at a fixed rate per ounce.

**2.** If two nations peg the value of their currencies relative to gold, then they also fix the exchange rate between the two currencies.

**3.** When a nation on the gold standard runs a deficit in its balance of payments, the result is an outflow of gold from official holdings. This can come about by sales to those wanting to exchange dollars for gold, or because the nation needs to buy its own currency in foreign-exchange markets to keep the exchange rate at its set level.

**4.** Under a gold-exchange standard, nations agree to hold reserves in securities denominated in one or more key currencies. The dollar was the dominant key currency during the gold-exchange era. Settlement of international debts was increasingly done in dollar-denominated securities rather than in gold.

**5.** As long as the key-currency nation maintained the commitment to buy and sell gold at a fixed rate, then reserves denominated in these currencies became the equivalent in value to gold.

**6.** The worldwide depression of the 1930s caused modifications in the international monetary system. After a brief period of floating exchange rates, the United States adopted a gold-bullion standard in which private purchases of gold by U.S. citizens were prohibited while purchases and sales to foreigners were retained, with payment being exclusively in bullion. In going on this standard, the United States retired all gold-based domestic money, and went off the gold standard domestically.

**7.** After World War II, the need was apparent for reformulations in the international monetary system. At Bretton Woods, major changes were made in the institutional structure of the system, most importantly involving the creation of the World Bank and the International Monetary Fund (IMF).

**8.** The IMF evolved into the agency that controls and manages the international monetary system on a continuous basis.

**9.** The IMF maintains a pool of national currencies that are available for lending to member nations that need to finance deficits.

**10.** In order for member nations to obtain credit beyond the limits of the available pool of currencies, the IMF introduced Special Drawing Rights (SDRs) as a form of IMF checks.

**11.** After World War II, the major western-world trading nations continued a gold-bullion standard, with dollar reserves playing a larger role in the supply of international money.

**Important Ideas in This Chapter**

**12.** In the late 1960s, a pattern of deficits in the U.S. payments position began to erode other nations' confidence in the dollar as a reserve currency.

**13.** Speculative runs on the dollar occurred on several occasions during the late 1960s and early 1970s, as private traders perceived that the U.S. commitment to hold the price of gold fixed could not be maintained.

**14.** After raising the price of gold proved unsuccessful in stabilizing the speculation against the dollar, the United States adopted a two-tier system in which gold had an official price among nations and a market price established on metals markets. The United States continued to fix the official price of gold.

**15.** The two-tier system proved to be a failure, as several important trading nations lost confidence in it, and further disruptions occurred in foreign-exchange markets.

**16.** To respond to the continuing crisis, the major nations of the world went off the gold standard and abandoned fixed exchange rates in early 1973, constructing a system of floating exchange rates.

**17.** Under the floating-exchange-rate system, all major European currencies are maintained in a fixed relationship with each other, but are allowed to jointly float against the dollar. The foreign-exchange market conditions of supply and demand thus determine the proper relationship between the dollar on the one hand and the entire group of European currencies on the other. Other currencies float directly against the dollar and against other currencies as well.

**18.** Gold, once the centerpiece of the world's money, has no role in the floating-rate system. International money has evolved into various currencies that are believed to be appropriate for reserve purposes, and SDRs. At present, the dollar is the dominant reserve currency.

**Discussion Questions**

**1.** Carefully distinguish between a gold standard, a gold-exchange standard, and a gold-bullion standard, noting the advantages and disadvantages you see in each system.

**2.** Why do you suppose it took the major trading nations of the world so long to evolve a floating-rate system? What are some of the disadvantages of a floating-rate system?

**3.** Professor Milton Friedman once argued that the problem with fixed exchange rates is that they are quite unstable, and the advantage of floating rates is that they are quite stable. Evaluate this argument based on what you have read here and elsewhere.

**4.** Examine the materials in a library that relate to the current activities of the IMF. From what you find, draw up a list of the most important continuing functions of the IMF at present.

**5.** Evaluate this statement: The reason the OPEC-related payments deficits did not destroy the system of international payments is that the oil-exporting nations had no choice but to hold financial assets denominated in a variety of currencies. To sell some on exchange markets in exchange for others would only have reduced the value of the remaining assets held in the weak currencies. Thus, floating rates were a great stabilizing force.

**For a good historical discussion of the IMF, see J. Carter Murphy,** *The International Monetary System, Beyond the First Stage of Reform,* Washington, D.C.: American Enterprise Institute, 1979. For an in-depth treatise on the post-World War II evolution of the international payments system, see Robert Solomon, *The International Monetary Systems, 1945–1976,* New York: Harper and Row, 1977. For a classic debate on the merits of fixed versus floating exchange rates, see Fritz Machlup, Gottfried Haberler, Henry C. Wallich, Peter B. Kenen, and Milton Friedman, "Round Table on Exchange Rate Policy," *American Economic Review, Papers and Proceedings,* 59, May 1969, pp. 357–69.

**Suggested Readings**

# FEATURE SECTION 6

## Accent on the Role of the Federal Reserve in the International Economy

Throughout our discussion of the Federal Reserve system (the Fed) and its function in financial markets and in banking, the concern has been with how the system interacts with and regulates the domestic economy. And properly so. After all, the Fed is the central bank of the United States. But, the Fed is also concerned with promoting stable conditions in international financial markets. The 1970s witnessed the evolution of an increasingly interrelated structure of money and capital markets in the western world. Today, it is not possible for a responsible U.S. central bank to remain aloof from financial problems elsewhere in the world. In this feature section, you can read about some of the ways in which the Fed is involved in international finance.

First, the Federal Reserve Bank of New York, acting as the agent for the U.S. Treasury, handles the day-to-day transactions that are necessary to transfer official reserves of governments from one account to another. Primary international reserves include gold, SDRs, and foreign-currency deposits of major nations with which the United States trades. Thus, a nation wishing to reduce its official reserve balance with the United States would deal with the Fed in carrying out the transactions necessary for this purpose.

Second, the Fed conducts its own foreign-currency operations to smooth out short-term fluctuations in exchange rates. The general policy of the Fed since the inception of the floating-rate system has been to allow the dollar to seek its own level. However, from time to time, unusual international events place heavy buying or selling pressures on the dollar. The Fed monitors this situation and reserves the right to intervene on a short-term basis to stabilize conditions.

Third, the Fed increasingly attempts to monitor the activities of foreign subsidiaries of U.S. banks. Even though such subsidiaries may be set up as separate corporations, their financial health and stability impact on the financial condition of the U.S. parent company or bank. This monitoring includes offshore banking (see the memo in chapter 26) as well as International Banking Facilities (IBFs). The growth of banking of this type has been explosive in recent years. Accordingly, the Fed's role in monitoring it is becoming more important and time-consuming as the 1980s progress.

Fourth, the Fed oversees the operations of foreign banks in the United States. Since passage of the 1978 International Banking Act, foreign banks operating in the United States are required to comply with most of the same regulations as domestic banks, which essentially means that the Fed is required to extend its regulatory structure to these banks.

Fifth, the Fed assumes broad responsibility for monitoring the general economic conditions in and the specific balance-of-payments condition of major trading-partner nations. The purpose of this monitoring is to formulate domestic monetary policy that is in harmony with international conditions as much as possible. For example, if the Fed sees the emergence of a recession in Japan, it can count on a reduced level of exports by U.S. firms to Japan, and can translate this into the effect on the U.S. balance-of-payments position. This in turn could generate a need for a change in the policies on money growth and interest-rate targets being followed by the Fed.

Similarly, by monitoring interest rates in other nations compared with those in the United States, the Fed can project the likely capital inflows or capital outflows that will result, and thus be in a position to offset the impact of these capital flows on reserves by its open-market policy.

As time passes, the United States is becoming more intertwined with its major trading partners. This growing interdependence will increase the need by the Fed to monitor and in some cases find ways to regulate the financial flows into and out of the domestic economy. Thus, it seems a sure bet that the role of the Fed in the international financial marketplace will increase over the decade of the 1980s.

*Note:* The numbers in parentheses just after each entry denote the chapter or chapters where the term is defined and discussed.

**Aftertax real wage (21)** real wages per hour minus taxes per hour

**Aggregate demand (13)** the total amount the public (including consumers, firms, governments, and net foreign demand) wants to buy.

**Aggregate demand and supply analysis (17)** an approach to determining prices. The amount demanded and the amount supplied determine the price level.

**Aggregate-supply function (16)** the relationship between prices and the amount firms are willing to produce.

**All-savers certificate (6)** a federally tax-exempt one-year note issued by thrift institutions whose interest rate is tied to a one-year Treasury bill.

**American Exchange (bonds) (24)** an organized exchange that lists bonds issued by the same types of corporations that are listed on the stock exchange of the same name.

**American Stock Exchange (Amex) (24)** the second largest stock exchange, where common stocks of private corporations are traded. It is located in New York City.

**Anticipated income (9)** an approach to bank-asset management that appeared after World War II and embraced the view that the security of any loan is ultimately determined by the ability of the borrower to repay.

**Arbitrage (26)** actions by market traders involving purchases and sales of financial contracts at prices that produce guaranteed short-term trading profits.

**Asking price (24)** in the over-the-counter market the dealer's offer to sell shares of stock at that price.

**Automatic Transfer Service (ATS) (6)** an account where funds are automatically transferred from an interest-bearing savings account to a checking account when a check is drawn.

**Autonomous spending (14)** spending that is independent of current economic activity and does not take place simply because people have more income.

**Balance on current account (27)** the difference between total dollar inflows resulting from exports and earnings and total outflows caused by imports, military, and other transfers.

**Balance sheet (2)** a financial statement showing the assets, liabilities, and net value of a business at a set point in time.

**Bank holding company (6)** a firm that owns one or more banks (holds all the shares) which constitute its main business

**Bank panic (3)** same as *bank run.*

**Bank run (7)** occurs when large numbers of depositors believe that their money is not safe in a certain bank and try to withdraw funds over a short period of time (a couple of days).

**Bank script (6, 7)** currency issued by a particular bank and backed by its own assets.

**Banker's acceptances (5, 26)** short-term fully discounted IOUs issued by corporations and backed by banks for a fee.

**Banking acts of 1933 and 1935 (10)** acts that modified the Federal Reserve act. Insituted the present structure of central governance of the Federal Reserve system with the creation of the seven-member, fourteen-year-term format of the Board of governors and established the centralized Federal Open-Market Committee.

**Banking institutions (2)** institutions that create checkable deposits, provide a safe place for depositors to store financial assets, and act as financial intermediaries.

**Barter system (1)** a system where goods trade for goods, with no medium of exchange.

**Bid-ask spread (24)** the point difference between the bid and the ask price, which becomes the compensation for the dealer on the over-the-counter market.

**Bid price (24)** in the over-the-counter market the dealer's offer to purchase shares of a stock at that price.

**Bill of exchange (26, 28)** a document that shows the transfer of goods and/or services in exchange for financial payment, and that closes an international transaction.

**Board of directors (5)** a committee elected by a firm's common-stock holders to represent them in top-level management decisions facing the firm.

**Board of Governors (10)** the seven-member decision-making body of the Federal Reserve.

**Bond (5)** a financial instrument having a set maturity date and a stated rate of interest. It is a debt obligation of the issuer.

**Borrowed liabilities (8)** funds that banks actively seek to borrow from the Federal Reserve, from nonbank financial institutions, and from abroad.

**Boston Exchange (24)** one of the four regional stock exchanges.

**Bracket creep (21)** the increasing income-tax rate that goes along with rising nominal (but not real) wage rates.

**Branch banks (6)** banks that have multiple offices from which the bank's business is conducted.

**Buyer's market (17)** a situation in which the level of supply exceeds the amount of aggregate demand, and the amount of purchasing power falls short of the amount of goods being sold.

$C + I + G + X$ curve (13) aggregate-demand function, which explains consumption, capital investment, government purchases, and net export expenditures.

Call option (24) a contract that gives the owner the right to buy shares of a stock at a preset price for a specified period of time.

Call price (5) the price at which a firm may retire a callable bond.

Callable bond (5) a bond that gives the issuing firm the option of retiring the bond prior to its maturity at a price stated in the bond.

Capital account (27) a statement showing the noncurrent capital flows of a nation.

Capital-account balance (27) the difference between capital inflows and capital outflows on the capital account statement.

Capital flow (27) a payment that occurs when a business investor in one nation invests in a new plant in another nation, or when a financial investor in one nation buys a security issued in another nation.

Capital goods (13) goods that add to the capital stock of business.

Capital markets (24) the markets where stocks, bonds, and other long-term securities are traded.

Capital stock (13) the factories, office buildings, machinery, equipment, and other long-lived assets used by business to produce its final products.

Certificate of deposit (5) commonly called a CD. The primary type of IOU issued by banks and savings and loan institutions.

Check-clearing process (2) the process of transferring reserves between banking institutions to settle claims arising from the normal practice of banks' honoring each other's checks.

Commercial banks (2, 6) state and federally chartered banks which traditionally have focused on the needs of commerce and business in their lending policies.

Commercial-loan theory (9) guidelines (for banks) stipulating that bank loans were to be short-term, self-liquidating, and "productive." Prevalent until about the end of the Civil War.

Commercial loans (6, 8) short-term, seasonal, inventory-financing loans made to business firms by commercial banks.

Commercial paper (5) a fully discounted corporation-issued short-term IOU having a maturity generally in the range of three to nine months.

Common stock (5) certificate of ownership of a corporation. Those who own the common stock of a corporation are collectively its legal owners.

Consumer asset (13) an asset that gives service in the present as well as in the future. It can be stored and is not used up upon purchase.

Consumer Price Index (CPI) (4) a measure of inflation calculated by the Bureau of Labor Statistics.

Consumption function (13) a curve showing the amount of consumer spending that associates with each GNP level.

Continual inflation (19) when one or more underlying influences on equilibrium prices steadily changes in a way that repeatedly pushes up the equilibrium price level.

Convertible bonds (5) a fixed coupon bond that can be converted into stock, based on a ratio of a unit of bonds for a set number of shares of common stock.

Corporate bonds (5) long-term IOUs issued by firms; they entitle the holder to regular interest payments and redemption of principal at a set maturity date.

Correspondent bank (7) a smaller bank that makes a deposit in a larger bank in exchange for services.

Cost of capital (13) the combined rate of return that a firm's stockholders, bondholders, and other financiers expect the firm to earn on the money they have jointly invested in it. The minimum investment standard.

Coupon equivalent yield (5) the yield for all non-coupon-bearing discounted securities, including T-Bills, commercial paper, and banker's acceptances. It is equivalent to the annual interest rate on coupon-bearing bonds.

Coupon rate (5) the set rate of interest of a bond, which the borrower pays at fixed intervals.

Credit instruments (5) vehicles by which a lender advances funds to a borrower in return for the borrower's IOU.

Credit lines (5) an arrangement between a bank and a firm authorizing the firm to overcharge on its checking account by an amount not to exceed a prearranged limit.

Credit market (18) the national financial arena where lenders bring funds to lend and borrowers come to borrow funds.

Credit-market equilibrium (18) the condition that exists when no net pressures are brought about to change either the interest rate or the volume of loanable funds. The supply of funds equals the demand for funds.

Credit unions (6) thrift institutions where the right to make deposits and borrow is restricted to people who belong to a related organization such as a trade union, religious group, firm, or profession.

Crowding out (15, 18) the depressing effect of increased government spending on private spending. Private spending is squeezed out of the credit market.

Currency (1) paper money. In present-day United States, nearly all outstanding currency is in the form of Federal Reserve Notes.

Currency Speculation (27) buying and selling deposits denominated in various currencies for the purpose of realizing speculative gains associated with fluctuations in exchange rates.

Cyclical GNP (4) the parts of the economy that have severe cyclical fluctuations. These include the production of capital goods and consumer durable goods, and the change in business inventories.

**Debenture (5)** a corporate bond not secured by any specific collateral but backed by the general assets of the firm that issues it.

**Default risk (2, 5)** risk that a debtor will not repay a debt.

**Defensive operations (12)** the Federal Open-Market Committee buys and sells from the Federal Reserve's portfolio in such a way as to offset the effect of uncontrollable factors on reserves.

**Deficient demand (18)** a condition where the level of aggregate demand is lower than the amount of production, so that some portion of current production goes unsold.

**Deflation (4)** a negative rate of inflation.

**Demand deposits (1, 2)** deposits that are redeemable on demand, which the public makes in financial institutions.

**Demand-for-labor curve (16)** the relationship between the real wage rate and the profit-maximizing amount of labor hours to be used by firms. The demand for labor is a negative function of the real wage.

**Demand for loanable funds (18)** the sum of business, government, and consumer borrowing plans. It is a downward-sloping function of the real rate of interest.

**Demand for money (15)** the amount of money people and firms want to hold.

**Demand-management policies (21)** policies that seek to manage the level of total demand in the economy by adjusting the government's part of it in such a way as to stabilize the total.

**Deposit multiplier (2)** the maximum amount by which demand deposits can expand for each dollar of new reserves, given by the expression $1/r_d$, where $r_d$ is the required reserve ratio.

**Depository-Institution Deregulation and Monetary Control Act of 1980 (10)** a law stating that all depository institutions—commercial banks, savings and loans associations, mutual savings banks, credit unions, and U.S. branches of foreign banks—are subject to the same reserve requirements on transaction-type (checkable) accounts and nonpersonal time deposits.

**Depository-institution reserve equation (11)** an expression showing the sources and uses of bank reserves in the U.S. banking system.

**Depository institutions (6)** financial institutions that hold checkable deposits. These include commercial banks, savings and loan associations, mutual savings banks, and credit unions.

**Depression (1)** a very severe recession.

**Discount rate (3)** the rate of interest on Federal Reserve loans to banks.

**Discount window (3)** a term that refers to the offer by the Federal Reserve system to loan funds to depository institutions on a short-term basis so the depository institutions can meet reserve requirements. Such lending is said to occur "through the discount window."

**Discretionary monetary policy (21)** a policy of the Fed-

eral Reserve for responding to a recession. It involves expanding the level of bank reserves when the economy weakens, thus enabling banking institutions to expand the money supply.

**Disintermediation (10)** occurs when savers bypass financial intermediaries and go directly to primary financial markets such as Treasury Bills or other short-term notes.

**Dollar inflow (27)** a reduction in the net dollar-denominated claims held by foreigners.

**Dollar outflow (27)** an increase in net dollar-denominated claims held by foreigners.

**Downwardly rigid wages (16)** a condition where wages do not adjust downward in response to an excess supply of labor.

**Dual-charter system (6, 7)** the banking system operating in the United States. A newly formed bank has the option of applying for either a state or federal charter, and an existing bank can apply to change its charter from one type to the other.

**Durable goods (4)** products that last longer than a year, are thought of as possessions by their owners, and include such goods as automobiles, motorcycles, and bicycles.

**Dynamic operations (12)** the Federal Reserve Bank of New York buys and sells from the Federal Reserve's (Fed's) portfolio to either increase or decrease the level of reserves to carry out the Fed's policy directives. In contrast, *defensive operations* are open-market changes that respond to outside influences rather than policy directives.

**Economic policy (21)** the guidelines, rules, and general dos and don'ts that apply to the economy; they are established by the presidential administration, and usually follow from applying theory.

**Edge Act corporations (26)** domestic bank subsidiaries located in the United States that must engage in strictly international operations. They are exempt from many domestic banking regulations.

**Efficient market (24)** a market in stocks or bonds where the prices of all securities remain continuously adjusted to changing information affecting their value.

**Equation of exchange (20)** an accounting identity that defines the nominal GNP in two different ways. It is stated as $(M)(V) = (P)(y)$, where $M$ is the money supply, $V$ is the income velocity of money (ratio of GNP to $M$), $P$ is the aggregate price level, and $y$ is the real GNP.

**Equilibrium price (17)** the price level that equates the amount of aggregate demand with the amount of aggregate supply. At equilibrium, no net forces are working to bring about a change in price.

**Equity instruments (5)** vehicles by which investors supply permanent financing to firms or other borrowers. The investors are part-owners of the firm in which they have placed their funds. Common stock is an example.

**Eurobond market (26)** the international market for long-term debt capital involving currencies of other nations.

**Eurodollar deposits (5,9)** various types of IOUs issued

by European and United Kingdom banks and held by both United States citizens and investors in other nations.

**Eurodollar loans (5)**   dollar-denominated loans made by European and United Kingdom banks.

**Eurodollar market (5)**   the market in which eurodollar lending takes place. It is the market for dollar-denominated deposits and loans held by and/or originated by mostly European financiers.

**European Monetary System (28)**   a structure that fixes European exchange rates against each other, but jointly floats this array of rates against the dollar.

**Exchange rate (27)**   the price of one nation's currency relative to that of another nation's currency. An *exchange rate* shows the number of units of one currency that is needed to buy a unit of the other currency.

**Expansion (4)**   occurs in the economy when the real GNP rises over two or more quarterly periods.

**Expectations theory (25)**   theory of the term structure of interest rates; it hypothesizes financial-market equilibrium will occur when forward interest rates are equal to expectations of future spot rates.

**Expected real rate (5)**   the real rate of interest anticipated by investors at the time financial contracts are negotiated. It is equal to the nominal rate of interest on a financial contract minus the rate of inflation anticipated to prevail over the contract's life.

**Export letter (26)**   a letter of credit guaranteeing payment in the exporter's currency.

**Federal Advisory Council (10)**   a twelve-person committee with one member from each Federal Reserve district. It has no authority but gives advice on monetary policy in the form of resolutions, papers, and memoranda.

**Federal-agency bonds and notes (5)**   long-term coupon-bearing IOUs issued by federal agencies such as the agricultural-support agencies, mortgage-assistance agencies, and other housing-related agencies.

**Federal Deposit Insurance Corporation (FDIC) (7)**   a government-formed entity that insures the deposits of commercial banks.

**Federal funds (9)**   banks' excess reserves which are borrowed by other banks with deficient reserves, with the transfer of funds arranged by the Federal Reserve system. In federal-funds markets, such lending of reserves occurs for periods of time ranging from overnight to several days.

**Federal Open-Market Committee (FOMC) (10)**   a twelve-person committee that oversees open-market operations, consisting of the seven members of the Board of Governors plus five other people.

**Federal Reserve Act of 1913 (10)**   the act that defined the original structure of the Federal Reserve system.

**Federal Reserve Board (2, 3)**   a governmental body composed of seven appointed officials who are responsible for deciding on the policies and regulatory actions to be implemented by the Federal Reserve system.

**Federal Reserve Bulletin (3)**   a monthly publication by the Federal Reserve that provides financial information to the banking and investment community.

**Federal Reserve districts (3)**   twelve geographic areas, each containing a regional Federal Reserve bank.

**Federal Reserve float (11)**   cash items in process of collection minus deferred-availability cash items.

**Federal Reserve Notes (11)**   the nation's active supply of currency.

**Federal Reserve system (3)**   the governmental agency that regulates the U.S. banking industry.

**Fiat money (1)**   an asset that has been decreed "money" by a government, after the Latin word *fiat*, meaning "Let it be done."

**Final sales (4)**   a measure of total sales of GNP products derived by subtracting from the GNP the amount of inventory change.

**Finance companies (6)**   financial institutions that make short-term loans to consumers for the purchase of durable goods such as automobiles, appliances, furniture, and televisions.

**Financial assets (23)**   assets that are either money or claims on money; they include checking accounts, savings accounts, bonds, stocks, and so forth.

**Financial instrument (5)**   an IOU written by a borrower and given to a lender in return for the lender's check.

**Financial intermediary (2)**   an institution such as a bank or thrift which creates deposit accounts that may be readily exchanged at face value for cash, and which uses depositors' funds to invest in the securities of business and government.

**Financial markets (5, 24)**   communication links by which borrowers and lenders conduct business. An arena where lenders and borrowers make deals for the funds that lenders want to lend and borrowers want to borrow.

**Fixed exchange rates (28)**   a system in which all major trading nations peg their currencies to gold. Exchange rates among these nations are defined by the combination of these pegged values.

**Float (2)**   the difference between the recorded demand deposits at a bank and the actual reserves at the Federal Reserve.

**Floating exchange rate (28)**   an exchange rate set by the forces of supply and demand, in contrast to fixed exchange rates which are set by governments.

**Flow-of-funds matrix (23)**   a matrix showing the sources and uses of funds for each major sector of the economy and for the economy as a whole. It shows explicitly how balance-sheet changes in household, business, and financial sectors interrelate.

**Foreign affiliate (26)**   a bank that is chartered and operated in a foreign country, but is owned by a U.S. bank holding company.

**Foreign branches (26)**   branches of U.S. banks that are located in foreign countries.

**Foreign correspondent banks (26)**   non-U.S. banks that

maintain deposits and other accounts in U.S. banks in exchange for banking services.

**Forward market in foreign exchange (26)** an exchange market where one country exchanges its domestic currency for another country's currency to be delivered at a later date.

**Full employment (4)** the level of employment where all job seekers are employed except those who are out of work for temporary reasons, those who are seasonally unemployed, those who lack sufficient training to compete for available jobs, and those who have marketable skills but are geographically immobile.

**Futures contract (24)** a contract that entitles the holder to buy a fixed quantity of either a commodity or a financial instrument at a price stated in the contract, at a time in the future specified by the contract.

**Futures markets (24)** markets where contracts are originated and traded that give the holder the right to buy something in the future, at a price specified by the contract.

**GNP deflator (4)** the index that converts or deflates the current-dollar GNP into the real GNP.

**Gold-bullion standard (28)** the international monetary standard in effect in the United States from 1934 to the early 1970s, whereby U.S. citizens were prohibited from buying gold while the government was still buying and selling gold for its international dealings.

**Gold certificates (11)** legal claims held by the Federal Reserve on gold that is physically held by the U.S. Treasury.

**Gold-exchange standard (28)** a modification of the gold standard whereby nations agree to make payments of international debts in one of several prominent currencies rather than in gold.

**Gold Reserve Act (28)** the 1934 act that designated gold bullion as the standard of exchange between nations.

**Gold standard (28)** a system of international payments in which a nation guarantees the free exchange of gold and paper money at a set price.

**Government spending (4)** a spending category of the GNP. It includes all the spending on goods and services bought from the private sector by federal, state, and local governmental units, plus the cost of all governmental units of the services they provide.

**Government transfer payment (13)** an incomelike payment by the government that is made without the recipient rendering a service or selling a product in return.

**Gresham's law (1)** undervalued money always drives overvalued money out of circulation.

**Gross National Product (GNP) (4)** the centerpiece of the National Income Accounting system that measures overall economic activity. It is the final value of domestically produced goods and services sold to final users.

**Gross Private Domestic Investment (4, 13)** a spending category of the GNP including all the spending by business on factories, machinery, and equipment; all the spending on new houses, apartments, and other residential structures; and the amount of inventory change.

**Hedging (24)** forming a structure of financial contracts in a way that insures they will have a set total value at a specified time in the future.

**Holding company (6)** see *bank holding company*.

**Household savings (18)** the difference between Disposable Personal Income and household expenditures on personal consumption goods and other personal outlays.

**Human capital (13)** the market value of consumers' labor skills.

*IS* **curve (15)** a curve showing all the combinations of interest rates and real GNP levels that equate aggregate demand with the amount of real GNP produced.

*IS–LM* **model (15)** the nominal IS curve and the LM curve on the same graph.

**Identity (20)** a mathematical statement that is true by definition.

**Import letter (26)** a letter of credit guaranteeing payment in the importer's currency.

**Income-expenditure multiplier (14)** also known as the *multiplier*. The multiplier shows that more production creates more income which leads to more spending. The simplest form of the multiplier is $1/(1 - b)$, where $b$ is the marginal propensity to consume.

**Income velocity of money (20)** the number of times per accounting period that money turns over in the form of GNP. It is the ratio of GNP to the money supply.

**Individual investors (24)** people who buy and sell stocks for their own account, using their own accumulated savings.

**Individual loans (8)** loans made to people as opposed to firms.

**Induced spending (14)** the type of spending that increases when people have more income.

**Inflation (1, 4)** a persistent and significant increase in the general level of prices.

**Inflation rate (20)** the percentage change in the price level.

**Installment loans (8)** loans with a periodic repayment schedule, used to finance purchases of automobiles or other durable goods.

**Institutional investors (24)** professionals who manage someone else's money. Included in this group are pension-fun managers, mutual-fund managers, trust-fund managers, and insurance-company investors.

**Insurance company (6)** a financial institution that receives inflows from premiums from policies and other contracts made with their customers, and has outflows in the form of claims made by policyholders and other contractual payments. Accumulated funds are invested in earning assets.

**Insurance-company investors (24)** institutional investors in the stock market who invest the insurance reserves amassed by the insurance companies.

**Intended inventory changes (14)** the additions to inventory that firms intend to make when sales rise.

**Interest-rate risk (2)** the risk of having to sell a bond or note at a loss before it matures.

**Intermittent inflation (19)** periods of inflation interrupted by periods of price stability or deflation.

**Internal rate of return (13)** same as *yield*. The rate of discount that equates the present value of a bond's stream of earnings with its market price.

**International Banking Act of 1978 (26)** under this act, foreign banks operating in the United States are required to comply with U.S. banking laws, with only minor exceptions.

**International Banking Facilities (IBFs) (26)** either a foreign bank or a foreign branch of a domestic bank that operates in the United States. They are regulated as though they were located abroad.

**International Monetary Fund (IMF) (28)** the agency that sets up and deals with changes in the rules governing foreign-exchange markets, and controls exchange rates in selected cases where exchange rates are fixed. The agency also arranges loans to member nations having financial problems.

**International Monetary System (28)** a system of rules for conducting international business, and the regulatory bodies that police the rules.

**Inventory-sales ratio (14)** the ratio of inventory levels to sales, which gives an indication of unintended buildups or drawdowns in inventories. This ratio can be an indicator of subsequent changes in production.

**Investment (13)** something for which you put some money down now in anticipation of a stream of returns later.

**Joint product market and monetary equilibrium (15)** the point on an IS-LM model where the IS and LM curves intersect.

**Keynesian (22)** An economist who adheres to the economic theory of John Maynard Keynes; the theory concerns the role of aggregate demand in setting the level of production.

**L (5)** a definition of money. M3 + eurodollar deposits (longer than overnight) + U.S. savings bonds + short-term Treasury securities + banker's acceptances + commercial paper.

**LM curve (15)** a curve showing all the combinations of interest rates and real GNP levels that produce monetary equilibrium when the real money supply is unchanged.

**Labor-force capacity (14)** the maximum amount of labor hours usable in the economy at a point in time.

**Laffer curve (21)** the net relationship between income-tax rates and total tax revenues collected. It arises from the effect of income-tax rates on the incentive to work.

**Large-denomination certificate of deposit (CD)(5,9)** a CD of $100,000 and up, bought predominantly by business and investment funds.

**Legal tender (7)** a legal means to settle debt.

**Letter of credit (26)** a document used in international trade that gives a bank's guarantee of payment for an international obligation.

**Liability management (9)** the strategy of raising funds for investment by actively seeking liabilities whenever attractive investment opportunities appear and market conditions permit.

**Liquidity trap (18)** the portion of the money-demand function where the demand for money becomes infinitely elastic. In the liquidity trap, the public is willing to hold more or less money balances with little or no change in the interest rate.

**Loan production office (LPO)(6)** a small facility that may be set up beyond a bank's chartered geographic area to market and service loans, primarily commercial loans.

**Loanable-funds theory (18)** a theory of how the real rate of interest is set, it focuses on the supply of and demand for loanable funds in credit markets.

**Long-term financial instruments (5)** financial instruments having maturities greater than one year.

**MI(1,5)** a definition of money. Currency + demand deposits + traveler's checks + other checkable deposits.

**M2 (5)** a definition of money. MI + overnight repurchase agreements and eurodollars + money-market mutual-fund shares held by individuals + savings accounts + small-denomination CDs.

**M3 (5)** a definition of money. M2 + large-denomination CDs + repurchase agreements (longer than overnight) + money-market mutual-fund shares held by institutions.

**MPL = W/P (16)** the point where the marginal product of labor equals the real wage. Profits are maximized at this point.

**Marginal product of labor (MPL) (16)** The additional production that an additional labor hour produces when other inputs to production are fixed.

**Medium of exchange (1)** an asset that may be exchanged or traded for another asset.

**Member bank (7)** a bank that belongs to the Federal Reserve system.

**Merchandise trade balance (27)** the difference between merchandise exports and merchandise imports.

**Midwest Exchange (24)** one of the four regional stock exchanges. It is located in Chicago.

**Monetarist (22)** an economist who attributes a central role to fluctuations in the money supply in the economy and is guided strongly by the quantity theory.

**Monetary base (12)** the portion of the money-supply-generating process over which the Federal Reserve has a strong measure of direct control. It consists of the level of bank reserves plus vault cash plus the currency in the hands of the nonbank public.

**Monetary equilibrium (15)** when the real demand for money equals the real amount of money outstanding.

**Money deposit (15)** any type of checkable account that can be directly used for transactions.

**Money growth (20)** the percentage change in the supply of money.

**Money-market certificates (5)** six-month $10,000 notes issued by banks, savings and loan associations, and other financial institutions. These notes carry rates of interest set in accordance with the six-month T-Bill rate.

**Money-market deposit account (5)** an account issued by banks and thrift institutions. It has no minimum maturity, allows limited check-writing privileges, and pays a rate of interest that compares with that paid by money-market mutual funds.

**Money-market mutual funds (5)** pools of funds invested in short-term financial instruments.

**Money markets (24)** financial markets where short-term notes such as Treasury Bills, commercial paper, and banker's acceptances are traded.

**Money multiplier (12)** a formula showing how much the money supply expands for each dollar of the monetary base. It is given by M1/monetary base.

**Mortgage bond (5)** a corporate note secured by the firm's buildings and equipment.

**Mortgage loans (8)** loans secured by a claim on real assets.

**Multiplier (14)** see income-expenditure multiplier.

**Municipal bonds (5)** coupon-bearing IOUs issued by state, county, and city governments, as well as other local governmental units. Maturities range from one to twenty or more years.

**Mutual-fund managers (24)** institutional investors who invest funds made available by individuals who buy shares in mutual funds as a way of participating in the stock market without the experience or confidence to do so by directly buying stocks.

**Mutual funds (6)** investment pools consisting of stocks, bonds, money-market instruments, gold, or any combination of these assets mutually owned by those who contribute money to them.

**Mutual savings bank (6)** a thrift institution that is legally owned by its depositors, who obtain ownership shares in the bank upon depositing funds.

**National Income Accounting (NIA) system (4)** various measures describing the level of total production, income, and spending in the United States. This system is used in making judgments about whether the economy is going down or up and what sectors are contributing to the trend.

**Natural-rate hypothesis (18)** the contention that the labor market is approximately fully adjusted most of the time so that the amount of employment and the rate of unemployment are usually at their equilibrium or natural levels.

**Natural rate of unemployment (18)** the unemployment rate corresponding to a fully adjusted labor market. It measures those who are unemployed as a result of skill barriers, seasonal factors, frictional factors, and geographic immobility.

**Negotiable (5)** a legal attribute of a financial contract that

enables it to be sold prior to maturity, by the party holding it. A negotiable contract is more liquid than a nonnegotiable contract.

**Negotiable Order of Withdrawal (NOW) (6)** an interest-bearing savings accunt upon which the holder can write an order of withdrawal of funds that can be transferred to a third party.

**Neoclassicist (22)** an economist who adheres to the classical system of economic thought that preceded Keynes. Neoclassicists believe that the natural-rate hypothesis is a good approximation of the way the world works, and feel the labor market is in equilibrium most of the time.

**Net exports (4)** a spending category of the GNP that includes the amount of U.S. production purchased by foreign consumers minus the amount of foreign production bought by U.S. consumers.

**Net worth (2,8,23)** total assets minus total liabilities. The net worth of a bank is the portion of commercial-bank assets financed by the ownership capital invested in the bank by shareholders, and retained in the firm by bank managers.

**New York Exchange (bonds) (24)** an organized exchange that lists bonds issued by the same type of corporations listed on the parallel stock exchange.

**New York Stock Exchange (NYSE) (24)** an organized exchange on Wall Street in New York City where common stocks of private corporations are traded. It is the largest exchange.

**Nominal GNP (4)** the GNP expressed in current prices, unadjusted for inflation.

**Nominal IS curve (15)** an IS curve with the interest rate on the vertical axis being a nominal rate and the GNP on the horizontal axis as usual.

**Nonborrowed reserves (12)** total reserves less borrowings from the Federal Reserve system. It is the guide to day-to-day actions by the open-market desk.

**Noncyclical GNP (4)** the parts of the economy that are insulated from recession. These include consumer nondurables and services plus government spending.

**Nondepository institution (6)** a financial institution that does not hold checkable deposits, such as an insurance company or a security broker.

**Nondurable goods (4)** goods that last a short period of time, generally less than one year. Nondurable goods include food, clothing, shoes, and drinks.

**Noninflationary (4)** a period of time in which no persistent rise in general prices occurs.

**Noninflationary money-growth rate (20)** a growth rate in money that equals the difference between the growth rate in the real GNP and the growth rate in the income velocity of money. According to the quantity theory, money growth at this rate will be noninflationary.

**Nonmember bank (7)** a bank that does not belong to the Federal Reserve system.

**Nonresidential fixed investment (13)** the part of the GNP measuring capital investment.

**One-bank holding company (6)** a holding company that

owns all the stock in one bank and owns no other banks or related firms.

**Open-market desk (12)** the place where the Federal Reserve Bank of New York carries out its open-market operations.

**Open-market operations (3)** the activities of buying and selling government securities from the Federal Reserve's portfolio.

**Open-market policy (3)** federal Reserve Board decisions on whether to buy or sell government securities at a particular time.

**Over-the-counter (24)** a vehicle for trading stocks where stocks are bought and sold from the inventory of a security broker or dealer at prices quoted by the dealer.

**Overnight repurchase agreements (5)** contracts between banks and nonfinancial firms that provide for the firm to buy an interest-earning deposit from the bank each afternoon and for the bank to buy back this deposit the next morning.

**Pacific Exchange (24)** one of the four regional stock exchanges. It is located in San Francisco.

**Pegging (28)** the guarantee by a government to buy and/or sell currency at a fixed price.

**Pension-fund managers (24)** institutional investors who invest funds contributed for retirement by employees in private and public organizations.

**Pension funds (6)** financial institutions that receive payments from workers over the lifetime of the workers' employment and then make payments to the pensioners upon their retirement. Accumulated funds are invested in financial assets.

**Perceived price level (22)** the price level that workers expect will prevail over the near future.

**Perfectly inelastic aggregate-supply (17)** a condition in which the aggregate production level is completely insensitive to the price level, so that a change in price level brings about no change in production.

**Permanent income (13)** a perception of a normal level of income consumers expect to earn over their working lives.

**Personal-consumption spending (4)** an expenditure category of the GNP. It includes the total consumers spending on durable goods, nondurables, and services.

**Philadelphia Exchange (24)** one of the four regional stock exchanges.

**Phillips curve (21)** the general relationship between inflation and the unemployment rate where the higher the unemployment rate, the lower the inflation rate, and the lower the unemployment rate, the higher the inflation rate.

**Plant capacity (14)** the maximum amount of usable capital equipment and facilities in the economy at a point in time.

**Preferred habitats (25)** particular types of securities and particular maturities that suit the objectives of institutional investors.

**Preferred stock (5)** a hybrid of bonds and common stock. Some is issued without provision for retirement whereas

other types have a specific redemption date and price. Preferred stock ordinarily does not carry voting rights as does common stock.

**Present value (5)** the present value of a future interest receipt is the amount of funds required today to reproduce that future interest receipt.

**Price-demand curve (16)** a curve showing the effect that price changes have on the amount of real GNP demanded.

**Price of Consumer Expenditures (PCE)(4)** an index formed by taking the GNP prices for consumer goods (durable, nondurable, and services) and weighting them by the amounts purchased in each category. It measures the prices paid for the consumer goods that people are buying as part of the GNP.

**Primary market (5,24)** a market where newly issued financial instruments are bought and sold.

**Primary reserves (9)** bank holdings of cash and reserve deposits.

**Prime commercial paper (5)** commercial paper with the lowest default risk and highest rating.

**Prime rate (5)** the rate on short-term borrowing that a bank's largest and most secure customers can obtain.

**Product-market equilibrium (14)** the point where aggregate demand $(C + I + G + X)$ **equals production.**

**Production function (14)** the broad relationship between the total use of labor, physical capital, materials, and technology and the resulting real GNP.

**Purchased funds (9)** liabilities that can be bought (borrowed) in the financial marketplace at the market rate of interest. Examples include federal funds, large CDs, and eurodollar accounts.

**Pure consumption goods (13)** goods that have no value as assets and are used up upon purchase.

**Put option (24)** a contract that gives the owner of shares of stock the right to sell the shares at a preset price for a specified period.

**Quantity theory (20)** a theory that holds that the primary reason for price changes is changes in the supply of money.

**Rational expectations (21)** a view held by a group of economists during 1972–1980 that assumes that the public takes all relevant information into account in the most efficient manner when forming their expectations.

**Real assets (23)** assets that are physical in nature and last longer than a single accounting period.

**"Real bills" doctrine (3)** a doctrine from the Federal Reserve that encouraged banks to invest in short-term self-liquidating loans that contributed directly to current production.

**Real Disposable Personal Income (DPI)(13)** the DPI is a statistical series measuring the income and transfer payments received by households net of the taxes paid by them. Real DPI is computed by dividing DPI by an index of prices.

**Real GNP (4)** the production of domestic final goods and services measured in constant dollars. Real GNP is derived by dividing the nominal GNP by the GNP deflator.

**Real growth rate (20)** the percentage change in the real GNP.

**Real interest rate (5)** the inflation-adjusted interest rate that shows how much the lender's purchasing power is expected to go up. The observed (or nominal) interest rate minus the rate of inflation expected over the period of interest.

**Real money demand (15)** the demand to hold an inventory of purchasing power.

**Real money supply (15)** the stock of money found by dividing the actual money supply by the general price level.

**Real wage (16)** the wage rate per hour divided by the price of the firm's product.

**Realized real rate (5, 13)** the real rate of return that actually materializes over the time period of a financial contract. It is the result of subtracting the actual inflation rate occurring over the life of the contract from the contract's nominal rate of interest.

**Recession (1, 4)** a period in which output, jobs, and spending fall off.

**Regional exchanges (24)** besides the NYSE and Amex, four other organized stock exchanges in the United States. They are the Pacific Exchange, the Boston Exchange, the Philadelphia Exchange, and the Midwest Exchange. These exchanges are smaller than the NYSE and the Amex, and list stocks that are too small for the Amex and stocks that are also listed on either the Amex or the NYSE.

**Regional Federal Reserve banks (3)** the part of the Federal Reserve system that carries out many of the actions decided on by the Federal Reserve Board. There are twelve such regional banks, each of which takes care of Federal Reserve business in its geographic area.

**Regulation Q (6)** a banking law stipulating that thrifts could pay a somewhat higher rate of interest on savings than banks could. Also, banks were prevented from accepting business savings deposits but were given the monopoly right to issue non-interest-bearing demand deposits.

**Relative price effect (27)** the effect that fluctuations in exchange rates have on the comparative prices of goods and services sold across borders of two trading nations.

**Repurchase agreement (5)** an arrangement with short-term IOUs that gives the holder of the note the option of selling it back to the issuer at a set price after part or all of the time period of the note has expired.

**Required reserve ratio (2)** the minimum value that banking institutions must maintain for their reserve ratio as established by the Federal Reserve Board.

**Reserve ratio (2)** vault cash plus reserves at the Federal Reserve divided by demand or other deposits.

**Rules policy (21)** a policy of the Federal Reserve in response to a recession. It involves taking no extraordinary action when the economy weakens, but instead continuing to expand bank reserves at a predetermined rate, set by a noninflationary rule.

**Savings account (5)** a special type of certificate of deposit in which money can be drawn out almost on demand by the depositor and which has not set maturity date.

**Savings and loan associations (6)** thrift institutions that seek to serve household financial needs as their primary goal. They are distinguished from mutual savings banks by the legal form of ownership. Savings and loans are owned by investors whereas mutual savings banks are owned by depositors.

**Say's law of markets (18)** a law supporting the natural-rate theory. It states that producing a real GNP of a certain size creates a level of aggregate demand equal to the real GNP produced.

**Scatter diagram (13)** a diagram displaying the relationship between two variables as a scatter of points.

**Secondary market (5, 24)** a market in which previously issued financial instruments are exchanged.

**Secondary reserves (9)** bank holdings of short-term readily marketable securities. Used to gauge the liquidity position of a bank.

**Segmented market (25)** a financial market where those demanding and/or supplying contracts fall into two or more heterogeneous groups regarding their demand and/or supply of contracts of varying maturities.

**Seller's market (17)** a situation in which the amount of purchasing power exceeds the products for sale.

**Services (4)** products used up immediately (or nearly so) upon production. Examples include medical treatment, recreational spending, rents, and transportation.

**Share draft (1, 6, 8)** a checklike document drawn on an account containing shares of an investment fund. It authorizes an agent to transfer share ownership to the person presenting it.

**Share-draft account (6, 8)** see share draft.

**Shift variable (13)** a variable that accounts for systematic shifts in a function displayed graphically in two dimensions.

**Shiftability theory (9)** a philosophy arising around 1900 that stipulated that a bank asset was acceptable if it could be "shifted" to another owner at no financial loss. In other words, it could be sold at little or no capital loss if the need arose to raise funds.

**Short-term financial instruments (5)** financial instruments having maturities of one year or less.

**Sight draft (26)** a bill of exchange that is payable upon receipt.

**Small-denomination CD (5)** a certificate of deposit that is less than $100,000 in amount and that is brought predominantly by households with savings.

**Smithsonian agreement (28)** a 1971 agreement in which the commitment of the United States to buy and sell gold to private foreign buyers or sellers was suspended. The United States retained a commitment for gold purchases and sales to and from foreign governments, thus creating a two-tier system of pricing.

**Sources of funds (23)** ways that firms have of raising

money. They are produced by increasing a liability, increasing net worth, or decreasing an asset.

**Special Drawing Rights (SDR) certificates (11, 27, 28)** claims held by the Federal Reserve on SDRs held by the Treasury. SDRs are paper assets created by the International Monetary Fund for allocation to all affiliated nations, they are used instead of gold for settlement of international transactions.

**Specialists (24)** professional market makers on the organized exchanges. They try to match buy and sell orders as much as possible by continually adjusting the market price of the stock. Often specialists will buy and/or sell for their own accounts in order to provide for an orderly market.

**Spot market in foreign exchange (26)** an exchange market where one country exchanges its domestic currency for another country's currency, to be delivered immediately.

**Stagflation (19)** a condition in the economy denoting the existence of both a recession and inflation.

**Stock of money or money supply (15)** the amount of money held in people's wallets and in the checkable deposits of individuals and firms.

**Store of value (1)** an attribute of money that indicates it can preserve monetary value from one time period to another.

**Striking price (24)** the preset price for a share of stock in a stock option.

**Structures (4)** structures such as houses and apartments, business factories, and office buildings often having useful lives of thirty years or more.

**Supply-of-labor curve (16)** the relationship between the amount of labor hours offered by the current population and the real wage rate. The supply of labor is a positive function of the real wage.

**Supply of loanable funds (18)** household savings as a source of funds that business and government can borrow.

**Supply-side economics (21)** an approach to government policy associated with the presidential administration of Ronald Reagan. It is a policy orientation toward the aggregate-supply function, which is as the key to growth in the economy. It emphasizes incentives to produce, invest, and save. People and firms are seen as responding to prices, wages, interest rates, and other incentives that affect the costs and benefits of their economic activities.

**Tax-wedge theory (21)** a supply-side philosophy proposing that because of taxes and other deductions, the earnings given to the worker for working are less than the cost to the firm for the worker's services.

**Term structure of interest rates (25)** the structure of yields that make up the yield curve.

**Theoretical statements (20)** theoretical statements in economics pertain to the behavior of people or firms. They are not true by definition; they are refutable. The consumption function is an example.

**Thrift institutions (6)** institutions that provide safe and interest-earning deposits that are primarily designed for household savers. Examples are mutual savings banks, savings and loan associations, and credit unions.

**Time draft (26)** a bill of exchange that specifies payment on a future date.

**Time value (5)** money has a time value. Current receipts are worth more than distant receipts.

**Total employment (4)** the civilian poulation over age sixteen who are employed.

**Total labor force (4)** the civilian population over age sixteen who are seeking jobs.

**Transactions demand for money (15)** the influence of the volume of transactions on the demand for money.

**Transitory income (13)** the difference between actual income and permanent income. It is income that is unexpected.

**Treasury Bills (5)** government-issued IOUs with maturities of between three months and one year.

**Treasury cash (11)** the amount of currency held by the U.S. Treasury.

**Treasury currency (11)** coins minted and issued by the U.S. Treasury, plus a small amount of Tresaury Notes.

**Trust-fund managers (24)** institutional investors who invest funds that have been placed in trust accounts by individuals who want the funds to be professionally managed.

**Two-tier system (28)** as a result of the Smithsonian agreement, the price of gold to foreign governments was fixed but the price to private buyers and sellers was not. It was free to fluctuate on world gold markets according to supply and demand.

**Unit banks (6)** banks that have one office where all their business is conducted. These banks are single organizational units.

**Unit of account (1)** an attribute of money that provides for the uniform assessment of value in terms of the monetary unit. Measuring everything in dollar value is an example of the use of the dollar as a unit of account.

**U.S. Treasury bonds (5)** long-term coupon-bearing IOUs issued by the federal government (Treasury Department) to finance federal budget deficits or to refinance prior debt issues.

**U.S. Treasury Notes (5)** long-term coupon-bearing IOUs issued by the federal government to finance public spending. They are very similar to U.S. Treasury bonds.

**Unemployed (4)** the number of people in the labor force minus total employment.

**Unemployment rate (4)** the fraction of the labor force that is unemployed.

**Uses of funds (23)** ways that firms have of using funds. They involve either increasing an asset or decreasing a liability.

**Velocity growth (20)** the percentage change in the velocity of money.

**World Bank (28)** an institution initially set up to facilitate the economic recovery of Western Europe after the devastation of World War II. Nations could receive loans from this institution to finance rebuilding. Now it provides capital for developing nations to use in their industrial development.

**Y = E (14)** shorthand notation for equilibrium in product markets in which real GNP produced (y) equals aggregate demand for products and services (E).

**Yield curve (25)** a curve showing interest rates on bonds plotted on the vertical axis, and showing time to maturity on the horizontal axis.

**Yield to maturity (5)** the earning rate (r) that makes the present value of a financial contract exactly equal to its market price.

**Zero-multiplier effect (17)** a circumstance where an autonomous change in aggregate demand produces no net change in overall output, because of complete crowding out. This condition occurs when interest rates and/or price effects are taken into account.

# INDEX